What's New in This Edition

Since the introduction of Visual Basic version 1.0 just a few years ago, Visual Basic has gone through quite an evolution! Naturally, *Sams Teach Yourself Visual Basic in 21 Days* follows this evolution.

As with previous editions of the book, this edition includes all the "standard" Visual Basic topics that enable you to write powerful Windows applications in a very short time. However, all the programs of this edition of the book are implemented with the new Visual Basic package, version 5.0.

Many of the new features that are incorporated in version 5 of Visual Basic are discussed in this book, including one of the main ones, which enables you to create your own OCX ActiveX controls.

SAMS
Teach Yourself

Visual Basic 5®

in 21 Days

FOURTH EDITION

Nathan Gurewich
Ori Gurewich

SAMS
Teach Yourself

Visual Basic 5®

in 21 Days

FOURTH EDITION

SAMS

A Division of Macmillan Computer Publishing
201 West 103rd Street, Indianapolis, Indiana, 46290 USA

Publisher and President   Richard K. Swadley
Publishing Manager   Greg Wiegand
Director of Editorial Services   Cindy Morrow
Assistant Marketing Managers   Kristina Perry, Rachel Wolfe

Acquisitions Editor
Chris Denny

Development Editor
Fran Hatton

Production Editor
Nancy Albright

Indexer
Erika Millen

Technical Reviewer
Jeff Perkins

Editorial Coordinator
Katie Wise

Technical Edit Coordinator
Lynette Quinn

Resource Coordinator
Deborah Frisby

Editorial Assistants
Carol Ackerman
Andi Richter
Rhonda Tinch-Mize

Cover Designer
Tim Amrhein

Book Designer
Gary Adair

Copy Writer
Peter Fuller

Production Team Supervisors
Brad Chinn
Charlotte Clapp

Production
Svetlana Dominguez
Dana Rhodes
Erich J. Richter
Anne Sipahimalani
Becky Stutzman

Overview

Contents

Acknowledgments

We would like to thank Chris Denny, the acquisitions editor of this book; Fran Hatton, the development editor; and Nancy Albright, the production editor.

We would also like to thank all the other people at Sams Publishing who contributed to this book.

Thanks also to Microsoft Corporation, which supplied us with technical information and various betas and upgrades of the software product.

About the Authors

Nathan Gurewich and **Ori Gurewich** are the authors of several best-selling books in the areas of Visual Basic, C/C++ programming, multimedia programming, database design and programming, and other topics.

Nathan Gurewich holds a master's degree in electrical engineering from Columbia University, New York, and a bachelor's degree in electrical engineering from Hofstra University, Long Island, New York. Since the introduction of the PC, the author has been involved in the design and implementation of commercial software packages for the PC. He is an expert in the field of PC programming and in providing consulting services in the area of local area networks, wide area networks, Internet technology, database management and design, and software marketing. Nathan Gurewich can be contacted by e-mail at the following address:

Nathan_Gurewich@msn.com

Ori Gurewich holds a bachelor's degree in electrical engineering from Stony Brook University, Stony Brook, New York. His background includes working as a senior software engineer and as a software consultant engineer for companies, and developing professional multimedia and Windows applications. He is an expert in the field of PC programming and network communications, and has developed various multimedia algorithms for the PC. Ori Gurewich can be contacted by e-mail at the following address:

Ori_Gurewich@msn.com

Tell Us What You Think!

As a reader, you are the most important critic and commentator of our books. We value your opinion and want to know what we're doing right, what we could do better, what areas you'd like to see us publish in, and any other words of wisdom you're willing to pass our way. You can help us make strong books that meet your needs and give you the computer guidance you require.

Do you have access to the World Wide Web? Then check out our site at http://www.samspublishing.com.

As the executive editor of the group that created this book, I welcome your comments. You can e-mail or write me directly to let me know what you did or didn't like about this book— as well as what we can do to make our books stronger. Here's the information:

E-mail: cdenny@mcp.com

Mail: Chris Denny
            Macmillan Computer Publishing
            201 W. 103rd Street
            Indianapolis, IN 46290

Introduction

This book teaches you how to use the Microsoft Visual Basic for Windows package. After reading this book, you'll be able to write advanced Windows programs using the Visual Basic programming language.

Basic Doesn't Mean Simple

The word *Basic* in Visual Basic may be misleading. You might think that all serious Windows applications should be written using the C/C++ compiler and SDK for Windows.

However, this is not the case. After reading this book you'll be able to write advanced Windows programs in a fraction of the time that it takes to write the same programs using other programming languages.

Visual Means Visual

As its name suggests, a big portion of the programming with Visual Basic is accomplished visually. This means that during design time, you are able to see how your program will look during runtime. This is a great advantage over other programming languages, because you are able to change and experiment with your design until you are satisfied with the colors, sizes, and images that are included in your program.

Using OCX ActiveX Controls

Perhaps the most powerful feature of Visual Basic is its capability of incorporating third-party controls (known as OCX ActiveX controls). If you are unfamiliar with the concept of OCX ActiveX controls, be patient—this topic is covered in the book. For now, however, just remember this: OCX ActiveX controls extend the capabilities of Visual Basic. No matter what application you are developing, if the programming feature you need is not included in the out-of-the-box Visual Basic package, you'll be able to add the feature by using an OCX ActiveX control. For example, in this book you'll learn how to use a third-party OCX ActiveX control to extend the capability of Visual Basic so your program will be able to play sound and display the map of the USA.

21 Chapters, 21 Days

The book is divided into 21 chapters, and you are expected to read and learn a chapter each day. However, many readers may feel confident enough to take two (or more) chapters in one day. The number of chapters you should read each day depends on your previous programming experience with Windows and/or any other programming language.

The book assumes no prior experience in Visual Basic. So, take your time when reading the chapters, and be sure to learn and enter the code of all the programs covered in each chapter. Once you understand the programs, experiment with them for a while. That is, change and modify the code to see what happens when you alter the programs in some way. Remember, the only way to learn a programming language is to actually write programs.

At the end of each chapter, you'll find quizzes and exercises. Be sure to perform these quizzes and exercises. (The solutions to the quizzes and exercises can be found at the end of each chapter.)

Device Independence

Windows is a very popular operating system. Why? Because it is a device-independent operating system. This means that no matter what printer you are using, as long as Windows accepted the printer (at the time you installed the printer), the printer should work fine with every program you design. In fact, you, the programmer, do not care which printer is used. Again, as long as Windows has accepted the printer, your program should work fine with the installed printer. This device-independent concept applies to other pieces of hardware. Therefore, no matter what sound card is used by your users, your programs will be able to work with the sound card without your knowing the name of the sound card's type. You'll realize this during the course of this book when you write a program that utilizes the sound card. That is, there will be no mention of the type of the sound card or who manufactured it.

Another thing that makes Windows so popular is the fact that the user interface is the same for all Windows applications. That is, the programs that you'll learn to design in this book are typical standard Windows programs that use regular Windows user interface. Therefore, you don't have to tell your user how to operate your programs, because the fact that your programs are Windows programs means that your user can use the Clipboard to cut, copy, and paste text and graphics, your user already knows how to minimize and maximize the windows of your programs, and your user can do other conventional Windows operations.

Final Words...

Visual Basic is interesting and fun, because it enables you to write sophisticated professional programs for Windows in a very short time.

So relax, and prepare yourself for a very enjoyable journey.

Week 1

At A Glance

During the course of this book, you'll write many Visual Basic programs. Therefore, you must install the Visual Basic package (if you haven't installed it yet).

Where You're Going

Okay, you've installed Visual Basic successfully. Now what? In Chapter 1, "Writing Your First Visual Basic 5 Program," you'll write your first Visual Basic program. This will give you insight into how easy it is to write a real Windows program with Visual Basic and why the package is called Visual Basic.

During the rest of the first week, you'll learn to write many more programs. Each program teaches you a new concept in Visual Basic and shows you how to apply the concept in your programs. As always, the only way to learn programming is to actually write programs, and Visual Basic is no exception.

1

2

3

4

5

6

7

Week 1

Day 1

Writing Your First Visual Basic 5 Program

In this chapter, you'll write your first Visual Basic program. Writing Visual Basic programs involves two steps:

- The visual programming step
- The code programming step

During the *visual programming step,* you design your programs by using the tools that come with the Visual Basic package. These tools let you design your programs by using the mouse and the keyboard.

To do visual programming, you don't have to do any code writing! All you have to know is how to operate and use the software tools of Visual Basic. As you'll soon see, the visual programming step amounts to a lot of clicking with your mouse, and it's a lot of fun! This chapter concentrates on learning how to use the visual tools of Visual Basic.

In the *code programming step,* you write programs using a text editor. The programs are composed of statements written in the Visual Basic programming language. Writing code with Visual Basic is similar to writing code for other programming languages. However, writing code with Visual Basic is easier than with many other programming languages.

About This Chapter

If you browse through subsequent chapters of this book, you may notice that this chapter is not a typical chapter. This chapter concentrates on the visual programming aspect of Visual Basic, so it mainly emphasizes teaching you how to use the Visual Basic software tools. It is the job of subsequent chapters to teach you how to write code with the Visual Basic programming language.

Creating the Working Directory

Before starting the process of writing your first Visual Basic program, you have to create a directory that will contain the files of your work. Throughout this chapter, it is assumed that you already have the directory C:\VB5PRG\CH01 on your hard drive. You will be instructed to save files into this directory.

The Hello Program

In this chapter you'll write a Visual Basic program called Hello. Before writing the Hello program yourself, let's review its specifications. This way, you'll gain a better understanding of what the Hello program is suppose to do.

When you start the program, the window shown in Figure 1.1 appears. As you can see, the window contains three command buttons (Display Hello, Clear, and Exit) and an empty text box.

Figure 1.1.
The Hello program.

☐ When you click the Display Hello button, the text Hello World! is displayed in the text box (see Figure 1.2).

Figure 1.2.

Displaying text in the text box.

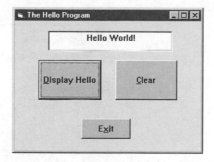

☐ When you click the Clear button, the Hello program clears the text in the text box.

☐ When you click the Exit button, the Hello program terminates.

Creating a New Project

Now that you know what the Hello program is supposed to do, you can write the program.

Note

The Hello program is a very simple program; nevertheless, you must understand how to write the Hello program yourself because it's a typical Visual Basic program. In fact, once you learn how to write the Hello program yourself, you can say that you know Visual Basic! Sure, there's plenty of other Visual Basic information you need to know, but writing the Hello program by yourself means that you know the essentials of Visual Basic.

The very first thing that you need to do is create a new project for the Hello program by using the following steps:

☐ Start Visual Basic. If you see the New Project dialog box shown in Figure 1.3, close this dialog box by clicking the Cancel button of this dialog box.

☐ Select New project from the File menu of Visual Basic.

Visual Basic responds by displaying the New Project dialog box shown in Figure 1.4.

Figure 1.3.

*The New Project
dialog box that
appears when you
start Visual Basic.*

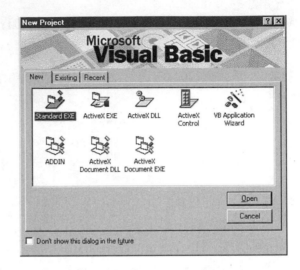

Figure 1.4.

*The New Project
dialog box that Visual
Basic displays after
you select New Project
from the File menu.*

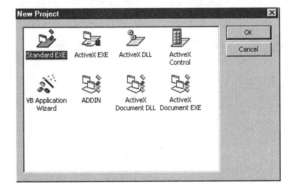

As you can see from Figure 1.4, the New Project dialog box lets you create various types of
projects. Currently, you want to create a standard EXE application. Tell Visual Basic you
want to create a standard EXE application as follows:

☐ Click the Standard EXE icon that appears in the New Project dialog box and then click
the OK button of the New Project dialog box.

  Visual Basic responds by displaying various windows on the desktop.

One of the windows that appears in the desktop of Visual Basic is a blank form with a caption,
Form1 (see Figure 1.5). Your job is to use the various tools of Visual Basic until the blank
form looks like the form shown in Figure 1.1.

Figure 1.5.
The blank form.

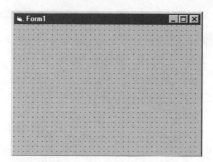

Saving the New Project

Although you haven't made any changes or modifications to the blank form yet, you should save the project at this early stage of the design. When you save the project, two files are saved:

■ The *project file* has the .VBP file extension, and it contains information Visual Basic uses for building the project.

■ The *form file* has the .FRM file extension, and it contains information about the form.

Now use the following steps to save the two files Hello.vbp (the project file) and Hello.frm (the form file):

☐ Make sure that the title of the Form1 window is highlighted and then select Save Form1 As from the File menu of Visual Basic. (When the title of Form1 is highlighted, it means that the form is selected.)

Visual Basic responds by displaying the Save File As dialog box.

☐ Use the Save File As dialog box to select the directory C:\VB5PRG\CH01 as the directory where the file will be saved. Change the default filename of the form from Form1.frm to Hello.frm (see Figure 1.6). Click the Save button of the Save File As dialog box.

Visual Basic responds by saving the form as Hello.frm in the C:\VB5PRG\CH01 directory.

Do	Don't

DON'T use the default name that Visual Basic supplies when saving a form. Instead, save the form by a name appropriate to the application you're designing. For example, now you are designing the Hello program. Therefore, it is appropriate to name the form of the program Hello.frm.

Figure 1.6.

Saving the form as Hello.frm.

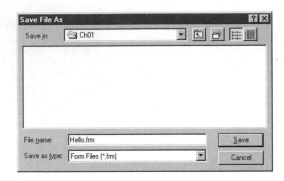

Next, you save the project file:

☐ Select Save Project As from the File menu of Visual Basic.

Visual Basic responds by displaying the Save Project As dialog box.

The default filename that Visual Basic supplies is Project1.vbp. However, you need to name the project file with a name that is more appropriate to the particular application you're developing:

☐ Use the Save Project As dialog box to save the project file as Hello.vbp in the C:\VB5PRG\CH01 directory.

Do	Don't

DON'T use the default name that Visual Basic supplies when you save a project file. Instead, save the file by a name appropriate to the application you're designing. For example, now you are designing a program that displays the text Hello. So an appropriate name for the project is Hello.vbp.

Now you have saved two files: Hello.vbp (the project file) and Hello.frm (the form file).

Examining the Project Window

At this point, your project is called Hello.vbp, and it consists of a single form file: the Hello.frm file. However, in subsequent chapters your project will contain more files.

One of the tools that Visual Basic offers is the Project window, which enables you to see the various files that are included in the project. (You'll learn to appreciate this feature as your projects get more complicated.)

1

Use the following steps to examine the Project window:

☐ Select Project Explorer from the View menu of Visual Basic.

The project window pops up, as shown in Figure 1.7.

Figure 1.7.
The Project window.

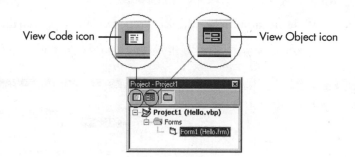

View Code icon

View Object icon

As indicated in the Project window, the project file is Hello.vbp. The Hello.vbp project includes a single form called Hello.frm. Again, for the simple Hello.vbp project, the Properties window does not look like an important tool. When your projects get more complex (many files in it), however, you'll find the Project window very helpful.

Changing the Caption Property of the Form

The blank form that was created by Visual Basic has the caption Form1, shown in Figure 1.5. This is the default caption that Visual Basic assigned to the new blank form. Although you may leave the caption of the form as Form1, it is a good idea to assign a friendlier caption to the form. As shown in Figure 1.1, the caption of the finished form should be The Hello Program.

Note

A form is also called a window. So, for example, Form1 in Figure 1.5 is called a form, and it is also called a window.

Here is how you change the caption of the blank form to The Hello Program:

☐ Make sure that the blank form is selected. You can easily recognize whether the form is selected by examining its caption. If the caption is highlighted, the form is selected. (In Visual Basic, the title of the window is also called the caption of the window.)

If the form is not selected, simply click anywhere in the form. Alternatively, you can select Project Explorer from the View menu to display the Project window, highlight the Hello.frm item in the Project window, and click the View Object icon that appears in the Project window. (Note in Figure 1.7 that the second icon from the right on the top of the Project window is called the View Object icon.)

☐ While the form is selected, select Properties Window from the View menu of Visual Basic.

Visual Basic responds by displaying the Properties window (see Figure 1.8).

Figure 1.8.

The Properties window.

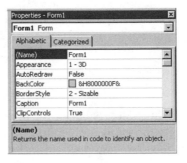

> **Note**
>
> In Visual Basic 5, you can move the various windows to various locations in the desktop of Visual Basic 5 by dragging the titles of the windows.
>
> Depending on the locations of the various windows in the desktop of Visual Basic, the windows may appear slightly different in different locations. Hence, depending on the particular location where your Properties window is located, your Properties window may look slightly different than the Properties window shown in Figure 1.8.
>
> In any case, you can easily identify the Properties window, because it has the word Properties in its title.

☐ Click the cell that appears to the right of the Caption cell in the Properties window.

☐ Currently, the cell to the right of the Caption has in it the text Form1. Use the Delete and arrow keys on your keyboard to delete the text Form1 and replace it by typing the text The Hello Program. The Properties window should now look like the one shown in Figure 1.9.

Congratulations! You have just completed changing the Caption property of the form. Take a look at the blank form (see Figure 1.10). Now its caption is The Hello Program.

Figure 1.9.
Changing the Caption property of the form.

Figure 1.10.
The Hello.frm form with its new Caption property.

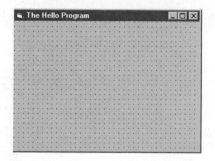

What Is a Property?

The Caption is just one of the properties of the form. As you can see from the Properties window, the form has many other properties. To understand what a property is, you have to understand that Visual Basic programs deal with objects, such as forms, command buttons, scroll bars, pictures, check boxes, and so on.

The properties of an object define how the object looks and behaves. For example, a form is an object. The Caption property of the form defines the text that appears in the title (caption) of the form.

Another property of the form object is BackColor, which defines the background color of the form. Use the following steps to change the form's BackColor property:

☐ Make sure that the form is selected by clicking anywhere in the form.

☐ To display the properties window, select Properties Window from the View menu.

☐ Click the cell to the right of the BackColor property in the Properties window.

When you click this cell, Visual Basic places a down-arrow icon in the cell (see Figure 1.11).

Figure 1.11.
The BackColor
property.

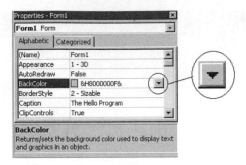

☐ Click the down-arrow icon that appears in the cell.

Visual Basic responds by displaying a pop-up dialog box like the one in Figure 1.12.

Figure 1.12.
The dialog box that
pops up when you
click the down-arrow
icon of the BackColor
property.

Note that the dialog box of Figure 1.12 has two tabs: Palette and System. In Figure 1.12, the System page is displayed.

☐ Click the Palette tab of the dialog box shown in Figure 1.12.

Visual Basic responds by displaying the Palette page (see Figure 1.13).

Figure 1.13.
The Palette page.

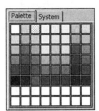

☐ Select the color of your choice by clicking on it in the Palette page. For now, select the color that appears as the square third column from the right and third row from the top. (If you do not like this color, select a different color.)

Do	Don't

DO examine the cell that appears to the right of the property cell that you want to set. If the cell has a down-arrow icon in it, clicking the arrow icon displays a window or a list that lets you select a value with the mouse.

Try a few colors by repeating the process until you are happy with your color selection.

Changing the Name Property of the Form

Each object in Visual Basic must have a name, which is defined in the Name property of the object. When you created the new form of the Hello program, Visual Basic automatically set the Name property of the form to Form1.

Now change the Name property of the form:

☐ Make sure the form is selected by clicking anywhere in it.

☐ Select Properties Window from the View menu.

Visual Basic responds by displaying the Properties window of Form1.

The Properties window has two tabs: Alphabetic and Categorized (refer to Figure 1.8). If you click the Alphabetic tab, the properties are sorted alphabetically, (except the Name property which appears first). If you click the Categorized tab, the properties are listed according to categories.

☐ Click the Alphabetic tab of the Properties window.

The Name property appears as the first property in the list of properties.

☐ Click in the cell that appears to the right of the Name property. Visual Basic now lets you edit the Name property.

☐ Replace the name Form1 by typing the name `frmHello`.

In the preceding step, you changed the Name property of the form from Form1 to frmHello. Throughout this book, the first three characters of the Name property of objects are three letters that indicate the type of object. Therefore, the first three characters of the Name property of a form are *frm*, as in frmHello.

Do	Don't

DO change the default names of objects so their names reflect their purposes in the program. For example, frmHello is the name of a form used by the Hello program.

By starting the name with the characters frm, you are making your program easier to understand and maintain. For example, take a look at the name frmHello. Because it starts with the characters frm, you (and anybody else who reads your program) can immediately tell that the frmHello object is a form.

This is not a Visual Basic requirement, but it will make the program easier to read and understand.

Saving Your Work

You haven't finished preparing the form yet. (Remember that upon completion, the form should look like the one shown in Figure 1.1.) Nevertheless, it's a good idea to save the work you have done so far, because you'll have to start designing the form all over again if your PC system collapses before you save your work. This is especially true when working in the Windows environment, where you can open windows of several applications. As you'll see in subsequent chapters, designing forms may involve opening and executing other Windows applications, such as Paintbrush and Word for Windows. If one of these other applications collapses, it may take down the whole system with it. So be safe—save your work from time to time.

Use the following step to save your work:

☐ Select Save Project from the File menu.

Visual Basic responds by saving all the changes that you made to the project file or to any of the files of the project (that is, the Hello.frm file).

Adding the Exit Button to the frmHello Form

As shown in Figure 1.1, the final form should have three command buttons in it: Display Hello, Clear, and Exit.

Note

In some Windows literature, command buttons are also referred to as pushbuttons. However, this book calls them command buttons, because this is the terminology used in Visual Basic.

To place a command button in your form, you have to pick it up from the toolbox window.

The Toolbox Window

The toolbox window contains icons of various objects. It is your job to "pick up" an object from the toolbox window and place it in your form:

☐ Display the toolbox window by selecting Toolbox from the View menu of Visual Basic.

Visual Basic responds by displaying the toolbox (see Figure 1.14).

Figure 1.14.

The toolbox.

Note

Depending on the particular location of the toolbox window in the desktop of Visual Basic, the toolbox window may appear slightly different from the window shown in Figure 1.14.

Depending on the particular edition of your Visual Basic 5 and on various other Visual Basic 5 settings, your toolbox window may include more (or fewer) icons in it.

One of the icons in the toolbox window—the command button—is shown magnified in Figure 1.15. You can easily recognize the various icons in the toolbox window by placing the mouse cursor (without clicking any of the mouse buttons) on the icon you want to examine. Visual Basic responds by displaying a small yellow rectangle with text in it. The text identifies the name of the object that the icon represents.

When you place the mouse cursor (without clicking any of the mouse buttons) on the command button icon in the toolbox, a yellow rectangle appears with the text CommandButton in it.

Figure 1.15.
The icon of the CommandButton in the toolbox window.

Placing the Exit Button in the Form

Use the following step to place a command button in the form:

☐ Double-click the icon of the CommandButton in the toolbox window. (Figure 1.15 shows the icon of the CommandButton in the toolbox window.)

Visual Basic responds by placing a CommandButton in the center of the form (see Figure 1.16).

Figure 1.16.
The form with the CommandButton in it.

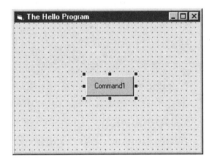

Visual Basic assigns various default properties to the CommandButton that you placed in the form. For example, the default Caption property of this command button is Command1.

Visual Basic also assigns the default name Command1 to the Name property of the command button that you placed in the form.

Changing the Name Property of the Exit Button

Because the CommandButton that you just placed in the form serves as the Exit button, change its Name property to cmdExit:

☐ Select Properties Window from the View menu of Visual Basic.

Visual Basic responds by displaying the Properties window.

☐ Make sure that the list box at the top of the Properties window displays this text: Command1 CommandButton (see Figure 1.17 for the location of the list box).

Figure 1.17.

The list box at the top of the Properties window is currently set to Command1 CommandButton.

This list box has the CommandButton selected in it.

Note

Currently, the form has two objects: the form frmHello and the command button Command1. The Properties window lists the properties of the object whose name currently appears in the list box at the top of the Properties window. To switch to another object, click on the down-arrow icon of the list box and select the desired object from the list that drops down.

☐ Change the Name property of Command1 from Command1 to cmdExit.

Note the name convention for the Name property of the CommandButton. Because the object is a command button, the first three characters of its name are *cmd*. Also, because this command button serves as the Exit button, its full name is cmdExit. This naming convention is not a Visual Basic requirement, but it makes your program easier to read and understand (that is, when you see the name cmdExit, you can immediately tell that this is the name of a command button, and that this command button serves as the Exit button).

Changing the Caption Property of the Exit Button

The default Caption that Visual Basic assigns to the command button is Command1. Because this command button is the Exit button, a more appropriate caption is Exit:

☐ Change the Caption property of cmdExit from Command1 to E&xit.

The & character (which you type by pressing Shift+7) before the *x* in E&xit causes Visual Basic to display the x underlined, as shown in Figure 1.1. When you execute the program, pressing Alt+x produces the same result as clicking the Exit button.

Note

> When setting the Caption property of a button, always insert an ampersand character (&) as a prefix before one of the characters in the caption's name. This underlines the prefixed character, and during execution time, your users will be able either to click the button or press Alt+*key* (where *key* is the underlined character).

Changing the Location of the Exit Button

As you can see from Figure 1.1, the Exit button should be near the bottom of the form.

☐ Drag the Exit button to the desired location by clicking anywhere in the Exit button and, without releasing the mouse's left button, moving the mouse.

Changing the Font Properties of the Exit Button

As shown in Figure 1.1, the font of the Exit button is different from the default font that Visual Basic assigned to the caption of the button that you placed in the form. Use the following steps to change the font of the cmdExit button:

☐ Click the cell to the right of the Font property of the cmdExit button. As you can see, the cell has an icon with three dots in it.

> *Clicking the three-dots icon will open a new dialog box that lets you select certain values from it.*

☐ Click the three-dots icon of the Font property of the cmdExit button.

> *Visual Basic responds by displaying the Font dialog box.*

☐ Change the font to System.

☐ Change the size of the font to 10.

☐ Click the OK button of the Font dialog box.

Take a look at the Exit button. Its caption has the text font you set with the Font dialog box!

Your form should now look like the one shown in Figure 1.18.

Figure 1.18.

The form with the Exit button in it.

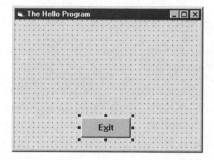

Note

One of the main advantages of Visual Basic is that you instantly see the results of your visual programming. Always experiment and try different options (that is, try different fonts, different sizes, different colors, and so on) until you are satisfied with the results.

Save your work:

☐ Select Save Project from the File menu of Visual Basic.

Adding the Other Buttons to the frmHello Form

Now it's time to add two more command buttons to the form: the Display Hello button and the Clear button.

Placing the Other Buttons in the Form

As shown in Figure 1.1, the form includes two other buttons: the Display Hello button and the Clear button. You'll now place these buttons in the form:

☐ Add the Display Hello button to the form by double-clicking the CommandButton icon in the toolbox window. Now drag the new command button to the left. (This button serves as the Display Hello button.)

☐ Double-click the command button icon in the toolbox window again, then drag the new command button to the right. (This button serves as the Clear button.)

Resizing the Buttons

The default sizes of the Display Hello and the Clear buttons are smaller than the size of the buttons shown in Figure 1.1.

☐ Enlarge the new buttons that you placed in the form. To enlarge or shrink an object, select the object by clicking on it. Once an object is selected, Visual Basic encloses the selected object with a rectangle. The rectangle has eight little black squares on it, which are called handles. Drag one of the handles until the object reaches the size you want. For example, to resize an object horizontally, drag one of its handles horizontally; to resize an object vertically, drag one of its handles vertically (see Figure 1.19).

Figure 1.19.

Resizing an object.

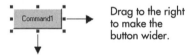

Drag to the right
to make the
button wider.

Drag downward to make the button higher.

Changing the Name Properties

The default names that Visual Basic assigned to the command buttons you just placed in the form are Command1 and Command2. More appropriate names are cmdHello and cmdClear.

☐ Change the Name property of the left command button to cmdHello.

☐ Change the Name property of the right command button to cmdClear.

Changing the Caption Properties

As shown in Figure 1.1, the left button should have the caption Display Hello, and the right button should have the caption Clear.

☐ Change the Caption property of the left button to &Display Hello.

☐ Change the Caption property of the right button to &Clear.

Changing the Font Properties

As shown in Figure 1.1, the Display Hello and Clear buttons should have a different font and font size from the default font that Visual Basic assigned to your command buttons.

☐ Change the Font property of the cmdHello button to System and the font size to 10.

☐ Change the Font property of the cmdClear button to System and the font size to 10.

After setting the font, you may discover that the button's area is too small. In this case, simply enlarge the size of the button by dragging its handles.

Your form should now look like the one shown in Figure 1.20.

Figure 1.20.
The form with the three buttons in it.

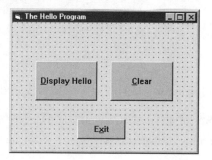

Save your work:

☐ Select Save Project from the File menu of Visual Basic.

Adding the Text Box Object to the frmHello Form

There is one more object to add to the form: the text box object. A text box object is a rectangular area in which text is displayed. In Windows terminology, a text box is also referred to as an edit box.

Placing the Text Box in the Form

In Figure 1.21, the icon of the text box is the second icon from the top in the left column of the toolbox window. Depending on your particular edition and setting of Visual Basic, the locations of the icons in the toolbox window may be different from the locations shown in Figure 1.21.

Note   When you place the mouse cursor (without clicking any of the mouse buttons) on the text box icon in the toolbox, a yellow rectangle appears with the text TextBox in it.

Figure 1.21.

The icon of the TextBox tool in the toolbox window.

Use the following steps to place the TextBox in the form:

☐ Double-click the icon of the TextBox in the toolbox window.

☐ Move and resize the text box until it looks like the text box shown in Figure 1.22.

Figure 1.22.

The form after placing the Text Box in it.

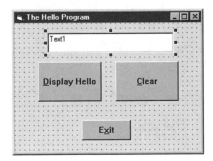

Changing the Properties of the Text Box

Use the following steps to modify several properties of the text box:

☐ Change the Name property of the text box from the default name Text1 to txtDisplay.

☐ The default Text property of the text box is Text1, so when you execute the Hello program, the text Text1 appears in the Text Box. Because you want the text box to be empty when you start the program, delete the text that appears in the cell to the right of the Text property of the txtDisplay object.

☐ Change the Font property of the txtDisplay Text Box to System and the font size to 10.

☐ The default Alignment property of the Text Box is 0-Left Justify, which means that the text in the Text Box is aligned to the left. Because you want the text to appear in the center of the Text Box, change the alignment property to 2-Center.

☐ As it turns out, Visual Basic refuses to place the text in the center of the Text Box unless the MultiLine property of the text box is set to True. So, besides setting the Alignment property to 2-Center, you must also change the MultiLine property to True. (If you set the MultiLine property to True, Visual Basic can display more than one line in the text box.) Change the MultiLine property of the txtDisplay text box to True.

Save your work:

☐ Select Save Project from the File menu of Visual Basic.

Note

As previously stated, it is very important to save your work from time to time. One way to save your work is to select Save Project from the File menu of Visual Basic (as you did so far in this chapter). Saving your work from time to time is so important, that Visual Basic lets you save your work in an easier manner. Take a look at Figure 1.23, which shows the toolbar of Visual Basic. (If the toolbar of Visual Basic is not displayed, you can display it by selecting Toolbars from the View menu of Visual Basic and then clicking the Standard item that appears in the menu that pops up.)

As shown in Figure 1.23, on the toolbar there is an icon that looks like a disk. If you place the mouse cursor (without clicking any of the mouse buttons) on this icon, a yellow rectangle appears with the text Save Project in it. Clicking this icon has the same effect as selecting Save Project from the File menu.

Yes, the designers of Visual Basic made it very easy for you to save your work. Just click this icon from time to time.

Figure 1.23.

The Save icon on the toolbar of Visual Basic.

Building Forms from Figures and Tables

The visual programming portion is now completed.

Throughout this book, you will be instructed to build many other forms. However, this book does not teach you to construct the form the same way you were taught to build the frmHello form. Instead, you'll have to build the form by looking at the figure of a completed form, such as Figure 1.1, and following a properties table. A *properties table* contains all the objects included in the form and lists objects' properties that are different from the default properties.

Your job is to follow the table, line by line, and change the properties' values to the values that appear in the table. Table 1.1 is the properties table of the frmHello Form.

Table 1.1. The properties table of the frmHello program.

Object	Property	Setting
Form	**Name**	**frmHello**
	BackColor	Blue
	Caption	The Hello Program
CommandButton	**Name**	**cmdExit**
	Caption	E&xit
	Font name	System
	Font size	10
CommandButton	**Name**	**cmdClear**
	Caption	&Clear
	Font name	System
	Font size	10
CommandButton	**Name**	**cmdHello**
	Caption	&Display Hello
	Font name	System
	Font size	10
TextBox	**Name**	**txtDisplay**
	Alignment	2-Center
	Font name	System
	Font size	10
	MultiLine	True

Attaching Code to the Objects

Because you placed the objects in the form and set their properties, the visual programming part of the job is completed. Now it's time to attach some code to the objects.

Visual Basic is an event-driven programming language. This means that code is executed as a response to an event. For example, if you click the Exit button during the execution of the Hello program, a Click event is automatically generated, and the code that corresponds to the Exit button's Click event is automatically executed.

Likewise, if you click the Display Hello button, a Click event is generated, and the code that corresponds to the Click event of the Display Hello button is automatically executed.

Your job is to write the appropriate code and attach it to the object and event. Does this sound complicated? Well, it's actually very easy! Start by attaching some code to the Click event of the Exit button.

Attaching Code to the Exit Button

Use the following steps to attach code to the cmdExit button:

☐ Double-click the cmdExit button.

> *Visual Basic responds by displaying the code window (you write code in this window) shown in Figure 1.24.*

Figure 1.24.

Attaching code to the cmdExit button in the code window.

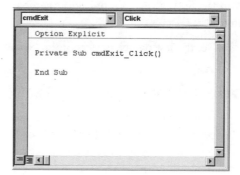

Visual Basic makes it very easy for you to recognize which code is currently being displayed in the code window. As shown in Figure 1.24, the top-left combo box displays the name of the object (cmdExit) and the top-right combo box displays the name of the event (Click).

As you can see from Figure 1.24, Visual Basic already placed two lines of code in the code window:

```
Private Sub cmdExit_Click ()
End Sub
```

You'll write your code between these two lines.

The First and Last Lines of the Code

The first line of code, which Visual Basic already wrote for you, starts with the words `Private Sub`. `Sub` is a keyword indicating that a procedure starts there. A *procedure* is a code dedicated for a particular event. The name of the procedure is `cmdExit_Click()`.

The last line of code, also written by Visual Basic, is `End Sub`, which marks the end of the procedure.

The Name of the Procedure

The name of the procedure is `cmdExit_Click()`. Why did Visual Basic assign this name to the procedure? Because you double-clicked the `cmdExit` button, Visual Basic knows that you are attempting to attach code to the Exit button. Therefore, the first half of the procedure name is `cmdExit`.

The second half of the procedure name is `Click`. Why did Visual Basic assign this name? Because the event you're writing code for is the `Click` event.

The first and second halves of the procedure name are separated with the underscore character (_), as in `cmdExit_Click()`.

As you can see, the last two characters of the procedure name are the parentheses ().

The Code of the `cmdExit_Click()` Procedure

What code should you write in the `cmdExit_Click()` procedure? Because this procedure is executed when you click the Exit button, the code to be inserted in this procedure should cause the program to terminate. The code that causes a Visual Basic program to terminate is the `End` statement.

☐ Type `End` in the `cmdExit_Click()` procedure. After typing the `End` statement, the `cmdExit_Click()` procedure should look as follows:

```
Sub cmdExit_Click()
    End
End Sub
```

That's all—you just completed attaching code to the `cmdExit_Click()` procedure.

Executing the Hello Program

Although you haven't finished attaching code to the rest of the objects, you can now execute the Hello program and see how the code that you attached to the Exit button works for you:

☐ Save your work by selecting Save Project from the File menu (or by clicking the Save Project icon on the toolbar of Visual Basic).

☐ Select Start from the Run menu of Visual Basic.

> *Visual Basic responds by executing your program. The window of the application pops up, as shown in Figure 1.1.*

You may now click the Display Hello button, but nothing will happen. Why? Because you haven't attached any code to this button. If you click the Clear button, nothing happens because you haven't attached any code to this object either.

Now click the Exit button. As a response to the clicking, the code of the procedure cmdExit_Click() is executed. Because the code in this procedure consists of code that causes the program to terminate, the Hello program terminates.

Attaching More Code to the cmdExit_Click() Procedure

Use the following steps to attach more code in the cmdExit_Click() procedure:

☐ Double-click the cmdExit button.

> *Visual Basic responds by displaying the cmdExit_Click() procedure ready to be edited by you.*

☐ Add the Beep statement before the End statement as follows:

```
Private Sub cmdExit_Click()
    Beep
    End
End Sub
```

☐ Save your work.

☐ Execute the Hello program by selecting Start from the Run menu of Visual Basic.

The Beep statement causes the PC to beep. So when you click the Exit button, the PC beeps and then the End statement is executed, causing the Hello program to terminate.

☐ Click the Exit button and verify that the program beeps and then the program terminates itself.

Attaching Code to the Display Hello Button

Use the following steps to attach code to the Display Hello button:

☐ Display the form and then double-click the Display Hello button. (Recall that you can display the form by selecting Project Explorer from the View menu, clicking the frmHello item in the Project window, and then clicking the View Object icon that appears as the second icon from the left at the top of the Project window.)

   After you double-click the Display Hello button, Visual Basic responds by displaying the cmdHello_Click() *procedure with two lines of code already written:*

```
Private Sub cmdHello_Click ()
End Sub
```

The preceding procedure is executed when you click the Display Hello button during the execution of the Hello program.

What code should you insert in this procedure? It depends on what you want to happen when you click the Display Hello button. In the Hello program, you want the program to display the words Hello World! in the text box.

☐ Type the following code in the cmdHello_Click() procedure:

```
     txtDisplay.Text = "Hello World!"
```

When you finish, the procedure should look like this:

```
Private Sub cmdHello_Click()
     txtDisplay.Text = "Hello World!"
End Sub
```

txtDisplay is the name of the TextBox object (the text box in which the words Hello World! will be displayed).

This statement:

```
txtDisplay.Text = "Hello World!"
```

assigns the value Hello World! to the Text property of txtDisplay. (The value of the Text property is the text that will be displayed in the txtDisplay TextBox.)

 Note

> To assign a new value to a property from within the program's code, use the following format:
>
> ```
> ObjectName.Property = "New value of the property"
> ```
>
> For example, to change the Text property of the txtDisplay TextBox to Hello World!, use the following code:

```
txtDisplay.Text = "Hello World!"
```

Note the dot (.) that appears between the name of the object (txtDisplay) and the name of the property (Text).

Attaching Code to the Clear Button

Use the following steps to attach code to the Click event of the Clear button:

☐ Display the form and then double-click the Clear button. (Recall that you can display the form by selecting Project Explorer from the View menu, clicking the frmHello item in the Project window, and then clicking the View Object icon that appears as the second icon from the left at the top of the Project window.)

After you double-click the Clear button, Visual Basic responds by displaying the code window with the cmdClear_Click() procedure in it.

The code of this procedure should clear the text box. In other words, the Text property of the txtDisplay text box should change to null. You do this by inserting the following statement in the procedure:

```
txtDisplay.Text = ""
```

☐ Type the following statement in the cmdClear_Click() procedure:

```
txtDisplay.Text = ""
```

When you finish, the procedure should look like this:

```
Private Sub cmdClear_Click()
    txtDisplay.Text = ""
End Sub
```

☐ Save your work by selecting Save Project from the File menu (or by clicking the Save Project icon on the Toolbar of Visual Basic).

Executing the Hello Program

The Hello program is complete. Use the following steps to execute the Hello program:

☐ Select Start from the Run menu of Visual Basic or press F5 to start the program.

Note

One of the main reasons that Visual Basic is such a popular programming language is the fact that you can develop your program a little, then run your application and see your development in action, then develop a little bit more, again run the application to test your development, and so on.

As previously stated, you execute the application from within Visual Basic by selecting Start from the Run menu of Visual Basic.

Because executing the application from within Visual Basic is such a frequent operation, the designers of Visual Basic included the Start icon on the toolbar of Visual Basic (see Figure 1.25). This way, you can execute the application with one click on the Start icon. If for some reason the toolbar is not displayed, you can display it by selecting Toolbars from the View menu of Visual Basic and then selecting Standard from the menu that pops up.

As stated, the fact that Visual Basic lets you execute programs that you develop from within Visual Basic is a very convenient feature. In a programming language such as Visual C++, you must first compile and link your program before you can execute the program.

Note

Visual Basic makes it very easy for you to execute the application that you develop. However, sometimes, due to an error in your code, the error will cause the collapse of the system, and you'll have to start Windows or Visual Basic again. This means that if you did not save your work, your work will be lost and you'll have to start developing the application again. So be wise, and make it a rule to save your work before you execute it. As previously stated, the toolbar also includes the Save Project icon. Make it a habit to first click the Save Project icon and then the Start icon. This way, if an error occurred during the execution of your program, you'll be able to start Visual Basic again and load your saved project. You'll correct your error and keep developing your project.

Figure 1.25.

The Start icon on the toolbar of Visual Basic.

☐ Click the Display Hello and Clear buttons to display and clear the words `Hello World!` in the text box. After clicking the Display Hello button, the window of the Hello program should look like the one shown in Figure 1.2. After clicking the Clear button, the window of the Hello program should look like the one shown in Figure 1.1.

☐ You may use the keys Alt+D and Alt+C to get the same results as clicking the Display Hello and Clear buttons (because you have the D underlined in the Display Hello caption of that button and you have the C underlined in the Clear caption of the Clear button).

☐ To terminate the program, click the Exit button (or press Alt+X).

Note that the text box displays the text centered in System font, because during the design time, you set the Font property to System and the Alignment property to 2-Center.

Other Events

The Hello program uses the `Click` event of the command buttons. (For example, during the execution of the Hello program, you clicked the Exit button, and as a result, the `Click` event of the cmdExit button occurs. This causes the automatic execution of the `cmdExit_Click()` procedure.) There are other events that a Visual Basic program may use. Each event has its own procedure.

The `KeyDown` Event

Let's look at the procedure that corresponds to the `KeyDown` event, which occurs when you press a key on the keyboard.

To see the `KeyDown` procedure of the Exit button do the following:

☐ Double-click the Exit button.

By default, Visual Basic displays the procedure that corresponds to the `Click` event.

☐ Because you want to look at the procedure that corresponds to the `KeyDown` event, switch to the `KeyDown` procedure by clicking the combo box that appears at the right side on the top of the code window.

Visual Basic responds by dropping down a list that contains all the possible events associated with the cmdExit object (see Figure 1.26).

☐ Click the KeyDown item in the list.

Visual Basic responds by displaying the cmdExit_KeyDown procedure:

```
Private Sub cmdExit_KeyDown(KeyCode As Integer, Shift As Integer)


End Sub
```

Figure 1.26.

*Displaying the events
of the cmdExit
button.*

The first line of the procedure that Visual Basic automatically writes for the KeyDown event is a little different from the first line for the Click event. That is, the parentheses of the cmdExit_Click() procedure do not have anything in them. However, the parentheses of the cmdExit_KeyDown() procedure do contain code. We'll discuss this difference in later chapters of this book.

At this point, do not add any code to the cmdExit_KeyDown() procedure. (You went through this exercise to become familiar with accessing the procedures of other events.)

Creating an Executable File (HELLO.EXE)

Earlier, you executed the Hello program by selecting Start from the Run menu. Naturally, you don't want your users to execute the program this way (your users may not even own the Visual Basic package).

To be able to distribute the Hello program, you need to generate the EXE file HELLO.EXE:

☐ Select Make Hello.EXE File from the File menu of Visual Basic.

   Visual Basic responds by displaying the Make dialog box. (Don't click the OK button in the dialog box yet.)

☐ Use the dialog box to save the file as HELLO.EXE in the C:\VB5PRG\CH01\HELLO.EXE directory.

   Visual Basic responds by saving the file HELLO.EXE in the directory C:\VB5PRG\CH01.

You may now execute HELLO.EXE just as you would any other Windows program! That is, you can use the Windows Explorer program to double-click the HELLO.EXE file and as a result, the Hello program will be executed.

Small EXE Filesize!

Take a look at the Hello.EXE file that now resides in the C:\VB5PRG\CH01 directory. How can a file that is only 8KB perform all the things that Hello.EXE can do? Think about it—the Hello.EXE program accomplishes a lot! The program lets you click buttons and drag the window of the program. It has a text box in it, and, in short, the 8KB has all the standard features of a Windows program. The reason for the small size of the Hello.EXE file is that the Hello.EXE program assumes that the System directory of your user already has a file in it called Msvbvm50.dll.

If your users use Windows 95 and Windows 95 is installed in the C:\Windows directory, the System directory is the C:\Windows\System directory. If your users use Windows NT and Windows NT is installed in the C:\WinNT directory, the System directory is the C:\WinNT\System32 directory. No matter which Windows your users use, to execute the Hello.EXE program, they need the Msvbvm50.dll in their System directories. You can take a look at your System directory and verify that you have this file already (it was installed when you installed Visual Basic 5).

The size of the Msvbvm50.DLL is about 1.3MB. This is a large file, but once your users have this file, they can execute powerful Windows programs that were written with Visual Basic 5. And the good news is that these powerful programs are very small in size. (You may also see the Hello.Vbw file in the directory where you saved the Hello.EXE file. The Hello.Vbw file is used by Visual Basic. You do not have to supply this file to your users.)

Note

> When you supply Windows programs, you have to also supply the corresponding DLL files of the programs. In the case of programs that were written with Visual Basic 5, the PC that executes these programs must have the Msvbvm50.DLL file in its System directory.

Summary

In this chapter you wrote your first Visual Basic program. You learned about the steps necessary to write a Visual Basic program: the visual programming step and the code programming step.

In the visual programming step, you place objects in the form and set their properties.

In the code programming step, you select a procedure by selecting the object and the event and then you insert code in the procedure. This code is executed during runtime when the event occurs.

Q&A

Q The title of this book is *Teach Yourself Visual Basic 5 in 21 Days*. Can I read and learn the book in fewer (or more) days?

A Yes. Some people work through a couple of chapters each day. You should learn at your own pace.

Q Can I write professional programs using Visual Basic?

A Yes. Visual Basic is designed so you can write fancy, advanced Windows applications in a very short time.

Q What is the difference between a command button and a pushbutton?

A Pushbuttons and command buttons are the same thing. Visual Basic literature refers to these objects as command buttons (other Windows literature sometimes calls them pushbuttons).

Q I get confused! There are many windows on the desktop: form, Project window, Properties window, toolbox window, and so on. Is there any good trick for finding and selecting a particular window?

A At any point during your design, you can select Project Explorer from the View menu. This pops up the Project window.

You can now highlight the Form item in the project window, then click either the View Object icon to display the form or the View Code icon to display the code window.

If you click Object icon while the Form is selected in the Project window, the form will be displayed.

Once the Form is displayed, you can display the Properties window by selecting Properties Window from the View menu. Alternatively, you can right-click the object whose properties you want to display and then click the Properties item from the menu that pops up.

After practicing for a while, you'll be able to maneuver among the various windows without any difficulty.

Quiz

1. What are the two steps in the design process of a Visual Basic program?
2. What is the first thing you have to do when writing a new Visual Basic program?
3. Give several examples of objects and their properties.

4. Which of the following is not a Visual Basic object?

    a. Command Button

    b. Form

    c. Variable

    d. Text Box

5. Describe how you attach code to an object.

6. BUG BUSTER. There is something wrong in the following statement:

```
txtDisplay.Text = Hi there!
```

What's wrong with it?

Exercise

Identify the icon of the Horizontal Scrollbar in the toolbox window.

Quiz Answers

1. These are the two steps:

   The visual programming step. In this step, you place objects in the form and set their properties.

   The code programming step. In this step, you write and attach code to objects and events.

2. The first thing you have to do when writing a new Visual Basic program is open a new project from the File menu.

3. A command button is an example of an object. Use the following steps to see its properties:

   ☐ Open a new Standard EXE project.

   ☐ Double-click the CommandButton icon in the toolbox.

       Visual Basic responds by placing the button in the form.

   ☐ Open the Properties window for the command button (that is, select Properties Window from the View menu) and browse through the properties of the command button. As you can see, the command button has many properties.

   Repeat the above process for other objects.

   During the course of this book you'll have a chance to set many properties of many objects.

4. c. A variable is not an object (variables are discussed in later chapters).

5. Here is how you attach code to an object:

☐ Double-click the object you placed in the form.

Visual Basic responds by displaying the code window for this object.

☐ Select the event from the combo box that appears on the right-top of the code window.

☐ You may now attach code to the object by typing it between the Private Sub and End Sub lines of the procedure.

6. This is the correct syntax:

```
txtDisplay.Text = "Hi there!"
```

That is, you must enclose the text within double quotation marks (" ").

Exercise Answer

Here is how you identify the Horizontal Scrollbar icon in the toolbox window:

☐ Display the toolbox window.

The icon of the Horizontal Scrollbar is shown in Figure 1.27.

Figure 1.27.

The icon of the Horizontal Scrollbar in the toolbox window.

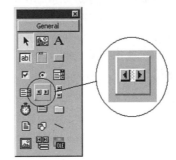

You can easily verify that you located the Horizontal Scrollbar icon: When you place the mouse cursor (without clicking any of the mouse buttons) on the Horizontal Scrollbar icon, a yellow rectangle appears with the text HScrollBar in it.

Week 1

Day 2

Properties, Controls, and Objects

This chapter focuses on Visual Basic controls, such as scroll bars, text boxes, option buttons, and command buttons. You'll learn how to include these controls in your programs, how to change their properties, and how to attach code to them.

Most programs output information to the user and get information from the user. The process of outputting and inputting information is called the user interface aspect of the program. Windows programs use controls to provide easy and pleasant user interface (that's one of the main reasons for the popularity of Windows). In this chapter you'll learn that implementing a fancy user interface is very easy in Visual Basic.

The Scroll Bar Control

The scroll bar is a commonly used control in Windows programs. Using this object enables the user to select a value by positioning the thumb (the square tab) of the scroll bar to a desired position (instead of typing the desired value).

Note

In Chapter 1, "Writing Your First Visual Basic 5 Program," the scroll bar was called an object. In this chapter and in the remaining chapters of this book, it will usually be referred to as a control.

In most cases, an object is also a control, but not always. For example, a form is an object, but it isn't a control. Typically, you call an object a control if the object can be placed in a form.

The Speed Program

The Speed program illustrates how a scroll bar is used for getting a value from the user.

The Speed program should do the following things:

■ When the Speed program is started, the window shown in Figure 2.1 should pop up. The thumb of the scroll bar should be positioned at the center of the scroll bar (the default position), and the text box should display a speed value of 50 mph (the default speed).

Figure 2.1.
The Speed program.

■ When you change the thumb's position of the scroll bar, the text box should reflect the change. For example, when the thumb is placed at the extreme left, the text box should display the value 0; when the thumb is placed at the extreme right, the text box should display the value 100.

☐ To exit the program, click the Exit button.

The Visual Implementation of the Speed Program

The Speed program uses the horizontal scroll bar control. To see which item in the toolbox window represents the horizontal scroll bar control, refer to Figure 2.2. The exact location of the icon of the horizontal scroll bar in the toolbox varies from version to version. When you place the mouse cursor (without clicking any of the mouse buttons) on the icon of the horizontal scroll bar, a yellow rectangle appears with the text HScrollBar in it. This way, you can verify that you located the icon of the horizontal scroll bar in the toolbox window.

☐ Start Visual Basic. If the New Project window appears, click its Cancel button to close this window. Then select New Project from the File menu of Visual Basic.

Visual Basic responds by displaying the New Project window.

☐ Select the Standard EXE icon in the New Project window, then click the OK button of the New Project window.

Visual Basic responds by creating a new project.

Figure 2.2.

The icon of the horizontal scroll bar in the toolbox window.

You'll now save the new project that you are creating:

☐ Create the C:\VB5Prg\Ch02 directory.

☐ Make sure that the Form1 window is the selected window, then select Save Form1 As from the File menu of Visual Basic.

Visual Basic responds by displaying the Save File As dialog box.

☐ Use the Save File As dialog box to save the form as Speed.Frm in the C:\VB5Prg\Ch02 directory.

☐ Select Save Project As from the File menu of Visual Basic, then use the Save Project As dialog box to save the project as Speed.Vbp in the C:\VBPrg\Ch02 directory.

☐ Modify Form1 according to Table 2.1.

When you complete modifying Form1, it should look like the one shown in Figure 2.3.

Figure 2.3.

The frmSpeed form in design mode.

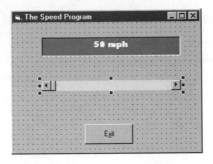

Table 2.1. The properties table of the frmSpeed form.

Object	Property	Setting
Form	**Name**	**frmSpeed**
	BackColor	Light gray
	Caption	The Speed Program
Command Button	**Name**	**cmdExit**
	Caption	E&xit
Horizontal Scroll Bar	**Name**	**hsbSpeed**
	Min	0
	Max	100
Text Box	**Name**	**txtSpeed**
	Alignment	2-Center
	MultiLine	True
	BackColor	Red
	ForeColor	White
	Font	(Select the font of your choice)
	Text	50 mph

☐ From Chapter 1 you should recall that to place a control in a form, you have to double-click the control's icon in the toolbox.

Visual Basic responds by placing the control in the middle of the form. You then move the control by dragging it with the mouse. You enlarge or shrink the control by dragging its handles.

□ To access the properties of the control, make sure that the control you placed in the form is selected and then select Properties Window from the View menu. Alternatively, you can right-click the control and then select Properties from the menu that pops up.

Visual Basic responds by displaying the Properties window for the control. You can then change the control's properties.

□ Save the project by selecting Save Project from the File menu of Visual Basic.

Entering the Code of the Speed Program

You'll now type the code of the Speed program:

□ Enter the following code in the cmdExit_Click() procedure of the frmSpeed form:

```
Private Sub cmdExit_Click()
       End
End Sub
```

The code that you typed is automatically executed when the user clicks the Exit button. This code terminates the program.

Note

> To enter the code, double-click the Exit button. Visual Basic responds by displaying the code window of the cmdExit_Click() procedure, where the cmdExit_Click() procedure is ready to be edited by you. (Make sure that the upper-left list box of the code window has the text cmdExit in it and that the upper-right list box of the code window has the text Click in it.)

□ Save the project by selecting Save Project from the File menu of Visual Basic.

Executing the Speed Program

Although you have not finished writing the code of the Speed program yet, execute the Speed program to see what you have accomplished so far:

□ Execute the Speed program (for example, press F5 and select Start from the Run menu).

The window of the Speed program pops up, as shown in Figure 2.4.

Figure 2.4.

*The window of the
Speed program.*

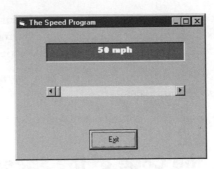

☐ Change the scroll bar's thumb position by clicking the right and left arrow icons of the scroll bar.

As you can see, nothing is happening in the text box! Why? Because you haven't attached any code that changes the contents of the text box in accordance with the scroll bar position.

☐ Click the Exit button to terminate the Speed program.

The Min, Max, and Value Properties of the Scroll Bar

The following sections describe some of the properties of the scroll bar.

The Min and Max Properties

A scroll bar represents a set of values. The Min property represents the minimum value, and the Max property represents the maximum value. As shown in Table 2.1, the Min property is set to 0, and the Max property is set to 100. This means that the scroll bar may be set to any value between 0 and 100.

The Value Property

The Value property of the scroll bar represents the current value of the scroll bar, so it may be any integer number between 0 and 100. When you execute the Speed program, the scroll bar's thumb is set to the position that corresponds to the Value property. During design time, you did not set the Value property of the scroll bar, so the default value of 0 is used. When you start the Speed program, the scroll bar's thumb is positioned at the extreme left position (which corresponds to the Value property equal to 0).

Because you want the default speed to be 50, you have to set the Value property of the scroll bar to 50:

☐ Set the Value property of the scroll bar to 50.

Now, if you execute the Speed program, the default thumb position of the scroll bar will be in the middle of the scroll bar (that is, midway between 0 and 100).

Note that the Text property of the text box is set to 50 mph in Table 2.1. When you start the program, the string displayed in the text box (50 mph) corresponds to the current setting of the scroll bar (Value=50).

The Keyboard Focus

While the program is running, you can press the Tab key on your keyboard to move the focus from control to control. Each time the Tab key is pressed, the focus shifts from one control to another. You can easily recognize which control has the focus because Windows gives a visual indication of it.

For example, when the text box has the focus, a cursor in the text box blinks; when the scroll bar has the focus, its thumb is blinking. When the Exit button has the focus, a dashed rectangle surrounds the button's caption.

What does it mean when a control has the focus? It means that you can use the keyboard to control it. To see the keyboard focus feature in action, try the following:

☐ Execute the Speed program. (Note that now the thumb of the scroll bar is in the middle, because you set the Value property of the scroll bar to 50.)

☐ Press the Tab key until the scroll bar has the focus (that is, until you see the scroll bar's thumb blinking).

☐ While the scroll bar has the focus, use the right-arrow and left-arrow keys of the keyboard to move the thumb of the scroll bar. Because the scroll bar now has the focus, pressing the arrow keys on the keyboard has the same effect as clicking the right-arrow and left-arrow icons of the scroll bar. Try to press the Home, End, Pg Up, and Pg Dn keys, and see the effects of these keys on the scroll bar.

☐ Press the Tab key until the Exit button has the focus.

☐ While the Exit button has the focus, press the space bar or the Enter key. Pressing the space bar or the Enter key while the button has the focus has the same effect as clicking the button.

See how much you can do with the Speed program! You can change the scroll bar position, shrink and enlarge the window of the program (by dragging the edges of the window), move the window of the program by dragging its caption, and perform many other standard Windows operations. The beauty of it is that you didn't have to write any code to incorporate these features. Indeed, this is one of the main advantages of writing Windows programs—the standard Windows features are already incorporated into your programs, and you don't need to write any code. Furthermore, a Windows user (the user of your program) is expected to know all these things. By being a "Windows user," your user is expected to know about all these Windows features (and your user expects your programs to include these features).

Enhancing the Speed Program

Now you'll enhance the Speed program by attaching more code to it.

☐ Display the hsbSpeed_Change() procedure by double-clicking the scroll bar control that you placed in the form. Make sure that the upper-left list box of the code window has the text hsbSpeed in it, and that the upper-right list box of the code window has the text Change in it.

☐ Type the following code in the hsbSpeed_Change() procedure:

```
Private Sub hsbSpeed_Change()
    txtSpeed.Text = Str(hsbSpeed.Value) + " mph"
End Sub
```

As implied by the name hsbSpeed_Change(), this procedure is executed when you change the position of the scroll bar. As you change the position of the scroll bar, the Value property of the scroll bar changes automatically. For example, if you place the scroll bar's thumb to the extreme left, the Value property of the scroll bar is automatically set to 0 (because this is the value you set for the Min property).

When you change the position of the scroll bar, the text box should display the new position of the scroll bar. In other words, you need to assign the Value property of the scroll bar to the Text property of the text box. You do this in the hsbSpeed_Change() procedure with the following statement:

```
txtSpeed.Text = Str(hsbSpeed.Value) + " mph"
```

For example, if the Value property of the scroll bar is 20, the Text property of the text box is set to 20 mph.

The Text property of the text box expects a string (text); however, the Value property of the scroll bar is a number. This means you must use the Str() function to convert the numeric value of the Value property to a string. In the parentheses of the Str() function you type the numeric value that you want to convert to a string. For example, to convert the number 11 to the string "11", you use Str(11); to convert the number 12345 to the string "12345", you use Str(12345). In this case, you want to convert the numeric hsbSpeed.Value to a string, so you use the following statement:

```
Str(hsbSpeed.Value)
```

Putting it all together, if the current position of the scroll bar is at 32 (that is, hsbSpeed.Value is equal to 32), this statement

```
txtSpeed.Text = Str(hsbSpeed.Value) + " mph"
```

fills the Text property of the text box with the following:

```
32 mph
```

Let's see your code in action:

☐ Save the project by selecting Save Project from the File menu.

☐ Execute the Speed program.

☐ Play with the scroll bar. As you change the scroll bar's thumb position, the content of the text box changes accordingly.

☐ Terminate the Speed program by clicking the Exit button.

Changing the Text Box While Dragging the Scroll Bar Thumb

You are almost finished with the Speed program. There is, however, one annoying problem to solve. To see the problem in action, follow these steps:

☐ Execute the Speed program.

☐ Try to drag the thumb of the scroll bar. As you drag the thumb, the text box content does not change! It changes only after you release the thumb.

It would be nice if the text box would change its content while you drag the scroll bar's thumb. To make this change, you have to type code in the hsbSpeed_Scroll() procedure. The hsbSpeed_Scroll() procedure is automatically executed when you drag the thumb of the scroll bar:

☐ Display the hsbSpeed_Scroll() procedure by double-clicking the scroll bar control that you placed in the form. Set the upper-left list box of the code window to hsbSpeed, and set the upper-right list box of the code window to Scroll.

☐ Type the following code in the hsbSpeed_Scroll() procedure:

```
Private Sub hsbSpeed_Scroll()
    hsbSpeed_Change
End Sub
```

☐ Select Save Project from the File menu of Visual Basic.

The code that you typed in the hsbSpeed_Scroll() procedure is the following:

hsbSpeed_Change

The preceding code causes the execution of the hsbSpeed_Change() procedure. The code that you previously typed in the hsbSpeed_Change() procedure sets the Text property of the text box control to the Value property of the scroll bar. So when the user drags the thumb of the scroll bar, the hsbSpeed_Scroll() procedure is executed automatically. The code that you typed in the hsbSpeed_Scroll() procedure executes the hsbSpeed_Change() procedure. This means that the code of the hsbSpeed_Change() procedure will be executed when you drag the thumb of the scroll bar, and this code will set the Text property of the text box control. Let's see this in action:

☐ Execute the Speed program.

☐ Drag the thumb of the scroll bar and verify that the text in the text box changes while you drag the thumb of the scroll bar.

☐ Click the Exit button to terminate the Speed program.

Note

You execute the hsbSpeed_Change() procedure from within the hsbSpeed_Scroll() position as follows:

```
Private Sub hsbSpeed_Scroll()
    hsbSpeed_Change
End Sub
```

That is, there are no parentheses after the word hsbSpeed_Change.

If you type the parentheses as follows:

hsbSpeed_Change()

you'll get an error. Actually, Visual Basic will display the code that has the error in it in red. This is a visual indication to you that you have an error in your code.

Final Words About the Speed Program

The Speed program illustrates how you can create an elegant user interface for entering numbers. Instead of telling the user to type an integer number between 0 and 100, you give your user a scroll bar. Your user can set any integer in the allowed range by using the scroll bar and gets visual feedback on the range of numbers that can be entered.

The Options Program

The Options program demonstrates how you can write programs that let your user select an option.

The Visual Implementation of the Options Program

The Options program uses the Option button control. To see which icon represents the Option button in the toolbox window, refer to Figure 2.5. The exact location of the Option icon in the toolbox varies from version to version. When you place the mouse cursor (without clicking any of the mouse buttons) on the icon of the Option button in the toolbox, a yellow rectangle appears with the text OptionButton in it.

Figure 2.5.
The icon of the Option button in the toolbox window.

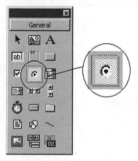

☐ Open a new project by selecting New Project from the File menu of Visual Basic. When the New Project window appears, select the Standard EXE icon and then click the OK button of the New Project window.

☐ Make sure that the Form1 window of the new project is the selected window, and then select Save Form1 As from the File menu of Visual Basic. Use the Save File As dialog box to save the file as Options.Frm in the C:\VB5PrgCh02 directory.

☐ Select Save Project As from the File menu of Visual Basic, and then use the Save Project As dialog box to save the project as Options.Vbp in the C:\VBPrg\Ch02 directory.

☐ Build the frmOptions form according to Table 2.2.

When you complete building the form, it should look like the one in Figure 2.6.

Figure 2.6.

*The frmOptions form
in design mode.*

Table 2.2. The properties table of the frmOptions form.

Object	Property	Setting
Form	**Name**	**frmOption**
	BackColor	Red
	Caption	The Options Program
Command Button	**Name**	**cmdExit**
	Caption	E&xit
Check Box	**Name**	**chkSound**
	BackColor	Red
	Caption	&Sound
	Font	(Select the font of your choice)
	ForeColor	White
Check Box	**Name**	**chkMouse**
	BackColor	Red
	Caption	&Mouse
	Font	(Select the font of your choice)
Check Box	**Name**	**chkColors**
	BackColor	Red
	Caption	&Colors
	Font	(Select the font of your choice)
	ForeColor	White

Object	Property	Setting
Option Button	**Name**	**optLevel1**
	BackColor	Red
	Caption	Level &1
	ForeColor	White
	Font	(Select the font of your choice)
Option Button	**Name**	**optLevel2**
	BackColor	Red
	Caption	Level &2
	ForeColor	White
	Font	(Select the font of your choice)
Option Button	**Name**	**optLevel3**
	BackColor	Red
	Caption	Level &3
	ForeColor	White
	Font	(Select the font of your choice)
Label	**Name**	**lblChoice**
	Alignment	2-Center
	BorderStyle	1-Fixed Single
	Font	(Select the font of your choice)

Note

When implementing the frmOptions per Table 2.2, you may have to increase the height of the form so that all the components will fit in the form. To increase the height of the form, drag the lower handle of the form window downward.

The General Declarations Area of the Form

You'll now enter code in the general declarations section of the frmOptions form, an area in the code window where you type various general statements.

The `Option Explicit` statement is an example of a general statement. The exact meaning of the `Option Explicit` statement is discussed later in this chapter. For now, you'll just learn how to examine the general declarations section and how to type code in it.

To examine the general declarations section do the following:

☐ Double-click in a free area of the frmOptions form to display the code window.

Visual Basic responds by displaying the code window.

☐ Click the down-arrow icon of the list box that is located on the upper-left corner of the code window. Then select the (General) item from the list.

☐ Click the down-arrow icon of the list box that is located on the upper-right corner of the code window. Then select the (Declarations) item from the list.

Your code window should now display the general declarations section, as shown in Figure 2.7.

In Figure 2.7, you see the following code:

```
Option Explicit
```

```
Private Sub Form_Load()
End Sub
```

In Figure 2.7, the general declarations section is the area above the `Form_Load()` procedure. As shown in Figure 2.7, Visual Basic may have already written the following code in the general declarations section:

```
Option Explicit
```

Figure 2.7.

Displaying the general declarations section of the code window.

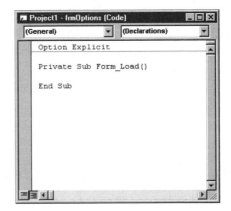

☐ You can now click in the general declarations section and type additional code in it. If you don't see the Option Explicit statement in the general declarations section, click in it and type the following code:

```
Option Explicit
```

Attaching Code to the Click Event of the Exit Button

You'll now attach code to the Click event of the cmdExit button:

☐ Enter the following code in the cmdExit_Click() procedure of the frmOptions form:

```
Private Sub cmdExit_Click()
    End
End Sub
```

☐ Select Save Project from the File menu of Visual Basic to save your work.

The code that you typed is automatically being executed when the user clicks the Exit button. This code terminates the Options program.

Executing the Options Program

Although you did not yet complete the design of the Options program, let's execute it:

☐ Execute the Options program.

☐ Click the Level 1 option button.

> *The program responds by selecting the Level 1 option button (a dot appears in the Level 1 option button).*

☐ Click the Level 2 option button.

> *The program responds by deselecting the Level 1 button (removing the dot from the Level 1 option button) and selecting the Level 2 button (placing a dot in the Level 2 option button).*

☐ Click the Level 3 option button.

> *The program responds by deselecting the Level 2 button and selecting the Level 3 button.*

Only one option button is selected at any time. Option buttons are used in programs when you want your user to select a single option out of several options. (Note that some Windows literature refers to an option button as a radio button.)

☐ Click the Sound check box.

> *The program responds by placing a check mark in the Sound check box.*

☐ Click the other check boxes.

As you can see, it is possible to check more than one check box. Check boxes are used when you want the user to be able to select various settings. For example, if the program is a game application, you may select to play with or without sound, with or without the mouse, and with or without colors.

However, the user can play the game with Level 1, Level 2, or Level 3. It does not make sense to have both Level 1 and Level 2 selected at the same time.

To deselect a check box, click it again. (When a check box is not selected, it does not have a check mark in it.)

☐ Terminate the program by clicking the Exit button.

Detecting Which Check Boxes and Option Button Are Selected

You'll now type code that detects which check boxes are selected and which option button is selected.

☐ Type the following code in the chkColors_Click() procedure of the frmOptions form:

```
Private Sub chkColors_Click()
    UpdateLabel
End Sub
```

☐ Enter the following code in the chkMouse_Click() procedure of the frmOptions form:

```
Private Sub chkMouse_Click()
    UpdateLabel
End Sub
```

☐ Enter the following code in the chkSound_Click() procedure of the frmOptions form:

```
Private Sub chkSound_Click()
    UpdateLabel
End Sub
```

☐ Enter the following code in the optLevel1_Click() procedure of the frmOptions form:

```
Private Sub optLevel1_Click()
    UpdateLabel
End Sub
```

☐ Enter the following code in the optLevel2_Click() procedure of the frmOptions form:

```
Private Sub optLevel2_Click()
    UpdateLabel
End Sub
```

☐ Enter the following code in the optLevel3_Click() procedure of the frmOptions form:

```
Private Sub optLevel3_Click()
    UpdateLabel
End Sub
```

What did you do in the preceding steps? You wrote the following statement:

UpdateLabel

in various procedures.

For example, you typed it in the optLevel3_Click() procedure. UpdateLabel is the name of a procedure you are going to write later in this chapter. So when the user clicks the Level 3 option button, the optLevel3_Click() procedure is automatically executed, which means the UpdateLabel procedure will be executed. The same thing happens when the user clicks the Level 2 option button, because you also typed the UpdateLabel statement in the optLevel2_Click() procedure. In short, when the user clicks any of the check boxes or any of the option buttons, the UpdateLabel procedure is executed.

Now use the following steps to add the UpdateLabel procedure to the form:

☐ Double-click in a free area of the form.

Visual Basic responds by displaying the code window.

☐ Select Add Procedure from the Tools menu of Visual Basic.

Visual Basic responds by displaying the Add Procedure dialog box.

☐ In the Name edit box of the Add Procedure dialog box type UpdateLabel (because this is the name of the new procedure you are now adding). Make sure that the option buttons of the Add Procedure dialog box are set as shown in Figure 2.8.

Figure 2.8.
Adding the
UpdateLabel
procedure.

☐ Click the OK button of the Add Procedure dialog box.

Visual Basic responds by displaying the code window with the UpdateLabel *procedure ready for you to edit.*

> **Note**
>
> Visual Basic inserted the UpdateLabel procedure in the General area of the frmOptions form. You can verify this as follows:
>
> ☐ Set the upper-left list box of the code window to (General).
>
> ☐ Click the down-arrow icon of the upper-right list box of the code window.
>
> As you can see, the right list box now has two items in it: (Declarations) and UpdateLabel. In the general declarations section, you have the Option Explicit statement.
>
> Procedures that you add to the form (such as the UpdateLabel procedure) are added to the General area. It is important to know where the procedure was added, because at a later time you may want to come back to the procedure, and modify it.
>
> Procedures that you added are added to the General area of the form. To access the procedure, set the upper-left list box of the code window to (General), and then select the procedure that you want to edit from the upper-right list box of the code window.

Visual Basic wrote the first and last lines of the new UpdateLabel procedure for you, but it is your responsibility to write the code of the UpdateLabel procedure:

☐ Type the following code in the UpdateLabel procedure:

```
Public Sub UpdateLabel()
    ' Declare the variables
    Dim Info
    Dim LFCR

    LFCR = Chr(13) + Chr(10)

    ' Sound
    If chkSound.Value = 1 Then
        Info = "Sound: ON"
    Else
        Info = "Sound: OFF"
    End If
```

```
' Mouse
If chkMouse.Value = 1 Then
    Info = Info + LFCR + "Mouse: ON"
Else
    Info = Info + LFCR + "Mouse: OFF"
End If

' Colors
If chkColors.Value = 1 Then
    Info = Info + LFCR + "Colors: ON"
Else
    Info = Info + LFCR + "Colors: OFF"
End If

' Level 1
If optLevel1.Value = True Then
    Info = Info + LFCR + "Level:1"
End If

' Level 2
If optLevel2.Value = True Then
    Info = Info + LFCR + "Level:2"
End If

' Level 3
If optLevel3.Value = True Then
    Info = Info + LFCR + "Level:3"
End If

lblChoice.Caption = Info
```

End Sub

☐ Save the project by selecting Save Project from the File menu.

Executing the Options Program

Before going over the code that you typed in the UpdateLabel procedure, let's execute the Options program and see your code in action:

☐ Execute the Options program.

☐ Click the various check boxes and option buttons.

The Options program responds by displaying the status of the check boxes and radio buttons in the lblChoice label (see Figure 2.9).

☐ Terminate the Options program by clicking its Exit button.

Figure 2.9.

The window of the Options program showing the current settings for the check boxes and option buttons.

How the Options Program Works

The Options program executes the UpdateLabel procedure when you click any of the check boxes or radio buttons.

The Code of the chkColors_Click() Procedure of the frmOptions Form

The chkColors_Click() procedure is automatically executed when you click the chkColors check box:

```
Private Sub chkColors_Click()
    UpdateLabel
End Sub
```

The code in the chkColors_Click() procedure executes the UpdateLabel procedure. The code of the UpdateLabel procedure is covered later in this chapter.

In a similar manner, when you click the other check boxes and other option buttons, the UpdateLabel procedure is executed (because you typed code that executes the UpdateLabel procedure in the corresponding procedures of the check boxes and option buttons).

The Code of the UpdateLabel Procedure

As discussed, when you click a check box or an option button, the UpdateLabel procedure is executed.

The UpdateLabel procedure is not an event procedure; you created the UpdateLabel procedure using the Add Procedure dialog box earlier in this chapter.

It is important to understand the difference between procedures such as the cmdExit_Click() procedure and the UpdateLabel procedure. The cmdExit_Click() procedure is executed automatically. You do not have to write any code that causes the execution of the `cmdExit_Click()` procedure. Why? Because that's how Visual Basic works! The moment the user clicks the Exit button, a `Click` event occurs, and as a result, the `cmdExit_Click()` procedure is executed.

On the other hand, the `UpdateLabel` procedure is not executed automatically. Your code has to cause the execution of the `UpdateLabel` procedure. Indeed, in various procedures you typed the statement:

`UpdateLabel`

The preceding statement causes the execution of the `UpdateLabel` procedure. In fact, you added the code that causes the execution of the `UpdateLabel` procedure in six places. So when the user clicks any of the check boxes or any of the option buttons, the `UpdateLabel` procedure is executed.

Declaring the `Info` **Variable**

The first statement that you typed in the `UpdateLabel` procedure declares the `Info` variable:

`Dim Info`

The word `Dim` is an instruction to Visual Basic that the following word—Info, in this case—is the name of a variable. The variable `Info` is used as a string variable during the execution of the `UpdateLabel` procedure.

You can also declare this variable as follows:

`Dim Info As String`

Fortunately, Visual Basic is liberal in this respect and does not force you to declare the type of variable at the time of the declaration. (Other programming languages, such as Visual C++, force you to declare the type of variable.)

If you have experience with other programming languages, you probably know that some programming languages don't require you to declare variables. However, it's a good programming habit to declare all variables. To see why, assume that your procedure includes the following calculations:

```
Time = 10
Velocity = 50
Distance = Velocity * Time
lblDistance.Caption = "Distance = " + Str(Distance)
```

The preceding four statements assign 10 to the `Time` variable, 50 to the `Velocity` variable, calculate the distance by multiplying `Velocity` by `Time`, and display the `Distance` by assigning its value to the Caption property of the lblDistance label.

Now suppose that by mistake you typed the following (that is, with a missing a after the t in Distance):

```
lblDistance.Caption = "Distance = " + Str(Distnce)
```

Visual Basic considers Distnce as a new variable, and it automatically assigns the value 0 to it. Therefore, the lblVelocity label displays the following:

```
Distance: 0
```

This, of course, is an error. You can avoid such foolish errors by instructing Visual Basic to complain when a variable is used in the program and yet the variable was not declared. In the preceding example, the statements that calculate and display the distance should be the following:

```
Dim Time
Dim Velocity
Dim Distance

Time = 10
Velocity = 50
Distance = Velocity * Time
lblDistance.Caption = "Distance = " + Str(Distnce)
```

If Visual Basic is set to complain when your code includes a variable that is not declared, Visual Basic will prompt you with an error message during the execution of the program, telling you that the Distnce variable is unknown. Visual Basic highlights the variable Distnce, letting you know that there is something wrong with it.

To instruct Visual Basic to complain when there is a variable in the code that is not declared, you have to place the following statement in the general declarations section of the form:

```
Option Explicit
```

This is the reason you were instructed earlier to type the Option Explicit statement in the general declarations section.

 Note

Always include the Option Explicit statement in the general declarations section of the form. This way, you tell Visual Basic not to accept variables that were not declared and save yourself many hours of debugging. Generally speaking, if you do not include the Option Explicit statement and you have a silly error such as misspelling the name of a variable, it could take you many hours of debugging to find your error. So be wise, and let Visual Basic find variables that you typed incorrectly.

Declaring the LFCR **Variable**

You also declared the LFCR variable in the UpdateLabel procedure:

```
Dim LFCR
```

and then you set the value of the LFCR variable as follows:

```
LFCR = Chr(13) + Chr(10)
```

Chr(13) is the carriage return character, and Chr(10) is the line feed character. As you'll soon see, the lblChoice label displays a long string that is spread over several lines. You'll spread the string over several lines by inserting the LFCR variable between the lines.

Checking the Value Property of the Check Box

The next statements that you typed in the UpdateLabel procedure were a block of If...Else...End If statements:

```
' Sound
If chkSound.Value = 1 Then
    Info = "Sound: ON"
Else
    Info = "Sound: OFF"
End If
```

In Visual Basic, you can insert comments in the code by using the apostrophe character (') or the Rem word. The following line:

```
' Sound
```

is identical to this line:

```
Rem Sound
```

This book uses the apostrophe as the character that starts a comment line. Comments also may be inserted in a line of code as follows:

```
MyVariable = 1 ' Initialize the variable.
```

It's a good programming habit to insert comments that give a brief description of the code; they make the program easier to read and debug. You can write anything you want after the ' character. Visual Basic simply ignores all the characters that follow the ' character.

The UpdateLabel procedure checks whether the Value property of the chkSound check box is equal to 1. If the Value property is equal to 1, the statements between the If line and the Else line are executed. In this case, you have only one statement between the If and the Else, so if the Value property of the chkSound box is equal to 1, the following statement is executed:

```
Info = "Sound: ON"
```

This statement assigns the string "Sound: ON" to the variable Info. Note that the Then word in the If statement must be included.

If the Value property of the Sound check box is equal to 1, it means that there is a check mark in the chkSound check box. Therefore, when there is a check mark in the chkSound check box, the variable Info is set to "Sound: ON".

The statements between the Else and End If lines are executed if the Value property of the chkSound Check property is not equal to 1. When there is no check mark in the check box, the Value property of the check box is equal to 0. If there is no check mark in the chkSound check box, the statement between Else and End If is executed, which sets the contents of the Info variable to the following:

"Sound: OFF"

To summarize, the Info variable is set to either

"Sound: ON"

or

"Sound: OFF"

In a similar way, the next If...Else...End If block checks the Value property of the chkMouse check box:

```
' Mouse
If chkMouse.Value = 1 Then
    Info = Info + LFCR + "Mouse: ON"
Else
    Info = Info + LFCR + "Mouse: OFF"
End If
```

For example, if the chkSound check box has a check mark in it and the chkMouse check box does not, the first two If...Else...End If blocks in the UpdateLabel procedure assign the following string to the Info variable:

"Sound: ON" + LFCR + "Mouse: OFF"

This is later displayed on two lines:

```
Sound: ON
Mouse: OFF
```

because of the LFCR that was inserted between the two strings.

The next If...Else...End If block in the UpdateLabel procedure checks the Value property of the chkColors check box and updates the Info variable accordingly:

```
' Colors
If chkColors.Value = 1 Then
    Info = Info + LFCR + "Colors: ON"
```

```
Else
   Info = Info + LFCR + "Colors: OFF"
End If
```

The next If…End If block in the UpdateLabel procedure checks the Value property of the optLevel1 option button:

```
' Level
If optLevel1.Value = True Then
   Info = Info + LFCR + "Level:1"
End If
```

Again, the Value property of the control specifies its status. However, for the option button control, a Value property that equals True means that the option button is selected and the Info variable is updated accordingly. If the Value property of the optLevel1 does not equal True, it means that this option button is not selected.

Note

The Value property of a check box may be 0, 1, or 2. The Value property of a check box that has a check mark in it is 1. The Value property of a check box that does not have a check mark in it is 0.

The Value property of a check box is 2 when the check box is grayed or dimmed.

Note

The Value property of an option button may be True or False. If the option button has a dot in it, the Value property is True. If the option button does not have a dot in it, the Value property is False.

The next two If…End If blocks update the Info variable according to the Value properties of the optLevel2 and optLevel3 option buttons:

```
If optLevel2.Value = True Then
   Info = Info + LFCR + "Level:2"
End If

If optLevel3.Value = True Then
   Info = Info + LFCR + "Level:3"
End If
```

The last statement in the UpdateLabel procedure updates the Caption property of the lblChoice label with the contents of the Info variable:

```
lblChoice.Caption = Info
```

This displays the contents of the Info variable in the lblChoice label, as shown in Figure 2.9.

What Else?

As you may realize by now, programming with Visual Basic amounts to understanding the meaning of each of the controls in the toolbox and the meaning and purpose of the controls' properties. The same property means different things for different controls. For example, the Caption property of the form contains the text displayed in the title of the form, and the Caption property of the label control contains the text displayed in the label. Likewise, the Value property of the check box indicates whether the check box has a check mark in it, and the Value property of the option button indicates whether the option button has a dot in it. The Value property of the scroll bar also indicates the current position of the scroll bar.

The toolbox contains the icons of the controls, and each control has its own set of properties. Some of the controls in the toolbox are standard Windows controls, such as horizontal scroll bars, vertical scroll bars, text boxes, labels, check boxes, option buttons, and command buttons.

One of the main things that makes Visual Basic a powerful programming language is that it enables you to add other icons in the toolbox and then place the controls that these icons represent in your form. The additional controls that you can add to the toolbox are called ActiveX controls. They are also known by the name OCX controls. You'll learn more about ActiveX/OCX controls later in this book.

Generally speaking, Visual Basic is not a difficult programming language to learn, but there is a lot to learn. The key to successful learning is practicing and experimenting. After writing and experimenting with the book's programs, you can master Visual Basic. After you enter the code of the book's programs and understand the code, experiment on your own. Try to change the properties of the control during design time (during the time you implement the visual portion of the program) and at runtime. Changing properties during runtime means that the value of the property changes from within the code of the program. For example, the last statement in the UpdateLabel procedures updates the Caption property of the lblChoice label during runtime:

```
lblChoice.Caption = Info
```

On the other hand, the Caption property of the form was set to The Options Program during design time.

Some properties can be changed during runtime or design time, but some properties may be set only during runtime. For example, the Caption property of the Label control may be set during design time as well as at runtime. During the course of this book, you'll learn about properties that can be changed only during runtime.

Chapter 3, "Programming Building Blocks," explores programming topics such as loops and decision statements. You'll make extensive use of these topics in subsequent chapters. The chapters that follow Chapter 3 discuss special controls, special properties, and special programming topics.

Naming Conventions Used in This Book

In this book, controls are named according to Table 2.3. For example, names of command buttons start with the characters *cmd* (as in cmdMyButton), and the names of text boxes start with the characters *txt* (as in txtMyTextBox).

Table 2.3. Naming conventions for controls.

Control	First 3 Characters of Name	Example
Form	frm	frmMyForm
Check Box	chk	chkSound
Combo box	cbo	cboSelection
Command Button	cmd	cmdExit
Directory List	dir	dirFiles
Drive List	drv	drvSource
File List	fil	filTarget
Frame	fra	fraChoices
Grid	grd	grdTV
Horiz Scroll Bar	hsb	hsbSpeed
Image	img	imgMyImage
Label	lbl	lblInfo
Line	lin	linDiagonal
List Box	lst	lstChapters
Menu	mnu	mnuFile
Option Button	opt	optLevel1
Picture Box	pic	picMyPicture
Shape	shp	shpMyShape
Text Box	txt	txtUserArea
Timer	tmr	tmrMoveIt
Vert Scroll Bar	vsb	vsbSpeed

Assigning names to the controls' Name properties according to Table 2.3 is not a Visual Basic requirement. For example, you assigned the name lblChoice to the Label control that displays information about the user's choice. However, you could have set the Name property of this label to Choice; if you had done this, the last statement in the UpdateLabel procedure would be this:

```
Choice.Caption = Info
```

However, because you set the Name property of the label to lblChoice, the last statement in UpdateLabel looks like this:

```
lblChoice.Caption = Info
```

Note that naming the controls according to Table 2.3 makes the program easy to read. For example, take a look at this statement:

```
Choice.Caption = Info
```

By just looking at this statement, you, or others who read your program, won't be able to tell that Choice is a label control. Therefore, the preceding statement might be misunderstood by someone reading the statement as updating the Caption property of a form whose Name property was set to Choice. On the other hand, look how easy it is to read this statement:

```
lblChoice.Caption = Info
```

Because you preceded the name of the label with *lbl,* someone reading the statement can figure out that lblChoice is a name of a label. Therefore, the statement means: "Update the Caption property of the label (whose Name property was set to lblChoice) to the value of the Info variable."

Statements that Cannot Fit on a Single Line in This Book

A statement can be typed so that it can be spread on more than one line. For example, this statement:

```
MyVariable = 1 + 2 + 3
```

can be typed this way:

```
MyVariable = 1 + _
             2 + 3
```

or this way:

```
MyVariable = 1 _
           + 2 _
           + 3
```

In Visual Basic, you can continue the statement on the following line if you end the current line with a space followed by the underscore (_) character.

> **Note**
>
> You can't "switch lines" in the middle of a string. For example, the statement
>
> ```
> lblMyLabel.Caption "This is my string"
> ```
>
> cannot be written as follows:
>
> ```
> ' This statement has an error in it.
> lblMyLabel.Caption "This is _
>                         my string"
> ```

2

Summary

In this chapter you jumped into the water! Yes, you actually built true Windows programs that include a scroll bar, a text box, a label, a command button, check boxes, and option buttons. You learned how to incorporate these controls into your Visual Basic programs, how to determine their Value properties, and how to insert code in the event procedures that correspond to these controls. In this chapter you also learned how to add a procedure to a form (as you did when you added the UpdateLabel procedure to the frmOptions form).

Q&A

Q The visual implementation portion took me a long time. Any suggestions?

A Yes. Practice. You should be fluent with the visual implementation portion of the programs, and the only way to be fluent is to practice.

Q I can't recognize the icons in the toolbox. Any suggestions?

A Yes. You can place the mouse cursor (without clicking any of the mouse buttons) on the icons of the toolbox window. After a second or two, Visual Basic will display a small yellow rectangle that tells you the icon's purpose.

Quiz

1. A certain statement appears in this book as follows:

```
Info = "ABC" + _
        + "DEF" + "GH"
```

How would you type it in your Visual Basic program?

    a. `Info = "ABC" + "DEF" + "GH"`

    b. Exactly as shown in the book

2. Suppose your program includes a vertical scroll bar with the name vsbVolume. Write a statement that places the thumb of the scroll bar at position 37.

3. Suppose your program includes a horizontal scroll bar with the name hsbDistance. How do you change the Min and Max properties of the scroll bar to 10 and 200, respectively?

Exercise

Enhance the Options program so it accomplishes the following: Currently, when you start the Options program, the text Label1 appears in the lblChoice label. Modify the program so that when you start it, there will be no text in the lblChoice label.

Quiz Answers

1. a or b. Both answers are correct. To spread a line of code on more than one line, type a space followed by the underscore character and continue the code on the next line.

2. To place the thumb of the vsbVolume scroll bar at position 37, use the following statement:

```
vsbVolume.Value = 37
```

3. You can change the Min and Max properties of the scroll bar at design time or runtime.

   Use the following steps to change the properties at design time:

   ☐ Right-click the scroll bar whose properties you want to change.

       As a response, a pop-up menu appears.

   ☐ Select the Properties item from the pop-up menu to display the Properties window of the scroll bar.

   ☐ Select the Min property and change its value to 10.

   ☐ Select the Max property and change its value to 200. Or you can set these properties at runtime by using the following statements:

```
hsbDistance.Min = 10
hsbDistance.Max = 200
```

Exercise Answer

Currently, the value of the Caption property of the lblChoice label is Label1.

☐ Display the Properties window of the lblChoice label and then set the Caption property of the lblChoice label to null (that is, delete the text of the Caption property).

☐ Execute the Options program, and notice that now when you start the program, there is no text in the lblChoice label.

2

Day 3

Programming Building Blocks

This chapter focuses on Visual Basic's programming building blocks. Just like any other programming language, Visual Basic uses programming building blocks such as procedures, functions, If statements, Do loops, variables, and other important programming language concepts.

The Multiply Program

The Multiply program that you'll design and implement next illustrates how to use procedures and functions in your programs.

The Visual Implementation of the Multiply Program

You'll now perform the visual implementation of the Multiply program:

☐ Create the C:\VB5Prg\Ch03 directory. You'll save your work into this directory.

☐ Open a new Standard EXE project, save the form of the project as Multiply.Frm in the C:\VB5Prg\Ch03 directory, and save the project file as Multiply.Vbp in the C:\VB5Prg\Ch03 directory.

☐ Build the frmMultiply form according to Table 3.1. When you complete implementing the form, it should look like the one in Figure 3.1.

Table 3.1. The properties table of the frmMultiply form.

Object	Property	Setting
Form	**Name**	**frmMultiply**
	Caption	The Multiply Program
Text Box	**Name**	**txtResult**
	Text	(Make it empty)
Command Button	**Name**	**cmdExit**
	Caption	E&xit
Command Button	**Name**	**cmdCalculate**
	Caption	&Calculate
Label	**Name**	**lblResult**
	Caption	Result:

Assign the font of your choice to the controls mentioned in Table 3.1.

Figure 3.1.

The frmMultiply form (design mode).

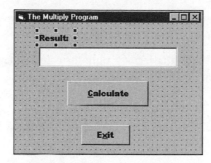

Entering the Code of the Multiply Program

You'll now type the code of the Multiply program:

☐ Double-click in the frmMultiply form to display the code window, set the upper-left list box of the code window to (General), and set the upper-right list box to (Declarations).

☐ Make sure that the general declarations section includes the Option Explicit statement. If it does not include the Option Explicit statement, add it as follows:

```
' All variables MUST be declared.
Option Explicit
```

From now on, you must declare a variable before you can use the variable in your program.

☐ Type the following code in the cmdCalculate_Click() procedure of the frmMultiply form:

```
Private Sub cmdCalculate_Click()
    Multiply 2, 3

End Sub
```

The code that you typed in the cmdCalculate_Click() procedure is automatically executed when the user clicks the Calculate button. This code executes the Multiply procedure. Later in this chapter, you'll add the Multiply procedure.

☐ Type the following code in the cmdExit_Click() procedure of the frmMultiply form:

```
Private Sub cmdExit_Click()
    End
End Sub
```

You'll now add a new procedure to the frmMultiply form and you'll name it Multiply. Here is how you accomplish this:

☐ Double-click the frmMultiply form to display the code window and then select Add Procedure from the Tools menu of Visual Basic.

    Visual Basic responds by displaying the Add Procedure dialog box.

☐ Type Multiply in the Name edit box of the Add Procedure dialog box.

☐ Set the Type of the procedure to Sub.

☐ Set the Scope of the procedure to Public.

Your Add Procedure dialog box should now look like the one shown in Figure 3.2.

Figure 3.2.

Adding the
`Multiply()`
procedure.

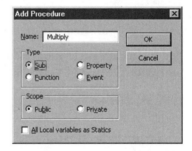

☐ Click the OK button of the Add Procedure dialog box.

    Visual Basic responds by adding the `Multiply()` *procedure to the general area of the frmMultiply form and displaying the code of the* `Multiply()` *procedure as follows:*

```
Public Sub Multiply()
End Sub
```

Now you need to change the first line of the Multiply procedure:

☐ Change the heading (the first line) of the `Multiply()` procedure so that it looks like this:

```
Public Sub Multiply(X As Integer, Y As Integer)
End Sub
```

That is, the default heading line of the procedure is the following:

```
Public Sub Multiply()
```

and you insert code between the parentheses so that it looks like this:

```
Public Sub Multiply(X As Integer, Y As Integer)
```

☐ Type the following code in the `Multiply()` procedure:

```
Public Sub Multiply(X As Integer, Y As Integer)
    Dim Z
    Z = X * Y
    txtResult.Text = Str(Z)
End Sub
```

☐ Select Save Project from the File menu of Visual Basic to save your work.

Executing the Multiply Program

Before going over the code that you typed so far, let's see your code in action:

☐ Execute the Multiply program.

☐ Click the Calculate button.

> *The program responds by displaying the number 6 in the text box. (When you press the Calculate button, the program multiplies 2 by 3 and displays the result in the text box.)*

How the Multiply Program Works

The Multiply program executes the `Multiply()` procedure to multiply two numbers.

The Code of the `cmdCalculate_Click()` Procedure

The `cmdCalculate_Click()` procedure is executed when the user clicks the cmdCalculate button. Here is the code that you already typed in the `cmdCalculate_Click()` procedure:

```
Private Sub cmdCalculate_Click()
    Multiply 2, 3
End Sub
```

The statement in this procedure executes the `Multiply()` procedure with two parameters: 2 and 3. That is, the `Multiply()` procedure needs to know which numbers to multiply. You supply the numbers 2 and 3 as the parameters, so now the `Multiply()` procedure knows that it should multiply 2 by 3.

The Code of the `Multiply()` Procedure

The `Multiply()` procedure has two parameters:

```
Public Sub Multiply(X As Integer, Y As Integer)
    Dim Z
    Z = X * Y
    txtResult.Text = Str(Z)
End Sub
```

The first parameter is called X, and it is declared As Integer. The second parameter is called Y and it is also declared As Integer.

The Multiply() procedure declares a variable called Z and then assigns to it the result of the X*Y multiplication.

The procedure then assigns the value of the Z variable to the Text property of the txtResult text box. The Str() function is used to convert the numeric value of Z to a string.

Note that the UpdateLabel procedure used in the Options program in Chapter 2, "Properties, Controls, and Objects," did not have any parameters, so its first line was as follows:

```
Public Sub UpdateLabel ()
...
...
...
End Sub
```

To execute the UpdateLabel procedure, the following statement was used:

```
UpdateLabel
```

On the other hand, the Multiply() procedure has two parameters (both are integers), so its first line is as follows:

```
Public Sub Multiply (X As Integer, Y As Integer)
...
...
...
End Sub
```

To execute the Multiply() procedure, you used the following statement in the cmdCalculate_Click() procedure:

```
Multiply 2, 3
```

In Visual Basic, you can also execute procedures using the Call statement. For example, you can rewrite the cmdCalculate_Click() procedure as follows:

```
Private Sub cmdCalculate_Click ()
   Call Multiply (2, 3)
End Sub
```

When using the Call statement, you must include the parameters in parentheses. (It doesn't matter which method you use to execute procedures; use whichever method is more convenient for you.)

Note

When you added the Multiply() procedure using the Add Procedure dialog box (refer to Figure 3.2), you set the scope of the procedure to Public. Therefore, Visual Basic declared the Multiply() procedure as public:

```
Public Sub Multiply()
```

If you had set the scope of the Multiply() procedure to Private, Visual Basic would have declared the Multiply() procedure as private:

```
Private Sub Multiply()
```

What's the difference between a public and private procedure? A *private* procedure can be used only by another procedure in the same file. For example, if you had declared the Multiply() procedure as private, then only procedures in the frmMultiply form (the Multiply.Frm file) could use the Multiply() procedure.

On the other hand, a *public* procedure can be used by any procedure in any file of the program. As you'll learn in later chapters in this book, a program can include several files (for example, several forms). When you declare a procedure as public, any procedure in any of the program's files can use the public procedure.

Using a Function in the Multiply Program

The Multiply() procedure is called a procedure because it does not return any value. A function is similar to a procedure, but a function does return a value. Next, you'll write code that demonstrates the use of a function. First, remove the Multiply() procedure from the Multiply program as follows:

☐ Display the code window by double-clicking in a free area in the frmMultiply form.

☐ Locate the Multiply() procedure in the code window. You'll find it in the general declarations section. You locate the Multiply() procedure by setting the upper-left list box to (General) and setting the upper-right list box to Multiply:

☐ Highlight the whole procedure (including its heading and last line) and press the Delete key on your keyboard.

That's it! You don't have the Multiply() procedure in your program anymore.

Use the following steps to add a new function to the Multiply program:

☐ Display the code window of the frmMultiply form.

☐ Select Add Procedure from the Tools menu of Visual Basic.

Visual Basic responds by displaying the Add Procedure dialog box.

☐ Set the Name edit box of the Add Procedure dialog box to Multiply.

☐ In the Add Procedure dialog box, select the Function radio button (because you are now adding a new function).

☐ In the Add Procedure dialog box, select the Public radio button.

Your Add Procedure dialog box should now look like the one in Figure 3.3.

Figure 3.3.

Adding the
Multiply()
function.

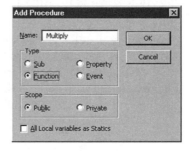

☐ Click the OK button of the Add Procedure dialog box.

Visual Basic responds by adding the Multiply() *function to the general declarations section area of the frmMultiply form and displaying the code window with the* Multiply() *function ready for editing:*

```
Public Function Multiply ()
End Function
```

☐ Change the first line of the Multiply() function so that it will look as follows:

```
Public Function Multiply (X As Integer, Y As Integer)
End Function
```

Now the Multiply() function has two parameters (both parameters are integers).

☐ Add the following code in the Multiply() function:

```
Public Function Multiply (X As Integer, Y As Integer)
    Dim Z
    Z = X * Y
    Multiply = Z
End Function
```

☐ Change the code in the cmdCalculate_Click() procedure so that it will look as follows:

```
Private Sub cmdCalculate_Click ()
    txtResult.Text = Str( Multiply(2, 3) )
End Sub
```

☐ Save the project by selecting Save Project from the File menu.

☐ Execute the Multiply program.

☐ Click the Calculate button.

As you can see, the program behaves in the same manner as it did when the Multiply() procedure was used.

☐ Click the Exit button of the Multiply program to terminate the program.

The Code of the Multiply() Function

The code of the Multiply() function declares the Z variable and assigns the result of the X*Y multiplication to it:

```
Public Function Multiply (X As Integer, Y As Integer)
    Dim Z
    Z = X * Y
    Multiply = Z
End Function
```

The last statement in the Multiply() function assigns the value of the Z variable to the Multiply variable:

```
Multiply = Z
```

Multiply is the returned value of the Multiply() function. That is, because the name of the function is Multiply, you must set the value of a variable called Multiply to the value that the function returns:

```
Multiply = Z
```

Whoever executes the Multiply() function can use the returned value of the Multiply() function, as explained in the next section.

The Code of the cmdCalculate_Click() Procedure

The code of the cmdCalculate_Click() procedure assigns the returned value from the Multiply() function to the Text property of the txtResult text box:

```
Private Sub cmdCalculate_Click ()
    txtResult.Text = Str( Multiply(2, 3) )
End Sub
```

As you can see, using a function is a little bit more complicated than using procedures. However, after using functions for a while, you'll get used to them; and you'll learn to appreciate them, because they make your program easier to read and understand. Consider the following statement:

```
txtResult.Text = Str( Multiply(2, 3) )
```

This statement says the following: "Execute the Multiply() function with two parameters, 2 and 3; convert the returned value of Multiply to a string (using the Str() function); and assign the string to the Text property of the txtResult text box." Therefore, the txtResult text box will have the string "6" in it (because 2*3=6).

Procedures, Functions, and Methods

As discussed earlier in this chapter, the difference between a procedure and a function is that a procedure does not return a value and a function does. In subsequent chapters of this book you will also encounter the term method. A method works similarly to how procedures and functions work. However, usually a method performs some type of functionality on a particular object. For example, the following statement clears the frmMyForm form:

```
frmMyForm.Cls
```

Note that in the preceding statement, Cls is the name of the method. From a programmer's point of view, methods can be seen as procedures or functions with a strange syntax. You'll have a chance to experiment with methods in subsequent chapters of this book.

Decision Makers' Statements

The following sections describe the main programming building blocks that are available in Visual Basic. The rest of this chapter shows you how to write programs that make use of these programming building blocks.

Specifying Controls

As you may have noticed by now, you can refer to a control's property by typing the name of the control, a dot (.), and then the name of the property. For example, this is how you refer to the Text property of the txtResult text box control:

```
txtResult.Text
```

You can also refer to the property by including the name of the form on which the control is located. For example, this is how you can refer to the Text property of the txtResult text box that is located in the frmMultiply form:

```
frmMultiply.txtResult.Text
```

In most cases, you can omit the name of the form (this saves you some typing). However, if your program includes more than one form, you may have to specify the name of the form. You'll see examples of situations where you must include the name of the form later in this book.

The If Statement

You already encountered the If…End If block of statements in Chapter 2. In the following If…End If block, the statements between the If line and the End If line are executed only if A is equal to 1:

```
If A = 1 Then

... This code is executed only if A
... is equal to 1.
End If
```

The following statements illustrate the If…Else…End If statements:

```
If A = 1 Then

    ... This code is executed only if A
    ... is equal to 1.
else
    ... This code is executed only if A
    ... is NOT equal to 1.
End If
```

The Select Case Statement

Select Case is sometimes more convenient to use than the If…Else…End If. The following block of statements illustrates how Select Case works:

```
Select Case X
      Case 0
           ... Write here code that will be ...
           ... executed if X = 0.          ...
           ....................................
      Case 1
           ....................................
           ... Write here code that will be ...
           ... executed if X = 1.          ...
           ....................................
```

```
        Case 2
        ....................................
        ... Write here code that will be ...
        ... executed if X = 2.           ...
End  Select
```

As you can see, Select Case works in a similar way to the If statement.

The Do While...Loop Method

The Do...Loop is used to execute statements until a certain condition is satisfied. The following Do...Loop counts from 1 to 1000:

```
Dim Counter
Counter = 1
Do While Counter < 1001
   Counter = Counter + 1
Loop
```

The variable Counter is initialized to 1, and then the Do While loop starts.

The first line of the loop checks whether the Counter variable is less than 1001. If it is, the statements between the Do While line and the Loop line are executed. In the preceding example, there is only one statement between these lines:

```
Counter = Counter + 1
```

which increases the Counter variable by 1.

The program then returns to the Do While line and examines the value of the Counter variable again. Now the variable Counter is equal to 2, so again the statement between the Do While line and the Loop line is executed. This process continues until Counter equals 1001. In this case, the Do While line finds that Counter is no longer less than 1001, and the program continues with the statement after the Loop line.

The Do...Loop While Method

The statements in the Do While...Loop described in the previous section may or may not be executed. For example, in the following Do While...Loop, the statements between the Do While line and the Loop line are never executed:

```
Dim Counter
Counter = 2000
Do While Counter < 1001
   Counter = Counter + 1
Loop
```

When the program reaches the Do While line, it discovers that Counter is equal to 2000; therefore, the statement between the Do While line and the Loop line is not executed.

Sometimes, you may want the program to enter the loop at least once. In this case, use the Do…Loop While statements:

```
Dim Counter
Counter - 2000
Do
      txtUserArea.Text = Str(Counter)
      Counter = Counter + 1
Loop While Counter < 1001
```

The program executes the statements between the Do line and the Loop While line in any case. Then the program determines whether Counter is less then 1001. If it is, the program again executes the statements between the Do line and the Loop While line.

When the program discovers that the Counter variable is no longer less than 1001, it continues by executing the statement that appears after the Loop While line.

The following Do…Loop While method counts from 50 to 300:

```
Dim Counter
Counter = 50
Do
      Counter = Counter + 1
Loop While Counter < 301
```

The For…Next **Method**

The For…Next loop is another way to make loops in Visual Basic. The following loop counts from 1 to 100:

```
Dim I
For I =1 to 100 Step 1

   txtMyTextArea.Text = Str(I)

Next
```

To count from 1 to 100 in steps of 2, you can use the following For…Next loop:

```
Dim I
For I =1 to 100 Step 2

   txtMyTextArea.Text = Str(I)

Next
```

This loop counts as follows: 1,3,5,….

If you omit the Step word, Visual Basic uses Step 1 as the default. So the following two For…Next blocks produce the same results:

```
Dim I
For I =1 to 100 Step 1

    txtMyTextArea.Text = Str(I)

Next


Dim I
For I =1 to 100

    txtMyTextArea.Text = Str(I)

Next
```

The Exit For Statement

You can exit a For…Next loop by using the Exit For statement as follows:

```
Dim I
For I = 1 To 1000
    txtResult.Text = Str(I)
    If I = 500 Then
        Exit For
    End If
Next
```

The preceding code counts in increments of 1, starting from 1. In each repetition of the loop, I is increased by 1.

When I equals 500, the condition of the inner If statement (If I=500) is satisfied; as a result, the Exit For statement is executed, which terminates the For…Next loop.

In other words, the inner If statement causes the For loop to terminate at I=500. (Without the inner If statement, the For loop would terminate when I=1000.)

The Exit Do Statement

The Do While…Loop may be terminated by using the Exit Do statement as follows:

```
Dim I
I = 1
Do While I < 10001
    txtResult.Text = Str(I)
    I = I + 2
    If I > 500 Then
        Exit Do
    End If
Loop
```

The preceding loop counts in increments of 2, starting from 1. When I is greater than 500, Do While...Loop terminates.

Oops...

Occasionally, you might make errors like the one shown in the following loop:

```
Dim I
I = 1
Do While I < 10001
   txtResult.Text = Str(I)
   If I > 500 Then
      Exit Do
   End If
Loop
```

That is, you might forget to include the following statement:

```
I = I + 2
```

In the preceding Do While...Loop, the Counter variable remains at its current value (Counter = 1), because you forgot to increment its value. In this case, the program stays in the loop forever, because I is always less than 10001 and is never greater than 500. In fact I is always equal to 1.

To get out of the loop, press Ctrl+Break to stop the program.

The With Statement

The With statement enables you to set several properties of an object without typing the name of the object for each property.

For example, the following With statement sets several properties of the cmdMyButton pushbutton:

```
With cmdMyButton
    .Height = 300
    .Width  = 900
    .Caption = "&My Button"
End With
```

This With statement has the same effect as the following statements:

```
cmdMyButton.Height = 300
cmdMyButton.Width = 900
cmdMyButton.Caption = "&My Button"
```

As you can see, the With statement saves you typing time. It lets you write code that sets several properties of a control without typing the name of the control for each property. You type the name of the control only at the first line of the With statement.

The Sum Program

You'll now design and implement a program called the Sum program.

The Sum program allows the user to select a number and then adds all the integers from 1 to the selected number. For example, if the user selects the number 5, the program makes the following calculation:

1 + 2 + 3 + 4 + 5 = 15

and displays the result.

As another example, if the user selects the number 4, the program makes the following calculation:

1 + 2 + 3 + 4 = 10

and displays the result.

The Visual Implementation of the Sum Program

You'll now perform the visual implementation of the Sum Program.

☐ Open a new Standard EXE project, save the form of the project as Sum.Frm in the C:\VB5Prg\Ch03 directory, and save the project file as Sum.Vbp in the C:\VB5Prg\CH03 directory.

☐ Build the frmSum form according to Table 3.2.

Once you complete implementing the frmSum form, it should look like the one in Figure 3.4.

Table 3.2. The properties table of the frmSum form.

Object	Property	Setting
Form	**Name**	**frmSum**
	Caption	The Sum Program
Command Button	**Name**	**cmdExit**
	Caption	E&xit
Text Box	**Name**	**txtResult**
	Alignment	2-Center
	MultiLine	-1-True
	Enabled	0-False
	Text	(Make it empty)

Object	Property	Setting
Vert. Scroll Bar	**Name**	**vsbNum**
	Max	500
	Min	1
	Value	1
Command Button	**Name**	**cmdSumIt**
	Caption	&Sum It
Label	**Name**	**lblNum**
	Caption	Selected Number: 1

You set the Enabled property of the txtResult text box to False. This means that the user will not be able to type text in the text box. Indeed, you want the program to update the string in the text box, but you do not want the user to be able to type text in the text box.

Figure 3.4.

The frmSum form.

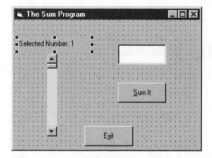

Entering the Code of the Sum Program

You'll now type the code of the Sum program:

☐ Make sure that the Option Explicit statement resides in the general declarations section of the frmSum form as follows:

```
' All variables MUST be declared.
Option Explicit
```

☐ Type the following code in the cmdExit_Click() procedure of the frmSum form:

```
Private Sub cmdExit_Click ()
    End
End Sub
```

☐ Type the following code in the `cmdSumIt_Click()` procedure of the frmSum form:

```
Private Sub cmdSumIt_Click ()
    Dim I
    Dim R
    For I = 1 To vsbNum.Value Step 1
        R = R + I
    Next
    txtResult.Text = Str(R)
End Sub
```

☐ Type the following code in the `vsbNum_Change()` procedure of the frmSum form:

```
Private Sub vsbNum_Change ()
    lblNum = "Selected number: " + Str(vsbNum.Value)
End Sub
```

☐ Type the following code in the `vsbNum_Scroll()` procedure of the frmSum form:

```
Private Sub vsbNum_Scroll ()
    vsbNum_Change
End Sub
```

☐ Select Save Project from the File menu of Visual Basic to save your work.

Executing the Sum Program

Before going over the code that you typed in the various procedures of the frmSum form, let's execute the Sum program:

☐ Execute the Sum program.

☐ Select a number by clicking the arrow icons of the vertical scroll bar or by dragging the thumb of the scroll bar.

   The program responds by displaying the selected number.

☐ Click the Sum It button.

   The program responds by making the calculations and displaying the result in the text box (see Figure 3.5).

For example, select the number 5 with the scroll bar and click the Sum It button. The program should display the number 15 (that is, 1+2+3+4+5=15).

☐ Terminate the Sum program by clicking its Exit button.

Figure 3.5.

The Sum program.

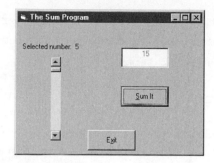

How the Sum Program Works

The Sum program uses a For...Next loop to perform the calculations.

The Code of the cmdSumIt_Click() Procedure

The cmdSumIt_Click() procedure is executed when the user clicks the cmdSumIt button:

```
Private Sub cmdSumIt_Click ()

    Dim I
    Dim R

    For I = 1 To vsbNum.Value Step 1
        R = R + I
    Next

    txtResult.Text = Str(R)

End Sub
```

The procedure declares two variables, I and R.

The For...Next loop then calculates the sum:

```
1 + 2 + 3 + ...+ vsbNum.Value
```

Initially, the R variable is equal to 0, because Visual Basic initializes variables to 0 at the time of the declaration. Some programmers like to include the following redundant statement:

```
R = 0
```

before the For statement to make the code easier to read.

The last statement in this procedure updates the Text property of the text box with the content of the R variable.

The Code of the `vsbNum_Change()` Procedure

The `vsbNum_Change()` procedure is executed when the user changes the scroll bar position:

```
Private Sub vsbNum_Change ()

    lblNum = "Selected number: " + Str(vsbNum.Value)

End Sub
```

The procedure updates the Caption property of the lblNum label with the Value property of the scroll bar so the user can read the position of the scroll bar.

Note that this statement:

```
lblNum = "Selected number: " + Str(vsbNum.Value)
```

is the same as this statement:

```
lblNum.Caption = "Selected number: " + Str(vsbNum.Value)
```

That is, when you set a label control to a value without specifying a property name, Visual Basic assumes that you want to set the value of the label's Caption property, because the Caption property is the default property for a label control.

Like the label control, other controls also have a default property. For example, the default property of the Text Box control is the Text property. Therefore, this statement:

```
txtMyTextBox = "Hello"
```

is the same as this statement:

```
txtMyTextBox.Text = "Hello"
```

As another example, this statement:

```
txtHerTextBox = "Have a nice day"
```

is the same as this statement:

```
txtHerTextBox.Text = "Have a nice day"
```

Again, the default property of the Text Box control is Text.

The Code of the `vsbNum_Scroll()` Procedure

The `vsbNum_Scroll()` procedure is executed when the user drags the thumb of the scroll bar:

```
Private Sub vsbNum_Scroll ()
    vsbNum_Change
End Sub
```

This procedure executes the vsbNum_Change() procedure, so while the user drags the thumb of the scroll bar, the vsbNum_Change() procedure is executed (and you already typed code in the vsbNum_Change() procedure that updates the label with the Value property of the scroll bar).

The Timer Program

You'll now implement the Timer program. The Timer program illustrates the concept of variable visibility. This program also introduces a new control: the Timer control.

The Visual Implementation of the Timer Program

The Timer program uses the Timer control. To see which icon in the toolbox window represents the Timer control, see Figure 3.6. When you place the mouse cursor on the Timer icon (without clicking any of the mouse buttons), a yellow rectangle appears with the text Timer in it. This way, you can verify that you located the icon of the Timer control in the toolbox window. Note that the locations of the icons in your toolbox window may be different than the one shown in Figure 3.6.

Figure 3.6.
The icon of the Timer control in the toolbox window.

☐ Open a new Standard EXE project, save the form of the project as Timer.Frm in the C:\VB5Prg\Ch03 directory, and save the project file as Timer.Vbp in the C:\VB5Prg\Ch03 directory.

☐ Build the frmTimer form according to Table 3.3.

When you complete implementing the frmTimer form, it should look like the one in Figure 3.7.

Table 3.3. The properties table of the frmTimer form.

Object	Property	Setting
Form	**Name**	**frmTimer**
	Caption	The Timer Program
Command Button	**Name**	**cmdExit**
	Caption	E&xit
Timer	**Name**	**tmrTimer**
	Enabled	True
	Interval	2000

Figure 3.7.

The frmTimer form.

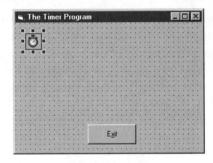

Entering the Code of the Timer Program

You'll now type the code of the Timer program.

☐ Make sure that the general declarations section of the frmTimer form as the Option Explicit statement in it as follows:

```
' All variables MUST be declared.
Option Explicit
```

☐ Type the following code in the cmdExit_Click() procedure of the frmTimer form:

```
Private Sub cmdExit_Click ()

    End

End Sub
```

☐ Type the following code in the `tmrTimer_Timer()` procedure of the frmTimer form:

```
Private Sub tmrTimer_Timer ()

    Beep

End Sub
```

☐ Select Save project from the File menu of Visual Basic to save your work.

Executing the Timer Program

Before going over the code that you typed, let's execute the Timer program:

☐ Execute the Timer program.

As you can hear, the Timer program beeps every 2 seconds. During the execution of the Timer program, the Timer control icon is not shown. As you'll see during the course of this book, some controls are invisible during runtime.

☐ Click the Exit button of the Timer program to terminate the program.

How the Timer Program Works

The Timer program uses the Timer control. The program automatically executes the `tmrTimer_Timer()` procedure every 2000 milliseconds (every 2 seconds).

The Code of the `tmrTimer_Timer()` Procedure

You set the Interval property of tmrTimer to 2000 at design time, so the `tmrTimer_Timer()` procedure is executed automatically every 2000 milliseconds (2 seconds):

```
Private Sub tmrTimer_Timer ()
   Beep
End Sub
```

Therefore, every 2 seconds the PC beeps.

Because the Timer control icon is not shown during the execution of the program, its position in the form is not important, and you may place it anywhere in the form.

Enhancing the Timer Program

You'll now enhance the Timer program:

☐ Add a CommandButton in the frmTimer form, as shown in Figure 3.8. The command
button should have the following properties: the Name property should be
cmdEnableDisable, and the Caption property should be &Enable.

Figure 3.8.

*Adding the Enable
button to the
frmTimer form.*

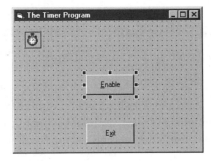

☐ Modify the general declarations section of the frmTimer form so that it will look as follows:

```
' All variables MUST be declared.
Option Explicit
' Declare the gKeepTrack variable
Dim gKeepTrack
```

The general declarations section of the frmTimer form should now look like the one in Figure
3.9. Note that due to a possible small bug in the editor program, you may have to increase
the area of the general declaration area by clicking the mouse at the *beginning* of the Option
Explicit line and then pressing the Enter key a few times on your keyboard. This will cause
the editor to insert a few new lines in the general declarations section. Now that you have a
few empty lines in the general declarations section, you can insert additional code in the
general Declarations area.

Figure 3.9.

*The general declara-
tions section of the
frmTimer form.*

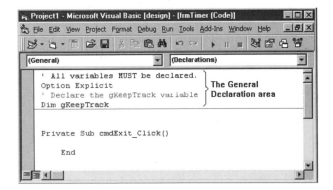

☐ Modify the `tmrTimer_Timer()` procedure so that it looks like the following:

```
Private Sub tmrTimer_Timer ()
    ' If the gKeepTrack variable is equal to 1,
    ' then beep.
    If gKeepTrack = 1 Then
        Beep
    End If

End Sub
```

☐ Add the following code in the `cmdEnableDisable_Click()` procedure:

```
Private Sub cmdEnableDisable_Click ()

    If gKeepTrack = 1 Then
        gKeepTrack = 0
        cmdEnableDisable.Caption = "&Enable"
    Else
        gKeepTrack = 1
        cmdEnableDisable.Caption = "&Disable"
    End If
```

☐ Select Save Project from the File menu of Visual Basic to save your work.

Executing the Timer Program

Before going over the code of the Timer program, let's see the code in action:

☐ Execute the Timer program.

The program does not beep every 2 seconds.

☐ To enable the beeping, click the Enable button.

As a response, the caption of the Enable button changes to Disable, and the program now beeps every 2 seconds (see Figure 3.10).

Figure 3.10.

The cmdEnableDisable button now has the Disable caption.

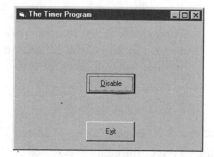

☐ Click the Disable button.

The caption of the Disable button changes back to Enable, and the program does not beep every 2 seconds.

☐ You can keep clicking the Enable/Disable button to enable or disable the beeping.

☐ Click the Exit button to terminate the program.

The Code of the General Declarations Section of the frmTimer Form

The code of the general declarations area of the frmTimer form includes the declaration of the gKeepTrack variable:

```
' Declare the gKeepTrack variable
Dim gKeepTrack
```

Why do you declare this variable in the general declarations section? You want this variable to be visible by all the procedures of the frmTimer form. If you declare this variable in the tmrTimer_Timer() procedure, you can access this variable from within the code of the tmrTimer_Timer() procedure, but you can't access it from any other procedure. By declaring this variable in the general declarations section of the frmTimer form, you make the variable accessible by all the procedures and functions that exist in the frmTimer form.

Note that the first letter of the gKeepTrack variable is g to signify that the gKeepTrack variable is declared in the general declarations section of the form. Including the g is not a Visual Basic requirement, but it is a good programming habit.

Note

> It's a good programming habit to make the first letter of a variable declared in the general declarations section g, because the program's code will be easier to understand.
>
> Whoever goes through the code of the form and encounters a variable whose first letter is g, such as gMyVariable, knows immediately that it is declared in the general declarations section of the form and is accessible by all the procedures of the form.

The Code of the tmrTimer_Timer() Procedure

The tmrTimer_Timer()procedure is executed every 2 seconds because you set the Interval property of the tmrTimer control to 2000:

```
Private Sub tmrTimer_Timer ()

  ' If the gKeepTrack variable is equal to 1,
  ' then beep.
  If gKeepTrack = 1 Then
     Beep
  End If

End Sub
```

If the variable gKeepTrack is equal to 1, the statement between the If line and the End If line is executed, and the Beep statement is executed. If, however, the variable gKeepTrack is not equal to 1, the Beep statement is not executed. Note that the gKeepTrack variable is not declared in this procedure; nevertheless, this procedure recognizes this variable because it was declared in the general declarations section of the form.

When you start the program, the variable gKeepTrack is created and its value is initialized to 0. (In other words, when you start the Timer program, the program creates the gKeepTrack variable, and it initials the value of this variable to 0.)

The Code of the cmdEnableDisable_Click() Procedure

The cmdEnableDisable_Click() procedure is executed when the user clicks the cmdEnableDisable button:

```
Private Sub cmdEnableDisable_Click ()

  If gKeepTrack = 1 Then
     gKeepTrack = 0
     cmdEnableDisable.Caption = "&Enable"
  Else
     gKeepTrack = 1
     cmdEnableDisable.Caption = "&Disable"
  End If

End Sub
```

If the current value of the gKeepTrack variable is 1, the statements between the If line and the Else line change the value of gKeepTrack to 0 and change the Caption property of the cmdEnableDisable button to &Enable.

If, however, the current value of the gKeepTrack variable is not equal to 1, the statements between the Else line and the End If line are executed. These statements toggle the value of the gKeepTrack variable to 1 and change the Caption property of the cmdEnableDisable button to &Disable.

The cmdEnableDisable_Click() procedure recognizes the gKeepTrack variable because this variable was declared in the general declarations section of the frmTimer form.

Modifying the Timer Program Again

The gKeepTrack variable was used to demonstrate how a variable is declared in the general declarations section so it can be accessed by all the procedures of the form. However, you can implement the Timer program without using the gKeepTrack variable. Use the following steps to see how this is accomplished:

☐ Remove the declaration of the gKeepTrack variable from the general declarations section of the frmTimer form (that is, the program will not use this variable). The only code that should now be in the general declarations section of the form is this:

```
' All variables MUST be declared.
Option Explicit
```

During the visual implementation of the frmTimer form, you were instructed to set the Enabled property of the tmrTimer control to True. Now change the setting of this property as follows:

☐ Change the Enabled property of the tmrTimer control to False.

When the Enabled property of the Timer control is set to False, the tmrTimer_Timer() procedure is not executed.

☐ Change the cmdEnableDisable_Click()procedure so that it looks like the following:

```
Private Sub cmdEnableDisable_Click ()

    If tmrTimer.Enabled = True Then
        tmrTimer.Enabled = False
        cmdEnableDisable.Caption = "&Enable"
    Else
        tmrTimer.Enabled = True
        cmdEnableDisable.Caption = "&Disable"
    End If

End Sub
```

☐ Change the tmrTimer_Timer() procedure so that it looks like the following:

```
Private Sub tmrTimer_Timer ()

    Beep

End Sub
```

☐ Save the project.

Executing the Timer Program

Let's see your code in action:

☐ Execute the Timer program and verify that it works the same way it worked when the gKeepTrack variable was used.

☐ Terminate the program by clicking its Exit button.

The Code of the tmrTimer_Timer() Procedure

The code of the tmrTimer_Timer() procedure is executed every 2000 milliseconds (2 seconds) if the Enabled property of the tmrTimer control is set to True. (Recall that the interval of the timer is 2000 milliseconds because in design time you set the Interval property of the tmrTimer control to 2000.)

At design time you set the Enabled property of the tmrTimer timer to False, so when you start the program, the tmrTimer_Timer() procedure is not executed every 2 seconds.

If the Enabled property of the tmrTimer control is set to True, the tmrTimer_Timer() procedure is executed, and the PC beeps every 2 seconds:

```
Private Sub tmrTimer_Timer ()

    Beep

End Sub
```

The Code of the cmdEnableDisable_Click() Procedure

The cmdEnableDisable_Click() procedure is executed when the user clicks the cmdEnableDisable button:

```
Private Sub cmdEnableDisable_Click ()

    If tmrTimer.Enabled = True Then
       tmrTimer.Enabled = False
       cmdEnableDisable.Caption = "&Enable"
    Else
       tmrTimer.Enabled = True
       cmdEnableDisable.Caption = "&Disable"
    End If

End Sub
```

The If statement checks the value of the Enabled property of the timer control. If the timer is enabled, the statements between the If line and the Else line are executed. These statements set the Enabled property of the timer to False and change the Caption property of the cmdEnableDisable button to Enable.

If, however, the current value of the Enabled property of the timer control is not True, the statements between the `Else` line and the `End If` line are executed. These statements set the Enabled property of the timer to True and change the Caption property of the cmdEnableDisable button to Disable.

Many Windows programs use the preceding technique for changing the Caption of the button according to the current status of the program.

> **Note**
>
> The Timer program uses a single button (the cmdEnableDisable button) to perform enable operations as well as disable operations.
>
> When the Timer is enabled, the caption of the button is Disable (so the user can click the button to disable the timer).
>
> When the Timer is disabled, the caption of the button is Enable (so the user can click the button to enable the timer).
>
> When the window of a program has many controls in it (for example, buttons, scrollbars, and text boxes), the user may get confused by all the controls that appear in the window. It's better to minimize the number of controls in the window—for example, by using the same button to perform two operations, such as enable/disable.
>
> Of course, you do not want to combine buttons that have completely different roles in the program. For example, do not combine the Exit button with the Enable/Disable button.

Summary

This chapter discusses the decision-maker statements of Visual Basic and the various loop statements. These statements are considered the programming building blocks of Visual Basic.

This chapter also focuses on the Timer control, the visibility (accessibility) of the variables, and procedures, functions, and methods.

Q&A

Q **The Timer program illustrates that I can run the program with or without the gKeepTrack variable declared in the general declarations section. Which way is preferred?**

A Generally speaking, designing a program without using variables declared in the general declarations section is the preferred way, because the program is easier to read and understand.

However, when writing programs, if you find that it is necessary to use such variables, use them. The problem with such variables is that if you have many variables declared in the general declarations section, you might lose track of their purpose, and the program will become difficult to read and understand.

Quiz

1. What's wrong with the following If…End If statement:

```
If B = 3
    B = 2
End If
```

2. Suppose that the variable MyVariable is currently equal to 3. What will be the contents of the lblMyLabel label after the following code is executed:

```
Select Case MyVariable
        Case 0
        lblMyLabel.Caption = "Hi, Have a nice day"
        Case 1
        lblMyLabel.Caption = ""
        Case 2
        lblMyLabel.Caption = "Are you having fun?"
        Case 3
        lblMyLabel.Caption = "Good-bye"
        Case 4
        lblMyLabel.Caption = "Good morning"
End  Select
```

3. What is wrong with the following function?

```
Public Function HowMuch (X As Integer)

    Dim Z
    Z = X * 100

End Function
```

Exercises

1. Change the Sum program so that it uses the Do While...Loop statements instead of the For...Next loop.

2. Enhance the Sum program as follows:

   Place a new CommandButton in the frmSum form, and set the following properties for this CommandButton: the Name should be cmdSqr, and the Caption should be &Square Root.

   Now add code that accomplishes the following: When the user clicks the Square Root button, the program should calculate and display the square root of the number selected by the scroll bar.

 Tip

> Use the Sqr() function of Visual Basic to calculate the square root of a number.

Quiz Answers

1. You must include the Then word. The correct syntax is as follows:

```
If B = 3 Then
    B = 2
End If
```

2. Because the current value of MyVariable is equal to 3, the statements under Case 3 are executed. In this example, there is only one statement under the Case 3 line:

```
Case 3
lblMyLabel.Caption = "Good-bye"
```

   The contents of the label will be Good-bye.

3. The HowMuch() function should look as follows:

```
Public Function HowMuch (X As Integer)
    Dim Z
    Z = X * 100
    HowMuch = Z
End Function
```

   That is, before terminating the HowMuch() function, you must assign the return value to a variable that has the same name as the function. The HowMuch() function must include the following statement:

```
HowMuch = Z
```

Exercise Answers

1. Change the cmdSumIt_Click() procedure so that it looks like the following:

```
Private Sub cmdSumIt_Click ()

    Dim I
    Dim R

    I = 1
    Do While I <= vsbNum.Value
        R = R + I
        I = I + 1
    Loop

    txtResult.Text = Str(R)

End Sub
```

The procedure initializes the variable I to 1 and starts the Do While…Loop. The statements between the Do While line and the Loop line are executed as long as I is less than or equal to (<=) the Value property of the vsbNum scroll bar.

2. Use the following steps:

   ☐ Add a CommandButton to the form.

   ☐ Set the Name property of the CommandButton to cmdSqr.

   ☐ Set the Caption property of the CommandButton to &Square Root.

   ☐ Add the following code in the cmdSqr_Click() procedure:

   ```
   Private Sub cmdSqr_Click ()

       txtResult.Text = Str( Sqr(vsbNum.Value) )

   End Sub
   ```

   ☐ Save the project.

   ☐ Execute the Sum program.

   ☐ Select the number 4 with the scroll bar.

   ☐ Click the Square Root button.

   The program responds by displaying the result (square root of 4 is 2).

   ☐ Terminate the program by clicking its Exit button.

3

The `cmdSqr_Click()` procedure is executed when the user clicks the Square Root button. The statement in this procedure executes the `Sqr()` function:

```
txtResult.Text = Str( Sqr(vsbNum.Value) )
```

The returned value of the `Sqr()` function is assigned to the Text property of the txtResult text box. The `Sqr()` function returns the square root of the number specified as its parameter. Note that the `Str()` function is used to convert the returned value of the `Sqr()` function from numeric to a string.

The `Sqr()` function is one of the many functions that Visual Basic includes, so you don't have to write the `Sqr()` function yourself.

Week 1

Day 4

The Mouse

Most Windows programs make heavy use of the mouse. In this chapter you'll learn how to detect and use events that occur in response to mouse movements, mouse clicking, and combining mouse clicking and keyboard pressing. You'll also learn about dragging and dropping objects with the mouse.

The Move Program

The Move program illustrates how to design programs that let the user move objects in the window of the program by using the mouse.

The Visual Implementation of the Move Program

As usual, you'll start with the visual implementation of the program:

☐ Create the C:\VB5Prg\Ch04 directory. You will save your work into this directory.

☐ Start a new Standard EXE project.

☐ Save the form of the project as Move.Frm in the C:\VB5Prg\Ch04 directory, and save the project file as Move.Vbp in the C:\VB5Prg\Ch04 directory.

☐ Build the frmMove form of the Move program according to Table 4.1. When you complete building the form, it should look like the one in Figure 4.1.

Table 4.1 instructs you to place three Image controls in the frmMove form. The icon of the Image control in the toolbox window is shown in Figure 4.2. When you place the mouse cursor (without clicking any of the mouse buttons) on the icon of the Image control in the toolbox window, a yellow rectangle appears with the text Image in it.

Figure 4.1.

*The frmMove form
(design mode).*

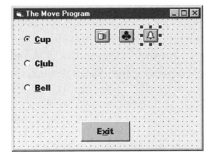

Figure 4.2.

*The icon of the Image
control in the toolbox
window.*

Table 4.1. The properties table of the Move program.

Object	Property	Setting
Form	Name	frmMove
	BackColor	Yellow
	Caption	The Move Program
Command Button	Name	cmdExit
	Caption	E&xit
Option Button	Name	optCup
	BackColor	Yellow
	Caption	&Cup
	Value	True
Option Button	Name	optClub
	BackColor	Yellow
	Caption	C&lub
Option Button	Name	optBell
	BackColor	Yellow
	Caption	&Bell
Image	Name	imgCup
	Picture	Cup.Bmp
Image	Name	imgClub
	Picture	Club.Bmp
Image	Name	imgBell
	Picture	Bell.Bmp

When you use Table 4.1, remember the following:

■ When you place the controls in the form, set their Font properties to the font of your choice.

■ Table 4.1 instructs you to set the Picture properties of the Image controls to various BMP files. Depending on the particular version of your Visual Basic, these BMP picture files may or may not have been supplied with your Visual Basic package. You may find these BMP files in one of the subdirectories under the directory where your Visual Basic was installed. Most likely, you'll find these BMP files in the \Bitmaps subdirectory. If you can't find these BMP files (because these

BMP files were not supplied with your Visual Basic package), use your own BMP picture files. Simply use the Paint program that comes with Windows to paint your own small BMP pictures, and save the pictures as BMP files.

Entering the Code of the Move Program

You'll now type the code of the Move program. As usual, let's start with the general declarations section of the form:

☐ Make sure that the Option Explicit statement resides in the general declarations section of the frmMove form as follows:

```
' All variables MUST be declared.
Option Explicit
```

☐ Type the following code in the Form_MouseDown() procedure:

```
Private Sub Form_MouseDown(Button As Integer, _
                           Shift As Integer, _
                           X As Single, _
                           Y As Single)

    ' Move the checked object to coordinate X,Y
    If optBell.Value = True Then
       imgBell.Move X, Y
    ElseIf optClub.Value = True Then
       imgClub.Move X, Y
    Else
       imgCup.Move X, Y
    End If

End Sub
```

☐ Type the following code in the cmdExit_Click() procedure:

```
Private Sub cmdExit_Click()

    End

End Sub
```

☐ Select Save Project from the File menu to save your work.

Executing the Move Program

Before going over the code that you typed, let's execute the Move program:

☐ Execute the Move program.

As shown in Figure 4.1, the Move program displays three images (a cup, a club, and a bell), and three option buttons are labeled Cup, Club, and Bell.

When you click the mouse in the window of the program, one of the images moves to the location where the mouse is clicked. You select which image moves by selecting one of the option buttons.

For example, if the bell's option button is currently checked, clicking the mouse anywhere in a free area of the form moves the bell image to the position where the mouse was clicked (see Figure 4.3).

☐ Terminate the Move program by clicking its Exit button.

Figure 4.3.

The Move program, after you move the bell.

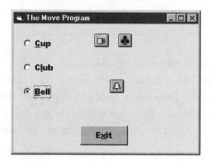

How the Move Program Works

During the discussion of the Move program, you'll encounter the term form coordinates, so the discussion of the Move program starts with this topic.

Form Coordinates

A form's coordinates may be specified in various units set by the ScaleMode property of the form. The default measurement unit that Visual Basic sets for this property is a twip (there are 1440 twips in 1 inch).

Note

The ScaleMode property may be set to any of the following units:

Twips (there are 1440 twips in 1 inch)

Points (there are 72 points in 1 inch)

Pixels (the number of inches per inch depends on your monitor's resolution)

Character (a character is defined as a rectangle with a width of 120 twips and a height of 240 twips)

Inches

Millimeters

Centimeters

The origin of the form coordinate system is defined by the ScaleTop and ScaleLeft properties of the form. The default value that Visual Basic assigns to the ScaleTop and ScaleLeft properties is 0. This means that the upper-left corner of the form's area has the coordinate 0,0. As you know, a form has borders and a title bar. However, the term form's area means the usable area of the form, which doesn't include its borders or title bar.

In short, when the ScaleTop property of the form is equal to 0 and the ScaleLeft property of the form is equal to 0, the upper-left corner of the form is at coordinates x=0, y=0. As you move to the right, the x coordinate increases. As you move downward, the y coordinate increases (see Figure 4.4).

Figure 4.4.

The Form's coordinates when ScaleTop=0 and ScaleLeft=0.

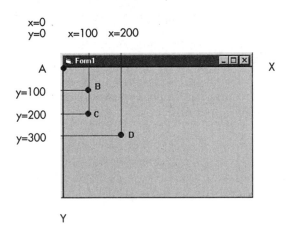

In Figure 4.4, point A is at coordinates x=0, y=0. Point B is at coordinates x=100, y=100. Point C is at coordinates x=100, y=20. Point D is at coordinates x=200, y=300.

> **Note**
>
> A form (window) includes the title of the window, the edges of the window, and the area that is enclosed by the title and edges of the window, which is called the client's area.

The Code of the cmdExit_Click() Procedure

When the user clicks the Exit button, the cmdExit_Click() procedure is executed. The End statement in this procedure causes the program to terminate:

```
Private Sub cmdExit_Click()

    End

End Sub
```

The Code of the Form_MouseDown() Procedure

Mouse devices may have one to three buttons. When you push any of the mouse buttons while the mouse cursor is in the client's area, the Form_MouseDown() procedure is automatically executed.

> **Note**
>
> *Pushing* the mouse button means pressing down the mouse button. *Clicking* the mouse means pushing and then releasing the mouse button. The Form_MouseDown() procedure is executed when you push the mouse button (while the mouse cursor is in the client's area). That is, the procedure is executed even before you release the mouse button.

Because the client's area doesn't include its title bar, this procedure is not executed if the mouse is clicked in the title bar of the window. The procedure is executed only if the mouse button is clicked in a free area of the client's area. For example, if the mouse button is clicked in the area of the option buttons or the Exit button, the Form_MouseDown() procedure is not executed.

The Parameters of the Form_MouseDown() Procedure

The Form_MouseDown() procedure has four parameters: Button, Shift, X, and Y. These parameters contain information about the mouse's condition when the mouse button is clicked:

```
Private Sub Form_MouseDown(Button As Integer, _
                           Shift As Integer, _
                           X As Single, _
                           Y As Single)
...
...
...
End Sub
```

(In your code window, you see the first line of the Form_MouseDown() procedure spread over a single line, not over four lines as in the preceding code. We spread the first line of the procedure over four lines because the line is too long to fit on this page width.)

The first parameter of the Form_MouseDown() procedure is an integer called Button. The value of this parameter indicates whether the pressed button was the left, right, or middle mouse button. The Move program doesn't care which button was clicked, so the value of this parameter is not used in the procedure.

The second parameter of the Form_MouseDown() procedure is an integer called Shift. The value of this parameter indicates whether the mouse button was simultaneously with the Shift key, Ctrl key, or Alt key. A better name for this parameter would be ShiftCtrlAlt, but you have to work with the name the designers of Visual Basic decided to use. The Move program doesn't care whether the mouse button was pressed simultaneously with any of these keys, so the value of the Shift parameter is not used in the procedure.

The third and fourth parameters of the Form_MouseDown() procedure are the X and Y variables. These variables contain the coordinates of the mouse cursor at the time the mouse button was pressed. Because the Form_MouseDown() procedure is automatically executed when the mouse button is pressed while the mouse cursor is in the client's area, the X,Y coordinates are referenced to the form. For example, suppose that the ScaleMode property of the frmMove form is set to twips, and the ScaleTop and ScaleLeft properties of the frmMove form are both set to 0. When the user presses any of the mouse buttons in the client's area and the Form_MouseDown() procedure reports that X=0 and Y=0, this means that the mouse button was pressed while the mouse cursor was on the upper-left corner of the client's area. X=10, Y=20 means that the mouse button was pressed while the mouse cursor was 10 twips from the left side of the form and 20 twips from the top of the form, and so on.

The If…Else **Statements of the** Form_MouseDown() **Procedure**

The If…Else statements in the Form_MouseDown() procedure check which option button is currently selected. For example, if the currently selected option button is the Bell button, the first If condition:

```
If optBell.Value = True Then
```

is met, and this statement:

```
imgBell.Move X, Y
```

is executed. This statement uses the Move method to move the bell image from its current position to the X,Y coordinate. X,Y are the coordinates of the mouse cursor when the mouse button was pressed. In short, the imgBell image will move to the point that has the X,Y coordinates. (Imagine that a rectangle encloses the Image control. The Move method moves the Image control so that the upper-left corner of the rectangle has the X, Y coordinates after the move.)

The Move **Method**

You use the Move method to move objects. Forms and controls are the objects you can move with the Move method.

To move the Cup object from its current location to a new location that has the X,Y coordinate, use this statement:

```
imgCup.Move X, Y
```

Note

After using this statement:

```
imgCup.Move X, Y
```

the new location of the upper-left corner of the image is at coordinate X,Y.

To move the image so that its center has the X,Y coordinate, use the following statement:

```
imgCup.Move(X-imgCup.Width/2), _
          (Y-imgCup.Height/2)
```

4

Important Information About Option Buttons

You have completed the Move program. However, there is one more thing you need to know about the option buttons.

In the Move program, you have three option buttons, but only one option button can be selected at any time. Therefore, you can select the cup, the bell, or the club, but you cannot select, for example, the cup and the bell together.

However, sometimes you'll need to have two or more groups of option buttons in the same form. You can add a second group of option buttons to the frmMove form as follows:

☐ Double-click the icon of the Frame control in the toolbox window. (See Figure 4.5 for the location of the Frame control's icon in the toolbox window.) When you place the mouse cursor (without clicking any of the mouse buttons) on the icon of the Frame control in the toolbox window, a yellow rectangle appears with the text Frame in it.

Visual Basic responds by placing the Frame control in the frmMove form.

Figure 4.5.

The icon of the Frame control in the toolbox window.

☐ Move the Frame control to the right and enlarge its area.

Your frmMove form should now look like the one shown in Figure 4.6.

Figure 4.6.

The frmMove form with the Frame control in it (design mode).

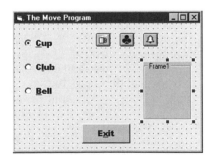

☐ Double-click the icon of the Frame control in the toolbox window again.

Visual Basic responds by placing a second Frame control in the frmMove form.

☐ Move and enlarge the second Frame control that you placed in the frmMove form.

Your frmMove form should now look like the one shown in Figure 4.7.

Figure 4.7.

The frmMove form with two Frame controls in it.

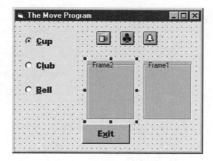

Now place two option buttons in the first Frame control that you added to the frmMove form:

☐ Click (do not double-click) the Option button icon in the toolbox window.

☐ Place the mouse cursor in the Frame control and drag the mouse.

Visual Basic responds by placing an option button in the Frame control.

Your frmMove form should now look like the one shown in Figure 4.8.

Figure 4.8.

The frmMove form with an option button added in the Frame control.

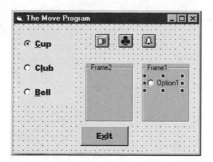

☐ Now repeat the steps for placing another option button in the frame. Remember not to double-click the icon of the option button in the toolbox window. Place a second option button in the first Frame control and place three option buttons in the second frame control.

When you're finished placing the option buttons, the frmMove form should look like the one shown in Figure 4.9.

Figure 4.9.

The frmMove form with option buttons in the two Frame controls.

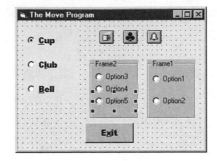

☐ Select Save Project from the File menu to save your work.

☐ Execute the Move program.

The important point to note is that the frmMove from has three independent option button groups. That is, when you select an option button in the Bell/Club/Cup group, it does not influence the other two groups. Also when you select Option1 or Option2, it does not influence the other groups. The same is true for the Option3/Option4/Option5 group. You can verify this as follows:

☐ Select the Option1, Option3, and Cup Option buttons (see Figure 4.10).

Figure 4.10.

Selecting option buttons in the three groups.

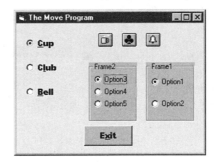

☐ Now change the selections in each of the option button groups and note that the other groups remain the same.

☐ Click the Exit button to terminate the Move program.

You have finished experimenting with the Move program. If you wish, you can delete the Frame1 and Frame2 and the Option1, Option2, Option3, Option4, and Option 5 option buttons. To remove an option button or a frame, select the control and then press Delete on your keyboard. You can delete each option button in the frame and later delete the frame itself, or you can just delete the frame, which will also delete all the controls in it.

The Draw Program

The Draw program illustrates how your program can use mouse events to implement a drawing program.

The Visual Implementation of the Draw Program

As usual, you'll start with the visual implementation of the form of the program:

☐ Start a new Standard EXE project.

☐ Save the form of the project as Draw.Frm in the C:\VB5Prg\Ch04 directory, and save the project file as Draw.Vbp in the C:\VB5Prg\Ch04 directory.

☐ Build the form of the Draw program according to Table 4.2.

When you complete implementing the form, it should look like the one shown in Figure 4.11.

Figure 4.11.
The frmDraw form
(design mode).

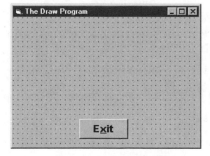

Table 4.2. The properties table of the frmDraw form.

Object	Property	Setting
Form	Name	frmDraw
	Caption	The Draw Program
Command Button	Name	cmdExit
	Caption	E&xit

Entering the Code of the Draw Program

You'll now enter the code of the Draw program:

☐ Make sure that the general declarations section of the frmDraw form has the Option Explicit statement in it as follows:

```
' All variables MUST be declared.
Option Explicit
```

☐ Type the following code in the Form_MouseDown() procedure:

```
Private Sub Form_MouseDown(Button As Integer, _
                           Shift As Integer, _
                           X As Single, _
                           Y As Single)

    ' Change CurrentX and CurrentY to the coordinates
    ' where the mouse button was just pressed.
    frmDraw.CurrentX = X
    frmDraw.CurrentY = Y

End Sub
```

☐ Type the following code in the Form_MouseMove() procedure:

```
Private Sub Form_MouseMove(Button As Integer, _
                           Shift As Integer, _
                           X As Single, _
                           Y As Single)

   ' If the left mouse button is currently pressed
   ' then draw a line.
    If Button = 1 Then
      Line (frmDraw.CurrentX, frmDraw.CurrentY)-(X, Y), _
           QBColor(0)
    End If

End Sub
```

☐ Type the following code in the cmdExit_Click() procedure:

```
Private Sub cmdExit_Click()

    End

End Sub
```

☐ Select Save Project from the File menu of Visual Basic to save your work.

Executing the Draw Program

Let's execute the Draw program:

☐ Execute the Draw program.

An empty window pops up, as shown in Figure 4.12.

☐ Push down the mouse button, and while holding down the button, move the mouse.

As a result, lines are drawn corresponding to the mouse's movement.

Releasing the mouse button stops the drawing process. In short, you can now draw in the same way you draw with the Paint program that comes with Windows. Figure 4.13 shows a drawing you can draw with the Draw program. Figure 4.14 shows that you can write with the Draw program by using the mouse.

Figure 4.12.
The window of the Draw program when you start the program.

Figure 4.13.
Drawing with the Draw program.

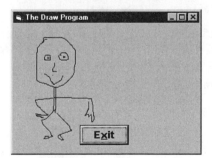

4

Figure 4.14.

*Writing with the
Draw program using
the mouse.*

☐ Draw something with the Draw program.

☐ Terminate the Draw program by clicking its Exit button.

How the Draw Program Works

The Draw program uses two graphics-related Visual Basic concepts: the `Line` method and the CurrentX and CurrentY properties. To understand the Draw program, you need to understand these concepts first.

The `Line` Method

To draw a line in a form, use the `Line` method. For example, to draw a line from the coordinate X=2000,Y=1500 to X=5000,Y=6000, use the following statement:

```
Line (2000,1500) - (5000,6000)
```

Figure 4.15 shows the line drawn by this `Line` method statement. The line starts 2000 twips from the left side of the form and 1500 twips from the top of the form (point A in Figure 4.15). The line ends 5000 twips from the left side of the form and 6000 twips from the top of the form (point B in Figure 4.15).

Figure 4.15.

*Drawing a line with
the* `Line` *method.*

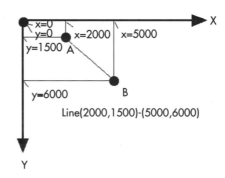

You may also specify the color for the line you draw by using the QBColor() function, which uses the numbers shown in Table 4.3.

Table 4.3. Numbers used in the QBColor() function.

Color	Number
Black	0
Blue	1
Green	2
Cyan	3
Red	4
Magenta	5
Yellow	6
White	7
Gray	8
Light blue	9
Light green	10
Light cyan	11
Light red	12
Light magenta	13
Light yellow	14
Bright white	15

For example, to draw the line in Figure 4.15 in black, use this statement:

```
Line (2000,1500) - (5000,6000), QBColor(0)
```

To draw the line in red, use this statement:

```
Line (2000,1500) - (5000,6000), QBColor(4)
```

The CurrentX and CurrentY Properties of a Form

If you examine the Properties window of a form, you won't find the CurrentX and CurrentY properties, because Visual Basic does not let you set these properties at design time. You can change the values of these properties only at runtime.

The CurrentX and CurrentY properties are automatically updated by the program after using various graphics methods. For example, after using the Line method to draw a line in a form, the program automatically assigns the coordinate of the line's endpoint to the CurrentX and CurrentY properties of the form on which the line was drawn. Therefore, after the following statement is executed, CurrentX equals 5000 and CurrentY equals 6000:

```
Line (2000,1500) - (5000,6000), QBColor(0)
```

The Code of the `Form_MouseDown()` Procedure

When the mouse button is pressed while the mouse cursor is in the client's area, the `Form_MouseDown()` procedure is automatically executed:

```
Private Sub Form_MouseDown(Button As Integer, _
                           Shift As Integer, _
                           X As Single, _
                           Y As Single)

    ' Change CurrentX and CurrentY to the coordinates
    ' where the mouse button was just pressed.
    frmDraw.CurrentX = X
    frmDraw.CurrentY = Y

End Sub
```

The `Form_MouseDown()` procedure assigns the values of the `X` and `Y` parameters to the CurrentX and CurrentY properties of the frmDraw form. Therefore, after you press down the mouse button, the CurrentX and CurrentY properties are updated with the coordinate of the mouse cursor at the time you pressed the mouse button.

The Code of the `Form_MouseMove()` Procedure

The procedure `Form_MouseMove()` is executed automatically when you move the mouse over the client's area.

The `X` and `Y` parameters of this procedure have the same meanings as the `X` and `Y` parameters of the `Form_MouseDown()` procedure (that is, X,Y are the mouse cursor's coordinates):

```
Private Sub Form_MouseMove(Button As Integer, _
                           Shift As Integer, _
                           X As Single, _
                           Y As Single)

   ' If the left mouse button is currently pressed
   ' then draw a line.
   If Button = 1 Then
     Line (frmDraw.CurrentX, frmDraw.CurrentY)-(X, Y), _
          QBColor(0)
   End If

End Sub
```

The code in the Form_MouseMove() procedure checks to see whether the left mouse button is currently being pressed by examining the value of the Button parameter. If the Button parameter is equal to 1, it means that the left mouse button is currently pressed down.

If the left button is pressed down, the Line method statement is executed:

```
Line (frmDraw.CurrentX, frmDraw.CurrentY)-(X, Y),
        QBColor(0)
```

This Line statement draws a black line from the location specified by the CurrentX and CurrentY properties to the current location of the mouse.

Remember, the program automatically updates the CurrentX and CurrentY properties with the line's endpoint after the Line method is executed. This means that the next time the Form_MouseMove() procedure is executed, the line's starting point is already updated. So on the next execution of the Form_MouseMove() procedure, a line is drawn starting from the endpoint of the previous line.

As you move the mouse, the program executes the Form_MouseMove() procedure; if the mouse button is held down, a new line is drawn from the end of the previous line to the current location of the mouse.

Note that as you move the mouse, the Form_MouseMove() procedure is executed again and again. If while you move the mouse the left button of the mouse is pressed down, each time the Form_MouseMove() procedure is executed, a new line is drawn. The line is drawn from the endpoint of the previous line to the current coordinates of the mouse cursor.

The Code of the cmdExit_Click() Procedure

When you click the Exit button, the cmdExit_Click() procedure is automatically executed. The End statement in this procedure causes the program to terminate:

```
Private Sub cmdExit_Click()

    End

End Sub
```

The AutoRedraw Property

There is a small flaw in the Draw program. Use the following steps to see the problem:

☐ Execute the Draw program and draw several lines with it.

☐ Minimize the window of the program. (Click the minus icon that appears on the upper-right corner of the window to minimize the window.)

The Draw program responds by displaying itself as an icon on the status bar of Windows.

☐ Restore the window of the Draw program. (Click the icon of the program that now resides on the status bar of Windows.)

As you can see, your drawing disappears!

The same problem occurs if you hide part of the Draw window by placing another window on top of it. To solve this problem, at design time simply set the AutoRedraw property of the frmDraw form to True.

☐ Set the AutoRedraw property of the frmDraw form to True.

☐ Select Save Project from the File menu of Visual Basic.

As implied by the name of this property, if it is set to True, Visual Basic automatically redraws the window when necessary. Let's see this in action:

☐ Execute the Draw program and draw several lines with it.

☐ Minimize the window of the program. (Click the minus icon that appears on the upper-right corner of the window to minimize the window.)

The Draw program responds by displaying itself as an icon on the status bar of Windows.

☐ Restore the window of the Draw program. (Click the icon of the program that now resides on the status bar of Windows.)

As you can see, your drawing appears!

You learned that setting the AutoRedraw property to True causes the program to automatically redraw the contents of the window when there is a need to do so. Although it is very convenient to use this feature, try not to use this feature. Why? Because this slows down the performances of the program. During the course of this book you'll learn other more efficient ways to refresh the window.

The HowOften Program

Your Visual Basic program cannot occupy itself by constantly executing the Form_MouseMove() procedure when the mouse is moved. If it did, your program couldn't execute any other procedure while you moved the mouse. Your Visual Basic program checks the status of the mouse only at fixed time intervals so it can execute other tasks while the mouse is moving. If your program finds that the mouse was moved since the last check, the Form_MouseMove() procedure is executed. The HowOften program illustrates how often Form_MouseMove() is executed.

The Visual Implementation of the HowOften Program

As usual, you'll start with the visual implementation of the form of the program:

☐ Start a new Standard EXE project.

☐ Save the form of the project as HowOften.Frm in the C:\VB5Prg\Ch04 directory and save the project file as HowOften.Vbp in the C:\VB5Prg\Ch04 directory.

☐ Implement the frmHowOften form according to Table 4.4.

When you complete implementing the form, it should look like the one shown in Figure 4.16.

Figure 4.16.
The frmHowOften form (in design mode).

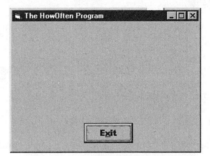

Table 4.4. The properties table of the HowOften program.

Object	Property	Setting
Form	Name	frmHowOften
	Caption	The HowOften Program
Command Button	Name	cmdExit
	Caption	E&xit

Entering the Code of the HowOften Program

You'll now enter the code of the HowOften program:

☐ Make sure that the general declarations section of the frmHowOften form has the Option Explicit statement in it as follows:

```
' All variables MUST be declared.
Option Explicit
```

☐ Type the following code in the Form_MouseMove() procedure:

```
Private Sub Form_MouseMove(Button As Integer, _
                           Shift As Integer, _
                           X As Single, _
                           Y As Single)

    ' Draw a circle with radius 40
    Circle (X, Y), 40

End Sub
```

☐ Type the following code in the cmdExit_Click() procedure:

```
Private Sub cmdExit_Click()

    End

End Sub
```

☐ Select Save Project from the File menu of Visual Basic to save your work.

Executing the HowOften Program

Let's see your code in action:

☐ Execute the HowOften program.

☐ Place the mouse cursor in the client's area, and then move the mouse.

As you move the mouse, the Form_MouseMove() procedure draws small circles at the current location of the mouse; however, you will notice that the Form_MouseMove() procedure is not executed for each and every movement of the mouse (see Figure 4.17).

Figure 4.17.

Moving the mouse in the client's area of the HowOften program.

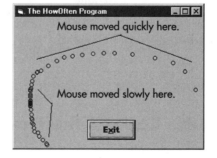

When you move the mouse quickly, the trail of circles that the Form_MouseMove() procedure draws is spaced widely along the path of the mouse. However, if you move the mouse slowly, the Form_MouseMove() procedure leaves a dense trail of circles.

Remember, each small circle is an indication that the MouseMove event occurred and the Form_MouseMove() procedure was executed.

How the HowOften Program Works

The HowOften program uses the Form_MouseMove() procedure for performing the work.

The Code of the Form_MouseMove() Procedure

When the program checks the mouse status and finds that the mouse moved since the last check, the Form_MouseMove() procedure is executed:

```
Private Sub Form_MouseMove(Button As Integer, _
                           Shift As Integer, _
                           X As Single, _
                           Y As Single)

    ' Draw a circle with radius 40
    Circle (X, Y), 40

End Sub
```

The Form_MouseMove() procedure simply draws a small circle at the mouse cursor's current location by using the Circle method.

The Circle Method

As implied by its name, the Circle method draws a circle. To draw a circle with a radius of 40 units at coordinate X,Y, use the following statement:

```
Circle (X, Y), 40
```

The Circle method uses the units indicated by the ScaleMode property. Because the ScaleMode property of the form is set to Twip, the Circle method uses twip units (that is, the radius is measured in units of twips, and the center is set at X,Y coordinates measured in units of twips).

4

The Code of the `cmdExit_Click()` Procedure

When you click the Exit button, the `cmdExit_Click()` procedure is executed. The `End` statement in this procedure causes the program to terminate:

```
Private Sub cmdExit_Click()

    End

End Sub
```

The Button Program

Now you'll write a program called Button that uses the `Button` parameter of the `Form_MouseDown()` and `Form_MouseUp()` procedures for determining which mouse button was pressed or released.

The Visual Implementation of the Button Program

You'll now build the form of the Button program:

☐ Start a new Standard EXE project.

☐ Save the form of the project as Button.Frm in the C:\VB5Prg\Ch04 directory, and save the project file as Button.Vbp in the C:\VB5Prg\Ch04 directory.

☐ Implement the frmButton form according to Table 4.5.

When you complete implementing the frmButton form, it should look like the one shown in Figure 4.18.

Figure 4.18.

The frmButton form (in design mode).

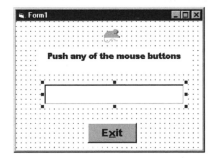

Table 4.5. The properties table of the frmButton form.

Object	Property	Setting
Form	**Name**	**frmButton**
	Caption	The Button Program
	BackColor	White
Command Button	**Name**	**cmdExit**
	Caption	E&xit
Text Box	**Name**	**txtResult**
	Alignment	2-Center
	MultiLine	True
	Enabled	0-False
	Text	(make it empty)
Label	**Name**	**lblInstruction**
	Caption	Push any of the mouse buttons
	Alignment	2-Center
	BackColor	White
Image	**Name**	**imgMouse**
	Picture	Mouse04.Ico
	Stretch	False

When using Table 4.5, remember the following: You were instructed to set the Picture property of the imgMouse Image control to Mouse04.Ico. The Mouse04.Ico file may have been supplied with your Visual Basic. You may find this file in the \Icons\Computer\ subdirectory which was installed under the directory where your Visual Basic was installed. If for some reason you do not have this file, set the Picture property of the imgMouse Image control to any icon file (*.ICO) that you may have. In any case, the only reason you are instructed to place this icon in the window of the program is for cosmetic reasons. That is, the subject of the Button program is mouse buttons, so an icon of a mouse is appropriate.

Entering the Code of the Button Program

You'll now type the code of the Button program:

☐ Make sure that the Option Explicit statement resides in the general declarations section of the frmButton form as follows:

```
' All variables must be declared
Option Explicit
```

☐ Type the following code in the Form_MouseDown() procedure:

```
Private Sub Form_MouseDown(Button As Integer, _
                            Shift As Integer, _
                            X As Single, _
                            Y As Single)

    ' Is the left mouse down?
    If Button = 1 Then
        txtResult.Text = "Left button is currently down"
    End If

    ' Is the right mouse down?
    If Button = 2 Then
        txtResult.Text = "Right button is currently down"
    End If

    ' Is the middle mouse down?
    If Button = 4 Then
        txtResult.Text = "Middle button is currently down"
    End If

End Sub
```

☐ Type the following code in the Form_MouseUp() procedure:

```
Private Sub Form_MouseUp(Button As Integer, _
                          Shift As Integer, _
                          X As Single, _
                          Y As Single)

    ' Clear the content of the text box
    txtResult.Text = ""

End Sub
```

☐ Type the following code in the cmdExit_Click() procedure:

```
Private Sub cmdExit_Click()

    End

End Sub
```

☐ Select Save Project from the File menu of Visual Basic to save your work.

Executing the Button Program

Let's see your code in action:

☐ Execute the Button program.

When you start the Button program, the window shown in Figure 4.19 appears.

Figure 4.19.

The window of the Button program.

When you press any of the mouse buttons in the client's area, the text box displays the name of the currently pressed button. For example, Figure 4.20 shows the content of the text box when the right button is pressed, and Figure 4.21 shows the content of the text box when the left button is clicked. The Button program displays the status of the mouse button only if the button is pressed in a free area of the form.

Figure 4.20.

The Button program when the right button of the mouse is down.

Figure 4.21.

The Button program when the left button of the mouse is down.

Note

An area in the form not covered by an enabled control is called a *free area*. For example, the Enabled property of the lblInstruction label is set to True. Therefore, the area that this label occupies is not considered a free area of the form.

On the other hand, the Enabled property of the txtResult text box is set to False, so the area that this text box occupies is considered a free area of the form.

When you click the lblInstruction Label in the window of the Button window, you are not clicking a free area. Hence, the Form_MouseDown() procedure is not executed. (It is not a free area, because the Enabled property of the lblInstruction is set to True.)

When you click the txtResult text box in the window of the Button window, you are clicking a free area (because you set the Enabled property of the txtResult text box to false). Hence, the Form_MouseDown() procedure is executed when you click this text box.

Even if your mouse has three buttons, if it isn't installed as a three-button mouse, the Button program does not respond to pressing the middle mouse button.

How the Button Program Works

The Button program responds to the MouseDown event in the Form_MouseDown() procedure and to the MouseUp event in the Form_MouseUp() procedure.

The Code of the Form_MouseDown() Procedure

When you press any of the mouse buttons while the mouse cursor is in a free area of the client's area, the Form_MouseDown() procedure is automatically executed. This procedure detects which button was pressed by examining the value of the Button parameter.

When the Button parameter equals 1, it means that the left button is being pressed; 2 means the right button is being pressed, and 4 means the middle button is being pressed:

```
Private Sub Form_MouseDown(Button As Integer, _
                           Shift As Integer, _
                           X As Single, _
                           Y As Single)

  ' Is the left mouse down?
  If Button = 1 Then
```

```
    txtResult.Text = "Left button is currently down"
End If

' Is the right mouse down?
If Button = 2 Then
  txtResult.Text = "Right button is currently down"
End If

' Is the middle mouse down?
If Button = 4 Then
  txtResult.Text = "Middle button is currently down"
End If

End Sub
```

The Code of the Form_MouseUp() Procedure

When the mouse button is released, the Form_MouseUp() procedure is automatically executed. The code in this procedure clears the content of the text box:

```
Private Sub Form_MouseUp(Button As Integer, _
                         Shift As Integer, _
                         X As Single, _
                         Y As Single)

    ' Clear the content of the text box
    txtResult.Text = ""

End Sub
```

The Button Parameter of the Form_MouseMove() Procedure

The Button parameter of the mouse procedures specifies which mouse button was pressed at the time of the event. As stated, the Button parameter of the Form_MouseDown() procedure may be 1, 2, or 4, but it *cannot* have any other values, which means you can't use the MouseDown event to detect whether more than one mouse button has been pressed.

The Button parameter of the Form_MouseMove() procedure, however, *can* have any value between 0 and 7, indicating all the possible combinations of pressing the mouse buttons. For example, when both the left and right buttons are pressed, the Button parameter of the Form_MouseMove() procedure is equal to 3, with the equivalent binary number 00000011 (see Figure 4.22).

Figure 4.22.

A visual representa-
tion of the Button
parameter of the
Form_MouseMove()
procedure.

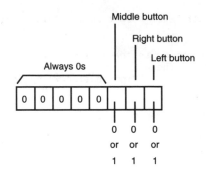

<table>
</table>

> **Note**
>
> Look over the following list if you're not familiar with the binary system:
>
> | Binary Notation | Decimal Notation |
> |---|---|
> | 00000000 | 0 |
> | 00000001 | 1 |
> | 00000010 | 2 |
> | 00000011 | 3 |
> | 00000100 | 4 |
> | 00000101 | 5 |
> | 00000110 | 6 |
> | 00000111 | 7 |
>
> For example, when the Button parameter is equal to 0, the binary value is 00000000. In Figure 4.22, it means that none of the mouse buttons is pressed. When the Button parameter is equal to 7, the binary value is 00000111, which means that all three mouse buttons are pressed. When the Button parameter is equal to 4, the binary value is 0000100, which means that only the middle button is pressed.

The Button2 Program

The Button2 program illustrates how to use the Button parameter of the Form_MouseMove() procedure.

The Visual Implementation of the Button2 Program

Let's start with the visual implementation of the Button2 program:

☐ Start a new Standard EXE project.

☐ Save the form as Button2.Frm in the C:\VB5Prg\Ch04 directory, and save the project file as Button2.Vbp in the C:\VB5Prg\Ch04 directory.

☐ Build the form of the Button2 program according to Table 4.6.

When you complete implementing the form, the form should look like the one shown in Figure 4.23.

Figure 4.23.

The frmButton2 form (in design mode).

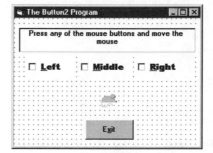

Table 4.6. The properties table of the frmButton2 form.

Object	Property	Setting
Form	**Name**	**frmButton2**
	BackColor	White
	Caption	The Button2 Program
Command Button	**Name**	**cmdExit**
	Caption	E&xit
Check Box	**Name**	**chkLeft**
	BackColor	White
	Caption	&Left
	Enabled	False
Check Box	**Name**	**chkMiddle**
	BackColor	White
	Caption	&Middle
	Enabled	False

continues

Table 4.6. continued

Object	Property	Setting
Check Box	**Name**	**chkRight**
	BackColor	White
	Caption	&Right
	Enabled	False
Label	**Name**	**lblInstruction**
	Alignment	2-Center
	BackColor	White
	BorderStyle	1-Fixed Single
	Caption	Press any of the mouse buttons and move the mouse
Image	**Name**	**imgMouse**
	Picture	Mouse04.Ico
	Stretch	False

When using Table 4.6, remember the following:

■ You were instructed to place the imgMouse Image control in the frmButton2 form and to set the Picture property of this Image control to the Mouse04.Ico file for cosmetic reasons only. If you do not have the \Icons\Computer\ subdirectory as one of the subdirectory of Visual Basic, use any other *.Ico file that you may have.

■ You were instructed to set the Stretch property of the Image control to False. This means that the Image control will not stretch the picture. So if, for example, you set the Picture property of the Image control to a picture that has the size 32 pixel by 32 pixels, and then you enlarge the size of the Image control, the picture will *not* stretch to fit the size of the Image control. Rather, the picture will be displayed in its original size.

■ You set the Enabled properties of the check boxes to False. This means that the user cannot check or uncheck these check boxes by clicking them. The reason you were instructed to disable the check boxes is because you want the code of the program to check or uncheck the check boxes based on the mouse buttons status (but you do not want the user to be able to check or uncheck the check boxes).

Entering the Code of the Button2 Program

You'll now enter the code of the Button2 program:

☐ Make sure that the Option Explicit statement resides in your general declarations section as follows:

```
' All variables MUST be declared.
Option Explicit
```

☐ Type the following code in the Form_MouseMove() procedure:

```
Private Sub Form_MouseMove(Button As Integer, _
                           Shift As Integer, _
                           X As Single, _
                           Y As Single)

    ' Is the left button down?
    If (Button And 1) = 1 Then
        chkLeft.Value = 1
    Else
        chkLeft.Value = 0
    End If

    ' Is the right button down?
    If (Button And 2) = 2 Then
        chkRight.Value = 1
    Else
        chkRight.Value = 0
    End If

    ' Is the middle button down?
    If (Button And 4) = 4 Then
        chkMiddle.Value = 1
    Else
        chkMiddle.Value = 0
    End If

End Sub
```

☐ Type the following code in the Form_MouseUp() event procedure:

```
Private Sub Form_MouseUp(Button As Integer, _
                         Shift As Integer, _
                         X As Single, _
                         Y As Single)

    ' Was the left button just released?
    If Button = 1 Then
        chkLeft.Value = 0
    End If

    ' Was the right button just released?
    If Button = 2 Then
        chkRight.Value = 0
```

4

```
          End If

          ' Was the middle button just released?
          If Button = 4 Then
              chkMiddle.Value = 0
          End If

      End Sub
```

☐ Type the following code in the `cmdExit_Click()` procedure:

```
      Private Sub cmdExit_Click()

          End

      End Sub
```

☐ Select Save Project from the File menu of Visual Basic to save your work.

Executing the Button2 Program

Before going over the code of the Button2 program, let's execute the program:

☐ Execute the Button2 program. As shown in Figure 4.24, the window of the Button2 program includes three check boxes: Left, Middle, and Right.

The Button2 program checks and unchecks the check boxes according to the status of the mouse buttons *while the mouse is moving*. For example, if you press down the left and right mouse buttons together and move the mouse, the program checks the Left and Right check boxes (see Figure 4.25).

Figure 4.24.

The window of the Button2 program.

Figure 4.25.

The Button2 program showing that the left and right buttons of the mouse are pressed (while moving the mouse).

How the Button2 Program Works

The Button2 program uses the `Button` parameter of the `Form_MouseMove()` procedure to report any combination of mouse buttons being clicked.

The Code of the `Form_MouseMove()` Procedure

When you move the mouse in the client's area of the frmButton2 form, the `Form_MouseMove()` procedure is automatically executed:

```
Private Sub Form_MouseMove(Button As Integer, _
                           Shift As Integer, _
                           X As Single, _
                           Y As Single)

    ' Is the left button down?
    If (Button And 1) = 1 Then
        chkLeft.Value = 1
    Else
        chkLeft.Value = 0
    End If

    ' Is the right button down?
    If (Button And 2) = 2 Then
        chkRight.Value = 1
    Else
        chkRight.Value = 0
    End If

    ' Is the middle button down?
    If (Button And 4) = 4 Then
        chkMiddle.Value = 1
    Else
        chkMiddle.Value = 0
    End If

End Sub
```

4

The code of this procedure checks and unchecks the check boxes based on the value of the Button parameter. For example, the first If…Else statement determines whether the left button is down by ANDing the Button parameter with 1. If the result of the AND operation is 1, the left button of the mouse is currently pressed. Similarly, if the result of ANDing Button with 2 is equal to 2, the right button of the mouse is currently pressed; if the result of ANDing Button with 4 is 4, the middle button of the mouse is currently pressed. Don't worry if you are not familiar with the AND operation and binary notation; you just need to know what results the code will have when pressing the mouse buttons while moving the mouse.

The Code of the `Form_MouseUp()` Procedure

When you release any of the mouse buttons, the Form_MouseUp() procedure is executed:

```
Private Sub Form_MouseUp(Button As Integer, _
                         Shift As Integer, _
                         X As Single, _
                         Y As Single)

    ' Was the left button just released?
    If Button = 1 Then
        chkLeft.Value = 0
    End If

    ' Was the right button just released?
    If Button = 2 Then
        chkRight.Value = 0
    End If

    ' Was the middle button just released?
    If Button = 4 Then
        chkMiddle.Value = 0
    End If

End Sub
```

This code checks which mouse button was released, then unchecks the corresponding check box. For example, if the mouse button that was just released is the left button, the first If condition is met and the Left check box is unchecked.

Pressing the Shift, Ctrl, and Alt Keys with the Mouse Buttons

The MouseDown, MouseUp, and MouseMove events have the Shift integer as their second parameter, which indicates whether the Shift, Ctrl, or Alt keys were pressed with the mouse buttons.

Figure 4.26 shows how the Shift parameter indicates which key was pressed.

Figure 4.26.

The Shift
parameter.

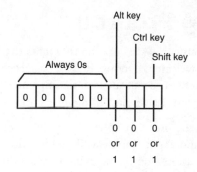

As shown in Figure 4.26, the three least significant bits of the Shift parameter (the three bits on the right side) represent the status of the Shift, Ctrl, and Alt keys at the time you pressed the mouse button(s).

Table 4.7 shows the meaning of the eight possible values that the Shift parameter can have.

Table 4.7. The Shift parameter.

Binary Value	Decimal Value	Alt Key	Ctrl Key	Shift Key
00000000	0	No	No	No
00000001	1	No	No	Yes
00000010	2	No	Yes	No
00000011	3	No	Yes	Yes
00000100	4	Yes	No	No
00000101	5	Yes	No	Yes
00000110	6	Yes	Yes	No
00000111	7	Yes	Yes	Yes

For example, when the Shift parameter of the Form_MouseDown(), Form_MouseUp(), or Form_MouseMove() procedures is equal to 6, it means that the mouse button is held down while pressing the Alt and Ctrl keys but not the Shift key.

Note that the Button parameter of the Form_MouseDown() procedure may have the value 1, 2, or 4. In contrast, the Shift parameter of the Form_MouseDown() procedure may have any of the values listed in Table 4.7.

The Drag Program

You have learned how to use mouse events that occur when you press the mouse button (MouseDown), release the mouse button (MouseUp), and move the mouse (MouseMove). You'll now learn how to use mouse events for implementing a mechanism that lets the user drag and drop controls in the window of the program.

Dragging is the process of pressing the left mouse button while the mouse cursor is on a control and moving the mouse while holding down the mouse button. The action of releasing the mouse button after the dragging is called dropping.

You'll now write a program called Drag; it illustrates how easy it is to accomplish a dragging mechanism in your programs.

The Visual Implementation of the Drag Program

You'll start with the visual implementation of the form of the Drag program:

☐ Start a new Standard EXE project.

☐ Save the form of the project as Drag.Frm in the C:\VB5Prg\Ch04 directory, and save the project file as Drag.Vbp in the C:\VB5Prg\Ch04 directory.

☐ Build the form of the Drag program according to Table 4.8.

When you complete implementing the form, it should look like the one shown in Figure 4.27.

Figure 4.27.

The frmDrag form (in design mode).

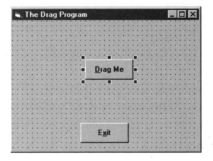

Table 4.8. The properties table of the Drag program.

Object	Property	Setting
Form	**Name**	**frmDrag**
	Caption	The Drag Program
Command Button	**Name**	**cmdExit**
	Caption	E&xit
Command Button	**Name**	**cmdDragMe**
	Caption	&Drag Me
	DragMode	1-Automatic

Entering the Code of the Drag Program

You'll now type the code of the Drag program:

☐ Make sure that the general declarations section of the frmDrag form has the `Option Explicit` statement in it as follows:

```
' All variables MUST be declared.
Option Explicit
```

☐ Type the following code in the `cmdExit_Click()` procedure:

```
Private Sub cmdExit_Click()

    End

End Sub
```

☐ Select Save Project from the File menu of Visual Basic to save your work.

Executing the Drag Program

During design time you set the DragMode property of the Drag Me button to 1-Automatic. This enables the user to drag the button during runtime.

Use the following steps to see how the Drag Me button is dragged:

☐ Execute the Drag program.

4

☐ Press the left mouse button while the mouse cursor is in the Drag Me button and hold the mouse button down while moving the mouse.

As you can see, a rectangle that has the size of the Drag Me button pops up and follows the mouse movements.

☐ Try to drag the Drag Me button outside the form.

The program responds by displaying the illegal icon, which is an indication that you dragged the control to a forbidden zone.

When you release the mouse button (called dropping), the rectangle disappears. Note that the Drag Me button remains in its original position.

☐ Click the Exit button of the Drag program to terminate the program.

Enhancing the Drag Program

In the Drag program, while you move a control with its DragMode property set to 1-Automatic, a rectangle that has the same size as the Drag Me button moves in response to the mouse movements. This rectangle enables you to see where the button is being dragged.

To produce a different image while the control is being dragged, use the following steps:

☐ Set the DragIcon property of the cmdDragMe button to Drag1Pg.Ico. (You will find the Drag1Pg.Ico file in the Icons\DragDrop\ subdirectory. This subdirectory was created when you installed your Visual Basic package. If you do not have DragPg1.Ico file, use any other *.ICO file.)

☐ Select Save project from the File menu of Visual Basic to save your work.

Use the following steps to see the effect of setting the DragIcon property:

☐ Execute the Drag program.

☐ Drag the Drag Me button.

The program responds by displaying the Drag1Pg.Ico icon while the Drag Me button is dragged (see Figure 4.28).

Now, as you move the mouse, the Drag1Pg.Ico moves according to the mouse movement instead of the rectangle.

Figure 4.28.
The Drag1Pg.Ico icon moves according to the mouse movement when you drag the Drag Me button.

The Drop Program

The Drop program illustrates how dropping, the action of releasing the mouse button after dragging, is used in a program.

The Visual Implementation of the Drop Program

You'll start with the visual implementation of the Drop program:

☐ Start a new Standard EXE project.

☐ Save the form of the project as Drop.Frm in the C:\VB5Prg\Ch04 directory, and save the project file as Drop.Vbp in the C:\VB5Prg\Ch04 directory.

☐ Build the form of the Drop program according to Table 4.9.

When you complete implementing the frmDrop form, it should look like the one in Figure 4.29.

Figure 4.29.
The frmDrop form (in design mode).

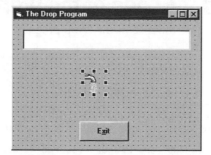

Table 4.9. The properties table of the Drop program.

Object	Property	Setting
Form	**Name**	**frmDrop**
	Caption	The Drop Program
Command Button	**Name**	**cmdExit**
	Caption	E&xit
Text Box	**Name**	**txtInfo**
	Alignment	2-Center
	Enabled	False
	MultiLine	True
	Text	(make it empty)
Image	**Name**	**imgWater**
	DragMode	1-Automatic
	Picture	Water.Ico
	Stretch	-1-True
	Tag	Water image

Table 4.9 instructs you to set the Picture property of the imgWater control to the Water.Ico icon. You may find this icon file in the \Icons\Elements subdirectory of your Visual Basic directory. If the Visual Basic version that you are using does not include this icon file, use a different icon.

Entering the Code of the Drop Program

You'll now type the code of the Drop program.

☐ Make sure that the general declarations section of the frmDrop form has the Option Explicit statement in it as follows:

```
' All variables MUST be declared.
Option Explicit
```

☐ Type the following code in the Form_DragOver() procedure:

```
Private Sub Form_DragOver(Source As Control, _
                          X As Single, _
```

```
                        Y As Single, _
                        State As Integer)

    Dim sInfo As String

    ' Display the dragging information.
    sInfo = "Now dragging "
    sInfo = sInfo + Source.Tag
    sInfo = sInfo + " over the Form."
    sInfo = sInfo + " State = "
    sInfo = sInfo + Str(State)
    txtInfo.Text = sInfo

End Sub
```

☐ Type the following code in the cmdExit_Click() event procedure:

```
Private Sub cmdExit_Click()

    End

End Sub
```

☐ Type the following code in the Form_DragDrop() procedure:

```
Private Sub Form_DragDrop(Source As Control, _
                          X As Single, _
                          Y As Single)

    ' Clear the text box.
    txtInfo.Text = ""
    ' Move the control.
    Source.Move X, Y

End Sub
```

☐ Type the following code in the cmdExit_DragOver() procedure:

```
Private Sub cmdExit_DragOver(Source As Control, _
                             X As Single, _
                             Y As Single, _
                             State As Integer)

    Dim sInfo As String

    ' Display the dragging information.
    sInfo = "Now dragging "
    sInfo = sInfo + Source.Tag
    sInfo = sInfo + " over the Exit button."
    sInfo = sInfo + " State = "
    sInfo = sInfo + Str(State)
    txtInfo.Text = sInfo

End Sub
```

☐ Select Save Project from the File menu of Visual Basic to save your work.

4

Executing the Drop Program

Let's see your work in action:

☐ Execute the Drop program.

☐ Drag the Water image.

> *As you drag the Water image, the text box displays a message that indicates the status of the dragging. Releasing the mouse button (dropping), causes the Water image to move to the point of the drop.*

☐ Terminate the program by clicking its Exit button.

How the Drop Program Works

The Drop program uses the `Form_DragOver()`, `cmdExit_DragOver()`, and `Form_DragDrop()` procedures.

The Code of the `Form_DragOver()` Procedure

In the Drop program the control being dragged is the Water image. Therefore, when you drag the Water image over the form, the `Form_DragOver()` procedure is executed. This procedure has four parameters: `Source`, `X`, `Y`, and `State`:

```
Private Sub cmdExit_DragOver(Source As Control, _
                             X As Single, _
                             Y As Single, _
                             State As Integer)

    . . .
    . . .
    . . .

End Sub
```

The `Source` parameter is the name of the control being dragged. Because the dragged control is the Water image, the `Source` parameter is automatically set to imgWater.

The `X` and `Y` parameters are the current X,Y coordinates of the mouse cursor (referenced to the form coordinate system).

The `State` parameter is an integer that has a value of 0, 1, or 2:

☐ When the `State` parameter equals 2, the Water image is dragged from one free point to another on the form.

☐ When the `State` parameter equals 1, the Water image is dragged from a free point on the form to an illegal point (such as to a point outside the form's free area).

☐ When the State parameter equals 0, the Water image is dragged from an illegal point to a free point in the form.

The Form_DragOver() procedure prepares a string called sInfo and displays this string in the txtInfo text box:

```
Dim sInfo As String

' Display the dragging information.
sInfo = "Now dragging "
sInfo = sInfo + Source.Tag
sInfo = sInfo + " over the Exit button."
sInfo = sInfo + " State = "
sInfo = sInfo + Str(State)
txtInfo.Text = sInfo
```

For example, when the Water image is dragged from one free point in the form to another, the content of the sInfo string is set as follows:

```
Now dragging The Water image over the Form. State=2.
```

The following statement is used in preparing the sInfo string:

```
sInfo = sInfo + Source.Tag
```

During design time, you set the Tag property of the Water image to Water image. Therefore, the value of Source.Tag is equal to Water image.

The Tag Property

The Tag property is often used as a storage area for data. For example, the Tag property of imgWater contains a string that identifies the control. In the Form_DragOver() procedure, you use this string to identify the dragged control. You can set the Tag property to anything you want, such as My Water.

The Code of the cmdExit_DragOver() Procedure

The cmdExit_DragOver() procedure is executed when you drag a control over the Exit button. Therefore, when you drag the Water image over the Exit button, this procedure is automatically executed.

The code of this procedure is similar to the code of the Form_DragOver() procedure, only now the sInfo string tells you that the Water image is being dragged over the Exit button:

```
Private Sub cmdExit_DragOver(Source As Control, _
                    X As Single, _
                    Y As Single, _
                    State As Integer)

    Dim sInfo As String
```

```
' Display the dragging information.
sInfo = "Now dragging "
sInfo = sInfo + Source.Tag
sInfo = sInfo + " over the Exit button."
sInfo = sInfo + " State = "
sInfo = sInfo + Str(State)
txtInfo.Text = sInfo
```

End Sub

For example, when dragging the Water image over the Exit button, sInfo is filled with the string

```
Now dragging Water image over the Exit button. State = 0
```

State is 0 in this string because the Water image is dragged from outside the Exit button into the Exit button. From the Exit button's point of view, any point outside the Exit button is an illegal point.

The Code of the Form_DragDrop() Procedure

The Form_DragDrop() procedure is executed when you drop the control in the form. There are two things to do when this occurs: clear the txtInfo text box and move the Water image to the drop point.

You use the following two statements to accomplish this:

```
Private Sub Form_DragDrop(Source As Control, _
                          X As Single, _
                          Y As Single)

    ' Clear the text box.
    txtInfo.Text = ""

    ' Move the control.
    Source.Move X, Y

End Sub
```

The Water image is moved to the drop point by using the Move method. The drop point is specified by the X and Y parameters of the procedure.

Summary

This chapter discusses mouse events. You have learned about the MouseDown, MouseUp, MouseMove, DragOver, and DragDrop events. The parameters of their procedures give you information about the state of the mouse at the time of the event. The Button parameter tells you which mouse button was pressed or released; the Shift parameter tells you whether the Shift, Ctrl, or Alt keys were pressed with the mouse button(s); and the X and Y parameters tell you where the mouse cursor was at the time of the event.

Q&A

Q **Dragging and dropping a control is nice. But where can I use it?**

A Suppose that you are developing a program that lets your user design forms. In such a program, the user should be able to drag and move controls. Of course, there are many other applications for the drag-and-drop features.

Q **During the execution of the Button program in this chapter, I clicked the mouse button on the lblInstruction label, but the program did not recognize this click. Why?**

A The `Form_MouseDown()` procedure is executed only if the mouse button is pressed while the mouse cursor is inside a free area of the client's area. During design time, you left the Enabled property of the label in its default value (True). This means that the area occupied by this label belongs to the label and is not considered part of the free area of the client's area.

Q **I assigned an icon to the DragIcon property of a control. Later I changed my mind about this icon. How do I take it off?**

A During design time, you may select the DragIcon property in the Properties window and then click on the three dots icon of this property; Visual Basic will then let you select another icon.

If you want to return the default icon (an empty rectangle), highlight the text (Icon) that appears as the value of this property, and then press the Delete key on your keyboard. The DragIcon property changes from (Icon) to (none).

4

Quiz

1. When is the `Form_MouseDown()` procedure executed?

   a. When the user clicks the mouse on the Exit button

   b. When any of the mouse buttons is pressed inside a free area of the form

   c. When the mouse moves inside a free area of the form

2. What is the ScaleMode property?

3. What method is used for moving objects during runtime?

   a. The `Move` method

   b. The `Line` method

   c. The `Circle` method

4. What is the meaning of the X and Y parameters in mouse event procedures?

5. When is the Form_MouseMove() procedure executed?

    a. When the user moves the mouse inside a free area of the form

    b. When any of the mouse buttons is released

    c. When the left mouse button is released

6. When is the Form_DragDrop() procedure executed?

    a. When the mouse drops on the floor

    b. When you release the mouse button over a free area of the form after dragging the mouse

    c. When a control is dragged outside the form

7. What is the value of the Source parameter of the Form_DragDrop() procedure?

    a. Source = 0

    b. Source = the Name property of the control that was dropped

    c. Source = the Tag property of the control that was dropped

Exercises

1. Enhance the Drag program so that when you drag the Drag Me button outside the free area of the form, the PC beeps.

2. Currently, the Draw program uses the left mouse button for drawing in black. Enhance the Draw program so that the right mouse button is used for drawing in red.

Quiz Answers

1. b

2. The ScaleMode property defines the units of the coordinate system of the object. For example, if the ScaleMode property of a form is set to twips, the width, height, and all other length-related properties are measured in twips. If the ScaleMode property of a form is set to pixels, the width, height, and all other length-related properties are measured in pixels, and so on.

3. a

4. The X and Y parameters contain the values of the mouse cursor location when the event occurred.

5. a

6. b

7. b

Exercise Answers

1. The program may detect that you dragged the control to a point outside the free area of the form by using the State parameter of the Form_DragOver() procedure. If the State parameter is equal to 1, the control was dragged outside the free area of the form:

```
Private Sub Form_DragOver(Source As Control, _
                          X As Single, _
                          Y As Single, _
                          State As Integer)

    If State = 1 Then
        Beep
    End If

End Sub
```

2. Modify the Form_MouseMove() procedure as follows:

```
Private Sub Form_MouseMove(Button As Integer, _
                           Shift As Integer, _
                           X As Single, _
                           Y As Single)

If Button = 1 Then
   ' Draw the line in black.
   Line(frmDraw.CurrentX, _
        frmDraw.CurrentY)-(X,Y),QBColor(0)
End If

If Button = 2 Then
   ' Draw the line in red.
   Line(frmDraw.CurrentX, _
        frmDraw.CurrentY)-(X,Y),QBColor(4)
End If

End Sub
```

The first If statement checks whether the left mouse button is currently pressed. If this is the case, a line is drawn in black.

The second If statement checks to see whether the right mouse button is currently pressed. If this is the case, a line is drawn in red.

4

Day 5

Menus

This chapter focuses on incorporating menus into your programs. You'll learn how to design the menus and attach code to them.

The Colors Program

You'll now write a program that includes a menu. The program, called Colors, lets you choose a color from a menu and paint the program's window with the selected color. The program also lets you select the size of the program's window from a menu.

Before you start writing the Colors program, you need to specify how the menu system of the program should look and what it should do:

☐ When you start the program, a menu bar with two menu titles appears: Colors and Size (see Figure 5.1).

Figure 5.1.
The Colors program.

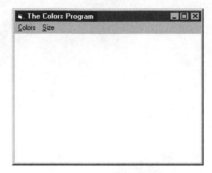

☐ The Colors menu has two items in it: Set Color and Exit (see Figure 5.2).

Figure 5.2.
The two items of the Colors menu.

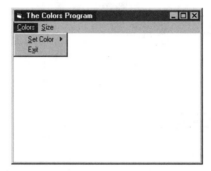

☐ The Size menu also has two items in it: Small and Large (see Figure 5.3).

Figure 5.3.
The Size menu.

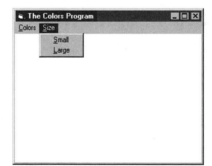

☐ When you select Set Color from the Colors menu, another menu pops up with a list of colors (see Figure 5.4). Once you select a color, the form of the program is filled with that color.

Figure 5.4.
*The submenu of the
Set Color menu item.*

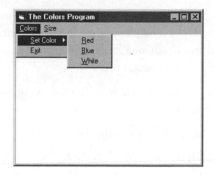

☐ When you select any of the sizes from the Size menu, the program window is sized to the selected size.

☐ When you select Exit from the Colors menu, the program terminates.

The Visual Implementation of the Colors Program

As usual, you'll start designing the program by implementing the form of the program:

☐ Create the C:\VB5Prg\Ch05 directory.

☐ Start a new Standard EXE project.

☐ Save the form of the project as Colors.Frm in the C:\VB5Prg\Ch05 directory, and save the project file as Colors.Vbp in the C:\VB5Prg\Ch05 directory.

☐ Build the form of the Colors program according to Table 5.1.

Table 5.1. The properties table of the Colors program.

Object	Property	Value
Form	Name	frmColors
	BackColor	White
	Caption	The Colors Program

Creating the Menu of the Colors Program

You'll now create the menus of the Colors program. In Visual Basic, a menu is attached to a form. So, before creating the menu, you must first select the form you want to attach it to:

□ Make sure that the frmColors form is the selected window. For the Colors program this step may seem redundant since the project has only one form, but when your project includes more than one form, this step is necessary because you have to attach the menu to the form you select.

Colors.Frm is now selected, so in the following steps, Visual Basic attaches the menu to the `Colors.Frm` form.

□ Select Menu Editor from the Tools menu.

Visual Basic responds by displaying the Menu Editor (see Figure 5.5).

You'll now use the Menu Editor window to create the menu system shown in Figures 5.1 through 5.4.

Figure 5.5.

The Menu Editor window.

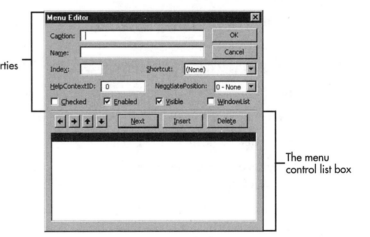

Creating Menu Controls

As you can see from Figure 5.5, the Menu Editor has two parts: the menu control list box (the lower part of the window) and the menu control properties (the upper part of the window).

When you finish creating the menus of the Colors program, the menu control list box will contain all the menu controls in the Colors program. What are menu controls? Menu controls could be menu titles (such as the Colors and Size menu titles shown in Figure 5.1) or menu items (such as the Set Color and Exit items shown in Figure 5.2).

The Colors program has two pull-down menus: the Colors menu shown in Figure 5.2 and the Size menu shown in Figure 5.3. As you can see from Figure 5.2, the Colors menu has three menu controls:

- Colors (the menu title)
- Set Color (a menu item)
- Exit (a menu item)

At this point, a blank row is highlighted in the menu control list box of the Menu Editor, as shown in Figure 5.5. This means that Visual Basic is ready for you to create a menu control.

Use the following steps to create the Colors menu title:

☐ In the Caption text box of the Menu Editor, type &Colors.

☐ In the Name text box of the Menu Editor, type mnuColors.

The & character in &Colors causes Visual Basic to underline the C in Colors (see Figure 5.1). When you run the program, pressing Alt+C has the same result as clicking the Colors menu title.

You have just created the menu title of the Colors menu. The Menu Editor should now look like the one shown in Figure 5.6.

Figure 5.6.

*Creating the Colors
menu title.*

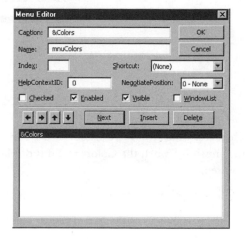

5

Next, create the two menu items of the Colors menu.

Use the following step to create the Set Color menu item:

☐ Click the Next button of the Menu Editor window.

   Visual Basic responds by highlighting the next row in the menu control list.

☐ In the Caption text box of the Menu Editor window, type &Set Color.

☐ In the Name text box of the Menu Editor window, type `mnuSetColor`.

Because Set Color is an item in the Colors menu, it must be indented. Use the following step to indent Set Color:

☐ Click the right-arrow button of the Menu Editor window.

As a response, the Set Color is shifted to the right (and three dots appears to the left of the Set Color item).

The Menu Editor should now look like the one shown in Figure 5.7.

Figure 5.7.

Creating the Set Color menu item.

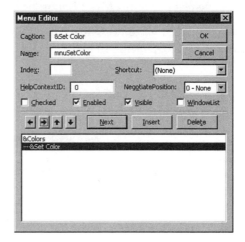

The & character of `&Set Color` causes Visual Basic to underline the `S`. When you run the program, pressing S when the Colors menu is displayed has the same result as clicking the Set Color item.

Use the following steps to create the second item in the Colors menu:

☐ Click the Next button of the Menu Editor window.

Visual Basic responds by highlighting the next row.

☐ In the Caption text box of the Menu Editor window, type `E&xit`.

☐ In the Name text box of the Menu Editor window, type `mnuExit`.

Visual Basic indented this item for you automatically, so you don't need to indent it.

That's it for the Colors menu.

Now create the Size menu. As you can see from Figure 5.3, the Size menu has three menu controls:

- Size (the menu title)
- Small (a menu item)
- Large (a menu item)

Use the following step to create the Size menu title:

☐ Click the Next button of the Menu Editor window.

Visual Basic responds by highlighting the next row in the menu control list.

☐ In the Caption text box of the Menu Editor window, type &Size.

☐ In the Name text box of the Menu Editor window, type mnuSize.

Visual Basic indented this item for you automatically, but since Size is a menu title, not a menu item, you need to remove the indent.

Use this step to remove the indent before Size:

☐ Click the left-arrow button of the Menu Editor window.

The Menu Editor should now look like the one shown in Figure 5.8.

Figure 5.8.

Creating the Size menu title.

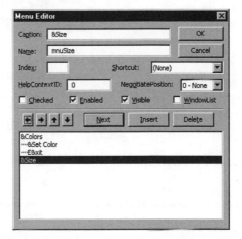

Now use the following steps to create the two menu items of the Size menu:

☐ Click the Next button of the Menu Editor window.

Visual Basic responds by highlighting the next row in the menu control list.

☐ In the Caption text box of the Menu Editor window, type &Small.

☐ In the Name text box of the Menu Editor window, type mnuSmall.

Because Small is an item of the Size menu, use this step to indent it:

☐ Click the right-arrow button of the Menu Editor window.

Use the following steps to create the second item in the Size menu:

☐ Click the Next button of the Menu Editor window.

☐ In the Caption text box of the Menu Editor window, type &Large.

☐ In the Name text box of the Menu Editor window, type mnuLarge.

Visual Basic indented this item for you automatically, so you don't need to indent it.

The Size menu is ready! The Menu Editor should now look like the one shown in Figure 5.9.

Figure 5.9.

Creating the items in the Size menu.

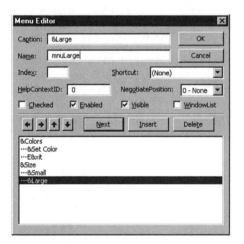

Although you did not complete designing the menu, let's see what you have accomplished so far:

☐ Click the OK button of the Menu Editor window.

☐ Select Save Project from the File menu of Visual Basic to save your work.

The frmColors in design mode now look like the one in Figure 5.10.

Figure 5.10.

*The frmColors form
with its menu bar
(design mode).*

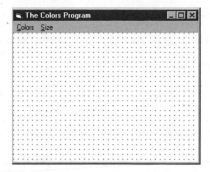

☐ Click the Colors item on the menu bar to pop up the Color menu (see Figure 5.11).

Figure 5.11.

*The Colors menu
(design mode).*

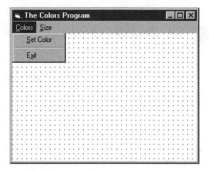

☐ Click the Size item on the menu bar to pop up the Size menu (see Figure 5.12).

Figure 5.12.

*The Size menu
(design mode).*

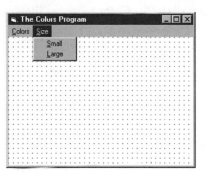

Let's execute the Colors program:

☐ Execute the Colors program.

> *The window of the Colors program appears. As you can see, the window has a menu bar with
> the Colors menu title and the Size menu title.*

☐ Click the Colors menu title.

The Colors program responds by displaying the Colors menu.

☐ Click the Size menu title.

The Colors program responds by displaying the Size menu.

Of course, you can click any of the menu items all you want, but nothing will happen. Why? Because you have not attached code to these menu items yet:

☐ Click the X icon that appears on the upper-right corner of the Colors program.

As a response, the Colors program terminates itself. (As yet, you have not attached code to the Exit menu item, so you can't click the Exit menu item to terminate the program.)

Creating a Submenu

You'll now continue with the visual design of the menu. Currently, one of the menu titles is Colors (see Figure 5.11). The Colors menu has two menu items:

■ Set Color

■ Exit

Later in this chapter, you'll attach code to the Exit menu item so that when the user will click the Exit menu item, the program will terminate itself. What will happen when the user clicks the Set Color item? Another menu (called a submenu) will pop up. You'll now build the submenu.

The contents of the Set Color submenu should be

■ Red

■ Blue

■ White

☐ While the window of the frmColors window is selected, select Menu Editor from the Tools menu.

Visual Basic responds by displaying the Menu Editor window.

The Red menu item is one of the menu items of the Set Color item. So you need to insert Red between Set Color and Exit. Here is how you do this:

☐ Select the Exit item (because you are about to insert an item in the line above the Exit item).

☐ Click the Insert button of the Menu Editor window.

Visual Basic responds by inserting a blank row below Set Color.

☐ In the Caption text box of the Menu Editor window, type &Red.

☐ In the Name text box of the Menu Editor window, type mnuRed.

Currently, Red is indented at the same level as Set Color, but it should be indented further because Red is an item in the Set Color submenu.

Use the following step to indent Red further:

☐ Click the right-arrow button of the Menu Editor window.

Use the following steps to insert the Blue item:

☐ Insert a blank row below the Red submenu item by selecting the Exit menu item and clicking the Insert button of the Menu Editor window.

☐ In the Caption text box of the Menu Editor window, type &Blue.

☐ In the Name text box of the Menu Editor window, type mnuBlue.

☐ Click the right-arrow button of the Menu Editor window to indent Blue at the same level as Red.

Use the following steps to insert the White submenu item:

☐ Insert a blank row below the Blue submenu item by selecting the Exit menu item and clicking the Insert button of the Menu Editor window.

☐ In the Caption text box of the Menu Editor window, type &White.

☐ In the Name text box of the Menu Editor window, type mnuWhite.

☐ Click the right-arrow button of the Menu Editor window to indent White at the same level as Red and Blue.

Congratulations! The menu of the Colors program is complete! The Menu Editor should now look like the one shown in Figure 5.13.

Use the following step to exit the Menu Editor:

☐ Click the OK button of the Menu Editor window.

Visual Basic responds by closing the Menu Editor, and the frmColors form is displayed. As you can see, the menu that you just designed is attached to the form.

The visual implementation of the Colors program is complete.

☐ Select Save Project from the File menu.

Figure 5.13.

The Menu Editor
after the Colors menu
is complete.

Following a Menu Table

Because the Colors program is your first menu program, the preceding instructions were a step-by-step tutorial of how to create a menu. However, later in this chapter and in subsequent chapters, you will be instructed to create other menus by following a menu table.

A menu table is made up of two columns. The left column lists the captions and indentation levels of the menu controls, and the right column lists the names of the menu controls.

A typical menu table is shown in Table 5.2. As you can see, it is the menu table of the Colors program.

Table 5.2. The menu table of the Colors program.

Caption	Name
&Colors	mnuColors
&Set Color	mnuSetColor
&Red	mnuRed
&Blue	mnuBlue
&White	mnuWhite
E&xit	mnuExit
&Size	mnuSize
&Small	mnuSmall
&Large	mnuLarge

Entering the Code of the Colors Program

Each of the menu controls that you designed has a `Click` event, which is executed when you select that menu item. For example, when you select the Exit item of the Colors menu, the event procedure `mnuExit_Click()` is automatically executed. The name of this event procedure starts with the characters `mnuExit_` because mnuExit is the name that you assigned to the Exit menu item in the Menu Editor window.

Although the event is called `Click`, this event procedure is executed whether you select the menu item by clicking or by using the keyboard.

As you can see, the program's menu is displayed during design time. To display the procedure of a menu item, simply click on the menu item. For example, to see the procedure that is executed when you select the Exit menu item, simply click this item.

Another way to display the procedure of a menu item is to display the form's code window by double-clicking anywhere in the form and selecting the desired menu object from the list boxes at the top of the code window.

Now enter the code of the Colors program.

☐ Make sure that the general declarations section of the frmColors form has the `Option Explicit` statement in it as follows:

```
' All variables MUST be declared.
Option Explicit
```

In the next step you are asked to type code in the `Form_Load()` procedure. To display the `Form_Load()` procedure you have to double-click the form. This displays the code window. Set the upper-left list box of the code window to Form. Set the upper-right list box of the code window to Load. This causes Visual Basic to display the `Form_Load()` procedure.

☐ Type the following code in the `Form_Load()` procedure:

```
Private Sub Form_Load ()

    'Because initially the window is white,
    'disable the White menu item.
    mnuWhite.Enabled = False

    'Because initially the window is small,
    'disable the Small menu item.
    mnuSmall.Enabled = False

End Sub
```

5

> **Note**
>
> In the next step you are instructed to type code in the mnuRed_Click()
> procedure. To display the mnuRed_Click() procedure, display the
> frmColors form, select the Set Color item in the Colors menu, and
> then select Red from the submenu that pops up.
>
> Or you can display the mnuRed_Click() procedure as follows:
>
> ☐ Display the code window.
>
> ☐ Set the left list box of the code window to mnuRed.
>
> ☐ Set the right list box of the code window to Click.

☐ Type the following code in the mnuRed_Click() procedure:

```
Private Sub mnuRed_Click ()

    ' Set the color of the form to red.
    frmColors.BackColor = QBColor(4)

    ' Disable the Red menu item.
    mnuRed.Enabled = False

    ' Enable the Blue and White menu items.
    mnuBlue.Enabled = True
    mnuWhite.Enabled = True

End Sub
```

☐ Type the following code in the mnuBlue_Click() procedure:

```
Private Sub mnuBlue_Click ()

    ' Set the color of the form to blue.
    frmColors.BackColor = QBColor(1)

    ' Disable the Blue menu item.
    mnuBlue.Enabled = False

    ' Enable the Red and White menu items.
    mnuRed.Enabled = True
    mnuWhite.Enabled = True

End Sub
```

☐ Type the following code in the mnuWhite_Click() procedure:

```
Private Sub mnuWhite_Click ()

    ' Set the color of the form to bright white.
    frmColors.BackColor = QBColor(15)

    ' Disable the White menu item.
    mnuWhite.Enabled = False
```

```
            ' Enable the Red and Blue menu items.
            mnuRed.Enabled = True
            mnuBlue.Enabled = True

       End Sub
```

☐ Type the following code in the mnuSmall_Click() procedure:

```
    Private Sub mnuSmall_Click ()

        ' Set the size of the form to small.
        frmColors.WindowState = 0

        ' Disable the Small menu item.
        mnuSmall.Enabled = False

        ' Enable the Large menu item.
        mnuLarge.Enabled = True

    End Sub
```

☐ Type the following code in the mnuLarge_Click() procedure:

```
    Private Sub mnuLarge_Click ()

        ' Set the size of the form to large.
        frmColors.WindowState = 2

        ' Disable the Large menu item.
        mnuLarge.Enabled = False

        ' Enable the Small menu item.
        mnuSmall.Enabled = True

    End Sub
```

☐ Type the following code in the mnuExit_Click() procedure:

```
    Private Sub mnuExit_Click ()

        End

    End Sub:
```

☐ Select Save Project from the File menu of Visual Basic to save your work.

Executing the Colors Program

Execute the Colors program and select the various items of the menu. While you run the program, notice the following features:

■ When you execute the program, the menu item White of the Set Color submenu is dimmed (that is, not available). This menu item is dimmed because the color of the form is already white, so it makes no sense to change white to white. Similarly, the Small menu item of the Size menu is dimmed because the form is already small.

- After you select Large from the Size menu, the form becomes large and the menu item Large is dimmed.

- After you select a color from the Set Color submenu, the form changes its color and the menu item of the selected color is dimmed.

☐ Select Exit from the Colors menu to terminate the Colors program.

How the Colors Program Works

The Colors program uses the Form_Load() procedure and the Click event of the various menu items.

The Code of the Form_Load() Procedure

When you start a Visual Basic program, one of the first procedures that is executed automatically is the Form_Load() procedure. You can use the Form_Load() procedure to perform various initialization tasks that you want the program to perform at the beginning of the execution.

In the case of the Colors program, you typed code in the Form_Load() procedure that disables the menu item White of the Set Color submenu and disables the menu item Small of the Size menu.

The Form_Load() procedure disables the White and Small menu items by setting their Enabled properties to False:

```
Private Sub Form_Load ()

    ' Because initially the window is white,
    ' disable the White menu item.
    mnuWhite.Enabled = False

    ' Because initially the window is small,
    ' disable the Small menu item.
    mnuSmall.Enabled = False

End Sub
```

The Code of the mnuRed_Click() Procedure

When you select Red from the Set Color submenu, the mnuRed_Click() procedure is executed, which changes the color of the form to red and disables the Red menu item:

```
Private Sub mnuRed_Click ()

    ' Set the color of the form to red.
    frmColors.BackColor = QBColor(4)
```

```
'Disable the Red menu item.
mnuRed.Enabled = False

'Enable the Blue and White menu items.
mnuBlue.Enabled = True
mnuWhite.Enabled = True
```

End Sub

After the procedure disables the Red menu item, the procedure enables the Blue and White menu items. The Blue and White menu items are enabled because now the form's color is red, and you should be able to change it to either blue or white.

The `mnuBlue_Click()` and `mnuWhite_Click()` procedures are similar to the `mnuRed_Click()` procedure.

The Code of the `mnuSmall_Click()` Procedure

When you select Small from the Size menu, the `mnuSmall_Click()` procedure is executed, which changes the size of the form to small and disables the Small menu item:

```
Private Sub mnuSmall_Click ()

    ' Set the size of the form to small.
    frmColors.WindowState = 0

    ' Disable the Small menu item.
    mnuSmall.Enabled = False

    ' Enable the Large menu item.
     mnuLarge.Enabled = True

End Sub
```

You change the size of the form by setting the WindowState property of the form. When the WindowState property of the form is set to 0, the form is sized to its default normal size (the size set at design time). When it is set to 2, the form is its maximum size.

After the procedure disables the Small menu item, it enables the Large menu item because when the form is small, you should be able to change it to large.

The `mnuLarge_Click()` procedure is similar to the `mnuSmall_Click()` procedure.

The Code of the `mnuExit_Click()` Procedure

When you select Exit from the Colors menu, the `mnuExit_Click()` procedure is executed, and this terminates the program:

```
Private Sub mnuExit_Click ()

    End

End Sub
```

5

Adding Shortcut Keys

You can enhance the Colors program by adding shortcut keys. Shortcut keys enable you to execute a menu item by pressing a combination of keys on the keyboard.

For example, in the Colors program you may assign the shortcut key Ctrl+R to the Red menu item of the Set Color submenu. By doing so, when you press Ctrl+R, the form will change its color to red.

Use the following steps to assign the shortcut key Ctrl+R to the Red menu item:

☐ Select the frmColors form.

☐ Select Menu Editor from the Tools menu.

   Visual Basic responds by displaying the Menu Editor.

☐ Highlight the Red menu item.

   Visual Basic responds by displaying the properties of the Red menu item on the upper portion of the Menu Editor window.

As you can see, the Shortcut combo box of the Red menu item is currently set to (none).

Use the following steps to set the shortcut to Ctrl+R:

☐ Click the down arrow of the Shortcut combo box of the Menu Editor window, and select the shortcut Ctrl+R.

☐ Click the OK button to close the Menu Editor.

Use the following steps to see the Ctrl+R shortcut that you attached to the Red menu item in action:

☐ Execute the Colors program.

☐ Press Ctrl+R.

   The Colors program responds by changing the color of the form to red.

☐ You repeat the preceding steps to assign the shortcut key Ctrl+B to the Blue menu item and the shortcut key Ctrl+W to the White menu item.

> **Note**
>
> Users know that they can press Ctrl+R and this will have an identical effect as selecting Red from the menu, because the text Ctrl+R appears to the right of the Red menu item. Similarly, the text Ctrl+B appears to the right of the Blue menu item, and the text Ctrl+W appears to the right of White item (see Figure 5.14).

Figure 5.14.

The shortcuts that appear to the right of the color menu items in the Set Color menu.

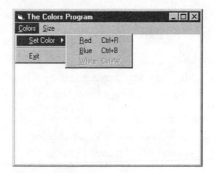

Adding a Separator Bar to a Menu

A separator bar is a horizontal line that separates menu items. Its only purpose is cosmetic. Figure 5.15 shows the Colors menu of the Colors program after a separator bar was inserted between the Set Color item and the Exit item.

Figure 5.15.

A separator bar.

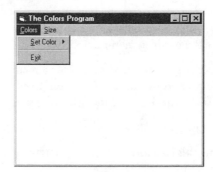

Use the following steps to insert a separator bar between the Set Color item and the Exit item:

☐ Select the frmColors form.

☐ Select Menu Editor from the Tools menu.

Visual Basic responds by displaying the Menu Editor.

☐ Highlight the Exit menu item and click the Insert button of the Menu Editor window.

Visual Basic responds by inserting a blank row above the Exit item.

☐ In the Caption text box of the Menu Editor window, type -.

☐ In the Name text box of the Menu Editor window, type mnuSep1.

☐ Click the OK button of the Menu Editor window to close the Menu Editor.

The hyphen character (-) that you typed in the Caption text box of the Menu Editor window is the symbol for a separator bar.

You named the separator bar mnuSep1. If you have to add more separator bars to the menu, you could name them mnuSep2, mnuSep3, and so on. Of course, you can give a separator bar any name you want, but it's a good idea to give it a name that distinguishes it as a separator.

You cannot select the separator bar during runtime, so the `mnuSep1_Click()` procedure is never executed. (Why do you need a name for a menu item that is never executed? Visual Basic requires that you name all menu items.)

☐ Execute the Colors program.

As you can see, the separator bar that you just created appears.

Making a Menu Control Invisible

In the Colors program, you enabled and disabled menu items at runtime by writing code that sets the Enabled property of the item to True or False. When the item is disabled (that is, the Enabled property is set to False), it becomes dimmed and you cannot select it. However, you can still see the disabled menu item.

In some programs you may need to hide a menu item completely, not just dim it. You use the Visible property to do this. For example, to make a menu item called mnuMyItem invisible during runtime, use the following statement:

```
mnuMyItem.Visible = False
```

After issuing this statement, the mnuMyItem menu item disappears, and all the menu items under it move up to fill its space.

To make a whole menu invisible, you need to set the Visible property of the menu's title to False. After making a menu invisible, it disappears and all the menus to its right move to the left to fill its space.

Using Check Marks

In some programs you may need to mark menu items. You can use check marks to do this. Figure 5.16 shows a menu item with a check mark next to it.

Figure 5.16.

A check mark to the left of a menu item.

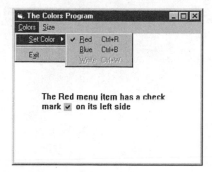

To place a check mark next to a menu item, set the Checked property to True; to remove the check mark, set the Checked property to False. For example, to place a check mark next to the Red menu item, you need to issue the following statement:

```
mnuRed.Checked = True
```

To uncheck the Red menu item, issue the following statement:

```
mnuRed.Checked = False
```

(The Colors program does not use the check marks of the menu items.)

Note that one of the check boxes that appear in the upper portion of the Menu Editor window is called Checked. If you place a check mark in this check box, the menu item that corresponds to the currently highlighted item in the lower part of the Menu Editor will appear with a check mark on its left. (You can remove the check mark from within the code of your program by setting the Checked property of this menu item to False.)

The Grow Program

You'll now write a program called Grow that illustrates how items can be added to or removed from a menu during runtime. Before you start writing the Grow program, let's specify what the program should do:

☐ When you start the program, a menu bar with the menu title Grow appears, as shown in Figure 5.17.

Figure 5.17.

The Grow program.

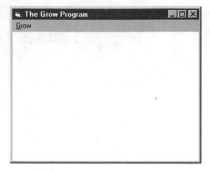

☐ The Grow menu initially has three menu items—Add, Remove, and Exit—and a separator bar (see Figure 5.18). Note that the Remove menu item is dimmed.

Figure 5.18.

The Grow menu
without added items.

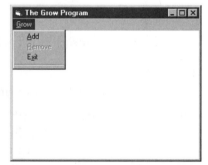

☐ Every time you select Add, a new item is added to the Grow menu. For example, after selecting Add three times, the Grow menu should look like the one shown in Figure 5.19.

Figure 5.19.

The Grow menu with
three added items.

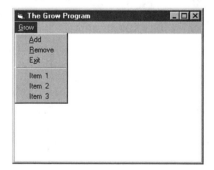

☐ Every time you select Remove, the last item of the Grow menu is removed.

☐ When you select one of the items that was added to the menu, a message box pops up with the name of the selected item. For example, if you select Item 2, the message box shown in Figure 5.20 appears.

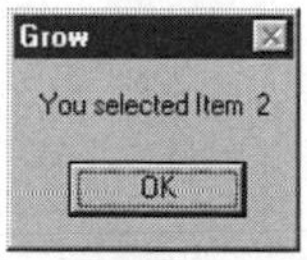

Figure 5.20.

The message box after you select Item 2 from the Grow menu.

The Visual Implementation of the Grow Program

As usual, you start by implementing the form of the program:

☐ Start a new Standard EXE project.

☐ Save the form of the project as Grow.Frm in the C:\VB5Prg\Ch05 directory, and save the project file as Grow.Vbp in the C:\VB5Prg\Ch05 directory.

☐ Build the form according to Table 5.3.

Table 5.3. The properties table of the frmGrow form.

Object	Property	Value
Form	Name	frmGrow
	Caption	The Grow Program
	BackColor	White

Creating the Menu of the Grow Program

You'll now attach a menu to the frmGrow form:

☐ Select the frmGrow form.

☐ Select Menu Editor from the Tools menu.

Visual Basic responds by displaying the Menu Editor.

☐ Design the menu according to Table 5.4. (In Table 5.4, the &Add menu item has three dots in front of it. This means that the &Add item is shifted to the right inside the Menu Editor window. Similarly, the &Remove, E&xit and separate bar (-) are shifted to the right in the Menu Editor window, just as the &Set Color, E&xit, &Small, and &Large items are shifted to the right in Figure 5.9.)

Table 5.4. The menu table of the frmGrow form.

Caption	Name
&Grow	mnuGrow
...&Add	mnuAdd
...&Remove	mnuRemove
...E&xit	mnuExit
...-	mnuItems

☐ Highlight the last item of the menu (the separator bar), and type 0 in the Index text box (see Figure 5.21).

☐ Click the OK button of the Menu Editor window.

The visual implementation of the Grow program is complete!

Figure 5.21.

Setting the Index property of the separator bar.

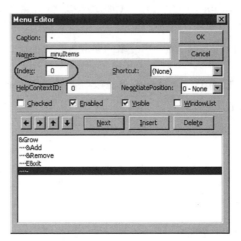

Creating a Menu Control Array

By setting the Index property of the separator bar to 0, you created a menu control array. Because you set the Name property to mnuItems, the control array you created is called mnuItems.

So far, the mnuItems array has only one element: the separator bar (that is, mnuItems(0) is the separator bar). During runtime, every time you select Add from the Grow menu, the program's code will add a new element to the mnuItems array. As a result, more menu items will appear below the separator bar.

Entering the Code of the Grow Program

Now type the code of the Grow program as follows:

☐ Type the following code in the general declarations section of the frmGrow form:

```
' All variables MUST be declared.
Option Explicit
' Declare the gLastElement variable.
Dim gLastElement As Integer
```

 Tip

> If you have problems adding code to the general declaration area, try the following: Place the mouse cursor at the beginning of the Option Explicit statement. Press the Enter key several times. As a result, a few empty lines are added to the general declarations section. Now you can type additional code in the general declarations section.

☐ Type the following code in the Form_Load() procedure:

```
Private Sub Form_Load ()

    ' Initially the last element in the
        ' mnuItems[] array is 0.
    gLastElement = 0

    ' Initially no items are added to the
    ' Grow menu, so disable the Remove option.
    mnuRemove.Enabled = False

End Sub
```

☐ Type the following code in the mnuAdd_Click() procedure:

```
Private Sub mnuAdd_Click ()

    ' Increment the gLastElement variable.
    gLastElement = gLastElement + 1

    ' Add a new element to the mnuItems[] array.
    Load mnuItems(gLastElement)

    ' Assign a caption to the item that
    ' was just added.
    mnuItems(gLastElement).Caption = _
                "Item "+Str(gLastElement)

    ' Because an element was just added to the
    ' mnuItems array, the Remove option should be
    ' enabled.
    mnuRemove.Enabled = True

End Sub
```

5

☐ Type the following code in the mnuRemove_Click() procedure:

```
Private Sub mnuRemove_Click ()

    ' Remove the last element of the mnuItems array.
    Unload mnuItems(gLastElement)

    ' Decrement the gLastElement variable.
    gLastElement = gLastElement - 1

    ' If only element 0 is left in the array,
    ' disable the Remove menu item.
    If gLastElement = 0 Then
       mnuRemove.Enabled = False
    End If

End Sub
```

☐ Type the following code in the mnuItems_Click() procedure:

```
Private Sub mnuItems_Click (Index As Integer)

    ' Display the item that was selected.
    MsgBox "You selected Item " + Str(Index)

End Sub
```

To access the mnuItems_Click() procedure, display the code window, set the upper-left list box of the code window to mnuItems, and set the upper-right list box of the code window to Click.

☐ Type the following code in the mnuExit_Click() procedure:

```
Private Sub mnuExit_Click ()

    End

End Sub
```

☐ Select Save Project from the File menu of Visual Basic to save your work.

Executing the Grow Program

Execute the Grow program and select the various items in the menu. While you run the program, notice the following features:

- When you execute the program, the menu item Remove is dimmed (that is, not available because no items have been added to the menu at this point, so there is nothing to remove).

- Every time Add is selected, a new item is added to the menu. When there is at least one added item in the menu, the Remove option is available.

■ Every time Remove is selected, the last added menu item is removed. When there
are no more added items in the menu, the Remove option is dimmed.

☐ Select Exit from the menu to terminate the Grow program.

How the Grow Program Works

The Grow program uses the variable gLastElement to keep count of the number of elements
in the mnuItems array. Because this variable should be visible in all the procedures of the form,
you declare the variable in the general declarations section of the form:

```
' All variables MUST be declared.
Option Explicit
' Declare the gLastElement variable.
Dim gLastElement As Integer
```

The Code of the Form_Load() Procedure

When you start the program, the Form_Load() procedure is automatically executed.

In this procedure, gLastElement is initialized to 0 and the Remove menu item is disabled:

```
Private Sub Form_Load ()

    ' Initially the last element in the
    ' mnuItems[] array is 0.
    gLastElement = 0

    ' Initially no items are added to the
    ' Grow menu, so disable the Remove option.
    mnuRemove.Enabled = False

End Sub
```

The first statement in this procedure initializes the gLastElement variable to 0 because the
mnuItems array has only one element in it: the 0th element. You created the 0th element of
the array (the separator bar) at design time.

The next statement in this procedure disables the Remove menu item because you haven't
added any items to the menu yet.

The Code of the mnuAdd_Click() Procedure

The mnuAdd_Click() procedure is executed when you select Add from the Grow menu. This
procedure is responsible for adding a new element to the mnuItems array and setting its
Caption property:

```
Private Sub mnuAdd_Click ()

   ' Increment the gLastElement variable.
   gLastElement = gLastElement + 1

   ' Add a new element to the mnuItems[] array.
   Load mnuItems(gLastElement)

   ' Assign a caption to the item that
   ' was just added.
   mnuItems(gLastElement).Caption = "Item "+Str(gLastElement)

   ' Because an element was just added to the
   ' mnuItems array, the Remove option should be
   ' enabled.
   mnuRemove.Enabled = True

End Sub
```

The first thing the procedure does is increment the value of the variable gLastElement:

```
gLastElement = gLastElement + 1
```

Then a new element is added to the mnuItems array with the Load statement:

```
Load mnuItems(gLastElement)
```

The Caption property of the new element is set with the following statement:

```
mnuItems(gLastElement).Caption = "Item "+Str(gLastElement)
```

Finally, the Remove menu item is enabled:

```
mnuRemove.Enabled = True
```

The Remove menu item is enabled because the procedure just added an item to the menu, and you should be able to remove it.

The Code of the mnuRemove_Click() Procedure

The mnuRemove_Click() procedure is executed when you select Remove from the menu:

```
Private Sub mnuRemove_Click ()

   ' Remove the last element of the mnuItems array.
   Unload mnuItems(gLastElement)

   ' Decrement the gLastElement variable.
   gLastElement = gLastElement - 1

   ' If only element 0 is left in the array,
   ' disable the Remove menu item.
   If gLastElement = 0 Then
      mnuRemove.Enabled = False
   End If

End Sub
```

In this procedure, the last element of the mnuItems array is removed with the Unload statement:

```
Unload mnuItems(gLastElement)
```

Then the variable gLastElement is decremented.

After removing the last element of the array, if it is left with only element 0, the Remove menu item is disabled:

```
If gLastElement = 0 Then
    mnuRemove.Enabled = False
End If
```

The Code of the mnuItems_Click() Procedure

The mnuItems_Click() procedure is executed when you select any of the added items from the Grow menu:

```
Private Sub mnuItems_Click (Index As Integer)

    ' Display the item that was selected.
    MsgBox "You selected Item " + Str(Index)

End Sub
```

The Index argument of this procedure indicates which item was selected. For example, if you selected Item 1, the Index argument is equal to 1 (that is, Item 1 is element number 1 in the mnuItems array). If you selected Item 2, the Index argument is equal to 2, and so on. The program automatically updates the Index argument for you.

Summary

This chapter teaches you how to write programs that include a menu, how to attach a menu to a form using the Menu Editor, and how to attach code to the menu controls. The different properties of the menu controls, such as the Visible property and the Checked property, give you the power and flexibility to change the appearance of the menu during runtime. By creating a menu control array, you can even add items to and remove them from a menu during runtime.

Q&A

Q In the Colors program, the Enabled properties of the White and Small menu items were set to False in the Form_Load() procedure. Can I set these properties at design time?

A Yes, you can set these properties during design time by using the Menu Editor dialog box. (Note that the Menu Editor window has the Enabled check box. When you place a check mark in the check box, the menu item that corresponds to the currently highlighted item in the lower part of the Menu editor will appear enabled. If there is no check mark in the Enabled check box, the menu item will appear disabled.)

Q I learned how to disable menu items during runtime from the examples of this chapter. How can I disable a complete menu?

A You need to set the Enabled property of the menu title to False to disable a complete menu. By doing so, the disabled title becomes dimmed, and the menu will not pop up. For example, to disable the Size menu of the Colors program you need to issue the following statement:

```
mnuSize.Enabled = False
```

The entire Size menu is disabled after issuing this statement.

Quiz

1. What is the difference between the Enabled property and the Visible property of a menu control?
2. How do you create a menu control array, and what is it used for?
3. What are shortcut keys and how do you create them?
4. What are check marks and how do you use them in a program?
5. What is a separator bar?

Exercises

1. Enhance the Colors program so that when a color is selected, a check mark is placed next to the selected color menu item.
2. Enhance the Grow program so that you will be limited to adding a maximum of 15 items to the Grow menu (at this point, you can add an unlimited number of items).

Quiz Answers

1. When the Enabled property of a menu item is set to False, the menu item is disabled (dimmed), but you can still see it. On the other hand, when the Visible property of a menu item is set to False, the menu item completely disappears.

2. A menu control array is created during design time by setting the Index property of a menu item to 0. This menu item becomes element number 0 of the array. During runtime, the program can add items to the menu by adding more elements to the array. (The items are added below the item created in design time.)

3. A shortcut key enables you to execute a menu item by pressing a combination of keys on the keyboard (for example, Ctrl+C, Ctrl+A). You assign a shortcut key to a menu item during design time by setting the Shortcut property to the desired key combination.

4. A check mark is used to mark menu items. To place a check mark next to a menu item during runtime, set the Checked property of the item to True. To remove a check mark, set the Checked property of the item to False.

5. A separator bar is a horizontal line used to separate menu items. The Caption property of a separator bar is the hyphen character (-).

Exercise Answers

1. To enhance the Colors program so that it will place a check mark next to the selected color menu item, modify the mnuRed_Click(), mnuBlue_Click(), and mnuWhite_Click() procedures as follows:

   ☐ Add the following statements to the mnuRed_Click() procedure:

   ```
   ' Put a check mark next to the Red menu item.
   mnuRed.Checked = True
   ' Uncheck the Blue and White menu items.
   mnuWhite.Checked = False
   mnuBlue.Checked = False
   ```

   ☐ Add the following statements to the mnuBlue_Click() procedure:

   ```
   ' Put a check mark next to the Blue menu item.
   mnuBlue.Checked = True
   ' Uncheck the White and Red menu items.
   mnuWhite.Checked = False
   mnuRed.Checked = False
   ```

   ☐ Add the following statements to the mnuWhite_Click() procedure:

   ```
   ' Put a check mark next to the White menu item.
   mnuWhite.Checked = True
   ' Uncheck the Blue and Red menu items.
   mnuBlue.Checked = False
   mnuRed.Checked = False
   ```

5

2. To limit the number of items that you can add to the Grow menu to 15, insert the following code at the beginning of the mnuAdd_Click() procedure:

```
Private Sub mnuAdd_Click ()

    ' If the last element is 15 then beep and end
    ' this procedure.
    If gLastElement = 15 Then
        Beep
        Exit Sub
    End If
    ..................................
    ... The rest of the procedure ...
    ... remains the same.         ...
    ..................................
End Sub
```

Day 6

Dialog Boxes

This chapter shows you how to incorporate dialog boxes into your programs. Dialog boxes are used to display and get information from your user. In Visual Basic there are three types of dialog boxes: predefined dialog boxes, custom dialog boxes, and common dialog boxes.

Predefined Dialog Boxes

As the name implies, predefined dialog boxes are predefined by Visual Basic. To display a predefined dialog box, you use a Visual Basic statement with parameters that specify how and when the dialog box should appear. You can display a predefined dialog box by using

- The `MsgBox` statement and `MsgBox()` function
- The `InputBox()` function

The Message Program

You can use the MsgBox statement and MsgBox() function to display messages to the user and to get the user's response to yes and no questions. The Message program shows how the MsgBox statement and MsgBox() function are used in a program.

The Visual Implementation of the Message Program

As usual, you'll start with the visual implementation of the form of the program:

☐ Create the C:\VB5Prg\Ch06 directory.

☐ Start a new Standard EXE project.

☐ Save the form of the project as Message.Frm in the C:\VB5Prg\Ch06 directory, and save the project file as Message.Vbp in the C:\VB5Prg\Ch06 directory.

☐ Build the form according to Table 6.1.

The completed form should look like the one shown in Figure 6.1.

Figure 6.1.

The frmMessage form (design mode).

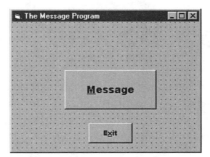

Table 6.1. The properties table of the frmMessage form.

Object	Property	Value
Form	**Name**	**frmMessage**
	Caption	The Message Program
Command Button	**Name**	**cmdMessage**
	Caption	&Message
Command Button	**Name**	**cmdExit**
	Caption	E&xit

Entering the Code of the Message Program

You'll now enter the code of the Message program:

☐ Make sure that the general declarations section of the frmMessage for includes the `Option Explicit` statement as follows:

```
' All variables MUST be declared.
Option Explicit
```

☐ Type the following code in the `cmdMessage_Click()` procedure:

```
Private Sub cmdMessage_Click()

    Dim Message As String
    Dim ButtonsAndIcons As Integer
    Dim Title As String

    ' The message of the dialog box.
    Message = "This is a sample message!"

    ' The dialog box should have an OK button and
    ' an exclamation icon.
    ButtonsAndIcons = vbOKOnly + vbExclamation

    ' The title of the dialog box.
    Title = "Dialog Box Demonstration"

    ' Display the dialog box.
    MsgBox Message, ButtonsAndIcons, Title

End Sub
```

☐ Type the following code in the `cmdExit_Click()` procedure:

```
Private Sub cmdExit_Click()

    Dim Message As String
    Dim ButtonsAndIcons As Integer
    Dim Title As String
    Dim Response As Integer

    ' The message of the dialog box.
    Message = "Are you sure you want to quit?"

    ' The dialog box should have Yes and No buttons,
    ' and a question icon.
    ButtonsAndIcons = vbYesNo + vbQuestion

    ' The title of the dialog box.
    Title = "The Message Program"

    ' Display the dialog box and get user's response.
    Response = MsgBox(Message, ButtonsAndIcons, Title)
```

6

```
' Evaluate the user's response.
If Response = vbYes Then
    End
End If

    End Sub
```

☐ Select Save Project from the File menu of Visual Basic to save your work.

Executing the Message Program

Let's execute the Message program and see your code in action:

☐ Execute the Message program.

While executing the Message program, note the following feature: When you click the Message button, a dialog box with a message, an OK button, and an exclamation point icon is displayed (see Figure 6.2). This dialog box is modal, which means that the program won't continue until you close the dialog box. For example, if you try to click the mouse on the Exit button while the dialog box is displayed, the program will not terminate (because the cmdExit_Click() procedure is not executed).

☐ Click the OK button of the dialog box.

As a response, the dialog box closes itself.

☐ Click the Exit button.

As a response, a dialog box with a question, a Yes button, a No button, and a question mark icon is displayed (see Figure 6.3). This dialog box asks you to confirm whether you want to exit the program. If you press the Yes button, the program terminates. If you press the No button, the dialog box closes and the program does not terminate. This dialog box is also modal (that is, you must click the Yes or No button before the program continues).

Figure 6.2.

A dialog box with an OK button and an exclamation point icon.

Figure 6.3.

A dialog box with Yes and No buttons and a question mark icon.

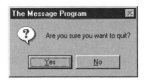

Note

> The message boxes that you implemented in the Message program are called application modal dialog boxes. That is, while the dialog box (the message box) is displayed, you can switch to other Windows programs. You cannot return to the window of the Message application unless you first close the dialog box.
>
> Another type of modality is the system modal dialog box, which does not let you return to the application and does not let you switch to other Windows applications. In other words, as long as the system modal dialog box is displayed, the user can work only with the dialog box (click the buttons of the dialog box and type text in a text box that resides in the dialog box).

How the Message Program Works

The Message program uses the MsgBox statement and MsgBox() function to display message boxes.

Displaying a Dialog Box with the MsgBox Statement

When the user clicks the Message button, the cmdMessage_Click() procedure is automatically executed. The code in this procedure uses the MsgBox statement to display a dialog box (message box) with an OK button and an exclamation point icon:

```
Private Sub cmdMessage_Click()

    Dim Message As String
    Dim ButtonsAndIcons As Integer
    Dim Title As String

    ' The message of the dialog box.
    Message = "This is a sample message!"

    ' The dialog box should have an OK button and
    ' an exclamation icon.
    ButtonsAndIcons = vbOKOnly + vbExclamation

    ' The title of the dialog box.
    Title = "Dialog Box Demonstration"

    ' Display the dialog box.
    MsgBox Message, ButtonsAndIcons, Title

End Sub
```

6

The statement that executes the MsgBox statement passes three parameters to the MsgBox statement:

- The message to be displayed (a string)
- The buttons and icons that will appear in the message box (a numeric value)
- The title of the dialog box (a string)

Before executing the MsgBox statement, the cmdMessage_Click() procedure updates three variables that will be used as the parameters of the MsgBox statement. The first variable that the cmdMessage() procedure updates is the string variable Message, which is updated with the message of the dialog box:

```
Message = "This is a sample message!"
```

Message is used as the first parameter of the MsgBox statement.

The second variable is an integer variable ButtonsAndIcons, which is updated with a number that determines the buttons and icons that will appear in the message box:

```
ButtonsAndIcons = vbOKOnly + vbExclamation
```

ButtonsAndIcons is used as the second parameter of the MsgBox statement. vbOKOnly and vbExclamation are Visual Basic constants. vbOKOnly is a constant that represents the OK button, and vbExclamation is a constant that represents the exclamation icon. By specifying ButtonsAndIcons as the sum of vbOKOnly and vbExclamation, you specify that the dialog box should have an OK button and an exclamation icon, as shown in Figure 6.2.

Tables 6.2 and 6.3 list all the button constants and icon constants that you can use for the second parameter of the MsgBox. For example, to specify a dialog box (message box) with an OK button and a critical icon, the second parameter of the MsgBox statement should be the sum of the two constants vbOKOnly and vbCritical.

Table 6.2. Button constants.

Constant Name	Value	Displayed Buttons
vbOKOnly	0	OK
vbOKCancel	1	OK, Cancel
vbAbortRetryIgnore	2	Abort, Retry, Ignore
vbYesNoCancel	3	Yes, No, Cancel
vbYesNo	4	Yes, No
vbRetryCancel	5	Retry, Cancel

Table 6.3. Icon constants.

Constant Name	Value	Displayed Icon
vbCritical	16	Critical icon
vbQuestion	32	Warning query icon
vbExclamation	48	Warning message icon
vbInformation	64	Information icon

The third variable that the code of the cmdMessage_Click() procedure updates is Title, which is updated with the title of the dialog box:

```
Title = "Dialog Box Demonstration"
```

Finally, the variables Message, ButtonsAndIcons, and Title are used as the parameters of the MsgBox statement:

```
MsgBox Message, ButtonsAndIcons, Title
```

As a result, the message box shown in Figure 6.2 is displayed.

Displaying a Dialog Box with the MsgBox() Function

When you click the Exit button, the cmdExit_Click() procedure is executed. The code in this procedure uses the MsgBox() function to display a dialog box with a question message, Yes and No buttons, and a question mark icon:

```
Private Sub cmdExit_Click()

    Dim Message As String
    Dim ButtonsAndIcons As Integer
    Dim Title As String
    Dim Response As Integer

    ' The message of the dialog box.
    Message = "Are you sure you want to quit?"

    ' The dialog box should have Yes and No buttons,
    ' and a question icon.
    ButtonsAndIcons = vbYesNo + vbQuestion

    ' The title of the dialog box.
    Title = "The Message Program"

    ' Display the dialog box and get user's response.
    Response = MsgBox(Message, ButtonsAndIcons, Title)

    ' Evaluate the user's response.
    If Response = vbYes Then
        End
    End If

End Sub
```

6

The MsgBox() function takes the same parameters as the MsgBox statement. The only difference between the MsgBox statement and the MsgBox() function is that the MsgBox() function returns a value. The returned value of the MsgBox() function indicates which button in the dialog box was clicked.

Before executing the MsgBox() function, the cmdExit_Click() procedure updates the three variables Message, ButtonsAndIcons, and Title:

```
Message = "Are you sure you want to quit?"
DialogType = vbYesNo + vbQuestion
Title = "The Message Program"
```

The variable ButtonsAndIcons is updated with the sum of the constants vbYesNo and vbQuestion, because the dialog box should have Yes and No buttons and a question mark icon.

Once the variables Message, ButtonsAndIcons, and Title are updated, the MsgBox() function is executed and its returned value is assigned to the variable Response:

```
Response = MsgBox(Message, DialogType, Title)
```

The returned value of the MsgBox() function indicates which button was clicked. Table 6.4 lists all possible constants that can be returned by the MsgBox() function. For example, if the returned value from the MsgBox() function is the constant vbYes, it means that the Yes button of the message box was clicked.

Table 6.4. Possible return values from the MsgBox() function.

Constant Name	Value	Clicked Button
vbOK	1	OK button
vbCancel	2	Cancel button
vbAbort	3	Abort button
vbRetry	4	Retry button
vbIgnore	5	Ignore button
vbYes	6	Yes button
vbNo	7	No button

To determine which button was clicked (the Yes button or the No button), the value of the Response variable is examined with an If statement:

```
If Response = vbYes Then
    End
End If
```

If you clicked the Yes button, Response is equal to vbYes and the program is terminated with the End statement. That is, you answered Yes to the question "Are you sure you want to quit?" and so the program ended.

Note

> The MsgBox statement in the cmdMessage_Click() procedure is executed as follows:
>
> MsgBox Message, ButtonsAndIcons, Title
>
> The MsgBox() function in the cmdExit_Click() procedure is executed as follows:
>
> Response = MsgBox(Message, DialogType, Title)
>
> When you use the MsgBox *statement*, you do *not* enclose the parameters in parentheses, but when you use the MsgBox() *function*, you *must* enclose the parameters in parentheses, and of course you must assign the returned value from the function to a variable.

The Dialogs Program

The Message program illustrated how you can use the MsgBox statement and MsgBox() function to display a dialog box with an OK button and a dialog box with Yes and No buttons. As shown in Table 6.2, you can display other standard buttons in the dialog box.

The Dialogs program illustrates how you can use the MsgBox() function to display various buttons in dialog boxes and how you can use the returned value of the MsgBox() function to determine which button was clicked.

The Visual Implementation of the Dialogs Program

You'll start with the visual implementation of the frmDialogs form:

☐ Start a new Standard EXE project.

☐ Save the form of the project as Dialogs.Frm in the C:\VB5Prg\Ch06 directory, and save the project file as Dialogs.Vbp in the C:\VB5Prg\Ch06 directory.

☐ Build the form according to Table 6.5 and Table 6.6. (Table 6.6 is the menu table of the frmDialogs form.)

The completed form should look like the one shown in Figure 6.4.

6

Figure 6.4.
The frmDialogs form
(design mode).

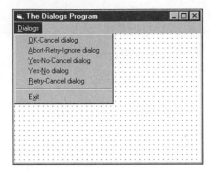

Table 6.5. The properties table of the frmDialogs form.

Object	Property	Value
Form	**Name**	**frmDialogs**
	BackColor	White
	Caption	The Dialogs Program
Menu	*(See Table 6.6)*	*(See Table 6.6)*

Table 6.6. The menu table of the frmDialogs form.

Caption	Name
&Dialogs	mnuDialogs
…&OK-Cancel dialog	mnuOkCancel
…&Abort-Retry-Ignore dialog	mnuAbortRetryIgnore
…&Yes-No-Cancel dialog	mnuYesNoCancel
…Yes-&No dialog	mnuYesNo
…&Retry-Cancel dialog	mnuRetryCancel
…-	mnuSep1
…E&xit	mnuExit

Entering the Code of the Dialogs Program

You'll now enter the code of the Dialogs program:

☐ Make sure that the Option Explicit statement resides in the general declarations section of the frmDialogs form:

```
' All variables MUST be declared.
Option Explicit
```

☐ Type the following code in the mnuAbortRetryIgnore_Click() procedure of the frmDialogs form:

```
Private Sub mnuAbortRetryIgnore_Click ()

    Dim DialogType As Integer
    Dim DialogTitle As String
    Dim DialogMsg As String
    Dim Response As Integer

    ' Dialog should have Abort, Retry, Ignore buttons,
    ' and an Exclamation icon.
    DialogType = vbAbortRetryIgnore + vbExclamation

    ' The dialog title.
    DialogTitle = "MsgBox Demonstration"

    ' The dialog message.
    DialogMsg = "This is a sample message!"

    ' Display the dialog box, and get user's response.
    Response = MsgBox(DialogMsg, DialogType, DialogTitle)

    ' Evaluate the user's response.
    Select Case Response
            Case vbAbort
                MsgBox "You clicked the Abort button!"
            Case vbRetry
                MsgBox "You clicked the Retry button!"
            Case vbIgnore
                MsgBox "You clicked the Ignore button!"
    End Select

End Sub
```

☐ Type the following code in the mnuExit_Click() procedure of the frmDialogs form:

```
Private Sub mnuExit_Click ()

    Dim DialogType As Integer
    Dim DialogTitle As String
    Dim DialogMsg As String
    Dim Response As Integer

    ' Dialog should have Yes & No buttons,
    ' and a Critical Message icon.
    DialogType = vbYesNo + vbCritical

    ' The dialog title.
    DialogTitle = "The Dialogs Program"

    ' The dialog message.
    DialogMsg = "Are you sure you want to exit?"

    ' Display the dialog box, and get user's response.
    Response = MsgBox(DialogMsg, DialogType, DialogTitle)
```

6

```
' Evaluate the user's response.
If Response = vbYes Then
    End
End If
```

End Sub

☐ Type the following code in the mnuOkCancel_Click() procedure of the frmDialogs form:

Private Sub mnuOkCancel_Click ()

```
Dim DialogType As Integer
Dim DialogTitle As String
Dim DialogMsg As String
Dim Response As Integer

' Dialog should have OK & Cancel buttons,
' and an Exclamation icon.
DialogType = vbOkCancel + vbExclamation

' The dialog title.
DialogTitle = "MsgBox Demonstration"

' The dialog message.
DialogMsg = "This is a sample message!"

' Display the dialog box, and get user's response.
Response = MsgBox(DialogMsg, DialogType, DialogTitle)

' Evaluate the user's response.
If Response = vbOK Then
    MsgBox "You clicked the OK button!"
Else
    MsgBox "You clicked the Cancel button!"
End If
```

End Sub

☐ Type the following code in the mnuRetryCancel_Click() procedure of the frmDialogs form:

Private Sub mnuRetryCancel_Click ()

```
Dim DialogType As Integer
Dim DialogTitle As String
Dim DialogMsg As String
Dim Response As Integer

' Dialog should have Retry & Cancel buttons,
' and an Exclamation icon.
DialogType = vbRetryCancel + vbExclamation

' The dialog title.
DialogTitle = "MsgBox Demonstration"

' The dialog message.
DialogMsg = "This is a sample message!"
```

```
' Display the dialog box, and get user's response.
Response = MsgBox(DialogMsg, DialogType, DialogTitle)

' Evaluate the user's response.
If Response = vbRetry Then
    MsgBox "You clicked the Retry button!"
Else
    MsgBox "You clicked the Cancel button!"
End If

End Sub
```

☐ Type the following code in the mnuYesNo_Click() procedure of the frmDialogs form:

```
Private Sub mnuYesNo_Click ()

Dim DialogType As Integer
Dim DialogTitle As String
Dim DialogMsg As String
Dim Response As Integer

' Dialog should have Yes & No buttons,
' and a question mark icon.
DialogType = vbYesNo + vbQuestion

' The dialog title.
DialogTitle = "MsgBox Demonstration"

' The dialog message.
DialogMsg = "Is this a sample message?"

' Display the dialog box, and get user's response.
Response = MsgBox(DialogMsg, DialogType, DialogTitle)

' Evaluate the user's response.
If Response = vbYes Then
    MsgBox "You clicked the Yes button!"
Else
    MsgBox "You clicked the No button!"
End If

End Sub
```

☐ Type the following code in the mnuYesNoCancel_Click() procedure of the frmDialogs form:

```
Private Sub mnuYesNoCancel_Click ()

Dim DialogType As Integer
Dim DialogTitle As String
Dim DialogMsg As String
Dim Response As Integer

' Dialog should have Yes, No, and Cancel buttons,
' and an Exclamation icon.
```

6

```
        DialogType = vbYesNoCancel + vbExclamation

        ' The dialog title.
        DialogTitle = "MsgBox Demonstration"

        ' The dialog message.
        DialogMsg = "This is a sample message!"

        ' Display the dialog box, and get user's response.
        Response = MsgBox(DialogMsg, DialogType, DialogTitle)

        ' Evaluate the user's response.
        Select Case Response
            Case vbYes
                MsgBox "You clicked the Yes button!"
            Case vbNo
                MsgBox "You clicked the No button!"
            Case vbCancel
                MsgBox "You clicked the Cancel button!"
        End Select

End Sub
```

☐ Select Save Project from the File menu of Visual Basic to save your work.

Executing the Dialogs Program

Let's see your code in action:

☐ Execute the Dialogs program.

Experiment with the various dialog boxes. For example, do this to display the Abort-Retry-Ignore dialog box:

☐ Select Abort-Retry-Ignore dialog from the Dialogs menu.

> *The program responds by displaying a dialog box with Abort, Retry, and Ignore buttons (see Figure 6.5).*

Figure 6.5.

A dialog box with Abort, Retry, and Ignore buttons.

☐ Click one of the buttons in the dialog box.

> *The program responds by displaying a message box that tells you the name of the button you clicked.*

Use the following steps to terminate the Dialogs program:

☐ Select Exit from the Dialogs menu.

> *The program responds by displaying a Yes/No dialog box, asking if you're sure you want to quit.*

☐ Click the Yes button.

> *The Dialogs program responds by terminating itself.*

How the Dialogs Program Works

The Dialogs program uses the MsgBox() function to display various dialog boxes with different buttons. The program uses the returned value of the MsgBox() function to determine which button was clicked.

The `mnuAbortRetryIgnore_Click()` Procedure

When you select Abort-Retry-Ignore dialog menu item from the Dialogs menu, the mnuAbortRetryIgnore_Click() procedure is executed. The code in this procedure uses the MsgBox() function to display a dialog box with Abort, Retry, and Ignore buttons:

```
Private Sub mnuAbortRetryIgnore_Click ()

    Dim DialogType As Integer
    Dim DialogTitle As String
    Dim DialogMsg As String
    Dim Response As Integer

    ' Dialog should have Abort, Retry, Ignore buttons,
    ' and an Exclamation icon.
    DialogType = vbAbortRetryIgnore + vbExclamation

    ' The dialog title.
    DialogTitle = "MsgBox Demonstration"

    ' The dialog message.
    DialogMsg = "This is a sample message!"

    ' Display the dialog box, and get user's response.
    Response = MsgBox(DialogMsg, DialogType, DialogTitle)

    ' Evaluate the user's response.
    Select Case Response
        Case vbAbort
            MsgBox "You clicked the Abort button!"
        Case vbRetry
            MsgBox "You clicked the Retry button!"
        Case vbIgnore
            MsgBox "You clicked the Ignore button!"
    End Select

End Sub
```

6

Before executing the MsgBox() function, the mnuAbortRetryIgnore_Click() procedure updates the variables DialogType, DialogMsg, and DialogTitle:

```
DialogType = vbAbortRetryIgnore + vbExclamation
DialogTitle = "MsgBox Demonstration"
DialogMsg = "This is a sample message!"
```

The variable DialogType is updated with the sum of vbAbortRetryIgnore and vbExclamation, because the dialog box should have Abort, Retry, and Ignore buttons and an exclamation point icon.

Once the variables Message, DialogType, and Title are updated, the MsgBox() function is executed, and its returned value is assigned to the variable Response:

```
Response = MsgBox(DialogMsg, DialogType, DialogTitle)
```

To determine which button was clicked (that is, the Abort button, the Retry button, or the Ignore button), the value of the Response variable is examined with a Select Case statement:

```
Select Case Response
      Case vbAbort
            MsgBox "You clicked the Abort button!"
      Case vbRetry
            MsgBox "You clicked the Retry button!"
      Case vbIgnore
            MsgBox "You clicked the Ignore button!"
End Select
```

If, for example, you clicked the Ignore button, the variable Response is equal to vbIgnore, and the statement under vbIgnore Case is executed. (The meanings of the vbAbort, vbRetry, and vbIgnore constants are listed in Table 6.4.)

The MsgBox statements under the Select Case statement specify only one parameter. For example, under the Case vbAbort line, the MsgBox statement is as follows:

```
MsgBox "You clicked the Abort button!"
```

When the second and third parameters of the MsgBox statement are not specified, the dialog box is displayed with an OK button and without any icon. The title of the dialog box is defaulted to the name of the program (which is the filename of the project).

The rest of the procedures of the Dialogs program are similar to the mnuAbortRetryIgnore_Click() procedure. They update the variables DialogMsg, DialogType, and DialogTitle and then use the MsgBox() function to display a dialog box. The returned value of the MsgBox() function is used to determine which button was clicked.

The InputBox() Function

You can use the InputBox() function to get information from the user. The InputBox() function displays a dialog box with a message, a text box, an OK button, and a Cancel button. The user can type text in the text box and then close the dialog box by clicking the OK button.

The first parameter of the InputBox() function is the message of the dialog box, and the second parameter is the title of the dialog box. The InputBox() function returns what the user typed in the text box. For example, the following statement displays a dialog box, shown in Figure 6.6, that asks the user to enter a name:

```
Name = _
 InputBox ("Enter your name:", "InputBox Demonstration")
```

Figure 6.6.

A dialog box that asks the user to enter a name.

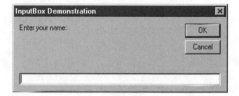

The user may type a name in the text box and then click OK to close the dialog box. In this example, the returned value of the InputBox() function is assigned to the variable Name. After the user clicks the OK button, the variable Name is updated with the user's name.

Now enhance the Dialogs program to see that you can use the InputBox() function to get a string, a number, and a date from the user.

☐ Add four new items with the following characteristics to the menu of the Dialogs program (insert them above the Exit menu item):

Caption	Name
…Get A String	mnuGetString
…Get A Number	mnuGetNumber
…Get A Date	mnuGetDate
…-	mnuSep2

After you insert these items, the menu table of the Dialogs program should look like the one shown in Table 6.7.

Table 6.7. The new menu table of the Dialogs program.

Caption	Name
Dialogs	mnuDialogs
…OK-Cancel dialog	mnuOkCancel
…Abort-Retry-Ignore dialog	mnuAbortRetryIgnore
…Yes-No-Cancel dialog	mnuYesNoCancel
…Yes-No dialog	mnuYesNo

continues

6

Table 6.7. continued

Caption	Name
...Retry-Cancel dialog	mnuRetryCancel
...-	mnuSep1
...Get A String	mnuGetString
...Get A Number	mnuGetNumber
...Get A Date	mnuGetDate
...-	mnuSep2
...Exit	mnuExit

☐ Type the following code in the mnuGetString_Click() procedure of the frmDialogs form:

```
Private Sub mnuGetString_Click ()

Dim UserInput

' Get a string from the user.
UserInput = InputBox("Type anything:", "InputBox Demo")

' If the user did not enter anything, or if the user
' pressed Cancel, exit the procedure.
If UserInput = "" Then
   MsgBox "You did not type anything or pressed Cancel."
   Exit Sub
End If

' Display whatever the user typed.
MsgBox "You typed: " + UserInput

End Sub
```

☐ Type the following code in the mnuGetNumber_Click() procedure of the frmDialogs form:

```
Private Sub mnuGetNumber_Click ()

Dim UserInput

' Get a number from the user.
UserInput = InputBox("Enter a number:", "InputBox Demo")

' If the user did not enter anything, or if the user
' pressed Cancel, exit the procedure.
If UserInput = "" Then
   MsgBox "You did not type anything or pressed Cancel."
   Exit Sub
End If

' If the user did not enter a number,
' exit the procedure.
```

```
If Not IsNumeric(UserInput) Then
   MsgBox "Invalid number!"
   Exit Sub
End If

' Display the number that the user entered.
MsgBox "You entered the number: " + UserInput
```

End Sub

☐ Type the following code in the mnuGetDate_Click() procedure of the frmDialogs form:

```
Private Sub mnuGetDate_Click ()

Dim UserInput, DayOfWeek, Msg

' Get a date from the user.
UserInput = InputBox("Enter a date:", "InputBox Demo")

' If the user did not enter anything, or if the user
' pressed Cancel, exit the procedure.
If UserInput = "" Then
   MsgBox "You did not type anything or pressed Cancel."
   Exit Sub
End If

' If the user did not enter a date, exit the procedure.
If Not IsDate(UserInput) Then
   MsgBox "Invalid date!"
   Exit Sub
End If

' Calculate the day of week of the entered date.
DayOfWeek = Format(UserInput, "dddd")

' Display the date that the user entered and the day
' of week of that date.
Msg = "You entered the date: " + UserInput
Msg = Msg + " Day of week of this date is: "+ DayOfWeek
MsgBox Msg
```

End Sub

☐ Select Save Project from the File menu of Visual Basic to save your work.

Execute the Dialogs program and experiment with the new menu items:

☐ Select Get A String from the menu.

The program responds by displaying the dialog box shown in Figure 6.7.

☐ Type anything in the dialog box and click the OK button.

The program responds by displaying a message box that tells you what you typed.

6

Figure 6.7.

The Get A String dialog box.

☐ Select Get A String again, but this time click the Cancel button instead of the OK button.

The program responds by displaying a message box telling you that you either typed nothing or pressed the Cancel button.

☐ Select Get A Number from the menu.

The program responds by displaying a dialog box that asks you to enter a number.

☐ Type any valid number, such as 1234, and click the OK button.

The program responds by displaying a message box with the number that you typed.

☐ Select Get A Number again, but this time type an invalid number, such as ABCD.

The program responds by displaying a message box, telling you that you entered an invalid number.

☐ Now experiment with the Get A Date menu item by entering both valid and invalid dates in the Get A Date dialog box. Valid dates might be, for example, January 1, 1994; July 4, 1776; and 01/01/94. Examples of invalid dates are 1234, ABCD, and 14/77/93.

Notice that after you enter a valid date in the Get A Date dialog box, the program displays a message box with the date you entered as well as the day of the week of that date. For example, if you enter the date July 4, 1776, the program responds by displaying this message:

```
You entered the date: July 4, 1776 Day of week of this date is: Thursday
```

The Code of the `mnuGetString_Click()` Procedure

When you select Get A String from the menu, the `mnuGetString_Click()` procedure is executed. The procedure begins by executing the `InputBox()` function:

```
UserInput = InputBox("Type anything:", "InputBox Demo")
```

This statement displays the dialog box shown in Figure 6.7. The returned value of the `InputBox()` function is assigned to the variable `UserInput`. If you pressed the Cancel button, the returned value of the `InputBox()` function is null. If, however, you typed something and clicked the OK button, the returned value of the `InputBox()` function is what you typed.

To see whether the Cancel button was clicked, an `If` statement is used:

```
If UserInput = "" Then
   MsgBox "You did not type anything or pressed Cancel."
   Exit Sub
End If
```

If you typed nothing or pressed the Cancel button, the condition `UserInput=""` is satisfied. As a result, the message `You did not type anything or pressed Cancel` is displayed, and the procedure is terminated with the `Exit Sub` statement.

If, however, the condition `UserInput=""` is not met, the last statement of the procedure is executed:

```
MsgBox "You typed: " + UserInput
```

This statement displays what you entered.

The Code of the `mnuGetNumber_Click()` Procedure

When you select Get A Number from the menu, the `mnuGetNumber_Click()` procedure is executed. The code of this procedure asks you to enter a number and then verifies that the number is valid.

The procedure begins by executing the `InputBox()` function:

```
UserInput = InputBox("Enter a number:", "InputBox Demo")
```

An `If` statement is used to determine whether you pressed Cancel:

```
If UserInput = "" Then
   MsgBox "You did not type anything or pressed Cancel."
   Exit Sub
End If
```

If you typed nothing and clicked the Cancel button, the condition `UserInput=""` is satisfied. As a result, the message `You did not type anything or pressed Cancel` is displayed, and the procedure is terminated with the `Exit Sub` statement.

After verifying that you typed something and didn't press Cancel, the procedure determines whether you typed a valid number by using the `IsNumeric()` function:

```
If Not IsNumeric(UserInput) Then
   MsgBox "Invalid number!"
   Exit Sub
End If
```

If the variable `UserInput` is filled with characters such as `ABC`, the condition `Not IsNumeric(UserInput)` is satisfied. As a result, the code under the `If` statement is executed. This code displays a message box with the message `Invalid number!`, and the procedure is terminated with the `Exit Sub` statement.

6

If, however, the variable UserInput is filled with characters such as 123, the condition Not IsNumeric(UserInput) is not satisfied, and the last statement of the procedure is executed:

```
MsgBox "You entered the number: " + UserInput
```

This statement displays the number you entered.

The Code of the mnuGetDate_Click() Procedure

When you select Get A Date from the menu, the mnuGetDate_Click() procedure is executed. The code of this procedure asks you to enter a date and then verifies whether the date is valid. The procedure begins by executing the InputBox() function:

```
UserInput = InputBox("Enter a date:", "InputBox Demo")
```

An If statement is used to determine whether you pressed Cancel:

```
If UserInput = "" Then
    MsgBox "You did not type anything or pressed Cancel."
    Exit Sub
End If
```

If you typed nothing or clicked the Cancel button, the condition UserInput="" is satisfied. As a result, the message You did not type anything or pressed Cancel is displayed, and the procedure is terminated with the Exit Sub statement.

After verifying that you typed something and didn't press Cancel, the procedure determines whether you typed a valid date by using the IsDate() function:

```
If Not IsDate(UserInput) Then
    MsgBox "Invalid date!"
    Exit Sub
End If
```

If the variable UserInput is filled with characters such as 123 or ABC, the condition Not IsDate(UserInput) is satisfied. As a result, a message box appears with the message Invalid date!, and the procedure is terminated with the Exit Sub statement. If, however, the variable UserInput is filled with characters such as 12/01/94, the condition Not IsDate(UserInput) is not satisfied, and the last four statements of the procedure are executed:

```
DayOfWeek = Format(UserInput, "dddd")
Msg = "You entered the date: " + UserInput
Msg = Msg + " Day of week of this date is: "+ DayOfWeek
MsgBox Msg
```

These statements display the date you entered (that is, UserInput) as well as the day of the week of that date (that is, DayOfWeek). The variable DayOfWeek is updated by using the Format() function. If, for example, UserInput is equal to July 4, 1776, Format(UserInput, "dddd") returns Thursday.

Using Other Parameters of the `InputBox()` Function

The Dialogs program used the `InputBox()` function with only two parameters (the message to be displayed and the title of the dialog box). You can also use other optional parameters of the `InputBox()` function. The third parameter specifies the default string that appears in the text box of the dialog box. The fourth and fifth parameters specify the X and Y positions (in units of twips) at which the dialog box appears.

For example, use the following statement:

```
MyNumber = InputBox("Enter a number:","Demo","7",100,200)
```

to display a dialog box with the following characteristics:

- The message is `Enter a number:`.
- The title is `Demo`.
- The default string in the text box is `7`.
- The left edge of the dialog box is 100 twips from the screen's left edge.
- The upper edge of the dialog box is 200 twips from the top of the screen.

As a result, the dialog box appears at the screen coordinate X=100,Y=200 and the default value in the text box is `7`.

The user can now click the OK button of the input dialog box (this means that the user wants the number 7), or the user can type another number (instead of the number 7) and then click the OK button of the input dialog box.

Custom Dialog Boxes

As the name implies, custom dialog boxes are customized by you (as opposed to the predefined dialog boxes that only let you customize limited things like buttons and icons in the dialog box). Designing a custom dialog box is the same as designing a form. In fact, a custom dialog box is a regular form used to display and get information. Once you design a custom dialog box, you can use it from any future Visual Basic programs that you design. In other words, you can design these dialog boxes so that they will be reusable in other programs that will need them.

To illustrate how to design a custom dialog box and use it in a program, you'll now enhance the Dialogs program further by designing a custom dialog box called GetMonth.Frm that lets your user select a month. After you finish designing the GetMonth.FRM dialog box, you'll add code to the Dialogs program that uses the GetMonth.FRM dialog box.

6

Designing a Custom Dialog Box

To design the GetMonth.FRM dialog box, use the following steps:

☐ While the Dialogs.Vbp project is the currently open project on the desktop of Visual Basic, select Add Form from the Project menu.

Visual Basic responds by displaying the Add Form window (see Figure 6.8).

Figure 6.8.

The Add Form window.

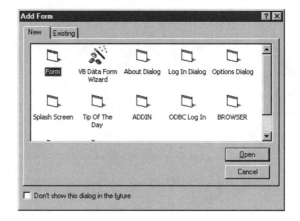

☐ Select the Form icon and then click the Open button of the Add Form window.

Visual Basic responds by adding a new form (called Form1) to the Dialogs.Vbp project.

☐ Save the new form as GetMonth.Frm (that is, select Save Form1 As from the File menu, and then use the Save File As dialog box to save the form as GetMonth.Frm in the C:\VB5Prg\Ch06 directory).

Before going any further, let's verify that the Dialogs.Vbp project now includes two forms in it:

☐ Select Project Explorer from the View menu of Visual Basic to display the Project window.

The Project window now appears like the one in Figure 6.9. Depending on the placement of the Project Window in the desktop of your Visual Basic, the Project window may appear in a slightly different window format than the one shown in Figure 6.9. However, the contents of the Project window will be the same no matter how the Project window is displayed.

☐ Build the GetMonth.Frm dialog box according to Table 6.8.

The completed dialog box should look like the one shown in Figure 6.10.

Figure 6.9.

The Project window shows that the project has two forms in it: Dialogs.Frm and GetMonth.Frm.

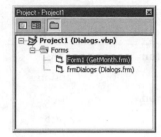

☐ Select Save Project from the File menu of Visual Basic to save your work.

When you select Save Project from the File menu, all new forms and modified forms are saved. If you made changes to the frmDialogs form or to the frmGetMonth form, the changes that you made are saved.

Figure 6.10.

The frmGetMonth form (design mode).

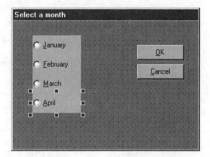

Table 6.8. The properties table of the GetMonth.FRM dialog box.

Object	Property	Value
Form	**Name**	**frmGetMonth**
	BackColor	Dark gray
	BorderStyle	1-Fixed Single
	Caption	Select a month
	ControlBox	False
	MaxButton	False
	MinButton	False
Option Button	**Name**	**optJan**
	Caption	&January

continues

6

Table 6.8. continued

Object	Property	Value
Option Button	**Name**	**optFeb**
	Caption	&February
Option Button	**Name**	**optMar**
	Caption	&March
Option Button	**Name**	**optApr**
	Caption	&April
Command Button	**Name**	**cmdOK**
	Cancel	False
	Caption	&OK
	Default	True
Command Button	**Name**	**cmdCancel**
	Cancel	True
	Caption	&Cancel
	Default	False

Note

Table 6.8 instructs you to place only four option buttons for four months, so the user will be able to select January, February, March, or April.

You are instructed to place only four option buttons because this will save you a lot of design time. At a later time, you can enhance the frmGetMonth form to include all twelve months.

Appropriate Properties of Dialog Boxes

A typical dialog box is designed so that you can't change its appearance during runtime. As you can see from Table 6.8, the properties of the frmGetMonth form (which will soon serve as a dialog box) are set so that you can't size, maximize, or minimize the frmGetMonth dialog box during runtime:

■ The Border Style property of the frmGetMonth dialog box is set to Fixed Single so you can't change the size of the dialog box during runtime.

- The Control Box property of the frmGetMonth dialog box is set to False so the dialog box is displayed without the Control Menu box. (The Control Menu box is the small icon that appears in the top-left corner of a form.)

- The Max Button property of the frmGetMonth dialog box is set to False so the dialog box is displayed without the Maximize button on its upper-right corner. This prevents you from maximizing the dialog box during runtime.

- The Min Button property of the frmGetMonth dialog box is set to False so the dialog box is displayed without the Minimize button on its upper-right corner. This prevents you from minimizing the dialog box during runtime.

The Cancel Property and Default Property of the Command Buttons

As you can see from Table 6.8, the Default property of the OK button is set to True, and the Cancel property of the Cancel button is set to True.

Setting the Default property of a command button to True makes this command button the Default button, which is the button that's considered clicked when you press Enter. Therefore, because the Default property of the OK button is set to True, when the frmGetMonth dialog box is displayed during runtime, pressing Enter has the same effect as clicking the OK button.

Setting the Cancel property of a command button to True makes this command button the Cancel button, which is the one that's selected when you press Esc. Therefore, because the Cancel property of the Cancel button is set to True, when the frmGetMonth dialog box is displayed during runtime, pressing Esc has the same effect as clicking the Cancel button.

Displaying and Hiding a Custom Dialog Box

To display a custom dialog box, use the Show method. The dialog box should be displayed as modal (the user must respond to the dialog box before the program continues). To display the dialog box as modal, use the Show method with its argument equal to 1. For example, to display the dialog box frmMyDialog as modal, use the following statement:

```
frmMyDialog.Show 1
```

To hide a dialog box, use the Hide method. For example, if the dialog box frmMyDialog is displayed, the following statement hides it from view:

```
frmMyDialog.Hide
```

6

To see the Show method and Hide method in action, add code to the Dialogs program. This code displays the frmGetMonth dialog box when the user selects the menu item Get A Month, and it hides the dialog box when the user responds to the dialog box by clicking the OK button or Cancel button in the dialog box.

☐ Add two new items with the following characteristics to the menu of the frmDialogs form (insert them above the Exit menu item):

Caption	Name
...Get A Month (custom dialog)	mnuGetMonth
...-	mnuSep3

After inserting these items, the complete menu table of the Dialogs program should look like the one shown in Table 6.9.

Note

Use the following steps to insert menu items in the frmDialogs form:

☐ Select the frmDialogs form.

☐ Select Menu Editor from the Tools menu.

> *Visual Basic responds by displaying the Menu Editor with the menu of the frmDialogs form displayed in the Menu Editor window.*

If the frmGetMonth form is currently selected and you don't select the frmDialogs form before selecting Menu Editor from the Tools menu, Visual Basic will "think" that you want to use the Menu Editor for editing the menu of the frmGetMonth form.

Table 6.9. The menu table of the Dialogs program after adding the Get Month item.

Caption	Name
Dialogs	mnuDialogs
...OK-Cancel dialog	mnuOkCancel
...Abort-Retry-Ignore dialog	mnuAbortRetryIgnore
...Yes-No-Cancel dialog	mnuYesNoCancel
...Yes-No dialog	mnuYesNo
...Retry-Cancel dialog	mnuRetryCancel
...-	mnuSep1
...Get A String	mnuGetString

Caption	Name
...Get A Number	mnuGetNumber
...Get A Date	mnuGetDate
...-	mnuSep2
...Get A Month (custom dialog)	mnuGetMonth
...-	mnuSep3
...Exit	mnuExit

☐ Type the following code in the mnuGetMonth_Click() procedure of the frmDialogs form:

```
Private Sub mnuGetMonth_Click ()

    ' Display the frmGetMonth dialog box.
    frmGetMonth.Show 1

    ' Display the month that the user selected (if any).
    If frmGetMonth.Tag = "" Then
       MsgBox "You canceled the dialog box!"
    Else
       MsgBox "You selected: " + frmGetMonth.Tag
    End If

End Sub
```

When you select Get A Month from the Dialogs menu, the mnuGetMonth_Click() procedure is executed. The code of this procedure uses the Show method to display the frmGetMonth dialog box and displays the month you selected by displaying the Tag property of the frmGetMonth dialog box. As you will soon see, the code of the frmGetMonth dialog box uses the Tag property of the frmGetMonth form (frmGetMonth.Tag) to store the name of the month you selected.

☐ Make sure that the Option Explicit statement resides in the general declarations section of the frmGetMonth form as follows:

```
' All variables must be declared.
Option Explicit
```

Note

To display the code window of the frmGetMonth form, double-click anywhere in the frmGetMonth form. Visual Basic then displays the code window of the frmGetMonth form.

You already have the Option Explicit statement in the general declaration area of the frmDialogs form. This means that before you can use

6

> a variable in the procedures of the frmDialogs form, the variable must be declared.
>
> In a similar manner, you have the Option Explicit statement in the general declarations section of the frmGetMonth form. This means that before you can use a variable in the procedures of the frmGetMonth form, the variable must be declared.
>
> You must include the Option Explicit statement for each of the forms.

☐ Type the following code in the cmdOK_Click() procedure of the frmGetMonth form:

```
Private Sub cmdOK_Click ()

    ' Update frmGetMonth.Tag with the month that the
    ' user selected. (frmGetMonth.Tag is used as the
    ' output of the form).
    If optJan = True Then frmGetMonth.Tag = "January"
    If optFeb = True Then frmGetMonth.Tag = "February"
    If optMar = True Then frmGetMonth.Tag = "March"
    If optApr = True Then frmGetMonth.Tag = "April"

    ' Hide the frmGetMonth form.
    frmGetMonth.Hide

End Sub
```

When you click the OK button of the frmGetMonth dialog box, the cmdOK_Click() procedure is executed. The code of this procedure uses a series of four If statements to see which option button is currently selected and accordingly updates the Tag property of the frmGetMonth form with the name of the selected month. After the four If statements, the procedure uses the Hide method to hide the frmGetMonth form from view.

The Tag property of the frmGetMonth dialog box is used as the output of the dialog box. That is, whoever displays the frmGetMonth window box can use frmGetMonth.Tag to know which month the user selected.

Here is the syntax of the If statement:

```
If optJan = True Then frmGetMonth.Tag = "January"
```

The preceding statement is identical to the following statement:

```
If optJan = True Then
    frmGetMonth.Tag = "January"
End If
```

Therefore, if you type the If statement on a single line, you do not have to type the End If line. This saves you some typing; more importantly, it makes your program easier to read and understand when you have a series of If statements.

☐ Type the following code in the cmdCancel_Click() procedure of the frmGetMonth dialog box:

```
Private Sub cmdCancel_Click ()

    ' Set frmGetMonth.Tag to null.
    frmGetMonth.Tag = ""

    ' Hide the frmGetMonth form.
    frmGetMonth.Hide

End Sub
```

When you click the Cancel button of the frmGetMonth window, the cmdCancel_Click() procedure is executed. The code of this procedure sets the Tag property of the form (frmGetMonth.Tag) to null and then uses the Hide method to hide the frmGetMonth dialog box from view. Setting frmGetMonth.Tag to null indicates that the user clicked the Cancel button.

☐ Select Save Project from the File menu of Visual Basic to save your work.

☐ Execute the Dialogs program, select Get A Month from the Dialogs menu, and experiment with the Get A Month custom dialog box.

In particular, note that if you click one of the option buttons, that option button becomes the control with the keyboard focus. You can now press the Esc key, and this has the same effect as clicking the Cancel button.

If one of the option buttons has the keyboard focus and you press the Enter key, this has the same effect as clicking the OK button, because you set the Default property of the OK button to True, and you set the Cancel property of the Cancel button to True.

☐ Terminate the Dialogs program by selecting Exit from the Dialogs menu.

Common Dialog Boxes

Visual Basic includes a control called Common Dialog. You can use it to display common dialog boxes during runtime by simply setting its properties. The common dialog box is frequently used as a dialog box that lets the user select and save files.

The Common Program

To illustrate how to use the Common Dialog control in a program, you'll now write the Common program to display two common dialog boxes: the Color Selection dialog box and the Open File dialog box.

The Visual Implementation of the Common Program

As usual, you'll start by implementing the form of the program.

☐ Start a new Standard EXE project.

☐ Save the form of the project as Common.Frm in the C:\VB5Prg\Ch06 directory, and save the project file as Common.Vbp in the C:\VB5Prg\Ch06 directory.

The CommandButton is an example of a control that always appears in the toolbox window. Similarly, the CheckBox, TextBox, and OptionButton are all examples of controls that always exist in the toolbox window.

On the other hand, the CommonDialog control is an example of a control that you can place in the toolbox window and can remove from the toolbox window. The common dialog box is called an OCX control. As stated in Chapter 1, "Writing Your First Visual Basic 5 Program," when you distribute your application, you also have to make sure that your users have the VBRun500.DLL in their System directory. The VBRun500.DLL file is a file that contains code that enables your EXE program to be executed. For example, this DLL file is the file that enables your program to use menus, the mouse, and all the other features that your small EXE file can have. One of the things that is included with the VBRun500.DLL file is these controls that are always seen in the toolbox window. Therefore, when you distribute an application that includes CommandButtons, CheckBoxes, and so on, you don't have to distribute additional files that correspond to these controls.

On the other hand, a control such as the CommonDialog control is not included in the VBrun500.DLL file. This means that when you distribute the EXE file, you have to include the VBrun500.DLL file, as well as the files that correspond to the OCX controls that your program uses. (Of course, before distributing OCX files, you must consult with the software license agreement of the OCX to see if you are allowed to distribute the OCX file.)

The file that corresponds to the CommonDialog control is Comdlg32.ocx. If you examine your System directory, you should see this file. (This file was installed when you installed your Visual Basic.)

Now let's see whether the CommonDialog control is already included in the Common.Vbp project:

☐ Select Custom Components from the Project menu of Visual Basic.

Visual Basic responds by displaying the Components dialog box (see Figure 6.11).

Figure 6.11.

*The Components
dialog box.*

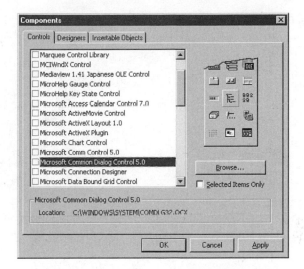

As shown in Figure 6.11, the Components window has three tabs on its top.

☐ Make sure that you are viewing the Controls page of the Components window (that is, click the Components tab).

☐ Scroll down the list of the Components window until you see the Microsoft Common Dialog Control 5.0 item (refer to Figure 6.11). If there is a check mark to the left of the Microsoft Common Dialog Control 5.0 item, it means that the CommonDialog control already resides in the toolbox window.

☐ If there is no check mark in the check box to the left of the Microsoft Common Dialog Control 5.0 item, place one there by clicking the check box.

☐ Click the OK button of the Component window.

As a result, the toolbox now includes the CommonDialog control.

To see the CommonDialog control in the toolbox window, you may have to drag the lower edge of the toolbox window to make this window larger. Figure 6.12 shows the CommonDialog control in the toolbox window. When you place the mouse cursor on the icon of the CommonDialog control in the toolbox (without clicking any of the mouse buttons), a yellow rectangle appears with the text CommonDialog in it. This way, you can verify that you located the icon of the CommonDialog control in the toolbox window.

6

Figure 6.12.

*The icon of the
CommonDialog
control in the toolbox
window.*

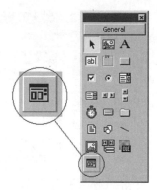

☐ Select the Common.Frm form by clicking anywhere in the Common.Frm form.

☐ Double-click the icon of the CommonDialog control in the toolbox window.

   *Visual Basic responds by placing the CommonDialog in the Common.Frm form. The
   default name that Visual Basic assigns to this control is CommonDialog1.*

☐ Build the Common.Frm form according to Table 6.10 and Table 6.11. (Table 6.11 is the
menu table of the frmCommon form.)

The completed form should look like the one shown in Figure 6.13.

Table 6.10. The properties table of the COMMON.FRM form.

Object	Property	Value
Form	**Name**	**frmCommon**
	Caption	The Common Program
Common Dialog	**Name**	**CommonDialog1**
	CancelError	True
Menu	*(See Table 6.11)*	*(See Table 6.11)*

Table 6.11. The menu table of the frmCommon form.

Caption	Name
&File	mnuFile
...&Color...	mnuColor
...&Open...	mnuOpen
...-	mnuSep1
...E&xit	mnuExit

Figure 6.13.

The frmCommon form of the Common program.

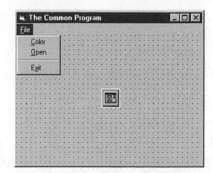

Entering the Code of the Common Program

You'll now enter the code of the Common program:

☐ Make sure that the general declarations section of the frmCommon form has the Option Explicit statement in it as follows:

```
' All variables must be declared.
Option Explicit
```

☐ Type the following code in the mnuColor_Click() procedure of the frmCommon form:

```
Private Sub mnuColor_Click ()

    ' Set an error trap to detect the pressing of the
    ' Cancel button of the Color dialog box.
    On Error GoTo ColorError

    ' Display the Color dialog box.
    CommonDialog1.Action = 3

    ' Change the color of the form to the color that the
    ' user selected in the color dialog box.
    frmCommon.BackColor = CommonDialog1.Color

    ' Exit the procedure.
    Exit Sub

ColorError:
    ' The user pressed the Cancel button of the Color
    ' dialog box.
    MsgBox "You canceled the dialog box!"
    Exit Sub

End Sub
```

☐ Type the following code in the mnuOpen_Click() procedure of the frmCommon form:

```
Private Sub mnuOpen_Click ()

    Dim Filter As String
```

6

```
                 ' Set an error trap to detect the pressing of the
                 ' Cancel key of the Open dialog box.
                 On Error GoTo OpenError

                 ' Fill the items of the File Type list box of
                 ' the Open dialog box.
                 Filter = "All Files (*.*)¦*.* ¦"
                 Filter = Filter + "Text Files (*.txt)¦*.txt ¦"
                 Filter = Filter + "Batch Files (*.bat)¦*.bat"
                 CommonDialog1.Filter = Filter

                 ' Set the default File Type to Text Files (*.txt).
                 CommonDialog1.FilterIndex = 2

                 ' Display the Open dialog box.
                 CommonDialog1.Action = 1

                 ' Display the name of the file that the user selected.
                 MsgBox "You selected: " + CommonDialog1.Filename

                 ' Exit the procedure.
                 Exit Sub

             OpenError:
                 ' The user pressed the Cancel key.
                 MsgBox "You canceled the dialog box!"
                 Exit Sub

         End Sub
```

☐ Type the following code in the mnuExit_Click() procedure of the frmCommon form:

```
         Private Sub mnuExit_Click ()

             End

         End Sub
```

☐ Select Save Project from the File menu of Visual Basic to save your work.

Executing the Common Program

Execute the Common program. Note that the common dialog custom control is invisible at runtime. The control comes to life as soon as you select Color or Open from the File menu.

☐ Select Color from the File menu.

The Common program responds by displaying the Color dialog box (see Figure 6.14).

☐ Select a color from the Color dialog box by clicking the desired color and pressing the OK button.

The Common program responds by closing the Color dialog box and changing the color of the program's window to the selected color.

Figure 6.14.

The Color dialog box.

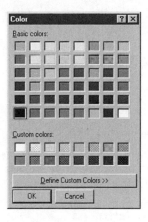

☐ Select Open from the File menu of the Common program.

The Common program responds by displaying the Open dialog box (see Figure 6.15).

Figure 6.15.

The Open dialog box.

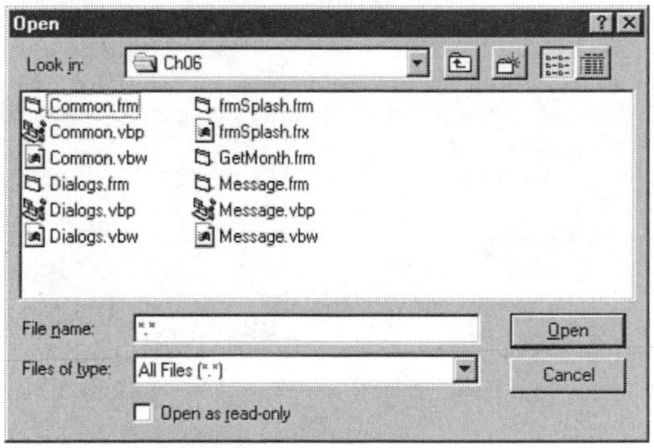

☐ Select a certain directory on your hard drive, set the File of Type list box to All Files (*.*), type *.* in the File name edit box, select a file, and then click the OK button of the Open dialog box (refer to Figure 6.15).

The Common program responds by displaying message box, telling you the name of the selected file.

☐ Experiment with the Common program and then terminate the program by selecting Exit from the File menu.

6

How the Common Program Works

The Common program uses the CommonDialog custom control to display a Color dialog box and an Open dialog box. The Color dialog box lets you select a color, and the Open dialog box lets you select a file.

The Color Dialog Box

When you select Color from the File menu, the mnuColor_Click() procedure is executed. The code of this procedure uses the CommonDialog custom control to display a Color dialog box:

```
Private Sub mnuColor_Click ()

    ' Set an error trap to detect the pressing of the
    ' Cancel button of the Color dialog box.
    On Error GoTo ColorError

    ' Display the Color dialog box.
    CommonDialog1.Action = 3

    ' Change the color of the form to the color that the
    ' user selected in the color dialog box.
    frmCommon.BackColor = CommonDialog1.Color

    ' Exit the procedure.
    Exit Sub

ColorError:
    ' The user pressed the Cancel button of the Color
    ' dialog box.
    MsgBox "You canceled the dialog box!"
    Exit Sub

End Sub
```

Before displaying the dialog box, the mnuColor_Click() procedure sets an error trap:

```
On Error GoTo ColorError
```

The purpose of this error trap is to detect an error during the display of the dialog box. Recall that during design time you set the CancelError property of the CommonDialog1 common dialog custom control to True. Therefore, if you click the Cancel button while the dialog box is displayed, an error is generated; as a result of the previous error trap, the program branches to the ColorError label.

After setting the error trap, the procedure displays the Color dialog box by setting the Action property of the CommonDialog1 common dialog custom control to 3:

```
CommonDialog1.Action = 3
```

If you click the Cancel button while the dialog box is displayed, an error is generated and, as a result, the code under the ColorError label is executed. The code under the ColorError label displays a message and terminates the procedure:

```
ColorError:
   MsgBox "You canceled the dialog box!"
   Exit Sub
```

However, if you don't click the Cancel button, but select a color from the dialog box and click the OK button, the procedure executes the following two statements:

```
frmCommon.BackColor = CommonDialog1.Color
Exit Sub
```

The first statement changes the BackColor property of the form to the color you selected, which is in the Color property of the CommonDialog1 control (CommonDialog1.Color). The second statement terminates the procedure.

The Open Dialog Box

When you select Open from the File menu, the mnuOpen_Click() procedure is executed. The code in this procedure uses the Common Dialog control to display an Open dialog box:

```
Private Sub mnuOpen_Click ()

   Dim Filter As String

   ' Set an error trap to detect the pressing of the
   ' Cancel key of the Open dialog box.
   On Error GoTo OpenError

   ' Fill the items of the File Type list box of
   ' the Open dialog box.
   Filter = "All Files (*.*)|*.* |"
   Filter = Filter + "Text Files (*.txt)|*.txt |"
   Filter = Filter + "Batch Files (*.bat)|*.bat"
   CommonDialog1.Filter = Filter

   ' Set the default File Type to Text Files (*.txt).
   CommonDialog1.FilterIndex = 2

   ' Display the Open dialog box.
   CommonDialog1.Action = 1

   ' Display the name of the file that the user selected.
   MsgBox "You selected: " + CommonDialog1.Filename

   ' Exit the procedure.
   Exit Sub
```

6

```
OpenError:
  ' The user pressed the Cancel key.
  MsgBox "You canceled the dialog box!"
  Exit Sub
```

End Sub

The first statement of the procedure sets an error trap:

```
On Error GoTo OpenError
```

As a result of this error trap, if you click the Cancel button while the Open dialog box is displayed, the procedure branches to the OpenError label.

After setting the error trap, the procedure uses the Filter property of the CommonDialog1 control to fill the items in the Files of type list box of the Open dialog box. The Files of type list box is filled with three file types:

```
Filter = "All Files (*.*)¦*.* ¦"
Filter = Filter + "Text Files (*.txt)¦*.txt ¦"
Filter = Filter + "Batch Files (*.bat)¦*.bat"
CommonDialog1.Filter = Filter
```

The preceding statements fill the Filter property of the CommonDialog1 control with a string that specifies the text of each of the items appearing in the Files of type list box, as well as the skeleton of the files that are displayed.

For example, the first item that appears in the Files of type list box is specified with the following string:

```
All Files (*.*)¦*.*
```

This string is made of two parts separated by the pipe character (¦). (You type the pipe character by pressing Shift+\.) The first part indicates the text that appears in the list box:

```
All Files (*.*)
```

The second part indicates the skeleton of the files that are displayed when this item is selected:

```
*.*
```

That is, when the first item of the Files of type list box is selected, the files with the skeleton *.* (that is, all the files) are displayed in the dialog box.

Notice that for clarity, the preceding statements fill the Filter property of the CommonDialog1 control in steps. First, the string variable Filter is filled:

```
Filter = "All Files (*.*)¦*.* ¦"
Filter = Filter + "Text Files (*.txt)¦*.txt ¦"
Filter = Filter + "Batch Files (*.bat)¦*.bat"
```

Then the Filter property of the CommonDialog1 control is set to the value of the `Filter` variable:

```
CommonDialog1.Filter = Filter
```

After the Files of type list box of the dialog box is filled, the default item that appears in the Files of type list box is set to item number 2. This is done by setting the FilterIndex property of CommonDialog1 to 2:

```
CommonDialog1.FilterIndex = 2
```

Because item number 2 of the Files of type list box is Text Files (*.txt), the default files listed in the Open dialog box are files with a TXT extension.

The procedure displays the Open dialog box by setting the Action property of the CommonDialog1 common dialog custom control to 1:

```
CommonDialog1.Action = 1
```

If you click the Cancel button while the dialog box is displayed, an error is generated and, as a result, the code under the OpenError label is executed. The code under the OpenError label displays a message and terminates the procedure:

```
OpenError:
   MsgBox "You canceled the dialog box!"
   Exit Sub
```

However, if you don't click the Cancel button but select a file from the dialog box, the name of the selected file is displayed and the procedure is terminated:

```
MsgBox "You selected: " + CommonDialog1.Filename
Exit Sub
```

The file you selected is in the FileName property of the CommonDialog1 control (`CommonDialog1.FileName`).

Other Common Dialog Boxes

The Common program used the common dialog custom control to display a Color dialog box and an Open dialog box. You may use the common dialog custom control to display other common dialog boxes. Table 6.12 lists the common dialog boxes that may be displayed and the values that should be assigned to the Action property of the common dialog custom control to display a particular dialog box. For example, to display the Save As common dialog box, you should set the Action property of the common dialog custom control to 2:

```
CommonDialog1.Action=2
```

Table 6.12. The common dialog boxes.

Displayed Common Dialog Box	Action Property
Open	1
Save As	2
Color	3
Font	4
Print	5

As with the Color and Open dialog boxes, you may use the properties of the common dialog custom control to determine the user's response to the dialog box.

Other Forms and Dialog Boxes

So far, you learned to create dialog boxes by using the MsgBox statement and the MsgBox() function by creating your own forms that will serve as dialog boxes, and by using the CommonDialog control. There is yet another way to create dialog boxes: by using preprepared forms. To see it in action, follow these steps:

☐ Create a new Standard EXE project.

You are not instructed to save this project, because the objective of this set of steps is just to show you how you can access the preprepared forms.

☐ Select Add From from the Project menu.

Visual Basic responds by displaying the Ad Form window (see Figure 6.16).

Figure 6.16.
The Add Form window.

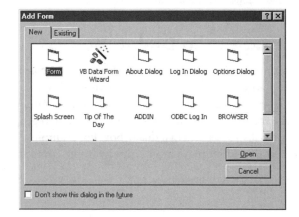

As you can see from Figure 6.16, there are various types of preprepared forms you can select. Earlier in this chapter, you added the frmGetMonth form by selecting Add Form from the Project menu and then selecting the Form icon from the Add Form window. You then implemented the frmGetMonth by placing controls in the form and attached code that displays or hides the frmGetMonth form.

Figure 6.17.

The Tip of the Day form (design mode).

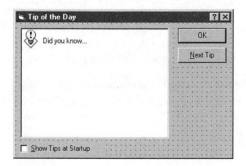

☐ Select the Tip of The Day icon from the Add Form window and then click the Open button of the Add Form window.

Visual Basic responds by displaying the Tip of the Day form in design mode (see Figure 6.17).

Basically, Visual Basic includes some preprepared forms that are commonly used in applications (such as the Tip of the Day form). You then continue with the design of the program in the same way you designed the frmGetMonth form. The only difference is that the Tip of The Day form was already prepared for you (and if you examine the code window of the form, you'll see that some code was also written for you). In short, you still have to keep working on the form (for example, you have to create the main form of the application also) and to write code that shows or hides the Tip of the Day form (just as you did with the frmGetMonth form). Using the preprepared forms is sometimes useful. For example, if you need a Tip of the Day form in your application, you might as well use the preprepared form (why reinvent the wheel?). Of course, you will be able to take full advantage of the preprepared forms after you know Visual Basic (this way, you'll be able to understand what the code that the preprepared form includes). For the time being, you will not use the preprepared forms. After you complete this book and experiment with building your own applications, go back to the Add Form window, and try to implement applications that use some of the preprepared forms.

☐ Terminate Visual Basic. There is no need to save the project or the forms of the project.

6

Summary

This chapter discusses dialog boxes. You have learned how to display predefined dialog boxes with the MsgBox statement, the MsgBox() function, and the InputBox() function. These dialog boxes are ideal for cases when you need to inform the user with short messages, get the user's response to yes and no questions, or get text data, such as a name, from the user.

You have also learned how to design your own custom dialog boxes and use them in a program. When you design a custom dialog box, there is no limit to the number of buttons or controls you can have in the dialog box.

This chapter also covers the common dialog custom control used to display common dialog boxes such as Open, Save As, Print, Color, and Font.

Q&A

Q This chapter covers three types of dialog boxes (predefined, custom, and common). Which type should I use?

A The advantage to designing your own custom dialog box, such as the frmGetMonth form, is that there is no limit to the buttons or controls you can place in the dialog box. For example, you can place pictures in the custom dialog box to improve the way it looks.

The disadvantage to designing your own custom control is that you need to spend some time designing it. If a predefined dialog box or a common dialog box can already do what your custom dialog box does, you will be "reinventing the wheel."

Remember that the common dialog boxes can be very powerful. For example, when you use a common dialog box to select a color, the control knows which color is supported by your PC, or when you a common dialog box to select a font, the control knows which fonts are available on your system.

Quiz

1. What is the difference between the MsgBox statement and MsgBox() function?

2. What does the following statement do?

```
MsgBox "File is missing!", vbOKOnly, "ERROR"
```

3. What does the following code do?

```
If MsgBox("Exit program?", vbYesNo, "DEMO") = vbYes Then
    End
End If
```

4. What does the following code do?

```
UserName = InputBox ("Enter your name:", "Demo")
If UserName<>"" Then
    MsgBox "Hello " + UserName
End If
```

5. Assume that you designed a custom dialog box called frmMyDialog. What does the following statement do?

```
frmMyDialog.Show 1
```

6. Assume that you designed a custom dialog box called frmMyDialog. What does the following statement do?

```
frmMyDialog.Hide
```

7. Assume that you have a common dialog custom control called CommonDialog1. What does the following statement do? (Use Table 6.12 to answer this question.)

```
CommonDialog1.Action = 2
```

Exercises

1. Write code that displays a dialog box with the title ERROR, the message Disk error!, an OK button, and an exclamation point icon.

2. Write code that displays a dialog box with the title QUESTION, the question message Are you sure you want to quit?, Yes and No buttons, and a question mark icon. If the user's response to the question is Yes (the user clicks the Yes button), terminate the program.

3. Write code that displays a dialog box asking the user to enter a number between 1 and 10. If the user enters a number in the range 1 to 10, the code should display a dialog box with the selected number. If, however, the user enters a number that is not in the range 1 to 10, (or the user enters nonnumeric characters), the code should display an error message. If the user presses the Cancel button of the dialog box, the code should not display anything. (*Hint:* This code is similar to the code in the mnuGetNumber_Click() procedure of the Dialogs program.)

Quiz Answers

1. The MsgBox statement and MsgBox() function take the same parameters and display the same dialog boxes. The only difference between them is that the MsgBox() function returns a value that represents the button selected in the dialog box. The MsgBox statement does not return any value.

2. This statement displays a message box with the title ERROR, the message File is missing!, and an OK button in the message box.

6

3. This code displays a message box with the title DEMO, the question message Exit program?, and Yes and No buttons. If you click the Yes button of the dialog box, the MsgBox() function returns the value vbYes, in which case the condition of the If statement is satisfied and the program is terminated by executing the End statement.

4. This code uses the InputBox() function to display a dialog box prompting you to enter a name. The returned value of the InputBox() function is assigned to the variable UserName. If you enter a name and don't press the Cancel button, the variable UserName is not null, in which case the condition of the If statement If UserName<>"" is satisfied and you are prompted with a Hello message displaying your name.

5. This statement uses the Show method to display the frmMyDialog dialog box as an application modal dialog. (The user cannot return to the application that displays the dialog box for as long as the dialog box is displayed.)

6. This statement uses the Hide method to hide the frmMyDialog dialog box from view. After executing this statement, the frmMyDialog dialog box disappears. Typically, this statement is used in the code of the terminating button of the dialog box. For example, after you respond to the dialog box by pressing the OK or Cancel button, use the Hide method to hide the dialog box from view.

7. This statement displays the Save As common dialog box.

Exercise Answers

1. To display such a dialog box, use the following statement:

```
MsgBox "Disk error!", vbOKOnly+vbExclamation, "ERROR"
```

2. To display such a dialog box, use the following code:

```
If MsgBox ( "Are you sure you want to quit?", _
           vbYesNo + vbQuestion, _
           "QUESTION" ) = vbYes Then
    End
End If
```

3. The following code is one possible solution:

```
Dim UserInput

' Get a number from the user.
UserInput = _
 InputBox("Enter a number between 1 and 10", "Demo")

' If the user did not enter anything, or if the user
' pressed Cancel, exit the procedure.
If UserInput = "" Then
    Exit Sub
End If
```

```
' If the user did not enter numeric characters,
' then display an error message and exit the procedure.
If Not IsNumeric(UserInput) Then
    MsgBox "Invalid number!"
    Exit Sub
End If

' If the number that the user entered is not in the range
' of 1 through 10, then display an error message and exit.
If UserInput<1 Or UserInput>10 Then
    MsgBox "The number is not between 1 and 10!"
    Exit Sub
End If

' Display the number that the user entered.
MsgBox "You entered the number: " + UserInput
```

6

Day 7

Graphics Controls

One of the advantages of using Visual Basic for Windows is that it enables you to easily create programs that include graphics. In this chapter you'll learn how to write programs that include graphics controls.

The Twip

In Visual Basic you can display graphic objects such as lines, circles, bitmap files, and so on. You need to specify the dimensions (such as length of line or radius of circle) for these objects. Although Visual Basic may use a variety of units for specifying the dimensions and locations of these graphic objects, the most commonly used unit is called a twip. There are 1440 twips in 1 inch.

Colors

An important characteristic of a graphic object is its color. You can use the RGB() function or QBColor() function to specify the color of objects.

Specifying Colors with the RGB() Function

The RGB() function enables you to specify colors. The letters RGB stand for red, green, and blue, because all colors that can be displayed are generated by mixing these three basic colors. The RGB() function has three parameters: the value of the first parameter represents the amount of red in the final color; the second parameter represents the amount of green in the final color; and the third parameter represents the amount of blue in the final color. For example, the following statement uses the RGB() function to return the color red:

```
RGB(255, 0, 0)
```

The maximum value of each parameter in the RGB() function is 255 and the minimum value is 0, so RGB(255,0,0) represents red, RGB(0,255,0) represents green, and RGB(0,0,255) represents blue.

For example, to change the BackColor property of a form called frmMyForm to blue, use the following statement:

```
frmMyForm.BackColor = RGB(0,0,255)
```

To generate yellow, use RGB(255,255,0). How can you tell that this combination of numbers yields the color yellow? If you have a Ph.D. in physics, you probably know the answer and can explain it in terms of wavelength and other light properties. Otherwise, you have to generate the color by trial and error. There are two RGB() combinations you should remember: RGB(255,255,255) represents white and RGB(0,0,0) represents black.

Specifying Colors with the QBColor() Function

Another easy way to specify colors is by using the QBColor() function. It has one parameter that may have any integer value between 0 and 15.

To change the BackColor property of the form frmMyForm to gray, use the following statement:

```
frmMyForm.BackColor = QBColor(8)
```

Table 4.3 in Chapter 4, "The Mouse," lists the 16 possible colors and their corresponding values.

The QBColor() function is easier to use than the RGB() function, but you can generate only 16 colors with it.

The Line Control

The line control is used for drawing lines. The Line program demonstrates how to use it in a program.

The Visual Implementation of the Line Program

Use the following steps to build the form of the Line program:

☐ Create the C:\Vb5Prg\Ch07 directory. You'll save your work in this directory.

☐ Create a new Standard EXE project by selecting New Project from the File menu.

☐ Save the form of the project as Line.Frm in the C:\VB5Prg\Ch07 directory and save the project file as Line.Vbp in the C:\VB5Prg\Ch07 directory.

☐ Build the form of the Line program according to the specifications in Table 7.1.

The completed form should look like the one in Figure 7.1.

7

Figure 7.1.

The form of the Line program.

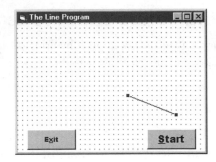

Table 7.1. The properties table of the frmLine form.

Object	Property	Setting
Form	**Name**	**frmLine**
	BackColor	White
	Caption	The Line Program
Command Button	**Name**	**cmdStart**
	Caption	&Start
Command Button	**Name**	**cmdExit**
	Caption	E&xit
Line	**Name**	**linLine**
	X1	2760
	X2	3960
	Y1	1800
	Y2	2280

When you place the mouse cursor (without clicking any of the mouse buttons) on the icon of the Line control in the toolbox window, a yellow rectangle appears with the text Line in it.

Entering the Code of the Line Program

You'll now enter the code of the Line program:

☐ Make sure that the general declarations section of the frmLine form has the Option Explicit statement in it:

```
' All variables MUST be declared.
Option Explicit
```

☐ Type the following code in the cmdExit_Click() procedure:

```
Private Sub cmdExit_Click()

    End

End Sub
```

☐ Type the following code in the cmdStart_Click() procedure:

```
Private Sub cmdStart_Click()

    ' Set the start and endpoints of the line
    ' control to random values.
    linLine.X1 = Int(frmLine.Width * Rnd)
    linLine.Y1 = Int(frmLine.Height * Rnd)
    linLine.X2 = Int(frmLine.Width * Rnd)
    linLine.Y2 = Int(frmLine.Height * Rnd)

End Sub
```

☐ Select Save Project from the File menu of Visual Basic to save your work.

Executing the Line Program

Let's see your code in action:

☐ Execute the Line program.

Click the Start button several times and notice that every time you click the button, the line control changes its location and its length. Because you set the Caption property of the Start button to &Start, you can press Alt+S on your keyboard. This will produce the same result as clicking the Start button.

How the Line Program Works

The Line program uses the cmdStart_Click() procedure to display the line control at a different location every time you click the Start button.

The Code of the cmdStart_Click() Procedure

The cmdStart_Click() procedure is executed when you click the Start button:

```
Private Sub cmdStart_Click()

    ' Set the start and endpoints of the line
    ' control to random values.
    linLine.X1 = Int(frmLine.Width * Rnd)
    linLine.Y1 = Int(frmLine.Height * Rnd)
    linLine.X2 = Int(frmLine.Width * Rnd)
```

7

```
    linLine.Y2 = Int(frmLine.Height * Rnd)
```

End Sub

The Rnd function returns a random number between 0 and 1, and the Width property represents the width of the frmLine form. Therefore, the result of the multiplication

```
frmLine.Width * Rnd
```

is equal to a number between 0 and the width of the form.

For example, if the Rnd function returns 0, the result equals 0. If the Rnd function returns 1, the result equals the width of the form. If the Rnd function returns 0.75, the result equals 3/4 the width of the form.

The Int() function converts its parameter to an integer. For example, Int(3.5) returns 3, and Int(7.999) returns 7. Therefore, the result Int(frmLine.Width * Rnd) returns a random integer between 0 and the width of the form.

The first statement in the cmdStart_Click() procedure assigns an integer to the X1 property of the line control. This integer is between 0 and the width of the form:

```
linLine.X1 = Int(frmLine.Width * Rnd)
```

The X1 property of the line control is the horizontal coordinate of the point where the line begins. Because the line is drawn on the form, the coordinate system is referenced to the form. Visual Basic's default coordinate system defines the coordinate X1=0,Y1=0 as the top-left corner of the form.

The second statement in the cmdStart_Click() procedure assigns a value to the Y1 property of the line control. The assigned value may be an integer between 0 and the height of the form:

```
linLine.Y1 = Int(frmLine.Height * Rnd)
```

The Y1 property of the line control is the vertical coordinate of the point where the line begins.

The last two statements of the cmdStart_Click() procedure assign values to the X2 and Y2 properties of the line control. The X2 and Y2 properties are the coordinates of the endpoints of the line control:

```
linLine.X2 = Int(frmLine.Width * Rnd)
linLine.Y2 = Int(frmLine.Height * Rnd)
```

When you click the Start button, the line moves to a new location that depends on random numbers. In other words, you are placing the line at a random location in the window.

More About the Properties of the Line Control

Experiment with some of the properties of the line control at design time:

☐ Select the line control at design time.

☐ Change the BorderColor property of the line control to red.

   Visual Basic responds by changing the color of the line to red.

☐ Change the BorderWidth property of the line control to 10.

   Visual Basic responds by changing the width of the line to 10 twips.

☐ Save the project by selecting Save Project from the File menu.

☐ Execute the Line program and then click the Start button several times.

   The Line program now displays the line control as a red line that is 10 twips wide (see Figure 7.2).

Figure 7.2.

The Line control as a 10-twips red line.

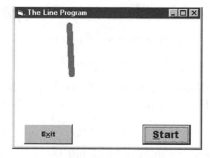

You can also change the color of the line and the size of the line at runtime:

☐ Insert the following statement at the beginning of the cmdStart_Click() procedure:

```
linLine.BorderColor=RGB(Int(255*Rnd), _
                        Int(255*Rnd), _
                        Int(255*Rnd))

linLine.BorderWidth = Int(100 * Rnd) + 1
```

The first statement assigns a new value to the BorderColor property of the line control. The new value is the returned value from the RGB() function in which all three parameters of the function are random numbers between 0 and 255, so the returned value from this RGB() function is a random color.

7

The second statement assigns a new value to the BorderWidth property of the line control. This new value is a random number between 0 and 100 plus 1. This means that the width of the line is assigned a new width between 1 and 101 twips. You add 1 to Int(100 * Rnd) because the minimum value for the BorderWidth cannot be 0.

☐ Execute the Line program.

As you can see, the line changes its color and its width every time you click the Start button or press Alt+S. Of course, if the random color is the same color as the form's background, you will not see the line.

The Shape Control

The shape control is used for drawing several shapes: rectangle, square, rounded rectangle, rounded square, circle, and oval. The Shape program illustrates how to display these shapes.

The Visual Implementation of the Shape Program

Use the following steps to build the form of the Shape program:

☐ Create a new Standard EXE project.

☐ Save the form of the project as Shape.Frm in the C:\VB5Prg\Ch07 directory, and save the project file of the project as Shape.Vbp in the C:\VB5Prg\Ch07 directory.

☐ Build the form of the Shape program according to Table 7.2.

The completed form should look like the one shown in Figure 7.3.

Figure 7.3.

The frmShape form.

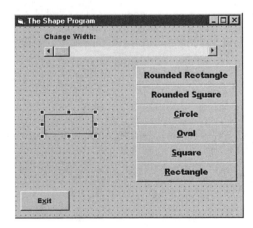

Table 7.2. The properties table of the Shape program.

Object	Property	Setting
Form	**Name**	**frmShape**
	Caption	The Shape Program
Horizontal Scroll Bar	**Name**	**hsbWidth**
	Max	10
	Min	1
	Value	1
CommandButton	**Name**	**cmdRndRect**
	Caption	Rounded Rectan&gle
CommandButton	**Name**	**cmdRndSqr**
	Caption	Rounded S&quare
CommandButton	**Name**	**cmdCircle**
	Caption	&Circle
Command Button	**Name**	**cmdOval**
	Caption	&Oval
CommandButton	**Name**	**cmdSquare**
	Caption	&Square
CommandButton	**Name**	**cmdRectangle**
	Caption	&Rectangle
CommandButton	**Name**	**cmdExit**
	Caption	E&xit
Label	**Name**	**lblInfo**
	Caption	Change Width:
Shape	**Name**	**shpAllShapes**

Entering the Code of the Shape Program

You'll now enter the code of the Shape program:

☐ Make sure that the Option Explicit statement resides in the general declarations section as follows:

```
' All variables MUST be declared.
Option Explicit
```

7

☐ Type the following code in the cmdExit_Click() procedure:

```
Private Sub cmdExit_Click()

    End

End Sub
```

☐ Type the following code in the cmdRectangle_Click() procedure:

```
Private Sub cmdRectangle_Click()

    ' The user clicked the Rectangle button,
    ' so set the Shape property of shpAllShapes to
    ' rectangle (0).
    shpAllShapes.Shape = 0

End Sub
```

☐ Type the following code in the cmdSquare_Click() procedure:

```
Private Sub cmdSquare_Click()

    ' The user clicked the Square button,
    ' so set the Shape property of shpAllShapes to
    ' square (1).
    shpAllShapes.Shape = 1

End Sub
```

☐ Type the following code in the cmdOval_Click() procedure:

```
Private Sub cmdOval_Click()

    ' The user clicked the Oval button,
    ' so set the Shape property of shpAllShapes to
    ' oval (2).
    shpAllShapes.Shape = 2

End Sub
```

☐ Type the following code in the cmdCircle_Click() procedure:

```
Private Sub cmdCircle_Click()

    ' The user clicked the Circle button,
    ' so set the Shape property of shpAllShapes to
    ' circle (3).
    shpAllShapes.Shape = 3

End Sub
```

☐ Type the following code in the cmdRndRect_Click() procedure:

```
Private Sub cmdRndRect_Click()

    ' The user clicked the Rounded Rectangle button,
    ' so set the Shape property of shpAllShapes to
```

```
' rounded rectangle (4).
shpAllShapes.Shape = 4
```

      End Sub

☐ Type the following code in the cmdRndSqr() procedure:

Private Sub cmdRndSqr_Click()

```
' The user clicked the Rounded Square button,
' so set the Shape property of shpAllShapes to
' rounded square (5).
shpAllShapes.Shape = 5
```

      End Sub

☐ Type the following code in the hsbWidth_Change() procedure:

Private Sub hsbWidth_Change()

```
' The user changed the scroll bar position,
' so set the BorderWidth property of
' shpAllShapes to the new value of the scroll
' bar.
shpAllShapes.BorderWidth = hsbWidth.Value
```

      End Sub

☐ Type the following code in the hsbWidth_Scroll() procedure:

Private Sub hsbWidth_Scroll()

```
' The user changed the scroll bar position,
' so set the BorderWidth property of
' shpAllShapes to the new value of the scroll
' bar.
shpAllShapes.BorderWidth = hsbWidth.Value
```

      End Sub

☐ Select Save Project from the File menu of Visual Basic to save your work.

Executing the Shape Program

When you execute the Shape program, the form shown in Figure 7.3 is displayed. When you click a button, the shape changes to the shape indicated by the button. For example, when you click the Circle button, the shape becomes a circle.

The width of the shape is changed when you change the scroll bar position. Figure 7.4 shows the shape after the Circle button was clicked and the scroll bar was set to its middle point.

7

Figure 7.4.
*Changing the shape to
a circle.*

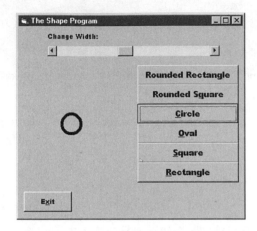

How the Shape Program Works

The code of the Shape program changes the shape and the width of the shpAllShapes control.

The Code of the `cmdRectangle_Click()` Procedure

The `cmdRectangle_Click()` procedure is executed when you click the Rectangle button. The statement in this procedure sets the Shape property of shpAllShapes to 0, which means a rectangle:

```
shpAllShapes.Shape = 0
```

In a similar manner, the `cmdSquare_Click()` procedure is executed when you click the Square button. The statement in the `cmdSquare_Click()` procedure sets the Shape property of shpAllShapes to 1, which means a square.

Table 7.3 lists the possible values the Shape property may have.

Table 7.3. Possible values for the Shape property of the shape control.

Value	Meaning
0	Rectangle
1	Square
2	Oval
3	Circle
4	Rounded rectangle
5	Rounded square

The Code of the `hsbWidth_Change()` Procedure

The `hsbWidth_Change()` procedure is executed when you change the scroll bar position. As indicated in the Properties table of the Shape program, the Min property of the scroll bar is 1 and the Max property is 10. Therefore, you can change the Value property of hsbWidth to a value between 1 and 10. This value is assigned to the BorderWidth property of shpAllShapes in the `hsbWidth_Change()` procedure as follows:

```
shpAllShapes.BorderWidth = hsbWidth.Value
```

Therefore, shpAllShapes changes its width according to the scroll bar position.

Other Properties of the Shape Control

The Shape program demonstrates only two properties of the shape control. You may experiment with other properties of the shape control by placing a shape in a form and changing its properties. Use the following steps as a guideline:

☐ Place a shape control in the form.

> *Visual Basic responds by assigning the default rectangle shape.*

☐ Change the Shape property to Circle.

> *Visual Basic responds by changing the shape from a rectangle to a circle.*

☐ Change the FillColor property to red.

> *Visual Basic does not fill the circle with red because the default FillStyle property of the shape is Transparent.*

☐ Change the FillStyle property to Solid.

> *Visual Basic responds by filling the circle with solid red.*

Pictures

The Line control and the Shape control are capable of drawing simple geometric shapes, such as lines, circles, squares, and so on. To display more complex shapes, you need to use a picture file. You can place picture files on a form, in an image control, or in a picture control.

To place a picture file in an object, you have to change the Picture property of the object. For example, to place a picture file in an image control, set the Picture property of the image control to the desired picture file.

7

You can create a picture file by using Paint to draw the picture, then saving your picture as a BMP file. If you don't think you have the talent to draw pictures yourself, you can buy professional pictures from a variety of vendors. These third-party picture products are called clip art. (Before purchasing clip-arts from a third-party vendor, read the software license agreement of the clip-art package to verify that you are allowed to distribute the pictures with your applications.)

Placing Pictures on a Form During Design Time

You may place pictures on a form during both design time and runtime.

Use the following steps to create a picture with the Paint program:

☐ Start the Paint program.

☐ Select Attributes from the Image menu of Paint.

> *Paint responds by displaying the Attributes dialog box.*

☐ Set the Units to Inches.

☐ Set the Width to 3.

☐ Set the Height to 3.

☐ Click the OK button of the Attributes dialog box.

> *Paint responds by displaying an empty picture 3 inches high and 3 inches wide.*

☐ Use the Paintbrush tools to draw your picture.

☐ Save your work by saving the file as MyPic.BMP in the C:\VB4Prg\Ch07 directory.

You now have a BMP picture file that you can place on a form:

☐ Create a new Standard Visual Basic project.

> *Visual Basic responds by displaying a blank form called Form1.frm.*

☐ Set the Picture property of Form1 to the MyPic.BMP file that you created.

> *The picture is placed on the form (see Figure 7.5).*

Figure 7.5.

Placing a picture created with Paint on a form.

As shown in Figure 7.5, the picture is displayed on the form with its upper-left corner at the X=0,Y=0 coordinate of the form. You cannot stretch or shrink the picture that you placed on the form. The picture has the same dimensions you specified in the Attributes dialog box of Paint.

The picture that is placed on the form serves as a background picture. To make the picture blend with the background, do the following:

☐ Set the BackColor property of Form1 to white.

> *Assuming that the background color of the MyPic.BMP picture that you created with Paint is also white, the picture blends nicely on Form1.*

☐ Drag the edges of Form1 so that the entire picture is displayed in Form1.

You can place command buttons and other controls directly on the picture. Figure 7.6 shows Form1 with several CommandButtons placed in the form.

Figure 7.6.

Placing buttons on the background picture of the form.

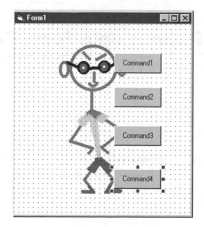

7

Now that the form has a background picture, you may want to prevent the user from stretching or shrinking the form (because if the user makes the window smaller or larger, the picture will not stretch or shrink).

☐ Set the BorderStyle property of Form1 to 1-Fixed Single.

☐ Execute the program.

> *As shown in Figure 7.7, the window of the program has a background picture (and the user cannot size the window, because you set the BorderStyle property of Form1 to Fixed Single).*

☐ Terminate the program. (You do not have to save the project. The only reason you were instructed to create this project is so that you can see the Picture property of the form in action.)

Figure 7.7.

The form with its BorderStyle property set to Fixed Single.

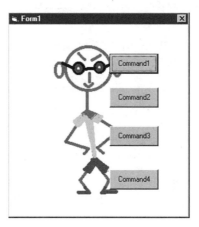

Placing Pictures on a Form During Runtime

You can also place pictures on a form during runtime. To load a picture called C:\VB5Prg\OurPic.BMP and place it on a form named frmOurForm form, use the following statement:

```
frmOurForm.Picture = _
    LoadPicture("C:\VB5Prg\OurPic.bmp")
```

Because only one picture may be placed on a form at any time, the LoadPicture() function replaces the current background picture (if there's already one on the form).

To clear a picture already on the form at runtime, use the following statement:

```
frmOurForm.Picture = LoadPicture("")
```

Once the preceding statement is executed, the form will not have a background picture.

The Image Control

You can also place BMP picture files that you create with Paint in the image control, which supports the Stretch property. This property enables you to stretch the picture to any desired size. (The form and the picture controls do not support the Stretch property.)

To load the picture C:\VB5Prg\Ch05\MyPic.BMP and place it in an image control called imgMyImage, use the following statement:

```
imgMyImage.Picture = _
      LoadPicture("C:\VB5Prg\Ch07\MyPic.BMP ")
```

Because only one picture may be placed in an image control at any time, the LoadPicture() function replaces the current picture if there's already one in the image control.

To clear a picture already in the image control at runtime, use the following statement:

```
imgMyImage.Picture = LoadPicture("")
```

To set the Stretch property of imgMyImage to True, use the following statement:

```
imgMyImage.Stretch = True
```

After you set the Stretch property to True, the picture file is automatically stretched so that the picture fills the entire area of the image control. In other words, Visual Basic automatically enlarges or shrinks the size of the picture. For example, if the image control holds the MyPic.BMP picture and the image control is 2 inches by 2 inches, then Visual Basic sizes the MyPic.BMP picture from its original size of 3 inches by 3 inches to 2 inches by 2 inches.

You can also set the Stretch property of the image control to True or False at design time.

The Picture Control

The picture control is very similar to the image control, except that it supports more properties, more events, and more methods than the image control does. However, the picture control does not support the Stretch property (only the image control supports the Stretch property).

The picture control supports the AutoSize property. If you set the AutoSize property of the picture control to True, Visual Basic adjusts the size of the picture control to the size of the picture file (that is, if the picture file is 3 inches by 2 inches, Visual Basic adjusts the size of the picture control to 3 inches by 3 inches). The form and the image control do not support the AutoSize property.

The image control uses fewer resources than the picture control uses, so it is repainted faster.

7

Incorporating the Picture Files into the EXE Files

As stated, the LoadPicture() function may be used to load a picture into an image control, a picture control, or a form at runtime. However, using the LoadPicture() function has a drawback: You must have the picture BMP file in the directory specified by the parameter of the LoadPicture() function. Therefore, your distribution disk (the disk that contains your complete program) must include the picture files that your program uses.

On the other hand, any picture file that was assigned to a picture holder control (form, picture control, or image control) during design time becomes an integral part of the final EXE file, so you don't have to distribute the picture file as a separate file. The picture files that are supported by Visual Basic are bitmap files, icon files, metafiles, and cursor files.

Bitmap Files

A bitmap file has either a BMP or DIB file extension. The bitmap file contains bytes that describe the locations and colors of the picture's pixels.

Icon Files

An icon file has an ICO file extension. Icon files are similar to BMP and DIB files, but icon files may represent images that have a maximum size of 32 pixels by 32 pixels.

Metafiles

A metafile has a WMF file extension. It contains a list of instructions that describe how to generate the picture.

Cursor Files

A cursor file has a CUR file extension and is similar to an icon file. It is a small file usually used to represent the mouse cursor, such as the familiar hourglass icon and arrow icon.

The MoveEye Program

You can move a control at runtime either by changing its Left and Top properties or by using the Move method.

You'll now write a program called MoveEye. This program illustrates how to move an object by changing its Left and Top properties.

The Visual Implementation of the MoveEye Program

As usual, you'll start with the visual implementation of the program:

☐ Create a new Standard EXE project by selecting New Project from the File menu of Visual Basic.

☐ Save the form of the project as MoveEye.Frm in the C:\VB5Prg\Ch07 directory, and save the project file as MoveEyc.Vbp in the C:\VB5Prg\Ch07 directory.

☐ Build the form of the MoveEye program according to Table 7.4.

The completed form should look like the one shown in Figure 7.8.

Figure 7.8.
The frmMoveEye form (design mode).

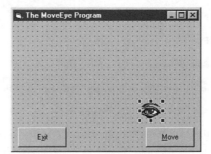

Table 7.4. The properties table of the MoveEye program.

Object	Property	Setting
Form	**Name**	**frmMoveEye**
	BackColor	Gray
	Caption	The MoveEye Program
CommandButton	**Name**	**cmdMove**
	Caption	&Move
CommandButton	**Name**	**cmdExit**
	Caption	E&xit
Image	**Name**	**imgEye**
	Picture	Eye.Ico
	Stretch	True

Table 7.4 instructs you to set the Picture property of the imgEye control to Eye.Ico. You may find this icon file in the \Icons\Misc sub-directory that was created when you installed Visual Basic. If your VB directory does not contain this ICO file, then use any other ICO file.

Entering the Code of the MoveEye Program

You'll now enter the code of the MoveEye program:

☐ Make sure that the general declarations section of the frmMoveEye from has the Option Explicit statement in it as follows:

```
' All variables MUST be declared.
Option Explicit
```

☐ Type the following code in the cmdExit_Click() procedure:

```
Private Sub cmdExit_Click()

    End

End Sub
```

☐ Type the following code in the cmdMove_Click() procedure:

```
Private Sub cmdMove_Click()

  ' Declare Counter as an integer.
  Dim Counter As Integer

  ' Execute the For loop 100 times.
  For Counter = 1 To 100 Step 1

     ' Raise the Top of the image 20 twips
     ' upward.
      imgEye.Top = imgEye.Top - 20

     ' Shift the Left edge of the image 20 twips
     ' to the left.
     imgEye.Left = imgEye.Left - 20

  Next Counter

End Sub
```

Executing the MoveEye Program

Let's see your code in action:

☐ Execute the MoveEye program.

As you click the Move button, the eye image is moved to a new location. You can keep clicking the Move button until the eye disappears from the form.

The Code of the MoveEye Program

The MoveEye program moves the image control by changing its Top and Left properties.

The Code of the cmdMove_Click() Procedure

When you click the Move button, the cmdMove_Click() procedure is automatically executed:

```
Private Sub cmdMove_Click()

    ' Declare Counter as an integer.
    Dim Counter As Integer

    ' Execute the For loop 100 times.
    For Counter = 1 To 100 Step 1

        ' Raise the Top of the image 20 twips
        ' upward.
        imgEye.Top = imgEye.Top - 20

        ' Shift the Left edge of the image 20 twips
        ' to the left.
        imgEye.Left = imgEye.Left - 20

    Next Counter

End Sub
```

The first statement in the For loop decreases the vertical coordinate of the top-left corner of the image by 20 twips:

```
imgEye.Top = imgEye.Top - 20
```

The second statement in the For loop decreases the horizontal coordinate of the top-left corner of the image by 20 twips:

```
imgEye.Left = imgEye.Left - 20
```

Figure 7.9 shows the effect of these two statements.

Figure 7.9.

Moving the image 20 twips up and 20 twips to the left.

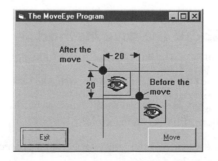

7

Because the For loop is executed 100 times, the image is moved 100 times, giving the illusion of continuous motion.

Moving a Control by Using the Move Method

The MoveEye program that was discussed in the previous section moves the image by changing its Top and Left properties. The Move method is another way to move the control.

☐ Replace the code of the cmdMove_Click() procedure with the following code:

```
Private Sub cmdMove_Click()

    ' Declare the variables.
    Dim Counter As Integer
    Dim LeftEdge As Single
    Dim TopEdge As Single

    ' Initialize the variables with the current
    ' location of the image.
    LeftEdge = imgEye.Left
    TopEdge = imgEye.Top

    ' Use the For loop to move the image 100
    ' times. In each Move, the image moves 20 twips
    ' upward and 20 twips to the left.
    For Counter = 1 To 100 Step 1
        LeftEdge = LeftEdge - 20
        TopEdge = TopEdge - 20
        imgEye.Move LeftEdge, TopEdge
    Next Counter

End Sub
```

The code of the procedure initializes the two variables, LeftEdge and TopEdge, to the current location of the top-left corner of the image, and the For loop is executed 100 times.

In each iteration of the For loop, the variables LeftEdge and TopEdge are decremented by 20. The Move method is used with the variable LeftEdge as the new horizontal coordinate and the variable TopEdge as the new vertical coordinate.

More About the Move Method

The full syntax of the Move method is as follows:

```
[Object name].Move. left, top, width, height
```

This means that you can also specify the new width and height that the object will have after the movement. Here is an example:

☐ Replace the code of the cmdMove_Click() procedure of the MoveEye program with the following code:

```
Private Sub cmdMove_Click()

    Dim Counter As Integer
    Dim LeftEdge As Single
    Dim TopEdge As Single
    Dim WidthOfImage As Single
    Dim HeightOfImage As Single
    imgEye.Stretch = True
    LeftEdge = imgEye.Left
    TopEdge = imgEye.Top
    WidthOfImage = imgEye.Width
    HeightOfImage = imgEye.Height
    For Counter = 1 To 100 Step 1
        LeftEdge = LeftEdge - 20
        TopEdge = TopEdge - 20
        WidthOfImage = WidthOfImage + 10
        HeightOfImage = HeightOfImage + 10
        imgEye.Move LeftEdge, TopEdge, _
                    WidthOfImage, HeightOfImage
    Next Counter

End Sub
```

☐ Execute the program and note how the eye moves and grows. After 100 moves, the form looks like the one shown in Figure 7.10.

Figure 7.10.

Using the Move *method to move and enlarge the eye.*

The first statement after the declaration statement is this:

```
imgEye.Stretch = True
```

This statement sets the Stretch property of imgEye to True, so that the program can stretch the image. (You already set the Stretch property of the imgEye image to True during design time. So why are you instructed to set this property again during runtime? To illustrate that the Stretch property can be set during runtime as well as design time.)

The variables WidthOfImage and HeightOfImage are initialized to the current width and height of the image:

```
WidthOfImage = imgEye.Width
HeightOfImage = imgEye.Height
```

7

Then the Move method is executed 100 times. In each iteration of the For loop, the WidthOfImage and HeightOfImage variables are increased by 10 twips.

The Move method specifies the new coordinates for the top-left corner of the image and the new width and height the image should have after the movement:

```
imgEye.Move LeftEdge, TopEdge, WidthOfImage, HeightOfImage
```

Comparing the Moving Techniques

If you compare the performance of the MoveEye program using both moving techniques—using the Move method and changing the Top and Left properties—you might notice that the Move method is better. Changing the Top and Left properties produces a jerky movement. However, if you are using a fast computer, such as a Pentium 200MHz, you may not notice any differences between the two moving techniques in the MoveEye program because the picture you're moving is a small picture.

However, while using the Move method, you may notice some flickering on the screen. In fact, the larger the image becomes, the more flickering you'll see. The flickering will occur even if a very fast PC is used. The flickering can be eliminated by using DirectX technology. In Chapter 19, "ActiveX—Sound Programming and DirectSound," you'll learn about this sophisticated graphic technology.

Moving a Picture Control

The previous program illustrated that using the Move method to move a control produces smoother motion than changing the Top and Left properties. You can get even better results by using a picture control instead of an image control. To see how you can use the picture control, change the frmMoveEye form as follows:

☐ Delete the imgEye Image control from the form by selecting the imgEye control and pressing Delete.

☐ Place a picture control in the form by double-clicking the picture control in the toolbox window. When you place the mouse cursor (without clicking any of the mouse buttons) on the icon of the picture control in the toolbox window, a yellow rectangle appears with the text PictureBox in it. This way, you can verify that you located the icon of the picture control in the toolbox window.

☐ Set the Name property of the picture control to picEye.

☐ Set the Picture property of picEye to Eye.ICO.

☐ Set the BorderStyle property of picEye to 0-None so that the picture will not be enclosed with a border.

☐ Set the Appearance property of the picEye control to 0-Flat so that the picture control will appear flat, not three-dimensional.

☐ Set the AutoSize property of the picEye control to True so that the picture control will resize itself to the size of the eye picture.

☐ Set the BackColor property of the picEye control to gray (so that the eye picture will have the same background color as the form).

☐ Replace the cmdMove_Click procedure with the following code:

```
Private Sub cmdMove_Click()

    ' Declare the variables.
    Dim Counter As Integer
    Dim LeftEdge As Single
    Dim TopEdge As Single

    ' Initialize the variables with the current
    ' location of the picture.
    LeftEdge = picEye.Left
    TopEdge = picEye.Top

    ' Use the For loop to move the image 100
    ' times. In each Move, the picture moves 20
    ' twips upward and 20 twips to the left.
    For Counter = 1 To 100 Step 1
        LeftEdge = LeftEdge - 20
        TopEdge = TopEdge - 20
        picEye.Move LeftEdge, TopEdge
    Next Counter

End Sub
```

☐ Select Save Project from the File menu of Visual Basic to save your work.

Let's see your code in action:

☐ Execute the program, click the Move button, and notice how the eye moves.

Control Arrays

A control array is an array that contains controls as its elements. For example, you can create an array whose elements are image controls.

The Moon Program

You'll now write a program called Moon. The Moon program makes use of arrays of images.

7

The Visual Implementation of the Moon Program

You'll now visually implement the form of the Moon program.

☐ Create a new Standard EXE project.

☐ Save the form of the project as Moon.Frm in the C:\VB5Prg\Ch07 directory and save the project file as Moon.Vbp in the C:\VB5Prg\Ch07 directory.

☐ Set the Name property of the form to frmMoon and set the Caption property of the form to The Moon Program.

☐ Place an image control in the frmMoon form by double-clicking the icon of the image control in the toolbox window.

   Visual Basic responds by placing the Image control in the frmMoon form.

☐ Drag the image control to the upper-left portion of the form.

☐ Set the Name property of the image control that you placed in the frmMoon form to imgMoon.

☐ Set the Visible property of the imgMoon image control to False.

☐ Make sure the Stretch property of imgMoon is set to False.

☐ Set the Picture property of imgMoon to Moon01.Ico. (The Moon01.Ico file resides in the \Icons\Elements subdirectory of the directory where you installed your Visual Basic. If you do not have this icon file, use another icon file.)

Your frmMoon form should now look like the one in Figure 7.11.

Figure 7.11.

The first element of the image control array.

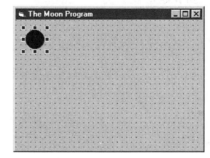

You have completed placing the image control in the form. This image will soon serve as element number 0 in the array of images. Currently, the image that you placed is a "regular" (nonarray) control. You can check this by examining the Index property of the imgMoon image. It should be blank.

Use the following steps to place the second element of the array of images:

☐ Double-click the icon of the image control in the toolbox window.

> *Visual Basic responds by placing a second image control in the frmMoon form. The form now contains two image controls.*

☐ Drag the second image control to the right of the first image control.

☐ Set the Visible property of the second image control to False.

☐ Make sure that the Stretch property of the second image is set to False.

☐ Set the Picture property of the second image control to Moon02.Ico.

Your frmMoon form should now look like the one in Figure 7.12.

Figure 7.12.

The first and second elements of the image control array.

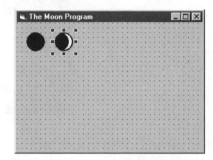

☐ Set the Name property of the second image to imgMoon and then click anywhere in the form.

> *Visual Basic responds by displaying the dialog box in Figure 7.13; that is, Visual Basic makes sure you intend to name the second image with the same name as the first image.*

☐ Click the Yes button of the dialog box shown in Figure 7.13.

Figure 7.13.

Creating a control array.

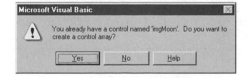

7

You are informing Visual Basic that you are creating a control array.

☐ Examine the Index properties of the first two image controls.

The Index property is 0 for the first image control and it is 1 for the second image control. This means that you now have a control array called imgMoon(). The first element of the array, imgMoon(0), is Moon01.Ico, which is the first image you placed in the form. The second element of the array is the image Moon02.Ico, the imgMoon(1) element.

☐ Now repeat this process and add six more elements to the control array. When you are finished, you should have a total of eight elements in the array, as shown in Figure 7.14 and Table 7.5. Don't forget to set the Name, Stretch, and Visible properties of the remaining six images. Note that when you add additional elements to the imgMoon() array, Visual Basic does not prompt you with the dialog box in Figure 7.13 because Visual Basic already knows that imgMoon is a control array. (If needed, make the frmMoon form wider so that all the moons will fit in the form.)

Figure 7.14.

The eight moons of the control array.

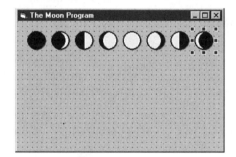

Table 7.5. The imgMoon() control array.

Element	Content of the Element
imgMoon(0)	Moon01.Ico
imgMoon(1)	Moon02.Ico
imgMoon(2)	Moon03.Ico
imgMoon(3)	Moon04.Ico
imgMoon(4)	Moon05.Ico
imgMoon(5)	Moon06.Ico
imgMoon(6)	Moon07.Ico
imgMoon(7)	Moon08.Ico

☐ Continue building the frmMoon form according to Table 7.6.

The completed form should look like the one shown in Figure 7.15.

Figure 7.15.
The frmMoon form.

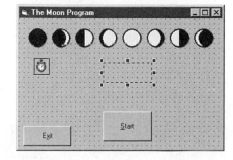

Table 7.6. The properties table of the Moon program.

Object	Property	Setting
Form	**Name**	**frmMoon**
	Caption	The Moon Program
Timer	**Name**	**tmrTimer**
	Interval	250
	Enabled	True
CommandButton	**Name**	**cmdStart**
	Caption	&Start
CommandButton	**Name**	**cmdExit**
	Caption	E&xit
Image	**Name**	**imgCurrentMoon**
	Visible	True
	Picture	(None)
	Stretch	False
Image Control	*(See Table 7.5)*	*(See Table 7.5)*

7

Note

Leave the Picture property of imgCurrentMoon at its default value (None). You'll assign a value to this property from within the program's code. This image control is *not* part of the imgMoon() image control array.

The Timer control is not visible during runtime, so it doesn't matter where you place it in the form.

Entering the Code of the Moon Program

You'll now enter the code of the Moon program:

☐ Type the following code in the general declarations section of the frmMoon form:

```
' All variables MUST be declared.
Option Explicit
' Declaration of variables that are visible from any
' procedure in the form.
Dim gRotateFlag As Integer
Dim gCurrentMoon As Integer
```

☐ Type the following code in the cmdExit_Click() procedure:

```
Private Sub cmdExit_Click()

    End

End Sub
```

☐ Type the following code in the cmdStart_Click() procedure:

```
Private Sub cmdStart_Click()

    ' Toggle the gRotateFlag, and toggle
    ' the caption of the Start/Stop button.
    If gRotateFlag = 0 Then
       gRotateFlag = 1
       cmdStart.Caption = "&Stop"
    Else
       gRotateFlag = 0
       cmdStart.Caption = "&Start"
    End If

End Sub
```

☐ Type the following code in the Form_Load() procedure:

```
Private Sub Form_Load()

    ' Initialize the flags.
```

```
            gRotateFlag = 0
            gCurrentMoon = 0

    End Sub
```

☐ Type the following code in the `tmrTimer_Timer()` procedure:

```
    Private Sub tmrTimer_Timer()

    If gRotateFlag = 1 Then
        imgCurrentMoon.Picture = _
                  imgMoon(gCurrentMoon).Picture
        gCurrentMoon = gCurrentMoon + 1

        If gCurrentMoon = 8 Then
            gCurrentMoon = 0
        End If

    End If

    End Sub
```

☐ Select Save Project from the File menu of Visual Basic to save your work.

Executing the Moon Program

Let's see the Moon program in action:

☐ Execute the Moon program.

☐ Click the Start button.

As you can see, the image of the moon seems to rotate around its axis.

☐ Click the Exit button to terminate the Moon program.

The Code of the Moon Program

The code of the Moon program uses a control array of images to display the elements (images) of the array one after the other, giving the illusion of a rotating moon.

The Code of the General Declarations Section

The code in the general declarations section declares two integers: `gRotateFlag` and `gCurrentMoon`. These variables are visible by all the procedures of the frmMoon form.

The Code of the `Form_Load()` Procedure

The `Form_Load()` procedure is automatically executed when you start the program, and it's a good place for performing various initializations. The two variables that were declared in the general declarations section are initialized to 0:

7

```
gRotateFlag = 0
gCurrentMoon = 0
```

> **Note**
>
> When you create variables, Visual Basic automatically initializes the variables to 0. However, including the initialization in the Form_Load() procedure makes the program easier to read().

The Code of the cmdStart_Click() Procedure

The cmdStart_Click() procedure is executed when you click the Start button. This procedure executes an If…Else statement. The If statement checks to see the current value of the gRotateFlag variable:

```
Private Sub cmdStart_Click()

    ' Toggle the gRotateFlag, and toggle
    ' the caption of the Start/Stop button.
    If gRotateFlag = 0 Then
        gRotateFlag = 1
        cmdStart.Caption = "&Stop"
    Else
        gRotateFlag = 0
        cmdStart.Caption = "&Start"
    End If

End Sub
```

If the current value of gRotateFlag is 0, it is changed to 1 and the caption of the cmdStart button changes to &Stop. If, however, the current value of gRotateFlag is 1, this procedure changes the value of gRotateFlag back to 0 and the caption of the cmdStart button is changed to back to &Start.

The gRotateFlag variable is used in the timer procedure discussed in the following section.

The Code of the tmrTimer_Timer() Procedure

Because you set the Interval property of the tmrTimer timer to 250, the tmrTimer_Timer() procedure is automatically executed every 250 milliseconds:

```
Private Sub tmrTimer_Timer()

    If gRotateFlag = 1 Then
        imgCurrentMoon.Picture = _
                imgMoon(gCurrentMoon).Picture
        gCurrentMoon = gCurrentMoon + 1

        If gCurrentMoon = 8 Then
```

```
        gCurrentMoon = 0
    End If

  End If

End Sub
```

If you haven't clicked the Start button, gRotateFlag is still equal to 0, and the statements in the If gRotateFlag = 1 block are not executed. If you have clicked the Start button, gRotateFlag is equal to 1, and the statements in the If gRotateFlag = 1 block are executed.

The code in the If statement assigns the Picture property of the control array of images to the Picture property of the imgCurrentMoon image:

```
imgCurrentMoon.Picture= _
    imgMoon(CurrentMoon).Picture
```

For example, when the gCurrentMoon variable is equal to 0, the Picture property of the 0th element in the control array is assigned to the Picture property of imgCurrentMoon. This causes the image Moon01.Ico to be displayed (because imgMoon(0).Picture contains the Moon01.Ico picture).

The next statement in the If block increases the variable gCurrentMoon:

```
gCurrentMoon = gCurrentMoon + 1
```

The next time the tmrTimer_Timer() procedure is executed (that is, after 250 milliseconds), the variable gCurrentMoon is already updated, pointing to the next element in the control array of images.

The next statements in the tmrTimer_Timer() procedure examine whether the value of gCurrentMoon is equal to 8. If it is, the 8th element in the array was displayed already, so you need to reset gCurrentMoon to 0:

```
If gCurrentMoon = 8 Then
    gCurrentMoon = 0
End If
```

Animation

The Moon program illustrates how easy it is to write animation programs in Visual Basic. You can enhance the Moon program so its animation performance is more impressive.

Enhancing the Moon Program

Enhance the Moon program as follows:

☐ Set the Interval property of the tmrTimer timer to 55.

7

☐ Add code to the general declarations section of the frmMoon form so that it will look as follows:

```
Option Explicit
Dim gRotateFlag As Integer
Dim gCurrentMoon As Integer
Dim gDirection As Integer
Dim gLeftCorner, gTopCorner As Single
Dim gWidthOfMoon, gHeightOfMoon
Dim gEnlargeShrink As Integer
```

☐ Modify the Form_Load() procedure so it will look as follows:

```
Private Sub Form_Load()

    gRotateFlag = 0
    gCurrentMoon = 0
    gDirection = 1
    gLeftCorner = imgCurrentMoon.Left
    gTopCorner = imgCurrentMoon.Top
    gWidthOfMoon = 1
    gHeightOfMoon = 1
    gEnlargeShrink = 1

    imgCurrentMoon.Stretch = True

End Sub
```

☐ Modify the tmrTimer_Timer() procedure so that it will look as follows:

```
Private Sub tmrTimer_Timer()

    If gRotateFlag = 1 Then
       imgCurrentMoon.Picture = _
                 imgMoon(gCurrentMoon).Picture
       gCurrentMoon = gCurrentMoon + 1
       If gCurrentMoon = 8 Then
          gCurrentMoon = 0
       End If
    Else
       Exit Sub
    End If
    ' Use the Move method to move the image.
    ' After the movement, the image will have new
    ' width (=gWidthOfMoon), and new Height
    ' (=gHeightOfMoon).
    imgCurrentMoon.Move gLeftCorner, gTopCorner, _
               gWidthOfMoon, gHeightOfMoon
    ' Change the variables that the Move method uses
    ' for the next execution of this procedure,
    gLeftCorner = gLeftCorner + 10 * gDirection
    gTopCorner = gTopCorner + 10 * gDirection
    gWidthOfMoon = gWidthOfMoon + 10 * gEnlargeShrink
    gHeightOfMoon = gHeightOfMoon + 10 * gEnlargeShrink
    ' Is width of image too large?
    If gWidthOfMoon > 700 Then
```

```
      gEnlargeShrink = -1
End If
' Is width of image too small?
If gWidthOfMoon < 10 Then
   gEnlargeShrink = 1
End If
' Image crosses bottom of frame?
If imgCurrentMoon.Top > frmMoon.ScaleHeight Then
   gDirection = -1
End If
 ' Image crosses top of frame?
If imgCurrentMoon.Top < 10 Then
   gDirection = 1
End If

End Sub
```

☐ Select Save Project from the File menu of Visual Basic to save your work

Executing the Enhanced Version of the Moon Program

Let's see the enhanced version of the Moon program in action:

☐ Execute the Moon program.

As you can see, the moon rotates on its axis and also seems to move in three dimensions!

The Code of the General Declarations Section

The general declarations section of the frmMoon form includes additional variable declarations of variables that are visible to all procedures in the form.

The Code of the `Form_Load()` Procedure

The code in the `Form_Load()` procedure initializes the variables.

The variables `gLeftCorner` and `gTopCorner` are initialized to the initial position of the upper-left corner of the imgCurrentMoon image:

```
gLeftCorner = imgCurrentMoon.Left
gTopCorner = imgCurrentMoon.Top
```

The Stretch property of the imgCurrentMoon image is set to True:

```
imgCurrentMoon.Stretch = True
```

This means that the size of the imgCurrentMoon image will change to fit within the control. This step is necessary because during the execution of the Moon program, the size of the imgCurrentMoon picture is enlarged and reduced.

7

The Code of the `tmrTimer_Timer()` **Procedure**

The first `If` block in the `tmrTimer_Timer()` procedure is the same as the earlier version, which displays one of the elements in the control array of images.

Once the image is displayed, the `Move` method is used to move the image so that the new location of the top-left corner of the image is at coordinate X=gLeftCorner, Y=gTopCorner.

The `Move` method also uses the optional width and height parameters:

```
imgCurrentMoon.Move gLeftCorner, gTopCorner, _
                gWidthOfMoon,gHeightOfMoon
```

After the movement, the image will have a new width and height.

The statements that follow the `Move` statement prepare the variables for the next time the `tmrTimer_Timer()` procedure is executed:

```
gLeftCorner = gLeftCorner + 10 * gDirection
gTopCorner = gTopCorner + 10 * gDirection
gWidthOfMoon = gWidthOfMoon + 10 * gEnlargeShrink
gHeightOfMoon = gHeightOfMoon + 10 * gEnlargeShrink
```

Depending on the values of the variables `gDirection` and `gEnlargeShrink`, the previous variables would either increase or decrease (that is, if `gDirection` is equal to 1, the value of `gLeftCorner` is increased by 10 twips; if `gDirection` is equal to -1, the value of `gLeftCorner` is decreased by 10 twips).

Next, the code examines the variable `gWidthOfMoon` to see whether it's too large or too small:

```
If gWidthOfMoon > 700 Then
   gEnlargeShrink = -1
End If

If gWidthOfMoon < 10 Then
   gEnlargeShrink = 1
End If
```

Then the code examines the current position of the top-left corner of the image to see whether the image crossed the bottom or the top of the form:

```
If imgCurrentMoon.Top > frmMoon.ScaleHeight Then
   gDirection = -1
End If

If imgCurrentMoon.Top < 10 Then
   gDirection = 1
End If
```

Summary

In this chapter you have learned how to use graphics controls: the line control and the shape control. You have also learned how to display picture files in image and picture controls and to create animation by displaying and moving pictures. As demonstrated, the control array is a useful technique often used in animation.

Q&A

Q In this chapter I learned how to use the Move method to move an image control and a picture control. Can I use the same technique to move other controls such as buttons?

A Yes. The Move method may be used to move any object except menus. Of course, some controls (for example, the Timer control) are invisible, and it doesn't make sense to move an invisible control.

Quiz

1. How many twips are in an inch?
   a. 1440
   b. 1
   c. There is no relationship between an inch and a twip.
2. The Min property of the horizontal scroll bar in the Shape program was set to 1 at design time. Why not leave it at the default value 0?
3. What is the AutoSize property?
4. What is the difference between the Stretch property and the AutoSize property?

Exercise

Modify the MoveEye program so that it beeps when the imgEye image reaches the top of the form.

7

Quiz Answers

1. a

2. In the code of the hsbWidth_Change() procedure of the Shape program, you set the BorderWidth property of the shape control to the current value of the scroll bar:

   ```
   shpAllShapes.BorderWidth = hsbWidth.Value
   ```

   If 0 is the minimum value the scroll bar may have, when the scroll bar is placed at its minimum position, the preceding statement assigns the value 0 to the BorderWidth property of the shpAllShapes control. However, a shape control must have a minimum width of 1. Assigning 0 to the BorderWidth property of a shape control causes a runtime error.

3. When the AutoSize property is set to True, the object sizes itself to the exact dimensions of the picture file.

4. The AutoSize property is supported by a picture control and by the label control. When this property is set to True, Visual Basic adjusts the size of the control so that the control fits its content.

   The Stretch property is supported by an image control. When this property is set to True, the size of the picture is stretched to fit the size of the image control.

Exercise Answer

The image reaches the top of the form when its Top property is equal to 0. You can detect it by inserting the following If statement in the For loop of the cmdMove_Click() procedure:

```
If picEye.Top <= 0 Then
   Beep
   Exit Sub
End If
```

This If statement checks the value of the Top property. If the value is equal to or less than 0, the control reached the top of the form. The Beep statement will be executed and the Exit Sub statement will end the procedure.

This technique is often used to write a bouncing program, in which an object moves in the form in straight lines. When the object hits the side of the form, it changes direction. The code detects that the object reached the edge of the form by examining the values of the Top and Left properties.

Week 2

At A Glance

You have completed your first week, and you now know how to write simple Visual Basic programs. This week you'll learn how to use more powerful features of Visual Basic by writing more programs that illustrate many more new concepts.

Where You're Going

In Chapter 8, "Graphics Methods," you'll learn to use the powerful graphics methods, and in Chapter 9, "Displaying Data in Tabular Formats," you'll learn to use the grid control. This week you'll also learn how to display and print data, how to interface with Windows, how to take advantage of Windows, and how to access files from within your Visual Basic programs.

Day 8

Graphics Methods

This chapter focuses on graphics methods, which are similar to the graphics controls discussed in Chapter 7, "Graphics Controls." Graphics methods are easier to use in some cases than graphic controls are.

The Points Program

The Points program, which draws points at random locations in a form, illustrates how to draw points by using the `Point` method.

The Visual Implementation of the Points Program

As usual, you'll start designing the program by implementing the form of the program:

☐ Create the C:\VB5Prg\Ch08 directory. You'll save your work in this directory.

☐ Create a new Standard EXE project, save the form of the project as Points.Frm in the C:\VB5Prg\Ch08 directory, and save the project file as Points.Vbp in the C:\VB5Prg\Ch08 directory.

☐ Build the frmPoints form according to Table 8.1.

The completed form should look like the one shown in Figure 8.1.

Figure 8.1.

The frmPoints form (design mode).

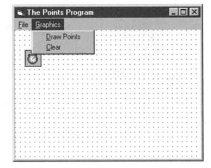

Table 8.1. The properties table of the frmPoints form.

Object	Property	Setting
Form	Name	frmPoints
	BackColor	White
	Caption	The Points Program
Timer	Name	tmrTimer
	Interval	60
	Enabled	True
Menu	(See Table 8.2)	(See Table 8.2)

Table 8.2. The menu table of the frmPoints form.

Caption	Name
&File	mnuFile
…E&xit	mnuExit
&Graphics	mnuGraphics
…&Draw Points	mnuDrawPoints
…&Clear	mnuClear

Entering the Code of the Points Program

You'll now enter the code of the Points program:

☐ Type the following code in the general declarations section of the frmPoints form:

```
' All variables MUST be declared.
Option Explicit

' A flag that determines if points will be drawn.
Dim gDrawPoints
```

☐ Type the following code in the Form_Load() procedure of the frmPoints form:

```
Private Sub Form_Load()

    ' Disable drawing.
    gDrawPoints = 0

End Sub
```

☐ Type the following code in the mnuClear_Click() procedure of the frmPoints form:

```
Private Sub mnuClear_Click()

    ' Disable drawing.
    gDrawPoints = 0

    ' Clear the form.
    frmPoints.Cls

End Sub
```

☐ Type the following code in the mnuDrawPoints_Click() procedure of the frmPoints form:

```
Private Sub mnuDrawPoints_Click()

    ' Enable drawing.
    gDrawPoints = 1

End Sub
```

☐ Type the following code in the mnuExit_Click() procedure of the frmPoints form:

```
Private Sub mnuExit_Click()

    End

End Sub
```

☐ Type the following code in the tmrTimer1_Timer() procedure of the frmPoints form:

```
Private Sub tmrTimer1_Timer()

    Dim R, G, B
    Dim X, Y
    Dim Counter
```

```
        ' Is it OK to draw?
        If gDrawPoints = 1 Then
            ' Draw 100 points.
            For Counter = 1 To 100 Step 1
                ' Get a random color.
                R = Rnd * 255
                G = Rnd * 255
                B = Rnd * 255
                ' Get a random (X,Y) coordinate.
                X = Rnd * frmPoints.ScaleWidth
                Y = Rnd * frmPoints.ScaleHeight
                ' Draw the point.
                frmPoints.PSet (X, Y), RGB(R, G, B)
            Next
        End If

    End Sub
```

☐ Select Save project from the File menu of Visual Basic to save your work.

Executing the Points Program

Let's see the Points program in action:

☐ Execute the Points program.

☐ Select Draw Points from the Graphics menu.

The program responds by displaying points with random colors at random locations in the form (see Figure 8.2).

Figure 8.2.

Drawing points in a form.

☐ Select Clear from the Graphics menu.

The program clears the form.

☐ Select Exit from the File menu to terminate the program.

How the Points Program Works

The Points program uses the PSet graphics method to draw a point in the form and the Cls method to clear the form.

The Code of the General Declarations Section

The general declarations section of the frmPoints form declares the gDrawPoints variable. This variable serves as a flag: When it is equal to 1, drawing is enabled; when it is equal to 0, drawing is disabled.

The Code of the Form_Load() Procedure

The Form_Load() procedure is automatically executed when the program is started:

```
Private Sub Form_Load()

    ' Disable drawing.
    gDrawPoints = 0

End Sub
```

This procedure initializes the gDrawPoints flag to 0 to disable drawing the points.

The Code of the mnuClear_Click() Procedure

The mnuClear_Click() procedure is executed when you select Clear from the Graphics menu:

```
Private Sub mnuClear_Click()

    ' Disable drawing.
    gDrawPoints = 0

    ' Clear the form.
    frmPoints.Cls

End Sub
```

This procedure disables the drawing by setting the gDrawPoints variable to 0 and then uses the Cls method to clear the form.

Do	Don't

DO use the Cls method to clear an object. The Cls method clears graphics generated during runtime with the graphics methods. For example, to clear the frmMyForm form, use frmMyForm.Cls.

The Code of the `mnuDrawPoints_Click()` **Procedure**

The `mnuDrawPoints_Click()` procedure is executed when you select Draw Points from the Graphics menu:

```
Private Sub mnuDrawPoints_Click()

    ' Enable drawing.
    gDrawPoints = 1

End Sub
```

This procedure sets the `gDrawPoints` flag to 1 to enable drawing.

The Code of the `tmrTimer1_Timer()` **Procedure**

Because you set the Interval property of the tmrTimer timer to 60, the `tmrTimer1_Timer()` procedure is automatically executed every 60 milliseconds:

```
Private Sub tmrTimer1_Timer()

    Dim R, G, B
    Dim X, Y
    Dim Counter

    ' Is it OK to draw?
    If gDrawPoints = 1 Then
        ' Draw 100 points.
        For Counter = 1 To 100 Step 1
            ' Get a random color.
            R = Rnd * 255
            G = Rnd * 255
            B = Rnd * 255
            ' Get a random (X,Y) coordinate.
            X = Rnd * frmPoints.ScaleWidth
            Y = Rnd * frmPoints.ScaleHeight
            ' Draw the point.
            frmPoints.PSet (X, Y), RGB(R, G, B)
        Next
    End If

End Sub
```

The `If` statement examines the value of the `gDrawPoints` flag. If this flag is equal to 1, it means you selected Draw Points from the Graphics menu, and the code in the `If` block is executed.

The `For` loop draws 100 points. Each point is drawn with a random color and at a random location. The `PSet` graphics method is used to draw each point:

```
frmPoints.PSet (X, Y), RGB(R, G, B)
```

8

The PSet **Graphics Method**

As demonstrated, the PSet method draws a point at the X,Y coordinate that is specified by its parameter.

The PSet method has an optional parameter called Step. When you're using the Step parameter, the point is drawn in relation to the CurrentX,CurrentY coordinate. For example, suppose that CurrentX is equal to 100 and CurrentY is equal to 50. Upon issuing the statement

```
frmPoints.PSet Step(10, 20), RGB(R, G, B)
```

a point is drawn at location 110,70. That is, the point is drawn 10 units to the right of CurrentX and 20 units below CurrentY. After the drawing, CurrentX and CurrentY are automatically updated—CurrentX is updated to 110, and CurrentY is updated to 70. (Recall from Chapter 4, "The Mouse," that CurrentX and CurrentY are automatically updated by Visual Basic to the endpoint of the last graphic that was drawn.)

☐ Replace the code in the tmrTimer1_Timer() procedure with the following code:

```
Private Sub tmrTimer1_Timer()

    Dim R, G, B
    Dim X, Y
    Dim Counter
    If gDrawPoints = 1 Then
        For Counter = 1 To 100 Step 1
            R = Rnd * 255
            G = Rnd * 255
            B = Rnd * 255
            frmPoints.PSet Step(1, 1), RGB(R, G, B)
            If CurrentX >= frmPoints.ScaleWidth Then
                CurrentX = Rnd * frmPoints.ScaleWidth
            End If
            If CurrentY >= frmPoints.ScaleHeight Then
                CurrentY = Rnd * frmPoints.ScaleHeight
            End If
        Next
    End If

End Sub
```

☐ Select Save Project from the File menu of Visual Basic.

☐ Execute the Points program, select Draw Points from the Graphics menu, and let the program run for a while.

The program now draws lines, as shown in Figure 8.3.

Figure 8.3.

Using the Step option of the PSet *graphics method.*

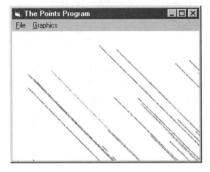

The code of the tmrTimer1_Timer() procedure uses the PSet method with the Step option:

```
frmPoints.PSet Step(1, 1), RGB(R, G, B)
```

Each point is drawn one unit to the right and one unit below the previous point. This explains why the points are drawn as straight diagonal lines, as shown in Figure 8.3.

The two If statements in this procedure check that the points are drawn within the boundaries of the form.

The Point Method

The Point method returns the color of a particular pixel. For example, to find the color of the pixel at location 30,40, use the following statement:

```
PixelColor = Point (30,40)
```

Although the Points program did not use the Point method, you may find some use for this method in your future projects.

Drawing Lines

You can draw lines using the Line method, which has the following syntax:

```
Line (x1,y1)-(x2,y2), color
```

where (x1,y1) is the coordinate of the starting point of the line, (x2,y2) is the coordinate of the ending point of the line, and color is the color of the line. If you omit the (x1,y1) parameter, the line is drawn starting at coordinate CurrentX, CurrentY.

To see the Line method in action, add the Lines menu item to the menu system of the Points program. Table 8.3 is the new menu table of the Points program.

Table 8.3. The new menu table of the frmPoints form.

Caption	Name
&File	mnuFile
...&Exit	mnuExit
&Graphics	mnuGraphics
...&Draw Points	mnuDrawPoints
...&Clear	mnuClear
...&Lines	mnuLines

☐ Add the following code in the mnuLines_Click() procedure of the frmPoints form:

```
Private Sub mnuLines_Click()

    Line -(Rnd * frmPoints.ScaleWidth, _
        Rnd * frmPoints.ScaleHeight), RGB(0, 0, 0)

End Sub
```

This procedure draws one line with random width, height, and color.

☐ Select Save Project from the File menu of Visual Basic to save your work.

☐ Execute the Points program.

☐ Select Lines from the Graphics menu.

A line is drawn in the form, as shown in Figure 8.4.

Figure 8.4.

Drawing a line with the Line method.

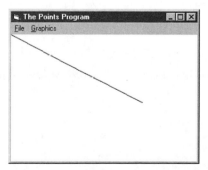

Because the (x1,y1) coordinate is omitted, the Line statement in the mnuLines_Click() procedure draws the line starting at coordinate CurrentX, CurrentY. The endpoint of the line is at a random location in the form. When you start the program, the initial values of CurrentX and CurrentY are 0—this explains why the line in Figure 8.4 starts at coordinate 0,0.

☐ Select Lines from the Graphics menu several times.

Each time you select Lines, a new line is drawn, starting from the endpoint of the previous line (see Figure 8.5).

Figure 8.5.

Drawing connected lines.

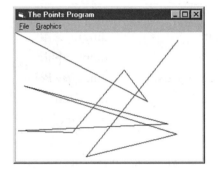

☐ Select Exit from the File menu of the Points program to terminate the program.

Now let's write code that draws several lines when you select Lines from the Graphics menu:

☐ Replace the code in the mnuLines_Click() procedure with the following code:

```
Private Sub mnuLines_Click()

    Dim Counter

    For Counter = 1 To 100 Step 1
        Line -(Rnd * frmPoints.ScaleWidth, _
               Rnd * frmPoints.ScaleHeight), RGB(0, 0, 0)

    Next

End Sub
```

☐ Execute the program.

☐ Select Lines from the Graphics menu.

The program draws 100 connected lines, as shown in Figure 8.6.

Figure 8.6.

Drawing 100 connected lines.

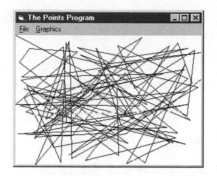

Using the Step Parameter in the Line Method

The optional Step parameter may be used with the Line method as follows:

```
Line (x1,y1)-Step (dX,dY), color
```

where (x1,y1) is the coordinate of the starting point, and Step (dX,dY) is an indication to Visual Basic that the endpoint of the line is at coordinate x1+dX, y1+dY. For example, the statement

```
Line (20,30)-Step(50,100), RGB(0,0,0)
```

draws a line with a starting point at coordinate 20,30 and an endpoint at coordinate 70,130.

The Step option may also be used to draw a box. The following statements draw the box shown in Figure 8.7:

```
' Line from left top corner to right top corner.
Line (100, 20)-(400,0)
' Line from right top corner to right bottom corner.
Line -Step(0, 400)
' Line from right bottom corner to left bottom ' corner.
Line -Step (-300, 0)
' Line from left bottom corner to left top corner.
Line -Step (0, -400)
```

Figure 8.7.

Drawing a box with the Line method.

As you can see, four `Line` statements are needed to draw a single box! An easier way to draw a box is to use the `Line` method with the `B` option as follows:

```
Line (100,20)- (400,420), RGB(0,0,0),B
```

The first coordinate (100,20) is the coordinate of the top-left corner of the box, and the second coordinate is the coordinate of the lower-right corner of the box. The `B` option instructs Visual Basic to draw a box with these two corners.

If you want to fill the box, use the `F` option:

```
Line (100,20)-(400,420),RGB(0,255,0),BF
```

This statement draws a box and fills the box with the color `RGB(0,255,0)`, which is green. There is no comma between the `B` and `F` options because you can't use the `F` option without the `B` option.

Filling the Box with the FillStyle Property

Another way to fill the box is to set the FillColor and FillStyle properties of the form and use the `Line` method with the `B` option and without the `F` option:

```
frmMyForm.FillStyle = 2
frmMyForm.FillColor = RGB(255,0,0)
frmMyForm.Line(100,20)-(400,420),RGB(0,0,0),B
```

The first statement sets the FillStyle property of the form to 2. The eight possible values of FillStyle are shown in Table 8.4. When the FillStyle property is equal to 2, the object is filled with horizontal lines. The second statement sets the FillColor property to `RGB(255,0,0)`, which means the box is filled with the color red. So the three statements draw a box filled with red horizontal lines.

Table 8.4. The eight possible values of the FillStyle property.

Value	Description
0	Solid
1	Transparent (default setting)
2	Horizontal lines
3	Vertical lines
4	Upward diagonal lines
5	Downward diagonal lines
6	Crosshatch
7	Diagonal crosshatch

8

To see the meaning of each of the different FillStyles in Table 8.4, do the following:

☐ Add the Draw Box menu to the menu system of the frmPoints form. The new menu table is shown in Table 8.5.

Table 8.5. Adding the Draw Box menu to the frmPoints form.

Caption	Name
&File	mnuFile
...&Exit	mnuExit
&Graphics	mnuGraphics
...&Draw Points	mnuDrawPoints
...&Clear	mnuClear
...&Lines	mnuLines
D&raw Box	mnuDrawBox
...R&ed	mnuRed
...Gree&n	mnuGreen
...&Blue	mnuBlue
...-	mnuSep1
...&Set Style	mnuSetStyle

☐ Add the following code in the mnuRed_Click() procedure of the frmPoints form:

```
Private Sub mnuRed_Click()

    ' Set the FillColor property of the form.
    frmPoints.FillColor = RGB(255, 0, 0)

    ' Draw the box.
    frmPoints.Line (100, 80)-Step(5000, 3000), _
            RGB(255, 0, 0), B

End Sub
```

☐ Add the following code in the mnuBlue_Click() procedure of the frmPoints form:

```
Private Sub mnuBlue_Click()

    ' Set the FillColor property of the form.to red
    frmPoints.FillColor = RGB(255, 0, 0)

    ' Draw the box.
    frmPoints.Line (100, 80)-Step(5000, 3000), _
            RGB(0, 0, 255), B

End Sub
```

☐ Add the following code in the mnuGreen_Click() procedure of the frmPoints form:

```
Private Sub mnuGreen_Click()

    ' Set the FillColor property of the form.
    frmPoints.FillColor = RGB(255, 0, 0)

    ' Draw the box.
    frmPoints.Line (100, 80)-Step(5000, 3000), _
                RGB(0, 255, 0), B

End Sub
```

☐ Add the following code in the mnuSetStyleClick() procedure of the frmPoints form:

```
Private Sub mnuSetStyle_Click()

    Dim FromUser
    Dim Instruction
    Instruction = "Enter a number between 0 and 7 " + _
                "for the FillStyle"

    ' Get from the user the desired FillStyle.
    FromUser = InputBox$(Instruction, _
                    "Setting the FillStyle")
    ' Clear the form.
    frmPoints.Cls

    ' Did the user enter a valid FillStyle?
    If Val(FromUser) >= 0 And Val(FromUser) <= 7 Then
        frmPoints.FillStyle = Val(FromUser)
    Else
        Beep
        MsgBox ("Invalid FillStyle")
    End If
    ' Draw the box.
    frmPoints.Line (100, 80)-Step(5000, 3000), _
                RGB(0, 0, 0), B

End Sub
```

☐ Select Save Project from the File menu of Visual Basic to save your work.

Executing the Points Program

Let's see your code in action:

☐ Execute the Points program.

☐ Select Set Style from the Draw Box menu.

The program responds by displaying an input box, as shown in Figure 8.8.

Figure 8.8.
Entering a value for
the FillStyle property.

☐ Type a number between 0 and 7 and click the OK button. This number represents the FillStyle.

The program displays the box and fills it with the FillStyle entered in the previous step. Figure 8.9 shows the box when the FillStyle is set to 2 (horizontal lines). (You may have to drag the left edge of the window to make the window wider.)

Figure 8.9.
Experimenting with
the FillStyle property.

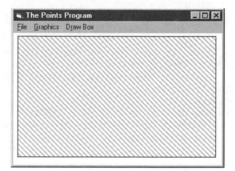

☐ Select the Red, Blue or Green color from the Draw Box menu.

The program draws the box with the selected color.

☐ Experiment with the Points program, then select Exit from its file menu to terminate the program.

The Code of the `mnuRed_Click()` Procedure

The `mnuRed_Click()` procedure is executed when you select Red from the Draw Box menu:

```
Private Sub mnuRed_Click()

    ' Set the FillColor property of the form.
    frmPoints.FillColor = RGB(255, 0, 0)

    ' Draw the box.
    frmPoints.Line (100, 80)-Step(5000, 3000), _
             RGB(255, 0, 0), B

End Sub
```

This procedure sets the value of the FillColor property to red, then the Line method with the B option is used to draw the box. The box is filled according to the current setting of the form's FillStyle property.

The mnuBlue_Click() and mnuGreen_Click() procedures of the frmPoints form work in a similar manner, setting the FillColor property in these procedures to blue and green.

The Code of the mnuSetStyleClick() Procedure

The mnuSetStyle_Click() procedure is executed when you select Set Style from the Draw Box menu:

```
Private Sub mnuSetStyle_Click()

    Dim FromUser
    Dim Instruction
    Instruction = "Enter a number between 0 and 7 " + _
                  "for the FillStyle"

    ' Get from the user the desired FillStyle.
    FromUser = InputBox$(Instruction, _
                   "Setting the FillStyle")
    ' Clear the form.
    frmPoints.Cls
    ' Did the user enter a valid FillStyle?
    If Val(FromUser) >= 0 And Val(FromUser) <= 7 Then
        frmPoints.FillStyle = Val(FromUser)
    Else
      Beep
      MsgBox ("Invalid FillStyle")
    End If
    ' Draw the box.
    frmPoints.Line (100, 80)-Step(5000, 3000), _
                   RGB(0, 0, 0), B

End Sub
```

This procedure uses the InputBox$() function to get a number between 0 and 7. The form is cleared with the Cls method, and the user's input is checked with the If statement to see whether the entered number is within the valid range. If the entered number is between 0 and 7, the FillStyle property is updated with this number.

The last statement in the procedure draws a box using the Line method with the B option. The box is drawn with the current setting of the FillColor and FillStyle properties of the form.

The Circles Program

Another important graphics method is the Circle method, used to draw circles. The Circles program illustrates how you can draw circles.

You can use the Circle method to draw circles in a form, as well as in the picture control.

The Visual Implementation of the Circles Program

As usual, you'll start with the visual implementation of the form of the Circles program:

☐ Create a new Standard EXE project, save the form of the project as Circles.Frm in the C:\VB5Prg\Ch08 directory, and save the project file as Circles.Vbp in the C:\VB5Prg\Ch08 directory.

☐ Build the frmCircles form according to Table 8.6.

The completed form should look like the one shown in Figure 8.10.

Figure 8.10.

The frmCircles form in design mode.

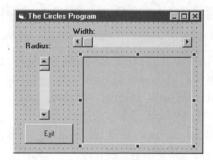

Table 8.6. The properties table of frmCircles form.

Object	Property	Setting
Form	Name	frmCircles
	Caption	The Circles Program
Picture Box	Name	picCircles
	BorderStyle	1-Fixed Single
Command Button	Name	cmdExit
	Caption	E&xit
Vertical Scroll Bar	Name	vsbRadius
	Max	100
	Min	1
	Value	1
Horizontal Scroll Bar	Name	hsbCircleWidth
	Max	10
	Min	1
	Value	1

continues

Table 8.6. continued

Object	Property	Setting
Label	Name	lblWidth
	Caption	Width:
Label	Name	lblRadius
	Caption	Radius:

Entering the Code of the Circles Program

You'll now enter the code of the Circles program:

☐ Make sure that the Option Explicit statement resides in the general declarations section as follows:

```
' All variables MUST be declared.
Option Explicit
```

☐ Type the following code in the cmdExit_Click() procedure of the frmCircles form:

```
Private Sub cmdExit_Click()

    End

End Sub
```

☐ Type the following code in the hsbCircleWidth_Change() procedure of the frmCircles form:

```
Private Sub hsbCircleWidth_Change()

    Dim X, Y, Radius

    ' Change the DrawWidth property of the picture
    ' control according to the horizontal
    ' scroll bar.
    picCircles.DrawWidth = hsbCircleWidth.Value


    ' Calculate the coordinate of the center of the
    ' circle.
    X = picCircles.ScaleWidth / 2
    Y = picCircles.ScaleHeight / 2
    ' Clear the picture box.
    picCircles.Cls
    picCircles.Circle (X, Y), vsbRadius.Value * 10, _
                RGB(255, 0, 0)


End Sub
```

☐ Type the following code in the hsbCircleWidth_Scroll() procedure of the frmCircles form:

```
Private Sub hsbCircleWidth_Scroll()

        hsbCircleWidth_Change

End Sub
```

☐ Type the following code in the vsbRadius_Change() procedure of the frmCircles form:

```
Private Sub vsbRadius_Change()

    Dim X, Y, Radius
    ' Calculate the coordinate of the center of the
    ' circle.
    X = picCircles.ScaleWidth / 2
    Y = picCircles.ScaleHeight / 2
    ' Clear the picture box.
    picCircles.Cls
    picCircles.Circle (X, Y), vsbRadius.Value * 10, _
            RGB(255, 0, 0)

End Sub
```

☐ Type the following code in the vsbRadius_Scroll() procedure of the frmCircles form:

```
Private Sub vsbRadius_Scroll()

        vsbRadius_Change

End Sub
```

☐ Select Save Project from the File menu of Visual Basic.

Executing the Circles Program

Let's see your code in action:

☐ Execute the Circles program.

☐ Change the vertical scroll bar.

> *The radius of the circle displayed in the picture control changes according to the setting of the vertical scroll bar (see Figure 8.11).*

☐ Change the horizontal scroll bar to set a new value for the circle line width.

> *The circle is now drawn with a different line width.*

Figure 8.11.
*Changing the radius
with the vertical
scroll bar.*

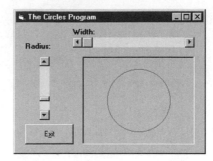

How the Circles Program Works

The Circles program uses the `Circle` method to draw the circle. The radius of the circle is changed according to the vertical scroll bar position, and the width of the circle is changed according to the horizontal scroll bar position.

The Code of the `vsbRadius_Change()` Procedure

The `vsbRadius_Change()` procedure is executed when you change the vertical scroll bar position:

```
Private Sub vsbRadius_Change()

    Dim X, Y, Radius

    ' Calculate the coordinate of the center of the
    ' circle.
    X = picCircles.ScaleWidth / 2
    Y = picCircles.ScaleHeight / 2

    ' Clear the picture box.
    picCircles.Cls

    picCircles.Circle (X, Y), vsbRadius.Value * 10, _
            RGB(255, 0, 0)

End Sub
```

This procedure calculates the coordinate of the center point (`X`, `Y`) of the circle by calculating the coordinate of the center of the picture control (that is, the center of the circle is placed at the center of the picture control).

Then the graphics content of the picture control is cleared with the `Cls` method (erasing the previous circle, if any), and finally the circle is drawn with the `Circle` method:

```
picCircles.Circle (X, Y), vsbRadius.Value * 10, _
            RGB(255, 0, 0)
```

The radius of the circle, drawn in red, is 10 times larger than the current setting of the vertical scroll bar.

Do	Don't

DO use the `Circle` method to draw a circle:

```
Object name.Circle _
    (X coord. of center, Y coord. of center), _
    Radius, Color
```

For example, to draw a blue circle in the frmMyForm form with the center at coordinate 1000,500 and the radius equal to 75, use the following:

```
frmMyForm.Circle (1000,500), 75, RGB(0,0,255)
```

In a similar way, the `vsbRadius_Scroll()` procedure draws a new circle when the radius vertical scroll bar is changed.

The Code of the `hsbCircleWidth_Change()` Procedure

The `hsbCircleWidth_Change()` procedure is executed when you change the horizontal scroll bar:

```
Private Sub hsbCircleWidth_Change()

    Dim X, Y, Radius

    ' Change the DrawWidth property of the picture
    ' control according to the horizontal
    ' scroll bar.
    picCircles.DrawWidth = hsbCircleWidth.Value

    ' Calculate the coordinate of the center of the
    ' circle.
    X = picCircles.ScaleWidth / 2
    Y = picCircles.ScaleHeight / 2
    ' Clear the picture box.
    picCircles.Cls
    picCircles.Circle (X, Y), vsbRadius.Value * 10, _
                RGB(255, 0, 0)


End Sub
```

This procedure changes the DrawWidth property of the picCircles picture control according to the position of the horizontal scroll bar. The value of the DrawWidth property of the picture control determines the width of the circle drawn in the picture control. As you can see, the code in this procedure is very similar to the code in the `hsbRadius_Change()` procedure. However, instead of the radius changing, the DrawWidth property of the picture control is updated:

```
picCircles.DrawWidth = hsbCircleWidth.Value
```

In a similar way, the hsbCircleWidth_Scroll() procedure draws a new circle when the circle width is changed with the horizontal scroll bar.

Enhancing the Circles Program

As you might expect, some impressive graphics effects can be created by adding several lines of code to the Circles program.

☐ Add the Draw Style button to the frmCircles form, as shown in Figure 8.12.

☐ Set the properties of the button as follows: The Name property should be cmdDrawStyle and the Caption property should be &Draw Style.

Figure 8.12.

Adding the Draw Style button to the Circles program.

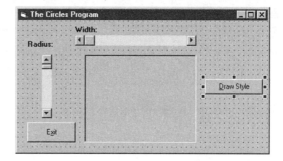

☐ Add the following code in the cmdDrawStyle_Click() procedure of the frmCircles form:

```
Private Sub cmdDrawStyle_Click()

    Dim TheStyle
    ' Get a number from the user.
    TheStyle = InputBox$("Enter DrawStyle (0-6):")

    ' Is the number between 0 and 6?
    If Val(TheStyle) < 0 Or Val(TheStyle) > 6 Then
        ' The entered number is not within the valid
        ' range.
        Beep
        MsgBox ("Invalid DrawStyle")
    Else
        ' The entered number is within the valid
        ' range, so change to DrawStyle property.
        picCircles.DrawStyle = Val(TheStyle)
    End If

End Sub
```

☐ Delete the horizontal scroll bar. (Make sure that the horizontal scroll bar is selected and press the Delete key.)

In the previous version of the Circles program, you wrote code in the hsbWidth_Change() procedure. Now that you have deleted this control, Visual Basic has placed the procedure in the General area of the frmCircles form. Therefore, after deleting the control, you can also remove its procedures from the General area.

☐ Delete the hsbWidth_Change() procedure from the General area. That is, highlight the whole procedure, including its first and last lines, and press the Delete key.

☐ Delete the hsbWidth_Scroll() procedure from the General area. That is, highlight the whole procedure, including its first and last lines, and press the Delete key.

☐ Delete the lblWidth label by selecting it and then press the Delete key.

☐ Set the BackColor property of the picCircles control to White. The circle will be drawn on a white background, so you'll be able to see the effects of the drawing styles better.

Executing the Circles Program

Let's see your code in action:

☐ Execute the Circles program.

☐ Click the Draw Style button.

The program responds by displaying a message box that asks you to enter a number between 0 and 6.

☐ Enter a number between 0 and 6, which represents the drawing style for the circle, and click the OK button.

☐ Play with the vertical scroll bar and see the effects that the different styles and radii have on the circle.

☐ Terminate the program by clicking the Exit button.

The DrawStyle Property

The cmdDrawStyle_Click() procedure is executed when you click the Draw Style button. You are asked to type a number between 0 and 6, which is assigned to the DrawStyle property of the picture control. Table 8.7 lists the seven possible values of the DrawStyle property and their meanings.

Table 8.7. The seven possible values of the DrawStyle property.

Value	Meaning
0	Solid (default value)
1	Dash (-)
2	Dot (…)
3	Dash-dot (-.-.)
4	Dash-dot-dot (_.._.._)
5	Invisible
6	Inside solid

If the DrawWidth property of the picture control is set to a value greater than 1, you will not be able to see the effects of the DrawStyle property when it's set to 2, 3, or 4. This explains why you were instructed to remove the scroll bar that changes the DrawWidth property (that is, to experiment with the DrawStyle property, the DrawWidth property must be equal to 1).

Enhancing the Circles Program Again

Now make an additional enhancement to the Circles program:

☐ Replace the code of the vsbRadius_Change() procedure with the following code:

```
Private Sub vsbRadius_Change ()

    Dim X, Y, Radius
    Static LastValue
    Dim R, G, B

    ' Generate random colors.
    R = Rnd * 255
    G = Rnd * 255
    B = Rnd * 255

    ' Calculate the coordinate of the center of the
    ' picture control.
    X = picCircles.ScaleWidth / 2
    Y = picCircles.ScaleHeight / 2

    ' If scroll bar was decrement, then clear the
    ' picture box.
    If LastValue > vsbRadius.Value Then
       picCircles.Cls
    End If
```

```
         ' Draw the circle.
         picCircles.Circle (X, Y), vsbRadius.Value * 10, _
                   RGB(R, G, B)

         ' Update LastValue for next time.
         LastValue = vsbRadius.Value

End Sub
```

☐ Select Save Project from the File menu of Visual Basic to save your work.

Executing the Enhanced Version of the Circles Program

Now you'll see some nice graphic effects:

☐ Execute the Circles program.

☐ Click the DrawStyle button.

> *The program responds by displaying the InputBox, which asks you to enter a number between 0 and 6.*

☐ Enter the number 2 and click the OK button.

☐ Increase the Radius scroll bar position by clicking several times on the down arrow at the bottom of the scroll bar.

> *The program responds by drawing the circles shown in Figure 8.13.*

Figure 8.13.

Drawing circles with the enhanced version of the Circles program.

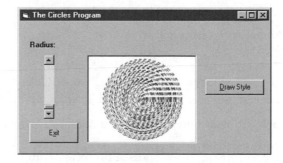

☐ Decrease the scroll bar position by clicking several times on the up arrow at the top of the scroll bar.

> *The program responds by drawing successively smaller circles.*

☐ Experiment with the Circles program, then terminate the program by clicking the Exit button.

The Code of the `vsbRadius_Change()` Procedure

The `vsbRadius_Change()` procedure is automatically executed when you change the scroll bar position. It starts by declaring several variables. The second variable is defined as `Static`:

```
Static LastValue
```

This means that the value of the `LastValue` variable is not initialized to 0 every time this procedure is executed (that is, this variable retains its value).

The procedure then prepares the three variables `R`, `G`, and `B`, updating the value of these variables with numbers that represent random colors:

```
' Generate random colors.
R = Rnd * 255
G = Rnd * 255
B = Rnd * 255
```

The procedure then calculates the coordinate of the center of the picture box control:

```
' Calculate the coordinate of the center of the
' picture control.
X = picCircles.ScaleWidth / 2
Y = picCircles.ScaleHeight / 2
```

This coordinate is used later in this procedure as the coordinate for the center of the circles.

The `LastValue` variable holds the Value property of the scroll bar before you changed the scroll bar position.

The `If` statement checks whether the current position of the scroll bar (specified by the Value property) is smaller than the last position of the scroll bar:

```
' If scroll bar was decremented, then clear the
' picture box.
If LastValue > vsbRadius.Value Then
    picCircles.Cls
End If
```

If the current Value property of the scroll bar is smaller than `LastValue`, you decremented the scroll bar. In this case, the `Cls` method is executed, which clears the picture box.

The procedure then draws the circle using the `Circle` method:

```
' Draw the circle.
picCircles.Circle (X, Y), vsbRadius.Value * 10, _
                   RGB(R, G, B)
```

The last thing this procedure does is update the `LastValue` variable.

The next time this procedure is executed, the value of `LastValue` represents the Value property of the scroll bar before the change:

```
' Update LastValue for next time.
LastValue = vsbRadius.Value
```

When the scroll bar is incremented, the Cls method is not executed. Thus, when incrementing the scroll bar, the already drawn circles remain onscreen.

The LastValue Static **Variable**

An important thing to note from the preceding discussion is that the variable LastValue is declared as a Static variable:

```
Static LastValue
```

When the vsbRadius_Change() procedure is executed for the very fist time, Visual Basic sets LastValue to 0. During the execution of the vsbRadius_Change() procedure, the value of LastValue is changed to another value. The next time hsbRadius_Change() is executed, the values of nonstatic variables such as X, Y, and Radius are initialized back to 0.

However, since LastValue is declared as a Static variable, its value is not changed from the last execution of the hsbRadius_Change() procedure.

You might note the similarity between a variable declared in the general declarations section and a variable declared as Static in a procedure. In both cases, the variable retains its value for as long as the program runs. However, there is an important difference between these two types of variables:

- A variable declared in the general declarations section of a form is accessible from within any procedure of the form.
- A variable declared as a static variable in a procedure is accessible only from within the procedure that declares this variable.

For example, if you try to access the LastValue variable from within the Form_Load() procedure, you'll get an error, because you can't access LastValue outside the vsbRadius_Change() procedure.

Also, you can declare another variable called LastValue in the Form_Load() procedure. This value can be declared as a static variable or a regular nonstatic local variable, but there is no connection between the LastValue variable of the Form_Load() procedure and the LastValue variable in the vsbRadius_Change() procedure.

As you can see, declaring a static variable is a good trick to use when you don't want to lose the value of a variable after a procedure is terminated.

Regular nonstatic local variables and static variables are stored in your PC in different ways. For example, compare how the Radius variable (a regular nonstatic local variable in the hsbRadius_Change() procedure) and the LastValue Static variable are stored. Once Visual Basic completes the execution of the hsbRadius_Change() procedure, the value of the Radius variable is gone forever, so the memory cells (RAM bytes) used to store the Radius variable are free. However, the memory cells used for storing the LastValue Static variable are never freed; they are occupied as long as the Circles program is running. A variable declared in the general declarations area also occupies memory cells as long as the program is running.

Drawing Ellipses and Arcs

To draw ellipses and arcs, use the Circle method. Its complete syntax is as follows:

```
[object.]Circle[Step](x,y), _
                radius, _
               [color], _
               [start], _
                 [end], _
              [aspect]
```

If you include the Step option, the x,y coordinate is referenced to the CurrentX, CurrentY point. For example, if CurrentX is 1000, and CurrentY is 3000, the statement

```
frmMyForm.Circle Step(10,20),80
```

draws a circle with a radius at 80 and a center at 1010,3020.

The aspect Parameter

The aspect parameter is a positive number that causes the Circle method to draw ellipses. For example, when the aspect ratio is equal to 1, the Circle method produces a perfect circle. When the aspect ratio is greater than 1, the Circle method produces an ellipse stretched along the vertical axis. When the aspect ratio is less than 1, the Circle method produces an ellipse stretched along the horizontal axis. Figures 8.14, 8.15, and 8.16 show three ellipses with three different aspects.

Figure 8.14.

The ellipse with the aspect *parameter equal to 1.*

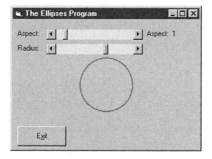

Figure 8.15.
The ellipse with the
aspect *parameter*
equal to 0.5.

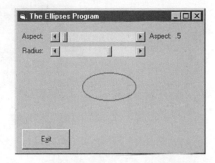

Figure 8.16.
The ellipse with the
aspect *parameter*
equal to 2.7.

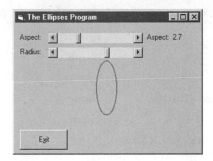

The Ellipses Program

The Ellipses program illustrates how to draw ellipses with different radii and aspects.

The Visual Implementation of the Ellipses Program

As usual, you'll start with the visual implementation of the form of the program.

☐ Create a new Standard EXE project, save the form of the project as Ellipses.Frm in the C:\VB5Prg\Ch08 directory, and save the project file as Ellipses.Vbp in the C:\VB5Prg\Ch08 directory.

☐ Build the frmEllipses form according to Table 8.8.

The completed form should look like the one shown in Figure 8.17.

Figure 8.17.

The frmEllipses form (design mode).

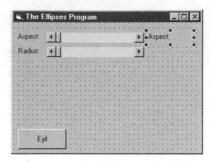

Table 8.8. The properties table of the frmEllipses form.

Object	Property	Setting
Form	Name	frmEllipses
	Caption	The Ellipses Program
CommandButton	Name	cmdExit
	Caption	E&xit
Horizontal Scroll Bar	Name	hsbAspect
	Max	100
	Min	1
	Value	1
Horizontal Scroll Bar	Name	hsbRadius
	Max	100
	Min	1
	Value	1
Label	Name	lblInfo
	Caption	Aspect:
Label	Name	lblAspect
	Caption	Aspect:
Label	Name	lblRadius
	Caption	Radius:

Entering the Code of the Ellipses Program

You'll now enter the code of the Ellipses program:

☐ Make sure that the Option Explicit statement resides in the general declarations section of the frmEllipses as follows:

```
' All variables MUST be declared.
Option Explicit
```

☐ Type the following code in the cmdExit_Click() procedure of the frmEllipses form:

```
Private Sub cmdExit_Click()

    End

End Sub
```

☐ Type the following code in the Form_Load() procedure of the frmEllipses form:

```
Private Sub Form_Load()

    ' Initialize the radius and aspect scroll bars.
    hsbRadius.Value = 10
    hsbAspect.Value = 10

    ' Initialize the info label.
    lblInfo.Caption = "Aspect: 1"

    ' Set the DrawWidth property of the form.
    frmEllipses.DrawWidth = 2

End Sub
```

☐ Type the following code in the hsbAspect_Change() procedure of the frmEllipses form:

```
Private Sub hsbAspect_Change()

    Dim X, Y
    Dim Info
    ' Calculate the center of the form.
    X = frmEllipses.ScaleWidth / 2
    Y = frmEllipses.ScaleHeight / 2

    ' Clear the form.
     frmEllipses.Cls

    ' Draw the ellipse.
    frmEllipses.Circle (X, Y), hsbRadius.Value * 10, _
            RGB(255, 0, 0), , , hsbAspect.Value / 10

    ' Prepare the Info string.
    Info = "Aspect: " + Str(hsbAspect.Value / 10)

    ' Display the value of the aspect.
    frmEllipses.lblInfo.Caption = Info

End Sub
```

☐ Type the following code in the `hsbAspect_Scroll()` procedure of the frmEllipses form:

```
Private Sub hsbAspect_Scroll()

        hsbAspect_Change

End Sub
```

☐ Type the following code in the `hsbRadius_Change()` procedure of the frmEllipses form:

```
Private Sub hsbRadius_Change()

    Dim X, Y
    Dim Info

    X = frmEllipses.ScaleWidth / 2
    Y = frmEllipses.ScaleHeight / 2

    frmEllipses.Cls
    frmEllipses.Circle (X, Y), hsbRadius.Value * 10, _
            RGB(255, 0, 0), , , hsbAspect.Value / 10

    Info = "Aspect: " + Str(hsbAspect.Value / 10)

    frmEllipses.lblInfo.Caption = Info

End Sub
```

☐ Type the following code in the `hsbRadius_Scroll()` procedure of the frmEllipses form:

```
Private Sub hsbRadius_Scroll()

    hsbRadius_Change

End Sub
```

Executing the Ellipses Program

Let's see the Ellipses program in action:

☐ Execute the Ellipses program.

☐ Change the position of the Radius scroll bar to draw circles and ellipses with different radii.

☐ Change the position of the Aspect scroll bar to draw ellipses with different aspects.

Note that the value of the current aspect is displayed to the right of the Aspect scroll bar. When the aspect parameter is equal to 1, the program draws a perfect circle. When the aspect parameter is less than 1, the program draws an ellipse stretched along the horizontal axis, as shown in Figure 8.15. When the aspect parameter is greater than 1, the program draws an ellipse stretched along its vertical axis, as shown in Figure 8.16.

How the Ellipses Program Works

The Ellipses program draws ellipses using the `Circle` method. The Value properties of the scroll bars are used as the parameters in the `Circle` method.

The Code of the `Form_Load()` Procedure

The `Form_Load()` procedure is executed when the frmEllipses form is loaded:

```
Private Sub Form_Load()

    ' Initialize the radius and aspect scroll bars.
    hsbRadius.Value = 10
    hsbAspect.Value = 10

    ' Initialize the info label.
    lblInfo.Caption = "Aspect: 1"

    ' Set the DrawWidth property of the form.
    frmEllipses.DrawWidth = 2

End Sub
```

This procedure initializes the Value properties of the scroll bars to 10 and displays the `lblInfo` label `Aspect: 1` to the right of the Aspect scroll bar. As you will see later, the program uses one-tenth of the Value property of the Aspect scroll bar as the aspect parameter in the `Circle` method.

For example, when the Value property of the Aspect scroll bar is 20, the `Circle` method uses 2 as the aspect parameter, which is why this procedure sets `lblInfo.Caption` with `Aspect: 1` after initializing the Aspect scroll bar to 10.

The last statement in this procedure sets the DrawWidth property of the form to 2:

```
frmEllipses.DrawWidth = 2
```

This causes the graphics to be drawn with a width equal to 2 units. Thus, when using the `Circle` method, the ellipses are drawn with a line 2 units wide. (Although the Ellipses program sets the DrawWidth property of the form, the caption of the lblInfo label, and the Value properties of the scroll bars from within the code, you could have set these properties during design time.)

The Code of the `hsbAspect_Change()` Procedure

The `hsbAspect_Change()` procedure is executed when you change the Aspect scroll bar:

```
Private Sub hsbAspect_Change()

    Dim X, Y
    Dim Info
```

```
' Calculate the center of the form.
X = frmEllipses.ScaleWidth / 2
Y = frmEllipses.ScaleHeight / 2

' Clear the form.
 frmEllipses.Cls

' Draw the ellipse.
frmEllipses.Circle (X, Y), hsbRadius.Value * 10, _
        RGB(255, 0, 0), , , hsbAspect.Value / 10

' Prepare the Info string.
Info = "Aspect: " + Str(hsbAspect.Value / 10)

' Display the value of the aspect.
frmEllipses.lblInfo.Caption = Info
```

End Sub

This procedure calculates the coordinate of the center of the form and assigns the calculated values to X and Y.

The procedure clears any previously drawn ellipses using the Cls method and draws the ellipse:

```
frmEllipses.Circle (X, Y), hsbRadius.Value * 10, _
        RGB(255, 0, 0), , , hsbAspect.Value / 10
```

The radius parameter is set to the current value of the Radius scroll bar multiplied by 10, and the aspect parameter is set as one-tenth the Value property of the Aspect scroll bar.

Note that because the two optional parameters (start and end) of the Circle method are not used, two commas are typed between the color parameter and the aspect parameter. The two commas indicate to Visual Basic that these two optional parameters are missing.

The Code of the hsbRadius_Change() Procedure

The hsbRadius_Change() procedure is automatically executed when you change the Radius scroll bar. It is identical to the hsbAspect_Change() procedure, displaying the ellipse and updating the lblInfo label.

Note that the code in the hsbRadius_Scroll() procedure executes the hsbRadius_Change() procedure, and the code in the hsbAspect_Scroll() procedure executes the hsbAspect_Change() procedure. (That is, you execute the procedures that correspond to the Change event when the Scroll event occurs.)

The Arcs Program

Now you'll write a program called Arcs. This program illustrates how to use the Circle method to draw arcs at different starting points and ending points. As stated, this is the complete syntax of the Circle method:

```
[object.]Circle[Step](x,y), _
                radius, _
               [color], _
               [start], _
                 [end], _
              [aspect]
```

The start and end parameters specify the starting point and ending point of the circle. For example, if the starting point is at 0 degrees and the endpoint is at 45 degrees, only this section of the circle is drawn. Figure 8.18 shows a portion of a circle, an arc, that was drawn using the Circle method with the start parameter equal to 0 degrees and the end parameter equal to 45 degrees. Similarly, Figure 8.19 shows an arc with the starting point at 23 degrees and the endpoint at 180 degrees.

Figure 8.18.

Drawing a 45-degree arc.

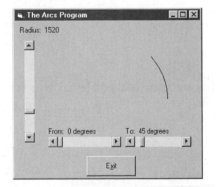

Figure 8.19.

Drawing an arc from 23 degrees to 180 degrees.

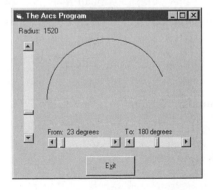

The Visual Implementation of the Arcs Program

You'll now design the form of the Arcs program.

☐ Create a new Standard EXE project, save the form of the project as Arcs.Frm in the C:\VB5Prg\Ch08 directory, and save the project file of the project as Arcs.Vbp in the C:\VB5Prg\Ch08 directory.

☐ Build the frmArcs form according to Table 8.9.

The completed form should look like the one shown in Figure 8.20.

Figure 8.20.

The frmArcs form.

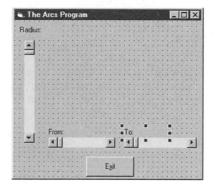

Table 8.9. The properties table of the frmArcs form.

Object	Property	Setting
Form	**Name**	**frmArcs**
	Caption	The Arcs Program
CommandButton	**Name**	**cmdExit**
	Caption	E&xit
Horizontal Scroll Bar	**Name**	**hsbFrom**
	Min	0
	Value	0
	Max	360
Horizontal Scroll Bar	**Name**	**hsbTo**
	Min	0
	Value	0
	Max	360

Object	Property	Setting
Vertical Scroll Bar	Name	**vsbRadius**
	Max	100
	Min	1
	Value	1
Label	Name	**lblFrom**
	Caption	From:
Label	Name	**lblTo**
	Caption	To:
Label	Name	**lblRadius**
	Caption	Radius:

Entering the Code of the Arcs Program

You'll now enter the code of the Arcs program:

☐ Make sure that the Option Explicit statement resides in the general declarations section of the frmArcs form as follows:

```
' All variables MUST be declared.
Option Explicit
```

☐ Create a new procedure called DrawArc in the General area of the frmArcs form. (Double-click the form to display the code window, select Add Procedure from the Tools menu, set the Type to Sub in the Add Procedure dialog box, set the Scope to Public, set the Name to DrawArc, and finally click the OK button.)

☐ Type the following code in the DrawArc() procedure that you created in the previous step:

```
Public Sub DrawArc()

    Dim X, Y

    Const PI = 3.14159265

    ' Calculate the center of the form.
    X = frmArcs.ScaleWidth / 2
    Y = frmArcs.ScaleHeight / 2

    ' Clear the form.
    frmArcs.Cls

    ' Draw an arc.
    Circle (X, Y), vsbRadius.Value * 20, , _
            hsbFrom * 2 * PI / 360, hsbTo * 2 * PI / 360
```

```
                ' Update the lblFrom label.
                lblFrom.Caption = "From: " + Str(hsbFrom.Value) + _
                                  " degrees"

                ' Update the lblTo label.
                lblTo.Caption = "To: " + Str(hsbTo.Value) + _
                                " degrees"

                ' Update the lblRadius label.
                lblRadius.Caption = "Radius: " + _
                                Str(vsbRadius.Value * 20)

        End Sub
```

☐ Type the following code in the cmdExit_Click() procedure of the frmArcs form:

```
        Private Sub cmdExit_Click()

            End

        End Sub
```

☐ Type the following code in the hsbFrom_Change() procedure of the frmArcs form:

```
        Private Sub hsbFrom_Change()

            ' Execute the DrawArc procedure to draw the arc.
            DrawArc

        End Sub
```

☐ Type the following code in the hsbFrom_Scroll() procedure of the frmArcs form:

```
        Private Sub hsbFrom_Scroll()

            hsbFrom_Change

        End Sub
```

☐ Type the following code in the hsbTo_Change() procedure of the frmArcs form:

```
        Private Sub hsbTo_Change()

            ' Execute the DrawArc procedure to draw the arc.
            DrawArc

        End Sub
```

☐ Type the following code in the hsbTo_Scroll() procedure of the frmArcs form:

```
        Private Sub hsbTo_Scroll()

            hsbTo_Change()

        End Sub
```

☐ Type the following code in the vsbRadius_Change() procedure of the frmArcs form:

```
Private Sub vsbRadius_Change()

    ' Execute the DrawArc procedure to draw the arc.
    DrawArc

End Sub
```

☐ Type the following code in the vsbRadius_Scroll() procedure of the frmArcs form:

```
Private Sub vsbRadius_Scroll()

    vsbRadius_Change

End Sub
```

☐ Select Save Project from the File menu of Visual Basic to save your work.

Executing the Arcs Program

Let's see the Arcs program in action:

☐ Execute the Arcs program.

☐ Increase the radius by changing the Radius scroll bar (the vertical scroll bar).

☐ Increase the To scroll bar (the right horizontal scroll bar).

☐ Increase the From scroll bar (the left horizontal scroll bar).

As you can see, an arc is drawn starting at a point specified by the From scroll bar and ending at a point specified by the To scroll bar.

Note that the arc is drawn counterclockwise. For example, Figure 8.19 shows an arc that starts at 23 degrees and ends at 180 degrees. In Figure 8.21, an arc is drawn starting at 180 degrees and ending at 23 degrees.

Figure 8.21.

An arc drawn from 180 degrees to 23 degrees.

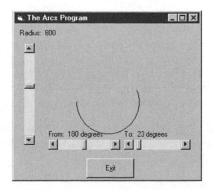

☐ Click the Exit button to terminate the program.

How the Arcs Program Works

The Arcs program uses the Circle method to draw the arcs.

The Value properties of the Radius scroll bar, From scroll bar, and To scroll bar are used as the parameters for the Circle method.

The Code of the DrawArc() Procedure

The DrawArc() procedure is executed when you change the Radius scroll bar, From scroll bar, or To scroll bar. It defines the PI constant as the numeric equivalent of pi:

```
Const PI = 3.14159265
```

The center of the form is calculated:

```
X = frmArcs.ScaleWidth / 2
Y = frmArcs.ScaleHeight / 2
```

and the form is cleared with the Cls method:

```
frmArcs.Cls
```

The arc is drawn using the Circle method:

```
Circle (X, Y), vsbRadius.Value * 20, , _
            hsbFrom* 2*PI/360, hsbTo*2*PI/360
```

Again, this is the complete syntax of the Circle method:

```
[object.]Circle[Step](x,y), _
                    radius, _
                   [color], _
                   [start], _
                     [end], _
                  [aspect]
```

The center of the arc is given by the (x,y) parameter, and the radius of the arc is given by the Value property of the vsbRadius scroll bar multiplied by 20.

At design time, the Min property of the vsbRadius scroll bar was set to 1, and its Max property was set to 100, so it takes 100 clicks to move the scroll bar position from its minimum position to its maximum position.

You multiply the Value property of the vbsRadius scrollbar by 20, and you supply this value to the radius parameter (the first parameter) of the Circle method; therefore, the radius can have any value between 20 and 2000.

The Color property is not supplied, so just type a comma indicating that the Circle method does not include the color parameter. The program therefore uses the ForeColor property of the form, which is black by default.

The next two parameters of the Circle method are the start and end parameters, which must be given in radians. At design time, the Min properties of the From and To scroll bars were set to 1, and the Max properties of these scroll bars were set to 360. Therefore, each of these scroll bars is divided into 360 parts with each part representing one degree. To convert degrees to radians, use this formula:

```
Radians = Degrees * 2 * PI /360
```

For example, 360 degrees is equivalent to

```
360*2*PI/360=2*PI=2*3.14159265=6.2831853 radians
```

This explains why this procedure supplies the start and end properties of the Circle method as the Value properties of the From and To scroll bars multiplied by $2*\pi/360$.

The last parameter of the Circle method is the optional aspect parameter, which isn't used in this procedure. Because the aspect parameter is the last parameter, there is no need to type a comma after the end parameter.

The last thing this procedure does is display the Radius label, the From label, and the To label:

```
lblFrom.Caption="From: "+hsbFrom.Value+ _
               " degrees"

lblTo.Caption = "To: " + hsbTo.Value+ _
               " degrees"

lblRadius.Caption = "Radius: " + _
               Str(vsbRadius.Value * 20)
```

This enables you to see the current values of the scroll bars.

The Code of the hsbFrom_Change() Procedure

The hsbFrom_Change() procedure is automatically executed when you change the From scroll bar:

```
Private Sub hsbFrom_Change()

    ' Execute the DrawArc procedure to draw the arc.
    DrawArc

End Sub
```

This procedure executes the DrawArc() procedure, which draws the arc according to the new value of the hsbFrom scroll bar.

In a similar manner, the `hsbTo_Change()` and the `vsbRadius_Change()` procedures of the frmArcs form execute the `DrawArc()` procedure when you change these scroll bars.

The `hsbFrom_Scroll()`, `hsbTo_Scroll()`, and `vsbRadius_Scroll()` procedures execute their corresponding `Change` procedures.

More About the `start` and `end` Parameters of the `Circle` Method

You may also supply negative values for the `start` and `end` parameters of the `Circle` method. When the `start` parameter is negative, Visual Basic draws a straight line from the center of the arc to the start point of the arc. And when the endpoint is negative, Visual Basic draws a straight line from the center of the arc to the endpoint of the arc. For example, Figure 8.22 shows an arc that was drawn with the following statement:

```
Circle(X,Y),1000, ,-25*2*PI/360,-45*2*PI/360
```

Figure 8.22.

Drawing an arc from -25 degrees to -45 degrees.

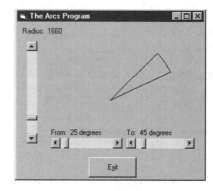

Figure 8.23 shows an arc that was drawn with the following statement:

```
Circle(X,Y),1000, ,-45*2*PI/360,-25*2*PI/360
```

Figure 8.23.

Drawing an arc from -45 degrees to -25 degrees.

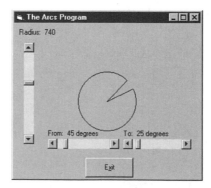

Figure 8.24 shows an arc that was drawn with the following statement:

```
Circle(X,Y),1000, ,45*2*PI/360,-25*2*PI/360
```

Figure 8.24.

*Drawing an arc from
-45 degrees to 25
degrees.*

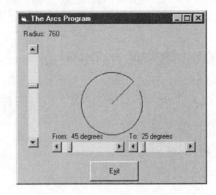

Figure 8.25 shows an arc that was drawn with the following statement:

```
Circle(X,Y),1000, ,-45*2*PI/360,25*2*PI/360
```

Figure 8.25.

*Drawing an arc from
45 degrees to -25
degrees.*

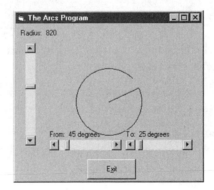

You can experiment with the start and end parameters of the Circle method in the DrawArc()
procedure as follows:

☐ To draw arcs as shown in Figures 8.22 and 8.23, change the Circle method in the
DrawArc() procedure to this:

```
Circle (X, Y), vsbRadius.Value * 20, , _
       -hsbFrom* 2^PI/360, -hsbTo*2*PI/360
```

☐ To draw arcs as shown in Figure 8.24, change the Circle method in the DrawArc()
procedure to this:

```
Circle (X, Y), vsbRadius.Value * 20, , _
       -hsbFrom* 2*PI/360, hsbTo*2*PI/360
```

☐ To draw arcs as shown in Figure 8.25, change the Circle method in the DrawArc() procedure to this:

```
Circle (X, Y), vsbRadius.Value * 20, , _
             hsbFrom* 2*PI/360, -hsbTo*2*PI/360
```

The AutoRedraw Property

The AutoRedraw property causes the graphics to be redrawn automatically when you need to do so. The default setting of the AutoRedraw property of the frmArcs is False.

Use the following steps to see the effects of the AutoRedraw property:

☐ Execute the Arcs program.

☐ Draw an arc by changing the Radius, From, and To scroll bars.

☐ Minimize the window of the Arcs program by clicking the minus icon on the top-right corner of the Arcs window.

The program responds by minimizing the window of the Arcs program and showing it as an icon.

☐ Restore the window of the Arcs program to its original size.

The Arcs window is displayed without the arc because the Redraw property of the form is currently set to False.

☐ Terminate the program and change the AutoRedraw property of the frmArcs form in the Properties window to True.

Now repeat the above experiment (draw an arc, minimize the window, and restore the original size of the window). As you can see, this time the program automatically redraws the arc because the AutoRedraw property of the form is set to True.

The Form_Paint() Procedure

You can use the Form_Paint() procedure to draw five horizontal lines as follows:

☐ Set the AutoRedraw property of the frmArcs form back to False.

☐ Add the following code in the Form_Paint() procedure of the frmArcs form:

```
Private Sub Form_Paint()

    ' Draw 5 horizontal lines
    frmArcs.Line (2000, 100)-(4000, 100)
    frmArcs.Line (2000, 200)-(4000, 200)
    frmArcs.Line (2000, 300)-(4000, 300)
```

```
frmArcs.Line (2000, 400)-(4000, 400)
frmArcs.Line (2000, 500)-(4000, 500)
```

End Sub

☐ Select Save Project from the File menu of Visual Basic to save your work.

☐ Execute the Arcs program and notice the five horizontal lines that are drawn in the window of the Arcs program.

☐ Minimize the window of the Arcs program, then restore the size of the window, and notice that the five horizontal lines are drawn.

☐ Cover the window of the Arcs program with a window of another application (so that the five horizontal lines are covered), then remove the window of the other application.

As you can see, the five horizontal lines are redrawn.

The Form_Paint() procedure is executed when Visual Basic needs to paint the form. Because Visual Basic paints the form when it's made visible at the program startup, the Form_Paint() procedure is executed when you start the program. If you drag the window of the Arcs program or cover it with a window of another application and then expose the Arcs window again, Visual Basic will automatically execute the Form_Paint() procedure because the window needs to be repainted.

In general, you can use the Form_Paint() procedure as a focal point in the program to perform the drawings, serving the same role as the AutoRedraw property. The advantage of setting AutoRedraw to True is that you don't have to insert code in the Form_Paint() procedure that redraws your drawings (that is, AutoRedraw does the redrawing automatically).

The disadvantage of setting the AutoRedraw property to True is that it consumes memory used to save current drawings; on slow PCs, the redrawing that occurs when AutoRedraw is set to True may cause noticeable delays in running the program.

Summary

In this chapter you have learned how to use the graphics methods PSet, Cls, Point, Line, and Circle. You have also learned how to draw ellipses and arcs.

Q&A

Q **What is the advantage and disadvantage of using graphics methods versus graphic controls?**

A The advantage of using graphics methods is that these methods enable you to draw complicated graphics with a small amount of code. For example, the graphics shown in Figure 8.13 are easy to do with graphics methods.

The disadvantage of using graphics methods is that you can examine the results only during runtime. When you use graphic controls, you can see how the form looks at design time.

Quiz

1. The last graphics method used in a hypothetical program was this:

   ```
   PSet (100,20) RGB(255,255,255)
   ```

   If the next statement executed in this program is this:

   ```
   PSet Step (-5,10) RGB(255,255,255)
   ```

   at what coordinate will the point be drawn?

2. BUG BUSTER. What is wrong with the following code?

   ```
   Line (100,20)-Step(300,400),RGB(0,255,0),F
   ```

3. The `Point` method is used for

   a. Drawing a point.
   b. There is no such thing as the `Point` method in Visual Basic.
   c. Finding the color of a pixel.

4. If you set the AutoRedraw property of a form to True, what happens?

Exercise

Write a program using the `Circle` method that displays circles at random locations all over the form when you start the program.

Quiz Answers

1. Because the last point was drawn at coordinate 100,20, after the drawing CurrentX is equal to 100 and CurrentY is equal to 20.

   Executing this statement:

   ```
   PSet Step (-5,10) RGB(255,255,255)
   ```

   causes the point to be drawn 5 units to the left of CurrentX. In the Y direction, the point is drawn 10 units below CurrentY. Therefore, the point is drawn at coordinate 100–5,20+10, or 95,30.

2. You can't use the `F` option without the `B` option. This is the correct syntax:

   ```
   Line (100,20)-Step(300,400),RGB(0,255,0),BF
   ```

3. c

4. The form on which a graphics method is drawn is automatically redrawn when there is need to redraw the form.

Exercise Answer

Use the following steps:

☐ Create a new Standard EXE project, save the form of the project as Circles2.Frm in the C:\VB5Prg\Ch08 directory, and save the project file of the project as Circles2.Vbp in the C:\VB5Prg\Ch08 directory.

☐ Build the frmCircles form according to Table 8.10.

Table 8.10. The properties table of frmCircles form.

Object	Property	Setting
Form	**Name**	**frmCircles2**
	Caption	The Circles2 Program

☐ Make sure that the Option Explicit statement resides in the general declarations section of the frmCircles form as follows:

```
'All variables MUST be declared.
Option Explicit
```

☐ Type the following code in the Form_Paint() procedure of the frmCircles form:

```
Private Sub Form_Paint()

    Dim I
    For I = 1 To 100 Step 1
        frmCircles2.DrawWidth = Int(Rnd * 10) + 1
        frmCircles2.ForeColor = _
            QBColor(Int(Rnd * 15))
      Circle (Rnd * frmCircles2.ScaleWidth, _
            Rnd * frmCircles2.ScaleHeight), _
            Rnd * frmCircles2.ScaleHeight / 2
    Next

End Sub
```

The Form_Paint() procedure draws 100 circles with random width and at random locations.

Day 9

Displaying Data in Tabular Formats

In some applications, it is necessary to display text in rows and columns (that is, in tables). You can do this by displaying the text line by line, calculating the required locations where the text should be displayed, and using the Print method to display the text. However, Visual Basic includes the grid control, which enables you to create tables easily. In this chapter you learn how to use the grid control.

The Table Program

You'll now write the Table program, which is an example of a program that uses the grid control.

☐ Create the C:\VB5Prg\Ch09 directory. You'll save your work in this directory.

☐ Create a new Standard EXE project, save the form of the project as Table.Frm in the C:\VB5Prg\Ch09 directory, and save the project file as Table.Vbp in the C:\VB5Prg\Ch09 directory.

Because the grid control is an OCX control, before you can place it in a form, you must first make sure it's included in your project.

The toolbox in Figure 9.1 shows the icon of the grid control. (The exact location of the grid icon in the toolbox window may be different on your system.) When you place the mouse cursor (without clicking any of the mouse buttons) on the icon of the grid control in the toolbox window, a yellow rectangle appears with the text MSFlexGrid in it. This way, you can verify that you located the icon of the grid control in the toolbox window.

Figure 9.1.

The icon of the grid control in the toolbox window.

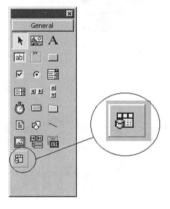

If the grid control does not appear in the toolbox window, add it as follows:

☐ Select Components from the Project menu of Visual Basic, and if needed, click the Controls tab to view the Controls page.

Visual Basic responds by displaying the Controls page of the Components dialog box.

Make sure that the Selected Items Only check box that appears in the Control page does not have a check mark in it (because you want to view the entire list of controls, not only these controls that are included already in the project).

☐ Scroll the list of custom controls until you see the Microsoft FlexGrid Control 5.0 item.

If there is an X in the check box to the left of the Microsoft FlexGrid Control 5.0 item, it means that the grid control already resides in the toolbox window. In this case, click the OK button of the Components dialog box.

9

If there is no X in the check box to the left of the Microsoft FlexGrid Control 5.0 item, it means that the grid control currently does not reside in the toolbox window. In this case, click the OK button of the Components dialog box.

If the Microsoft FlexGrid Control 5.0 item does not appear in the list, add it to the list as follows:

☐ Click the Browse button of the Controls page in the Components dialog box.

   As a result, the Add ActiveX Control dialog box appears.

☐ Select the MSFlxGrd.OCX file from your System directory and then click the Open button.

   As a result, the Microsoft FlexGrid Control 5.0 item appears as one of the items in the list of controls.

☐ Make sure that there is an X in the check box to the left of the Microsoft FlexGrid Control 5.0 item and then click the OK button.

The Microsoft FlexGrid Control 5.0 item in the Controls page of the Components window is shown in Figure 9.2.

Figure 9.2.
The Microsoft FlexGrid Control 5.0 item in the Controls page of the Components window.

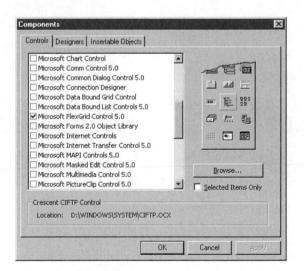

> **Note**
>
> If your Windows 95 is installed in your C:\Windows directory, your System directory is C:\Windows\System.
>
> If your Windows NT is installed in your C:\WinNT directory, your System directory is C:\WinNT\System32.

Note

Visual Basic 5 comes in various editions (for example, Learning Edition, Professional Edition, Enterprise Edition). If the particular Visual Basic version that you are using does not include the MSFlxGrd.OCX file, you will not be able to implement the Table program (because the Table program makes use of this OCX control). Nevertheless, it is highly recommended that you keep reading the discussion of the Table program in this chapter, because you'll learn about the grid control and how you use it in a program.

☐ Double-click the icon of the grid control in the toolbox.

As a result, the grid control appears in the form, as shown in Figure 9.3.

Figure 9.3.

Placing the Microsoft grid control in the form (design mode).

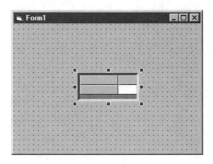

Implement the form as follows:

☐ Set the Name property of the form to frmTable.

☐ Set the Caption property of the frmTable form to The Table Program.

☐ Set the Name property of the grid control to grdTable.

☐ Set the Rows property of grdTable to 13.

☐ Set the Cols property of grdTable to 5.

☐ Enlarge the grdTable vertically and horizontally by dragging its handles.

The enlarged grid control should look like the one shown in Figure 9.4.

☐ Enlarge the frmTable form and place a CommandButton in the frmTable form below the grid control.

☐ Set the Name property of the CommandButton that you placed in the from in the previous step to cmdExit and set the caption of the CommandButton to E&xit.

Figure 9.4.

The enlarged grid control.

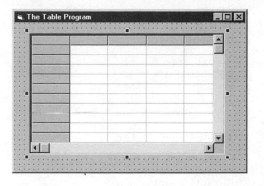

9

☐ Make sure that the Option Explicit statement resides in the general declarations section of the frmTable form:

```
' All variables MUST be declared.
Option Explicit
```

☐ Type the following code in the Form_Load() procedure of the frmTable form:

```
Private Sub Form_Load ()

    ' Set the current row to row #0.
    grdTable.Row = 0

    ' Write into Row #0, Col #1
    grdTable.Col = 1
    grdTable.Text = "Electricity"

    ' Write into Row #0, Col #2
    grdTable.Col = 2
    grdTable.Text = "Water"

    ' Write into Row #0, Col #3
    grdTable.Col = 3
    grdTable.Text = "Transportation"

    ' Write into Row #0, Col #4
    grdTable.Col = 4
    grdTable.Text = "Food"

    ' Set the current Column to column #0.
    grdTable.Col = 0

    ' Write into Row #1, Col #0
    grdTable.Row = 1
    grdTable.Text = "Jan."

    ' Write into Row #2, Col #0
    grdTable.Row = 2
    grdTable.Text = "Feb."
```

```
         ' Write into Row #3, Col #0
         grdTable.Row = 3
         grdTable.Text = "Mar."

         ' Write into Row #4, Col #0
         grdTable.Row = 4
         grdTable.Text = "Apr."

         ' Write into Row #5, Col #0
         grdTable.Row = 5
         grdTable.Text = "May."

         ' Write into Row #6, Col #0
         grdTable.Row = 6
         grdTable.Text = "Jun."

         ' Write into Row #7, Col #0
         grdTable.Row = 7
         grdTable.Text = "Jul."

         ' Write into Row #8, Col #0
         grdTable.Row = 8
         grdTable.Text = "Aug."

         ' Write into Row #9, Col #0
         grdTable.Row = 9
         grdTable.Text = "Sep."

         ' Write into Row #10, Col #0
         grdTable.Row = 10
         grdTable.Text = "Oct."

         ' Write into Row #11, Col #0
         grdTable.Row = 11
         grdTable.Text = "Nov."

         ' Write into Row #12, Col #0
         grdTable.Row = 12
         grdTable.Text = "Dec."

End Sub
```

☐ Type the following code in the cmdExit_Click() procedure of the frmTable form:

```
Private Sub cmdExit_Click ()

    End

End Sub
```

☐ Select Save Project from the File menu of Visual Basic to save your work.

Although you have not finished writing the Table program, execute it:

☐ Execute the Table program.

The program displays the grid control, as shown in Figure 9.5.

Figure 9.5.
The Table program.

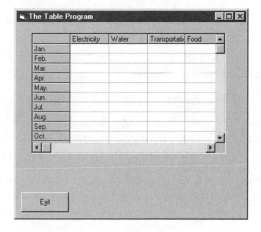

☐ Click the horizontal and vertical scroll bars of the grid control to scroll the table and use the arrow keys of your keyboard to move from cell to cell in the table.

As you can see, the grid control has a total of 13 rows (including the top heading row) and a total of 5 columns (including the left heading column). That's because during design time you set the Rows property of grdTable to 13 and you set the Cols property of grdTable to 5.

☐ Terminate the program by clicking the Exit button.

You can make the grid lines of the table more impressive as follows:

☐ Set the GridLines property of the grdTable control to 2-flexGridInset.

☐ Make sure that the BackColor property of the grdTable control is set to White.

The Code of the `Form_Load()` Procedure

The `Form_Load()` procedure is executed when the frmTable form is loaded at startup. The code in this procedure sets the current row to 0:

```
' Set the current row to row #0.
grdTable.Row = 0
```

Note

> The grid control has a property called Row and a property called Row*s*.
> When typing code, be sure not to confuse Row with Rows.
>
> The grid control also has a property called Col and a property called
> Col*s*. When typing code, be sure not to confuse Col with Cols.

Once the current row is set to 0, the procedure writes into the cell Row #0, Col #1 as follows:

```
' Write into Row #0, Col #1
grdTable.Col = 1
grdTable.Text = "Electricity"
```

That is, the procedure makes Row #0 the current row (or active row), sets Column #1 as the active column, and sets the Text property of the grid control to Electricity. As a result, the text Electricity will be placed in the cell at Row #0,Col #1.

In a similar manner, the procedure sets the Text properties of Row #0,Col #2, Row #0,Col #3, and Row #0,Col #4 to Water, Transportation, and Food, respectively. For example, to set the Text property of the cell in Row #0,Col #4, the following statements are used:

```
' Write into Row #0, Col #4
grdTable.Col = 4
grdTable.Text = "Food"
```

There is no need to set the Row property to 0 again, because it retains its value unless your code sets the Row property to a different value.

Once the four row headings are written, the procedure sets the Text property of the left column. For example, to set the Text property of the cell at Row #1,Col #0, the following statements are used:

```
' Set the current Column to column #0.
grdTable.Col = 0
' Write into Row #1, Col #0
grdTable.Row = 1
grdTable.Text = "Jan."
```

In a similar manner, the rest of the cells in the left column are filled with the rest of the months.

Note

> The grid control displays information in a tabular format. You can
> move from cell to cell by using the arrow keys or the scroll bars, but
> you can't enter information directly into the cells from the keyboard.

Changing the Cell Width

Depending on the font that you are using, the cells of the table may not be wide enough. For example, the word Electricity does not fit within its cell (refer to Figure 9.5). You can use the following steps to widen the cell during runtime:

☐ Add a procedure to the frmTable form by double-clicking the frmTable (to display the code window) and select Add Procedure from the Tool menu of Visual Basic.

As a result, Visual Basic displays the Add Procedure dialog box.

☐ Set the Name edit box of the Add Procedure dialog box to SetColWidth.

☐ Make sure that the Sub option button of the Add Procedure dialog box is selected.

☐ Make sure that the Public option button of the Add Procedure dialog box is selected.

☐ Click the OK button of the Add Procedure dialog box.

Visual Basic creates a new procedure called SetColWidth *in the General area of the frmTable form.*

☐ Type the following code in the SetColWidth() procedure:

```
Public Sub SetColWidth ()

    Dim Counter

    For Counter = 0 To 4 Step 1
        grdTable.ColWidth(Counter) = 1300
    Next

End Sub
```

The code that you typed in the SetColWidth() procedure uses a For loop to change the ColWidth property of each of the columns to 1,300 twips. As implied by its name, the ColWidth property determines the width of the column. That is, grdTable.ColWidth(0) determines the width of column 0, grdTable.ColWidth(1) determines the width of column 1, grdTable.ColWidth(2) determines the width of column 2, and so on.

☐ Add the SetColWidth statement to the end of the Form_Load() procedure. The Form_Load() procedure should now look as follows:

```
Sub Form_Load ()

    .................................................
    ... No change to this section of the procedure ...
    .................................................

    SetColWidth

End Sub
```

☐ Select Save Project from the File menu of Visual Basic to save your work.

☐ Execute the Table program.

The window of the Table program now looks like the one shown in Figure 9.6.

Figure 9.6.

Making the columns wider.

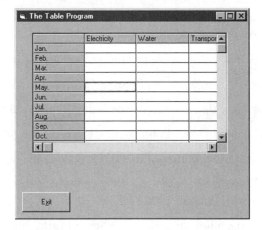

☐ Use the arrow keys or the scroll bars to move from cell to cell.

As you can see from Figure 9.7, all the columns changed their widths, and they are now wider than the original width.

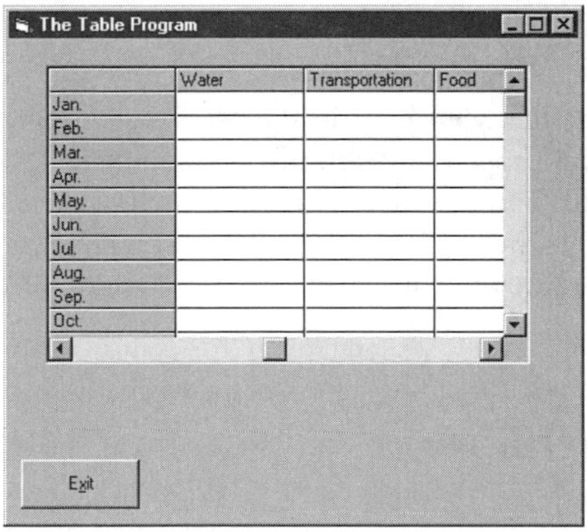

Figure 9.7.

Widening all the columns.

☐ Terminate the program by clicking its Exit button.

☐ Enlarge the grdTable grid control by dragging its handles until it looks like the one shown in Figure 9.8.

> *As you can see, the total area of the grid control is larger, but the cell widths are still at their default widths. This is because you can widen the cell only during runtime.*

Figure 9.8.

Enlarging the size of the grid control at design time.

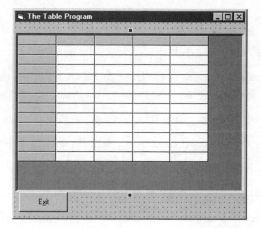

☐ Execute the Table program.

> *The grid control now looks like the one shown in Figure 9.9. As you can see, the total area of the grid control is larger and the width of each of the cells is greater.*

Figure 9.9.

The enlarged grid control with widened cells at runtime.

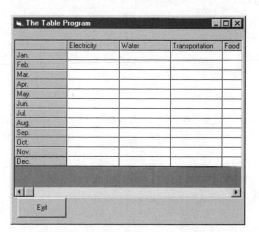

☐ Experiment with the grid control by using the arrow keys or the scroll bars to move from cell to cell.

☐ Terminate the Table program by clicking its Exit button.

☐ Make the size of the grid control smaller (so that there will be no empty space below the December row).

Changing the Cell Height

You'll now write code that changes the height of the cells during runtime:

☐ Add a procedure to the frmTable form by double-clicking the frmTable (to display the code window) and then select Add Procedure from the Tool menu of Visual Basic.

As a result, Visual Basic displays the Add Procedure dialog box.

☐ Set the Name edit box of the Add Procedure dialog box to SetRowHeight.

☐ Make sure that the Sub option button of the Add Procedure dialog box is selected.

☐ Make sure that the Public option button of the Add Procedure dialog box is selected.

☐ Click the OK button of the Add Procedure dialog box.

Visual Basic creates a new procedure called SetRowHeight *in the General area of the frmTable form.*

☐ Type the following code in the SetRowHeight() procedure:

```
Public Sub SetRowHeight ()

    Dim Counter

    For Counter = 0 To 12 Step 1
        grdTable.RowHeight(Counter) = 500
    Next

End Sub
```

The RowHeight property determines the height of the cell. The SetRowHeight() procedure uses a For loop to set the height of each of the rows to 500 twips.

☐ Type code that executes the SetRowHeight from within the Form_Load() procedure as follows:

```
Private Sub Form_Load ()

    ..................................................
    ... No change to this section of the procedure ...
    ..................................................
```

```
SetColWidth
SetRowHeight
```

End Sub

☐ Select Save Project from the File menu of Visual Basic to save your work.

☐ Execute the Table program.

The cells of the grid control now look like the ones shown in Figure 9.10.

Figure 9.10.

Increasing the height of rows.

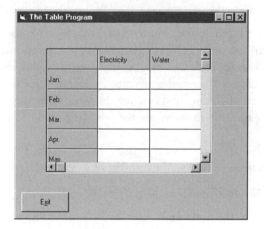

The Scroll Bars of the Grid Control

You have probably noticed that Visual Basic automatically adds horizontal and vertical scroll bars when the cells won't fit within the area of the grid control. This is because you left the default value of the ScrollBars property of the grdTable grid control to 3-flexScrollBarBoth. If you don't want these scroll bars to appear, either set the ScrollBars property of the grid control to 3-flexScrollBarNone at design time or issue the following statement from within the program:

```
grdTable.ScrollBars = 0
```

If you want the grid to have only a horizontal scroll bar, either set the ScrollBars property of the grid control to 1-flexScrollBarHorizontal at design time or issue the following statement from within the program:

```
grdTable.ScrollBars = 1
```

If you want the grid control to have only a vertical scroll bar, set the ScrollBars property to 2-flexScrollBarVertical.

Note
No matter how you set the ScrollBars property of the grid control, you are always able to move from cell to cell using the arrow keys.

Setting the Rows and Cols Properties During Runtime

During design time, you set the Rows property of the grid control to 13 and the Cols property to 5 so the grid control has a total of 5 columns and 13 rows.

Sometimes, the number of rows and columns is known only during runtime. For example, you can set up the Table program to give you the option of displaying only the electricity and water bills for each month. If you choose to display only these two columns, your program has to change the number of columns to three (one for the left column heading, one for the Electricity heading, and one for the Water heading). To change the number of columns during runtime to three, use the following statement:

```
grdTable.Cols = 3
```

If you need to change the number of rows during runtime, use the following statement:

```
grdTable.Rows = n
```

where *n* is the number of rows (including the top heading row).

Filling the Rest of the Cells of the Table Program

Use the following steps to fill the rest of the cells of the Table program:

☐ Add a new procedure to the General area of the frmTable form.

☐ Name the new procedure FillCells.

Visual Basic responds by adding the FillCells() procedure to the General area.

☐ Type the following code in the FillCells() procedure:

```
Public Sub FillCells ()

    Dim RowCounter, ColCounter

    For ColCounter = 1 To 4 Step 1
        grdTable.Col = ColCounter
        For RowCounter = 1 To 12 Step 1
            grdTable.Row = RowCounter
            grdTable.Text = "Unknown"
        Next
    Next

End Sub
```

☐ Add code to the end of the Form_Load() procedure that executed the FillCells statement. The Form_Load() procedure should now look as follows:

```
Private Sub Form_Load ()

    ...........................................
    ... No change to this section of the procedure ...
    ...........................................

    SetColWidth
    SetRowHeight
    FillCells

End Sub
```

The Code of the FillCells() Procedure

In the FillCells procedure you execute two For() loops:

```
For ColCounter = 1 To 4 Step 1
    grdTable.Col = ColCounter
    For RowCounter = 1 To 12 Step 1
        grdTable.Row = RowCounter
        grdTable.Text = "Unknown"
    Next
Next
```

The two For loops set the Text property for each of the cells of the grdTable to Unknown. The outer For loop counts from 1 to 4, and the inner For loop counts from 1 to 12. These two For loops set the Text property of all the cells in the grid (except the left heading column and the top row heading) to Unknown.

☐ Select Save Project from the File menu of Visual Basic to save your work.

☐ Execute the Table program.

The cells of the grid control are all filled with the text Unknown (see Figure 9.11).

☐ Terminate the Table program by clicking its Exit button.

☐ Now add code to the FillCells() procedure that fills cells with specific data. After you add the code, the FillCells() procedure should look as follows:

```
Public Sub FillCells ()

    ...........................................
    ... No change to this section of the procedure ...
    ...........................................

    ' Fill the Electricity bill for January.
    grdTable.Row = 1
    grdTable.Col = 1
    grdTable.Text = "$100.00"
```

```
' Fill the Electricity bill for February.
grdTable.Row = 2
grdTable.Col = 1
grdTable.Text = "$50.00"

' Fill the Water bill for February.
grdTable.Row = 2
grdTable.Col = 2
grdTable.Text = "$75.00"

End Sub
```

Figure 9.11.

Filling the cells of the grid control with text.

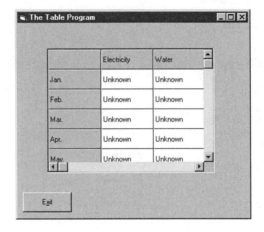

The code that you added to the FillCells() procedure fills three cells in the grid control by setting the Row and Col properties with the required row number and column number, then setting the Text property of the cell with the desired text.

☐ Execute the Table program.

As you can see, the three cells are filled with the text $100.00, $50.00, and $75.00 (see Figure 9.12).

☐ Add a Clear button to the frmTable form, as shown in Figure 9.13. Set the properties of the CommandButton as follows: Name should be cmdClear, and Caption should be &Clear.

The frmTable form should now look like the one in Figure 9.13.

Figure 9.12.

Filling three cells in the grid.

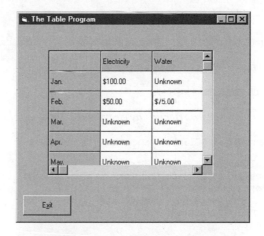

Figure 9.13.

Adding a Clear button.

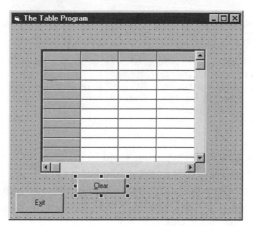

☐ Type the following code in the cmdClear_Click() procedure of the frmTable form:

```
Private Sub cmdClear_Click ()

    Dim RowCounter, ColCounter

    For ColCounter = 1 To 4 Step 1
        grdTable.Col = ColCounter
        For RowCounter = 1 To 12 Step 1
            grdTable.Row = RowCounter
            grdTable.Text = ""
        Next
    Next

End Sub
```

The code that you typed clears all the data cells.

☐ Select Save Project from the File menu of Visual Basic to save your work.

☐ Execute the Table program.

☐ Click the Clear button.

   The program responds by clearing all the data cells in the grid control.

In the cmdClear_Click() procedure you execute the For() loop as follows:

```
For ColCounter = 1 To 4 Step 1
    grdTable.Col = ColCounter
    For RowCounter = 1 To 12 Step 1
        grdTable.Row = RowCounter
        grdTable.Text = ""
    Next
Next
```

That is, you specified 4 as the upper limit of the outer For() loop, and you specified 12 as the upper limit of the inner For() loop. A better technique would be to use the following code:

```
For ColCounter = 1 To grdTable.Cols - 1 Step 1
    grdTable.Col = ColCounter
    For RowCounter = 1 To grdTable.Rows - 1 Step 1
        grdTable.Row = RowCounter
    grdTable.Text = ""
    Next
Next
```

That is, instead of specifying 4 and 12 as the upper limits of the For() loops, you use the Cols and Rows properties of the grid control. This way, if you change the number of rows and columns of the table when you develop your program, you do not have to change the code of the procedure (because the procedure uses the properties of the table instead of the hard-coded numbers 4 and 12).

Aligning Text in the Cells

The cells in Row #0 (the top row) are used to store the headings of the columns, and the cells in the left column are used to store the heading of the rows. These cells are called fixed rows and fixed columns because as you scroll in the grid control, these cells are always fixed in their position. However, you can scroll up and down or scroll left and right in all the other cells of the grid control. Appropriately, these cells are called *non-fixed cells*.

To align the non-fixed columns in a grid control, use the ColAlignment property. The possible settings of the ColAlignment property are shown in Table 9.1.

Table 9.1. Possible setting of data in a cell.

Value	Description
0	Left top
1	Left center (default for strings)
2	Left bottom
3	Center top
4	Center center
5	Center bottom
6	Right top
7	Right center (default for numbers)
8	Right bottom
9	General

For example, to place the contents of the cell on the right side of the bottom of the cell, set the ColAlignment property of the cell to 8. To place the contents of the cell on the right side of the top of the cell, set the ColAlignment property of the cell to 6.

Use the following steps to see the ColAlignment property in action:

☐ Add the Align CommandButton to the frmTable form, as shown in Figure 9.14.

☐ Set the properties of the Align button as follows: Name should be cmdAlign, and Caption should be &Align.

Figure 9.14.

Adding the Align button.

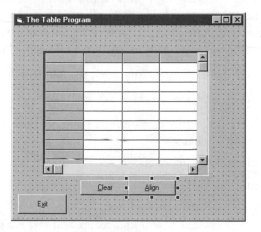

☐ Type the following code in the cmdAlign_Click() procedure of the frmTable form:

```
Private Sub cmdAlign_Click ()

    Dim ColCounter

    ' Center the text in the cells.
    For ColCounter = 1 To (grdTable.Cols - 2) Step 1
        grdTable.ColAlignment(ColCounter) = 4
    Next

End Sub
```

This procedure sets the ColAlignment property to 4 for all the non-fixed columns except the extreme right column. As specified in Table 9.1, when the ColAlignment property is set to 4, the text is centered in the horizontal as well as vertical direction of the cell.

☐ Execute the Table program.

☐ Click the Align button.

As you can see, the text is centered in all the non-fixed cells except the ones in the extreme right column.

The reason for not centering the text in the extreme right column when you develop your program column is to demonstrate that you can assign different values to the ColAlignment property for different columns (that is, in this example, the non-fixed columns 1 to 11 have their ColAlignment property set to 4); the ColAlignment property for column 12 remains at its default alignment.

To align the fixed columns and fixed rows, you have to use the FixedAlignment property. You can use the FixedAlignment property to align the text in a fixed column to a different alignment than the non-fixed cells below the heading. For example, if you set the FixedAlignment property of column 1 to 1 (left, center), the text alignment of the cells below this heading can be set with the ColAlignment property to any of the values listed in Table 9.1.

To center the text in the extreme left column (column 0), use the following statement:

```
grdTable.FixedAlignment(0) = 1
```

To center the Electricity, Water, and Food headings (columns 1, 2, and 3, respectively), use the following statements:

```
grdTable.FixedAlignment(1) = 4
grdTable.FixedAlignment(2) = 4
grdTable.FixedAlignment(3) = 4
```

You can experiment with the various alignment settings by adding the preceding code to the end of the cmdAlign_Click() procedure and observing the results.

Summary

In this chapter you learned how to use the grid control, a control that lets you present data in a tabular format.

Q&A

Q Can I place more than one grid control in a form?

A Yes. You can place many grid controls in a form—just as you can place many CommandButtons and other controls in a form.

Q The properties table of the grid control includes the properties FixedRows and GridLines. What do these properties do?

A The default settings of these properties are 1s. This causes the grid control to appear with one fixed column and one fixed row. A typical table has one fixed heading row on its top and one fixed column on the left side of the table. However, if you set the FixedRows property to 2, for example, the table will appear with two fixed rows at the top of the table. If you set the FixedCols to 3, for example, there will be three fixed columns on the left side. (Try it.)

Quiz

1. The height of the cells can be changed only during runtime.

    a. True
    b. False

2. The width of the cells can be changed only during runtime.

    a. True
    b. False

3. Which property should you set to change the height of a cell?

    a. RowHeight
    b. ColWidth
    c. You can't change the height of a cell.

4. Which property should you set to change the width of a cell?

    a. RowHeight
    b. ColWidth
    c. You can't change the width of a cell.

Exercise

Write a program that displays a multiplication table.

Quiz Answers

1. a
2. a
3. a
4. b

Exercise Answer

There are several ways to build such a program. The grid control should appear as follows:

```
        0    1    2    3    . . .
0       0    0    0    0    . . .
1       0    1    2    3    . . .
2       0    1    4    6    . . .
3       0    3    6    9    . . .
.       .    .    .    .    . . .
.       .    .    .    .    . . .
.       .    .    .    .    . . .
```

Try to write the program by yourself. When implementing the program, calculate the Text property of the nonfixed cells by doing the multiplication. For example, the text that may be placed in the cell Row #2,Col #3 can be calculated as follows:

```
Dim X, Y
grdMultiply.Row = 2
grdMultiply.Col = 0
X = Val(grdMultiply.Text)
grdMultiply.Row = 0
grdMultiply.Col = 3
Y = Val(grdMultiply.Text)
grdMultiply.Row = 2
grdMultiply.Col = 3
grdMultiply.Text = X*Y
```

Try to implement a loop that goes through all the rows and columns and fills all the cells of the grid control.

Day 10

Displaying and Printing

In this chapter you'll learn how to display and print information, how to display text in different fonts, how to format numbers, dates, and times, and how to send data (text and graphics) to the printer.

Fonts

There are two types of fonts: scaleable and nonscaleable. A scaleable font is created using mathematical formulas. For example, the basic B character is defined only once. All other sizes of the B character are produced from the basic character by enlarging or shrinking the basic B. On the other hand, a nonscaleable font is stored as a bitmap. Larger and smaller fonts of the same character are stored as different bitmaps. Depending on the font, sometimes a font that is displayed as a scaled font (enlarged or shrinked), does not look nice.

Using Different Fonts in Your Programs

When you display text in a form, you have to choose its font. Selecting the proper font is an important job. Will your users have this type of font on their systems? If the user of your program does not have the font installed, Windows chooses a font that most closely resembles the required font. However, if your user doesn't have a large selection of fonts, Windows might choose a font that is larger than the font you intended to use, which could mess up your form by producing overlapped text. In some cases, Windows will try to select the most closely resembled font by using a font that exists on the user's machine and scaling it. This also can mess up the beauty of your forms.

The easiest way to overcome this problem is to use only the most common fonts, such as the fonts shipped with the original Windows package. Your program also can examine the file WIN.INI in the Windows directory. This file has a section that starts with the heading [fonts]. All the currently installed fonts are listed under this heading. Your program can examine this section and decide which font should be used.

The FontTransparent Property

The form and the picture control support the FontTransparent property. When FontTransparent is False (the default), the text is displayed with a background indicated by the BackColor property of the object on which the text is displayed. For example, if the BackColor property of a form is set to blue, the text is displayed on the form with a blue background.

Figure 10.1 shows a form with a bitmap picture in it. That is, the Picture property of the form was set so that the form has a BMP picture in it (the BMP picture consists of solid circles).

Figure 10.1.

*The frmMyForm form
with the BMP picture
of solid circles on the
surface of the form.*

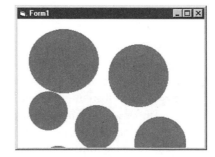

You can display text in the form by using the Print method. The following Form_Click() procedure is automatically executed when you click in the form:

```
Private Sub Form_Click()

' Set the FontTransparent property to True.
frmMyForm.FontTransparent = True

' Display text.
frmMyForm.Print "Testing with FontTransparent = True"

' Set the FontTransparent property to False.
frmMyForm.FontTransparent = False

' Display text.
frmMyForm.Print "Testing with FontTransparent = False"

End Sub
```

The code in this procedure sets the FontTransparent property of the form to True and uses the Print method to display the text:

```
Testing with FontTransparent = True
```

The procedure then sets the FontTransparent property of the form to False and displays this text:

```
Testing with FontTransparent = False
```

Figure 10.2 shows the form after clicking the form several times (after each click, two lines of text are displayed).

So the first, third, fifth, and seventh lines of text are text that was displayed with the FontTransparent property of the form set to True. The second, fourth, sixth, and eighth lines of text are text that was displayed with the FontTransparent property of the form set to False.

Note that the text that was displayed with FontTransparent set to True "accepts" whatever color it is displayed on. The third line of text in Figure 10.2 demonstrates it best.

On the other hand, text that was displayed with FontTransparent set to False, will always have white as its background color (because the BackColor property of the form is set to white). The fourth line of text in Figure 10.2 demonstrates this best.

10

Figure 10.2.

Text is displayed on the form of Figure 10.1. Some of the text is displayed with FontTransparent set to True and some with FontTransparent set to False.

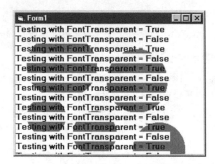

The ShowFont Program

The ShowFont program illustrates the various font properties available in Visual Basic.

The Visual Implementation of the ShowFont Program

As usual, you'll start with the visual implementation of the form of the program.

☐ Create the C:\VB5Prg\Ch10 directory. You'll save your work in this directory.

☐ Create a new Standard EXE project, save the form of the project as ShowFont.Frm in the C:\VB5Prg\Ch10 directory and save the project file as ShowFont.Vbp in the C:\VB5Prg\Ch10 directory.

☐ Build the frmShowFont form according to Table 10.1.

The completed form should look like the one shown in Figure 10.3.

Figure 10.3.

The frmShowFont form (design mode).

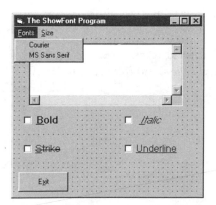

Table 10.1. The properties table of frmShowFont form.

Object	Property	Setting
Form	**Name**	**frmShowFont**
	Caption	The ShowFont Program
TextBox	**Name**	**txtTest**
	MultiLine	True
	ScrollBars	3-Both
	Text	(make it empty)
CommandButton	**Name**	**cmdExit**
	Caption	E&xit
CheckBox	**Name**	**chkBold**
	Caption	&Bold
	Font	(Make it a bold font)
CheckBox	**Name**	**chkItalic**
	Caption	&Italic
	Font	(Make it italic font)
CheckBox	**Name**	**chkStrike**
	Caption	&Strike
	Font	(Make it a strikeout font)
CheckBox	**Name**	**chkUnderline**
	Caption	&Underline
	Font	(Make it an underline font)
Menu	*(See Table 10.2)*	*(See Table 10.2)*

Table 10.2. The menu table of the frmShowFont form.

Caption	Name
&Fonts	mnuFonts
…Courier	mnuCourier
…MS Sans Serif	mnuMSSansSerif
&Size	mnuSize
…1&0 Points	mnu10Points
…1&2 Points	mnu12Points

10

Entering the Code of the ShowFont Program

You'll now enter the code of the ShowFont program:

☐ Type the following code in the general declarations section of the frmShowFont form:

```
' All variables MUST be declared.
Option Explicit
```

☐ Type the following code in the chkBold_Click() procedure of the frmShowFont form:

```
Private Sub chkBold_Click()

' Update the FontBold property of the text
' box with the Value property of the
' chkBold check box.
txtTest.FontBold = chkBold.Value

End Sub
```

☐ Type the following code in the chkItalic_Click() procedure of the frmShowFont form:

```
Private Sub chkItalic_Click()

    ' Update the FontItalic property of the
    ' text box with the Value property
    ' of the chkItalic check box.
    txtTest.FontItalic = chkItalic.Value

End Sub
```

☐ Type the following code in the chkStrike_Click() procedure of the frmShowFont form:

```
Private Sub chkStrike_Click()

    ' Update the FontStrikethru property
    ' of the text box with the  Value property
    ' of the chkStrike check box.
    txtTest.FontStrikethru = chkStrike.Value

End Sub
```

☐ Type the following code in the chkUnderline_Click() procedure of the frmShowFont form:

```
Private Sub chkUnderline_Click()

    ' Update the FontUnderline property
    ' of the text box with the Value
    ' property of the chkUnderline check box.
    txtTest.FontUnderline = chkUnderline.Value

End Sub
```

☐ Type the following code in the cmdExit_Click() procedure of the frmShowFont form:

```
Private Sub cmdExit_Click()

    End

End Sub
```

☐ Type the following code in the mnu10Points_Click() procedure of the frmShowFont form:

```
Private Sub mnu10Points_Click()

    ' Set the size of the font to 10 points.
    txtTest.FontSize = 10

End Sub
```

☐ Type the following code in the mnu12Points_Click() procedure of the frmShowFont form:

```
Private Sub mnu12Points_Click()

    ' Set the size of the font to 12 points.
    txtTest.FontSize = 12

End Sub
```

☐ Type the following code in the mnuCourier_Click() procedure of the frmShowFont form:

```
Private Sub mnuCourier_Click()

    ' Set the font name to Courier.
    txtTest.FontName = "Courier"

End Sub
```

☐ Type the following code in the mnuMSSansSerif_Click() procedure of the frmShowFont form:

```
Private Sub mnuMSSansSerif_Click()

    ' Set the font name to MS Sans Serif.
    txtTest.FontName = "MS Sans Serif"

End Sub
```

☐ Select Save Project from the File menu of Visual Basic to save your work.

Executing the ShowFont Program

Let's see your code in action:

☐ Execute the ShowFont program.

☐ Type something in the text box (see Figure 10.4).

The text you typed appears with the default font (the font set during design time).

10

Figure 10.4.

*The default font of the
ShowFont program.*

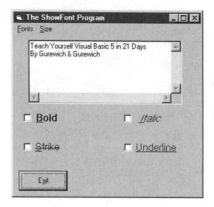

☐ Place a check mark in the Bold check box.

The program responds by changing the font in the text box to bold (see Figure 10.5).

Figure 10.5.

*Checking the Bold
check box.*

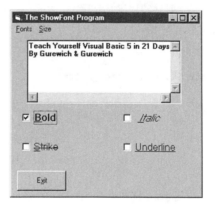

☐ Place a check mark in the Italic check box.

*The program responds by changing the text in the text box to italic. Since the Bold check box
is also checked, the text is bold and italic (see Figure 10.6).*

☐ Click the Bold check box and the Italic check box to uncheck them.

The program responds by removing the bold and italic from the text in the text box.

☐ Place a check mark in the Strike check box.

*The program responds by displaying the text in the text box as strikethrough text (see Figure
10.7).*

Figure 10.6.

Checking the Bold and Italic check boxes.

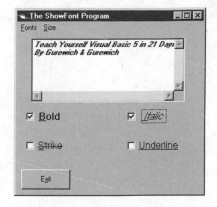

Figure 10.7.

Checking the Strike check box.

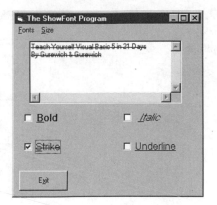

☐ Click the Strike check box to uncheck this check box.

   The program responds by removing the strikethrough font from the text.

☐ Place a check mark in the Underline check box.

   The program responds by underlining the text in the text box (see Figure 10.8).

☐ Change the font name by selecting a font from the Fonts menu.

   The program responds by changing the text in the text box to the font you selected.

☐ Change the font size by selecting a size from the Size menu.

   The program responds by changing the text in the text box to the point size you selected. Figure 10.9 shows the text box after setting the size to 12 points.

☐ Click the Exit button to terminate the program.

10

Figure 10.8.
*Checking the Under-
line check box.*

Figure 10.9.
*Setting the FontSize
property to 12 points.*

How the ShowFont Program Works

The ShowFont program changes the font properties of the text box according to your
selections.

The Code of the chkBold_Click() Procedure

The chkBold_Click() procedure is automatically executed when you click the chkBold check
box:

```
Private Sub chkBold_Click()

    ' Update the FontBold property of the
    ' text box with the Value
    ' property of the chkBold check box.
    txtTest.FontBold = chkBold.Value

End Sub
```

When the Value property of chkBold is True (that is, checked), the FontBold property of the text box is set to True; when the Value property of chkBold is False (that is, unchecked), the FontBold property of the text box is set to False.

The chkItalic_Click(), chkStrike_Click(), and chkUnderline_Click() procedures work the same way to change the txtTest text box:

The chkItalic_Click() procedure sets the FontItalic property to True or False.

The chkStrike_Click() procedure sets the FontStrike property to True or False.

The chkUnderline_Click() procedure sets the FontUnderline property to True or False.

The Code of the mnu10Points_Click() Procedure

The mnu10Points_Click() procedure is executed when you select 10 Points from the Size menu:

```
Private Sub mnu10Points_Click()

    ' Set the size of the font to 10 points.
    txtTest.FontSize = 10

End Sub
```

This procedure sets the FontSize property of the txtTest text box to 10. The mnu12Points_Click() procedure works the same way to set the FontSize property of the text box to 12.

The Code of the mnuCourier_Click() Procedure

The mnuCourier_Click() procedure is executed when you select Courier from the Font menu:

```
Private Sub mnuCourier_Click()

    ' Set the font name to Courier.
    txtTest.FontName = "Courier"

End Sub
```

This procedure sets the FontName property of the txtTest text box to Courier. The mnuMSSansSerif_Click() procedure works the same way to set the FontName property to MS Sans Serif.

WYSIWYG

WYSIWYG is an abbreviation for "what you see is what you get." WYSIWYG refers to the capability of a program to produce a hard copy on the printer that is an exact replica of what's on the screen. Producing 100 percent WYSIWYG programs requires careful programming because users can have different printers, monitors, fonts, and so forth.

The Fonts Program

The Fonts program illustrates how your program can make a decision about the available fonts in the system. The technique used by the Fonts program can be used to produce programs with WYSIWYG capability.

The Visual Implementation of the Fonts Program

As usual, you'll start with the visual implementation of the program:

☐ Create a Standard EXE project, save the form of the program as Fonts.Frm in the C:\VB5Prg\Ch10 directory and save the project file as Fonts.Vbp in the C:\VB5Prg\Ch10 directory.

☐ Build the frmFonts form according to Table 10.3.

The completed form should look like the one shown in Figure 10.10.

Figure 10.10.

The frmFonts form (design mode).

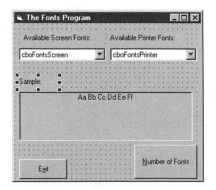

Table 10.3. The properties table of the frmFonts form.

Object	Property	Setting
Form	**Name**	**frmFonts**
	Caption	The Fonts Program

Object	Property	Setting
CommandButton	**Name**	**cmdExit**
	Caption	E&xit
ComboBox	**Name**	**cboFontsScreen**
	Sorted	True
	Style	2-Dropdown List
ComboBox	**Name**	**cboFontsPrinter**
	Sorted	True
	Style	2-Dropdown List
CommandButton	**Name**	**cmdNumberOfFonts**
	Caption	&Number of Fonts
Label	**Name**	**lblScreen**
	Caption	Available Screen Fonts:
Label	**Name**	**lblPrinter**
	Caption	Available Printer Fonts:
Label	**Name**	**lblSample**
	Caption	Aa Bb Cc Dd Ee Ff
	Alignment	2-Center
	BorderStyle	1-Fixed Single
Label	**Name**	**lblSampleInfo**
	Caption	Sample:

Table 20.3 instructs you to place two ComboBoxes in the frmFonts form. When you place the mouse cursor on the icon of the ComboBox in the toolbox window, a yellow rectangle appears with the text ComboBox in it. This way, you can verify that you located the icon of the ComboBox in the toolbox window.

Entering the Code of the Fonts Program

You'll now enter the code of the Fonts program:

☐ Type the following code in the general declarations section of the frmFonts form:

```
' All variables MUST be declared.
Option Explicit
Dim gNumOfScreenFonts
Dim gNumOfPrinterFonts
```

☐ Type the following code in the cboFontsScreen_Click() procedure of the frmFonts form:

```
Private Sub cboFontsScreen_Click()

    ' User selected a new screen font. Change the
    ' font of the label in accordance with the
    ' user's font selection.
    lblSample.FontName = cboFontsScreen.Text

End Sub
```

☐ Type the following code in the cmdNumberOfFonts_Click() procedure of the frmFonts form:

```
Private Sub cmdNumberOfFonts_Click()

    'Display the number of screen fonts in the
    ' system.
    MsgBox "Number of Screen fonts:" + _
          Str(gNumOfScreenFonts)

    'Display the number of printer fonts in the
    ' system.
    MsgBox "Number of Printer fonts:" + _
          Str(gNumOfPrinterFonts)

End Sub
```

☐ Type the following code in the Form_Load() procedure of the frmFonts form:

```
Private Sub Form_Load()

    Dim I

    ' Calculate the number of screen fonts.
    gNumOfScreenFonts = Screen.FontCount - 1

    ' Calculate the number of printer fonts.
    gNumOfPrinterFonts = Printer.FontCount - 1

    ' Fill the items of the combo box with the
    ' screen fonts.
    For I = 0 To gNumOfScreenFonts - 1 Step 1
        cboFontsScreen.AddItem Screen.Fonts(I)
    Next

    ' Fill the items of the combo box with the
    ' printer fonts.
    For I = 0 To gNumOfPrinterFonts - 1 Step 1
        cboFontsPrinter.AddItem Printer.Fonts(I)
    Next

    ' initialize the text of the Screen combo box
    ' to item #0.
    cboFontsScreen.ListIndex = 0
    ' Initialize the label font to value of the
    ' combo box.
```

```
lblSample.FontName = cboFontsScreen.Text

' initialize the text of the Printer combo box
' to item #0.
cboFontsPrinter.ListIndex = 0
```

End Sub

☐ Type the following code in the cmdExit_Click() procedure of the frmFonts form:

```
Private Sub cmdExit_Click()

    End

End Sub
```

☐ Select Save Project from the File menu of Visual Basic to save your work.

Executing the Fonts Program

Let's see your code in action:

☐ Execute the Fonts program.

☐ Click the Number of Fonts button.

> *The program responds by displaying the number of available screen fonts and the number of available printer fonts.*

☐ Click the down-arrow icon of the combo box on the left and select a font from the list. As indicated by the label above the left combo box, the list in the box includes all the available screen fonts on your system.

> *As a response, the sample label at the bottom of the form changes its font according to your selection (see Figure 10.11).*

Figure 10.11.

Choosing the Arial Black screen font.

10

☐ Select a font from the combo box on the right.

> *As indicated by the label above this combo box, the list in the box includes all the available printer fonts in your system.*

> *The program responds by displaying all the available printer fonts (see Figure 10.12).*

Figure 10.12.
Displaying the printer fonts.

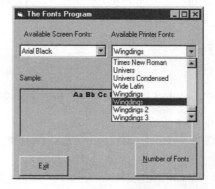

Note

The text in the Sample label doesn't change when you select new fonts from the combo box on the right, because the right combo box represents the printer fonts.

How the Fonts Program Works

The Fonts program extracts the available screen and printer fonts and displays them in combo boxes.

The Code of the General Declarations Section

The code in the general declarations section of the frmFonts form declares two variables:

```
Dim gNumOfScreenFonts
Dim gNumOfPrinterFonts
```

These variables represent the number of available screen fonts and printer fonts. Because these variables are declared in the general declarations section, they are visible in all the procedures of the form.

The Code of the `Form_Load()` Procedure

The `Form_Load()` procedure is executed when the form is loaded:

```
Private Sub Form_Load()

    Dim I

    ' Calculate the number of screen fonts.
    gNumOfScreenFonts = Screen.FontCount - 1

    ' Calculate the number of printer fonts.
    gNumOfPrinterFonts = Printer.FontCount - 1

    ' Fill the items of the combo box with the
    ' screen fonts.
    For I = 0 To gNumOfScreenFonts - 1 Step 1
        cboFontsScreen.AddItem Screen.Fonts(I)
    Next

    ' Fill the items of the combo box with the
    ' printer fonts.
    For I = 0 To gNumOfPrinterFonts - 1 Step 1
        cboFontsPrinter.AddItem Printer.Fonts(I)
    Next

    ' initialize the text of the Screen combo box
    ' to item #0.
    cboFontsScreen.ListIndex = 0
    ' Initialize the label font to value of the
    ' combo box.
    lblSample.FontName = cboFontsScreen.Text

    ' initialize the text of the Printer combo box
    ' to item #0.
    cboFontsPrinter.ListIndex = 0

End Sub
```

You extract the number of available screen fonts of the PC on which the Fonts program is executed by using the FontCount property of the screen:

```
' Calculate the number of screen fonts.
gNumOfScreenFonts = Screen.FontCount
```

Similarly, you extract the number of available printer fonts by using the FontCount property of the printer:

```
' Calculate the number of printer fonts.
gNumOfPrinterFonts = Printer.FontCount -1
```

10

Do — **Don't**

DO use the FontCount property to find the number of available screen fonts. For example, to assign the number of available screen fonts to the variable gNumOfScreenFonts, use the following:

```
gNumOfScreenFonts = Screen.FontCount
```

Do — **Don't**

DO use the FontCount property to find the number of available printer fonts. For example, to assign the number of available printer fonts to the variable gNumOfPrinterFonts, use the following:

```
gNumOfPrinterFonts = Printer.FontCount
```

The Form_Load() procedure then fills the item of the cboFontsScreen combo box with the screen fonts:

```
' Fill the items of the combo box with the
' screen fonts.
For I = 0 To gNumOfScreenFonts - 1 Step 1
 cboFontsScreen.AddItem Screen.Fonts(I)
Next
```

The procedure then fills the items of the cboFontsPrinter combo box with the printer fonts:

```
' Fill the items of the combo box with the
' printer fonts.
For I = 0 To gNumOfPrinterFonts - 1 Step 1
 cboFontsPrinter.AddItem Printer.Fonts(I)
Next
```

The available fonts are extracted by using the Fonts property.

Note

To extract the screen fonts, use the Fonts property. For example, to assign the first available font of the screen to a string variable called CurrentScreenFont, use the following:

```
CurrentScreenFont = Screen.Fonts(0)
```

Note

> To extract the printer fonts, use the Fonts property. For example, to assign the ninth available font of the printer to a string variable called CurrentPrinterFont, use the following:
>
> CurrentPrinterFont = Printer.Fonts(8)

The procedure then initializes the cboFontScreen combo box to the first item:

```
cboFontsScreen.ListIndex = 0
```

The text font in the lblSample label is changed according to the Text property of the screen's font combo box:

```
lblSample.FontName = cboFontsScreen.Text
```

Finally, the procedure initializes the cboFontPrinter combo box to the first item:

```
cboFontsPrinter.ListIndex = 0
```

The Code of the cboFontsScreen_Click() Procedure

The code in the cboFontsScreen_Click() procedure is executed when you select a new screen font from the cboFontsScreen combo box (the Available Screen Fonts combo box on the left):

```
Private Sub cboFontsScreen_Click()

    ' User selected a new screen font. Change the
    ' font of the label in accordance with the
    ' user's font selection.
    lblSample.FontName = cboFontsScreen.Text

End Sub
```

The procedure changes the font of the lblSample label to the font you selected.

The Code of the cmdNumberOfFonts_Click() Procedure

The cmdNumberOfFonts_Click() procedure is automatically executed when you click the Number of Fonts button:

```
Private Sub cmdNumnerOfFonts_Click()

    'Display the number of screen fonts in the
    'system.
    MsgBox "Number of Screen fonts:" + _
          Str(gNumOfScreenFonts)

    'Display the number of printer fonts in the
    ' system.
```

```
MsgBox "Number of Printer fonts:" + _
        Str(gNumOfPrinterFonts)
```
End Sub

The procedure displays the number of available screen fonts and the number of available printer fonts using the MsgBox statements. The number of available fonts is stored in the variables gNumOfScreenFonts and gNumOfPrinterFonts. These variables were updated in the Form_Load() procedure.

The Print Method

The Print method can be used to print in a form or in a picture control. To display the text Testing... in the frmMyForm form, use the following statement:

```
frmMyForm.Print "Testing..."
```

To display the text Testing... in the picMyPicture picture control, use the following statement:

```
picMyPicture.Print "Testing..."
```

The semicolon (;) is used to instruct Visual Basic to place the text on the same line. For example, use the following two statements:

```
frmMyForm.Print "This is line number 1 and ";
frmMyForm.Print "it continues..."
```

to produce this output:

```
This is line number 1 and it continues...
```

The following statement produces the same output:

```
frmMyForm.Print _
 "This is line ";"number 1";" and it continues"
```

Clearing Text

You can use the Cls method to clear text that was written in a form or in a picture control. For example, to clear the frmMyForm form, use the following:

```
frmMyForm.Cls
```

To clear the picMyPicture picture control, use the following:

```
picMyPicture.Cls
```

The Cls method clears text as well as graphics drawn with a graphics method (for example, Line. Circle).

Placing Text at a Specified Location

To place text at a specified location, update the CurrentX and CurrentY properties. For example, to place the text Testing in the frmMyForm form at column 5, row 6, use the following:

```
frmMyForm.CurrentX = 5
frmMyForm.CurrentY = 6
frmMyForm.Print "Testing"
```

Similarly, to place the text Testing in the picMyPicture picture control at column 11, row 10 use the following:

```
picMyPicture.CurrentX = 11
picMyPicture.CurrentY = 10
picMyPicture.Print "Testing"
```

The Index Program

The Index program illustrates how you can use the TextHeight and TextWidth properties to display text at any desired location. These properties are used to determine the height and width of text. For example, the height of the text AaBbCc is assigned to the variable HeightOfabc as follows:

```
HeightOfabc = frmMyForm.TextHeight("AaBbCc")
```

The returned value of the TextHeight property is given in the same units as indicated by the ScaleMode property. Imagine that the text AaBbCc is enclosed by a rectangle. The preceding statement assigns the height of the rectangle to the HeightOfabc variable. The height of the rectangle is determined by the highest character among the characters A, a, B, b, C, and c.

The TextHeight property is useful when you want to calculate the CurrentY property for a certain line. For example, suppose that you displayed nine lines. After displaying the nine lines, you want to draw a horizontal line below the ninth line. You need to calculate the y coordinate of the 10th line and assign this value to CurrentY. Here is how you calculate CurrentY in this case:

```
CurrentY = frmMyForm.TextHeight("AaBbCc")*9
```

The TextWidth property returns the width of the text. For example, to calculate the width of the text Index, use this statement:

```
WidthOfIndex = frmMyForm.TextWidth("Index")
```

Again, imagine the text Index as enclosed by a rectangle. The preceding statement updates the variable WidthOfIndex with the width of the imaginary rectangle.

The TextHeight and TextWidth properties return the height and width of the text according to the current value of the FontSize property.

The Visual Implementation of the Index Program

As usual, you start designing the program by implementing the form of the program:

☐ Create a new Standard EXE project, save the form as Index.Frm in the C:\VB5PrG\Ch10 directory, and save the project file as Index.Vbp in the C:\VB5PrgCh10 directory.

☐ Implement the frmIndex form according to Tables 10.4 and 10.5.

The completed form should look like the one shown in Figure 10.13.

Figure 10.13.

*The frmIndex form
(design mode).*

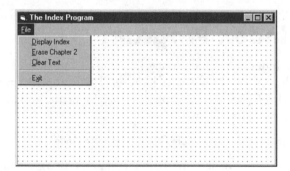

Table 10.4. The properties table of frmIndex form.

Object	Property	Setting
Form	Name	frmIndex
	BackColor	White
	Caption	The Index Program
Menu	*(See Table 10.5)*	*(See Table 10.5)*

Table 10.5. The menu table of the frmIndex form.

Caption	Name
&File	mnuFile
...&Display Index	mnuDisplayIndex
...&Erase Chapter 2	mnuEraseCh2
...&Clear Text	mnuClearText

Caption	Name
...-	mnuSep1
...E&xit	mnuExit

Entering the Code of the Index Program

You'll now enter the code of the Index program:

☐ Type the following code in the general declarations section of the frmIndex form:

```
' All variables MUST be declared.
Option Explicit
Dim gDots
```

☐ Type the following code in the Form_Load() procedure of the frmIndex form:

```
Private Sub Form_Load()

    gDots = String$(84, ".")

End Sub
```

☐ Type the following code in the mnuClear_Click() procedure of the frmIndex form:

```
Private Sub mnuClear_Click()

    ' Clear the form.
    frmIndex.Cls

End Sub
```

☐ Type the following code in the mnuDisplayIndex_Click() procedure of the frmIndex form:

```
Private Sub mnuDisplayIndex_Click()

    frmIndex.Cls

    ' Heading should be displayed 100 twips from
    ' the top.
    CurrentY = 100

    ' Place the heading at the center of the row.
    CurrentX = (frmIndex.ScaleWidth - _
               frmIndex.TextWidth("Index")) / 2
    frmIndex.FontUnderline = True

    frmIndex.Print "Index"

    ' Display the chapters.
    frmIndex.FontUnderline = False
    CurrentY = frmIndex.TextHeight("VVV") * 2
    CurrentX = 100
```

10

```
Print "Chapter 1" + gDots + "The world"
CurrentY = frmIndex.TextHeight("VVV") * 3
CurrentX = 100
Print "Chapter 2" + gDots + "The chair"
CurrentY = frmIndex.TextHeight("VVV") * 4
CurrentX = 100
Print "Chapter 3" + gDots + "The mouse"
CurrentY = frmIndex.TextHeight("VVV") * 5
CurrentX = 100
Print "Chapter 4" + gDots + "The end"

End Sub
```

☐ Type the following code in the mnuEraseCh2_Click() procedure of the frmIndex form:

```
Private Sub mnuEraseCh2_Click()

    Dim LengthOfLine
    Dim HeightOfLine

    ' Erase the line by placing a box with white
    ' background over the line.
    CurrentY = frmIndex.TextHeight("VVV") * 3
    CurrentX = 100
    LengthOfLine = frmIndex.TextWidth("Chapter 2" + _
                   gDots + "The chair")
    HeightOfLine = frmIndex.TextHeight("C")
    frmIndex.Line -Step(LengthOfLine, HeightOfLine), _
                   RGB(255, 255, 255), BF

End Sub
```

☐ Enter the following code in the mnuExit_Click() procedure of the frmIndex form:

```
Private Sub mnuExit_Click()

    End

End Sub
```

☐ Select Save Project from the File menu of Visual Basic to save your work.

Executing the Index Program

Let's see your code in action:

☐ Execute the Index program.

☐ Select Display Index from the File menu.

The program responds by displaying the index shown in Figure 10.14.

☐ Select Erase Chapter 2 from the File menu.

The program responds by erasing the Chapter 2 line (see Figure 10.15).

Figure 10.14.
Displaying the index.

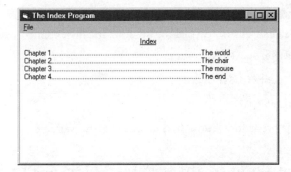

Figure 10.15.
Erasing Chapter 2.

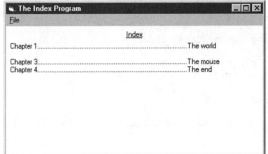

☐ Select Clear Text from the File menu.

> *The program responds by erasing the text from the form.*

☐ Select Exit from the File menu to terminate the Index program.

How the Index Program Works

The Index program displays text with the Print method. You can display the text at any location by updating the CurrentX and CurrentY properties.

The Code of the General Declarations Section

The code in the general declarations section of the frmIndex form declares the variable gDots. This variable, therefore, is visible in all the procedures of the frmIndex form.

The Code of the `Form_Load()` **Procedure**

The `Form_Load()` procedure is automatically executed when the frmIndex form is loaded:

```
Private Sub Form_Load()

    gDots = String$(84, ".")

End Sub
```

This procedure stores 84 dots in the `gDots` variable.

The Code of the `mnuClear_Click()` **Procedure**

The `mnuClear_Click()` procedure is automatically executed when you select Clear Text from the File menu:

```
Private Sub mnuClear_Click()

    ' Clear the form.
    frmIndex.Cls

End Sub
```

This procedure uses the `Cls` method to clear the form.

The Code of the `mnuDisplayIndex_Click()` **Procedure**

The `mnuDisplayIndex_Click()` procedure is automatically executed when you select Display Index from the File menu. The code of this procedure clears the text (if any) from the form and then updates CurrentY with 100:

```
frmIndex.Cls
CurrentY = 100
```

Because CurrentY is now equal to 100, text that will be displayed with the `Print` method will be displayed 100 twips from the top. Because the text `Index` should be displayed at the center of the form (refer to Figure 10.15), the CurrentX property is updated as follows:

```
CurrentX = (frmIndex.ScaleWidth - _
           frmIndex.TextWidth("Index")) / 2
```

The following procedure sets the FontUnderline property to True and uses the `Print` method to display the text `Index`:

```
frmIndex.FontUnderline = True
frmIndex.Print "Index"
```

The rest of the text is displayed as non-underlined text, so the FontUnderline property is set to False:

```
frmIndex.FontUnderline = False
```

The CurrentY property is updated for the Chapter 1 line as follows:

```
CurrentY = frmIndex.TextHeight("VVV") * 2
```

and the CurrentX property is updated to 100 twips so that the line starts 100 twips from the left of the form:

```
CurrentX = 100
```

Now that CurrentX and CurrentY are updated, the Print method is used to display the text:

```
Print "Chapter 1" + Dots + "The world"
```

The rest of the lines are displayed in a similar manner.

If you omit the name of the object before the Print method, the Print method displays text in the currently active form. Therefore, this statement:

```
frmIndex.Print "Index"
```

produces the same result as this statement:

```
Print "Index"
```

Similarly, in this procedure the CurrentX and CurrentY properties were updated without preceding these properties with the form name. When you omit the name of the object, Visual Basic updates the properties of the currently active form. For example, if the currently active form is frmIndex, the following two statements are identical:

```
frmIndex.CurrentY = 100
```

```
CurrentY = 100
```

The Code of the `mnuEraseCh2_Click()` Procedure

The mnuEraseCh2_Click() procedure is executed when you select Erase Chapter 2 from the File menu:

```
Private Sub mnuEraseCh2_Click()

    Dim LengthOfLine
    Dim HeightOfLine

    ' Erase the line by placing a box with white
    ' background over the line.
    CurrentY = frmIndex.TextHeight("VVV") * 3
    CurrentX = 100
    LengthOfLine = frmIndex.TextWidth("Chapter 2" + _
                    gDots + "The chair")
    HeightOfLine = frmIndex.TextHeight("C")
    frmIndex.Line -Step(LengthOfLine, HeightOfLine), _
                RGB(255, 255, 255), BF

End Sub
```

This procedure sets the CurrentX and CurrentY properties to the location where the Chapter 2 line starts and then draws a box with a white background. The width of the box is calculated using the TextWidth property.

Displaying Tables

You can use the Print method to display tables in a form or a picture control. Complete the following steps to see how to do this:

☐ Add the Table menu and Display Table menu item to the menu of the Index program. The new menu table is shown in Table 10.6.

Table 10.6. The menu table of the frmIndex form.

Caption	Name
&File	mnuFile
...&Display Index	mnuDisplayIndex
...&Erase Chapter 2	mnuEraseCh2
...&Clear text	mnuClear
...-	mnuSep1
...E&xit	mnuExit
&Table	mnuTable
...&Display Table	mnuDisplayTable

☐ Type the following code in the mnuDisplayTable_Click() procedure of the frmIndex form:

```
Private Sub mnuDisplayTable_Click()

    ' Clear the form.
    frmIndex.Cls
    ' Set the FontName and FontSize properties.
    frmIndex.FontName = "MS Sans Serif"
    frmIndex.FontSize = 10
    ' Display the heading.
    frmIndex.Print "Chapter", "Description", "Page"
    ' Display a blank line.
    frmIndex.Print
    ' Display the table.
    frmIndex.Print "1", "The world", "1"
    frmIndex.Print "2", "The chair", "12"
    frmIndex.Print "3", "The mouse", "42"
    frmIndex.Print "4", "The end", "100"

End Sub
```

☐ Select Save Project from the File menu of Visual Basic.

Executing the Enhanced Version of the Index Program

Let's see your code in action:

☐ Execute the enhanced version of the Index program.

☐ Select Display Table from the table menu.

The program responds by displaying the table shown in Figure 10.16.

Figure 10.16.

Displaying the table of the Index program.

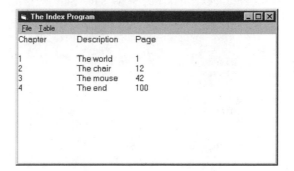

10

☐ Select Exit from the File menu to terminate the program.

The code of the mnuDisplayTable_Click() procedure uses the Print method with commas:

```
frmIndex.Print "Chapter", "Description", "Page"
```

This causes the first string ("Chapter") to be displayed starting at column 0. The second string ("Description") is displayed starting at column 14, and the third string ("Page") is displayed starting at column 28. The commas are an indication to Visual Basic to change printing zones. By default, Visual Basic defines each printing zone as 13 characters.

> **Note**
>
> To print strings that start at different printing zones, use the Print method and type commas between the strings. For example, use the following statements:
>
> ```
> Print "abc", "def", "ghj"
> Print "nop", "qrs", "tuv"
> Print "ABC", "DEF", "GHI"
> ```
>
> to produce the following output:
>
> ```
> abc     def     ghj
> nop     qrs     tuv
> ABC     DEF     GHI
> ```

Defining New Printing Zones

You can define new printing zones by using the Tab() function.

☐ Replace the code in the mnuDisplayTable_Click() procedure with the following code:

```
Private Sub mnuDisplayTable_Click()

    ' Clear the form.
    frmIndex.Cls

    ' Set the FontName and FontSize properties.
    frmIndex.FontName = "MS Sans Serif"
    frmIndex.FontSize = 10
    frmIndex.Print Tab(5); "Chapter"; Tab(20); _
            "Description"; Tab(50); "Page"

    ' Display a blank line.
    frmIndex.Print

    ' Display the table.
    frmIndex.Print Tab(5); "1"; Tab(20); _
                "The world"; Tab(50); "1"

    frmIndex.Print Tab(5); "2"; Tab(20); _
                "The chair"; Tab(50); "12"

    frmIndex.Print Tab(5); "3"; Tab(20); _
                "The mouse"; Tab(50); "42"

    frmIndex.Print Tab(5); "4"; Tab(20); _
                "The end"; Tab(50); "100"

End Sub
```

☐ Execute the Index program.

☐ Select Display Table from the Table menu.

The program responds by displaying the table, as shown in Figure 10.17.

Figure 10.17.
The window of the Index program.

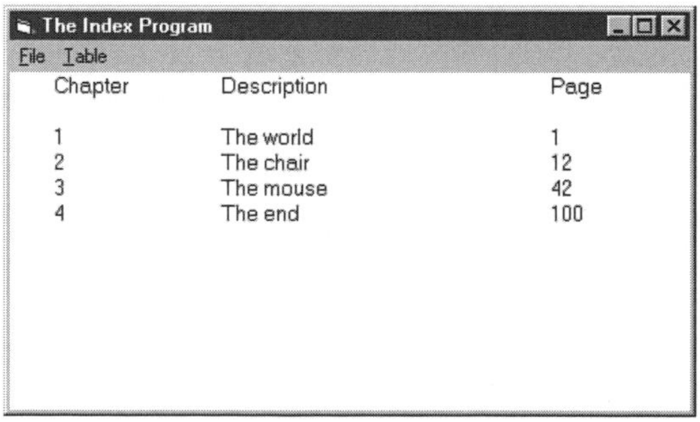

The Tab() function causes the text to be displayed at the columns indicated by the parameter of the Tab() function. For example, the following statement displays the Chapter 1 line:

```
frmIndex.Print Tab(5); "1"; Tab(20); _
           "The world"; Tab(50); "1"
```

The first parameter of the Print method is Tab(5); this sets CurrentX at column 5. The semicolon (;) instructs Visual Basic to stay on the current line.

The second parameter of the Print method is "1"; this causes the text 1 to be displayed at column 5.

The third parameter of the Print method is Tab(20); this sets CurrentX to column 20. The semicolon (;) instructs Visual Basic to stay on the same line. Therefore, the fourth parameter (the string "The world") is displayed starting at column 20.

As you can see, the Tab() function enables you to display text at any column you want.

Formatting Numbers, Dates, and Times

The Format$() function is used to display numbers, dates, and times in different ways. The next two sections explain how the Format$() function works.

Formatting Numbers

You can have control over the way Visual Basic displays numbers by using the Format$() function. The Format$() function has two parameters: the first parameter is the number to be displayed, and the second parameter serves as a format instruction. For example, to display the number 45.6 with leading and trailing zeros, use the following statement:

```
Print Format$(45.6, "000000.00")
```

This is the result:

```
000045.60
```

That is, the number 45.6 contains two digits to the left of the decimal point and one digit to the right of the decimal point. The second parameter contains 000000.00. This means there should be six digits to the left of the decimal point and two digits to the right of the decimal point. Because 45.6 has two digits to the left of the decimal point, Visual Basic inserts four leading zeros. And because 45.6 has one digit to the right of the decimal point, Visual Basic inserts one trailing zero.

10

This feature is used to display numbers in a column where the decimal points are placed one under the other as in the following:

```
000324.45
000123.40
123546.67
000004.90
132123.76
```

Formatting Dates and Times

You can use the following statement to display today's date:

```
Print Format$(Now, "m/d/yy")
```

For example, if today's date is July 4, 1997, the preceding statement produces this output:

```
7/4/97
```

The Now function is used in the first parameter of the Format$() function to supply the date, and "m/d/yy" is supplied as the format indicator to format the date to month/day/year. Note that Now is being updated according to the setting of your PC's date and time.

You can display the date in other formats. For example, use the following statement:

```
Print Format$(Now, "dddd, mmmm dd, yyyy")
```

to produce this output:

```
Sunday, April 11, 1999
```

and use the following statement:

```
Print Format$(Now, "mmmm-yy")
```

to produce this output:

```
April-99
```

The Now function can also be used to display the current time. For example, you can use this statement:

```
Print Format$(Now, "h:mm:ss a/p")
```

to produce this output:

```
4:23:00 a
```

The Print Program

The Print program demonstrates how easy it is to send data to the printer with the PrintForm method.

The Visual Implementation of the Print Program

As usual, you'll start with the visual implementation of the form of the program:

☐ Create a new Standard EXE project, save the form of the project as Print.Frm in the C:\VB5Prg\Ch10 directory, and save the project file as Print.Vbp in the C:\VB5Prg\Ch10 directory.

☐ Build the frmPrint form according to Table 10.7.

The completed form should look like the one shown in Figure 10.18.

Figure 10.18.
*The frmPrint form
(design mode).*

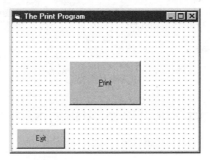

Table 10.7. The properties table of frmPrint form.

Object	Property	Setting
Form	**Name**	**frmPrint**
	BackColor	Make it white
	Caption	The Print Program
CommandButton	**Name**	**cmdExit**
	Caption	E&xit
CommandButton	**Name**	**cmdPrint**
	Caption	&Print

Entering the Code of the Print Program

You'll now enter the code of the Print program:

☐ Type the following code in the general declarations section of the frmPrint form:

```
' All variables MUST be declared.
Option Explicit
```

☐ Type the following code in the cmdExit_Click() procedure of the frmPrint form:

```
Private Sub cmdExit_Click()

    End

End Sub
```

☐ Type the following code in the cmdPrint_Click() procedure of the frmPrint form:

```
Private Sub cmdPrint_Click()

    ' Print.
    Printer.Print "Testing…1 2 3…Testing"
    Printer.EndDoc

End Sub
```

☐ Select Save Project from the File menu of Visual Basic to save your work.

Executing the Print Program

Execute the Print program:

☐ Make sure that your printer is ready to print.

☐ Execute the Print program.

☐ Click the Print button.

> *The program responds by using the printer to print this text:*

```
"Testing… 1 2 3…Testing"
```

How the Print Program Works

The Print program uses the Print method to send data to the printer. The EndDoc method sends the "start printing" command to the printer device.

The Code of the `cmdPrint_Click()` Procedure

The `cmdPrint_Click()` procedure is executed when you click the Print button:

```
Private Sub cmdPrint_Click()

    ' Print.
    Printer.Print "Testing… 1 2 3…Testing"
    Printer.EndDoc

End Sub
```

The `Print` method is used with the `Printer` object. The parameter of the `Print` method, `Testing… 1 2 3…Testing`, is printed as soon as the `EndDoc` method is executed.

Enhancing the Print Program

10

The `Print` method sends the text that appears as its parameter to the printer. Now enhance the Print program so that the Print program will print the contents of the frmPrint form:

☐ Replace the `cmdPrint_Click()` procedure with the following code:

```
Private Sub cmdPrint_Click()

    ' Print the form's contents.
    frmPrint.PrintForm
    Printer.EndDoc

End Sub
```

☐ Select Save Project from the File menu of Visual Basic to save your work.

Executing the Enhanced Version of the Print Program

Let's see your code in action:

☐ Execute the enhanced version of the Print program.

☐ Click the Print button.

The program responds by printing the form's contents.

☐ Click the Exit button to terminate the program.

The Code of the Enhanced Version of the `cmdPrint_Click()` Procedure

The `PrintForm` method sends to the printer the content of the form, pixel by pixel:

```
frmPrint.PrintForm
```

The last thing that this procedure does is execute the `EndDoc` method, causing the printer to print the data it received.

Do	Don't

DO use the `PrintForm` method to send the content of the form to the printer. For example, to send the contents of the frmMyForm to the printer, use the following statement:

```
frmMyForm.PrintForm
```

In previous versions of Visual Basic, the AutoDraw property of the form you want to print must be set to True for the `PrintForm` method to work properly.

Printing Several Pages

You can print several pages using the NewPage property. Visual Basic keeps track of the number of pages printed by updating the Page property. Use the following steps to print several pages:

☐ Replace the code in the `cmdPrint_Click()` procedure with the following code:

```
Private Sub cmdPrint_Click()

    Printer.Print "This is page number " + Str(Printer.Page)
    Printer.NewPage
    Printer.Print "This is page number " + Str(Printer.Page)
    Printer.EndDoc

End Sub
```

☐ Execute the Print program.

☐ Click the Print button.

The program responds by printing two pages. The first page is printed with This is page number 1 *and the second page is printed with* This is page number 2.

☐ Click the Exit button to terminate the program.

The `cmdPrint_Click()` *procedure prints the following string:*

```
This is page number + Printer.Page
```

The Page property contains the current page number. Because this is the first printed page, Visual Basic automatically updates this property with 1.

The procedure then declares a new page by using the `NewPage` method:

```
Printer.NewPage
```

and sends this string to the printer:

```
This is page number + Printer.Page
```

Because the value of the Page property is currently 2, the printer prints the text:

```
This is page number 2
```

10

Printing Images, Picture Controls, and Graphics

To print pictures, you can place bitmaps in image controls and picture controls and then print the form with the `PrintForm` method. In other words, whatever is placed in the form will be sent to the printer.

Printing with Better Quality

The Print program illustrates how easy it is to send data to the printer with the `Print` method (text) and the `PrintForm` method (contents of the form). Your monitor's resolution determines the best resolution that the hard copy produced by `PrintForm` can have. To get a better resolution, your program can use the `PSet`, `Line`, and `Circle` methods described next.

Generally, you draw in the `Printer` object just as you draw in a form. Therefore, you can set the CurrentX and CurrentY properties of the `Printer` object, as in this statement:

```
Printer.CurrentX = 0
Printer.CurrentY = 0
```

and you can use properties such as the following:

```
Printer.ScaleLeft
Printer.ScaleTop
Printer.Width
Printer.Height
```

To help you position text at specific locations, your program can use the TextHeight and TextWidth properties:

☐ Replace the code in the cmdPrint_Click() procedure with the following code:

```
Private Sub cmdPrint_Click()

    Printer.DrawWidth = 4
    Printer.Line (1000, 1000)-Step(1000, 1000)
    Printer.Circle (3000, 3000), 1000
    Printer.EndDoc

End Sub
```

The procedure sets the DrawWidth property of the printer to 4, draws a line and a circle, and then executes the EndDoc method. The output is shown in Figure 10.19.

As you can see, the preceding code is no different from the code that draws in a form or in a picture control.

Figure 10.19.

Drawing a line and a circle with the Printer *object.*

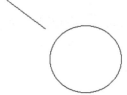

Summary

In this chapter you learned how to set text to the desired font by changing the FontName, FontSize, FontBold, FontItalic, FontStrike, FontUnderline, and FontTransparent properties.

You also learned how to extract the Screen and Printer fonts with the Fonts property, how to extract the number of available fonts with the FontCount property, and how to use the TextWidth and TextHeight properties and the Tab() function.

This chapter discusses how to send data (text and graphics) to the printer using two techniques:

■ The PrintForm method, which sends the contents of the form, pixel by pixel, to the printer.

■ The Print and graphics methods, such as:

```
Printer.Print "Abc"
Printer.Line -(1000.1000)
Circle (400,500),800
Printer.EndDoc
```

Q&A

Q I want to write a program that has the WYSIWYG capability. How can I make sure that the user chooses only those screen fonts that have corresponding printer fonts?

A The Fonts program illustrates how you can extract the screen and printer fonts using the Fonts property. To achieve WYSIWYG, you must make sure that the screen fonts you use are available for the printer. This is easily accomplished by building a list that contains the screen fonts using the Fonts property of the screen. Then build another list that contains the printer fonts by using the Fonts property of the printer. Now that you have the two lists, you can create a third list that contains only the fonts that appear in both lists. Your program should let the user choose a font from the third list only.

10

Quiz

1. When you set the FontTransparent property to True and then display text in a form with the `Print` method, which of the following happens?

    a. The text will be drawn in white.
    b. The text will not be visible.
    c. The text is displayed with the same background as the form.

2. The FontCount property is used to do which of the following?

    a. Assign a counting number to the fonts.
    b. There's no such thing.
    c. Extract the number of available fonts.

3. The Fonts property is used to do which of the following?

    a. Extract the names of available fonts.
    b. Assign a new font.
    c. Remove a font.

4. WYSIWYG means having the capability to do which of the following?

    a. Speak a foreign language.
    b. Print a hard copy that is an exact replica of the screen.
    c. No meaning, just rubbish.

5. What does the TextHeight property return?

6. What does the TextWidth property return?

7. Which of the following should you use to print the contents of a form?

   a. The Print screen key
   b. The `Print` method
   c. The `PrintForm` method

Exercise

Write a program that asks users to enter their date of birth. The program should respond by displaying the day of the week when this happy event occurred.

Quiz Answers

1. c
2. c
3. a
4. b
5. The TextHeight property returns the height of the characters specified in the parameter.
6. The TextWidth property returns the width of the characters specified in the parameter.
7. c

Exercise Answer

One possible solution is the following:

☐ Build a form with a CommandButton called Enter Birthday and a CommandButton called Find Day Of Week.

The code in the `cmdEnterBirthday_Click()` should display an input box that asks the user to enter the data. For example, the following statement can be used:

```
UserDate = InputBox("Enter date")
```

The code in the `cmdFindDayOfWeek_Click()` should include the statement

```
Print "Day of Week:", Format$(UserDate, "dddd")
```

Day 11

Interfacing with Windows

The programs you write with Visual Basic are Windows programs, so you are entitled to use the standard Windows features. In this chapter you'll learn to use two of them: the Clipboard interface and idle loops.

The Clipboard Object

Your Visual Basic programs can use the Windows Clipboard. The Clipboard is used to transfer data, which can be text or pictures.

The Clip Program

You'll now write a program called Clip, which enables you to type text in a text box and perform the standard Windows editing manipulations. The program has a standard Edit menu that you can use to copy, cut, and paste text.

The Visual Implementation of the Clip Program

As usual, you'll start with the visual implementation of the form of the program.

☐ Create the C:\VB5Prg\Ch11 directory. You'll save your work in this directory.

☐ Start a new Standard EXE project.

☐ Save the form of the project as Clip.Frm in the C:\VB5Prg\Ch11 directory and save the project file as Clip.Vbp in the C:\VB5Prg\Ch11 directory.

☐ Build the form of the Clip program according to Tables 11.1 and 11.2.

The completed form should look like the one shown in Figure 11.1.

Figure 11.1.

The frmClip form.

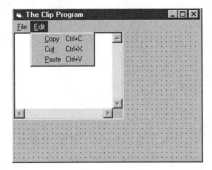

Table 11.1. The properties table of the Clip program.

Object	Property	Setting
Form	**Name**	**frmClip**
	Caption	The Clip Program
Text Box	**Name**	**txtUserArea**
	MultiLine	True
	ScrollBars	3-Both
	Text	(Make it empty)
	Left	0
	Top	0
Menu	*(See Table 11.2)*	*(See Table 11.2)*

You are instructed to set the Left and Top properties of the text box to 0. This places the upper-left corner of the Text box at the upper-left corner of the client's area. The reason for placing the text box in this manner is discussed during the course of this chapter.

Table 11.2. The menu table of the Clip program.

Caption	Name	Shortcut
&File	mnuFile	None
...E&xit	mnuExit	None
&Edit	mnuEdit	None
...&Copy	mnuCopy	Ctrl+C
...Cu&t	mnuCut	Ctrl+X
...&Paste	mnuPaste	Ctrl+V

Entering the Code of the Clip Program

You'll now enter the code of the Clip prorgam:

☐ Enter the following code in the general declarations section of the frmClip form:

```
' All variables MUST be declared.
Option Explicit
```

☐ Enter the following code in the Form_Resize() procedure:

```
Private Sub Form_Resize()

    ' Make the text box cover the entire form area.
    txtUserArea.Width = frmClip.ScaleWidth
    txtUserArea.Height = frmClip.ScaleHeight

End Sub
```

☐ Enter the following code in the mnuCopy_Click() procedure:

```
Private Sub mnuCopy_Click()

    ' Clear the clipboard.
    Clipboard.Clear
    ' Transfer to the clipboard the currently
    ' selected text of the text box.
    Clipboard.SetText txtUserArea.SelText

End Sub
```

☐ Enter the following code in the mnuCut_Click() procedure:

```
Private Sub mnuCut_Click()

    ' Clear the clipboard.
    Clipboard.Clear
    ' Transfer to the clipboard the currently
    ' selected text of the text box.
```

11

```
Clipboard.SetText txtUserArea.SelText
' Replace the currently selected text of the
' text box with null.
txtUserArea.SelText = ""
```

   End Sub

☐ Enter the following code in the `mnuPaste_Click()` procedure:

   Private Sub mnuPaste_Click()

```
' Replace the currently selected area of the
' text box with the content of the clipboard.
' If nothing is selected in the text box,
' transfer the text of the clipboard to the text
' box at the current location of the cursor.
txtUserArea.SelText = Clipboard.GetText()
```

   End Sub

☐ Enter the following code in the `mnuExit_Click()` procedure:

   Private Sub mnuExit_Click()

```
End
```

   End Sub

☐ Select Save Project from the File menu of Visual Basic to save your work.

Executing the Clip Program

Let's see your code in action:

☐ Execute the Clip program and note its many features (even though you wrote only a small amount of code).

☐ Experiment with the copy, cut, and paste operations of the program. Try to copy text from one part of the text box to another. Try to copy text to and from another Windows program. For example, try to copy text to and from Word for Windows or WordPad (WordPad is a word processing program that is shipped with Windows).

☐ Select Exit from the File menu to terminate the program.

How the Clip Program Works

The Clip program uses the `Form_Resize()` procedure to fill the entire client's area with the text box. The code in the `mnuCopy_Click()`, `mnuCut_Clip()`, and `mnuPaste_Click()` procedures performs standard editing manipulations.

The Code of the `Form_Resize()` Procedure

The `Form_Resize()` procedure is automatically executed when the form is displayed for the first time (upon starting the program) and when the size of the form changes (for example, when the user drags the edges of the program's window to change the size of the window).

Throughout the program, the text box should fill the entire client's area of the form. Therefore, the `Form_Resize()` procedure is a good place to put the code that causes the text box to cover the entire client's area. You accomplish this by changing the Width and Height properties of the ext box to the ScaleWidth and ScaleHeight properties of the form:

```
Private Sub Form_Resize()

    ' Make the text box cover the entire form area.
    txtUserArea.Width = frmClip.ScaleWidth
    txtUserArea.Height = frmClip.ScaleHeight

End Sub
```

Recall that during design time you set the Left and Top properties of the Text box to 0. So the upper-left corner of the text box is at the upper-left corner of the form. When the form is resized, the code in the `Form_Resize()` procedure is executed, and this code sets the Width and Height properties of the Text box to the width and height of the form. Thus, the text box fills the entire client's area of the form.

11

The Code of the `mnuCopy_Click()` Procedure

The `mnuCopy_Click()` procedure is executed when the user selects Copy from the Edit menu:

```
Private Sub mnuCopy_Click()

    ' Clear the clipboard.
    Clipboard.Clear
    ' Transfer to the clipboard the currently
    ' selected text of the text box.
    Clipboard.SetText txtUserArea.SelText

End Sub
```

Copy means copy the highlighted text of the text box into the Clipboard.

The first statement in this procedure clears the Clipboard:

```
Clipboard.Clear
```

Then the selected area in the text box is copied to the Clipboard:

```
Clipboard.SetText txtUserArea.SelText
```

Do	Don't

DO use the Clear method to clear the Clipboard:

```
Clipboard.Clear
```

DO copy selected text from a text box to the Clipboard by using the following:

```
Clipboard.SetText Name of text box.SelText
```

For example, to copy the highlighted (selected) text of the txtUserArea text box to the Clipboard, use the following:

```
Clipboard.SetText txtUserArea.SelText
```

The Code of the mnuCutClick() Procedure

The mnuCut_Click() procedure is executed when the user selects Cut from the Edit menu:

```
Private Sub mnuCut_Click()

    ' Clear the clipboard.
    Clipboard.Clear
    ' Transfer to the clipboard the currently
    ' selected text of the text box.
    Clipboard.SetText txtUserArea.SelText
    ' Replace the currently selected text of the
    ' text box with null.
    txtUserArea.SelText = ""

End Sub
```

Cut means copy the highlighted text to the Clipboard and delete the highlighted text.

The first statement in this procedure clears the Clipboard:

```
Clipboard.Clear
```

Then the highlighted text of the text box is copied to the Clipboard:

```
Clipboard.SetText txtUserArea.SelText
```

The last thing the procedure does is delete the currently highlighted text in the text box:

```
txtUserArea.SelText = ""
```

The Code of the mnuPaste_Click() Procedure

The mnuPaste_Click() procedure is executed when the user selects Paste from the Edit menu:

```
Private Sub mnuPaste_Click()

    ' Replace the currently selected area of the
```

```
' text box with the content of the clipboard.
' If nothing is selected in the text box,
' transfer the text of the clipboard to the text
' box at the current location of the cursor.
txtUserArea.SelText = Clipboard.GetText()
```

End Sub

Paste means replace the highlighted area of the text box with the contents of the Clipboard. If the text box doesn't have highlighted text in it, the contents of the Clipboard are inserted in the text box at the current cursor location. This is accomplished with the following statement:

```
txtUserArea.SelText = Clipboard.GetText()
```

Do	Don't

DO use the following statement to paste the contents of the Clipboard to a text box:

```
Name of text box.SelText = Clipboard.GetText()
```

For example, to paste the contents of the Clipboard to a text box called txtUserArea, use the following:

```
txtUserArea.SelText = Clipboard.GetText()
```

11

The SelLength Property

The SelLength property is defined as a Long variable, and it contains the number of characters that are currently highlighted. Although the Clip program doesn't use this property, you might find a use for it in your future Visual Basic projects.

For example, to determine the number of characters that are currently selected in the txtMyTextBox text box, use the following statement:

```
NumberOfCharacters = txtMyTextBox.SelLength
```

Transferring Pictures to and from the Clipboard: The AnyData Program

The Clip program demonstrates how to transfer text between the Clipboard and a text box. The Clipboard is also capable of accepting pictures from picture holder controls. The AnyData program illustrates this capability.

The Visual Implementation of the AnyData Program

As usual, you'll start with the visual implementation of the form of the program:

☐ Start a new Standard EXE project.

☐ Save the form of the project as AnyData.Frm in the C:\VB5Prg\Ch11 directory, and save the project file as AnyData.Vbp in the C:\VB5Prg\Ch11 directory.

☐ Build the form according to Tables 11.3 and 11.4.

The completed form should look like the one shown in Figure 11.2.

Figure 11.2.

The frmAnyData form.

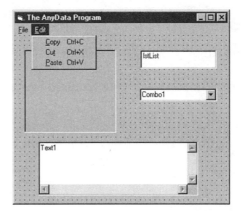

Table 11.3. The properties table of the frmAnyData Form.

Object	Property	Setting
Form	**Name**	**frmAnyData**
	Caption	The AnyData Program
PictureBox	**Name**	**picMyPicture**
ListBox	**Name**	**lstList**
ComboBox	**Name**	**cboList**
	Text	(Make it empty)
TextBox	**Name**	**txtUserArea**
	MultiLine	True
	ScrollBars	3-Both
	Text	(Make it empty)
Menu	*(See Table 11.4)*	*(See Table 11.4)*

Table 11.4. The menu table of the frmAnyData form.

Caption	Name	Shortcut
&File	mnuFile	None
...E&xit	mnuExit	None
&Edit	mnuEdit	None
...&Copy	mnuCopy	Ctrl+C
...Cu&t	mnuCut	Ctrl+X
...&Paste	mnuPaste	Ctrl+V

Entering the Code of the AnyData Program

You'll now enter the code of the AnyDate program:

☐ Type the following code in the general declarations section of the frmAnyData form:

```
' All variables must be declared.
Option Explicit
```

☐ Type the following code in the Form_Load() procedure:

```
Private Sub Form_Load()

    ' Fill three items inside the combo box.
    cboList.AddItem "Clock"
    cboList.AddItem "Cup"
    cboList.AddItem "Bell"

    ' Fill three items inside the list control.
    lstList.AddItem "One"
    lstList.AddItem "Two"
    lstList.AddItem "Three"

End Sub
```

☐ Type the following code in the picMyPicture_GotFocus() procedure:

```
Private Sub picMyPicture_GotFocus()

    ' Change the BorderStyle so that user will be
    ' able to tell that the picture control got the
    ' focus (i.e., selected).
    picMyPicture.BorderStyle = 1

End Sub
```

11

☐ Type the following code in the picMyPicture_LostFocus() procedure:

```
Private Sub picMyPicture_LostFocus()

    ' Change the BorderStyle so that user will be
    ' able to tell that the picture control lost the
    ' focus (i.e., not selected).
    picMyPicture.BorderStyle = 0

End Sub
```

☐ Type the following code in the mnuCopy_Click() procedure:

```
Private Sub mnuCopy_Click()

    ' Clear the clipboard.
    Clipboard.Clear
    ' Find which is the currently active control, and
    ' copy its highlighted content to the clipboard.
    If TypeOf Screen.ActiveControl Is TextBox Then
        Clipboard.SetText Screen.ActiveControl.SelText
    ElseIf TypeOf Screen.ActiveControl Is ComboBox Then
        Clipboard.SetText Screen.ActiveControl.Text
    ElseIf TypeOf Screen.ActiveControl Is PictureBox Then
        Clipboard.SetData Screen.ActiveControl.Picture
    ElseIf TypeOf Screen.ActiveControl Is ListBox Then
        Clipboard.SetText Screen.ActiveControl.Text
    Else
        ' Do nothing
    End If

End Sub
```

☐ Type the following code in the mnuCut_Click() procedure:

```
Private Sub mnuCut_Click()

    'Execute the mnuCopy_Click() procedure
    mnuCopy_Click
    ' Find which is the currently highlighted control,
    ' and remove its highlighted content.
    If TypeOf Screen.ActiveControl Is TextBox Then
        Screen.ActiveControl.SelText = ""
    ElseIf TypeOf Screen.ActiveControl Is ComboBox Then
        Screen.ActiveControl.Text = ""
    ElseIf TypeOf Screen.ActiveControl Is PictureBox Then
        Screen.ActiveControl.Picture = LoadPicture()
    ElseIf TypeOf Screen.ActiveControl Is ListBox Then
        If Screen.ActiveControl.ListIndex >= 0 Then
            Screen.ActiveControl.RemoveItem _
                    Screen.ActiveControl.ListIndex
        End If
    Else
        ' Do nothing
    End If

End Sub
```

☐ Type the following code in the mnuPaste_Click() procedure:

```
Private Sub mnuPaste_Click()

    ' Find which is the currently active control and
    ' paste the content of the clipboard to it.
    If TypeOf Screen.ActiveControl Is TextBox Then
        Screen.ActiveControl.SelText = Clipboard.GetText()
    ElseIf TypeOf Screen.ActiveControl Is ComboBox Then
        Screen.ActiveControl.Text = Clipboard.GetText()
    ElseIf TypeOf Screen.ActiveControl Is PictureBox Then
        Screen.ActiveControl.Picture = Clipboard.GetData()
    ElseIf TypeOf Screen.ActiveControl Is ListBox Then
        Screen.ActiveControl.AddItem Clipboard.GetText()
    Else
        ' Do nothing
    End If

End Sub
```

☐ Type the following code in the mnuExit_Click() procedure:

```
Private Sub mnuExit_Click()

    End

End Sub
```

☐ Select Save Project from the File menu of Visual Basic to save your work.

Executing the AnyData Program

Let's see your work in action:

☐ Execute the AnyData program.

The AnyData program lets you copy, cut, and paste data from and to the Clipboard. The data can be either text or pictures.

Use the following steps to copy a picture from Paint to the picture box of the AnyData program:

☐ Start Paint while AnyData is still running.

☐ Draw something in the desktop of Paint.

☐ Copy a portion of your drawing from Paint to the Clipboard by selecting it and then choosing Copy from the Edit menu of Paint. (For example, in Figure 11.3, the portion of the picture that includes the man's head was copied to the Clipboard.)

☐ Switch to the AnyData program.

☐ Make the picMyPicture picture control the active control by clicking the picture. You can tell that the picture box is selected by observing its borders. If it has a border, it is selected.

11

☐ Select Paste from the Edit menu.

The AnyData program responds by copying the picture that resides in the Clipboard into picMyPicture (see Figure 11.4).

Figure 11.3.

Using Paint to draw a picture that will be copied to the AnyData program.

Figure 11.4.

Copying a picture to the AnyData program.

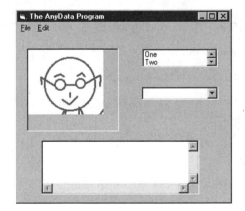

☐ The AnyData program also lets you copy, cut, and paste text to and from the text box, list box, and combo box controls of the program. Experiment with these controls for a while. You can't paste pictures into the text box, list box, or combo box, and you can't paste text in the picture box.

Before pasting data into an object, you must select the object by clicking it. You can tell which object is selected as follows:

☐ When a text box is selected, Visual Basic places a blinking cursor in it.

☐ When a combo box is selected, Visual Basic places a blinking cursor on the currently selected item.

☐ When a list box is selected, Visual Basic places a dashed rectangle around the selected item in the list box.

How the AnyData Program Works

The AnyData program uses the mnuCopy_Click(), mnuCut_Click(), and mnuPaste_Click() procedures to transfer text and pictures to or from the Clipboard.

The Code of the Form_Load() Procedure

The Form_Load() procedure is automatically executed when you start the program:

```
Private Sub Form_Load()

    ' Fill three items inside the combo box.
    cboList.AddItem "Clock"
    cboList.AddItem "Cup"
    cboList.AddItem "Bell"

    ' Fill three items inside the list control.
    lstList.AddItem "One"
    lstList.AddItem "Two"
    lstList.AddItem "Three"

End Sub
```

The code in this procedure fills three items in the combo box and three items in the list box.

The Code of the picMyPicture_GotFocus() Procedure

The picMyPicture_GotFocus() procedure is executed when the picture box gets the focus (that is, when you select the picture):

```
Private Sub picMyPicture_GotFocus()

    ' Change the BorderStyle so that user will be
    ' able to tell that the picture control got the
    ' focus (i.e., selected).
    picMyPicture.BorderStyle = 1

End Sub
```

11

When you select the picture box, Visual Basic doesn't automatically give you any visible indication that the picture box has been selected, as it does for the text box, combo box, and list box. The code you typed in the picMyPicture_GotFocus() procedure changes the BorderStyle property of the picture box so you can tell that the picture box is selected. Setting the BorderStyle property of the picture box to 1 places a border around the picture control.

The Code of the `picMyPicture_LostFocus()` Procedure

The picMyPicture_LostFocus() procedure is executed when the picture box is not selected (that is, loses the focus):

```
Private Sub picMyPicture_LostFocus()

    ' Change the BorderStyle so that user will be
    ' able to tell that the picture control lost the
    ' focus (i.e., not selected).
    picMyPicture.BorderStyle = 0

End Sub
```

The code in this procedure sets the BorderStyle property to 0, which removes the border around the picture control; this shows you that the picture box is not selected.

The Code of the `mnuCopy_Click()` Procedure

The mnuCopy_Click() procedure is executed when the user selects Copy from the Edit menu. The code in this procedure clears the Clipboard and copies the highlighted contents of the control to the Clipboard:

```
Private Sub mnuCopy_Click()

    ' Clear the clipboard.
    Clipboard.Clear
    ' Find which is the currently active control, and
    ' copy its highlighted content to the clipboard.
    If TypeOf Screen.ActiveControl Is TextBox Then
        Clipboard.SetText Screen.ActiveControl.SelText
    ElseIf TypeOf Screen.ActiveControl Is ComboBox Then
        Clipboard.SetText Screen.ActiveControl.Text
    ElseIf TypeOf Screen.ActiveControl Is PictureBox Then
        Clipboard.SetData Screen.ActiveControl.Picture
    ElseIf TypeOf Screen.ActiveControl Is ListBox Then
        Clipboard.SetText Screen.ActiveControl.Text
    Else
        ' Do nothing
    End If

End Sub
```

The Clipboard is cleared with the following statement:

```
' Clear the clipboard.
Clipboard.Clear
```

To copy the contents of the control to the Clipboard, you must first decide which control is currently active. You do this with a series of If TypeOf statements.

The first If TypeOf statement checks whether the currently active control is the text box. If this is the case, the contents of the highlighted text in the text box are copied to the Clipboard:

```
Clipboard.SetText Screen.ActiveControl.SelText
```

If the currently active control is the combo box, the highlighted text of the combo box is copied to the Clipboard:

```
Clipboard.SetText Screen.ActiveControl.Text
```

If the currently active control is the picture box, the picture in the picture box is copied to the Clipboard:

```
Clipboard.SetData Screen.ActiveControl.Picture
```

Finally, if the currently active control is the list box, the highlighted text in the list box is copied to the Clipboard:

```
Clipboard.SetText Screen.ActiveControl.Text
```

11

> **Note**
>
> The value Screen.ActiveControl represents the currently active control. During the execution of the program, the program automatically updates this variable for you. As you can see, Screen.ActiveControl is useful when you need to perform operations on the currently active control.

The Code of the mnuCut_Click() Procedure

The mnuCut_Click() procedure is executed when you select Cut from the Edit menu:

```
Private Sub mnuCut_Click()

    'Execute the mnuCopy_Click() procedure
    mnuCopy_Click
    ' Find which is the currently highlighted control,
    ' and remove its highlighted content.
    If TypeOf Screen.ActiveControl Is TextBox Then
        Screen.ActiveControl.SelText = ""
    ElseIf TypeOf Screen.ActiveControl Is ComboBox Then
        Screen.ActiveControl.Text = ""
    ElseIf TypeOf Screen.ActiveControl Is PictureBox Then
        Screen.ActiveControl.Picture = LoadPicture()
    ElseIf TypeOf Screen.ActiveControl Is ListBox Then
        If Screen.ActiveControl.ListIndex >= 0 Then
```

```
                Screen.ActiveControl.RemoveItem _
                      Screen.ActiveControl.ListIndex
        End If
    Else
          ' Do nothing
    End If
```

End Sub

Cut is defined as copying the selected data to the Clipboard and deleting the data that was copied. Therefore, the first statement in this procedure executes the mnuCopy_Click() procedure:

```
'Execute the mnuCopy_Click() procedure
mnuCopy_Click
```

To delete the data, a series of If TypeOf statements is executed. Each If TypeOf statement determines the currently active control and clears the data that was copied.

If the currently active control is the text box, the text copied from this control is cleared with the following statement:

```
Screen.ActiveControl.SelText = ""
```

Similarly, the text copied from the combo box is cleared with the following statement:

```
Screen.ActiveControl.Text = ""
```

To clear the picture box, the LoadPicture() function is used:

```
Screen.ActiveControl.Picture = LoadPicture()
```

LoadPicture() loads a picture into the picture box. The argument of LoadPicture() specifies which picture file to load. Because the preceding statement did not specify the name of the picture file to be loaded, the LoadPicture() function clears the current picture from the picture box, which is exactly what you want it to do.

If the currently active control is the list box, the copied text (which is the highlighted item in the list) is cleared with the RemoveItem statement:

```
ElseIf TypeOf Screen.ActiveControl Is ListBox Then
If Screen.ActiveControl.ListIndex >= 0 Then
Screen.ActiveControl.RemoveItem _
      Screen.ActiveControl.ListIndex
End If
```

Before removing the item, the code checks that ListIndex is greater or equal to 0. ListIndex is the currently selected item in the list, and you want to make sure that there is currently a selected item in the list box (that is, when ListIndex is equal to -1, no item is currently selected in the list box).

The Code of the `mnuPaste_Click()` Procedure

The `mnuPaste_Click()` procedure is executed when the user selects Paste from the Edit menu:

```
Private Sub mnuPaste_Click()

    ' Find which is the currently active control and
    ' paste the content of the clipboard to it.
    If TypeOf Screen.ActiveControl Is TextBox Then
        Screen.ActiveControl.SelText = Clipboard.GetText()
    ElseIf TypeOf Screen.ActiveControl Is ComboBox Then
        Screen.ActiveControl.Text = Clipboard.GetText()
    ElseIf TypeOf Screen.ActiveControl Is PictureBox Then
        Screen.ActiveControl.Picture = Clipboard.GetData()
    ElseIf TypeOf Screen.ActiveControl Is ListBox Then
        Screen.ActiveControl.AddItem Clipboard.GetText()
    Else
        ' Do nothing
    End If

End Sub
```

Like the `mnuCopy_Click()` and `mnuCut_Click()` procedures, this procedure determines the currently active control with a series of `If TypeOf` statements.

If the currently active control is the text box, the text of the Clipboard is copied into the text box:

```
Screen.ActiveControl.SelText = Clipboard.GetText()
```

If the currently active control is the combo box, the text of the Clipboard is copied into the combo box:

```
Screen.ActiveControl.Text = Clipboard.GetText()
```

If the currently active control is the picture box, the picture in the Clipboard is copied to the picture box using `GetData()`:

```
Screen.ActiveControl.Picture = Clipboard.GetData()
```

Finally, if the currently active control is the list box, the text in the Clipboard is added as a new item to the list:

```
Screen.ActiveControl.AddItem Clipboard.GetText()
```

Using `GetFormat()` to Determine the Type of Data in the Clipboard

As demonstrated, the Clipboard is capable of holding text as well as pictures. To examine what type of data the Clipboard currently holds, you can use the `GetFormat()` function.

11

For example, the following statement determines whether the data in the Clipboard is text:

```
If Clipboard.GetFormat(vbCFText) Then
... GetFormat() returned True, so indeed ...
... the clipboard holds text.          ...
End If
```

If the Clipboard currently holds text, `GetFormat(vbCFText)` returns True.

To decide whether the Clipboard currently holds a bitmap, use the following:

```
If Clipboard.GetFormat(vbCFBitmap) Then
... GetFormat() returned True, so indeed ...
... the clipboard holds bit map.        ...
End If
```

`GetFormat(vbCFBitmap)` returns True if the Clipboard currently holds a bitmap.

Idle Time

During the execution of your Visual Basic programs, there are many times when no code of your program is executed. These periods of time are called idle time. For example, suppose you write a program called the Beep program that has a Beep button in it. When you click this button, the program beeps 100 times. Until you click the button, your program is sitting idle, not executing any of your code. Once you click the button, the corresponding procedure is executed. During the execution of this procedure, your program is not in idle time any more. Upon completing the execution of the event procedure, your program is again in idle time, waiting for you to press the Beep button again (or press a different button or select a menu item).

During idle times, you are able to switch to other Windows programs. For example, in the Beep program discussed, when the program is in idle time, you can switch to another Windows program. But if you click the beep button, you cannot switch to other Windows programs while the program is beeping 100 times.

The Count Program

Now you'll write the Count program, a program that counts numbers from 1 to 999.

The Visual Implementation of the Count Program

As usual, you'll start with the visual implementation of the form of the program:

☐ Start a new Standard EXE project.

☐ Save the form of the project as Count.Frm in the C:\VB5Prg\Ch11 directory and save the project as Count.Vbp in the C:\VB5Prg\Ch11 directory.

☐ Build the form of the Count program according to the specifications in Table 11.5.

The completed form should look like the one shown in Figure 11.5.

Figure 11.5.

The frmCount form.

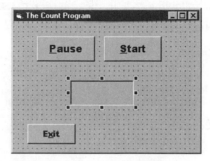

Table 11.5. The properties table of the Count program.

Object	Property	Setting
Form	Name	frmCount
	Caption	The Count Program
CommandButton	Name	cmdExit
	Caption	E&xit
CommandButton	Name	cmdPause
	Caption	&Pause
CommandButton	Name	cmdStart
	Caption	&Start
Label	Name	lblResult
	Alignment	2-Center
	BorderStyle	1-Fixed Single
	Caption	(Make it empty)

Entering the Code of the Count Program

You'll now enter the code of the Count program:

☐ Type the following code in the general declarations section of the frmCount form:

```
' All variables MUST be declared.
Option Explicit
```

☐ Type the following code in the cmdExit_Click() procedure:

```
Private Sub cmdExit_Click()

    End

End Sub
```

☐ Type the following code in the cmdStart_Click() procedure:

```
Private Sub cmdStart_Click()

    Dim Counter As Integer
    Counter = 1
    ' Count from 1 to 999
    Do While Counter < 1000
        lblResult.Caption = Str$(Counter)
        Counter = Counter + 1
    Loop

End Sub
```

☐ Select Save Project from the File menu of Visual Basic to save your work.

Note

> At this point, you are not instructed to attach any code to the cmdPause_Click() procedure.

Executing the Count Program

Let's see your code in action:

☐ Execute the Count program.

☐ Click the Start button.

> *The program seems to do nothing for a while, and then the number 999 is displayed. Depending on how fast your PC is, it may take several seconds until it displays the number 999.*

By reading the code in the cmdStart_Click() procedure, you might expect to see the program display all the numbers from 1 to 999 during the counting. To understand why the program doesn't do this, look at the statements that are supposed to display the numbers:

```
Private Sub cmdStart_Click()

    Dim Counter As Integer
    Counter = 1
    ' Count from 1 to 999
```

```
Do While Counter < 1000
    lblResult.Caption = Str$(Counter)
    Counter = Counter + 1
Loop
```

End Sub

This is the statement responsible for changing the caption of the label:

```
lblResult.Caption = Str$(Counter)
```

However, Visual Basic is able to refresh the screen (repainting the screen) only during idle time (that is, after the procedure is completed and the program returns to idle time). This is why the label doesn't display the numbers while counting is in progress.

Keep in mind that clicking the Exit button during the counting does not terminate the program because your program can recognize clicking only during idle times. Once the counting is done, your program returns to idle time and responds to the clicking on the Exit button.

Note

Your PC might be so fast that, to appreciate the previous discussion, you'll have to replace the statement

```
Do While Counter < 1000
```

in the cmdStart_Click() procedure with the statement

```
Do While Counter < 10000
```

That is, a fast computer will be able to execute the Do While loop 1,000 times in a very short time, and you will not be able to see that the loop was executed.

Modifying the Count Program

Use the following steps to modify the Count program so that the label displays each number from 1 to 999 during the counting:

☐ Add the following statement to the cmdStart_Click() procedure:

```
lblResult.Refresh
```

Now the cmdStart_Click() procedure looks like this:

Private Sub cmdStart_Click()

```
Dim Counter As Integer
```

```
Counter = 1
' Count from 1 to 999
Do While Counter < 1000
    lblResult.Caption = Str$(Counter)

    lblResult.Refresh

    Counter = Counter + 1
Loop

End Sub
```

The Refresh method causes an immediate refreshing of the screen.

Do   **Don't**

DO use the Refresh method to cause immediate paint refreshing of an object:

`object.Refresh`

For example, to refresh the lblResult object, use the following statement:

`lblResult.Refresh`

Executing the Modified Count Program

Let's see your code in action:

☐ Execute the modified version of the Count program.

Now the label displays each number from 1 to 999 during the counting. Notice that clicking the Exit button during the counting still does not terminate the program. Why? During the execution of the cmdStart_Click() procedure, your program is not in idle time (and hence the program can respond to the clicking of the Exit button).

More Enhancement to the Count Program

Now enhance the Count program so that it will respond to mouse clicking during the counting. You will need to write a procedure called Main(), which will be the first procedure executed when you start the program.

Instruct Visual Basic to execute the Main() procedure on startup as follows:

☐ Select Project1 Properties from Project menu.

Visual Basic responds by displaying the Project 1 - Project Properties dialog box.

☐ Click the General tab to display the General page in the Project Properties dialog box.

Take a look at the Startup Object ComboBox that appears in the General page. Currently, the Startup Object field is set to frmCount. However, you want the Main() procedure to be the first procedure executed when you start the Count program. Change the Startup Object field to Main() as follows:

☐ Set the Startup Object field of the Project Properties dialog box to Sub Main and then click the OK button (see Figure 11.6).

Figure 11.6.

Setting the Startup Form field to Sub Main.

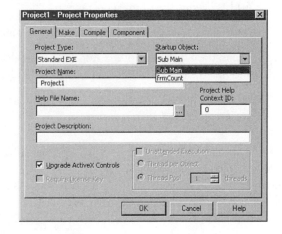

When you start the Count program, the first procedure that will be executed is Main().

Now write the Main() procedure. Visual Basic requires Main() to be in a separate module (that is, not in the frmCount form). Add a new module to the project:

☐ Select Add Module from the Project menu.

   Visual Basic responds by displaying the Add Module dialog box.

☐ Select Module icon in the New Page of the Add Module dialog box and then click the Open button.

   Visual Basic responds by adding a new module to the project window. The default name of the newly added module is Module1.bas. (Examine the project window by selecting Project Explorer from the View menu.)

Now save the newly added module as CountM.Bas:

☐ Make sure that Module1.bas is highlighted in the project window and select Save Module1 As from the File menu of Visual Basic.

   Visual Basic responds by displaying the Save File As dialog box.

☐ Save the newly added module file as CountM.Bas in the C:\VB5Prg\Ch11 directory.

Your project window should now contain the Count.Frm and CountM.Bas files.

Now add a procedure called Main() in the module CountM.Bas:

☐ Make sure CountM.Bas is highlighted in the Project window.

☐ Click the View Code icon that appears as the leftmost icon on the toolbar of the project window (because you are about to add a procedure in the CountM.Bas module).

☐ Select Add Procedure from the Tools menu.

Visual Basic responds by displaying the Add Procedure dialog box.

☐ Type Main in the Name field of the Add Procedure dialog box, make sure the Type is set to Sub and that the Scope is set to Public (see Figure 11.7), and finally click the OK button.

Visual Basic responds by adding the Main() procedure in the CountM.Bas module. The Main() procedure is shown in Figure 11.8.

Figure 11.7.

Adding the Main() *procedure to the COUNTM.BAS module.*

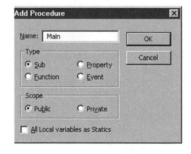

Figure 11.8.

The Main() *procedure.*

☐ Add the following code in the general declarations section of the CountM.Bas module:

```
' All variables MUST be declared.
Option Explicit
' Declare a global variable so that it is visible in
' all the procedures of all the modules and forms.
Global ggFlag As Integer
```

☐ Type the following code in the Main() procedure of the CountM.Bas module:

```
Public Sub Main()

    Dim Counter As Integer

    ' Show the form.
    frmCount.Show

    ' Count from 1 to 999, then start counting
    ' all over again.
    Do While DoEvents()
       If ggFlag = 1 Then
          Counter = Counter + 1
          frmCount.lblResult.Caption = Str$(Counter)
          If Counter = 999 Then
             Counter = 1
          End If
       End If
    Loop

End Sub
```

11

☐ Type the following code in the cmdPause_Click() procedure of the frmCount form by selecting Project Explorer from the View menu, selecting the frmCount form in the project window, clicking the View Form button, and finally double-clicking the Pause button of the frmCount form:

```
Private Sub cmdPause_Click()

    ' Set the flag to 0 to disable counting.
    ggFlag = 0

End Sub
```

☐ Change the code in the cmdStart_Click() procedure of the frmCount form so that it looks like the following:

```
Private Sub cmdStart_Click()

    ' Set the flag to 1 to enable counting.
    ggFlag = 1

End Sub
```

☐ Add the following code in the Form_Load() procedure of the frmCount form:

```
Private Sub Form_Load()

    ' Set the flag to 0 to disable counting.
    ' (You must click the Start button to start
    ' counting).
    ggFlag = 0

End Sub
```

☐ Select Save project from the File menu of Visual Basic to save your work.

Executing the Enhanced Count Program

Let's see your code in action:

☐ Execute the enhanced Count program.

   The program counts from 1 to 999 and then starts counting again. Each number is displayed in the label during counting.

☐ Click the Pause button.

   As you can see, you can click the Pause button to pause the counting!

☐ Click the Start button to continue counting.

☐ While the Count program is counting, start Paint and manipulate and resize the windows of Paint and the Count programs so that the Count form is shown with the Paint window onscreen (see Figure 11.9).

Figure 11.9.

Executing the Count program and Paint together.

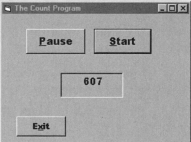

As you can see, you can draw with Paint, and the Count program continues to count.

The `Main()` Procedure

The `Main()` procedure is the first procedure that is executed when you start the program. Therefore, the first statement in this procedure is responsible for showing the frmCount form:

```
' Show the form.
frmCount.Show
```

Do	Don't

DO use the Show method as the first statement in the `Main()` procedure to show the form. Because the `Main()` procedure is the first procedure that is executed when you start the program, the form isn't loaded automatically.

The `Do While DoEvents()` loop in `Main()` is called the *idle loop*:

```
Do While DoEvents()
    If ggFlag = 1 Then
    Counter = Counter + 1
    frmCount.lblResult.Caption = Str$(Counter)
        If Counter = 999 Then
            Counter = 1
        End If
    End If
Loop
```

The logic flow diagram of the `Do While DoEvents()` loop is shown in Figure 11.10. Notice that the program stays in an endless loop.

Terminating the Endless Loop

The top block in Figure 11.10 is the `DoEvents()` block. This function returns the number of the currently open forms. If you close the frmCount form, there are no open forms in the program, and `DoEvents()` returns 0. This causes the loop to terminate, which terminates the program.

11

Figure 11.10.
The Do While
DoEvents() *loop.*

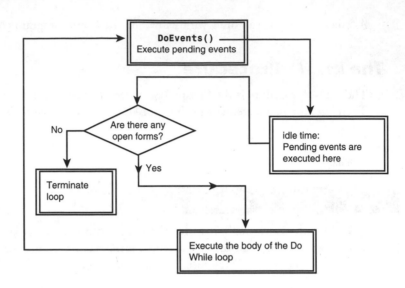

Executing the Body of the Do While DoEvents() Loop

As shown in Figure 11.10, if there is an open form, the body of the Do While DoEvents() loop is executed.

The first statement in the loop is an If statement that checks the value of ggFlag. Assuming that you already clicked the Start button, which sets the value of this flag to 1, the statements of the If block are executed, increasing the Counter variable and updating the Caption property of the lblResult label.

During the execution of the body of the Do While loop, the program is not in idle time. This means that the program can't act on certain events that occur during the execution of the body of the Do While loop. For example, if you click the Pause button during the execution of the Do While loop, the program can't respond to this event. Events that occur while the program is not in idle time are called pending events. For example, clicking the Pause button while the program executes the body of the Do While loop causes a pending event.

The Do While loop contains the following statement:

```
frmCount.lblResult.Caption = Str$(Counter)
```

This statement causes a pending event, because the Caption of the lblResult label can be refreshed only during idle time.

As shown in Figure 11.10, once the body of the Do While loop is executed, the program again executes the DoEvents() function.

The DoEvents() **Function**

To cause the program to act on the pending events, you must force the program to be in idle time; you do this by using the DoEvents() function.

The program acts on any pending events while it's in idle time. Refreshing the lblResult label is a pending event that occurred while the program executed the body of the Do While loop. If you click the Pause button during the execution of the Do While loop, the program acts on this pending event. Once the program finishes acting on the pending events, it returns to the Do While loop and the whole process starts again.

 Note

The DoEvents() function in the Do While DoEvents() loop serves two purposes:

☐ The returned value from DoEvents() is the number of currently open forms. The loop is terminated when there are no more open forms.

☐ The DoEvents() function forces the program to be in idle time so Windows can act on all pending events.

11

The Code of the General Declarations Section of the CountM.Bas Module

The code in the general declarations section of the CountM.Bas module includes the following statement:

```
' Declare a global variable that is visible in
' all procedures in all the modules and forms.
Global ggFlag As Integer
```

Declaring the ggFlag variable in the general declarations section of the CountN.Bas module means that this variable is visible by all procedures in all modules and forms. Indeed, the ggFlag variable is updated in the procedures Form_Load(), cmdStart_Click(), and cmdPause_Click() of the frmCount form and this variable is also used in the Main() procedure of the CountM.Bas module.

The Code of the cmdPause_Click() Procedure

The cmdPause_Click() procedure of the frmCount form is executed during idle time if you click the Pause button during the execution of the Do While DoEvents() loop. The code in this procedure sets the global variable ggFlag to 0 so that the counting process in the Main() procedure is disabled:

```
Private Sub cmdPause_Click()

    ' Set the flag to 0 to disable counting.
    ggFlag = 0

End Sub
```

The Code of the cmdStart_Click() Procedure

The code in the cmdStart_Click() procedure sets ggFlag to 1 to enable the counting process in the Main() procedure.

Summary

In this chapter you learned how your Visual Basic program can take advantage of the standard Windows features. You learned how to copy, cut, and paste text and pictures to and from the Clipboard; how to use the Refresh method to request an immediate refreshing of objects; and how to write code that is executed during idle time.

Q&A

Q I understand the usefulness of copy, cut, and paste as explained in this chapter. Can I use copy, cut, and paste in a slightly different way?

A You can use them any way you like. However, the programs that you write with Visual Basic are designed to work in the Windows environment. As such, your users expect the copy, cut, and paste operations to work in a certain known and acceptable manner, as described in this chapter.

Quiz

1. What does the value Screen.ActiveControl represent?

2. GetFormat() is used to do which of the following?

    a. Find the type of data that the Clipboard currently holds
    b. Format the hard drive
    c. Format the disk (floppy or hard drive)

3. What does the Refresh method do?

Exercise

As demonstrated in the AnyData program, if the Clipboard contains text, you can't paste its contents to the picture box; if the Clipboard contains a picture, you can't paste its contents to the text box, list box, or combo box.

Enhance the AnyData program so that the Paste item in the Edit menu is disabled when the paste operation doesn't make sense.

Quiz Answers

1. The currently active control.
2. a
3. It causes an immediate refreshing of the screen.

Exercise Answer

The code of the program needs to determine whether to enable/disable the paste operation. A good focal point to insert such code is in the mnuEdit_Click() procedure.

The following code enables or disables the Paste item in the Edit menu by comparing the data type of the Clipboard contents with the data type of the currently active control:

```
Private Sub mnuEdit_Click()

    ' Start by enabling the Cut and Copy menus.
    mnuCut.Enabled = True
    mnuCopy.Enabled = True

    ' Initially, disable the Paste menu.
    mnuPaste.Enabled = False

    ' Is the currently active control a text box?
    If TypeOf Screen.ActiveControl Is TextBox Then
        ' Does the clipboard hold text?
        If Clipboard.GetFormat(vbCFText) Then
            ' It is Ok to paste.
            mnuPaste.Enabled = True
        End If

    ' Is the currently active control a combo box?
    ElseIf TypeOf Screen.ActiveControl Is ComboBox Then
        ' Does the clipboard hold text?
        If Clipboard.GetFormat(vbCFText) Then
            ' It is OK to paste.
            mnuPaste.Enabled = True
        End If

    ' Is the currently active control a list box?
```

11

```
ElseIf TypeOf Screen.ActiveControl Is ListBox Then
' Does the clipboard hold text?
   If Clipboard.GetFormat(vbCFText) Then
      ' It is OK to paste.
      mnuPaste.Enabled = True
   End If

' Is the currently active control a picture box?
ElseIf TypeOf Screen.ActiveControl Is PictureBox Then
      ' Does the clipboard hold bit map?
   If Clipboard.GetFormat(vbCFBitmap) Then
      ' It is OK to paste.
      mnuPaste.Enabled = True
   End If
Else
' We checked all the valid possibilities!
' The user is trying to paste incompatible data types!
' Paste should be disabled!
' Do nothing (i.e., leave the Paste menu gray.

End If
```

End Sub

It's a good idea to include such code in your programs. If you don't, your user might try to paste text into a picture box and will not understand why the paste operation isn't working. Adding this procedure prevents your user from trying to perform paste operations that don't make sense.

Day 12

The Keyboard

In this chapter, you'll learn how your program can respond to keyboard events, how to detect whether a key was pressed or released, and how to manipulate the input data that comes from the keyboard.

The Keyboard Focus

As stated in previous chapters, the current object that has the keyboard focus is the object that responds to keyboard input. When a control has the keyboard focus, it changes its appearance in some way. For example, when a command button has the focus, a dashed rectangle appears around its caption. When a scroll bar has the focus, its thumb blinks.

The Keyboard Events

Three keyboard events correspond to keyboard activities: KeyDown, KeyUp, and KeyPress.

The KeyDown Event

The KeyDown event occurs when you press down any of the keys on the keyboard. For example, if you press a key while a command button called cmdPushMe has the focus, the cmdPushMe_KeyDown() procedure is automatically executed.

The KeyUp Event

The KeyUp event occurs when you release any of the keys on the keyboard. For example, if you release a key while a command button called cmdPushMe has the focus, the cmdPushMe_KeyUp() procedure is automatically executed.

The KeyPress Event

The KeyPress event occurs when you press a key that has a corresponding ASCII character. For example, if you press the A key while a command button called cmdPushMe has the focus, the cmdPushMe_KeyPress() procedure is executed. If you press F1, the KeyPress event does not occur because the F1 key has no corresponding ASCII character.

The Keys Program

The Keys program illustrates how the three keyboard events are used in a program.

The Visual Implementation of the Keys Program

As usual, you'll start by implementing the form of the program:

☐ Create the C:\VB5Prg\Ch12 directory. You'll save your work in this directory.

☐ Open a new Standard EXE project, save the form of the project as Keys.Frm in the C:\VB5Prg\Ch12 directory, and save the project file as Keys.Vbp in the C:\VB5Prg\Ch12 directory.

☐ Build the form of the project according to Table 12.1.

The completed form should look like the one shown in Figure 12.1.

Figure 12.1.

*The frmKeys form
(design mode).*

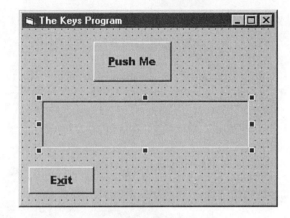

Table 12.1. The properties table of the frmKeys form.

Object	Property	Setting
Form	Name	frmKeys
	Caption	The Keys Program
Command Button	Name	cmdExit
	Caption	E&xit
Command Button	Name	cmdPushMe
	Caption	&Push Me
Label	Name	lblInfo
	Alignment	2-Center
	BorderStyle	1-Fixed Single
	Caption	(Make it empty)

12

Entering the Code of the Keys Program

You'll now enter the code of the Keys program:

☐ Type the following code in the general declarations section of the frmKeys form:

```
' All variables MUST be declared.
Option Explicit
```

☐ Type the following code in the cmdExit_Click() procedure of the frmKeys form:

```
Private Sub cmdExit_Click ()

    End
End Sub
```

☐ Type the following code in the cmdPushMe_KeyDown() procedure of the frmKeys form:

```
Private Sub cmdPushMe_KeyDown (KeyCode As Integer, _
                            Shift As Integer)

    lblInfo.Caption = "A key was pressed. KeyCode=" + _
                    Str(KeyCode) + " Shift=" + _
                    Str(Shift)

End Sub
```

☐ Select Save Project from the File menu of Visual Basic.

Executing the Keys Program

Let's see your code in action:

☐ Execute the Keys program.

☐ Click the Push Me button.

> *The Keys program responds by placing a dashed rectangle around the caption of the Push Me button, indicating that the Push Me button now has the keyboard focus (because you clicked this button in the previous step).*

☐ Make sure that the Push Me button has the focus, then press the A key.

> *The Keys program responds by displaying the ASCII code of the A key in the lblInfo label, as shown in Figure 12.2.*

Figure 12.2.

Pressing the A key.

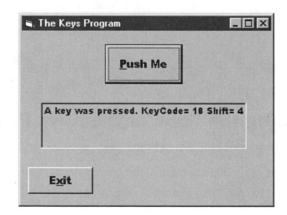

☐ Press other keys on the keyboard and notice that the lblInfo label displays the code of the key that was pressed.

☐ Press the Num Lock key and notice that the program reports that the key corresponding to the value 144 was pressed. The correlation between the displayed numbers and the pressed keys is explained later in this chapter.

☐ While holding down the Shift key, press the Ctrl key, and then press the Alt key (while holding down the Shift and Ctrl keys).

The lblInfo label reports that Shift is equal to 1, 3, and then 7. The correlation between these numbers and the Shift, Ctrl, and Alt keys is explained later in this chapter.

☐ Click the Exit button to terminate the Keys program.

How the Keys Program Works

The Keys program uses the KeyDown event to respond to keys that are pressed on the keyboard.

The Code of the cmdPushMe_KeyDown() Procedure

The cmdPushMe_KeyDown() procedure is executed when the Push Me button has the focus and you press any key on the keyboard:

```
Private Sub cmdPushMe_KeyDown (KeyCode As Integer, _
                               Shift As Integer)

  lblInfo.Caption = "A key was pressed. KeyCode=" + _
                    Str(KeyCode) + " Shift=" + _
                    Str(Shift)

End Sub
```

The cmdPushMe_KeyDown() procedure has two parameters. The first parameter, called KeyCode, is an integer that represents the pressed key. The second parameter represents the state of the Shift, Ctrl, and Alt keys.

To determine which key was pressed, you can compare the value of the first parameter (KeyCode) with Visual Basic keyboard constants. For example, if the user pressed the Num Lock key, the value of KeyCode will equal the constant vbKeyNumlock. Similarly, if the user pressed the F1 key, the value of KeyCode will equal vbKeyF1; if the user pressed the Z key, the value of KeyCode will be vbKeyZ; if the user pressed the Home key, the value of KeyCode will be vbKeyHome, and so on.

Table 12.2 lists the meanings of the values for the cmdPushMe_KeyDown() procedure's second parameter. For example, when the value of the second parameter is equal to 3, it means that both the Shift and the Ctrl keys are pressed and the Alt key is not pressed.

12

Table 12.2. The possible values of the second parameter of the `cmdPushMe_KeyDown()` procedure.

Second Parameter	Alt Status	Ctrl Status	Shift Status
0	Not pressed	Not pressed	Not pressed
1	Not pressed	Not pressed	Pressed
2	Not pressed	Pressed	Not pressed
3	Not pressed	Pressed	Pressed
4	Pressed	Not pressed	Not pressed
5	Pressed	Not pressed	Pressed
6	Pressed	Pressed	Not pressed
7	Pressed	Pressed	Pressed

The code in the `cmdPushMe_KeyDown()` procedure assigns a string representing the values of the two parameters to the Caption property of the lblInfo label:

```
lblInfo.Caption = "A key was pressed. KeyCode=" + _
                  Str(KeyCode) + " Shift=" + _
                  Str(Shift)
```

The `Str()` function is used because the Caption property is a string and the `KeyCode` and `Shift` variables are integers. `Str(KeyCode)` converts the integer `KeyCode` to a string, and `Str(Shift)` converts the integer `Shift` to a string.

Detecting a Released Key

As you have seen, you can use the two parameters of the `KeyDown` event to detect any pressed key. The `KeyUp` event has the same two parameters as the `KeyDown` event; however, the `KeyDown` event occurs when you press a key down, and the `KeyUp` event occurs when you release the key. The `KeyPress` event can also be used to detect a pressed key, but it detects only ASCII keys.

To see the `KeyUp` event in action, type the following code in the `cmdPushMe_KeyUp()` procedure of the `frmKeys` form:

```
Private Sub cmdPushMe_KeyUp (KeyCode As Integer, _
                             Shift As Integer)

  lblInfo.Caption = "A key was released. KeyCode=" + _
                    Str(KeyCode) + " Shift=" + _
                    Str(Shift)

End Sub
```

☐ Select Save Project from the File menu of Visual Basic.

☐ Execute the Keys program.

☐ Click the Push Me button.

The Keys program responds by displaying a dashed rectangle around the Push Me button, indicating that this button now has the keyboard focus.

☐ Press a key.

The Keys program responds by displaying a number corresponding to the key pressed.

☐ Release the key.

The Keys program responds by displaying the value of the released key.

☐ Click the Exit button to terminate the Keys program.

The cmdPushMe_KeyUp() procedure has the same parameters as the cmdPushMe_KeyDown() procedure, but cmdPushMe_KeyDown()'s parameters report which key was pressed down, and cmdPushMe_KeyUp()'s parameters report which key was released.

Detecting an ASCII Key

To detect that the user pressed an ASCII key, you can use the KeyPress event. To see the KeyPress event in action, follow these steps:

☐ Type the following code in the cmdPushMe_KeyPress() procedure of the frmKeys form:

```
Private Sub cmdPushMe_KeyPress (KeyAscii As Integer)

   Dim Char

   Char = Chr(KeyAscii)

   lblInfo.Caption = "KeyAscii ="  + _
                     Str(KeyAscii) + _
                     " Char=" + Char

End Sub
```

☐ Comment out the code in the cmdPushMe_KeyDown() procedure (that is, type an apostrophe at the beginning of the statements in the cmdPushMe_KeyDown() procedure).

☐ Execute the Keys program.

☐ Click the Push Me button.

The Keys program responds by displaying a dashed rectangle around the Push Me button, indicating that this button now has the keyboard focus.

12

☐ Press the A key and keep holding it down.

The Keys program responds to the pressing of the A key by displaying the ASCII value of the key, which is 97 for lowercase a or 65 for uppercase A.

☐ Press F1 and keep holding it down.

The Keys program does not display any value in the lblInfo label because F1 does not have an ASCII code, so the KeyPress event doesn't occur when you press the F1 key.

☐ Click the Exit button to terminate the Keys program.

The Code of the cmdPushMe_KeyPress() Procedure

The cmdPushMe_KeyPress() procedure is executed when you press an ASCII key. This procedure has one parameter, which represents the ASCII value of the pressed key.

The Chr() function converts the integer KeyAscii to a character:

```
Char = Chr(KeyAscii)
```

Now the variable Char holds the character of the key that was pressed. For example, if the user pressed the Z key, now Char holds the character Z. The last statement in the cmdPushMe_KeyPress() procedure assigns a string to the Caption property of the lblInfo label:

```
lblInfo.Caption = "KeyAscii ="  + _
                  Str(KeyAscii) + _
                  " Char=" + Char
```

Therefore, the user sees the character that was typed, as well as the ASCII value of the character.

Intercepting Keys with the Form_KeyPress() Procedure

A form can have the keyboard focus if there are no controls in it or if its controls are disabled. However, in most programs, a form does have some enabled controls in it, so the Form_KeyDown(), Form_KeyUp(), and Form_KeyPress() procedures are not executed.

To force the execution of these procedures even when the form does not have the keyboard focus, set the KeyPreview property of the form to True. To see the effect of the KeyPreview property, follow these steps:

☐ Set the KeyPreview property of the frmKeys form to True.

☐ Comment out the code in the cmdPushMe_KeyDown(), cmdPushMe_KeyUp(), and cmdPushMe_KeyPress() procedures.

☐ Enter the following code in the Form_KeyPress() procedure:

```
Private Sub Form_KeyPress (KeyAscii As Integer)

    Dim Char

    Char = Chr(KeyAscii)

    lblInfo.Caption = "KeyAscii =" + _
                       Str(KeyAscii) + _
                       " Char=" + Char

End Sub
```

☐ Save your work.

☐ Execute the Keys program.

☐ Press any ASCII key and note that the lblInfo label displays the pressed key no matter which control has the keyboard focus. (That's because earlier you set the KeyPreview property of the frmKeys form to True.)

In a similar way, you can use the Form_KeyDown() procedure and the Form_KeyUp() procedure to trap pressed keys, even if the form doesn't have the keyboard focus. However, don't forget to set the KeyPreview property of the form to True.

The KeyPreview property enables the program to preview (or trap) the keyboard events. This enables you to write code that responds to key pressing regardless of which control has the keyboard focus.

12

The Upper Program

The Upper program illustrates how your program can trap ASCII keys.

The Visual Implementation of the Upper Program

You'll now implement the form of the program:

☐ Open a new Standard EXE project, save the form of the project as Upper.Frm in the C:\VB5Prg\Ch12 directory, and save the project file as Upper.Vbp in the C:\VB5Prg\Ch12 directory.

☐ Build the frmUpper form according to Table 12.3.

The completed form should look like the one shown in Figure 12.3.

Table 12.3. The properties table of the frmUpper form.

Object	Property	Setting
Form	Name	frmUpper
	Caption	The Upper Program
Text Box	Name	txtUserArea
	ScrollBars	3-Both
	Text	(empty)
Command Button	Name	cmdExit
	Caption	E&xit

Figure 12.3.

The frmUpper form.

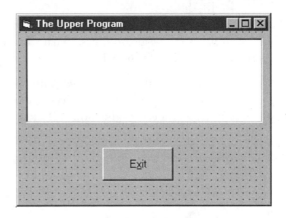

Entering the Code of the Upper Program

You'll now enter the code of the Upper program:

☐ Enter the following code in the general declarations section of the frmUpper form:

```
' All variables MUST be declared.
Option Explicit
```

☐ Enter the following code in the cmdExit_Click() procedure of the frmUpper form:

```
Private Sub cmdExit_Click ()

    End

End Sub
```

Executing the Upper Program

Let's see your code in action:

☐ Execute the Upper program.

☐ Type something in the text box.

☐ Try to press the Enter key to move to the next line.

> *As you can see, the Upper program refuses to move to the next line in the text box because the MultiLine property of the txtUserArea text box is currently set to False. Note that every time you press Enter, the PC beeps, alerting you that you pressed an illegal key.*

☐ Click the Exit button to exit the program.

Trapping the Enter Key

As demonstrated, the PC beeps when you press an illegal key. You can trap the event and fool the Upper program as follows:

☐ Enter the following code in the txtUserArea_KeyPress() procedure of the frmUpper form:

```
Private Sub txtUserArea_KeyPress (KeyAscii As Integer)

    ' If the user pressed the Return key (the Enter key),
    ' change the value of KeyAscii to 0 (null character).
    If KeyAscii = vbKeyReturn Then
       KeyAscii = 0
    End If

End Sub
```

☐ Execute the Upper program.

☐ Type something in the text box.

☐ Press Enter.

> *As you can see, the text box does not let you move to the next line, but the PC doesn't beep when you press Enter.*

☐ Terminate the Upper program by clicking the Exit button.

The Code in the txtUserArea_KeyPress() Procedure

The txtUserArea_KeyPress() procedure is executed when you press an ASCII key. The code in this procedure checks whether you pressed the Return key (the Enter key). If you pressed

12

the Enter key, the code in this procedure changes the value of the KeyAscii parameter to 0 (the null character). Therefore, the txtUserArea text box "thinks" you pressed the 0 (null) key. This is why the PC doesn't beep when you press Enter.

The code in the txtUserArea_KeyPress() procedure demonstrates that this procedure is executed before the text box has a chance to process the pressed key.

Modifying the Upper Program

Modify the Upper program as follows:

☐ Change the MultiLine property of the txtUserArea text box to True.

☐ Execute the Upper program.

☐ Type something in the text box and press Enter.

> *As you can see, the text box does not let you move to the next line because the Enter key is blocked by the code in the txtUserArea_KeyPress() procedure. That is, when you press the Enter key, the code you wrote in the txtUserArea_KeyPress() procedure changes the value of the KeyAscii parameter to 0, which makes the text box think you didn't press a key.*

☐ Click the Exit button to terminate the Upper program.

Converting ASCII Characters to Uppercase

In some programs, you may want the text that the user types to appear in uppercase or lowercase only. To see how you accomplish this, change the code in the txtUserArea_KeyPress() procedure so that it looks like the following:

```
Private Sub txtUserArea_KeyPress (KeyAscii As Integer)

    Dim Char

    Char = Chr(KeyAscii)
    KeyAscii = Asc(UCase(Char))

End Sub
```

☐ Execute the Upper program.

☐ Type something in the text box.

> *As you can see, whatever you type appears in uppercase letters regardless of the status of the Shift or Caps Lock keys.*

☐ Click the Exit button to terminate the Upper program.

The code in the txtUserArea_KeyPress() procedure uses the Chr() function to convert the pressed key to a character:

```
Char = Chr(KeyAscii)
```

Then the character is converted to uppercase using the UCase() function, which returns the uppercase character of its parameter. For example, the returned value of UCase("a") is A, and the returned value of UCase("A") is also A.

The txtUserArea_KeyPress() procedure converts the returned value of UCase() to an integer using the Asc() function:

```
KeyAscii = Asc( UCase(Char) )
```

The Asc() function returns an integer that represents the ASCII value of its parameter.

The parameter of the txtUserArea_KeyPress() procedure contains an integer that represents the ASCII value of the pressed key. This integer is converted to a character, the character is converted to uppercase, and the ASCII value of the uppercase character is assigned to the KeyAscii parameter. Therefore, the text box thinks the user pressed an uppercase key.

The Cancel Property

The Cancel property is used to provide a response to pressing the Esc key. To see the Cancel property in action, follow these steps:

☐ Execute the Upper program.

☐ Press the Esc key.

> As you can see, no matter what has the keyboard focus, the Upper program does not respond to the Esc key.

☐ Click the Exit button to exit the Upper program.

☐ Change the Cancel property of the Exit button to True.

☐ Execute the Upper program.

☐ Press the Esc key on your keyboard.

> No matter which control has the focus, the program responds to the Esc key as if the Exit key was pressed. This is because you set the Cancel property of the Exit button to True.

In a similar manner, if you set the Default property of the Exit button to True, the program responds to pressing the Enter key the same way it responds to clicking the Exit button, regardless of which control has the focus.

12

The Tab Program

Windows programs let you move from control to control by pressing the Tab key (that is, moving the keyboard focus from control to control by pressing Tab). Pressing Shift+Tab moves the keyboard focus in the reverse order. The Tab program illustrates how the Tab order works.

☐ Start a new Standard EXE project, save the form of the project as Tab.Frm in the C:\VB5Prg\Ch12 directory, and save the project file as Tab.Vbp in the C:\VB5Prg\Ch12 directory.

☐ Implement the frmTab form according to Table 12.4.

The completed form should look like the one shown in Figure 12.4.

Table 12.4. The properties table of the frmTab form.

Object	Property	Setting
Form	**Name**	**frmTab**
	Caption	The Tab Program
Command Button	**Name**	**Command1**
	Caption	Command1
	TabIndex	0
Command Button	**Name**	**Command2**
	Caption	Command2
	TabIndex	1
Command Button	**Name**	**Command3**
	Caption	Command3
	TabIndex	2
Command Button	**Name**	**Command4**
	Caption	Command4
	TabIndex	3
Command Button	**Name**	**Command5**
	Caption	Command5
	TabIndex	4

Object	Property	Setting
Command Button	**Name**	**Command6**
	Caption	Command6
	TabIndex	5
Command Button	**Name**	**Command7**
	Caption	Command7
	TabIndex	6
Command Button	**Name**	**Command8**
	Caption	Command8
	TabIndex	7
Command Button	**Name**	**Command9**
	Caption	Command9
	TabIndex	8
Command Button	**Name**	**Command10**
	Caption	Command10
	TabIndex	9
Command Button	**Name**	**cmdExit**
	Caption	E&xit
	TabIndex	10
Check Box	**Name**	**Check1**
	Caption	Check1
	TabIndex	11
Check Box	**Name**	**Check2**
	Caption	Check2
	TabIndex	12
Check Box	**Name**	**Check3**
	Caption	Check3
	TabIndex	13
Horizontal Scroll Bar	**Name**	**HScroll1**
	Max	50
	TabIndex	14

12

Figure 12.4.
The frmTab form.

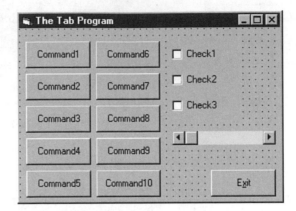

Entering the Code of the Tab Program

You'll now enter the code of the Tab program:

☐ Type the following code in the general declarations section of the frmTab form:

```
' All variables MUST be declared.
Option Explicit
```

☐ Type the following code in the cmdExit_Click() procedure of the frmTab form:

```
Private Sub cmdExit_Click ()

    End

End Sub
```

Executing the Tab Program

Experiment with the Tab program as follows:

☐ Execute the Tab program.

☐ Move the focus from one control to another by pressing the Tab key or the arrow keys. Note that when the scroll bar has the focus, the left- and right-arrow keys are used for changing the thumb's position on the scroll bar.

☐ Click the Exit button to terminate the program.

The TabIndex Property

The TabIndex property determines the order in which controls receive the keyboard focus. For example, if the keyboard focus is currently on a control that has its TabIndex property set to 5, pressing Tab moves the keyboard focus to the control that has its TabIndex set to 6. If the keyboard focus is currently on a control that has its TabIndex property set to 5, pressing Shift+Tab moves the keyboard focus back to the control that has its TabIndex set to 4.

The Tab order works in a circular manner: if the control that currently has the keyboard focus is the control with the highest TabIndex value, pressing Tab moves the keyboard focus to the control that has its TabIndex property set to 0. Similarly, if the control that currently has the keyboard focus is the control that has its TabIndex property set to 0, pressing Shift+Tab moves the keyboard focus to the control with the highest TabIndex. Some controls, such as a label control, cannot accept the keyboard focus.

Visual Basic sets the TabIndex property with sequential numbers. That is, the TabIndex property of the first control placed in the form is set to 0, the TabProperty of the second control placed in the form is set to 1, and so on. However, you can change the value of the TabIndex property so that the Tab order is appropriate to your program.

The Focus Program

The Focus program demonstrates how your program can detect when a control gets or loses the keyboard focus.

12

The Visual Implementation of the Focus Program

As usual, you'll start with the visual implementation of the program's form:

☐ Start a new Standard EXE project, save the form of the project as Focus.Frm in the C:\VB5Prg\Ch12 directory, and save the project file as Focus.Vbp in the C:\VB5Prg\Ch12 directory.

☐ Build the frmFocus form according to Table 12.5.

The completed form should look like the one shown in Figure 12.5.

Table 12.5. The properties table of the frmFocus form.

Object	Property	Setting
Form	**Name**	**frmFocus**
	Caption	The Focus Program
Command Button	**Name**	**cmdExit**
	Caption	E&xit
Text Box	**Name**	**txtUserArea**
	MultiLine	True
	Text	(empty)
Command Button	**Name**	**cmdLoad**
	Caption	&Load
Command Button	**Name**	**cmdSave**
	Caption	&Save
Label	**Name**	**lblInfo**
	Alignment	2-Center
	BorderStyle	1-Fixed Single
Label	**Name**	**lblTitle**
	Caption	Lost or Got the Focus?

Figure 12.5.

The frmFocus form.

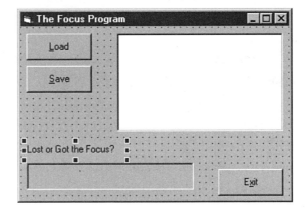

Entering the Code of the Focus Program

You'll now enter the code of the Focus program:

☐ Enter the following code in the general declarations section of the frmFocus form:

```
' All variables must be declared.
Option Explicit
```

☐ Enter the following code in the cmdExit_Click() procedure of the frmFocus form:

```
Private Sub cmdExit_Click ()

   End

End Sub
```

☐ Enter the following code in the txtUserArea_GotFocus() procedure of the frmFocus form:

```
Private Sub txtUserArea_GotFocus ()

   lblInfo.Caption = "txtUserArea got the focus"

End Sub
```

☐ Enter the following code in the txtUserArea_LostFocus() procedure of the frmFocus form:

```
Private Sub txtUserArea_LostFocus ()

   lblInfo.Caption = "txtUserArea lost the focus"

End Sub
```

Executing the Focus Program

Experiment with the Focus program as follows:

☐ Execute the Focus program.

☐ Move the keyboard focus to the textUserArea text box by clicking in the text box or using the Tab key or arrow keys.

When you move the focus to the text box, the lblInfo label displays the following message:

```
txtUserArea got the focus
```

12

☐ Move the keyboard focus away from the txtUserArea text box by clicking the Save or Load buttons or using the Tab or arrow keys.

When you move the focus away from the text box, the lblInfo label displays the following message:

```
txtUserArea lost the focus
```

☐ Exit the program by clicking the Exit button.

How the Focus Program Works

The Focus program uses the GotFocus and LostFocus events to detect whether the text box got or lost the keyboard focus.

The Code in the txtUserArea_GotFocus() Procedure

The txtUserArea_GotFocus() procedure is executed when you move the focus to the text box:

```
Private Sub txtUserArea_GotFocus ()

  lblInfo.Caption = "txtUserArea got the focus"

End Sub
```

This procedure sets the Caption property of the lblInfo label to a string indicating that the text box got the focus.

The Code in the txtUserArea_LostFocus() Procedure

The txtUserArea_LostFocus() procedure is executed when you move the focus away from the text box:

```
Private Sub txtUserArea_LostFocus ()

  lblInfo.Caption = "txtUserArea lost the focus"

End Sub
```

This procedure sets the Caption property of the lblInfo label to a string indicating that the text box lost the focus.

Summary

In this chapter, you learned how to determine which key was pressed, using the KeyDown, KeyUp, and KeyPress events. You learned that when the KeyPreview property of a form is set to True, the Form_KeyDown(), Form_KeyUp(), and Form_KeyPress() procedures are executed no matter which control in the form has the focus.

You have also learned that the Tab order is determined by the TabIndex property and that the GotFocus and LostFocus events occur when a control loses or gets the keyboard focus.

Q&A

Q Which event should I use to trap key pressing: KeyDown or KeyPress?

A If your code is written to trap ASCII keys, you should use the KeyPress event, because this event occurs only when an ASCII key is pressed. If your code is written to trap any key (ASCII or non-ASCII), you need to use the KeyDown event.

Quiz

1. The KeyPress event occurs when you do what?
2. The KeyDown event occurs when you do what?
3. The KeyUp event occurs when you do what?
4. What happens once the KeyPreview property of a form is set to True?

Exercises

1. Change the Upper program so that when you press a or A on the keyboard, the text box thinks you pressed the b or B keys.
2. Add code to the Tab program so it is terminated when you press Shift+Alt+F1.

12

Quiz Answers

1. When you press an ASCII key on the keyboard.
2. When you press any key on the keyboard.
3. When you release a key.
4. Once the KeyPreview property of a form is set to True, the various keyboard event procedures of the form, such as Form_KeyDown(), Form_KeyUp(), and Form_KeyPress(), are executed (no matter which control in the form has the focus).

Exercise Answers

1. The solution to this exercise is as follows:

   ☐ Enter the following code in the txtUserArea_KeyPress() procedure of the frmUpper form:

   ```
   Private Sub txtUserArea_KeyPress (KeyAscii As Integer)

        If KeyAscii = Asc("a") Then
           KeyAscii = Asc("b")
        End If

        If KeyAscii = Asc("A") Then
           KeyAscii = Asc("B")
        End If

   End Sub
   ```

   ☐ Save the project.

   ☐ Execute the Upper program.

   ☐ Type the word Alabama in the text box.

   The text that you'll see in the text box is B1bbbmb. (Each A is replaced with B, and each a is replaced with b.)

   ☐ Click the Exit button to terminate the program.

   The first If statement checks whether the pressed key is the A key, and if so, it changes the KeyAscii value to the ASCII value of B. Similarly, the second If statement checks whether the pressed key is the a key. If it is, the value of KeyAscii is changed to the ASCII value of b.

2. The solution to this exercise is as follows:

   ☐ Set the KeyPreview property of the frmTab form to True.

   ☐ Enter the following code in the Form_KeyDown() procedure:

   ```
   Private Sub Form_KeyDown (KeyCode As Integer, _
                             Shift As Integer)

        If Shift = 5 And KeyCode = vbKeyF1 Then
           End
        End If

   End Sub
   ```

   ☐ Save the project.

☐ Execute the Tab program.

☐ Press Shift+Alt+F1 to terminate the program.

The `Form_KeyDown()` procedure is executed when you press down a key.

The `If` condition in the following code is satisfied when you press the Shift, Alt, and F1 keys simultaneously:

```
If Shift = 5 And KeyCode = vbKeyF1 Then
```

That is, when `Shift` is equal to 5, it means that the Shift key and the Alt key are currently pressed (refer to Table 12.2); when `KeyCode` is equal to `vbKeyF1`, the F1 key is pressed. The `End` statement under the `If` condition terminates the program.

12

Week 2

Day 13

File-System Controls

This chapter focuses on using file-system controls to write a program that lets you select a file from a drive. There are three file-system controls: the Drive list box, the Directory list box, and the File list box.

In a typical program that allows you to select files from drives, these three controls are used in combination. When you need to select a file, a dialog box including the three controls is displayed onscreen (see Figure 13.1). You can then select the desired file by selecting a drive from the Drive list box, a directory from the Directory list box, and a file from the File list box.

Figure 13.1.

The three file-system controls.

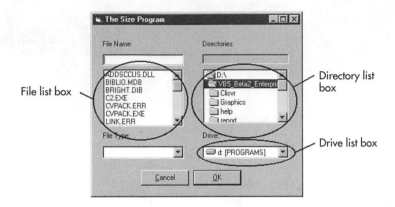

File list box

Directory list box

Drive list box

Note

In Chapter 6, "Dialog Boxes," you learned how to use the Common Dialog control to display an Open File dialog box and a Save As dialog box. As you know from Chapter 6, incorporating the Common Dialog control in your programs is very easy and convenient.

So why should you learn how to use the file-system controls? As you'll see in this chapter, they give more control over how the dialog box that displays the directories and files looks and performs.

The Size Program

You'll now write a program called Size that includes the three file-system controls in it. You can use it to select a file from a drive and display the size of the selected file.

The Size program should do the following:

■ When you start the program, a file selection form is displayed onscreen, as shown in Figure 13.2. As you also can see in Figure 13.2, the Size program's window also includes a combo box, called File Type, below the File list box. This combo box lets you select a file type from a list.

■ When you select a drive from the Drive list box, the Directory list box displays that drive's directories.

■ When you select a directory from the Directory list box, the File list box displays that directory's files.

■ When you select a file from the File list box, the selected filename is displayed in the File Name text box.

Figure 13.2.

The Size program.

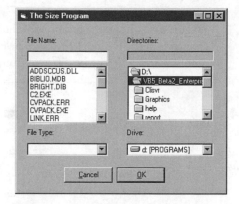

- When you click the OK button, the size of the selected file is displayed (see Figure 13.3).

Figure 13.3.

Displaying the size of the selected file.

- When you click the Cancel button, the program terminates.
- When you select a file type from the File Type combo box, the File list box displays only files of the type you selected. For example, if you select Text files (*.TXT), only files with the extension TXT are displayed in the File list box.

The Visual Implementation of the Size Program

As usual, you'll start with the implementation of the form of the program:

☐ Create the C:\VB5Prg\Ch13 directory. You'll save your work in this directory.

☐ Start a new Standard EXE project.

☐ Save the form of the project as Sise.Frm in the C:\VB5Prg\Ch13 directory and save the project file as Size.Vbp in the C:\VB5Prg\Ch13 directory.

☐ Build the form according to Table 13.1.

The completed form should look like the one shown in Figure 13.2.

13

Note

Figure 13.4 shows the locations of the icons of the three file-system controls in the toolbox window. The exact locations of the icons in your toolbox window may be different from those shown in Figure 13.4.

Figure 13.4.

The icons of the file-system controls in the toolbox window.

Table 13.1. The properties table of the Size program.

Object	Property	Value
Form	**Name**	**frmSize**
	Caption	The Size Program
Label	**Name**	**lblFileName**
	Caption	File Name:
Text Box	**Name**	**txtFileName**
	Text	(Make it empty)
File List Box	**Name**	**filFiles**
Label	**Name**	**lblFileType**
	Caption	File Type:
Combo Box	**Name**	**cboFileType**
	Style	2-Dropdown List
Label	**Name**	**lblDirectories**
	Caption	Directories:
Label	**Name**	**lblDirName**
	Caption	(empty)
	BorderStyle	1-Fixed Single
Directory List Box	**Name**	**dirDirectory**

Object	Property	Value
Command Button	**Name**	**cmdOK**
	Caption	&OK
	Default	True
Label	**Name**	**lblDrive**
	Caption	Drive:
Drive List Box	**Name**	**drvDrive**
Command Button	**Name**	**cmdCancel**
	Caption	&Cancel
	Cancel	True

Entering the Code of the Size Program

You'll now enter the code of the Size program:

☐ Enter the following code in the general declarations section of the frmSize form:

```
' All variables MUST be declared.
Option Explicit
```

☐ Type the following code in the Form_Load() procedure:

```
Private Sub Form_Load ()

    ' Fill the cboFileType combo box.
    cboFileType.AddItem "All files (*.*)"
    cboFileType.AddItem "Text files (*.TXT)"
    cboFileType.AddItem "Doc files (*.DOC)"

    ' Initialize the cboFileType combo box to
    ' item #0. (i.e. All files *.*)
    cboFileType.ListIndex = 0

    ' Update the lblDirName label with the path.
    lblDirName.Caption = dirDirectory.Path

End Sub
```

☐ Type the following code in the drvDrive_Change() procedure:

```
Private Sub drvDrive_Change ()

    ' The next statement may cause an error so we
    ' set an error trap.
    On Error GoTo DriveError

    ' Change the path of the directory list box to
```

13

```
                          ' the new drive.
                          dirDirectory.Path = drvDrive.Drive
                          Exit Sub

                  DriveError:
                          ' An error occurred! So tell the user and
                          ' restore the original drive.
                          MsgBox "Drive error!", vbExclamation, "Error"
                          drvDrive.Drive = dirDirectory.Path
                          Exit Sub

                  End Sub
```

☐ Type the following code in the dirDirectory_Change() procedure:

```
  Private Sub dirDirectory_Change ()

          ' A directory was just selected by the user so
          ' update the path of the file list box
          ' accordingly.
          filFiles.Path = dirDirectory.Path

          ' Also update the lblDirName label.
          lblDirName.Caption = dirDirectory.Path

  End Sub
```

☐ Type the following code in the cboFileType_Click() procedure:

```
  Private Sub cboFileType_Click ()

          ' Change the Pattern of the file list box
          ' according to the File Type that the user
          ' selected.
          Select Case cboFileType.ListIndex
          Case 0
              filFiles.Pattern = "*.*"
          Case 1
              filFiles.Pattern = "*.TXT"
          Case 2
              filFiles.Pattern = "*.DOC"
          End Select

  End Sub
```

☐ Type the following code in the filFiles_Click() procedure:

```
  Private Sub filFiles_Click ()

          ' Update the txtFileName text box with the file
          ' name that was just selected.
          txtFileName.Text = filFiles.FileName

  End Sub
```

☐ Type the following code in the cmdOK_Click() procedure:

```
Private Sub cmdOK_Click ()

Dim PathAndName As String
Dim FileSize As String
Dim Path As String

' If no file is selected, tell the user and
' exit this procedure.
If txtFileName.Text = "" Then
    MsgBox "You must first select a file!"
    Exit Sub
End If

'Make sure that Path ends with backslash (\).
If Right(filFiles.Path, 1) <> "\" Then
    Path = filFiles.Path + "\"
Else
    Path = filFiles.Path
End If

'Extract the Path and Name of the selected file.
If txtFileName.Text = filFiles.FileName Then
    PathAndName = Path + filFiles.FileName
Else
    PathAndName = txtFileName.Text
End If

' The next statement may cause an error so we
' set an error trap.
On Error GoTo FileLenError

'Get the file size of the file.
FileSize = Str(FileLen(PathAndName))

'Display the size of the file.
MsgBox "Size of "+PathAndName+": "+FileSize+" bytes"
Exit Sub

FileLenError:
' There was an error, so display error message
' and exit.
MsgBox "Cannot find size of " + PathAndName
Exit Sub

End Sub
```

☐ Type the following code in the filFiles_DblClick() procedure:

```
Private Sub filFiles_DblClick ()

' Update the txtFileName text box with the file
' name that was just double clicked.
txtFileName.Text = filFiles.FileName
```

13

```
'Execute the cmdOK_Click() procedure.
cmdOK_Click
```

End Sub

☐ Type the following code in the cmdCancel() procedure:

```
Private Sub cmdCancel_Click ()

    End

End Sub
```

☐ Select Save Project from the File menu of Visual Basic.

Executing the Size Program

Let's execute the Size program:

☐ Execute the Size program and experiment with the various controls that appear onscreen.

While you run the program, notice the following features:

■ As soon as you select a drive from the Drive list box, its directories appear in the Directory list box.

■ If you choose a drive that is not ready, an error message appears and the Drive list box is restored to its original value. For example, if the Drive list box currently displays the C: drive and you try to change it to the A: drive while there is no disk in the A: drive, an error message appears and the Drive list box is restored to its original value (C:).

■ To select a directory from the Directory list box, you need to double-click the desired directory.

■ As soon as you select a directory from the Directory list box, its files appear in the File list box and the directory name appears above the Directory list box.

■ As soon as you highlight a file in the File list box, its filename is displayed in the File Name text box.

■ After you select a file type from the File Type combo box, the File list box displays only files of the type you selected. You cannot type in the text area of the combo box because the Style property of the combo box was set to Dropdown list at design time.

■ When you click the OK button, a message appears that displays the file size of the selected file.

■ Instead of selecting a file from the File list box, you can type its filename in the File Name text box.

- Pressing Enter is the same as clicking the OK button because you set the Default property of the OK button to True at design time.
- Pressing Esc is the same as pushing the Cancel button because you set the Cancel property of the Cancel button to True at design time.

☐ Click the Cancel button to terminate the Size program.

How the Size Program Works

Like other controls, the file-system controls have event procedures. The code in these procedures determines how the controls interact with each other.

The Code of the `Form_Load()` Procedure

When you start the program, the `Form_Load()` procedure is automatically executed. In this procedure, the cboFileType combo box and the lblDirName label are initialized:

```
Private Sub Form_Load ()

    ' Fill the cboFileType combo box.
    cboFileType.AddItem "All files (*.*)"
    cboFileType.AddItem "Text files (*.TXT)"
    cboFileType.AddItem "Doc files (*.DOC)"

    ' Initialize the cboFileType combo box to
    ' item #0. (i.e. All files *.*)
    cboFileType.ListIndex = 0

    ' Update the lblDirName label with the path.
    lblDirName.Caption = dirDirectory.Path

End Sub
```

The AddItem method is used three times to fill the cboFileType combo box with three items: All files (*.*), Text files (*.TXT), and Doc files (*.DOC).

Then the ListIndex property of the cboFileType combo box is set to 0. This sets the currently selected item of the combo box to item 0, or All files (*.*).

Finally, the caption of the lblDirName label is set to the Path property of the Directory list box. The initial value of the Path property is the current directory, so when you start the program, the lblDirName label displays the name of the current directory.

The Code of the `drvDrive_Change()` Procedure

When you change a drive in the Drive list box, the `drvDrive_Change()` procedure is automatically executed. The code in this procedure updates the Path property of the Directory list box with the new drive that was selected:

13

```
Private Sub drvDrive_Change ()

   ' The next statement may cause an error so we
   ' set an error trap.
   On Error GoTo DriveError

   ' Change the path of the directory list box to
   ' the new drive.
   dirDirectory.Path = drvDrive.Drive
   Exit Sub

DriveError:
   ' An error occurred! So tell the user and
   ' restore the original drive.
   MsgBox "Drive error!", vbExclamation, "Error"
   drvDrive.Drive = dirDirectory.Path
   Exit Sub

End Sub
```

Before the procedure executes the statement that changes the Path property of the Directory list box, an error trap is set. The error trap is required because changing the path of the Directory list box may cause an error. For example, if you changed the Drive list box to drive A:, and drive A: is not ready, changing the path of the Directory list box to A: will cause an error. To avoid a runtime error, an error trap is set with the following statement:

```
On Error Goto DriveError
```

If an error occurs now during the execution of this statement:

```
dirDirectory.Path = drvDrive.Drive
```

Visual Basic gives control to the code below the DriveError label. The code below the DriveError label displays an error message and restores the original value of the drive with the following statement:

```
drvDrive.Drive = dirDirectory.Path
```

Note that dirDirectory.Path still contains the original drive value because the statement that caused the error was not executed.

If the drive you selected is ready, no error occurs. The path of the Directory list box is changed to the selected drive, and as a result, the Directory list box lists the directories of the selected drive.

The Code of the dirDirectory_Change() Procedure

When you change a directory in the Directory list box, the dirDirectory_Change() procedure is executed. The code in this procedure updates the Path property of the File list box and the Caption property of the lblDirName label with the new directory:

```
Private Sub dirDirectory_Change ()

    ' A directory was just selected by the user so
    ' update the path of the file list box
    ' accordingly.
    filFiles.Path = dirDirectory.Path

    ' Also update the lblDirName label.
    lblDirName.Caption = dirDirectory.Path

End Sub
```

As a result of updating the Path property of the File list box with the selected directory, the File list box displays the files of that directory.

The Code of the cboFileType_Click() Procedure

When you make a selection from the cboFileType combo box, the cboFileType_Click() procedure is executed. The code in this procedure updates the Pattern property of the File list box according to the file type you selected:

```
Private Sub cboFileType_Click ()

    ' Change the Pattern of the file list box
    ' according to the File Type that the user
    ' selected.
    Select Case cboFileType.ListIndex
    Case 0
        filFiles.Pattern = "*.*"
    Case 1
        filFiles.Pattern = "*.TXT"
    Case 2
        filFiles.Pattern = "*.DOC"
    End Select

End Sub
```

To determine which item in the cboFileType combo box you selected, a Select Case is used. Recall that the Form_Load() procedure filled the cboFileType combo box with three items: All files (*.*), Text files (*.TXT), and Doc files (*.DOC). Depending on which item you select from the combo box, a different Case statement is executed. For example, if you select the second item in the combo box—Text files (*.TXT)—the following statement is executed:

```
filFiles.Pattern = "*.TXT"
```

As a result, the File list box displays only files with the TXT extension.

13

The Code of the `filFiles_Click()` Procedure

When you highlight a file in the filFiles File list box, the `filFiles_Click()` procedure is executed. The code in this procedure updates the txtFileName text box with the name of the selected file:

```
Private Sub filFiles_Click ()

    ' Update the txtFileName text box with the file
    ' name that was just selected.
    txtFileName.Text = filFiles.FileName

End Sub
```

The Code of the `cmdOK_Click()` Procedure

When you click the OK button, the `cmdOK_Click()` procedure is executed. The code of this procedure displays the file size of the currently selected file:

```
Private Sub cmdOK_Click ()

Dim PathAndName As String
Dim FileSize As String
Dim Path As String

' If no file is selected, tell the user and
' exit this procedure.
If txtFileName.Text = "" Then
    MsgBox "You must first select a file!"
    Exit Sub
End If

'Make sure that Path ends with backslash (\).
If Right(filFiles.Path, 1) <> "\" Then
    Path = filFiles.Path + "\"
Else
    Path = filFiles.Path
End If

'Extract the Path and Name of the selected file.
If txtFileName.Text = filFiles.FileName Then
    PathAndName = Path + filFiles.FileName
Else
    PathAndName = txtFileName.Text
End If

' The next statement may cause an error so we
' set an error trap.
On Error GoTo FileLenError

'Get the file size of the file.
FileSize = Str(FileLen(PathAndName))

'Display the size of the file.
```

```
   MsgBox "Size of "+PathAndName+": "+FileSize+" bytes"
   Exit Sub

FileLenError:
 ' There was an error, so display error message
 ' and exit.
 MsgBox "Cannot find size of " + PathAndName
 Exit Sub

End Sub
```

The first thing the procedure does is check whether you selected a file by comparing the Text property of the txtFileName text box with null. If txtFileName.Text is null, a message is displayed and the procedure is terminated:

```
If txtFileName.Text = "" Then
   MsgBox "You must first select a file!"
   Exit Sub
End If
```

After your code makes sure that the user selected a file, the Path variable is updated with the path of the selected file. The Right() function is used to make sure the rightmost character of the selected file's path is the backslash (\). If it isn't, a backslash is added to the Path variable:

```
If Right(filFiles.Path, 1) <> "\" Then
   Path = filFiles.Path + "\"
Else
   Path = filFiles.Path
End If
```

After the Path variable is ready, the PathAndName variable can be updated. As implied by its name, the PathAndName variable should contain the full name of the file (that is, path and name). The PathAndName variable is updated with an If statement:

```
If txtFileName.Text = filFiles.FileName Then
   PathAndName = Path + filFiles.FileName
Else
   PathAndName = txtFileName.Text
End If
```

This If statement checks whether the currently highlighted file in the File list box is the same as the contents of the File Name text box.

If the filename in the text box is not the same as the currently highlighted file, it means that you manually typed the path and name of the file, so the PathAndName variable is updated with whatever you typed. However, if the filename in the text box is the same as the currently highlighted file, the variable PathAndName is updated with the string Path + filFiles.FileName.

After the PathAndName variable is updated, the FileLen() function can be used to find the size of the file. However, because the FileLen() function may cause a runtime error (for example, if you typed a name of a file that doesn't exist), an error trap is set with the following statement:

13

```
On Error GoTo FileLenError
```

If an error occurs during the execution of the following statement:

```
FileSize = Str(FileLen(PathAndName))
```

Visual Basic gives control to the statement below the `FileLenError` label, which displays an error message and terminates the procedure:

```
FileLenError:
   MsgBox "Cannot find size of " + PathAndName
   Exit Sub
```

However, if the `FileLen()` function does not cause an error, the size of the file is displayed onscreen and the procedure is terminated:

```
MsgBox "Size of "+PathAndName+": "+FileSize+" bytes"
Exit Sub
```

The Code of the `filFiles_DblClick()` Procedure

When you double-click on a file in the File list box, the `filFiles_DblClick()` procedure is executed. The code of this procedure updates the File Name text box with the name of the file that was doubled-clicked and executes the `cmdOK_Click()` procedure:

```
Private Sub filFiles_DblClick ()

   ' Update the txtFileName text box with the file
   ' name that was just double clicked.
   txtFileName.Text = filFiles.FileName

   'Execute the cmdOK_Click() procedure.
   cmdOK_Click

End Sub
```

The Code of the `cmdCancel_Click()` Procedure

When you click the Cancel button, the `cmdCancel_Click()` procedure is executed. The code of this procedure terminates the program:

```
Private Sub cmdCancel_Click ()

   End

End Sub
```

The Attribute Properties of the File List Box

A file can have any of the following four attributes:

- ■ Read-only: When the read-only attribute of a file is set, the file can only be read (that is, it cannot be erased or overwritten).

- Hidden: When the hidden attribute of a file is set, the DIR command of DOS does not display the file.

- System: DOS system files (files that are part of the operating system) have their system attribute set. A system file cannot be erased or overwritten.

- Archive: When the DOS BACKUP command (and other backup utilities) backs up a file, the archive attribute of the file is set. This attribute is used as a flag to indicate that the file was backed up. As soon as the file is modified, the archive attribute is automatically reset by DOS to indicate that the file was modified and therefore needs to be backed up. The archive attribute can be used by a backup utility to perform incremental backup (that is, to back up only files that were modified since the last backup).

The attribute properties of a File list box determine which files are displayed in the File list box, depending on the attributes of the files. The attribute properties of a File list box are ReadOnly, Archive, Normal, System, and Hidden. Each of these properties can be set to either True or False. For example, to display just the read-only files, you need to set the attribute properties of the filMyFiles File list box as follows:

```
filMyFiles.ReadOnly = True
filMyFiles.Archive = False
filMyFiles.Normal = False
filMyFiles.System = False
filMyFiles.Hidden = False
```

The Select Program

The Size program illustrates how to create a form that lets you select files from a drive. Because many programs need such a form, it is a good idea to create a general-purpose Select a file dialog box form that could be used by many projects. The Select program illustrates how to create and use a general-purpose Select a file dialog box.

Before you start writing the Select program, let's specify what it should do:

- When you start the program, a menu bar with a File menu title appears (see Figure 13.5).

- The File menu has two items: Select File and Exit (see Figure 13.6).

- When you choose Select File from the File menu, the Select a file dialog box appears (see Figure 13.7).

- After selecting a file from the Select a file dialog box, the dialog box closes and the name of the selected file is displayed.

- When you select Exit from the File menu, the program terminates.

13

Figure 13.5.

The Select program.

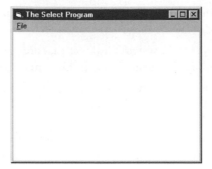

Figure 13.6.

The File menu of the Select program.

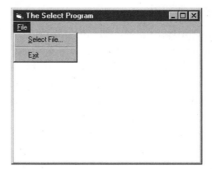

Figure 13.7.

The Select a file dialog box.

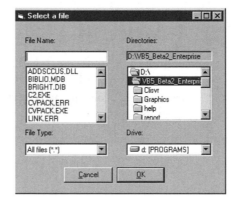

The Visual Implementation of the Select Program

As usual, you'll start with the visual implementation of the form of the Select program:

☐ Start a new Standard EXE project.

☐ Save the form of the project as Select.Frm in the C:\VB5Prg\Ch13 directory and save the project file as Select.Vbp in the C:\VB5Prg\Ch13 directory.

☐ Build the form according to Table 13.2.

The completed form should look like the one shown in Figure 13.5.

Table 13.2. The properties table of the frmSelect form.

Object	Property	Value
Form	**Name**	**frmSelect**
	BackColor	White
	Caption	The Select Program
Menu	*(See Table 13.3)*	*(See Table 13.3)*

Table 13.3. The menu table of the frmSelect form.

Caption	Name
&File	mnuFile
…&Select File	mnuSelectFile
…-	mnuSep1
…E&xit	mnuExit

You now have to create another form and name it GetFile.Frm—it will be used as a general-purpose Select a file dialog box.

The GetFile.Frm form is almost identical to the Size.Frm form that you designed earlier in the Size program. Instead of creating the GetFile.Frm form from scratch, you copy the Size.Frm file onto GetFile.Frm and then add the GetFile.Frm form to the Select.Vbp project. Here is how you do that:

☐ Use the Windows Explorer program of Windows to copy the file Size.Frm onto GetFile.Frm. (In Windows 95 for example, after you copy Size.Frm into the C:\VB5Prg\ Ch13 directory, the resultant file is Copy of Size.Frm. You now have to rename the Copy of Size.Frm file to GetFile.Frm.)

Now the directory C:\VB5Prg\Ch13 has in it the Size.Frm file and the GetFile.Frm file.

Add the GetFile.Frm file to the Select.Vbp project as follows:

☐ Switch back to Visual Basic.

☐ Select Add Form from the Project menu.

☐ Visual Basic responds by displaying the Add Form dialog box.

13

☐ Click the Existing tab of the Add Form dialog box (because you want to add an existing form to the project).

☐ Use the Existing page of the Add Form dialog box to select the GetFile.Frm file from the C:\VB5Prg\Ch13 directory and then click the Open button.

> *Visual Basic responds by adding the GetFile.Frm file to the Select.Vbp project. You can display the Project window and verify that the Select.Vbp project now includes two forms: Select.Frm and GetFile.Frm.*

At this point, the GetFile.Frm form is identical to the Size.Frm form. You have to change the Name property and Caption property of the GetFile.Frm form as follows:

☐ Select the GetFile.Frm form by highlighting GetFile.Frm item in the Project window and then clicking the View Object button.

☐ Change the Name property of the GetFile.Frm form from frmSize to frmGetFile.

☐ Change the Caption property of the GetFile.Frm form from The Size Program to Select a file.

> *The visual implementation of the frmGetFile form is completed. The frmGetFile form should now look like the one shown in Figure 13.7.*

Entering the Code of the Select Program

The Select program has two forms: frmSelect and frmGetFile. In the following sections you'll enter code in the procedures of these forms. (Note that the frmGetFile form already has code in its procedures. You typed the code when you designed the frmSize form.)

Entering the Code of the frmSelect Form

☐ Enter the following code in the general declarations section of the frmSelect form:

```
' All variables MUST be declared.
Option Explicit
```

☐ Type the following code in the Form_Load() procedure of the frmSelect form:

```
Private Sub Form_Load ()

    ' Load the frmGetFile dialog box
    '(without displaying it).
    Load frmGetFile

    ' Initialize the cboFileType combo box of the
    ' frmGetFile dialog box.
    frmGetFile.cboFileType.AddItem "All files (*.*)"
```

```
        frmGetFile.cboFileType.AddItem "Text files (*.TXT)"
        frmGetFile.cboFileType.AddItem "Doc files  (*.DOC)"
        frmGetFile.cboFileType.ListIndex = 0

    End Sub
```

☐ Type the following code in the mnuSelectFile_Click() procedure of the frmSelect form:

```
    Private Sub mnuSelectFile_Click ()

        ' Set the Caption property of frmGetFile.
        frmGetFile.Caption = "Select a file"

        ' Display the frmGetFile form as a modal dialog
        ' box.
        frmGetFile.Show 1

        ' Display the name of the selected file on the
        ' screen.
        If frmGetFile.Tag = "" Then
            MsgBox "No file was selected!"
        Else
            MsgBox "You selected " + frmGetFile.Tag
        End If

    End Sub
```

☐ Type the following code in the mnuExit_Click() procedure of the frmSelect form:

```
    Private Sub mnuExit_Click ()

        End

    End Sub
```

Entering the Code of the frmGetFile Form

As stated, the frmGetFile form already has code in it (because you created the frmGetFile form from the frmSize form when you copied the file Size.Frm onto the file GetFile.Frm). You'll now type additional code and modify the code of the procedures in the frmGetFile form:

☐ Edit the code in the Form_Load() procedure of the frmGetFile form so that it looks as follows:

```
    Private Sub Form_Load ()

        ' Update the Directory lblDirName label with the
        ' path value of the directory list box.
        lblDirName.Caption = dirDirectory.Path

    End Sub
```

13

☐ The code of the drvDrive_Change() procedure of the frmGetFile form is the same as the code in the frmSize form, so you don't have to modify it. Just make sure that it looks as follows:

```
Private Sub drvDrive_Change()

    ' The next statement may cause an error so we
    ' set an error trap.
    On Error GoTo DriveError

    ' Change the path of the directory list box to
    ' the new drive.
    dirDirectory.Path = drvDrive.Drive
    Exit Sub

DriveError:
    ' An error occurred! So tell the user and
    ' restore the original drive.
    MsgBox "Drive error!", vbExclamation, "Error"
    drvDrive.Drive = dirDirectory.Path
    Exit Sub

End Sub
```

☐ The code of the dirDirectory_Change() procedure of the frmGetFile form is the same as the code in the frmSize form, so you don't have to modify it. Just make sure that it looks as follows:

```
Private Sub dirDirectory_Change()

    ' A directory was just selected by the user so
    ' update the path of the file list box
    ' accordingly.
    filFiles.Path = dirDirectory.Path

    ' Also update the lblDirName label.
    lblDirName.Caption = dirDirectory.Path

End Sub
```

☐ Edit the code in the cboFileType_Click() procedure of the frmGetFile form so that it will look as follows:

```
Private Sub cboFileType_Click ()

    Dim PatternPos1 As Integer
    Dim PatternPos2 As Integer
    Dim PatternLen As Integer
    Dim Pattern As String

    ' Find the start position of the pattern in the
    ' cbboFileType combo box.
    PatternPos1 = InStr(1, cboFileType.Text, "(") + 1

    ' Find the end position of the pattern in the
```

```
' cbboFileType combo box.
PatternPos2 = InStr(1, cboFileType.Text, ")") - 1

' Calculate the length of the Pattern string.
PatternLen = PatternPos2 - PatternPos1 + 1

' Extract the Pattern portion of the cboFileType
' combo box.
Pattern=Mid(cboFileType.Text,PatternPos1,PatternLen)

' Set the Pattern of the filFiles file listbox to the
' selected pattern.
filFiles.Pattern = Pattern

End Sub
```

☐ The code in the `filFiles_Click()` procedure of the frmGetFile form is the same as the code in the frmSize form, so you don't have to modify it. Just make sure that it looks as follows:

```
Private Sub filFiles_Click()

' Update the txtFileName text box with the file
' name that was just selected.
txtFileName.Text = filFiles.FileName

End Sub
```

☐ Edit the code in the `cmdOK_Click()` procedure of the frmGetFile form so that it will look as follows:

```
Private Sub cmdOK_Click ()

Dim PathAndName As String
Dim Path As String

' If no file is selected, tell the user and
' exit this procedure.
If txtFileName.Text = "" Then
 MsgBox "No file is selected!", vbExclamation, "Error"
 Exit Sub
End If

' Make sure that Path ends with backslash (\).
If Right(filFiles.Path, 1) <> "\" Then
   Path = filFiles.Path + "\"
Else
   Path = filFiles.Path
End If

' Extract the Path and Name of the selected
' file.
If txtFileName.Text = filFiles.FileName Then
   PathAndName = Path + filFiles.FileName
Else
   PathAndName = txtFileName.Text
End If
```

13

```
' Set the tag property of the frmGetFile dialog
' box to the selected file path and name.
frmGetFile.Tag = PathAndName

' Hide the frmGetFile dialog box.
frmGetFile.Hide
```

End Sub

☐ The code of the filFiles_DblClick() procedure of the frmGetFile form is the same as the code in the frmSize form, so you don't have to modify it. Just make sure that it looks as follows:

```
Private Sub filFiles_DblClick()

    ' Update the txtFileName text box with the file
    ' name that was just double clicked.
    txtFileName.Text = filFiles.FileName

    'Execute the cmdOK_Click() procedure.
    cmdOK_Click

End Sub
```

☐ Edit the code in the cmdCancel_Click() procedure of the frmGetFile form so that it looks as follows:

```
Private Sub cmdCancel_Click ()

    ' Set the tag property of the form to null.
    frmGetFile.Tag = ""

    ' Hide the frmGetFile dialog box.
    frmGetFile.Hide

End Sub
```

☐ Select Save Project from the File menu of Visual Basic to save your work.

Executing the Select Program

Let's see your code in action:

☐ Execute the Select program.

After you choose Select File from the File menu, the Select a file dialog box appears onscreen as a modal form. So as long as the dialog box is open, you can't select other forms in the program. If you click the mouse in the frmSelect form while the dialog box is displayed, you hear a beep.

☐ Experiment with the various controls of the Select a file dialog box.

☐ Terminate the Select program by selecting Exit from the File menu.

How the Select Program Works

The Select program uses the frmGetFile form as a modal dialog box. The program's code displays the frmGetFile form when it needs a filename from you.

The frmSelect Form's Procedures

The next two sections explain the code of the Form_Load() and mnuSelectFile_Click() procedures for the frmSelect form.

The Code of the Form_Load() Procedure

When you start the program, the Form_Load() procedure of the frmSelect form is executed. In this procedure, the frmGetFile dialog box is loaded, and the cboFileType combo box of the dialog box is initialized:

```
Private Sub Form_Load ()

    ' Load the frmGetFile dialog box
    '(without displaying it).
    Load frmGetFile

    ' Initialize the cboFileType combo box of the
    ' frmGetFile dialog box.
    frmGetFile.cboFileType.AddItem "All files (*.*)"
    frmGetFile.cboFileType.AddItem "Text files (*.TXT)"
    frmGetFile.cboFileType.AddItem "Doc files  (*.DOC)"
    frmGetFile.cboFileType.ListIndex = 0

End Sub
```

The frmGetFile dialog box is loaded into memory with the Load statement. Loading the form does not display it. The form is loaded into memory so that later other procedures can show the dialog box without delays.

After the frmGetFile dialog box is loaded, the procedure initializes the cboFileType combo box of the frmGetFile dialog box. The cboFileType combo box is filled with three items: All files (*.*), Text files (*.TXT), and Doc files (*.DOC); later when the frmGetFile dialog box is displayed, you can set the File Type combo box to either *.*, *.TXT, or *.DOC.

The Code of the mnuSelectFile_Click() Procedure

When you choose Select File from the File menu, the mnuSelectFile_Click() procedure is executed. The code in this procedure displays the frmGetFile form as a modal dialog box, then uses the output of the dialog box to find which file you selected from the dialog box. The output of the dialog box (that is, the name of the selected file) is provided in the Tag property of the frmGetFile form:

13

```
Private Sub mnuSelectFile_Click ()

    ' Set the Caption property of frmGetFile.
    frmGetFile.Caption = "Select a file"

    ' Display the frmGetFile form as a modal dialog
    ' box.
    frmGetFile.Show 1

    ' Display the name of the selected file on the
    ' screen.
    If frmGetFile.Tag = "" Then
        MsgBox "No file was selected!"
    Else
        MsgBox "You selected " + frmGetFile.Tag
    End If

End Sub
```

The first statement of the procedure sets the Caption property of the frmGetFile form to
Select a file:

```
frmGetFile.Caption = "Select a file"
```

Then the frmGetFile form is displayed onscreen as a modal dialog box by using the Show
method with its style equal to 1:

```
frmGetFile.Show 1
```

The code in the frmGetFile form updates the Tag property of frmGetFile with the name
of the file that you select. If you don't select a file (for example, you push the Cancel button),
the code of the frmGetFile sets the Tag property of frmGetFile to null.

After you select a file from the frmGetFile form, the name of the selected file, if any, is
displayed with a message box:

```
If frmGetFile.Tag = "" Then
    MsgBox "No file was selected!"
Else
    MsgBox "You selected " + frmGetFile.Tag
End If
```

If frmGetFile.Tag is null, you didn't select a file, and the message No file was selected! is
displayed. However, if frmGetFile.Tag is not null, the selected file (that is, frmGetFile.Tag)
is displayed.

The frmGetFile Form's Procedures

The following sections explain the code in the frmGetFile form's procedures.

The Code of the `Form_Load()` Procedure

When the frmGetFile form is loaded, the `Form_Load()` procedure of the frmGetFile form is executed. The code of this procedure updates the lblDirName label with the path value of the Directory list box:

```
Private Sub Form_Load ()

    ' Update the Directory lblDirName label with the
    ' path value of the Directory list box.
    lblDirName.Caption = dirDirectory.Path

End Sub
```

The Code of the `drvDrive_Change()` Procedure

The code in this procedure is the same as the code in the Size program's `drvDrive_Change()` procedure.

The Code of the `dirDirectory_Change()` Procedure

The code in this procedure is the same as the code in the Size program's `drvDirectory_Change()` procedure.

The Code of the `cboFileType_Click()` Procedure

When you make a selection from the cboFileType combo box, the `cboFileType_Click()` procedure is executed. The code in this procedure updates the Pattern property of the File list box:

```
Private Sub cboFileType_Click ()

    Dim PatternPos1 As Integer
    Dim PatternPos2 As Integer
    Dim PatternLen As Integer
    Dim Pattern As String

    ' Find the start position of the pattern in the
    ' cbboFileType combo box.
    PatternPos1 = InStr(1, cboFileType.Text, "(") + 1

    ' Find the end position of the pattern in the
    ' cbboFileType combo box.
    PatternPos2 = InStr(1, cboFileType.Text, ")") - 1

    ' Calculate the length of the Pattern string.
    PatternLen = PatternPos2 - PatternPos1 + 1

    ' Extract the Pattern portion of the cboFileType
    ' combo box.
    Pattern=Mid(cboFileType.Text,PatternPos1,PatternLen)
```

13

```
' Set the Pattern of the filFiles file listbox to the
' selected pattern.
filFiles.Pattern = Pattern
```

```
End Sub
```

The Text property of the cboFileType combo box (cboFileType.Text) contains the file type you selected. To find the pattern of the selected file type, the procedure extracts the pattern portion from cboFileType.Text. For example, if cboFileType.Text is equal to Text files (*.TXT), the pattern portion is *.TXT.

The procedure finds the position of the first character of the pattern portion from cboFileType.Text by locating the first parenthesis and adding 1 to it:

```
PatternPos1 = InStr(1, cboFileType.Text, "(") + 1
```

Similarly, the procedure finds the position of the last character of the pattern portion by locating the second parenthesis and subtracting 1 from it:

```
PatternPos2 = InStr(1, cboFileType.Text, ")") - 1
```

The length of the Pattern string is calculated by subtracting PatternPos1 from PatternPos2 and adding 1 to the result:

```
PatternLen = PatternPos2 - PatternPos1 + 1
```

Finally, the pattern portion is extracted by using the Mid() function:

```
Pattern= Mid(cboFileType.Text, PatternPos1, PatternLen)
```

The last statement of the procedure assigns the extracted pattern to the Pattern property of the filFiles File list box:

```
filFiles.Pattern = Pattern
```

As a result, the File list box displays only files with the same pattern as the extracted pattern.

The Code of the filFiles_Click() Procedure

The code in this procedure is the same as the code in the Size program's filFiles_Click() procedure.

The Code of the cmdOK_Click() Procedure

When you push the OK pushbutton, the cmdOK_Click() procedure is executed:

```
Private Sub cmdOK_Click ()

Dim PathAndName As String
```

```
Dim Path As String

' If no file is selected, tell the user and
' exit this procedure.
If txtFileName.Text = "" Then
 MsgBox "No file is selected!", vbExclamation, "Error"
 Exit Sub
End If

' Make sure that Path ends with backslash (\).
If Right(filFiles.Path, 1) <> "\" Then
    Path = filFiles.Path + "\"
Else
    Path = filFiles.Path
End If

' Extract the Path and Name of the selected
' file.
If txtFileName.Text = filFiles.FileName Then
    PathAndName = Path + filFiles.FileName
Else
    PathAndName = txtFileName.Text
End If

' Set the tag property of the frmGetFile dialog
' box to the selected file path and name.
frmGetFile.Tag = PathAndName

' Hide the frmGetFile dialog box.
frmGetFile.Hide

End Sub
```

As you can see, this procedure is very similar to the Size program's cmdOK_Click() procedure. The first thing it does is check whether you selected a file by comparing the Text property of the txtFileName text box with null. If txtFileName.Text is null, a message is displayed and the procedure is terminated:

```
If txtFileName.Text = "" Then
  MsgBox "No file is selected!", vbExclamation, "Error"
  Exit Sub
End If
```

After the code makes sure that the user selected a file, the Path variable is updated with the path (directory name) of the selected file. The Right() function is used to make sure the rightmost character of the selected file's path is the backslash (\). If it isn't, the backslash is added to the Path variable:

```
If Right(filFiles.Path, 1) <> "\" Then
    Path = filFiles.Path + "\"
Else
    Path = filFiles.Path
End If
```

13

The preceding If statement is necessary because when you select a file from the root directory of a drive, `filFiles.Path` contains the letter drive of the selected root directory and the backslash character (for example, `C:\`). However, when you select a file that isn't in the root directory, `filFiles.Path` contains the pathname of the selected directory without the backslash character at the end (for example, `C:\TRY` instead of `C:\TRY\`). Therefore, the preceding If statement ensures that no matter which directory you select, the `Path` variable will always terminate with the backslash character.

After the `Path` variable is ready, the `PathAndName` variable can be updated. As implied by its name, the `PathAndName` variable should contain the full name of the file (that is, path and name). The `PathAndName` variable is updated with an If statement:

```
If txtFileName.Text = filFiles.FileName Then
    PathAndName = Path + filFiles.FileName
Else
    PathAndName = txtFileName.Text
End If
```

This If statement checks whether the currently highlighted file in the File list box is the same as the contents of the File Name text box. If the filename in the text box is not the same as the currently highlighted file, it means that you manually typed the path and name of the file, so the `PathAndName` variable is updated with whatever you typed. However, if the filename in the text box is the same as the currently highlighted file, the variable `PathAndName` is updated with the string `Path + filFiles.FileName`.

Once the variable `PathAndName` is updated, its value is assigned to the Tag property of the frmGetFile form:

```
frmGetFile.Tag = PathAndName
```

The Tag property of the form is used to store the output of the frmGetFile form. The procedure that displayed the frmGetFile form "knows" which file you selected by using `frmGetFile.Tag`.

The last statement in the procedure removes the frmGetFile form from the screen by using the `Hide` method:

```
frmGetFile.Hide
```

After executing this statement, the frmGetFile is removed from the screen, and control is given back to the procedure that displayed the frmGetFile form.

The Code of the `filFiles_DblClick()` Procedure

The code in this procedure is the same as the code in the Size program's `filFiles_DblClick()` procedure.

The Code of the `cmdCancel_Click()` Procedure

When you click the Cancel button, the `cmdCancel_Click()` procedure is executed:

```
Private Sub cmdCancel_Click ()

   ' Set the tag property of the form to null.
   frmGetFile.Tag = ""

   ' Hide the frmGetFile dialog box.
   frmGetFile.Hide

End Sub
```

Recall that the Tag property of the frmGetFile form is used to store the path and name of the file you selected. Because you clicked the Cancel button, this procedure assigns null to the Tag property:

```
frmGetFile.Tag = ""
```

The last statement in the procedure removes the frmGetFile form from the screen by using the `Hide` method:

```
frmGetFile.Hide
```

After executing this statement, the frmGetFile is removed from the screen, and control is given back to the procedure that displayed the frmGetFile form.

Summary

In this chapter you learned how to use the file-system controls to write programs that let you select files. You also learned how to write a general-purpose GetFile form that can be used by any program that requires you to select files.

Q&A

13

Q How can I add the GetFile.Frm form of the Select program to other projects?

A Suppose you have a project called AnyProj. Use the following steps to add the GetFile.Frm form to the AnyProj project:

☐ Open the AnyProj project.

☐ Add the GetFile.Frm file to the project in the same manner you added this file to the Select.Vbp project. The point to note is that the GetFile form is available for all your future projects. That's one of the main advantages of using an object-oriented programming language such as Visual Basic—you can reuse code.

Quiz

1. What is the purpose of the first line in the following code?

```
On Error GoTo DriveError
dirDirectory.Path = "A:"
Exit Sub
DriveError:
    MsgBox "Drive error!", 48, "Error"
    drvDrive.Drive = dirDirectory.Path
    Exit Sub
```

2. What happens after the following statement is executed?

```
filFiles.Pattern = "*.BAT"
```

3. What happens after the following statement is executed?

```
filFiles.Path = dirDirectory.Path
```

4. What happens after the following statement is executed?

```
dirDirectory.Path = "D:"
```

Exercise

Enhance the Select program so that the File Type combo box of the GetFile dialog box also includes the file type Batch Files (*.BAT).

Quiz Answers

1. The purpose of the first line of this code:

```
On Error GoTo DriveError
```

   is to set an error trap so that if a runtime error occurs on the following lines, the error will be trapped.

2. After the statement `filFiles.Pattern = "*.BAT"` is executed, the filFiles File list box displays only files that have the BAT extension.

3. After the statement `filFiles.Path = dirDirectory.Path` is executed, the filFiles list box displays the files of the directory currently selected in the dirDirectory Directory list box.

4. After the statement `dirDirectory.Path = "D:"` is executed, the dirDirectory Directory list box displays the directories of the D drive.

Exercise Answer

To enhance the Select program so that the File Type combo box of the Select a File dialog box includes the file type Batch Files (*.BAT), you need to add the following statement to the Form_Load() procedure of the frmSelect form:

```
frmGetFile.cboFileType.AddItem "Batch files (*.BAT)"
```

After adding this statement, the Form_Load() procedure should look like the following:

```
Private Sub Form_Load ()

    ' Load the frmGetFile dialog box
    '(without displaying it).
    Load frmGetFile

    ' Initialize the File Type combo box of the
    ' frmGetFile dialog box.
    frmGetFile.cboFileType.AddItem "All files (*.*)"
    frmGetFile.cboFileType.AddItem "Text files (*.TXT)"
    frmGetFile.cboFileType.AddItem "Doc files  (*.DOC)"
    frmGetFile.cboFileType.AddItem "Batch files (*.BAT)"
    frmGetFile.cboFileType.ListIndex = 0

End Sub
```

13

Week 2

Day 14

Accessing Files

Many programs need to read and write data to disk files. In this chapter, you'll learn how to create files, how to read data from files, and how to write data to files.

There are three ways to access files in Visual Basic:

■ Random access
■ Sequential access
■ Binary access

This chapter teaches you how to use each of these file access techniques to manipulate files.

Random Access Files

A *random access file* is like a database. It is made up of records of identical size. Each record is made up of fields that store data. Figure 14.1 shows a random access file with two fields per record. The first field is a 5-byte string that corresponds to a person's name. The second field is a 2-byte string that corresponds to a person's age. Each record in this file is 7 bytes—the first sequence of 7 bytes makes up the first record, the second sequence of 7 bytes makes up the second record, and so on. Each record stores data about a specific person (that is, the person's name and age).

Figure 14.1.
A random access file.

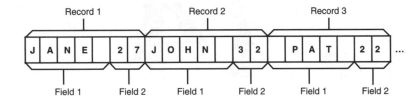

The Phone Program

The Phone program illustrates how to create and manipulate random access files. The program lets you maintain a database file called PHONE.DAT that keeps records of people and their phone numbers.

The Visual Implementation of the Phone Program

☐ Start a new Standard EXE project.

☐ Save the form of the project as PHONE.FRM in the C:\VB5PRG\CH14 directory and save the project file as PHONE.VBP in the C:\VB5PRG\CH14 directory.

☐ Build the form according to the specifications in Table 14.1.

The completed form should look like the one shown in Figure 14.2.

Table 14.1. The properties table of the Phone program.

Object	Property	Value
Form	**Name**	**frmPhone**
	Caption	(empty)
	MaxButton	False

Object	Property	Value
Text Box	**Name**	**txtName**
	Text	(empty)
	MaxLength	40
Text Box	**Name**	**txtPhone**
	Text	(empty)
	MaxLength	40
Text Box	**Name**	**txtComments**
	Text	(empty)
	MaxLength	100
	MultiLine	True
	ScrollBars	2-Vertical
Command Button	**Name**	**cmdNew**
	Caption	New
Command Button	**Name**	**cmdNext**
	Caption	Next
Command Button	**Name**	**cmdPrevious**
	Caption	Previous
Command Button	**Name**	**cmdExit**
	Caption	Exit
Label	**Name**	**lblComments**
	Caption	Comments:
Label	**Name**	**lblPhone**
	Caption	Phone:
Label	**Name**	**lblName**
	Caption	Name:

Entering the Code of the Phone Program

14

As you'll soon see, besides the PHONE.FRM form that you designed, the Phone program also needs a program module (you'll soon see what it's for). Therefore, you need to create a program module. Here is how you do that:

☐ Select Add Module from the Project menu.

Visual Basic responds by displaying the Add Module dialog box.

☐ Select the Module icon in the New tab of the Add Module dialog box and click the Open button of the Add Module dialog box.

Visual Basic responds by creating a new module and displaying its code window. As you can see from the title of the new module's code window, Visual Basic named the new module Module1.

Save the new module as PHONE.BAS:

☐ Select Save Module1 As from the File menu and save the file as PHONE.BAS in the C:\VB5PRG\CH14 directory.

Now the Module1 module is saved in the file PHONE.BAS:

☐ Enter the following code in the general declarations section of the Module1 module:

```
' All variables must be declared.
Option Explicit

' Declare a user-defined type that corresponds to a
' record in the file PHONE.DAT.
Type PersonInfo
    Name      As String * 40
    Phone     As String * 40
    Comments  As String * 100
End Type
```

Figure 14.2.

The form of the Phone program.

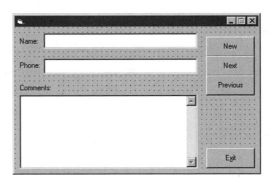

That's all the code you need to type in the Module1 module. In the following steps you'll enter code in the frmPhone form:

☐ Enter the following code in the general declarations section of the frmPhone form:

```
' All variables must be declared.
Option Explicit
```

```
' Declare variables that should be visible in all
' the procedures of the form.
Dim gPerson As PersonInfo
Dim gFileNum As Integer
Dim gRecordLen As Long
Dim gCurrentRecord As Long
Dim gLastRecord As Long
```

☐ Create a new procedure in the frmPhone form (by selecting Add Procedure from the Tools menu) and name it SaveCurrentRecord.

☐ Enter the following code in the SaveCurrentRecord() procedure:

```
Public Sub SaveCurrentRecord ()

    ' Fill gPerson with the currently displayed data.
    gPerson.Name = txtName.Text
    gPerson.Phone = txtPhone.Text
    gPerson.Comments = txtComments.Text

    ' Save gPerson to the current record.
    Put #gFileNum, gCurrentRecord, gPerson

End Sub
```

☐ Create a new procedure in the frmPhone form and name it ShowCurrentRecord.

☐ Enter the following code in the ShowCurrentRecord() procedure:

```
Public Sub ShowCurrentRecord ()

    ' Fill gPerson with the data of the current
    ' record.
    Get #gFileNum, gCurrentRecord, gPerson

    ' Display gPerson.
    txtName.Text = Trim(gPerson.Name)
    txtPhone.Text = Trim(gPerson.Phone)
    txtComments.Text = Trim(gPerson.Comments)

    ' Display the current record number in the
    ' caption of the form.
    frmPhone.Caption= "Record " + _
                    Str(gCurrentRecord) + "/" + _
                    Str(gLastRecord)

End Sub
```

☐ Enter the following code in the Form_Load() procedure:

```
Private Sub Form_Load ()

    ' Calculate the length of a record.
    gRecordLen = Len(gPerson)

    ' Get the next available file number.
    gFileNum = FreeFile
```

14

```
' Open the file for random-access. If the file
' does not exist then it is created.
Open "PHONE.DAT" For Random As gFileNum Len = gRecordLen

' Update gCurrentRecord.
gCurrentRecord = 1

' Find what is the last record number of
' the file.
gLastRecord = FileLen("PHONE.DAT") / gRecordLen

' If the file was just created
' (i.e. gLastRecord=0) then update gLastRecord
' to 1.
If gLastRecord = 0 Then
   gLastRecord = 1
End If

' Display the current record.
ShowCurrentRecord
```

End Sub

☐ Enter the following code in the cmdNew_Click() procedure:

Private Sub cmdNew_Click ()

```
' Save the current record.
SaveCurrentRecord

' Add a new blank record.
gLastRecord = gLastRecord + 1
gPerson.Name = ""
gPerson.Phone = ""
gPerson.Comments = ""
Put #gFileNum, gLastRecord, gPerson

' Update gCurrentRecord.
gCurrentRecord = gLastRecord

' Display the record that was just created.
ShowCurrentRecord

' Give the focus to the txtName field.
txtName.SetFocus
```

End Sub

☐ Enter the following code in the cmdNext_Click() procedure:

Private Sub cmdNext_Click ()

```
' If the current record is the last record,
' beep and display an error message. Otherwise,
' save the current record and skip to the
' next record.
```

```
    If gCurrentRecord = gLastRecord Then
       Beep
       MsgBox "End of file!", vbExclamation
    Else
       SaveCurrentRecord
       gCurrentRecord = gCurrentRecord + 1
       ShowCurrentRecord
    End If

    ' Give the focus to the txtName field.
    txtName.SetFocus

End Sub
```

☐ Enter the following code in the cmdPrevious_Click() procedure:

```
Private Sub cmdPrevious_Click ()

    ' If the current record is the first record,
    ' beep and display an error message. Otherwise,
    ' save the current record and go to the
    ' previous record.
    If gCurrentRecord = 1 Then
       Beep
       MsgBox "Beginning of file!", vbExclamation
    Else
       SaveCurrentRecord
       gCurrentRecord = gCurrentRecord - 1
       ShowCurrentRecord
    End If

    ' Give the focus to the txtName field.
    txtName.SetFocus

End Sub
```

☐ Enter the following code in the cmdExit_Click() procedure:

```
Private Sub cmdExit_Click ()

    ' Save the current record.
    SaveCurrentRecord

    ' Close the file.
    Close #gFileNum

    ' End the program.
    End

End Sub
```

14

Executing the Phone Program

Let's see your code in action:

☐ Execute the Phone program.

While you run the program, notice the following features:

■ The first time you execute the program, the database is empty and a blank record appears onscreen. This record is record 1 of 1, as indicated in the caption of the program's window. The program lets you type the person's name and phone number and comments about the person (see Figure 14.3). You can move from one field to another by using the mouse or pressing the Tab key.

■ To add a new record, click the New button and a new blank record will appear. The form's caption displays the new record's record number and the total number of records (see Figure 14.4).

■ Once you have a few records in the database, you can move from one record to another by using the Next and Previous buttons. When you click the Next button, the next record is displayed; clicking the Previous button displays the previous record.

Figure 14.3.

The first record in the Phone program.

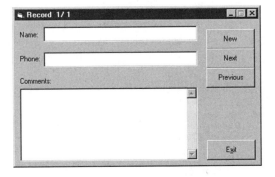

Figure 14.4.

The Phone program after you add a new record.

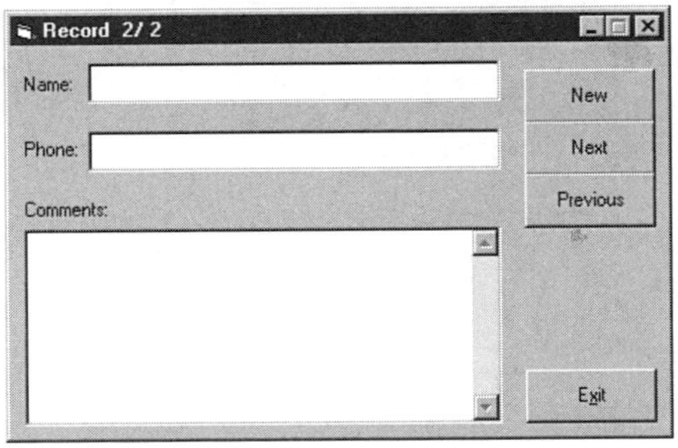

☐ Click the Exit button to terminate the Phone program.

All the records you added to the database are stored in the file PHONE.DAT. If you execute the program again, you will see the records you entered.

As you can see, you can't delete a record or search for a record in the Phone program. Later in this chapter, you will enhance the program so you can delete records and search for records.

How the Phone Program Works

The Phone program opens the file PHONE.DAT as a random access file with the fields Name, Phone, and Comments. If the file does not exist, the program creates it.

Declaring a User-Defined Type

The code you typed in the general declarations section of the Module1 module declares a user-defined type that corresponds to the fields of a record in the PHONE.DAT file:

```
' Declare a user-defined type that corresponds to a
' record in the file PHONE.DAT.
Type PersonInfo
     Name       As String * 40
     Phone      As String * 40
     Comments   As String * 100
End Type
```

The declared type is called PersonInfo, and it is made up of three variables: Name (a 40-character string), Phone (a 40-character string), and Comments (a 100-character string). Each of these strings corresponds to a field in the PHONE.DAT file.

Later, the Phone program will use a variable of the type PersonInfo to write (and read) data to the PERSON.DAT file.

Note that PersonInfo is declared in the general declarations section of the Module1 module, not in the general declarations section of the frmPhone form.

The General Declarations Section of the frmPhone Form

In the general declarations section of the frmPhone form, the variables that should be visible in all the form's procedures are declared:

```
' Declare variables that should be visible in all
' the procedures of the form.
Dim gPerson As PersonInfo
Dim gFileNum As Integer
Dim gRecordLen As Long
Dim gCurrentRecord As Long
Dim gLastRecord As Long
```

14

The variable gPerson is declared as type PersonInfo. Because the user-defined type PersonInfo consists of three variables (that is, Name, Phone, and Comments), the variable gPerson also consists of three variables: gPerson.Name, gPerson.Phone, and gPerson.Comments. The variable gPerson is used to hold a record's data.

Opening the PHONE.DAT File

Before data can be written to or read from a file, the file must be opened. The code responsible for opening the PHONE.DAT file is in the Form_Load() procedure:

```
Private Sub Form_Load ()

  ' Calculate the length of a record.
  gRecordLen = Len(gPerson)

  ' Get the next available file number.
  gFileNum = FreeFile

  ' Open the file for random-access. If the file
  ' does not exist then it is created.
  Open "PHONE.DAT" For Random As gFileNum Len = gRecordLen

  ' Update gCurrentRecord.
  gCurrentRecord = 1

  ' Find what the last record number of
  ' the file is.
  gLastRecord = FileLen("PHONE.DAT") / gRecordLen

  ' If the file was just created
  ' (i.e. gLastRecord=0) then update gLastRecord
  ' to 1.
  If gLastRecord = 0 Then
     gLastRecord = 1
  End If

  ' Display the current record.
  ShowCurrentRecord

End Sub
```

When you open a file for random access, you need to specify the record size of the file and a file number. So before opening the file, the Form_Load() procedure extracts these values with the following two statements:

```
RecordLen = Len(gPerson)
gFileNum = FreeFile
```

The first statement uses the Len() function to extract the length of the variable gPerson. Because the variable gPerson corresponds to the fields of the PHONE.DAT file, its length is the same as the length of a record.

The second statement uses the FreeFile function to get a file number that is not already in use. As stated previously, when you open a file, you need to specify a file number used to identify the opened file. Subsequent statements that perform operations on this file need this file number to tell Visual Basic which file to perform the operation on.

Now that the variables gRecordLen and gFileNum are updated, the procedure opens the PHONE.DAT file for random access with the following statement:

```
Open "PHONE.DAT" For Random As FileNum Len = RecordLen
```

If the PHONE.DAT file does not exist, the Open statement creates it. So the first time you execute the Phone program, the file PHONE.DAT is created in the same directory the Phone program is executed from. When you finish developing the Phone program, you'll create the file PHONE.EXE. If you save the PHONE.EXE file in, for example, the C:\TRY directory and then later execute the PHONE.EXE program from the C:\TRY directory, the PHONE.DAT file will be created in the C:\TRY directory. However, during design time (when you execute the Phone program from Visual Basic), the PHONE.DAT file is created in the Visual Basic directory.

After the file PHONE.DAT is opened, the procedure updates the variables gCurrentRecord and gLastRecord.

The variable gCurrentRecord is used to store the record number of the currently displayed record. Because initially record number 1 should be displayed, gCurrentRecord is initialized to 1:

```
gCurrentRecord = 1
```

The variable gLastRecord is used to store the record number of the last record in the file (that is, the total number of records). This value is calculated by dividing the total file length by the length of a record:

```
gLastRecord = FileLen("PHONE.DAT") / gRecordLen
```

However, there is one special case for which this calculation does not work. If the file was just created, FileLen() returns 0 and the above calculation yields a value of 0 for gLastRecord. To make sure that gLastRecord is not assigned a value of 0, use an If statement:

```
If gLastRecord = 0 Then
   gLastRecord = 1
End If
```

This If statement checks to see whether gLastRecord is 0. If it is, the If statement changes it to 1.

The last statement in the Form_Load() procedure executes the procedure ShowCurrentRecord():

```
' Display the current record.
ShowCurrentRecord
```

The procedure ShowCurrentRecord displays the data of the record specified by the variable gCurrentRecord. Because gCurrentRecord is now equal to 1 after executing the preceding statement, the data of record number 1 is displayed.

14

The Code of the `ShowCurrentRecord()` Procedure

The code in the `ShowCurrentRecord()` procedure displays the data of the record specified by the variable gCurrentRecord:

```
Public Sub ShowCurrentRecord ()

  ' Fill gPerson with the data of the current
  ' record.
  Get #gFileNum, gCurrentRecord, gPerson

  ' Display gPerson.
  txtName.Text = Trim(gPerson.Name)
  txtPhone.Text = Trim(gPerson.Phone)
  txtComments.Text = Trim(gPerson.Comments)

  ' Display the current record number in the
  ' caption of the form.
   frmPhone.Caption= "Record " + _
                    Str(gCurrentRecord) + "/" + _
                    Str(gLastRecord)

End Sub
```

The first statement of the procedure uses the Get statement to fill the variable gPerson with the data of the current record:

```
Get #FileNum, CurrentRecord, Person
```

The Get statement takes three parameters: the first parameter specifies the file number of the file (the number specified when the file was opened), the second parameter specifies the record number of the record to be read, and the third parameter specifies the name of the variable that is filled with the data read from the record.

For example, if gCurrentRecord is currently equal to 5 after executing the preceding statement, the variable gPerson contains the data of record number 5. That is, gPerson.Name, gPerson.Phone, and gPerson.Comments contain the data stored in the fields Name, Phone, and Comments of record number 5.

After the variable gPerson is filled with the data of the current record, its contents are displayed by updating the txtName, txtPhone, and txtComments text boxes:

```
txtName.Text = Trim(gPerson.Name)
txtPhone.Text = Trim(gPerson.Phone)
txtComments.Text = Trim(gPerson.Comments)
```

Note that the text boxes are assigned with the trimmed values of the gPerson variable. That's because the text boxes shouldn't contain any trailing blanks. For example, if the current record in the database contains the name JOHN SMITH in the Name field, after you execute the Get statement the variable gPerson.Name contains these characters:

```
"JOHN SMITH.............................".
```

Because the Name field was defined as 40 characters and JOHN SMITH is only 10 characters, Visual Basic added 30 trailing blanks to the field when the record was stored. These trailing blanks should not appear in the text box, so the Trim() function was used.

The last statement of the procedure displays the current record number in the form's caption:

```
frmPhone.Caption= "Record " + _
                 Str(gCurrentRecord) + "/" + _
                 Str(gLastRecord)
```

For example, if the current value of gCurrentRecord is 5 and the value of gLastRecord is 15, the preceding statement sets the form's caption to Record 5/15.

The Code of the cmdNext_Click() Procedure

When you click the Next button, the cmdNext_Click() procedure is executed. The code in this procedure is responsible for displaying the contents of the next record:

```
Private Sub cmdNext_Click ()

  ' If the current record is the last record,
  ' beep and display an error message. Otherwise,
  ' save the current record and skip to the
  ' next record.
  If gCurrentRecord = gLastRecord Then
     Beep
     MsgBox "End of file!", vbExclamation
  Else
     SaveCurrentRecord
     gCurrentRecord = gCurrentRecord + 1
     ShowCurrentRecord
  End If

  ' Give the focus to the txtName field.
  txtName.SetFocus

End Sub
```

The first statement of the procedure is an If statement that checks whether gCurrentRecord is equal to gLastRecord. If gCurrentRecord is equal to gLastRecord (that is, there is no next record), your PC beeps and displays a message—End of File!—informing you that the current record is the end of the file:

```
Beep
MsgBox "End of file!", vbExclamation
```

If, however, gCurrentRecord is not equal to gLastRecord, the following statements are executed:

```
SaveCurrentRecord
gCurrentRecord = gCurrentRecord + 1
ShowCurrentRecord
```

14

The first statement executes the SaveCurrentRecord procedure, which saves the contents of the text boxes txtName, txtPhone, and txtComments in the PHONE.DAT file. The second statement increments the variable gCurrentRecord by 1 so it points to the next record. The third statement executes the procedure ShowCurrentRecord() so the text boxes txtName, txtPhone, and txtComments display the record that equals the new value of gCurrentRecord.

The last statement of the procedure uses the SetFocus method to set the keyboard focus to the txtName text box:

```
txtName.SetFocus
```

After the preceding statement is executed, the cursor appears in the txtName text box.

The Code of the SaveCurrentRecord() Procedure

The SaveCurrentRecord() procedure is responsible for saving the contents of the text boxes txtName, txtPhone, and txtComments in the record specified by gCurrentRecord:

```
Public Sub SaveCurrentRecord ()

    ' Fill gPerson with the currently displayed data.
    gPerson.Name = txtName.Text
    gPerson.Phone = txtPhone.Text
    gPerson.Comments = txtComments.Text

    ' Save gPerson to the current record.
    Put #gFileNum, gCurrentRecord, gPerson

End Sub
```

The first three statements of the procedure fill the gPerson variable with the contents of the three text boxes:

```
gPerson.Name = txtName.Text
gPerson.Phone = txtPhone.Text
gPerson.Comments = txtComments.Text
```

After the gPerson variable is filled, the procedure executes the Put statement to store the contents of the gPerson variable in record number gCurrentRecord of the file:

```
Put #gFileNum, gCurrentRecord, gPerson
```

The Put statement takes three parameters: The first parameter specifies the file number of the file (the number specified when the file was opened), the second parameter specifies the record number that is being saved, and the third parameter specifies the name of the variable whose contents will be saved in the record.

Adding a New Record to the PHONE.DAT File

The cmdNew_Click() procedure is responsible for adding a new record to the PHONE.DAT file. It is executed when you click the New button:

```
Private Sub cmdNew_Click ()

  ' Save the current record.
  SaveCurrentRecord

  ' Add a new blank record.
  gLastRecord = gLastRecord + 1
  gPerson.Name = ""
  gPerson.Phone = ""
  gPerson.Comments = ""
  Put #gFileNum, gLastRecord, gPerson

  ' Update gCurrentRecord.
  gCurrentRecord = gLastRecord

  ' Display the record that was just created.
  ShowCurrentRecord

  ' Give the focus to the txtName field.
  txtName.SetFocus

End Sub
```

The first statement of the procedure executes the SaveCurrentRecord() procedure so the current record (that is, the contents of the text boxes) is saved in the PHONE.DAT file. After saving the current record, the procedure adds a new blank record to the file with the following statements:

```
gLastRecord = gLastRecord + 1
gPerson.Name = ""
gPerson.Phone = ""
gPerson.Comments = ""
Put #gFileNum, gLastRecord, gPerson
```

The first statement increments gLastRecord so it points to the number of the new record, then the gPerson variable is set to null, and finally the Put statement is used to create the new record. The number of the new record is gLastRecord, and its contents are the contents of the gPerson variable (that is, null).

After creating the new blank record, the gCurrentRecord variable is updated so it points to the new record:

```
gCurrentRecord = gLastRecord
```

14

Then the ShowCurrentRecord() procedure is executed so the record that was just created is displayed:

```
ShowCurrentRecord
```

The last statement of the procedure uses the SetFocus method to set the keyboard focus to the txtName text box:

```
txtName.SetFocus
```

After the preceding statement is executed, the cursor appears in the txtName text box.

The Code of the cmdPrevious_Click() Procedure

When you click the Previous button, the cmdPrevious_Click() procedure is executed. The code in this procedure is responsible for displaying the contents of the previous record:

```
Private Sub cmdPrevious_Click ()

  ' If the current record is the first record,
  ' beep and display an error message. Otherwise,
  ' save the current record and go to the
  ' previous record.
  If gCurrentRecord = 1 Then
    Beep
    MsgBox "Beginning of file!", vbExclamation
  Else
    SaveCurrentRecord
    gCurrentRecord = gCurrentRecord - 1
    ShowCurrentRecord
  End If

  ' Give the focus to the txtName field.
  txtName.SetFocus

End Sub
```

The first statement of the procedure is an If statement that checks whether gCurrentRecord is equal to 1. If it is (that is, there is no previous record), your PC beeps and displays a message—Beginning of file!—informing you that the current record is the beginning of the file:

```
Beep
MsgBox "Beginning of file!", vbExclamation
```

If, however, gCurrentRecord is not equal to 1, the following statements are executed:

```
SaveCurrentRecord
gCurrentRecord = gCurrentRecord - 1
ShowCurrentRecord
```

The first statement executes the SaveCurrentRecord() procedure to save the contents of the text boxes txtName, txtPhone, and txtComments in the PHONE.DAT file. The second statement decrements the variable gCurrentRecord by 1 so it points to the previous record. The third statement executes the procedure ShowCurrentRecord so the text boxes txtName, txtPhone, and txtComments display the record that equals the new value of gCurrentRecord.

The last statement of the procedure uses the SetFocus method to set the keyboard focus to the txtName text box:

```
txtName.SetFocus
```

After executing this statement, the cursor appears in the txtName text box.

The Code of the cmdExit_Click() Procedure

The cmdExit_Click() procedure is executed when you click the Exit button. The code in this procedure saves the current record in the PHONE.DAT file, closes the PHONE.DAT file, and terminates the program:

```
Private Sub cmdExit_Click ()

    ' Save the current record.
    SaveCurrentRecord

    ' Close the file.
    Close #gFileNum

    ' End the program.
    End

End Sub
```

The Close statement, Close #gFileNum, closes the file. As you can see, it takes one parameter that specifies the file number of the file to be closed.

You really don't have to use the Close statement in the cmdExit_Click() procedure because the last statement in the cmdExit_Click() procedure is End, which closes all files, if any, that were opened with the Open statement. As you know, the End statement also terminates the program. The Close statement was included in the cmdExit_Click() procedure to illustrate how you can close a file without using the End statement (that is, without terminating the program).

Enhancing the Phone Program

You'll now enhance the Phone program by adding a Search button and a Delete button. The Search button enables you to search for a particular name, and the Delete button enables you to delete records:

14

☐ Add a command button to the frmPhone form and set its properties as follows:

Object	Property	Value
Command Button	**Name**	**cmdSearch**
	Caption	Search

☐ Add another command button to the frmPhone form and set its properties as follows:

Object	Property	Value
Command Button	**Name**	**cmdDelete**
	Caption	Delete

When you finish setting the properties of the two new buttons, the frmPhone form should look like the one shown in Figure 14.5.

Figure 14.5.

The frmPhone form after you add the Search and Delete buttons.

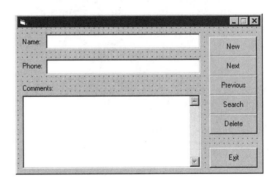

☐ Enter the following code in the cmdSearch_Click() procedure:

```
Private Sub cmdSearch_Click ()

Dim NameToSearch As String
Dim Found As Integer
Dim RecNum As Long
Dim TmpPerson As PersonInfo

' Get the name to search from the user.
NameToSearch = InputBox("Search for:", "Search")

' If the user did not enter a name, exit
' from this procedure.
If NameToSearch = "" Then
   ' Give the focus to the txtName field.
   txtName.SetFocus
   ' Exit this procedure.
   Exit Sub
End If
```

```
' Convert the name to be searched to upper case.
NameToSearch = UCase(NameTosearch)

' Initialize the Found flag to False.
Found = False

' Search for the name that the user entered.
For RecNum = 1 To gLastRecord
   Get #gFileNum, RecNum, TmpPerson
   If NameToSearch=UCase(Trim(TmpPerson.Name)) Then
      Found = True
      Exit For
   End If
Next

' If the name was found, display the record
' of the found name.
If Found = True Then
   SaveCurrentRecord
   gCurrentRecord = RecNum
   ShowCurrentRecord
Else
   MsgBox "Name " + NameToSearch + " not found!"
End If

' Give the focus to the txtName field.
txtName.SetFocus
```

End Sub

☐ Enter the following code in the cmdDelete_Click() procedure:

```
Private Sub cmdDelete_Click ()

Dim DirResult
Dim TmpFileNum
Dim TmpPerson As PersonInfo
Dim RecNum As Long
Dim TmpRecNum As Long

' Before deleting get a confirmation from the user.
If MsgBox("Delete this record?", vbYesNo) = vbNo Then
   ' Give the focus to the txtName field.
   txtName.SetFocus
   ' Exit the procedure without deleting.
   Exit Sub
End If

' To physically delete the current record of PHONE.DAT,
' all the records of PHONE.DAT, except the
' current record, are copied into a temporary file
' (PHONE.TMP) and then the file PHONE.TMP is copied into
' PHONE.DAT:

' Make sure that PHONE.TMP does not exist.
If Dir("PHONE.TMP") = "PHONE.TMP" Then
```

14

```
    Kill "PHONE.TMP"
End If

' Create PHONE.TMP with the same format
' as PHONE.DAT.
TmpFileNum = FreeFile
Open "PHONE.TMP" For Random As TmpFileNum Len = gRecordLen

' Copy all the records from PHONE.DAT
' to PHONE.TMP, except the current record.
RecNum = 1
TmpRecNum = 1
Do While RecNum < gLastRecord + 1
    If RecNum <> gCurrentRecord Then
        Get #gFileNum, RecNum, TmpPerson
        Put #TmpFileNum, TmpRecNum, TmpPerson
        TmpRecNum = TmpRecNum + 1
    End If
    RecNum = RecNum + 1
Loop

' Delete PHONE.DAT.
Close gFileNum
Kill "PHONE.DAT"

' Rename PHONE.TMP into PHONE.DAT.
Close TmpFileNum
Name "PHONE.TMP" As "PHONE.DAT"

' Re-open PHONE.DAT.
gFileNum = FreeFile
Open "PHONE.DAT" For Random As gFileNum Len = gRecordLen

' Update the value of LastRecord.
gLastRecord = gLastRecord - 1

' Make sure that gLastRecord is not 0.
If gLastRecord = 0 Then gLastRecord = 1

' Make sure gCurrentRecord is not out of range.
If gCurrentRecord > gLastRecord Then
    gCurrentRecord = gLastRecord
End If

' Show the current record.
ShowCurrentRecord

' Give the focus to the txtName field.
txtName.SetFocus

End Sub
```

☐ Execute the Phone program and experiment with the Search and Delete buttons.

The Code of the `cmdSearch_Click()` Procedure

When you click the Search button, the `cmdSearch_Click()` procedure is executed. This procedure lets you search for a particular name.

The procedure begins by using the `InputBox()` function to get a name from you. The name you enter is stored in the variable `NameToSearch`:

```
NameToSearch = InputBox("Search for:", "Search")
```

The `InputBox()` function returns null if you click the Cancel button of the Search Input Box, so an `If` statement is used. If you click the Cancel button, the procedure is terminated:

```
If NameToSearch = "" Then
    ' Give the focus to the txtName field.
    txtName.SetFocus
    ' Exit this procedure.
    Exit Sub
End If
```

After the variable `NameToSearch` is updated, the `UCase()` function is used to convert it to uppercase:

```
NameToSearch = UCase(NameTosearch)
```

This conversion is necessary because the search for the name shouldn't be case sensitive (that is, even if you type john, the record containing the name JOHN should be found).

To search for the name you entered, a `For` loop is used:

```
' Initialize the Found flag to False.
Found = False

' Search for the name that the user entered.
For RecNum = 1 To gLastRecord
   Get #gFileNum, RecNum, TmpPerson
   If NameToSearch=UCase(Trim(TmpPerson.Name)) Then
      Found = True
      Exit For
   End If
Next
```

This `For` loop uses the `Get` statement to read the records of the file, record after record, into the variable `TmpPerson`. After it reads each record, an `If` statement is used to see whether the record that was just read contains the name being searched for. The `If` statement compares the value of the variable `NameToSearch` with the value of `UCase(Trim(TmpPerson.Name))`. The `UCase()` function is used so the search won't be case sensitive, and the `Trim()` function gets rid of leading or trailing blanks in the Name field.

14

Note

The LTrim() function returns a string without the leading spaces.

The RTrim() function returns a string without the trailing spaces.

The Trim() function returns a string without the leading and trailing spaces.

For example, consider the following code:

```
ToBeWorkedOn = "   Testing    "
```

If you execute the statement

```
ResultOfLTrim = LTrim(ToBeWorkedOn)
```

then ResultOfLTrim will be equal to "Testing   ".

If you execute the statement

```
ResultOfRTrim = RTrim(ToBeWorkedOn)
```

then ResultOfRTrim will be equal to "   Testing".

If you execute the statement

```
ResultOfTrim = Trim(ToBeWorkedOn)
```

then ResultOfTrim will be equal to "Testing".

If a record with its Name field equal to NameToSearch is found, the variable Found is set to True and the For loop is terminated. After the For loop ends, the procedure displays the results of the search:

```
If Found = True Then
    SaveCurrentRecord
    gCurrentRecord = RecNum
    ShowCurrentRecord
Else
    MsgBox "Name " + NameToSearch + " not found!"
End If
```

If the search was successful, the current record is saved and the found record is displayed. If, however, the search failed, a not found! message is displayed.

The Code of the cmdDelete_Click() Procedure

When you click the Delete button, the cmdDelete_Click() procedure deletes the current record. It uses the following four steps to delete the current record from the PHONE.DAT file:

1. Create an empty temporary file (PHONE.TMP).

2. Use a For loop to copy all the records in PHONE.DAT (record after record), except the current record, into the file PHONE.TMP.

3. Erase the file PHONE.DAT.

4. Rename the file PHONE.TMP as PHONE.DAT.

Sequential Access Files

Random files are accessed record by record, but *sequential files* are accessed line by line. That is, when you write data into a sequential file, you write lines of text into the file. When you read data from a sequential file, you read lines of text from the file. The fact that sequential files are accessed line by line makes them ideal for use in applications that manipulate text files.

You can open a sequential file in one of three ways: output, append, or input.

Opening a Sequential File for Output

To create a sequential file, you need to open a file for output. After the file is created, you can use output commands to write lines to the file. The following sample code creates the file TRY.TXT:

```
' Get a free file number.
FileNum = FreeFile

' Open the file TRY.TXT for output (i.e. create it).
Open "TRY.TXT" For Output As FileNum
```

If the file TRY.TXT does not exist, this code creates it. If the file does exist, this code erases the old file and creates a new one.

Note that in the preceding code, the file to be opened, TRY.TXT, was specified without a path. When a path isn't specified, the file is opened in the current directory. For example, if the current directory is C:\PROGRAMS, the following two statements will do the same thing:

```
Open "TRY.TXT" For Output As FileNum
Open "C:\PROGRAMS\TRY.TXT" For Output As FileNum
```

Because opening a file for output creates the file, it will be empty. To write text into the file, you can use the Print # statement. The following example creates the file TRY.TXT and writes the contents of the text box txtMyText into the file:

```
' Get a free file number.
FileNum = FreeFile

' Open TRY.TXT for output (i.e. create TRY.TXT).
Open "TRY.TXT" For Output As FileNum

' Write the contents of the text box txtMyText into the file TRY.TXT.
Print #FileNum, txtMyText.Text
```

14

```
' Close the file.
Close FileNum
```

In the preceding code, two parameters are passed to the Print# statement: The first parameter is the file number, and the second parameter is the string to be written into the file.

Opening a Sequential File for Append

Opening a sequential file for append is similar to opening it for output; however, when you open a file for append, it isn't erased if the file already exists. Rather, subsequent output commands append new lines to the opened file. For example, suppose that the file TRY.TXT already exists and contains the following two lines:

```
THIS IS LINE NUMBER 1
THIS IS LINE NUMBER 2
```

To append a new line to the file TRY.TXT, you can use the following code:

```
' Get a free file number.
FileNum = FreeFile

' Open TRY.TXT for append.
Open "TRY.TXT" For Append As FileNum

' Add new text to the file.
Print #FileNum, "THIS IS A NEW TEXT"

' Close the file.
Close FileNum
```

After executing this code, the file TRY.TXT contains three lines:

```
THIS IS LINE NUMBER 1
THIS IS LINE NUMBER 2
THIS IS A NEW TEXT
```

If you execute the same code again, the file TRY.TXT will contain four lines:

```
THIS IS LINE NUMBER 1
THIS IS LINE NUMBER 2
THIS IS A NEW TEXT
THIS IS A NEW TEXT
```

Opening a Sequential File for Input

To read the contents of a sequential file, you need to open a file for input. Once a file is opened for input, you can use the Input() function to read the entire contents of the file into a text box or a string variable.

The following example opens the file TRY.TXT for input and uses the Input() function to read the contents of the file into the text box txtMyText:

```
' Get a free file number.
FileNum = FreeFile

' Open TRY.TXT for input.
Open "TRY.TXT" For Input As FileNum

' Read all the contents of the file into the text
' box txtMyText.
txtMyText.Text = Input(LOF(FileNum), FileNum)

' Close the file.
Close FileNum
```

The Input() function takes two parameters: The first parameter specifies the number of bytes to be read from the file, and the second parameter specifies the file number.

Because the purpose of the preceding code is to read the entire contents of the file, the first parameter of the Input() function was specified as LOF(FileNum). The LOF() function returns the total length of the file in bytes.

The Write # and Input # Statements

In the preceding examples, the Input() function and the Print # statement were used to read data from and write data to a sequential file, but you can also use the Write # and Input # statements.

The Write # statement lets you write a list of variables (strings or numeric) to a file. The following example creates the file TRY.TXT and stores the contents of the string variable MyString and the contents of the numeric variable MyNumber into the file:

```
' Get a free file number.
FileNum = FreeFile

' Create the file TRY.TXT.
Open "TRY.TXT" For Output As FileNum

' Write the contents of the variables MyString, and
' MyNumber into the file.
Write #FileNum, MyString, MyNumber

' Close the file.
Close FileNum
```

14

The first parameter of the Write # statement is the file number. The rest of the parameters are the variables that will be written into the file. Because only two variables are written into the file in the preceding example, there are only two parameters after the first parameter.

The `Input #` statement lets you read data from a file that contains the contents of a list of variables. The following code reads the contents of the file created in the preceding example:

```
' Get a free file number.
FileNum = FreeFile

' Open the file TRY.TXT for input.
Open "TRY.TXT" For Input As FileNum

' Read the contents of the file into the variables
' MyString, and MyNumber.
Input #FileNum, MyString, MyNumber

' Close the file.
Close FileNum
```

The first parameter of the `Input #` statement is the file number. The rest of the parameters are the variables that will be filled with the contents of the file. The order in which the variables are placed in the `Input #` statement must match the order in which they were originally stored in the file with the `Write #` statement.

Binary Access Files

Random files are accessed record by record and sequential files are accessed line by line, but *binary files* are accessed byte by byte. Once you open a file for binary access, you can read from and write to any byte location in the file. This ability to access any desired byte in the file makes binary access the most flexible.

Opening a File for Binary Access

Before you can access a file in a binary mode (byte by byte), you must first open a file for binary access. The following sample code opens the file TRY.DAT for binary access:

```
' Get a free file number.
FileNum = FreeFile

' Open the file TRY.DAT for binary access.
Open "TRY.DAT" For Binary As FileNum
```

If the file TRY.DAT does not already exist, the preceding `Open` statement creates it.

Writing Bytes into a Binary File

After a file is opened for binary access, the `Put #` statement can be used to write bytes to any byte location in the file. The following sample code writes the string THIS IS A TEST into the file TRY.DAT, starting at byte location 100:

```
' Fill the string variable MyString with the
' string "THIS IS A TEST".
MyString = "THIS IS A TEST"

' Get a free file number.
FileNum = FreeFile

' Open the file TRY.DAT for binary access.
Open "TRY.DAT" For Binary As FileNum

' Write the string variable MyString, starting at
' byte location 100.
Put #FileNum,100, MyString

' Close the file.
Close FileNum
```

The Put # statement takes three parameters: The first parameter is the file number, the second parameter is the byte location where the writing starts, and the third parameter is the name of the variable whose contents will be written into the file. In the preceding example, the variable whose contents are written into the file is a string variable, but you could use other types of variables, such as numeric.

After the Put # statement is executed, the position of the file is automatically set to the next byte after the last byte that was written. For example, in the preceding sample code, after the 14 characters of the string THIS IS A TEST are written into the file starting at position 100, the position of the file is automatically set to 114. So if another Put # statement is executed without specifying the byte location, the writing of this new Put # statement starts at byte location 114. The following sample code illustrates how the file position is updated automatically after a Put # statement:

```
' Get a free file number.
FileNum = FreeFile

' Open the file TRY.DAT for binary access.
Open "TRY.DAT" For Binary As FileNum

' Write the string "12345" starting at byte
' location 20 of the file.
MyString = "12345"
Put #FileNum, 20, MyString

' At this point the file position is set at byte
' location 25, so if the next Put # statement will
' not specify a byte location, then the writing of
' the next Put # statement will be performed at byte
' location 25.

' Write the string "67890" without specifying a byte
' location.
MyString = "67890"
Put #FileNum, , MyString
```

14

```
' Close the file.
Close FileNum
```

Note that the second Put # statement in the preceding code did not specify a byte location (that is, the second parameter is not specified—there is a blank between the first comma and second comma).

Reading Bytes from a Binary File

After a file is opened for binary access, the Get # statement can be used to read bytes from any byte location in the file. The following sample code reads 15 characters, starting at byte location 40, of the file TRY.DAT:

```
' Get a free file number.
FileNum = FreeFile

' Open the file TRY.DAT for binary access.
Open "TRY.DAT" For Binary As FileNum

' Initialize the MyString string to 15 blanks. '
MyString = String(15, " ")

' Read 15 characters from the file, starting at byte
' location 40.
Get #FileNum, 40, MyString

' Close the file.
Close FileNum
```

As you can see, the Get # statement takes three parameters: The first parameter is the file number, the second parameter is the byte location where the reading will start, and the third parameter is the name of the variable that will be filled with the data from the file. The number of bytes read from the file is determined by the size of the variable filled with the data. Because the variable MyString was initialized to 15 blanks in the preceding code, the Get # statement reads only 15 characters.

Summary

In this chapter you learned how to create files, how to write data to files, and how to read data from files. You also learned that there are three types of files: random, sequential, and binary. Random files are accessed record by record and are useful in database applications. Sequential files are accessed line by line and are ideal for use with text files. Binary files are the most flexible because they are accessed byte by byte.

Q&A

Q Why are random files considered random?

A The word *random* is used because once a file is opened for random access, the program can access any record in the file. In other words, the program can read and write records in a random order (first record 7, then record 3, then record 9, and so on).

Q In the Phone program, the file PHONE.DAT was opened for random access with the following statement:

```
Open "PHONE.DAT" For Random As FileNum Len = RecordLen
```

The name of the file, PHONE.DAT, was specified without a path. In what directory is the file opened?

A Because no path was specified, the file is opened in the current directory. The question is, "What is the current directory?" Suppose that you create an EXE file PHONE.EXE from the Phone program and save the file PHONE.EXE in the C:\MYDIR directory. When you execute the C:\MYDIR\PHONE.EXE program, the current directory is C:\MYDIR by default. This means that the file PHONE.DAT is opened in C:\MYDIR.

Quiz

1. Assume there is a user-defined data type that is defined as follows:

```
Type EmployeeInfo
   Name As String * 40
   Age  As Integer
End Type
```

Then what does the following code do?

```
Dim FileNum As Integer
Dim Employee As EmployeeInfo
FileNum = FreeFile
Open "EMPLOYEE.DAT" For Random As FileNum Len=Len(Employee)
Employee.Name = "JOHN SMITH"
Employee.Age = 32
Put FileNum, 5, Employee
```

2. Assume there is a user-defined data type that is defined as follows:

```
Type EmployeeInfo
   Name As String * 40
   Age  As Integer
End Type
```

14

Then what does the following code do?

```
Dim FileNum As Integer
Dim Employee As EmployeeInfo
FileNum = FreeFile
Open "EMPLOYEE.DAT" For Random As FileNum Len=Len(Employee)
Get #FileNum, 10, Employee
MsgBox "The age of  "+ _
        Trim(Employee.Name)+ _
        " is " + Str(Employee.Age)
```

3. What does the following code do?

```
FileNum = FreeFile
Open "TRY.TXT" For Output As FileNum
Print #FileNum, txtMyText.Text
Close FileNum
```

4. What do the following statements do?

```
FileNum = FreeFile
Open "C:\TRY\TRY.TXT" For Append As FileNum
```

5. What does the following code do?

```
FileNum = FreeFile
Open "INFO.TXT" For Append As FileNum
Print #FileNum, txtMyText.Text
Close FileNum
```

6. What does the following code do?

```
FileNum = FreeFile
Open "TRY.TXT" For Input As FileNum
txtMyText.Text = Input(LOF(FileNum), FileNum)
Close FileNum
```

7. What does the following code do?

```
FileNum = FreeFile
Open "TRY.DAT" For Binary As FileNum
MyString = "THIS IS A TEST"
Put #FileNum, 75, MyString
Close FileNum
```

8. What does the following code do?

```
FileNum = FreeFile
Open "TRY.DAT" For Binary As FileNum
MyString = String(20, " ")
Get #FileNum, 75, MyString
MsgBox "MyString="+MyString
Close FileNum
```

Exercises

1. Wave (*.WAV) files are standard sound files used in Windows. The sampling rate of a WAV file is saved as an integer value starting at byte location 25 of the file.

Write a program that displays the sampling rate of the file C:\WINDOWS\ TADA.WAV. (The file TADA.WAV is included with Windows.) *Hint:* Use binary access.

2. Write a program that displays the contents of the file C:\AUTOEXEC.BAT in a text box. *Hint:* Use sequential access.

Quiz Answers

1. The code stores the name "JOHN SMITH" and his age (32) in record number 5 of the file EMPLOYEE.DAT:

```
' Declare variables.
Dim FileNum As Integer
Dim Employee As EmployeeInfo
' Get a free file number.
FileNum = FreeFile

' Open the file EMPLOYEE.DAT.
Open "EMPLOYEE.DAT" For Random As FileNum Len=Len(Employee)

' Fill the variable Employee.
Employee.Name = "JOHN SMITH"
Employee.Age = 32

' Store the contents of the variable Employee in
' record number 5 of the file.
Put FileNum, 5, Employee
```

2. The code displays the name of the person and his age from record number 10:

```
Dim FileNum As Integer
Dim Employee As EmployeeInfo

' Get a free file number.
FileNum = FreeFile

' Open the file EMPLOYEE.DAT.
Open "EMPLOYEE.DAT" For Random As FileNum Len=Len(Employee)

' Fill the variable Employee with the contents of
' record number 10 of the file.
Get #FileNum, 10, Employee

' Display the contents of the Employee variable.
MsgBox "The age of  "+ Trim(Employee.Name)+ " is "+Str(Employee.Age)
```

3. The code creates the file TRY.TXT and writes the contents of the txtMyText text box into the file:

```
NL' Get a free file number.
FileNum = FreeFile

' Create the file TRY.TXT.
Open "TRY.TXT" For Output As FileNum
```

14

```
' Write the contents of the text box txtMyText into
' the file TRY.TXT.
Print #FileNum, txtMyText.Text

' Close the file.
Close FileNum
```

4. These statements open the file C:\TRY\TRY.TXT for sequential append. If the file does not exist, it is created. If it does exist, subsequent output statements append new data to the file.

5. The code appends the contents of the txtMyText text box to the file INFO.TXT:

```
' Get a free file number.
FileNum = FreeFile

' Open the file INFO.TXT for append.
Open "INFO.TXT" For Append As FileNum

' Add the contents of the text box txtMyText to the
' end of INFO.TXT.
Print #FileNum, txtMyText.Text

' Close the file.
Close FileNum
```

6. The code reads the contents of the file TRY.TXT into the txtMyText text box:

```
' Get a free file number.
FileNum = FreeFile

' Open the file TRY.TXT for input.
Open "TRY.TXT" For Input As FileNum

' Read all the contents of TRY.TXT into the text
' box txtMyText.
txtMyText.Text = Input(LOF(FileNum), FileNum)

' Close the file.
Close FileNum
```

7. The code writes the string THIS IS A TEST into the file TRY.DAT, starting at byte location 75:

```
' Get a free file number.
FileNum = FreeFile

' Open the file TRY.DAT for binary access.
Open "TRY.DAT" For Binary As FileNum

' Fill the string variable MyString.
MyString = "THIS IS A TEST"

' Write the string variable MyString into the file,
' starting at byte location 75.
Put #FileNum, 75, MyString
```

```
' Close the file.
Close FileNum
```

8. The code reads 20 bytes from the file TRY.DAT, starting at byte location 75. The code then displays these 20 bytes:

```
' Get a free file number.
FileNum = FreeFile

' Open the file TRY.DAT for binary access.
Open "TRY.DAT" For Binary As FileNum

' Initialize the MyString string to 20 blanks.
MyString = String(20, " ")

' Read 20 characters from the file, starting at byte
' location 75. Only 20 characters are read because
' the length of MyString is 20 characters.
Get #FileNum, 75, MyString

' Display MyString.
MsgBox "MyString="+MyString

' Close the file.
Close FileNum
```

Exercise Answers

1. One possible solution to this exercise is to open the TADA.WAV file for binary access and read an integer value starting at byte number 25 of the file. After the value is read into an integer variable, the value of the variable can be displayed using a message box. The following code does this:

```
Dim SamplingRate As Integer
Dim FileNum As Integer

' Get a free file number.
FileNum = FreeFile

' Open the file C:\WINDOWS\MEDIA\TADA.WAV for binary access.
' NOTE: It is assumed that the TADA.WAV file
' resides in C:\WINDOWS\MEDIA
Open "C:\WINDOWS\MEDIA\TADA.WAV" For Binary As FileNum

' Read the sampling rate into the integer variable
' SamplingRate, starting at byte location 25.
Get #FileNum, 25, SamplingRate

' Close the file.
Close FileNum

' Display the sampling rate.
MsgBox "The sampling rate of TADA.WAV is " + _
       Str(SamplingRate)
```

14

You can place this code in the Click event procedure of a command button. After you run the program and click the command button, the following message should be displayed (assuming that your TADA.WAV was recorded at a sampling rate of 22050Hz):

```
The sampling rate of TADA.WAV is 22050
```

2. Because the file C:\AUTOEXEC.BAT is a text file, a good way to open it is with sequential access. The following code opens the file C:\AUTOEXEC.BAT for input and reads the contents of the file into a text box. The Name property of the text box should be set to txtMyText and the Multiline property of the text box should be set to TRUE. The code is placed in the Form_Load() procedure of the program's form:

```
Private Sub Form_Load ()

    ' Get a free file number.
    FileNum = FreeFile

    ' Open the file C:\AUTOEXEC.BAT for input.
    Open "C:\AUTOEXEC.BAT" For Input As FileNum

    ' Read all the contents of AUTOEXEC.BAT into the
    ' text box txtMyText.
    txtMyText.Text = Input(LOF(FileNum), FileNum)

    ' Close the file.
    Close FileNum

End Sub
```

Week 3

At A Glance

This is your final week! This week you'll learn about some of the most sophisticated features of Visual Basic—features that make it famous.

Where You're Going

This week, you'll learn how to use the data control, which enables your Visual Basic programs to interface with databases. You'll also learn how to create multiple-document interface (MDI) applications, how to use popular powerful OCX ActiveX controls, and more.

In Chapter 20, "Using Windows API," you'll learn how to write programs that use Windows API functions.

In Chapter 21, "Building Your Own OCX ActiveX Controls," you'll learn how to write and implement your own OCX ActiveX controls.

15

16

17

18

19

20

21

Day 15

Arrays, OLE, and Other Topics

In this chapter you'll learn about miscellaneous topics in Visual Basic that have not been covered in previous chapters.

ASCII Files

As you develop your programs, you might find it useful to print a hard copy of the form's properties table and the program's code. Visual Basic saves the properties table and the code in the form file. For example, the form file MYFORM.FRM contains the properties table and the code of the form frmMyForm.

Take a look at the OPTION.FRM file that you developed in Chapter 2, "Properties, Controls, and Objects."

☐ Start a text editor program that is capable of loading ASCII files (such as Notepad or WordPad).

In the following discussion, it is assumed that you use Notepad as your Text Editor program. (As stated, you can use any text editor or Word processor program that lets you load text files.)

☐ Select Open from the File menu of Notepad and load the fileC:\VB5PRG\CH02\ OPTION.FRM.

The OPTION.FRM file looks like this:

```
VERSION 5.00
Begin VB.Form frmOptions
   BackColor       =    &H000000FF&
   Caption         =    "The Options Program"
   ClientHeight    =    4185
   ClientLeft      =    60
   ClientTop       =    345
   ClientWidth     =    4680
   LinkTopic       =    "Form1"
   ScaleHeight     =    4185
   ScaleWidth      =    4680
   StartUpPosition =    3    'Windows Default
   Begin VB.OptionButton optLevel3
      BackColor       =    &H000000FF&
      Caption         =    "Level &3"
      BeginProperty Font
         Name          =    "MS Sans Serif"
         Size          =    9.75
         Charset       =    0
         Weight        =    700
         Underline     =    0    'False
         Italic        =    0    'False
         Strikethrough =    0    'False
      EndProperty
      ForeColor       =    &H00FFFFFF&
      Height          =    495
      Left            =    2760
      TabIndex        =    6
      Top             =    1560
      Width           =    1215
   End
   Begin VB.OptionButton optLevel2
      BackColor       =    &H000000FF&
      Caption         =    "Level &2"
      BeginProperty Font
         Name          =    "MS Sans Serif"
         Size          =    9.75
         Charset       =    0
         Weight        =    700
         Underline     =    0    'False
```

```
            Italic          =   0    'False
            Strikethrough   =   0    'False
      EndProperty
      ForeColor       =     &H00FFFFFF&
      Height          =     495
      Left            =     2760
      TabIndex        =     5
      Top             =     960
      Width           =     1215
   End
   Begin VB.OptionButton optLevel1
      BackColor       =     &H000000FF&
      Caption         =     "Level &1"
      BeginProperty Font
         Name         =     "MS Sans Serif"
         Size         =     9.75
         Charset      =     0
         Weight       =     700
         Underline    =     0    'False
         Italic       =     0    'False
         Strikethrough =    0    'False
      EndProperty
      ForeColor       =     &H00FFFFFF&
      Height          =     495
      Left            =     2760
      TabIndex        =     4
      Top             =     360
      Width           =     1215
   End
   Begin VB.CheckBox chkColors
      BackColor       =     &H000000FF&
      Caption         =     "&Colors"
      BeginProperty Font
         Name         =     "MS Sans Serif"
         Size         =     9.75
         Charset      =     0
         Weight       =     700
         Underline    =     0    'False
         Italic       =     0    'False
         Strikethrough =    0    'False
      EndProperty
      ForeColor       =     &H00FFFFFF&
      Height          =     495
      Left            =     600
      TabIndex        =     3
      Top             =     1320
      Width           =     1215
   End
   Begin VB.CheckBox chkMouse
      BackColor       =     &H000000FF&
      Caption         =     "&Mouse"
      BeginProperty Font
         Name         =     "MS Sans Serif"
         Size         =     9.75
         Charset      =     0
         Weight       =     700
```

```
                    Underline       =    0    'False
                    Italic          =    0    'False
                    Strikethrough   =    0    'False
                EndProperty
                ForeColor       =    &H00FFFFFF&
                Height          =    495
                Left            =    600
                TabIndex        =    2
                Top             =    840
                Width           =    1215
            End
            Begin VB.CheckBox chkSound
                BackColor       =    &H000000FF&
                Caption         =    "&Sound"
                BeginProperty Font
                    Name            =    "MS Sans Serif"
                    Size            =    9.75
                    Charset         =    0
                    Weight          =    700
                    Underline       =    0    'False
                    Italic          =    0    'False
                    Strikethrough   =    0    'False
                EndProperty
                ForeColor       =    &H00FFFFFF&
                Height          =    495
                Left            =    600
                TabIndex        =    1
                Top             =    360
                Width           =    1215
            End
            Begin VB.CommandButton cmdExit
                Caption         =    "E&xit"
                Height          =    495
                Left            =    1680
                TabIndex        =    0
                Top             =    3600
                Width           =    1215
            End
            Begin VB.Label lblChoice
                BorderStyle     =    1    'Fixed Single
                BeginProperty Font
                    Name            =    "MS Sans Serif"
                    Size            =    8.25
                    Charset         =    0
                    Weight          =    700
                    Underline       =    0    'False
                    Italic          =    0    'False
                    Strikethrough   =    0    'False
                EndProperty
                Height          =    1215
                Left            =    600
                TabIndex        =    7
                Top             =    2160
                Width           =    3255
            End
        End
    End
```

```
Attribute VB_Name = "frmOptions"
Attribute VB_GlobalNameSpace = False
Attribute VB_Creatable = False
Attribute VB_PredeclaredId = True
Attribute VB_Exposed = False
Option Explicit

Private Sub chkColors_Click()

    UpdateLabel

End Sub

Private Sub chkMouse_Click()

    UpdateLabel

End Sub

Private Sub chkSound_Click()

    UpdateLabel

End Sub

Private Sub cmdExit_Click()

    End

End Sub

Private Sub optLevel1_Click()

    UpdateLabel

End Sub

Private Sub optLevel2_Click()

    UpdateLabel

End Sub

Private Sub optLevel3_Click()

    UpdateLabel

End Sub

Public Sub UpdateLabel()

    ' Declare the variables
    Dim Info
    Dim LFCR
```

```
    LFCR = Chr(13) + Chr(10)

    ' Sound
    If chkSound.Value = 1 Then
        Info = "Sound: ON"
    Else
        Info = "Sound: OFF"
    End If

    ' Mouse
    If chkMouse.Value = 1 Then
        Info = Info + LFCR + "Mouse: ON"
    Else
        Info = Info + LFCR + "Mouse: OFF"
    End If

    ' Colors
    If chkColors.Value = 1 Then
        Info = Info + LFCR + "Colors: ON"
    Else
        Info = Info + LFCR + "Colors: OFF"
    End If

  ' Level 1
  If optLevel1.Value = True Then
      Info = Info + LFCR + "Level:1"
  End If

  ' Level 2
  If optLevel2.Value = True Then
      Info = Info + LFCR + "Level:2"
  End If

    ' Level 3
    If optLevel3.Value = True Then
        Info = Info + LFCR + "Level:3"
    End If

    lblChoice.Caption = Info

End Sub
```

As you can see, OPTION.FRM is a regular ASCII file (text file).

The first line of the ASCII file OPTION.FRM indicates which version of Visual Basic was used to generate the file:

```
VERSION 5.00
```

The next lines describe the form and the controls in the form (that is, the properties table). The lines after the properties table are the code of the program. The ASCII file of the form can be useful for documenting programs.

Understanding the format of the ASCII files can also be useful for programmers who write programs that generate the ASCII files automatically. (That is, you can write a program that asks your user several questions, and based on your user's answers, the program generates the ASCII file of the form.) Naturally, Visual Basic has no way of knowing who generated the ASCII file. However, the file must be in strict compliance with the format that Visual Basic expects.

Arrays

If your program uses arrays, it must declare them. The declaration of the array specifies the array's name and the number of elements it can hold. As with other variables, if you declare an array in the general declarations section of a form, the array is visible by all procedures and functions in the form. If you declare an array in a separate module and precede the declaration statement with the Global keyword, the array is visible by all the forms of the project.

Data Types

As you might have noticed by now, Visual Basic supports several data types. Table 15.1 lists the various data types and the range of values of the data Visual Basic supports. For example, when you declare a variable as an integer, you can use the following statement:

```
Dim Counter As Integer
```

The following statement yields identical results:

```
Dim Counter%
```

That is, the character % is a short notation for As Integer. An integer variable has the range of -32,768 to 32,767. Each integer occupies 2 bytes of memory.

Similarly, you can declare the long variable Number as follows:

```
Dim Numbers As Long
```

The following statement is another syntax notation for declaring the Number variable As Long:

```
Dim Numbers&
```

That is, the character & is a short notation for As Long. A long variable has the range -2,147,483,648 to 2,147,483,647. Each long variable occupies 4 bytes of memory.

The double variable MyVariable is declared as follows:

```
Dim MyVariable As Double
```

which is the same as this:

```
Dim MyVariable#
```

A double variable can be a positive or negative number and occupies 8 bytes of memory. The ranges of positive and negative values for each data type are specified in Table 15.1.

Table 15.1. The data types that Visual Basic supports.

Data Type	Number of Bytes	Shortcut Notation	Range
Integer	2	%	-32,768 to 32,767
Long	4	&	-2,147,483,648 to 2,147,483,647
Single-positive	4	!	1.401298E-45 to 3.402823E38
Single-negative	4	!	-3.402823E38 to -1.401298E-45
Double-positive	8	#	4.94065645841247D-24 to 1.79769313486232D308
Double-negative	8	#	1.79769313486232D308 to -4.94065645841247D-324
Currency	8	@	-922337203685477.5808 to 922337203685466.5807
String	Depends	$	In Windows 3.1 or earlier, a string can hold up to approximately 65,000 characters. In other newer operating systems, strings can support up to 2 billion characters.
Variant	Date, time, floating point, or string.	(none)	Range of date: from January 1, 0000 to December 31, 9999

Note that the last item in Table 15.1 describes a variable of the type Variant, which can be a date, time, floating point (for example, 1234.5678), or string. When you declare a variable as follows:

```
Dim I As Integer
```

Visual Basic creates a variable called I as an integer. However, if you declare a variable as follows:

```
Dim I
```

Visual Basic creates this variable as a variant variable. That is, Visual Basic doesn't know whether the I variable will serve as a string, an integer, a long, or other type. Later in the program, Visual Basic will figure out how to treat the variable by looking at the statement that uses the variable. For example, if Visual Basic encounters this statement:

```
I = "My String"
```

Visual Basic knows the variable should be treated as a string. However, if Visual Basic encounters this statement:

```
I = 2 + 3
```

Visual Basic knows the variable should be treated as an integer.

The advantage of using variant variables is that the same variable can serve as several types of data. For example, it is OK to have the following statements in the same procedure:

```
Dim I
I = 2 + 3
I = "My String"
```

That is, as a variant data type, I serves as an integer and then as a string.

The disadvantage of using variant data types is that Visual Basic programs that use them can sometimes run more slowly than programs that specifically indicate the variables' data types. For example, a For loop will be executed faster when the counter variable of the loop is declared as an integer. Of course, if the For loop has to count more than 32,767 times, you must use a long variable in the For counter (because an integer variable has a maximum value of 32,767). A For loop with a long variable as its counter variable will be executed a bit slower than a For loop with an integer.

You can write the For loop with a variant variable. In this case, the For loop will be executed slower than it would with an integer or a long variable. To declare a variable as variant, you use a statement such as this:

```
Dim HisVariant
```

However, you can also use the following statement to declare a variant variable:

```
Dim HisVariant As Variant
```

The Arrays Program

The Arrays program illustrates how you declare arrays in Visual Basic.

The Visual Implementation of the Arrays Program

Start by implementing the arrays program:

☐ Create the C:\VB5PRG\CH15 directory. You'll save your work in this directory.

☐ Open a new project, save the form of the project as ARRAYS.FRM in the C:\VB5PRG\CH15 directory, and save the project file as ARRAYS.VBP in the C:\VB5PRG\CH15 directory.

☐ Build the frmArrays form according to the specifications in Table 15.2.

The completed form should look like the one shown in Figure 15.1.

Table 15.2. The properties table of the frmArrays form.

Object	Property	Setting
Form	**Name**	**frmArrays**
	Caption	The Arrays Program
Command Button	**Name**	**cmdArray1**
	Caption	Array&1
Command Button	**Name**	**cmdArray2**
	Caption	Array&2
Command Button	**Name**	**cmdExit**
	Caption	E&xit

Figure 15.1.

The frmArrays form.

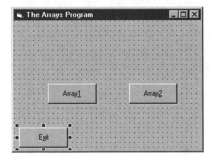

Entering the Code of the Arrays Program

Start by entering the code of the arrays program:

☐ Enter the following code in the general declarations section of the frmArrays form:

```
' All variables MUST be declared.
Option Explicit
' Declare  the array.
```

```
' The first element of the array is gArray2(10).
' The last element of the array is gArray2(20).
Dim gArray2(10 To 20)  As Integer
```

☐ Enter the following code in the cmdArray1_Click() procedure of the frmArrays form:

```
Private Sub cmdArray1_Click()

    Dim Counter

    ' Declare the array.
    ' The first element of the array is Array1(1).
    ' The last element of the array is Array1(10).
    Static Array1(1 To 10)  As String

    ' Fill 3 elements of the array.
    Array1(1) = "ABC"
    Array1(2) = "DEF"
    Array1(3) = "GHI"

    ' Clear the form.
    frmArrays.Cls

    ' Display 3 elements of the array.
    Print "Here are the elements of Array1[]:"
    For Counter = 1 To 3 Step 1
        Print "Array1(" + Str(Counter) + ") =" + _
                  Array1(Counter)
    Next

End Sub
```

☐ Enter the following code in the cmdArray2_Click() procedure of the frmArrays form:

```
Private Sub cmdArray2_Click()

    Dim Counter

    ' Fill 3 elements of the array.
    gArray2(11) = 234
    gArray2(12) = 567
    gArray2(13) = 890

    ' Clear the form.
    frmArrays.Cls

    ' Display 3 elements of the array.
    Print "Here are the elements of gArray2[]:"
    For Counter = 11 To 13 Step 1
        Print "gArray2(" + Str(Counter) + ") = "; _
                  Str(gArray2(Counter))
    Next

End Sub
```

☐ Enter the following code in the cmdExit_Click() procedure of the frmArrays form:

```
Private Sub cmdExit_Click()

    End

End Sub
```

Executing the Arrays Program

Then execute the arrays program:

☐ Execute the Arrays program.

☐ Click the Array1 button.

The Arrays program responds by displaying the elements of Array1() (see Figure 15.2).

☐ Click the Array2 button.

The Arrays program responds by displaying the elements of gArray2() (see Figure 15.3).

☐ Click the Exit button to exit the Arrays program.

Figure 15.2.

Displaying the elements of Array1().

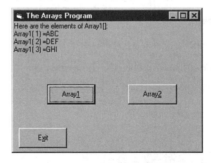

Figure 15.3.

Displaying the elements of gArray2().

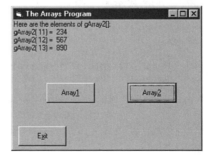

How the Arrays Program Works

The Arrays program declares the arrays Array1() and gArray2(). When you click the Array1 button, the program fills three elements of the Array1() array and displays them; when you click the Array2 button, the program fills three elements of the gArray2() array and displays them.

The Code of the General Declarations Section

The code in the general declarations section declares the gArray2() array:

```
Dim gArray2(10 To 20)  As Integer
```

The array is declared As Integer, which means that its elements are integers. The numbers in the parentheses indicate that the first element of the array is gArray(10), the second element is gArray(11), and so on. The last element of the array is gArray(20).

Because the gArray2() array is declared in the general declarations section of the form, it is visible in all procedures and functions of the form.

The Code of the cmdArray1_Click() Procedure

The cmdArray1_Click()procedure is automatically executed when you click the Array1 button:

```
Private Sub cmdArray1_Click()

    Dim Counter

    ' Declare the array.
    ' The first element of the array is Array1(1).
    ' The last element of the array is Array1(10).
    Static Array1(1 To 10)  As String

    ' Fill 3 elements of the array.
    Array1(1) = "ABC"
    Array1(2) = "DEF"
    Array1(3) = "GHI"

    ' Clear the form.
    frmArrays.Cls

    ' Display 3 elements of the array.
    Print "Here are the elements of Array1[]:"
    For Counter - 1 To 3 Step 1
        Print "Array1(" + Str(Counter) + ") =" + _
                Array1(Counter)
    Next

End Sub
```

This procedure declares the `Array1()` array as follows:

```
Static Array1(1 To 10) As String
```

Note that because `Array1()` is declared in a procedure, you must declare it as `Static`. That is, an array must be declared either in the general declarations section or as static in a procedure.

The first element of the array is `Array1(1)`, the second element of the array is `Array1(2)`, and so on. The last element of the array is `Array1(10)`.

The procedure then fills three elements in the array and clears the form with the `Cls` method:

```
Array1(1) = "ABC"
Array1(2) = "DEF"
Array1(3) = "GHI"
frmArrays.Cls
```

Finally, the procedure displays the first three elements of the array with a `For` loop:

```
Print "Here are the elements of Array1[]:"
For Counter = 1 To 3 Step 1
    Print "Array1(" + Str(Counter) + ") =" + _
          Array1(Counter)
Next
```

The Code of the `cmdArray2_Click()` Procedure

The `cmdArray2_Click()` procedure is executed when you click the Array2 button:

```
Private Sub cmdArray2_Click()

    Dim Counter

    ' Fill 3 elements of the array.
    gArray2(11) = 234
    gArray2(12) = 567
    gArray2(13) = 890

    ' Clear the form.
    frmArrays.Cls

    ' Display 3 elements of the array.
    Print "Here are the elements of gArray2[]:"
    For Counter = 11 To 13 Step 1
        Print "gArray2(" + Str(Counter) + ") = "; _
                  Str(gArray2(Counter))
    Next

End Sub
```

This procedure is similar to the `cmdArray1_Click()` procedure. Because the `gArray2()` array is declared in the general declarations section of the form, this array is visible from all procedures in the project.

15

The Upper and Lower Bounds of Arrays

As illustrated in the Arrays program, the first and last elements of the array are specified in the declaration of the array. For example, this declaration declares an array of long numbers:

```
Dim MyArray (0 to 35) As Long
```

The first element (the lower bound) is MyArray(0), and the last element (the upper bound) in the array is MyArray(35). As a shortcut, you can also declare arrays as follows:

```
Dim MyArray(35) As long
```

The preceding notations are interpreted by Visual Basic as follows: The first element of the array is MyArray(0), the second element is MyArray(1), and so on. The last element of the array is MyArray(35). The disadvantage of using this shortcut notation for the declaration is that the lower bound of the array is 0 by default. In other words, you have to remember that element number 0 is the first element, element number 1 is the second element, and so on.

The Array's Size

Basically, the maximum size of the array depends on the operating system. As you know, Windows uses virtual memory. That is, when all the available memory (RAM) is used, Windows starts using the hard drive as RAM. When space in the hard drive is used as RAM, that portion of the hard drive is called virtual memory.

For example, if a PC with 16 megabytes of RAM used all 16MB, Windows will start using hard drive space as RAM. As you know, RAM uses integrated circuit chips that store bytes electronically, so storing data to RAM and reading data from RAM is performed very fast. On the other hand, the hard drive is a mechanical device and requires an actual mechanical rotation of its parts. This means that storing and reading data from the hard drive is much slower than storing and reading data from RAM. If you are using huge arrays and your PC has used all the available RAM, Windows will start using hard drive space as RAM and the program will slow down. Again, your program will experience performance problems only if your PC has used all the available RAM.

Multidimensional Arrays

The Arrays program used a one-dimensional array. In Visual Basic, you can declare multidimensional arrays. For example, the following statement declares a two-dimensional array:

```
Static MyArray (0 To 3, 1 To 4 )
```

These are the elements of the preceding array:

```
MyArray(0,1) MyArray(0,2) MyArray(0,3) MyArray(0,4)
MyArray(1,1) MyArray(1,2) MyArray(1,3) MyArray(1,4)
MyArray(2,1) MyArray(2,2) MyArray(2,3) MyArray(2,4)
MyArray(3,1) MyArray(3,2) MyArray(3,3) MyArray(3,4)
```

In a similar way, you can declare a three-dimensional array:

```
Dim MyArray ( 1 To 3, 1 To 7, 1 To 5)
```

The following code uses two For loops to fill all the elements of a two-dimensional array with the value 3:

```
Static MyArray (1 To 10, 1 To 10) As Integer
Dim Counter1, Counter2
For Counter1 = 1 To 10
    For Counter2 = 1 To 10
        MyArray(Counter1, Counter2) = 3
    Next Counter2
Next Counter1
```

Typically, you'll use one-dimensional arrays, although you may find that two-dimensional arrays are more convenient to use in some situations. Occasionally, you might even find that using three-dimensional arrays is useful. However, using an array with more than three dimensions makes the program very hard to understand and debug.

Dynamic Arrays

When declaring arrays, you have to be careful not to consume too much memory. For example, this declaration declares an array with 10,001 elements:

```
Static MyArray (10000) As long
```

Because each element is defined as long, and a long variable occupies four bytes of memory (as shown in Table 15.1), the MyArray() array requires 40,004 (10,001×4) bytes of memory. This might not sound like a lot of memory, but if you have 10 such arrays in your program, these arrays consume 400,040 (40,004×10) bytes of memory! Therefore, always try to set the size of your arrays to the minimum your program requires. Sometimes, however, the size of the arrays can be determined only during runtime. In these cases, you can use the ReDim (redimensioning) statement that Visual Basic supports. An array that changes its size during runtime is called a *dynamic array*.

The following code illustrates how to redimension an array:

```
Private Sub Command1_Click()

    Dim Counter
```

```
' Declare Array1 as a dynamic array.
Dim Array1() As Integer

' Assign the size of the dynamic array.
ReDim Array1(1 To 15) As Integer

For Counter = 1 To 15 Step 1
    Array1(Counter) = Counter
Next Counter

' Assign a new size to the dynamic array.
ReDim Array1(1 To 5) As Integer
```

End Sub

The procedure declares Array1() as a dynamic array. Note that the declaration of a fixed array is different from the declaration of a dynamic array. That is, when you declare a dynamic array, its size isn't specified in the declaration.

The next statement in the preceding code assigns a size to the array by using the ReDim statement:

```
ReDim Array1(1 To 15) As Integer
```

This ReDim statement assigns 15 elements to the array. The elements in the array are defined as integers.

The For loop fills the 15 elements of the array; then the ReDim statement is used again to redimension the array:

```
ReDim Array1(1 To 5)  As Integer
```

After executing the second ReDim statement, the Array1() array has only five elements. Therefore, you can use this technique to change the size of your arrays during runtime and conserve memory. In the preceding code, Array1() required 30 (15×2) bytes. However, after the execution of the second ReDim statement, the size of Array1() was changed to five elements, and from that point on, Array1() occupied only 10 (5×2) bytes.

It is important to understand that once the ReDim statement is executed, the values that were stored in the array are lost forever! If you want to preserve some of the values of the array, you must use the Preserve keyword. The Arrays2 program illustrates how you can accomplish this.

The Arrays2 Program

You'll now implement the Arrays2 program. The Arrays2 program illustrates how you can redimension arrays from within your Visual Basic programs.

The Visual Implementation of the Arrays2 Program

Start by implementing the Arrays2 program:

☐ Start a new Standard EXE project, save the new form of the form as ARRAYS2.FRM in the C:\VB5PRG\CH15 directory, and save the project file as ARRAYS2.VBP in the C:\VB5PRG\CH15 directory.

☐ Build the frmArray form according to the specifications in Table 15.3.

The completed form should look like the one shown in Figure 15.4.

Table 15.3. The properties table of the frmArray form.

Object	Property	Setting
Form	**Name**	**frmArray**
	Caption	The Arrays2 Program
Command Button	**Name**	**cmdFill10**
	Caption	Fill &10 Elements
Command Button	**Name**	**cmdOnly5**
	Caption	Cut to &5 Elements
Combo Box	**Name**	**cboElements**
	Text	(Make it empty)
	Style	0-Drop Down Combo
Command Button	**Name**	**cmdExit**
	Caption	E&xit

Figure 15.4.

The frmArray form of the Arrays2 program.

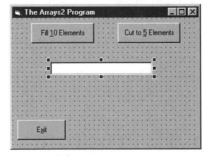

Entering the Code of the Arrays2 Program

Next, enter the code:

☐ Enter the following code in the general declarations section of the frmArray form:

```
' All variables MUST be declared.
Option Explicit
' Declare a dynamic array.
Dim gTheArray() As Integer
```

☐ Enter the following code in the cmdExit_Click() procedure of the frmArray form:

```
Private Sub cmdExit_Click()

    End

End Sub
```

☐ Enter the following code in the cmdFill10_Click() procedure of the frmArray form:

```
Private Sub cmdFill10_Click()

    ' Set the size of the array.
    ReDim gTheArray(1 To 10) As Integer
    Dim Counter
    ' Fill the elements of the array.
    For Counter = 1 To 10 Step 1
        gTheArray(Counter) = Counter
    Next Counter
    ' Clear the combo box.
    cboElements.Clear
    ' Fill the items of the combo box.
    For Counter = 0 To 9 Step 1
        cboElements.AddItem _
                Str(gTheArray(Counter + 1))
    Next Counter

End Sub
```

☐ Enter the following code in the cmdOnly5_Click() procedure of the frmArray form:

```
Private Sub cmdOnly5_Click()

    ' Set the size of the array.
    ReDim Preserve gTheArray(1 To 5) As Integer
    Dim Counter
    ' Clear the combo box.
    cboElements.Clear
    ' Fill the items of the combo box.
    For Counter = 0 To 4 Step 1
        cboElements.AddItem _
                Str(gTheArray(Counter + 1))
    Next Counter

End Sub
```

Executing the Arrays2 Program

Then execute the program:

☐ Execute the Arrays2 program.

☐ Click the down-arrow icon of the Combo box to verify that currently, there are no items in the Combo box.

☐ Click the Fill 10 Elements button.

> *The Arrays2 program responds by filling the combo box with 10 elements. You can see these 10 elements by clicking the down-arrow button of the combo box to drop down the list (see Figure 15.5).*

☐ Click the Cut to 5 Elements button.

> *The Arrays2 program responds by eliminating five elements in the combo box. You can see the five elements that are left in the combo box by clicking the down-arrow button of the combo box to drop down the list (see Figure 15.6).*

Figure 15.5.

Filling the combo box with 10 items.

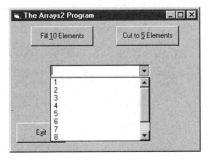

Figure 15.6.

Preserving five elements of the array.

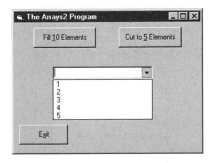

☐ Click the Exit button to exit the program.

How the Arrays2 Program Works

The Arrays2 program fills an array and then fills the items in the combo box with the elements of the array. As you'll soon see, the array is then redimensioned with the Preserve keyword, which retains the values of the elements that remain in the array.

The Code of the General Declarations Section

The code in the general declarations section of the frmArray form declares a dynamic array:

```
Dim gTheArray() As Integer
```

Visual Basic interprets this statement as a declaration of a dynamic array, because the parentheses that follow the name of the array are empty.

The Code of the cmdFill10_Click() Procedure

The cmdFill10_Click() procedure is automatically executed when you click the Fill 10 Elements button:

```
Private Sub cmdFill10_Click()

    ' Set the size of the array.
    ReDim gTheArray(1 To 10) As Integer
    Dim Counter
    ' Fill the elements of the array.
    For Counter = 1 To 10 Step 1
        gTheArray(Counter) = Counter
    Next Counter
    ' Clear the combo box.
    cboElements.Clear
    ' Fill the items of the combo box.
    For Counter = 0 To 9 Step 1
        cboElements.AddItem _
            Str(gTheArray(Counter + 1))
    Next Counter

End Sub
```

The procedure uses the ReDim statement to set the size of the array to 10 elements:

```
ReDim gTheArray(1 To 10) As Integer
```

The elements of the array are filled using a For loop:

```
For Counter = 1 To 10 Step 1
    gTheArray(Counter) = Counter
Next Counter
```

The elements in the combo box are cleared; then a For loop is used to fill 10 items in the combo box. The items in the combo box correspond to the elements of the array:

```
cboElements.Clear
For Counter = 0 To 9 Step 1
    cboElements.AddItem _
        Str(gTheArray(Counter + 1))
Next Counter
```

Note that the first item in the combo box is item number 0, and the first element of the array is element number 1. The last item of the combo box is item number 9, and the last element of the array is element number 10.

The Code of the cmdOnly5_Click() Procedure

The cmdOnly5_Click()procedure is automatically executed when you click the Cut to 5 Elements button:

```
Private Sub cmdOnly5_Click()

    ' Set the size of the array.
    ReDim Preserve gTheArray(1 To 5) As Integer
    Dim Counter
    ' Clear the combo box.
    cboElements.Clear
    ' Fill the items of the combo box.
    For Counter = 0 To 4 Step 1
        cboElements.AddItem _
            Str(gTheArray(Counter + 1))
    Next Counter

End Sub
```

The procedure uses the ReDim statement to change the size of the array to five elements:

```
ReDim Preserve gTheArray(1 To 5) As Integer
```

The Preserve keyword causes the first five elements of the array to retain their original values. The procedure then clears the items in the combo box and fills five elements in the combo box:

```
cboElements.Clear
For Counter = 0 To 4 Step 1
    cboElements.AddItem _
        Str(TheArray(Counter + 1))
Next Counter
```

Use the following steps to see the effect of the Preserve keyword:

☐ Remove the Preserve keyword from the ReDim statement. That is, change the ReDim statement in the cmdOnly5_Click() procedure so that it looks like this:

```
ReDim gTheArray(1 To 5) As Integer
```

☐ Execute the Arrays2 program and check its proper operation. That is, click the Fill 10 Elements button, open the combo list, and check whether the list is filled with 10 items (each item corresponds to an element of the array). Click the Cut to 5 Elements button, open the combo list, and check whether the list is filled with five items (each item corresponds to an element of the array). Because you removed the Preserve keyword, the elements of the array are all zeros.

☐ Click the Exit button to terminate the Arrays2 program.

Arrays that Exceed 64KB

The size of the arrays can exceed 64KB. An array that exceeds 64KB is called a *huge array*. You do not have to use any special declaration for huge arrays. Generally speaking, huge arrays are handled the same way as non-huge arrays—the only exception is that if the huge array is declared as a string, all the elements in the array must have the same number of characters in each element.

The Vary Program

As you saw in previous chapters, sometimes you create your own procedures and functions in your projects by selecting Add Procedure from the Tools menu of Visual Basic. When you create your own procedure or function, you can design it so that it has parameters. (In programming literature, a parameter is also called an *argument*.)

In Visual Basic, you can pass parameters to a function by one of two methods: by reference or by value. The difference between these two methods is illustrated with the Vary program.

The Visual Implementation of the Vary Program

Start by implementing the Vary program:

☐ Start a new Standard EXE project, save the form of the project as VARY.FRM in the C:\VB5PRG\ CH15 directory, and save the project file as VARY.VBP in the C:\VB5PRG\CH15 directory.

☐ Build the frmVary form according to the specifications in Table 15.4.

The completed form should look like the one shown in Figure 15.7.

Table 15.4. The properties table of the frmVary form.

Object	Property	Setting
Form	**Name**	**frmVary**
	Caption	The Vary Program
Command Button	**Name**	**cmdDoIt**
	Caption	&Do It
Command Button	**Name**	**cmdExit**
	Caption	E&xit
Label	**Name**	**lblInfo**
	Alignment	2-Center
	BorderStyle	1-Fixed Single
	Caption	(Make it empty)

Figure 15.7.

The frmVary form.

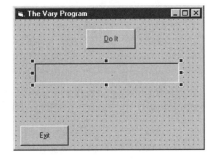

Entering the Code of the Vary Program

Next, enter the code:

☐ Enter the following code in the general declarations section of the frmVary form:

```
' All variables MUST be declared.
Option Explicit
```

☐ Enter the following code in the cmdDoIt_Click() procedure of the frmVary form:

```
Private Sub cmdDoIt_Click()

    Dim V As Integer
    Dim Result As Integer
```

15

```
      V = 3
      Result = VSquare(V)
      lblInfo.Caption = "V=" + Str(V) + "     4*4=" _
                                      + Str(Result)
```

End Sub

☐ Enter the following code in the cmdExit_Click() procedure of the frmVary form:

```
Private Sub cmdExit_Click()

    End

End Sub
```

☐ Create a new function in the frmArray form and name it VSquare. That is, display the code window, display the Add Procedure dialog box by selecting Add Procedure from the Tools menu, set the Type option to Function, set the Name to VSquare, and click the OK button.

Visual Basic responds by adding the VSquare() function.

☐ Change the first line of the VSquare() function as follows:

```
Public Function VSquare(ByVal V As Integer)

End Function
```

☐ Enter the following code in the VSquare() function:

```
Public Function VSquare(ByVal V As Integer)

    V = 4
    VSquare = V * V

End Function
```

Executing the Vary Program

Then execute the program:

☐ Execute the Vary program.

☐ Click the Do It button.

The Vary program responds by displaying the values in the lblInfo label, as shown in Figure 15.8.

☐ Click the Exit button to exit the Vary program.

Figure 15.8.

*The Vary program,
when passing the* V
variable to the ByVal
function.

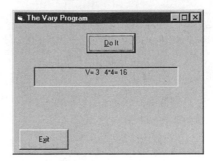

How the Vary Program Works

The Vary program passes a variable to a function by value (ByVal), which is explained in the
following sections.

The Code of the cmdDoIt_Click() Procedure

The cmdDoIt_Click() procedure is automatically executed when you click the Do It button:

```
Private Sub cmdDoIt_Click()

    Dim V As Integer
    Dim Result As Integer

    V = 3
    Result = VSquare(V)
    lblInfo.Caption = "V=" + Str(V) + "    4*4=" _
                                  + Str(Result)

End Sub
```

The procedure sets the value of the V variable to 3, then executes the VSquare() function.
VSquare() returns the result of 4×4.

The procedure then displays the value of V and the returned value from VSquare() in the
lblInfo label.

The Code of the VSquare() Function

The VSquare() function is called by the cmdDoIt_Click() procedure:

```
Public Function VSquare(ByVal V As Integer)

    V = 4
    VSquare = V * V

End Function
```

15

This function sets the value of V to 4, then sets the value of VSquare to V×V. The important thing to note is that the V variable is passed to the function ByVal. This means that this procedure creates a new copy of a variable called V. There are no connections between the variable V in the calling procedure cmdDoIt_Click() and the variable V in the VSquare() function. This explains why the value of V displayed in the lblInfo label is 3 and not 4 (refer to Figure 15.8). When you pass a variable to a function ByVal, the value of the passed variable doesn't change in the calling procedure.

Modifying the Vary Program

Now modify the Vary program:

☐ Change the VSquare() function so that it looks like the following (note that the first line of the function is modified):

```
Public Function VSquare(V As Integer)

    V = 4
    VSquare = V * V

End Function
```

☐ Execute the Vary program.

☐ Click the Do It button.

The Vary program responds by displaying values in the lblInfo label, as shown in Figure 15.9.

Figure 15.9.

The Vary program when passing the variable V by reference.

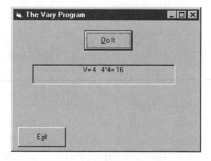

Note that now the variable is not passed by value to the VSquare() function; it is passed by reference. Passing a parameter by reference means that the passed variable is the same variable in the calling procedure and the called function. Therefore, when passing V by reference, the V variable in the cmdDoIt_Click() procedure is the same V variable used in the VSquare() function. This explains why the value of V is displayed in the lblInfo label as 4 (refer to Figure 15.9).

Readers familiar with the C programming language may recognize that passing a parameter by reference is the equivalent of passing the address of the variable in C. If you are not familiar with C and find the concept a little confusing, just note the difference between the two methods of passing parameters:

■ When you're passing a parameter by value (ByVal), the called function is not able to change the value of the passed variable in the calling procedure. For example, in the Vary program, even though the VSquare() function sets the value of V to 4, the value of V in cmdDoIt_Click() procedure remains 3.

■ When you're passing a parameter by reference, the called function and the calling procedure use the same variable. For example, in the modified version of the Vary program, the VSquare() function sets the value of V to 4, and this value is displayed in the lblInfo label by the cmdDoIt_Click() procedure.

Modifying the Vary Program Again

Let's modify the Vary program further:

☐ Change the first line of the VSquare() function and the contents of the VSquare() function so that it looks like this:

```
Public Function VSquare(VV As Integer)

    VV = 4
    VSquare = VV * VV

End Function
```

☐ Execute the Vary program.

☐ Click the Do It button.

The Vary program again responds, as shown in Figure 15.9.

☐ Terminate the program by clicking the Exit button.

As you can see, you changed the name of the variable in the VSquare() function from V to VV. However, this did not affect the way the program works because the variable V was passed by reference! So, although the variable is called VV in the VSquare() function, it is the same variable passed by the calling procedure (that is, V and VV are the same variable). As you can see, passing variables by reference can be tricky.

Note

To further understand the concept of passing variables by reference, take a look at Figure 15.10.

In Figure 15.10, certain cells in RAM are used for storing the v variable of the cmdDoIt_Click() procedure. Because the cmdDoIt_Click() passed the v variable by reference to the VSquare() function, the VSquare() function uses the passed variable by using the same cells in the RAM.

So, the cmdDoIt_Click() procedure uses the RAM area that stores the v variable, and the VSquare() function uses the RAM area that stores the vv variable; but in either case, v and vv are the same variable.

Figure 15.10.

Passing variables by reference.

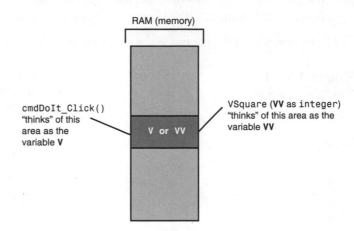

OLE is the abbreviation for object linking and embedding. A program that includes OLE capability can communicate data (text and graphics) to other Windows applications that are OLE-based.

OLE

Object linking and embedding (OLE) is an important Windows topic available in Visual Basic. (The topic of OLE deserves a whole book.)

OLE is so powerful that you can think of it as a separate software package included with your Visual Basic package. The rest of this chapter serves as a brief introduction to OLE.

What Is OLE?

OLE is the abbreviation for object linking and embedding. A program that includes OLE capability can communicate data (text and graphics) to other Windows applications that are OLE-based.

To see an example of OLE in action, suppose that you have to tell your user to modify a certain BMP file. One way to do this (although not the best way) is to write a Visual Basic program that lets your user draw and modify BMP pictures. However, writing your own graphics program can take a long time and you'll have to teach your user how to use your graphics program for drawing and modifying BMP files.

The solution is to tell your user to load the BMP picture by using a well-known drawing program such as Paint and then modifying the picture. Because your user is using Windows, he or she will most likely know how to use Paint or another drawing program that comes with Windows.

How do you tell your user to use Paint? You can write a simple Visual Basic program that lists a sequence of steps telling your user to start Paint, load a certain BMP file, and then modify the BMP picture by using the Paint tools. A more elegant way to tell your user to use Paint is to use OLE control, as the UsePaint program demonstrates.

The icon of the OLE control in the tools window of Visual Basic is shown in Figure 15.11.

Figure 15.11.
The OLE control.

The UsePaint Program

The UsePaint program illustrates how an OLE-based Visual Basic program can be used as a *front-end application*, which is an application used in front of all the other applications. That is, when you start the front-end application, you see menus and icons that enable you to perform word processing, spreadsheet work, and other common tasks. When you click the word processor icon, a word processor program starts as if the word processor's icon were clicked from the Explorer program of Windows. The UsePaint program lets your user use Paint for loading a BMP picture and modifying it.

The Visual Implementation of the UsePaint Program

Start by implementing the UsePaint program:

☐ Start a new standard EXE project, save the form of the project as USEPAINT.FRM in the C:\VB4PRG\CH15 directory, and save the project file as USEPAINT.VBP in the C:\VB4PRG\CH15 directory.

☐ Change the properties of the form as follows: the Name property should be frmUsePaint, and the Caption property should be The UsePaint Program.

Adding the OLE Control to the frmUsePaint Form

Now add the OLE control to the frmUsePaint form:

☐ Double-click the OLE icon in the toolbox.

Visual Basic responds by placing the OLE control in the form and displaying the Insert Object dialog box (see Figure 15.12).

Figure 15.12.

The Insert Object dialog box.

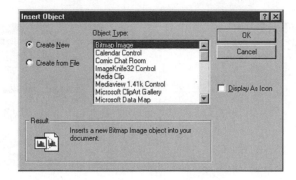

As you can see, the Insert Object dialog box displays a list of objects that can be embedded in the UsePaint program.

☐ Select the item Bitmap Image from the list of objects, then click the OK button.

☐ Save the project.

Executing the UsePaint Program

Execute the UsePaint program and see OLE in action:

☐ Execute the UsePaint program.

The window of the UsePaint program appears, as shown in Figure 15.13.

Figure 15.13.
*The UsePaint
program.*

☐ Double-click the OLE control in the window of the UsePaint program.

> *The program responds by letting you draw in the OLE control, as you can draw in Paint
> (see Figure 15.14). Note that you can perform other Paint operations by using the menu that
> now appears on the top of the UsePaint window.*

Figure 15.14.
*Drawing in the OLE
control.*

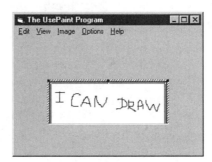

☐ Draw something with the Paint program.

☐ Terminate the UsePaint program.

Summary

In this chapter you learned about the FRM file that contains the description of the form in
an ASCII format, how to declare and use arrays, and how to pass parameters by reference and
ByVal. This chapter also introduces the OLE topic.

Q&A

Q Should I pass parameters ByVal or by reference?

A Sometimes it is not up to you to decide whether a variable should be passed ByVal
or by reference. When you use functions written by others, you must pass the
parameters as specified by the authors of the functions.

15

When you write your own Visual Basic functions, you can design them in such a way that the variables must be passed ByVal or by reference. Generally speaking, the easiest and safest way to pass parameters to a function is by value (ByVal). However, there are applications in which passing parameters by reference might be more convenient.

Quiz

1. A file with the FRM file extension is which of the following?

    a. A file that describes the form and its procedures in an ASCII format.
    b. A file that comes with Notepad.

2. The following declaration is used to declare an array:

    ```
    Dim OurArray (7) As integer
    ```

    Is the following statement correct?

    ```
    OurArray(12) = 32
    ```

3. Is the variable MyVariable in the following statement passed ByVal or by reference?

    ```
    Result = Calculate( MyVariable)
    ```

    a. ByVal
    b. By reference
    c. There is no way to answer this question just by looking at this statement.

4. Is the variable MyVariable in the following function passed ByVal or by reference?

    ```
    Function Calculate (MyVariable)
            ..........
            ..........
            ..........
    End Function
    ```

    a. By reference
    b. ByVal
    c. There is no way to answer this question just by looking at this statement.

5. Is the variable MyVariable in the following function passed ByVal or by reference?

    ```
    Function Calculate (ByVal MyVariable)
            ..........
            ..........
            ..........
    End Function
    ```

    a. By reference
    b. ByVal
    c. There is no way to answer this question just by looking at this statement.

Exercise

Write a loop that declares a two-dimensional array. The loop should fill the elements of the array with an integer that represents the multiplication of its two indexes. For example, the element (3,5) should contain the value 3×5 = 15.

Quiz Answers

1. a

2. No; the subscript of the array can be any value between 0 and 7.

3. c

4. a

5. b

Exercise Answer

Here is one possible solution:

```
Static TheArray (1 To 5, 1 To 5 )As Integer
Dim I, J
For I = 1 To 5 Step 1
    For J = 1 To 5 Step 1
        TheArray(I,J) = I*J
    Next J
Next I
```

Day 16

The Data Control and SQL

This chapter shows you how to use the data control, a powerful control supplied with the Visual Basic package. *Data controls* enable you to write programs that access databases such as Microsoft Access, dBASE, Btrieve, Paradox, and FoxPro.

This chapter also shows you how to use SQL statements to manipulate databases.

The Data Program

The Data program illustrates how easy it is to access data from within your Visual Basic programs, using the data control. Figure 16.1 shows the icon of the data control in the toolbox window. In your toolbox window, the icon of the data control may appear in a different location than the one shown in Figure 16.1. When you place the mouse cursor on the icon of the data control in the toolbox window, a yellow rectangle appears with the text Data in it. This way, you can verify that you located the data control.

Figure 16.1.

The data control.

Creating the Database and the Table

The Data program that you'll design next communicates with a database. Therefore, to see the data control in action, you must first create a database. In this chapter you'll create a database by using a software utility called the Data Manager. The Data Manager utility comes with Visual Basic.

In particular, you'll use the Data Manager of Visual Basic to design a database called Test.MDB. A database is a collection of tables. For example, a company may have a database that consists of the following tables: Parts (a table that includes a list of parts that the company manufacturers), Vendors (a table that includes a list of vendors that sell raw material to the company), Customers (a table that includes a list of customers), and so on. For simplicity, the Test.MDB database that you'll now design will include only one table in it, the Parts table:

☐ Create the C:\Vb5Prg\Ch16 directory. You'll save your work into this directory.

☐ Select Visual Data Manager from the Add Ins menu of Visual Basic.

☐ Visual Basic may display a dialog box asking you if you want to add SYSTEM.MD to the INI file. Click the No button.

Visual Basic responds by displaying the VisData window shown in Figure 16.2.

Figure 16.2.

The Data Manager window.

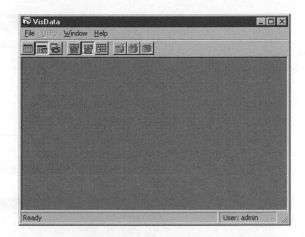

☐ Select New from the File menu of the VisData window, select Microsoft Access, and then select Version 7.0 MDB (see Figure 16.3).

Figure 16.3.

The VisData window.

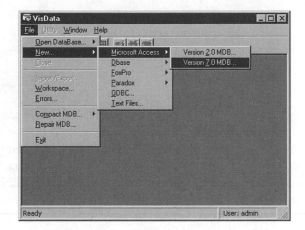

The Data Manager responds by displaying the Select Microsoft Access Database to Create dialog box (see Figure 16.4). This dialog box lets you create a new Microsoft Access database.

☐ Use the Select Microsoft Access Database to Create dialog box to save the new database as Test.MDB in the C:\Vb5Prg\Ch16 directory.

The Data Manager responds by saving the new database as an Access database file called Test.MDB, and the window shown in Figure 16.5 is displayed.

Figure 16.4.
The Select Microsoft Access Database to Create dialog box.

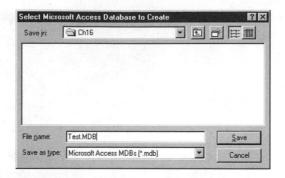

Figure 16.5.
The Test.MDB database window.

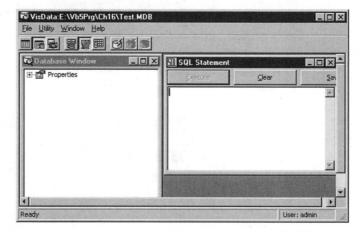

If you are unfamiliar with databases and tables, just remember that a database is a collection of data. For example, a factory can store its inventory data in a database. The database itself is a collection of tables. For example, the database INVENTRY.MDB may include a table called Parts, which lists parts numbers in the inventory; another table called Shipping, which lists shipping transactions; and so on.

The Test.MDB database should include one or more tables. As shown in Figure 16.5, the Test.MDB database does not include any tables right now, so your job is to create a new table called Parts.

☐ Right-click in the Database Window.

As a response, a menu pops up. The pop-up menu has two items in it: the Refresh List item and the New Table item.

☐ Select the New Table item (because you now want to create a new table for the Test.MDB database).

As expected, Visual Basic responds by displaying the Table Structure window shown in Figure 16.6.

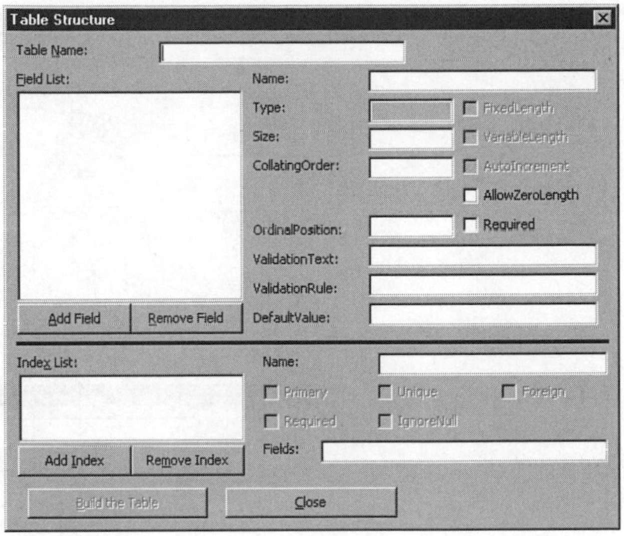

Figure 16.6.

The Table Structure window.

You'll now use the Table Structure window shown in Figure 16.6 to construct the Parts table.

☐ In the Table Name box, type Parts (this is the name of the table).

Add the fields of the Parts table:

☐ Click the Add Field button.

As a response, the Add Field dialog box appears (see Figure 16.7).

☐ In the Name box, type PartNum (this is the name of the first field in the Parts table).

☐ Set the type list box to Text, because the PartNum field is composed of text.

☐ Set the size to 10. (The PartNum field can hold a maximum of 10 characters.)

The Add Field window should now look like the one in Figure 16.7.

☐ Click the OK button of the Add Field window.

☐ Click the Close button of the Add Field window.

> *As you can see in Figure 16.8, now the Field List of the Parts table includes the PartNum field.*

Now it's time to add a second field to the Parts table:

☐ Click the Add Field button of the Table Structure window.

> *As a response, the Add Field window appears.*

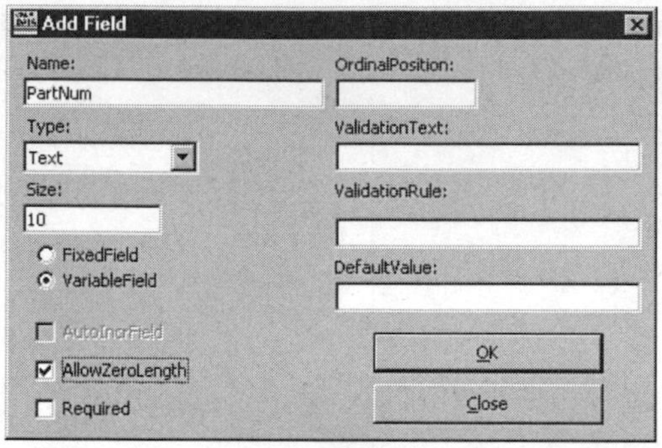

Figure 16.7.

Designing the first field of the Parts table.

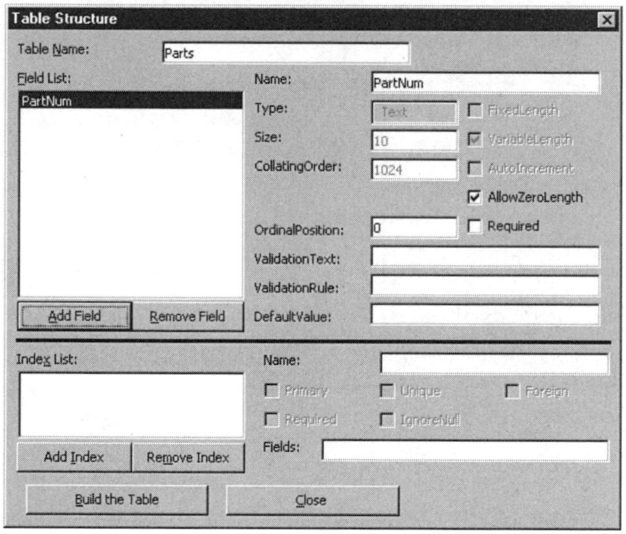

Figure 16.8.

The Parts table now has the PartNum field in it.

☐ In the Name box, type Description.

☐ Set the type to Text.

☐ Set the size to 20.

The Add Field window should now look like the one in Figure 16.9.

☐ Click the OK button of the Add Field window.

☐ Click the Close button of the Add Field window.

As you can see in Figure 16.10, the Parts table now has two fields.

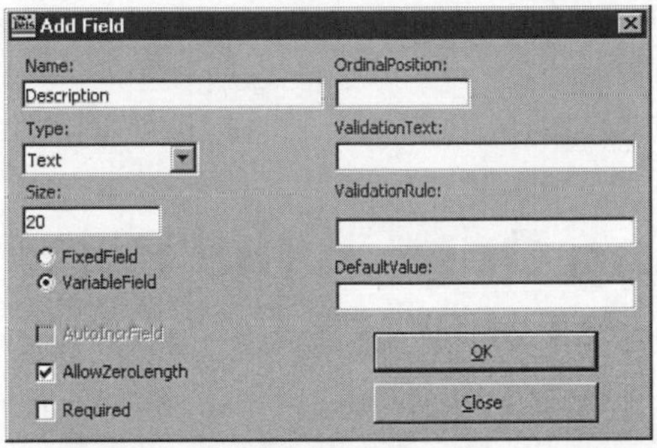

Figure 16.9.

Adding the Description field.

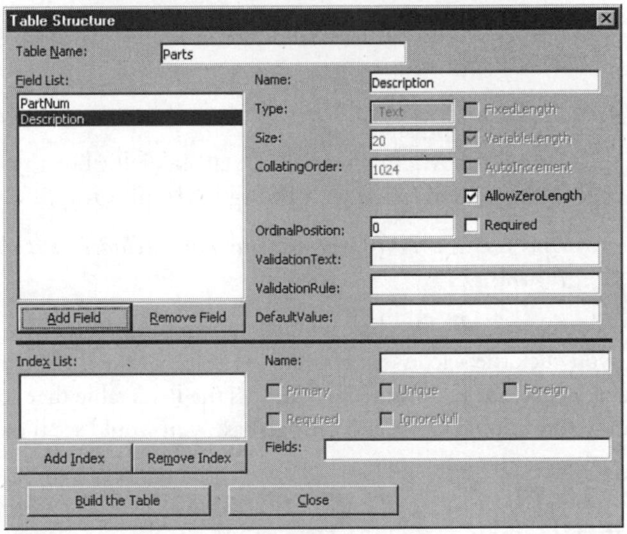

Figure 16.10.

The Parts table with the two fields in it.

You have finished designing the Parts table.

☐ Click the Build the Table button of the Table Structure window.

☐ Select Exit from the File menu of the VisData window.

So far, you accomplished the following:

■ You created an Access database called Test.MDB.

■ You created one table called Parts in the database.

■ The Parts table includes the following fields:

Field Name	Type	Size
PartNum	Text	10
Description	Text	20

Entering Data in the Parts Table

Now add data to the Parts table:

☐ Select Visual Data Manager from the Add-Ins menu of Visual Basic.

As a result, the VisData window appears.

☐ Select Open Database from the File menu of the VisData window and then select Microsoft Access.

As a result, the Open Microsoft Access Database dialog box appears.

☐ Use the Open Microsoft Access Database dialog box to select the Test.MDB file that you previously saved in the C:\VB5Prg\Ch16 directory.

As a result, the VisData window now includes in it the Test.MDB database shown in Figure 16.11.

As you can see, the Database window in Figure 16.11 has two items in it: Properties and Parts. If you click the + icon that appears to the left of the Properties item, you see the properties of the database. The Parts item represents the Parts table that you previously created. If you had added additional tables into the database, you would see these listed in the Database window.

Figure 16.11.

The Test.MDB database with the Parts table included.

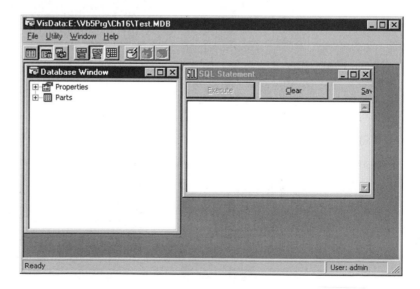

☐ Click the + icon that appears to the left of the Parts item.

As a result, a list of items appears under the Parts item.

One of the items that appears under the Parts item is the Fields item.

☐ Click the + icon that appears to the left of the Fields item.

As a result, a list of fields in the Parts table appears. These are the fields that you designed when you created the Parts table—the PartNum and Description items.

Now enter data to the Parts table. Here is how you accomplish this:

☐ Double-click the Parts item in the Database window.

As a result, the Dynaset:Parts window appears, as shown in Figure 16.12. You enter data in the table by using this dialog box.

Figure 16.12.

The Dynaset:Parts window.

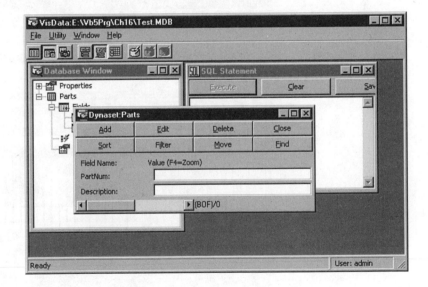

☐ Click the Add button of the Dynaset:Parts dialog box (because you now want to add a record to the Parts table).

As a result, the window shown in Figure 16.13 appears.

☐ Type PC100 in the PartNum field.

☐ Type PC 100 megahertz in the Description field.

The first record of the table should now look like the one in Figure 16.14.

Figure 16.13.

The window used to add a record to the table.

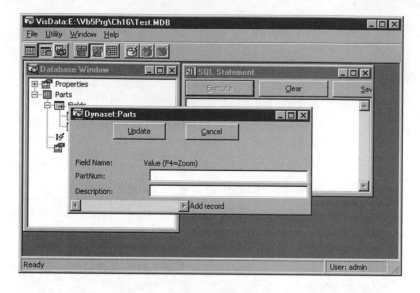

Figure 16.14.

The first record of the Parts table.

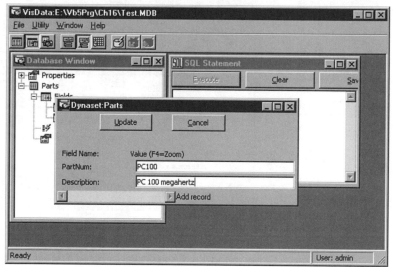

Figure 16.14 shows a record. That is, the Parts table is composed of records, and the first record contains the PC100 part number.

☐ Click the Update button to actually enter the data into the table.

☐ Click the Add button to display the next record (that is, record number 2, which is currently empty).

☐ Type RAM40 in the PartNum field of record number 2.

☐ Type 40 nanoseconds RAM in the Description field of record number 2.

☐ Click the Update button.

The last record you'll enter is record number 3:

☐ Click the Add button.

The Data Manager responds by displaying record number 3, ready for you to edit.

☐ Type KEY101 in the PartNum field.

☐ Type 101 keys keyboard in the Description field.

☐ Click the Update button.

☐ Click the Close button.

☐ Select Exit from the Data Manager's File menu.

What have you accomplished so far? You have created the Test.MDB database in the C:\Vb5Prg\Ch16 directory, and you have attached a table called Parts to the Test.MDB database. The Parts table consists of two fields: PartNum and Description. You have also added three records to the Parts table.

The Visual Implementation of the Data Program

Start by implementing the data program:

☐ Start a new Standard EXE project in Visual Basic, save the form of the project as C:\Vb5Prg\Ch16\Data.FRM, and save the project file of the project as C:\Vb5Prg\Ch16\ Data.VBP.

☐ Double-click the icon of the data control in the toolbox window.

As a response, the form now has the data control in it, as shown in Figure 16.15.

You can move, enlarge, and shrink the data control just as you would any other control:

☐ Move the data control to the lower part of the form and enlarge the data control by dragging its handles. The enlarged data control is shown in Figure 16.16.

The default name that Visual Basic assigns to the data control is Data1.

☐ Change the Name property of the form to frmData and the Caption property of the form to The Data Program.

Figure 16.15.
*The form with the
data control in it.*

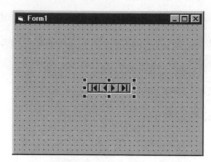

Figure 16.16.
*Enlarging the data
control.*

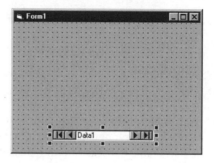

Specifying an Access Database

Now enter the name and path of the database file that will communicate with the Data1 data control. Specifying a non-Access database is a little different from specifying an Access database. The Test database you created with the Data Manager at the beginning of this chapter is an Access database. (That is, the files generated by Visual Basic's Data Manager are compatible with the Microsoft Access database manager program.)

Use the following steps to enter the name and path of an Access database:

☐ Make sure the data control is selected and select Properties Window from the View menu.

Visual Basic responds by displaying the Properties window of the data control.

☐ Click the DatabaseName property in the Properties table of the data control and then click the three-dots icon on the DatabaseName property line.

Visual Basic responds by displaying the DatabaseName dialog box shown in Figure 16.17.

☐ Use the DatabaseName dialog box to select the C:\VB5PRG\CH16\Test.MDB file that you created with the Data Manager and click the Open button.

Now the Data1 control knows it should control the Test.MDB database.

Figure 16.17.

The DatabaseName dialog box.

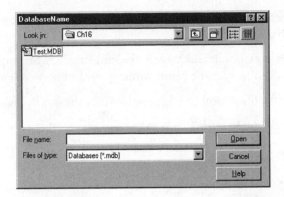

16

☐ Click the data control's RecordSource property in the Properties table, then click the down-arrow icon to display a list of all the tables in the Test database.

> *Visual Basic responds by letting you select from a list box a table that contains all the tables in the Test database. Because you created just one table, the Parts table, the list contains only that table. However, if the Test database had several tables, the drop-down list would show all of them and you would select one from the list.*

☐ Select the Parts table from the RecordSource property list.

Placing a Text Box to Hold the Data

Next, you'll place a text box in the frmData form. This text box serves as a placeholder for the PartNum field:

☐ Place a text box control in the frmData form, as shown in Figure 16.18.

☐ Set the text box's Name property to txtPartNumber and set its Text property to empty.

☐ Place a label control in the frmData form, as shown in Figure 16.18.

Figure 16.18.

Placing a text box, a label, and a command button in the frmData form.

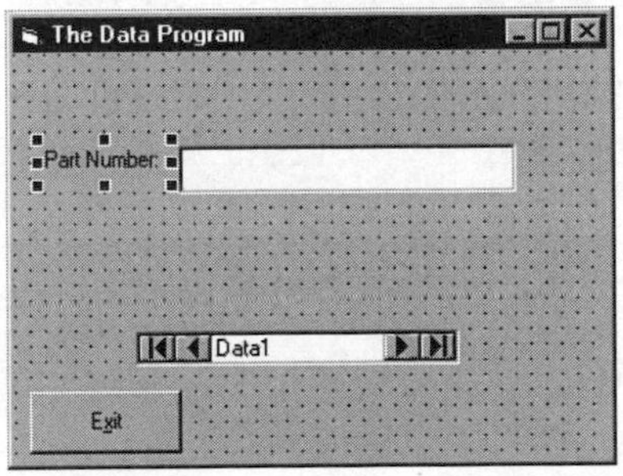

☐ Set the label's Name property to lblPartNumber and its Caption property to Part Number:.

☐ Add a CommandButton to the frmData form. Set the Caption property of the button to E&xit and set the Name property of the button to cmdExit.

The frmData form should now look like the one in Figure 16.18.

☐ Add the following code to the cmdExit_Click() procedure of the frmData form:

```
Private Sub cmdExit_Click()

    End

End Sub
```

The txtPartNumber text box you placed in the form will be used to display and edit the contents of the PartNum field. Now tell Visual Basic which data control is associated with this text box:

☐ Set the DataSource property of the txtPartNumber text box in the Properties window to Data1. (Recall that Data1 is the name of the data control.)

Because you have only one data control in the form, the DataSource property's drop-down list contains only one item: Data1.

Now tell Visual Basic that this text box should hold the contents of the PartNum field:

☐ Set the DataField property of the txtPartNumber text box to PartNum.

☐ Select Save Project from the File menu of Visual Basic to save your work.

Do	Don't

DO save your work, because if you had made an error in the preceding steps, it might cause Windows to crash, and all the work that you had done so far would be lost. However, if you save your work you can restart Windows, start Visual Basic, load the DATA.VBP project, and correct the mistake. This advice is valid for any project, but it is particularly valid for projects that include databases, OLE, DDE, and other powerful Visual Basic/Windows features.

Executing the Data Program

Let's execute the Data program and see your work in action:

☐ Execute the Data program.

The Data program responds by displaying the window shown in Figure 16.19. As you can see, the part number you entered in the Parts table appears in the text box!

Figure 16.19.

The Data program displaying the first record of the Parts table.

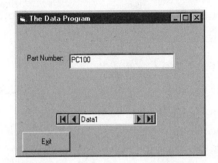

☐ Click the arrow icons of the Data1 data control and notice that the contents of the text box change with the contents of the PartNum field. Each click of the inner-right arrow of the Data1 data control causes the record in the table to advance one record; each click of the inner-left arrow of the Data1 data control causes the record to retreat one record. Clicking the rightmost arrow of the Data1 control causes the text box to display the PartNum contents of the very last record, and clicking the leftmost arrow of the Data1 control causes the text box to display the PartNum contents of the very first record.

☐ Experiment with the Data program, then click the Exit button to terminate the Data program.

As shown in Figure 16.19, the text in the Data1 data control displays the text Data1. This is the default name of the Caption property of Data1. You can set the Caption property of Data1 at design time to Test.MDB or any other text appropriate to your application, or you can change the Caption property of Data1 during runtime. For example, you can set the Caption property of Data1 to Database:TEST Table:Parts with the following statement:

```
Data1.Caption = "Database:TEST Table:Parts"
```

Disabling the Text Box

Note that the text box holding the contents of the PartNum field is currently enabled. That is, you can click in the text box and change its contents. For example, try the following experiment:

☐ Execute the Data program.

☐ Change the PartNum contents of the first record from PC100 to PC200.

☐ Click the inner-right arrow icon of the data control to display the second record.

☐ Click the inner-left arrow icon of the data control to display the first record.

As you can see, you are able to change the contents of the table!

☐ Click the Exit button to terminate the Data program.

☐ Execute the Data program again.

As you can see, the PartNum field contains the data you modified in the previous steps.

☐ Change the contents of the PartNum field back to PC100.

☐ Click the inner-right arrow icon to advance to the next record, then click the inner-left arrow icon to display the first record and check that the PartNum field now contains the value PC100.

☐ Click the Exit button to terminate the program.

There are additional "database considerations" that must be incorporated into a Visual Basic program that includes the data control. For example, during the design of your tables, you can design the table so that the PartNum field is the key field. This means that the Parts table must not have more than one record with the same value for PartNum; the value of the PartNum field must be unique. Because this chapter concentrates on Visual Basic programming and not on database design, simplify the Data program by disabling the text box containing the contents of the PartNum field:

☐ Set the Enabled property of the txtPartNumber text box to False.

☐ Save the project.

☐ Execute the Data program.

☐ Check that the txtPartNumber text box displays the contents of the PartNum field and that the contents cannot be modified.

☐ Experiment with the Data program, then click the Exit button to terminate the program.

Enhancing the Data Program

Now enhance the Data program by adding to the frmData form another text box, shown in Figure 16.20, that will contain the contents of the Description field:

☐ Add a label to the frmData form. Set the Name property of the label to lblDescription and set the Caption property of the label to Description:.

☐ Add a text box to the frmData form and set its properties as follows: the Name property should be txtDescription, the Text property should be empty, and the Enabled property should be False.

Figure 16.20.

*The Data program
with the Description
text box added.*

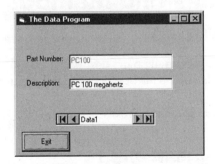

16

Of course, if you execute the Data program now, only the txtPartNumber text box will display the contents of its field. The txtDescription text box will not display the contents of its field in the Parts table because you haven't instructed Visual Basic to associate the text box with the corresponding field in the Parts table.

☐ Set the DataSource property of the txtDescription text box to Data1.

☐ Set the DataField property of the txtDescription text box to Description.

☐ Select Save Project from the File menu of Visual Basic.

Executing the Enhanced Data Program

Now execute the program:

☐ Execute the Data program.

The Data program appears, as shown in Figure 16.21.

Figure 16.21.

*The Data program
with two text boxes
that correspond to
two fields.*

☐ Click the arrows of the Data1 data control to move from record to record.

As you can see, the contents of the two text boxes correspond to the contents of the two fields in the Parts table.

☐ Click the Exit button to terminate the program.

Adding Logical Fields to the Table of the Database

In a similar manner, you can design the Parts table with a boolean (logical) field. For example, you could add the field InStock. When the value of the InStock field is True, it means that the part number is available in stock. If InStock is equal to False, the part number is not in stock.

You can then place a check box in the form and correlate its Value property with the InStock field of the Parts table (just as you correlated the Part Number and Description text boxes with the fields of the Parts table).

Remember to use the following steps when correlating a check box with a field of the Parts table:

☐ Set the DataSource property of the check box to Data1.

☐ Set the DataField property of the check box to the logical field of the Parts table.

Using Bound Controls

The Data program illustrates how a text box is used to bind the data of a table. A control used to display the contents of a field is called a *bound control.* Therefore, a text box control and a check box control can be used in a program as bound controls. In a similar manner, you can add a field to the Parts table that contains a BMP file, then add a picture control or an image control to the frmData form that corresponds to the picture field in the Parts table. Picture controls and image controls can also serve as bound controls.

Properties and Methods of the Data Control

The Data program illustrates how your Visual Basic program can display the contents of a table's fields. As you might expect, the data control has many more properties and methods that enable you to manipulate the database in almost any conceivable way. Some of these properties and methods are discussed in the following sections.

The Refresh Method

You can use the Refresh method to update the bound controls with the most recent values of the table's fields. For example, if the database is in a file server connected to your PC through a LAN (local area network), and another user on a different station changed a field's values in the table, the current values on your screen haven't been updated with those changes. To update the screen with the most recent values, use the following statement:

```
Data1.Refresh
```

The Exclusive Property

If you want your program to be the only program that can access the database, you have to set the Exclusive property of the data control to True, as shown in the following statement:

```
Data1.Exclusive = True
```

Setting the Exclusive property to True prevents all other programs from accessing the database.

The default value of the Exclusive property is False. To return to its default value, use the following statement:

```
Data1.Exclusive = False
```

If the database is already open and you change the Exclusive property, you must execute the `Refresh` method to make the change effective:

```
Data1.Exclusive = False
Data1.Refresh
```

Working with a database with the Exclusive property set to True makes access to the database much faster (at the expense of other users, who have to wait until you are kind enough to set the Exclusive property back to False).

The ReadOnly Property

Once you modify the contents of a field, you can click the arrows of the Data1 data control to move to the next record. The changes you made to the previous record are automatically saved. To see the automatic saving in action, try the following experiment:

☐ Execute the Data program.

☐ Change the contents of any of the fields of the first record.

☐ Click the inner-right arrow of the Data1 data control to move to the next record, which saves the new data.

☐ Click the Exit button to terminate the Data program.

☐ Start the Data program again.

As you can see, the record appears with the value you updated. This means that the changes you made to the database in the previous execution of the Data program were saved.

If you want your program to just read records, set the ReadOnly property of the data control to True. For example, modify the Form_Load() procedure so that it looks like this:

```
Private Sub Form_Load()

    Data1.ReadOnly = True
    Data1.Refresh

End Sub
```

☐ Enable the text box that holds the contents of the PartNum field.

☐ Save the project.

☐ Execute the Data program.

☐ Change the contents of any of the fields in the first record.

The program responds by changing the contents of the field, but as you'll see in the next step, it does not change the value in the table.

☐ Click the inner-right arrow of the Data1 data control to move to the next record.

☐ Click the inner-left arrow of the Data1 data control to return to the previous record.

The field was not changed because the ReadOnly property was set to True.

To set the ReadOnly property back to its default value of False, change the Form_Load() procedure so that it looks like this:

```
Private Sub Form_Load()

    Data1.ReadOnly = False
    Data1.Refresh

End Sub
```

☐ Try the previous experiment again and notice that now you can change the contents of the fields in the table.

Again, if you change properties (such as the ReadOnly property) after the database is already open, you must use the Refresh method to make the change to the property effective.

Note

You must set the ReadOnly property of Data1 to False to perform the experiments with the properties and methods described in the next sections.

Typically, you'll design the application so that the bound control's Enabled property matches the ReadOnly property. For example, if the table is set as read-only, you must set the Enabled property of the bound controls to False to let your user know that the database is in a read-only state. If you enable the bound controls and the database is read-only, your users might not realize that the data they are modifying on the screen isn't being transferred to the database.

16

Using SQL (Structured Query Language) Statements

Your program can use SQL statements to select only a set of records that comply with a certain condition. Do the following steps to see an SQL statement in action:

☐ Add the Select command button, as shown in Figure 16.22.

Figure 16.22.
Adding the Select button.

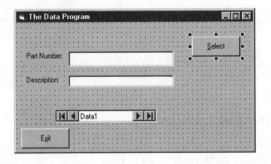

☐ Set the Name property of the Select button to cmdSelect and the Caption property to &Select.

☐ Add the following code in the cmdSelect_Click() procedure of the frmData form:

```
Private Sub cmdSelect_Click()

    Data1.RecordSource = "Select * from Parts where PartNum = 'PC100' "

    Data1.Refresh

End Sub
```

The preceding procedure uses the standard SQL Select statement to select all the records from the Parts table that satisfy the condition PartNum = 'PC100'. To make the SQL request effective, the Refresh method is executed:

☐ Save the project.

☐ Execute the Data program.

☐ Make sure the PartNum of the first record is PC100.

☐ Click the arrows of the Data1 data control to browse from record to record.

As you can see, you are able to browse through all the records.

☐ Click the Select button.

Because there is only one record that satisfies the SQL statement, the Data program displays only this record, as shown in Figure 16.23.

Figure 16.23.
Clicking the Select button to select the PC100 record.

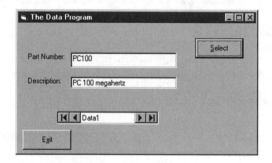

Clicking the arrow of the Data1 data control doesn't display any other records, because only one record satisfies the SQL selection. The SQL statement filtered out all the records that didn't satisfy the SQL requirement.

☐ Exit the Data program by clicking the Exit button.

You can use SQL statements to select any group of records. For example, suppose you added the InStock field to the Parts field (a field that indicates whether the part number exists in stock). You can then change the cmdSelect_Click() procedure so that it looks like this:

```
Private Sub cmdSelect_Click()

    Data1.RecordSource = "Select * from Parts where InStock = True "
    Data1.Refresh

End Sub
```

When you click the Select button, the Data program will display only those records that have their InStock field equal to True.

Generally speaking, the syntax of the SQL statements is simple, but this book does not teach SQL syntax. You should know, however, that SQL statements can manipulate databases and tables in almost any conceivable way.

The AddNew **Method**

You can add a new record at runtime by using the AddNew method:

☐ Add the Add Record button, as shown in Figure 16.24. Set its Name property to cmdAddRecord and its Caption property to &Add Record.

Figure 16.24.

Adding the Add Record button to the frmData form.

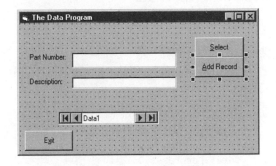

☐ Add the following code in the cmdAddRecord_Click() procedure of the frmData form:

```
Private Sub cmdAddRecord_Click()

    Data1.Recordset.AddNew

End Sub
```

The AddNew method is applied to the RecordSet property of Data1. (The RecordSet property is discussed later in this chapter.)

In the following experiment, you are going to fill the fields of the Parts table with data:

☐ Set the Enable property of the txtPartNumber text box to True.

☐ Set the Enable property of the txtDescription text box to True.

☐ Save the project.

☐ Execute the Data program.

☐ Click the Add Record button.

> *The Data program responds by displaying a blank record (that is, all the bound controls are empty).*

☐ Fill the contents of the bound controls with new values, but remember that if the PartNum field is a key field, you should not add a part number that already exists in the table.

The data control saves the new record once you move the record pointer (that is, click the inner arrow of the Data1 data control to the next or previous record).

☐ Exit the program by clicking the Exit button.

The Delete Method

To delete a record, you can use the Delete method:

☐ Add the Delete button and place this button below the Add Records button.

☐ Set the Delete button's Name property to cmdDelete and its Caption property to &Delete.

☐ Add the following code in the cmdDelete_Click() procedure of the frmData form:

```
Private Sub cmdDelete_Click()

    Data1.Recordset.Delete
    Data1.Recordset.MoveNext

End Sub
```

☐ Save the project.

☐ Execute the Data program.

☐ Use the arrow buttons of the Data1 data control to move the record pointer to the record you want to delete.

☐ Click the Delete button.

The Data program responds by deleting the record.

☐ Practice with the Delete and Add Record buttons for a while, then click the Exit button to terminate the Data program.

Like the AddNew method, the Delete method is used on the RecordSet property of the Data1 data control.

> **Note**
>
> In the Data program, you can delete records very easily! You simply click the Delete button.
>
> Naturally, in a real-world application you have to use a verification step. When you click the Delete button, a message box pops up, asking whether you really want to delete the record. The record will be deleted if you click the Yes button in the message box.

The `MoveNext` **Method**

In the `cmdDelete_Click()` procedure, the `MoveNext` method was executed after the `Delete` method:

```
Data1.RecordSet.MoveNext
```

The `MoveNext` method moves the record pointer to the next record. The `MoveNext` method has the same effect as clicking the inner-right arrow of the data control.

The `MovePrevious` **Method**

The `MovePrevious` method moves the record pointer to the previous record. You can use the `MovePrevious` method as follows:

```
Data1.RecordSet.MovePrevious
```

The `MovePrevious` method has the same effect as clicking the inner-left arrow of the data control.

The `MoveLast` **Method**

The `MoveLast` method moves the record pointer to the very last record. You can use the `MoveLast` method as follows:

```
Data1.RecordSet.MoveLast
```

The `MoveLast` method has the same effect as clicking the rightmost arrow of the data control.

The `MoveFirst` **Method**

The `MoveFirst` method moves the record pointer to the very first record. You can use the `MoveFirst` method as follows:

```
Data1.RecordSet.MoveFirst
```

The `MoveFirst` method has the same effect as clicking the leftmost arrow of the data control.

The RecordSet Property

You can think of the RecordSet property of the data control as the current record your program can access. For example, if you don't set a filter by issuing an SQL statement, the RecordSet property represents all the records in the Parts table. Because the data control can represent a database with several tables, you can use SQL statements to create a RecordSet that represent records from several tables.

16

As demonstrated in the previous sections, many of the methods are applied to the RecordSet property (for example, `Data1.RecordSet.Delete`, `Data1.RecordSet.AddNew`, and `Data1.RecordSet.MoveNext`).

The following steps illustrate how your program can determine the number of records in the RecordSet:

☐ Add the Count Records button, as shown in Figure 16.25.

Figure 16.25.

Adding the Count Records button to the frmData form.

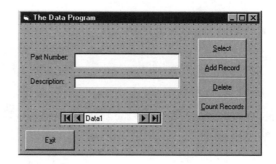

☐ Set the Name property of the Count Records button to cmdCountRecords and its Caption property to &Count Records.

☐ Add the following code in the `cmdCountRecords_Click()` procedure:

```
Private Sub cmdCountRecords_Click()

    Data1.RecordSet.MoveLast
    MsgBox Data1.Recordset.RecordCount

End Sub
```

The `cmdCountRecords_Click()` procedure moves the record pointer to the last record of the RecordSet, then the `RecordCount` method counts all the records up to the current record. Because the `MoveLast` method moved the record pointer to the last record of the RecordSet (which represents the Parts table), `RecordCount` returns the total number of records in the Parts table.

☐ Save the project.

☐ Execute the Data program.

☐ Click the Count Records button.

The Data program responds by displaying the total number of records in the RecordSet (which represents the total number of records in the Parts table).

☐ Delete and add records by clicking the Add Record and Delete buttons, and then click the Count Records button to see whether the number of total records in the table increases and decreases accordingly.

☐ Terminate the Data program by clicking the Exit button.

Note

> You should be aware of certain "standard" database users' interfaces. Once you add a new record, a blank record is created. If you then fill the contents of the key field, the new record will indeed be added to the table. However, if you just added a new record and then moved the record pointer to a different record, the blank record won't be added to the table.
>
> Also, once you modify a record, the change will take effect only after you move the record pointer.

The Value Property

You can extract the contents of the fields by examining the corresponding properties of the bound controls. For example, you can determine the contents of the PartNum field of the current record by examining the Text property of the txtPartNumber text box. The following steps illustrate how to display the contents of the current record's PartNum field when you click the form:

☐ Add the following code in the Form_Click() procedure of the frmData form:

```
Private Sub Form_Click()

    MsgBox "Part number: " + txtPartNumber.Text

End Sub
```

☐ Save the project.

☐ Execute the Data program.

☐ Click the form.

The Data program responds by displaying the contents of the current record's PartNum field.

☐ Click the Exit button to terminate the program.

Sometimes you might want to know the contents of a field that doesn't have a corresponding bound control in the form. In these cases, you can use the Value property. To see how it works, do the following:

☐ Change the code in the Form_Click() procedure so that it looks like this:

```
Private Sub Form_Click()

    Dim MyString As String

    MyString = Data1.Recordset.Fields("PartNum").Value
    MsgBox MyString

End Sub
```

☐ Save the project.

☐ Execute the Data program.

☐ Click the form.

The Data program responds by displaying a message box with the contents of the current record's PartNum field.

☐ Click the Exit button to terminate the program.

The code in the Form_Click() procedure assigns the Value property of the current record's PartNum field to the MyString variable. Then this string is displayed by using the MsgBox statement.

In a similar manner, you can extract the Value property of the other fields in the database. For example, to assign the Value property of the current record's Description field to the MyString variable, you can use the following statement:

```
MyString = Data1.RecordSet.Fields("Description").Value
```

The EOF and BOF Properties

Your program can use the EOF (end of file) and BOF (beginning of file) properties to determine whether the current record is valid. For example, while your program is displaying a particular record, another workstation (another PC in the LAN) could delete that record. In this case, the record pointer would be pointing to an invalid record. Your program can determine the validity of the pointer as follows:

```
If Data1.RecordSet.EOF = False AND Data1.RecordSet.BOF=False Then
    ................................
    ... The record pointer points ...
    ... to a valid record.        ...
    ................................
End If
```

The above If...End If block of statements checks whether the record pointer is pointing to a valid record by checking whether both the EOF and the BOF properties are False.

As shown in Table 16.1, any other combination of values for the EOF and BOF properties, such as both properties being True, means that the record pointer is pointing to an invalid record.

Table 16.1. The BOF and EOF properties.

BOF	EOF	Comment
False	False	Valid record
False	True	Invalid record
True	False	Invalid record
True	True	Invalid record

What Else Can the Data Control Do?

The properties and methods this chapter introduces are the basic properties and methods of the data control, and you can use them to display and modify the contents of the tables' fields. However, the data control supports many more features that enable Visual Basic to manipulate databases in almost any way (for example, building a database or modifying the structures of tables). In fact, Visual Basic's data control is so powerful that you could think of it as a separate programming package included with the Visual Basic package. Although the data control can handle databases other than the Access database, it uses the same software engine that powers the Access program, so it makes sense to assume that for faster, bug-free operations, the Access database is the easiest database platform to use.

Summary

In this chapter you learned about the data control supplied with the Visual Basic package, how to assign properties to the data control, and how to assign properties to the bound controls that display the contents of the tables' fields.

You also learned how to refresh the data, issue SQL statements, and delete and add records to the tables.

Q&A

Q Is it possible to place more than one data control in a form?

A Yes. You can place several data controls in a form. Make sure to set the DatabaseName and RecordSource properties of each of the data controls to the corresponding database and tables each of them represents.

Quiz

1. When using an Access database, the DatabaseName property of a data control is a string that specifies which of the following?
    a. The name of the required table
    b. The name of the required database
    c. The name of the bound control

2. When using an Access database, the RecordSource property of a data control is a string that specifies which of the following?
    a. The name of the required table in the database
    b. The contents of the SQL statement
    c. The name of the field

3. A scroll bar can be a bound control.
    a. False
    b. True

4. What is the ReadOnly property used for?

5. What is the `AddNew` method used for?

6. What is the `Delete` method used for?

7. What is the `MoveNext` method used for?

Exercise

Suppose that the Parts table includes the InStock Boolean field. Write an SQL statement so the Data1 control accesses only those records that have their InStock fields equal to No.

Quiz Answers

1. b.
2. Both a and b.
3. a.
4. The ReadOnly property is used to prevent your program from changing the contents of the table's field from within your Visual Basic program.
5. The AddNew method is used for adding a record.
6. The Delete method is used for deleting a record.
7. The MoveNext method is used for moving the record pointer to the next record.

Exercise Answer

☐ Change the code in the cmdSelect_Click() procedure so it looks like the following:

```
Private Sub cmdSelect_Click()

    Data1.RecordSource = "Select * from Parts where InStock = False "
    Data1.Refresh

End Sub
```

☐ Execute the Data program.

☐ Click the Select button.

☐ Click the arrows of the Data1 data control.

As you can see, only those records that have their InStock field equal to No are displayed.

16

Day 17

Multiple-Document Interface

This chapter focuses on developing multiple-document interface (MDI) programs. An *MDI program* contains several documents, each with its own window, contained in a single parent form. Some well-known MDI applications are programs such as Word for Windows, Microsoft Excel, and others.

Your First MDI Program: The Picture Program

The Pictures program illustrates how to create an MDI program. The key to designing impressive MDI programs with Visual Basic is understanding how to manipulate the various forms of the program.

Creating the Pictures Project

You'll now build an MDI project called Pictures.vbp that consists of a parent form called Pictures.frm and three child forms: Picture1.frm, Picture2.frm, and Picture3.frm.

☐ Create the C:\VB5Prg\Ch17 directory. You'll save your work in this directory.

To create the Pictures project, follow these steps:

☐ Create a new Standard EXE project.

> *Visual Basic responds by opening a new project and displaying a blank form. So far, this is no different from creating a typical new (non-MDI) project.*

☐ Select Save Form1 As from the File menu of Visual Basic and save the form as Form1.frm in the C:\VB5Prg\Ch17 directory. Select Save Project As from the File menu of Visual Basic and save the project as Pictures.Vbp in the C:\VB5Prg\Ch16 directory.

Every MDI program has one parent form. Use the following step to create the parent form:

☐ Select Add MDI Form from the Project menu.

> *Visual Basic responds by displaying the Add MDI Form dialog box.*

☐ Select the MDI Form icon in the Add MDI Form dialog box and then click the Open button.

> *Visual Basic responds by displaying a blank form with the default name MDIForm1 (see Figure 17.1). This blank form is the parent form.*

Figure 17.1.

The blank MDI form.

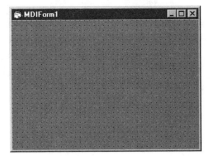

Let's see how the Project window looks at this point:

☐ Select Project Explorer from the View menu.

Visual Basic responds by displaying the Project window shown in Figure 17.2. As shown, the Project window contains the following: Form1.frm (a standard non-MDI blank form), and MDIForm1.frm (the blank parent form).

Figure 17.2.

The Project window with the Form1 and MDIForm1 forms in it.

17

Note the little icons to the left of each form in the Project window. These icons are indicators of the type of form. The standard form (Form1.frm) has an icon that looks like a form standing on its edge. The parent form's (MDIForm1.frm) icon looks like a form standing on its edge with a little form next to it.

Your Visual Basic program can have only one parent form. Use the following steps to see this for yourself:

☐ Select the Project menu.

As you can see, the Add MDI Form item is gray (not available), because you already have a parent MDI window in the project.

So, what do you have so far? As indicated by the project window, you have one parent form (MDIForm1.frm) and one standard form (Form1.frm). Use the following steps to convert the standard form to a child form:

☐ Highlight Form1.frm in the project window.

☐ Click the View Object icon that appears at the top of the Project window.

As a result, Form1 becomes the active form.

☐ Change the MDIChild property of Form1 to True.

Now take a look at the project window (select Project Explorer from the View menu). Form1.frm now appears as a child form (it has the MDI icon next to its name in the Project window). To tell the difference between the parent form and the child form, look at their icons. Both have an icon of a large form standing on its edge next to a little form. However, the little form is dimmed in the parent form's icon (MDIForm1.frm), and the large form is dimmed in the child form's icon (Form1.frm) (see Figure 17.3).

Figure 17.3.

The difference between the parent form's icon and the child form's icon.

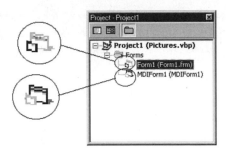

The MDI program that you are currently building is called Pictures. Therefore, a more appropriate name for the child form is Picture1.frm. Use the following steps to change its name from Form1.frm to Picture1.frm:

☐ Highlight Form1.frm in the Project window.

☐ Select Save Form1 As from the File menu.

   Visual Basic responds by displaying the Save File As dialog box.

☐ Save the file as C:\VB5Prg\Ch17\Picture1.frm.

Now that Visual Basic has saved the child form as Picture1.frm, take a look at the Project window. The child form's name was changed to Picture1.frm.

Currently, the name of the parent form is MDIForm1.frm. Use the following steps to change its name to Pictures.frm:

☐ Highlight MDIForm1.frm in the Project window.

☐ Select Save MDIForm1 As from the File menu.

   Visual Basic responds by displaying the Save File As dialog box.

☐ Save the parent form as C:\VB5Prg\Ch17\Pictures.frm.

Take a look at the project window. The parent form's name MDIForm1.frm was changed to Pictures.frm.

MDI programs usually have more than one child form. Use the following steps to add two more child windows:

☐ Select Add Form from the Project menu.

   Visual Basic responds by displaying the Add Form window.

☐ Select the Form icon and then click the Open button.

Visual Basic responds by adding a standard form called Form2.frm to the project window (see the Project window shown in Figure 17.4).

Figure 17.4.

The Project window now has a parent form and two child forms.

☐ Select Add Form from the Project menu and add a Form to the project again.

Visual Basic responds by adding a standard form called Form3.frm to the project window.

The project window now has one parent form (Pictures.frm), one child form (Picture1.frm), and two new standard forms (Form2.frm and Form3.frm). Of course, you need these two new standard forms to be child forms, not standard forms, so change Form2.frm and Form3.frm from standard forms to child forms:

☐ Highlight Form2.frm in the project window and click the View Object icon in the Project window.

☐ Change the MDIChild property of Form2.frm to True.

☐ Highlight Form3.frm in the Project window and click the View Object button in the Project window.

☐ Change the MDIChild property of Form3.frm to True.

Currently, the two newly added child forms are called Form2.frm and Form3.frm (the default names that Visual Basic assigned to these forms). Use the following steps to change their filenames:

☐ Highlight Form2.frm in the Project window.

☐ Select Save Form2 As from the File menu and save the form as C:\VB5Prg\Ch17\ Picture2.frm.

☐ Highlight Form3.frm in the Project window.

☐ Select Save Form3 As from the File menu and save the form as C:\VB5Prg\Ch17\ Picture3.frm.

17

You now have a project called Pictures.vbp, with a parent form called Pictures.frm and three child forms: Picture1.frm, Picture2.frm, and Picture3.frm. The complete project window is shown in Figure 17.5.

Figure 17.5.

The complete Project window of the Pictures project.

Use the following step to save the project:

☐ Select Save Project from the File menu.

Changing the Properties of the Child Forms

Now you will change several properties of the forms. Use the following steps to change the properties of the child form Picture1.frm:

☐ Select the Picture1 form by highlighting Picture1.frm in the Project window, then click the View Object button in the Project window. Now select Properties Window from the View menu to display the Properties window of the Picture1 form.

☐ Set the properties of the Picture1 form as follows: set the Caption property of Picture1.frm to The Picture 1 Child. Set the Name property of Picture1.frm to frmPicture1.

Now change the properties of the other child forms:

☐ Set the Caption property of Picture2.frm to The Picture 2 Child.

☐ Set the Name property of Picture2.frm to frmPicture2.

☐ Set the Caption property of Picture3.frm to The Picture 3 Child.

☐ Set the Name property of Picture3.frm to frmPicture3.

Changing the Properties of the Parent Form

To change the properties of Pictures.frm (the parent form), highlight Pictures.frm in the Project window and then click the View Object button. Then select Properties Window from the View menu (this gives you access to the Properties window of Pictures.frm).

☐ Set the Caption property of Pictures.frm to I am the parent window.

☐ Change the Name property of Pictures.frm to frmPictures.

☐ To save the work that you've done so far, select Save project from the File menu.

The Visual Implementation of the Pictures Program

An MDI program has several properties tables: one for the parent form and one for each of the child forms.

The Visual Implementation of the Parent Form

Start by implementing the Parent form:

☐ Build the frmPictures form according to its properties table (Table 17.1) and menu table (Table 17.2).

The completed form should look like the one shown in Figure 17.6.

Table 17.1. The properties table of the parent form Pictures.frm.

Object	Property	Setting
Form	Name	frmPictures
	Caption	I am the parent window
Menu	(See Table 17.2)	(See Table 17.2)

Note

You already set the properties of the parent form according to Table 17.1 in the previous steps, so build the menu of the parent form according to Table 17.2. Make sure to attach the menu of Table 17.2 to the Pictures form. That is, select the Pictures form, then select Menu Editor from the Window menu.

Table 17.2. The menu table of the parent form Pictures.frm.

Caption	Name
&File	mnuFile
...E&xit	mnuExit
&Show Pictures	mnuShow

continues

Table 17.2. continued

Caption	Name
...Show Picture &1	mnuShowPicture1
...Show Picture &2	mnuShowPicture2
...Show Picture &3	mnuShowPicture3
...- (separator)	mnuSep1
...Show &All Pictures	mnuShowAll
...&Clear All Pictures	mnuClearAll

Figure 17.6.

The parent form in design mode.

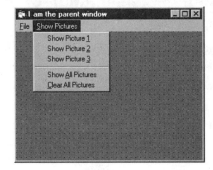

The Visual Implementation of the Child Forms

Because the Pictures project contains three child forms, there are three separate properties tables.

The Visual Implementation of frmPicture1

First, implement frmPicture1:

☐ Build the frmPicture1 form according to the specifications in its properties table (Table 17.3) and menu table (Table 17.4).

The completed form should look like the one shown in Figure 17.7.

Note

You already set some of the properties listed in Table 17.3 in the previous steps.

Note

Table 17.3 instructs you to set the Picture property of the imgClub image control to Club.Bmp.

If your Visual Basic directory doesn't contain this BMP file, use a different BMP file. For example, you can use Paint or other drawing programs to draw your own small BMP pictures.

17

Table 17.3. The properties table of the frmPicture1 form.

Object	Property	Setting
Form	**Name**	**frmPicture1**
	MDIChild	True
	Caption	The Picture 1 Child
	BackColor	Yellow
Image	**Name**	**imgClub**
	Picture	CLUB.BMP
	Stretch	False
Command Button	**Name**	**cmdClose**
	Caption	&Close
Menu	*(See Table 17.4)*	*(See Table 17.4)*

Table 17.4. The menu table of the frmPicture1 form.

Caption	Name
&File	mnuFile
… Close	mnuClose
&Beep	mnuBeep
…Beep &Once	mnuBeepOnce
…Beep &Twice	mnuBeepTwice

Figure 17.7.

The frmPicture1 form in design mode.

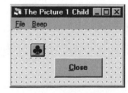

The Visual Implementation of frmPicture2

Next, implement frmPicture2:

☐ Build the frmPicture2 form according to the specifications in its properties table. (See Table 17.5.)

The completed form should look like the one shown in Figure 17.8.

 Note | The frmPicture2 form does not have a menu.

Table 17.5. The properties table of the frmPicture2 form.

Object	Property	Setting
Form	**Name**	**frmPicture2**
	MDIChild	True
	Caption	The Picture 2 Child
	BackColor	Yellow
Image	**Name**	**imgCup**
	Picture	CUP.BMP
	Stretch	False
Command Button	**Name**	**cmdClose**
	Caption	&Close

Figure 17.8.

The frmPicture2 form in design mode.

The Visual Implementation of frmPicture3

Finally, implement frmPicture3:

☐ Build the frmPicture3 form according to the specifications in its properties table. (See Table 17.6.)

The completed form should look like the one shown in Figure 17.9.

Note   The frmPicture3 form does not have a menu.

Table 17.6. The properties table of the frmPicture3 form.

Object	Property	Setting
Form	Name	frmPicture3
	MDIChild	True
	Caption	The Picture 3 Child
	BackColor	Yellow
Image	Name	imgBell
	Picture	BELL.BMP
	Stretch	False
Command Button	Name	cmdClose
	Caption	&Close

Figure 17.9.

The frmPicture3 form in design mode.

Your parent form (Picture.frm) and the three child forms (Picture1.frm, Picture2.frm, and Picture3.frm) are now ready.

As previously stated, the parent window will contain the three windows of the child forms in it. Thus, for cosmetic reasons, make the size of the three child forms smaller and make the size of the parent form larger.

☐ Drag the handles of the forms to make the forms larger and smaller.

Entering the Code of the Pictures Program

You'll now enter the code of the Pictures program in the various forms (parent form and child forms). Type the code of the parent form in the procedures of frmPictures, the code of the Picture1 child form in the procedures of frmPicture1, and so on.

Entering the Code of the Parent Form

Start by entering the code:

☐ Enter the following code in the general declarations section of the frmPictures form:

```
' Each variable MUST be declared.
Option Explicit
```

☐ Enter the following code in the MDIForm_Load() procedure of the frmPictures form:

```
Private Sub MDIForm_Load()

    ' Upon starting the program, show the three
    ' children.
    frmPicture1.Show
    frmPicture2.Show
    frmPicture3.Show

End Sub
```

☐ Enter the following code in the mnuExit_Click() procedure of the frmPictures form:

```
Private Sub mnuExit_Click()

    ' The user selected Exit from the menu,
    ' so terminate the program.
    End

End Sub
```

☐ Enter the following code in the mnuShowAll_Click() procedure of the frmPictures form:

```
Private Sub mnuShowAll_Click()

    ' The user selected Show All from the menu,
    ' so show all the children.
    frmPicture1.Show
    frmPicture2.Show
    frmPicture3.Show

End Sub
```

☐ Enter the following code in the mnuShowPicture1_Click() procedure of the frmPictures form:

```
Private Sub mnuShowPicture1_Click()

    ' The user selected Show Picture 1 from the
    ' menu, so show PICTURE1.
    frmPicture1.Show

End Sub
```

☐ Enter the following code in the mnuShowPicture2_Click() procedure of the frmPictures form:

```
Private Sub mnuShowPicture2_Click()

    ' The user selected Show Picture 2 from
    ' the menu, so show PICTURE2.
    frmPicture2.Show

End Sub
```

☐ Enter the following code in the mnuShowPicture3_Click() procedure of the frmPictures form:

```
Private Sub mnuShowPicture3_Click()

    ' The user selected Show Picture 3 from the
    ' menu, so show PICTURE3.
    frmPicture3.Show

End Sub
```

☐ Enter the following code in the mnuClearAll_Click() procedure of the frmPictures form:

```
Private Sub mnuClearAll_Click()

    ' The user selected Clear All from the Show
    ' Picture menu, so unload the children.
    Unload frmPicture1
    Unload frmPicture2
    Unload frmPicture3

End Sub
```

Entering the Code of the frmPicture1 Form

First, enter the code of the frmPicture1 form:

☐ Enter the following code in the general declarations section of the frmPicture1 form:

```
' Each variable MUST be declared.
Option Explicit
```

☐ Enter the following code in the cmdClose_Click() procedure of the frmPicture1 form:

```
Private Sub cmdClose_Click()

    ' The user clicked the Close button of PICTURE1,
    ' so unload PICTURE1.
    Unload frmPicture1

End Sub
```

17

☐ Enter the following code in the `mnuBeepOnce_Click()` procedure of the frmPicture1 form:

```
Private Sub mnuBeepOnce_Click()

    ' The user selected Beep Once from the menu,
    ' so beep once.
    Beep

End Sub
```

☐ Enter the following code in the `mnuBeepTwice_Click()` procedure of the frmPicture1 form:

```
Private Sub mnuBeepTwice_Click()

    ' First beep.
    Beep

    MsgBox "Beep Again"

    ' Second beep.
    Beep

End Sub
```

☐ Enter the following code in the `mnuClose_Click()` procedure of the frmPicture1 form:

```
Private Sub mnuClose_Click()

    Unload frmPicture1

End Sub
```

Entering the Code of the frmPicture2 Form

Then, enter the code of the frmPicture2 form:

☐ Enter the following code in the general declarations section of the frmPicture2 form:

```
' Each variable MUST be declared.
Option Explicit
```

☐ Enter the following code in the `cmdClose_Click()` procedure of the frmPicture2 form:

```
Private Sub cmdClose_Click()

    ' The user clicked the Close button,
    ' so unload PICTURE2.
    Unload frmPicture2

End Sub
```

Entering the Code of the frmPicture3 Form

Finally, enter the code of the frmPicture3 form:

☐ Enter the following code in the general declarations section of the frmPicture3 form:

```
' Each variable MUST be declared.
Option Explicit
```

☐ Enter the following code in the cmdClose_Click() procedure of the frmPicture3 form:

```
Private Sub cmdClose_Click()

    ' The user clicked the Close button,
    ' so unload PICTURE3.
    Unload frmPicture3

End Sub
```

Executing the Pictures Program

Now execute the Pictures program:

☐ Execute the Pictures program.

When you execute the Pictures program, the parent window pops up, as shown in Figure 17.10. The child forms are contained in the parent form.

☐ Drag the child windows by dragging the title of the windows.

As you can see, the child windows can be dragged anywhere in the parent form, but they cannot be dragged outside the parent form.

Users can minimize each child form as they would minimize any standard form (by clicking the minus icon on the upper-right corner of each child window or by clicking the icon that appears on the upper-left corner of the window and then selecting Minimize from the system menu that pops up). Figure 17.11 shows the Pictures program after minimizing two child forms, Picture1 and Picture2. As shown, the minimized forms appear as icons at the bottom of the parent form.

Figure 17.10.

The Pictures program.

Figure 17.11.
Minimizing children in an MDI program.

The Menus of the Parent and Child Forms

Experiment with the Pictures program and note that the menu bar of the parent form is displayed and available as long as the currently active child form doesn't have a menu. To see how this works, try the following experiments:

☐ Make Picture2 the active form by clicking in its form or selecting Show Picture 2 from the Show Pictures menu.

  Because Picture2 doesn't have a menu, the menu bar displays the parent form's menu.

☐ Make Picture3 the active form by clicking in its form or selecting Show Picture 3 from the Show Pictures menu.

  Because Picture3 does not have a menu, the menu bar displays the parent form's menu.

However, if the currently active child form has a menu, the menu bar that appears contains the child form's menu:

☐ Make Picture1 the active form by clicking in its form or selecting Show Picture 1 from the Show Picture menu.

  Because Picture1 has its own menu, the menu bar that appears in the parent form is the menu of Picture1 (see Figure 17.12).

Compare Figure 17.11 with Figure 17.12. In Figure 17.11, Picture3, which doesn't have a menu, is the active window, so the menu bar displays the parent form's menu.

Figure 17.12.
The menu of the parent form when frmPicture1 is the active form.

☐ Play with the Pictures program and study its features and behavior: minimize and maximize the child forms, select items from the various menus, and so forth. Then terminate the Picture program.

The Code of the Parent Form

The code in the procedures of the parent form contains the code corresponding to events related to the parent form. For example, selecting Show All Pictures from the Show Pictures menu of the parent form causes the execution of the mnuShowAll_Click() procedure.

The Code in the MDIForm_Load() Procedure

The Pictures program consists of an MDI parent form and three child forms. When you start the program, the form that is loaded is the parent MDI form frmPictures. The procedure that corresponds to loading the parent form is called MDIForm_Load():

```
Private Sub MDIForm_Load()

    ' Upon starting the program, show the three
    ' children.
    frmPicture1.Show
    frmPicture2.Show
    frmPicture3.Show

End Sub
```

Because the Pictures program is an MDI program, the MDI parent form is loaded when you start the program. You can take advantage of this and perform initializations and start-up tasks in the MDIForm_Load() procedure.

The code in the MDIForm_Load() procedure of the frmPictures form displays the three child forms by using the Show method. For example, to display the frmPicture1 child form, the MDIForm_Load() procedure uses the following statement:

```
frmPicture1.Show
```

The Code in the mnuClearAll_Click() Procedure

The mnuClearAll_Click() procedure of the frmPictures parent form is executed when you select Clear All Pictures from the Show Pictures menu:

```
Private Sub mnuClearAll_Click()

    ' The user selected Clear All from the Show
    ' Picture menu, so unload the children.
    Unload frmPicture1
    Unload frmPicture2
    Unload frmPicture3

End Sub
```

To remove a child form, use the Unload statement. For example, to remove the frmPicture1 child form, the mnuClearAll_Click() procedure uses the following statement:

```
Unload frmPicture1
```

The Code in the mnuExit_Click() Procedure

The mnuExit_Click() procedure of the frmPictures parent form is executed when you select Exit from the File menu. This procedure terminates the program by executing the End statement.

The Code in the mnuShowAll_Click() Procedure

The mnuShowAll_Click() procedure of the frmPictures parent form is executed when you select Show All Pictures from the Show Pictures menu:

```
Private Sub mnuShowAll_Click()

    ' The user selected Show All Pictures from the menu,
    ' so show all the children.
    frmPicture1.Show
    frmPicture2.Show
    frmPicture3.Show

End Sub
```

This procedure uses the Show method for each of the child forms.

The Code in the mnuShowPicture1_Click() Procedure

The mnuShowPicture1_Click() procedure of the frmPictures parent form is executed when you select Show Picture 1 from the Show Pictures menu:

```
Private Sub mnuShowPicture1_Click()

    ' The user selected Show Picture 1 from the
    ' menu, so show PICTURE1.
    frmPicture1.Show

End Sub
```

This procedure uses the Show method to display the frmPicture1 child form.

In a similar manner, the mnuShowPicture2_Click() and mnuShowPicture3_Click() procedures are executed when you select Show Picture 2 and Show Picture 3 from the Show Pictures menu. Again, these procedures use the Show method for displaying the corresponding child form.

The Code in the frmPicture1 Child Form

The procedures of the frmPicture1 child form contain the code corresponding to events related to the frmPicture1 form. For example, clicking the Close button (cmdClose) of frmPicture1 causes the execution of the `cmdClose_Click()` procedure.

The Code in the `mnuBeepOnce_Click()` Procedure

The `mnuBeepOnce_Click()` procedure is executed when you select Beep Once from the Beep menu of the frmPicture1 form. Therefore, this procedure contains the `Beep` statement:

```
Private Sub mnuBeepOnce_Click()

    ' The user selected Beep Once from the menu,
    ' so beep once.
    Beep

End Sub
```

The Code in the `mnuBeepTwice_Click()` Procedure

The `mnuBeepTwice_Click()` procedure is executed when you select Beep Twice from the Beep menu of the frmPicture1 form. Therefore, this procedure contains two `Beep` statements. Between the beeps, a message box is inserted:

```
Private Sub mnuBeepTwice_Click()

    ' First beep.
    Beep

    MsgBox "Beep Again"

    ' Second beep.
    Beep

End Sub
```

The Code in the `cmdClose_Click()` Procedure

The `cmdClose_Click()` procedure is executed when you click the Close button in the frmPicture1 form:

```
Private Sub cmdClose_Click()

    ' The user clicked the Close button of PICTURE1,
    ' so unload PICTURE1.
    Unload frmPicture1

End Sub
```

17

The form is unloaded with the following statement:

```
Unload frmPicture1
```

The Code in the frmPicture2 and frmPicture3 Child Forms

Child forms frmPicture2 and frmPicture3 each have a Close button. When you click it, the cmdClose_Click() procedure is executed. To close the frmPicture2 and frmPicture3 forms, the cmdClose_Click() procedure uses the Unload statement. This statement is used to close frmPicture2:

```
Unload frmPicture2
```

And this statement is used to close frmPicture3:

```
Unload frmPicture3
```

Which Form Is Loaded First?

The Pictures program comprises an MDI parent form and its three child forms. As previously stated, a Visual Basic program can contain only one MDI form; however, it's possible to design a program that has one MDI form and several standard forms. Add a standard form to the Pictures program:

☐ Select Add Form from the Project menu.

  Visual Basic responds by displaying the Add Form window.

☐ Select the Form icon, and then click the Open button.

  Visual Basic responds by adding a standard form to the project window.

Use the following steps to save the newly added standard form:

☐ Make sure the new form is the selected window.

☐ Select Save Form1 As from the File menu.

  Visual Basic responds by displaying the Save File As dialog box.

☐ Save the newly added form as C:\VB5Prg\Ch17\Standard.frm.

☐ Build the Standard.frm form according to the specifications in Table 17.7.

The completed form should look like the one shown in Figure 17.13.

☐ Select Save Project from the File menu to save your work.

Table 17.7. The properties table of Standard.frm.

Object	Property	Setting
Form	Name	frmStandard
	Caption	I am a standard form
	BackColor	Light gray
Command Button	Name	cmdExit
	Caption	E&xit
Command Button	Name	cmdSwitch
	Caption	&Switch to the MDI form

Figure 17.13.

The frmStandard form.

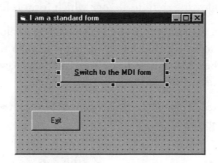

☐ Add the following code to the cmdSwitch_Click() procedure of the frmStandard form:

```
Private Sub cmdSwitch_Click()

    ' Show the parent form.
    frmPictures.Show

End Sub
```

☐ Add the following code to the cmdExit_Click() procedure of the frmStandard form:

```
Private Sub cmdExit_Click()

    End

End Sub
```

The Pictures.vbp project now contains the following forms:

■ An MDI parent form (Pictures.frm) and its three child forms (Picture1.frm, Picture2.frm, Picture3.frm)

■ The frmStandard form

Which form is loaded when you start the program: the MDI parent form or the frmStandard form? At design time, you decide which form will be loaded by updating the Project Options window.

Use the following step to tell Visual Basic which form should be loaded first:

☐ Select Project1 Properties from the Project menu.

> *Visual Basic responds by displaying the Project Properties dialog box (see Figure 17.14). As shown in Figure 17.14, the content of the Startup Object is frmPicture1. This means that the child form frmPicture1 is loaded when you start the program. However, because frmPicture1 is a child of frmPictures, both the parent form frmPictures and the child form frmPicture1 are loaded.*

Use the following steps to change which form is loaded when you start the program:

☐ Change the content of the Startup Object field of the Project Properties dialog box to frmStandard. (Click the down-arrow icon to the right of the Startup Object field and select the frmStandard form from the drop-down list.) Then click the OK button of the Properties dialog box.

☐ Now execute the Pictures program. As you can see, frmStandard is loaded when you start the program.

Figure 17.14.

The Project Properties dialog box with the General tab selected.

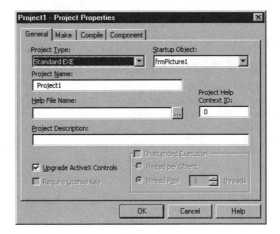

Switching Between Forms at Runtime

At runtime, you can switch between the frmStandard and frmPictures forms by clicking the cmdSwitch button in the frmStandard form. The code in the `cmdSwitch_Click()` procedure is executed when you click this button:

```
Private Sub cmdSwitch_Click()

    ' Show the parent form.
    frmPictures.Show

End Sub
```

The statement `frmPictures.Show` in this procedure displays the MDI parent form.

☐ Execute the program.

As you can see, the frmStandard form is loaded when you start the program.

☐ Switch to the MDI form by clicking the Switch to the MDI form button.

The program responds by displaying the MDI form.

In a similar way, you can add code to the MDI parent form or any of the child forms that would cause the program to switch from the MDI form to the standard form. For example, you can add a command button in the frmPicture1 form with the caption Switch to the Standard Form and insert the following statement in the button's `Click` procedure:

```
frmStandard.Show
```

The Window List Menu

Many professional MDI programs include a Window menu. If you own the Word for Windows program, take a look at its Window menu (see Figure 17.15). The Window menu contains a list of all the child forms that the parent form currently contains. If you don't have the Word for Windows program, look at any other MDI application you have (for example, Excel, Access).

Figure 17.15.

The Window menu of Word for Windows.

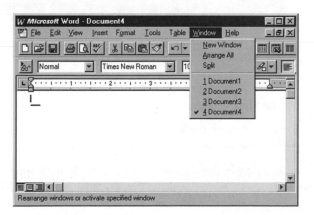

Adding a Window List Menu to the Parent Window

Now you'll add a Window list menu to the parent window frmPictures of the Pictures program with the following steps:

☐ Select the frmPictures parent form and add a menu item called Window. (Make sure the frmPictures parent form is selected. Select Menu Editor from the Tools menu and add the Window item, as shown in Figure 17.16.) The Caption of the menu is &Window. The Name is mnuWindow.

☐ Place a check mark in the WindowList check box in the Menu Editor dialog box, as shown in Figure 17.16. Before you do this, make sure the Window menu item is selected, because that's where you want to add the WindowList feature.

That's all! The frmPictures parent form now has a Window list menu.

Figure 17.16.

Adding a Window list menu.

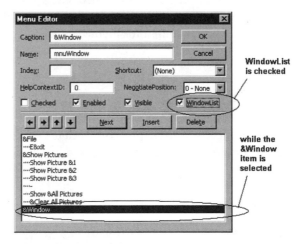

☐ Click the OK button of the Menu Editor window, then select Save Project from the File menu of Visual Basic to save your work.

☐ Execute the Pictures program and select the Window menu. The Window menu should list the three child forms (see Figure 17.17).

☐ Experiment with the Window menu. For example, close the frmPicture1 child and note that the list in the Window menu is updated.

Note also that in the Window menu, a check mark appears next to the child form that is currently active. For example, in Figure 17.17, frmPicture3 has a check mark next to it in the window list, so it is the active window.

Figure 17.17.
The Window menu of the Pictures program.

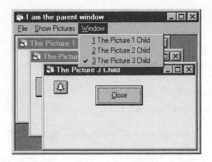

Adding a Window List Menu to a Child Form

In the preceding steps, you added a Window list menu to the frmPictures parent form. A Window list menu can also be added to a child form. In many applications, it is convenient to have the Window menu in the child forms as well as in the parent form. Use the following steps to add a Window list menu to the frmPicture1 child form:

☐ Select the frmPicture1 form and add a menu item called Window. (Select the frmPicture1 form, select Menu Editor from the Tools menu, and add the Window item to the menu of frmPicture1.) Set the Caption to &Window and set the Name to mnuWindow.

☐ Make sure the Window menu item is selected, then place a check mark in the WindowList check box in the Menu Editor dialog box (see Figure 17.18). Then click the OK button of the Menu Editor window.

Figure 17.18.
Adding the Window list menu to the frmPicture1 form.

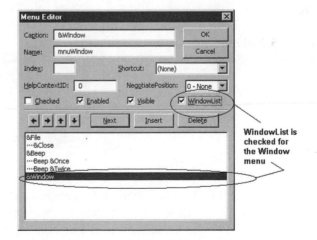

☐ Select Save project from the File menu.

☐ Execute the Pictures program.

☐ Click the Switch to the MDI button.

The Pictures program responds by displaying the MDI form.

☐ Make the frmPicture3 child form the active form.

As you can see from Figure 17.19, the menu that appears is the menu of the frmPictures parent form, because the frmPicture3 child form doesn't have a menu of its own.

☐ Make the frmPicture1 child form the active form.

As you can see from Figure 17.20, the menu that appears is the menu of the frmPicture1 child form, because the frmPicture1 child form does have its own menu. Note that the Window menu you added to the menu of frmPicture1 appears in Figure 17.20.

Figure 17.19.

The menu of the Pictures program when frmPicture3 is the active window.

Figure 17.20.

The menu of the Pictures program when frmPicture1 is the active window.

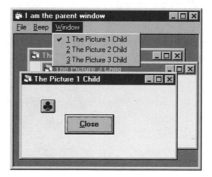

Note

The Window menu feature can save you a lot of programming work. Each item in it represents a child form, and the active child form has a check mark next to it. The items in the Window menu also are updated automatically. For example, if you close a child form, the corresponding menu item in the Window menu is removed. And the beauty of it is that you didn't have to write a single line of code to do all this! All you had to do was place a check mark in the WindowList check box when you designed the Window menu.

Adding Cascade, Tile, and Arrange Icons Items to the Window Menu

Sometimes it is useful to add items to the Window menu of an MDI application that help you arrange the child windows. The following sections explain how to add the Cascade, Tile, and Arrange Icons items to the Window menu.

The Visual Implementation of the Window Menu

Start by implementing the Window menu:

☐ Add the Cascade, Tile, and Arrange Icons items to the Window menu of the frmPictures parent form, as shown in Table 17.8. The Menu Editor dialog box is shown in Figure 17.21.

Table 17.8. The menu table of the Window menu.

Caption	Name	Shortcut
&Cascade	mnuCascade	Shift+F5
&Tile	mnuTile	Shift+F4
&ArrangeIcons	mnuArrangeIcons	none

Figure 17.21.

Adding items to the Window menu.

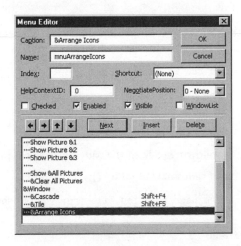

☐ Click the OK button of the Menu Editor window. Then save the project and execute the Pictures program.

☐ Make the frmPicture2 child form the active menu.

> *As you can see in Figure 17.22, the Window menu now contains the Cascade, Tile, and Arrange Icons items. Of course, none of these items functions, because you haven't written any code yet that accomplishes these tasks.*

☐ Terminate the Pictures program by selecting Exit from the File menu.

Figure 17.22.

The Window menu of the Pictures program.

Attaching Code to the Cascade, Tile, and Arrange Icons Menu Items

You'll now add code that is executed when you select Cascade, Tile, or Arrange Icons from the Window menu.

☐ Add the following code to the mnuCascade_Click() procedure of the frmPictures parent form:

```
Private Sub mnuCascade_Click()

    ' The user selected Cascade from the Window menu.
    frmPictures.Arrange vbCascade

End Sub
```

☐ Add the following code to the mnuTile_Click() procedure of the frmPictures form:

```
Private Sub mnuTile_Click()

    ' The user selected Tile from the Window menu.
    frmPictures.Arrange vbTileHorizontal

End Sub
```

☐ Add the following code to the mnuArrangeIcons_Click() procedure of the frmPictures form:

```
Private Sub mnuArrangeIcons_Click()

    ' The user selected Arrange Icons from the
    ' Window menu.
    frmPictures.Arrange vbArrangeIcons

End Sub
```

How the Window Menu Items Work

The mnuCascade_Click() procedure is executed when you select Cascade from the Window menu of the Pictures program. The code in this procedure consists of the following statement:

```
frmPictures.Arrange vbCascade
```

It uses the Arrange method with vbCascade as the parameter to cascade the child forms.

Similarly, when you select the Tile item from the Window menu, the Arrange method is executed with vbTileHorizontal as the parameter.

```
frmPictures.Arrange vbTileHorizontal
```

When you select the Arrange Icons item from the Window menu, the Arrange method is executed with vbArrangeIcons as the parameter:

```
frmPictures.Arrange vbArrangeIcons
```

☐ Select Save Project from the File menu.

☐ Execute the Pictures program, click the Switch to the MDI form button, and resize and rearrange the three child forms by dragging their captions and the edges of their windows.

After scrambling the child forms, the Pictures program should look like the one in Figure 17.23.

Figure 17.23.

The child forms after you've scrambled them in the MDI parent form.

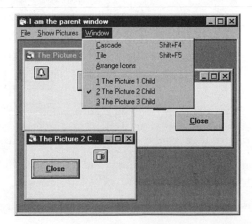

☐ Make frmPicture2 or frmPicture3 the active form so the menu of the frmPictures parent form will appear.

☐ Select Cascade from the Window menu.

The Pictures program responds by cascading the child forms, as shown in Figure 17.24.

Figure 17.24.

The child forms after you've cascaded Cascade from the Window menu.

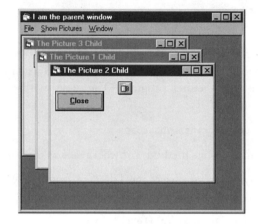

☐ Select Tile from the Window menu.

The Pictures program responds by tiling the child forms, as shown in Figure 17.25.

Figure 17.25.

The child forms after you've selected Tile from the Window menu.

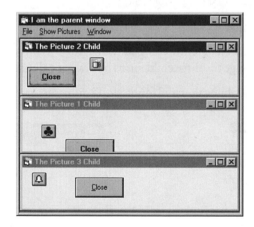

To see the Arrange Icons feature in action, follow these steps:

☐ Minimize the three child forms, and place them (by dragging them) at different locations in the parent window.

The three minimized child forms are shown in Figure 17.26.

Figure 17.26.

The three minimized child forms.

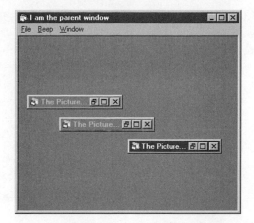

☐ Make sure the frmPicture1 icon isn't highlighted, then select Arrange Icons from the Window menu.

The Pictures program responds by arranging the minimized child forms, as shown in Figure 17.27.

Figure 17.27.

The three minimized child forms after selecting the Arrange Icons menu item from the Window menu.

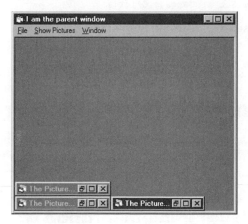

☐ Experiment with the Pictures program and then terminate the program.

The vbTileVertical **Constant**

In the preceding section, you learned that the Arrange method can be executed with the vbCascade, vbTileHorizontal, and vbArrangeIcons parameters.

There is also a fourth parameter, vbTileVertical. When the Arrange method is used with the vbTileVertical parameter, the child forms are arranged as shown in Figure 17.28.

Figure 17.28.

Arranging the child forms vertically.

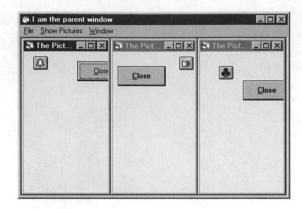

You added the Cascade, Tile, and Arrange Icons items to the Window menu of the parent form. Of course, because the frmPicture1 has its own Window menu, you have to add these menu items and their codes to the frmPicture1 child form.

For example, you can add the Cascade item to the Window menu of the frmPicture1 form, then add the following code to the mnuCascade_Click() procedure of the frmPicture1 form:

```
Private Sub mnuCascade_Click()

    ' The user selected Cascade from the Window menu.
    frmPictures.Arrange vbCascade

End Sub
```

Designing a Text Editor Program

Now you'll build an MDI program called TextEd. This program illustrates how a text editor program can be designed as an MDI program in which each child form represents a new document.

The Visual Implementation of the TextEd Program

First, implement the program:

☐ Create a Standard EXE project (from the File menu of Visual Basic).

☐ Select Save Form1 As from the File menu of Visual Basic and then save the form as Template.frm in the C:\VB5Prg\Ch17 directory.

☐ Select Save Project As from the File menu of Visual Basic and then save the project as TextEd.Vbp in the C:\VB5Prg\Ch17 directory.

☐ Create an MDI parent form by selecting Add MDI Form from the Project menu (then select the Form icon from the Add MDI Form window, and click the Open button of the Add MDI Form window).

Your project window should now contain a standard form (Template.frm) and an MDI parent form (see Figure 17.29).

Figure 17.29.

The Project window of the TextEd.vbp project.

17

☐ While the MDI parent form is the selected form, select Save MDIForm1 As from the File menu and save the parent form as TextEd.frm in the C:\VB5Prg\Ch17 directory.

Your Project window should now contain the following items:

- A standard form Template.frm
- An MDI parent form TextEd.frm

Now you'll convert the non-MDI form Template.frm to an MDI child form and change its properties:

☐ Build the Template.frm form according to the specifications in Table 17.9.

The completed form should look like the one shown in Figure 17.30.

Figure 17.30.

The frmTemplate form in design mode.

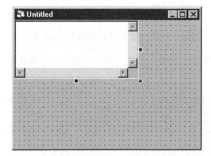

Note that once you change the MDIChild property of Template.frm to True (as specified in Table 17.9), the icon that appears in the project window to the left of Template.frm indicates that this form is a child form.

Table 17.9. The properties table of the Template.frm child form.

Object	Property	Setting
Form	**Name**	**frmTemplate**
	MDIChild	True
	Caption	Untitled
Text Box	**Name**	**txtUserArea**
	Text	(Make it empty)
	MultiLine	True
	ScrollBars	3-Both
	Top	0
	Left	0

Now build the parent form of the project:

☐ Build the MDI parent form according to the specifications in Table 17.10.

The completed form should look like the one shown in Figure 7.31.

Table 17.10. The properties table of the MDI parent form frmTextEd.

Object	Property	Setting
Form	**Name**	**frmTextEd**
	Caption	My Text Editor
Menu	*(See Table 17.11)*	*(See Table 17.11)*

Table 17.11. The menu table of the MDI parent form TextEd.frm.

Caption	Procedure Name
&File	mnuFile
...&New	mnuNew
...E&xit	mnuExit

Figure 17.31.
*The frmTextEd form
in design mode.*

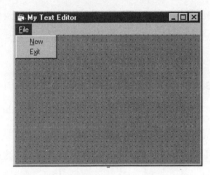

You'll now set the startup form to be the frmTextEd form:

☐ Select Project1 Properties from the Project menu.

>   *Visual Basic responds by displaying the Properties dialog box.*

☐ Click the General tab of the Properties dialog box, set the Startup Object to frmTextEd, and then click the OK button of the Properties window.

☐ Save the project by selecting Save Project from the File menu.

Entering the Code of the TextEd Program

You'll now enter the code of the TextEd program. Remember that the project has two forms (TextEd.Frm and Template.Frm). In the following sections, make sure you are entering the code to the proper form as instructed.

☐ Enter the following code in the general declarations section of the frmTextEd parent form:

```
' Variables MUST be declared.
Option Explicit
```

☐ Enter the following code in the mnuNew_Click() procedure of the frmTextEd parent form:

```
Private Sub mnuNew_Click()

    ' Declare a variable for the instance form
    ' as a copy of the form frmTemplate.
    Dim frmNewForm As New frmTemplate
    ' Show the instance form.
    frmNewForm.Show

End Sub
```

☐ Enter the following code in the `mnuExit_Click()` procedure of the frmTextEd form:

```
Private Sub mnuExit_Click()

    End

End Sub
```

☐ Save the project by select Save Project from the File menu.

Executing the TextEd Program

The TextEd program isn't finished yet, but see what you have accomplished so far:

☐ Execute the TextEd program.

The parent form frmTextEd pops up (see Figure 17.32).

Figure 17.32.

The TextEd program with no documents in it.

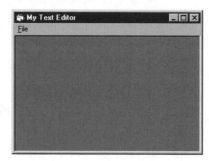

☐ Select New from the File menu.

A new child form pops up (see Figure 17.33). You can now type text in the text box. As you can see, the text box area isn't big enough! But don't worry about it—you'll fix this problem soon.

Figure 17.33.

The TextEd program with one document in it.

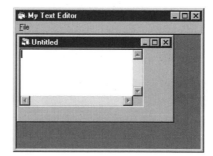

☐ Select New from the File menu several more times.

The program displays the child forms, as shown in Figure 17.34.

Figure 17.34.
The TextEd program with several documents in it.

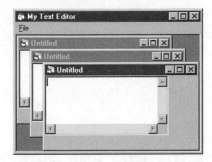

☐ Terminate the program by selecting Exit from the File menu.

The Code of the `mnuNew_Click()` Procedure

The `mnuNew_Click()` procedure is executed when you select New from the File menu:

```
Private Sub mnuNew_Click()

    ' Declare a variable for the instance form
    ' as a copy of the form frmTemplate.
    Dim frmNewForm As New frmTemplate
    ' Show the instance form.
    frmNewForm.Show

End Sub
```

This is the first statement in the procedure:

```
Dim frmNewForm As New frmTemplate
```

This statement declares a variable called `frmNewForm` as a new *instance*, or copy, of the child form frmTemplate. This means that, for all purposes, you can refer to frmNewForm as a form with the same properties as the frmTemplate form you designed at design time. In other words, you create a copy of the frmTemplate form. Once the frmNewForm is created, you can use it in the program just like any other form.

For example, the second statement in the `mnuNew_Click()` procedure causes the newly created form to pop up by using the following statement:

```
frmNewForm.Show
```

Every time you select New from the File menu, a new instance is created that is a copy of the frmTemplate form.

Adjusting the Text Box Size According to the Form Size

The text box should fill the entire child form area. Therefore, no matter how big or small the child form is, the text box should always cover the whole child form. You can do this by using the Resize event.

The Resize Event

The Resize event occurs when the form pops up and when the size of the form is changed. Therefore, the Form_Resize() procedure is a focal point that is executed when the form size changes. This is a good place to resize the text box according to the form size.

☐ Enter the following code in the Form_Resize() procedure of the frmTemplate child form:

```
Private Sub Form_Resize()

    Me.txtUserArea.Height = Me.ScaleHeight
    Me.txtUserArea.Width = Me.ScaleWidth

End Sub
```

The first statement in the Form_Resize() procedure assigns the ScaleHeight property of the current form to the Height property of the text box. Similarly, the second statement of the Form_Resize() procedure assigns the ScaleWidth property of the current form to the Width property of the text box. Therefore, the text box has the size of the current form.

The Me Reserved Word

The Me reserved word used in the two statements of Form_Resize() is a Visual Basic reserved word. It is a variable containing the name of the form where the code is currently executed.

For example, in the TextEd program, there may be several instances of the frmTemplate form in the parent form. When the size of one of these forms is changed, the TextEd program executes the `Form_Resize()` procedure and automatically updates the `Me` variable with the name of the instance that was resized. Again, the program automatically maintains and updates the value of the `Me` variable with the instance where code is currently executed (so you do not have to write code that accomplishes this).

Interestingly enough, if you omit the `Me` word in the statements of the `Form_Resize()` procedure, the program still works, because when you omit the name of the form, it has the same effect as substituting `Me` for the name of the form.

Changing the Caption Property of a Form

17

Another useful feature in Visual Basic is the ActiveForm property, which specifies the currently active form. If there is currently no active child form, the ActiveForm property specifies the most recently active child form.

To illustrate how useful the ActiveForm property is, enhance the TextEd program so that you can change the Caption property of the child forms at runtime.

☐ Add the Assign Name menu to the parent form, as shown in Figure 17.35. (In the Menu Editor, set the Caption to &Assign Name and set the Name to mnuAssignName.)

Figure 17.35.

Adding the Assign Name menu to the parent form.

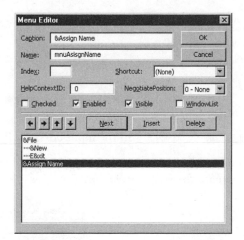

Entering the Code in the `mnuAssignName_Click()` Procedure

Enter the code:

☐ Enter the following code in the `mnuAssignName_Click()` procedure of the frmTextEd parent form:

```
Private Sub mnuAssignName_Click()

    ' Declare a string variable
    Dim DocumentName As String

    ' Get from the user the name of the document
    DocumentName = InputBox("Document name:", "Assign Name")

    ' Change the Caption property of the currently
    ' active (or last active)form.
    frmTextEd.ActiveForm.Caption = DocumentName

End Sub
```

Executing the TextEd Program Again

Next, execute the program again:

☐ Execute the TextEd program.

☐ Select New from the File menu.

A new child document appears.

☐ Select the Assign Name menu.

The program responds by displaying the input box, as shown in Figure 17.36.

Figure 17.36.
*Entering the docu-
ment name by using
an input box.*

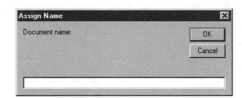

☐ Type Document Number 1 in the input box and click the OK button.

*The program responds by changing the Caption property of the currently active child form
from Untitled to Document Number 1 (see Figure 17.37).*

Figure 17.37.
*The new document
with its new caption.*

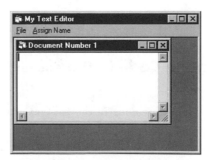

☐ Add several more new documents by selecting New from the File menu.

☐ You can switch to other child documents and change their names by selecting the Assign Name menu.

The Code in the `mnuAssignName_Click()` Procedure

The `mnuAssignName_Click()` procedure is automatically executed when you select the Assign Name menu:

```
Private Sub mnuAssignName_Click()

    ' Declare a string variable
    Dim DocumentName As String

     ' Get from the user the name of the document
     DocumentName = InputBox("Document name:", "Assign Name")

    ' Change the Caption property of the currently
    ' active (or last active)form.
    frmTextEd.ActiveForm.Caption = DocumentName

End Sub
```

The first statement in this procedure declares `DocumentName` as a string variable. The second statement displays the input box shown in Figure 17.36. Your input is assigned to the `DocumentName` string variable:

```
DocumentName = InputBox("Enter Document name:", "Assign Name")
```

The last statement in the procedure assigns the contents of the `DocumentName` variable to the Caption property of the currently active child form:

```
frmTextEd.ActiveForm.Caption = DocumentName
```

Visual Basic automatically maintains and updates the `ActiveForm` variable. When the `mnuAssignName_Click()` procedure is executed, `ActiveForm` is already updated with the value of the currently active form (to which you're assigning a new name).

 Note

> The properties of the currently active or the most recently active child form can be changed by using the ActiveForm property as follows:
>
> ```
> [ParentForm].ActiveForm.[Property to be changed] = Value
> ```
>
> For example, to change the Caption property of the currently active child form of the frmTextEd parent form to DocumentName, use this statement:
>
> ```
> frmTextEd.ActiveForm.Caption = DocumentName
> ```

Note

> The TextEd program currently has a little bug in it. Can you tell what it is?
>
> If you execute the program and select the AssignName menu without selecting New from the File menu, the program crashes. Why? There aren't any child forms in the parent form. The `mnuAssignName_Click()` procedure tries to change the Caption property of a child form that doesn't exist.
>
> The answer to the second exercise at the end of this chapter tells you how to fix this bug.

Creating a Toolbar

Many Windows programs include a toolbar, which is an area containing controls you can select. Figure 17.38 shows the toolbar of the popular Microsoft Word for Windows program. Typically, the controls on the toolbar are included in programs to provide quick access to the most commonly used operations. The controls on the toolbar may be images, command buttons, scroll bars, and so on. For example, clicking the disk image on the toolbar of Word for Windows has the same effect as selecting Save from the File menu of the Word program.

Figure 17.38.

The toolbar of Microsoft Word for Windows.

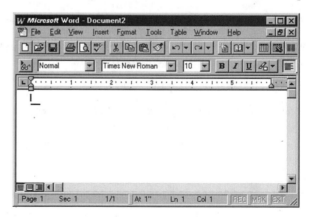

| Note | In some Windows literature, the toolbar is called a ribbon bar or a control bar. |

The Visual Implementation of the Toolbar and the Status Bar

Now you'll add a toolbar and a status bar to the TextEd program. The complete TextEd form with its toolbar and status bar is shown in Figure 17.39.

Figure 17.39.

The toolbar and the status bar in the TextEd program.

☐ Select the MDI parent form.

☐ Double-click the icon of the image control in the toolbox window.

   Visual Basic responds by displaying an error box (see Figure 17.40).

Why is Visual Basic unhappy with your action? Because you tried to place a control that doesn't support the Align property in the MDI parent form. (If you examine the properties window of the image control, you'll see that this control doesn't support the Align property.) The only control that supports the Align property is the picture control.

Figure 17.40.

The error message displayed when you try to place a control in the MDI parent form.

☐ Click the OK button of the error message.

☐ Double-click the icon of the picture control in the toolbox window.

Visual Basic responds by placing the picture control in the MDI form, as shown in Figure 17.41. You will place the toolbar icons in this picture control. If you try to drag the picture control to another location in the MDI parent form, Visual Basic refuses to honor your request.

Figure 17.41.

Placing the toolbar in the MDI parent form.

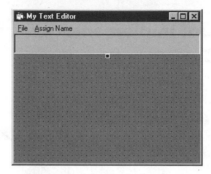

Now you'll prepare the area where the icons of the status bar are located. (The status bar serves the same purpose as the toolbar, but the toolbar is at the top of the form and the status bar is at the bottom.)

☐ Double-click the icon of the Picture icon in the toolbox window again.

Visual Basic responds by placing a picture control below the picture control you placed in the previous step (see Figure 17.42).

Figure 17.42.

Placing a second picture control in the MDI parent form.

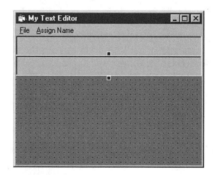

As shown in Figure 17.39, the status bar is located at the bottom of the form, so you need to reposition the second picture control you placed:

☐ Make sure the second picture control is selected and change its Align property to 2-Align Bottom.

Visual Basic responds by positioning the picture control at the bottom of the form (see Figure 17.43).

Figure 17.43.

Placing the status bar in the MDI parent form.

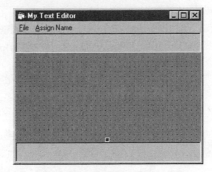

Now you'll place controls on the toolbar and the status bar, as shown in Figure 17.39. Use the following steps to place the disk image on the toolbar:

☐ Click (do not double-click) the icon of the image control in the toolbox window.

Visual Basic responds by highlighting the icon of the image control in the toolbox window.

☐ Place the mouse cursor in the toolbar area (the top picture control) and click and hold the left mouse button while you move the mouse.

Visual Basic responds by placing the image control in the toolbar area.

☐ Change the Picture property of the image control to C:\VB\ICONS\COMPUTER\ DISK03.ICO. (If your VB directory doesn't have this ICO file, use any other ICO file.)

☐ Change the Stretch property of the image control to True.

☐ Change the Name property of the Image to imgSave.

☐ Enlarge the area of the toolbar (which is the picture control) so that you see the entire area of the imgSave image control.

You can now place the other controls shown in Figure 17.39 in the toolbar and the status bar. (The globe shown on the status bar in Figure 17.39 is an image control with its Picture property set to C:\VB\ICONS\ELEMENTS\EARTH.ICO.) Again, if you don't have this ICO file, use a different one. Remember not to double-click the icons in the toolbox window. Rather, click the icon of a control, then move the mouse cursor in the area of the toolbar (or status bar), and drag the mouse.

☐ Change the Name property of the CommandButton on the toolbar to cmdExit.

☐ Change the Caption property of the cmdExit button to E&xit.

The visual implementation of the toolbar and status bar is complete. Now you'll attach code to some of the controls on the toolbar.

Note

> You haven't been instructed to change the properties of the other controls that you placed on the toolbar and status bar. You have been instructed to place these controls on the toolbar and the status bar just so you could see how this task is done.

Do   **Don't**

DON'T double-click the control when you want to place controls in the toolbar and in the status bar. Simply click the icon of the control in the toolbox, then click the left mouse button where you want the control and drag the mouse.

Entering the Code of the Toolbar Icons

Attaching code to the icons and controls of the toolbar and status bar is done the same way as attaching code to regular controls.

The Code in the imgSave_Click() Procedure

Use the following steps to enter code in the imgSave_Click() procedure, which is automatically executed when you click the disk icon on the toolbar:

☐ Make sure the parent form is selected.

☐ Double-click the disk image on the toolbar.

Visual Basic responds by displaying the imgSave_Click() *procedure.*

☐ Enter the Beep statement in this procedure:

```
Private Sub imgSave_Click()

    Beep

End Sub
```

Saving files is the subject of another chapter, so for simplicity, the concept is demonstrated by inserting the Beep statement instead of statements that save files. In other words, during the execution of the program, when you click the disk icon, you'll hear a beep instead of actually saving the file.

☐ Double-click the Exit button and add the following code in the `cmdExit_Click()` procedure:

```
Private Sub cmdExit_Click()

    End

End Sub
```

☐ Select Save Project from the File menu to save the TextEd project.

Executing the TextEd Program After Adding the Toolbar and Status Bar

Now let's see what you've got:

☐ Execute the TextEd program.

The TextEd form should pop up, as shown in Figure 17.44.

Figure 17.44.

*The TextEd program
with no documents
in it.*

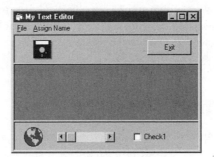

☐ Click the disk icon on the toolbar.

The program beeps when you click this icon.

☐ Select New from the File menu several times.

The program responds by creating a new document (a new child form) every time you click the New item (see Figure 17.45).

☐ Click the Exit button to terminate the program.

Figure 17.45.

*The TextEd program
with new documents
in its parent window.*

Attaching Code to the Other Controls of the Toolbar and Status Bar

You can now attach code to the other controls on the toolbar and status bar. You type code in the procedures of the scroll bar just as you would for procedures of regular scroll bars in non-MDI forms.

It is possible to have more than one toolbar or status bar. For example, in Figure 17.38, Word for Windows is shown with two toolbars. The top toolbar contains icons such as the disk icon, and the lower toolbar contains tools such as a list box for font styles. Take a look at Figure 17.42—before you converted the second toolbar to a status bar, you had two toolbars in the program.

Summary

In this chapter you learned how to write multiple-document interface (MDI) programs. MDI programs include one parent form and at least one child form. You learned how to display (show) the child forms, how to unload child forms, and how to use the powerful Window list menu that helps you maneuver and arrange child forms in the parent form.

You also learned how to create instances (copies) of a child form at runtime, how to change the properties of the instances at runtime, how to build a toolbar and status bar, and how to attach code to the controls of these bars.

Q&A

Q I want to design an MDI program that doesn't load any of its child forms when I start the program. Is it possible?

A Yes. By default, Visual Basic initializes the Startup Object of the Project Properties window with the name of the first child form. For example, in the Pictures program, the default Startup Object is the frmPicture1 form. When you start the program, the MDI parent form and the child form frmPicture1 are loaded. If you want only the parent MDI form to be loaded, set the Startup Form field to the parent MDI form.

You can try this procedure by making the following changes to the Pictures program:

☐ Set the Startup Object field of the Pictures project to frmPictures by selecting Project Properties from the Project Menu, clicking the General tab, and then setting the Startup Object field.

☐ Remove the statements in the MDIForm_Load() procedure. (These statements cause all the child forms to be displayed.)

> *When you start the Pictures program, the parent form is shown without any of its child forms.*

Q If the currently active child form has a menu, the menu of the parent form changes to the child form's menu. Is it possible to design the program so that the menu of the parent form remains unchanged, and the child form's menu appears on the window of the child form?

A No. That's how MDI programs work! Generally speaking, it is best to accept the rules and standards of MDI, because your users expect the MDI program to work in an acceptable, known way. After all, one of the main advantages of using Windows programs is that the user-interface aspect of all Windows programs is well known and accepted by millions of happy users.

Quiz

1. How many MDI parent forms can a Visual Basic program have?

    a. 255
    b. No limit
    c. 1
    d. Depends on the number of child forms

2. A program contains the following forms: an MDI parent form and its child forms and two standard forms. Which form is loaded when you start the program?

    a. The MDI parent form
    b. The form mentioned in the Startup object of the Project Properties window
    c. Depends on the code in the Form_Load() procedure

3. What is the difference between a toolbar and a status bar?

    a. They're the same thing—it's just different terminology.
    b. The toolbar is at the top of the MDI parent form, and the status bar is at the bottom.
    c. Status bars are not supported by Visual Basic. (They are supported by Word for Windows only.)

17

Exercises

1. Enhance the Window menu of the Pictures program by adding the Tile Vertical item.

2. Enhance the TextEd program as follows:

    ■ Add a new menu to the TextEd parent form called Color. This menu should have two items in it: Green and Gray.

    ■ When you select Green or Gray from the Color menu, the currently active child document should change its background color to the selected color.

Quiz Answers

1. c
2. b
3. b

Exercise Answers

1. To enhance the Pictures program, perform the following steps:

    ☐ Highlight the frmPictures parent form and select Menu Editor from the Tools menu.

    ☐ Add the menu item Tile Vertical to the Window menu of the frmPictures form. (Set Caption to Tile &Vertical, set Name to mnuTileVertical.)

    ☐ Add the following code in the mnuTileVertical_Click() procedure of the frmPictures form:

    ```
    Private Sub mnuTileVertical_Click()

        ' The user selected Tile from the Window menu.
        frmPictures.Arrange vbTileVertical

    End Sub
    ```

    The mnuTileVertical_Click() procedure causes the child forms to be arranged vertically, as shown in Figure 17.28.

2. To enhance the TextEd program, perform the following steps:

    ☐ Add the following items to the menu of the TextEd parent form:

Caption	Procedure name
&Color	mnuColor
...&Green	mnuGreen
...G&ray	mnuGray

☐ Enter the following code in the mnuGray_Click() procedure:

```
Private Sub mnuGray_Click()

    frmTextEd.ActiveForm.txtUserArea.BackColor = _

                            QBColor(8)

End Sub
```

☐ Enter the following code in the mnuGreen_Click() procedure:

```
Private Sub mnuGreen_Click()

    frmTextEd.ActiveForm.txtUserArea.BackColor = _
                        QBColor(2)
End Sub
```

(Note that the ActiveForm property is used as a substitute for the child form name in the preceding two procedures.)

☐ Save the project.

☐ Execute the program.

☐ Select New from the File menu several times.

☐ Change the color of the currently active child form by selecting an item from the Color menu.

☐ Experiment with the program, then select Exit from the File menu to terminate the program.

This implementation is not finished, because if you select a color from the Color menu while there is no child document in the parent form, the program will crash. One solution is to declare a variable called ggNumberOfChildren in the general declarations section of a new module as follows:

☐ Select Add Module from the Project menu, Select the Module icon that appears in the Add Module window, and then click the Open button.

> *Visual Basic responds by adding a new module to the project. The default name that Visual Basic assigns to the new module is Module1.bas.*

☐ Make sure that the code window of the new module is the selected window, then select Save Module 1 As from the File menu of Visual Basic, and save the new module file as C:\VB5Prg\Ch17\TextEd.bas.

☐ Add the following statement in the general declarations section of the TextEd.bas module:

```
Option Explicit
Public ggNumberOfChildren
```

This statement declares the ggNumberOfChildren public variable in a separate module, so it is visible by all the other modules (if any) and forms of this project. The objective is to maintain the value of ggNumberOfChildren, so that this variable will always indicate the number of child forms in the parent form.

☐ Modify the code in the mnuNew_Click() procedure of the frmTextEd parent form as follows:

```
Private Sub mnuNew_Click()

    ' Declare a variable for the instance form
    ' as a copy of the form frmTemplate.
    Dim frmNewForm As New frmTemplate

    ' Show the instance form.
    frmNewForm.Show


    ' For exercise #2 chapter 17
    ggNumberOfChildren = ggNumberOfChildren + 1

End Sub
```

When you select New from the File menu, the code in the mnuNew_Click() procedure should increase ggNumberOfChildren. Initially, ggNumberOfChildren is 0, but every time you select New from the File menu, it is increased by one.

☐ Also, you have to add code to the mnuForm_Unload() procedure of the frmTemplate child form as follows:

```
Private Sub Form_Unload(Cancel As Integer)

    ggNumberOfChildren = ggNumberOfChildren - 1

End Sub
```

The Form_Unload() procedure of the frmTemplate child form is automatically executed when you unload a child form. For example, if you select New from the File menu three times, the current value of ggNumberOfChildren is 3. Now suppose that you click the system icon of one of the child forms and select Close to close the child form. Visual Basic automatically executes the Form_Unload() procedure of the frmTemplate child form, which means that the value of ggNumberOfChildren is now 3-1=2.

☐ Now modify the mnuGreen_Click() and the mnuGray_Click() procedures of the frmTextEd parent form so that they will look like this:

```
Private Sub mnuGreen_Click()
    If ggNumberOfChildren > 0 Then
        frmTextEd.ActiveForm.txtUserArea.BackColor = _
                                QBColor(2)
    End If
End Sub
```

```
Private Sub mnuGray_Click()
    If ggNumberOfChildren > 0 Then
        frmTextEd.ActiveForm.txtUserArea.BackColor = _
                                    QBColor(8)
    End If

End Sub
```

As you can see, an If statement is executed to check whether ggNumberOfChildren is greater than 0. If it isn't, the background color of the child form is not changed (because there is no child form in the parent form).

As this chapter explains, you have to use the same If statement (with the ggNumberOfChildren variable) for determining whether the code in the mnuAssignName_Click() procedure of the frmTextEd parent form should be executed. That is, if there is no child form in the parent form, then the statements in the mnuAssignName_Click() procedure shouldn't be executed.

☐ Therefore, modify the mnuAssignName_Click() procedure of the frmTextEd parent form as follows:

```
Private Sub mnuAssignName_Click()

    ' Declare a string variable
    Dim DocumentName As String

If ggNumberOfChildren > 0 Then
        ' Get from the user the name of the document
    DocumentName = InputBox("Document name:", "Assign Name")
    ' Change the Caption property of the currently
    ' active (or last active)form.
    frmTextEd.ActiveForm.Caption = DocumentName
End If

End Sub
```

17

Day 18

Sending Keystrokes

In this chapter you'll learn how to send keystrokes from within your program to other Windows programs, and you'll also learn how to send keystrokes to yourself. These features are helpful when building demo programs and other applications.

Emulating Keystrokes: The Source and Dest Programs

You can write a Visual Basic program that sends keystrokes to another Windows application. You'll now write two programs: Source.EXE and Dest.EXE. As implied by their names, Source.EXE serves as the *source program* where keystrokes are generated, and Dest.EXE is the *destination program* that receives the keystrokes.

The Visual Implementation of the Source Program

First, implement the source program:

☐ Start a new Standard EXE project, and save the project form as C:\VB5PRG\CH18\ SOURCE.FRM and the project file as C:\VB5PRG\CH18\SOURCE.VBP.

☐ Build the frmSource form according to the specifications in Table 18.1.

The completed form should look like the one shown in Figure 18.1.

Table 18.1. The properties table of the frmSource form.

Object	Property	Setting
Form	**Name**	**frmSource**
	Caption	The Source Program
Text Box	**Name**	**txtUserArea**
	MultiLine	True
	ScrollBars	3-Both
Command Button	**Name**	**cmdSend**
	Caption	&Send
Command Button	**Name**	**cmdExit**
	Caption	E&xit

Figure 18.1.
The frmSource form in design mode.

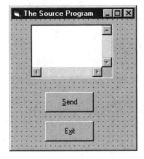

Entering the Code of the frmSource Program

Enter the code of the frmSource program:

☐ Enter the following code in the general declarations section of the frmSource form:

```
' All variables MUST be declared.
Option Explicit
```

☐ Enter the following code in the `Form_Load()` procedure of the frmSource form:

```
Private Sub Form_Load()

    Dim ID

    ' Execute the destination program.
    ID = Shell("DEST.exe", 1)

End Sub
```

☐ Enter the following code in the `cmdSend_Click()` procedure of the frmSource form:

```
Private Sub cmdSend_Click()

    ' Make the destination program the active program.
    AppActivate "The Dest Program"

    ' Send characters to the destination program.
    SendKeys txtUserArea.Text, True

End Sub
```

☐ Enter the following code in the `cmdExit_Click()` procedure of the frmSource form:

```
Private Sub cmdExit_Click()

    End

End Sub
```

☐ Save the project.

☐ Create the Source.EXE file by selecting Make Source.EXE from the File menu of Visual Basic and saving the file as Source.EXE in the C:\VB5PRG\EXE directory.

You cannot execute the Source.EXE program yet! Why? The Source.EXE program requires the Dest.EXE program to work.

The Visual Implementation of the Dest Program

Implement the Dest.EXE program:

☐ Start a new Standard EXE project, save the new form as DEST.FRM in the C:\VB5PRG\ CH18 directory, and save the new project file as DEST.VBP in the C:\VB5PRG\CH18 directory.

☐ Build the frmDest form according to the specifications in Table 18.2. When you finish building the form, it should look like the one shown in Figure 18.2.

18

Table 18.2. The properties table of the frmDest form.

Object	Property	Setting
Form	**Name**	**frmDest**
	Caption	The Dest Program
Command Button	**Name**	**cmdDisplayMessage**
	Caption	&Display Message
Command Button	**Name**	**cmdExit**
	Caption	E&xit

Figure 18.2.

The frmDest form in design mode.

Entering the Code of the Dest Program

Next, enter the code of the Dest program:

☐ Type the following code in the general declarations section of the frmDest form:

```
' All variables must be declared
Option Explicit
```

☐ Type the following code in the cmdDisplayMessage_Click() procedure of the frmDest form:

```
Private Sub cmdDisplayMessage_Click()

    MsgBox "Display Message was clicked"

End Sub
```

☐ Type the following code in the cmdExit_Click() procedure of the frmDest form:

```
Private Sub cmdExit_Click()

    End

End Sub
```

You'll now create the Dest.EXE program:

☐ Select Make Dest.EXE from the File menu of Visual Basic and save the program as Dest.EXE in the C:\VB5PRG\EXE directory. Make sure the Source.EXE program is in the same directory as the Dest.EXE program.

Executing the Source and Dest Programs

Now execute the Dest.EXE program:

☐ Terminate Visual Basic by selecting Exit from the File menu of Visual Basic.

☐ Execute the Dest.EXE program by displaying the C:\VB5PRG\EXE directory and double-clicking the Dest.EXE item.

> *Windows responds by executing the Dest.EXE program, and the window shown in Figure 18.3 is displayed.*

Figure 18.3.
*The Dest.EXE
program.*

☐ Click the Display Message button of the Dest.EXE program.

> *Dest.EXE responds by displaying the message box shown in Figure 18.4.*

Figure 18.4.
*The message box
displayed after you
click the Display
Message button.*

☐ Click the Exit button of the Dest.EXE program to terminate the program.

As you can see, the Dest program is very simple—you click its Display Message button to display a message box. The point of the Source and Dest programs is to illustrate how you can click the Display Message button of the Dest program from within the Source program! Use the following steps to see how this is accomplished:

☐ Make sure that the Dest.EXE program isn't running.

☐ Execute the Source.EXE program.

> *Windows responds by executing the Source.EXE program, and the windows shown in Figure 18.5 are displayed. As soon as you execute Source.EXE, Windows executes the Dest.EXE program as well.*

☐ Minimize all programs except the Source.EXE and Dest.EXE programs so you can see their windows better.

18

Figure 18.5.
The Source.EXE and
Dest.EXE programs.

☐ Type %{D} in the Source.EXE text box.

☐ Click the Send button of the Source.EXE program.

> *As you can see, the Dest.EXE program responds as if you had clicked its Display Message*
> *button; in other words, you clicked the Display Message button of the Dest.EXE program*
> *from within the Source.EXE program.*

☐ Experiment with the Source and Dest programs and then terminate them.

How the Source Program Works

The code in the Source program executes the Dest program by using the Shell() function
and the SendKeys statement to send characters to the Dest program.

The Code of the Form_Load() Procedure

The Form_Load() procedure is executed when the frmSource form is loaded:

```
Private Sub Form_Load()

    Dim ID
    ' Execute the destination program.
    ID = Shell("DEST.exe", 1)

End Sub
```

This procedure uses the Shell() function to execute the Dest program. The first argument
of the Shell() function is a string containing the name of the program to be executed.

The second argument is an optional argument that specifies the window style of the program
to be executed. A value of 1 means that the program to be executed will be shown with a
normal window. The preceding Shell() function assumes that the Dest.EXE program is in
either the current directory or a directory mentioned in the DOS path.

The Code of the `cmdSend_Click()` Procedure

The `cmdSend_Click()` procedure is executed when you click the Send button:

```
Private Sub cmdSend_Click()

    ' Make the destination program the active program.
    AppActivate "The Dest Program"

    ' Send characters to the destination program.
    SendKeys txtUserArea.Text, True

End Sub
```

This procedure makes the Dest program the active application with the `AppActivate` statement:

```
AppActivate "The Dest Program"
```

The argument of the `AppActivate` statement is the title of the program to be activated. You must supply this argument exactly as it appears in the window title of the program to be activated. When you start the Dest program, the window title that appears is `The Dest Program`.

For example, if you supply `The Dest.EXE Program` as the argument of the `AppActivate` statement, you get a runtime error because the text `.EXE` doesn't appear in the Dest program's title.

However, the `AppActivate` argument is not case-sensitive. For example, you could use the following statement to activate the Dest program:

```
ThE DeSt PrOgRaM
```

The second statement in the `cmdSend_Click()` procedure sends characters to the currently active application with the `SendKeys` statement:

```
SendKeys txtUserArea.Text, True
```

The characters that are sent are the contents of the `txtUserArea`. It is important to understand that these characters are transferred to the currently active application. This explains why you activated the Dest program before issuing the `SendKeys` statement.

After sending the keys to Dest.EXE, the active program is still the Dest program. You can add the following statement after the `SendKeys` statement in the `cmdSend_Click()` procedure of the frmSource form:

```
AppActivate "The Source Program"
```

This statement makes Source.EXE the active program.

18

The SendKeys **Statement**

As demonstrated in the Source and Dest programs, the SendKeys statement is used to send characters to the currently active program. The True argument causes these keys to be processed before the program returns to the cmdSend_Click() procedure. This means that the Source program yields to the program receiving the characters, letting it execute its code. If you supply False as the second argument of the SendKeys statement, control is returned to the Source program immediately after the characters are sent.

You can send special keys using the codes specified in Table 18.3. For example, to send the Alt+D key, use %{D}.

When you press Alt+D in Dest, you get the same result as when you click the Display Message button (because the Caption property of the Display Message button was set at design time to &Display Message).

Table 18.3. The code for special keys when used with the SendKeys statement.

Key	Use in SendKeys
Shift	+
Ctrl	^ (Above the 6 key)
Alt	%
Backspace	{BACKSPACE}
Break	{BREAK}
CapsLock	{CAPLOCKS}
Clear	{CLEAR}
Del	{DELETE}
Down Arrow	{DOWN}
End	{END}
Enter	{ENTER}
Esc	{ESCAPE}
Help	{HELP}
Home	{HOME}
Ins	{INSERT}
Left Arrow	{LEFT}

Key	Use in SendKeys
Num Lock	{NUMLOCK}
Page Down	{PGDN}
Page Up	{PGUP}
Print Screen	{PRTSC}
Right Arrow	{RIGHT}
Scroll Lock	{SCROLLLOCK}
Tab	{TAB}
Up Arrow	{UP}
F1	{F1}
...	...
F16	{F16}

Sending Keystrokes to Yourself: The MySelf Program

18

The SendKeys statement sends the keys to the currently active program. What happens when the currently active program is the Source program? As you might expect, the keys are sent to themselves!

Does sending keystrokes to your program have any practical uses? Sure. For example, you can build a demo program or a tutorial program that demonstrates what happens when a sequence of keystrokes is pressed. The MySelf program demonstrates how a Visual Basic program can send keystrokes to itself.

The Visual Implementation of the MySelf Program

First, implement the Dest.EXE program:

☐ Start a new Standard EXE project and save the project form as C:\VB5PRG\CH18\ MYSELF.FRM and the project file as C:\VB5PRG\CH18\MYSELF.VBP.

☐ Build the frmMySelf form according to the specifications in Table 18.4.

The completed form should look like the one shown in Figure 18.6.

Table 18.4. The properties table of the frmMySelf form.

Object	Property	Setting
Form	**Name**	**frmMySelf**
	Caption	The MySelf Program
Command Button	**Name**	**cmdBeep**
	Caption	&Beep
Command Button	**Name**	**cmdSend**
	Caption	&Send
Text Box	**Name**	**txtUserArea**
	MultiLine	True
	Text	(empty)
Command Button	**Name**	**cmdExit**
	Caption	E&xit

Figure 18.6.

*The frmMySelf form
in design mode.*

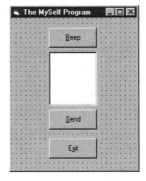

Entering the Code of the frmMySelf Program

Now enter the code of the frmMySelf program:

☐ Enter the following code in the general declarations section of the frmMySelf form:

```
' All variables MUST be declared.
Option Explicit
```

☐ Enter the following code in the cmdSend_Click() procedure of the frmMySelf form:

```
Private Sub cmdSend_Click()

    ' Make sure this program is the active program.
    AppActivate "The MySelf Program"
```

```
                    ' Send the text to this program that is
                    ' currently in the text box.
                    SendKeys txtUserArea.Text, True

            End Sub
```

☐ Enter the following code in the cmdBeep_Click() procedure of the frmMySelf form:

```
        Private Sub cmdBeep_Click()

            Beep
            MsgBox "The Beep button was clicked"

        End Sub
```

☐ Enter the following code in the cmdExit_Click() procedure of the frmMySelf form:

```
        Private Sub cmdExit_Click()

            End

        End Sub
```

Executing the MySelf Program

Execute the MySelf program:

☐ Select Make MySelf.EXE from the File menu of Visual Basic and save the program as MySelf.EXE in the C:\VB5PRG\EXE directory.

☐ Select Exit from the File menu of Visual Basic to terminate Visual Basic.

☐ Execute the MySelf.EXE program.

☐ Click the Beep button.

The PC should beep.

☐ Press Alt+B.

The PC should beep because the caption of the Beep button is &Beep.

☐ Type %{B} in the text box of the MySelf program and click the Send button.

The PC should beep!

☐ Experiment with the MySelf.EXE program and then terminate the program.

18

The Code of the `cmdSend_Click()` Procedure

The `cmdSend_Click` procedure is executed when you click the Send button:

```
Private Sub cmdSend_Click()

    ' Make sure this program is the active program.
    AppActivate "The MySelf Program"

    ' Send the text to this program that is
    ' currently in the text box.
    SendKeys txtUserArea.Text, True

End Sub
```

The first statement in this procedure makes sure the currently active program is the MySelf program. (This statement is really not necessary, because even if you omit this statement, the currently active program is the MySelf program. This statement is included to emphasize that you are sending keystrokes to yourself.)

The second statement in this procedure executes the `SendKeys` statement to send whatever characters are in the text box.

If you type `%{B}` in the text box, this text is translated as Alt+B (as shown in Table 18.3), which is the same as clicking the &Beep button.

The code in the `cmdBeep_Click()` procedure contains the `Beep` and `MsgBox` statements, which causes the PC to beep and display a message box.

Summary

In this chapter, you learned how to use the `Shell()` function to execute the destination application from within the source application, how to send data from the source application to the destination application, and how to send keystrokes to yourself.

Q&A

Q When will I want to use the feature of one application sending keystrokes to another application?

A There are many situations in which this capability of sending keystrokes from one application to another is useful. For example, you can build a very complicated program that uses other pieces of hardware, such as a CD-ROM drive, sound card, scanner, and so on. Because of its complexity, you may have to test the program by trying different ways to execute it. In such a case, you might consider using another program that will serve as the source program. The source program will periodically send keystrokes to the destination program, so instead of hiring someone to test the destination program, you can build a tester program that will do the testing for you automatically.

Other applications might send keystrokes to a destination program for educational or demo purposes. For example, an automatic Demo program that serves as the destination program is executed according to keystrokes sent to it from a source program.

Quiz

1. What does the `Shell()` function provide?

   a. A good seafood dinner.
   b. A means to execute any program from within a Visual Basic program.
   c. There is no such thing.

2. What does the `AppActivate` statement do?

Exercise

18

What should you type in the text box of the MySelf program so that clicking the Send button terminates the program?

Quiz Answer

1. b

2. The `AppActivate` statement activates the window of a program. For example, the statement

   ```
   AppActivate "My Program"
   ```

   activates the window of the program whose window's title is My Program.

Exercise Answer

Use the following steps to terminate the program:

☐ Type `&{x}` in the text box.

☐ Click the Send button.

   The sequence `%{x}` is translated to Alt+X (refer to Table 18.3).

The caption of the Exit button is E&xit, so pressing Alt+X terminates the program. Typing `%{x}` in the text box and clicking the Send button causes the program to send the Alt+X keystroke to itself, which has the same effect as clicking the Exit button.

Week 3

Day 19

ActiveX—Sound Programming and DirectSound

So far in this book you learned the essentials of Visual Basic. You learned how to design forms, place objects in the forms, and attach code to the objects that you placed in the forms. This chapter concentrates on designing Windows applications with Visual Basic and ActiveX technology. In particular, in this chapter you'll see how a professional Windows application is designed from start to finish. The two main aspects of this chapter are

■ *Using ActiveX controls.* During the implementation of the application, you'll be instructed to use ActiveX controls for implementing certain features of the application. As you'll soon see, using these ActiveX controls will save you a lot of design time.

■ *Sound programming.* The application that you'll build plays sound.

At the end of this chapter, you'll read about the powerful DirectSound technology.

OCX ActiveX Technology

OCX ActiveX technology is a very important Windows technology. Basically, this technology enables you to plug software modules into your programs. As an example, suppose that you want to display 3-dimensional pictures (3-D pictures) and to enable your user to "travel" to different parts of the 3-D picture by using the mouse or the keyboard. Furthermore, as your user travels in the 3-D picture, you want your user to move from room to room, open doors, see views of other rooms and halls through transparent windows, encounter animated pictures of people and objects, pick up tools and use the tools to do some tasks, and so on. Designing such a program by yourself with Visual Basic could take you a very long time. A better approach is to use the powerful OCX ActiveX technology. When using ActiveX technology to design such a program, all the hard work is already prepared for you. That is, the mechanism that displays the 3-D picture, the mechanism that lets the user move in the 3-D pictures, the mechanism that creates animated objects, and so on—all these features are already included as an integral part of the OCX ActiveX control.

As an analogy, let's see how things are done when you use a simple control such as a CommandButton. When you use a CommandButton in your program, you are basically using a pre-prepared CommandButton. This means that when you design your Visual Basic program, you can assume that pressing the button with the mouse will cause the CommandButton to appear pushed down, and releasing the mouse button will cause the CommandButton to come back to its original state. Of course, all the other standard features of a Windows button are already implemented in the CommandButton control (for example, generating the Click event when the CommandButton is clicked). Thanks to the CommandButton control, you do not have to spend time designing all these features. As the designer of your program, you concentrate on designing the features of your program, rather than spending time designing code that is already available as part of the CommandButton.

Visual Basic comes with several standard controls—for example, CommandButton, Scrollbar, OptionButton, CheckBox, and so on. As you know by now, it makes sense to use these controls in your program rather than design them by yourself. In a similar manner, when you need to perform more complex operations and tasks, you'd better use a control (OCX ActiveX control) that is available as an inexpensive off-the-shelf component. In many cases, the time that you'll spend researching for an off-the-shelf ActiveX control that accomplishes the feature that you need in your program will be much less than the time it will take you to implement the features with pure Visual Basic code.

Let's summarize the advantages of using an ActiveX control:

■ *Develop your project faster.* Using ActiveX controls that accomplish what you need saves you design time. Instead of spending time on the design of a feature that is already available, you spend your time designing your program. This way, you can complete your project faster. In other words, you are not spending your time reinventing the wheel.

- *Reliability.* ActiveX controls that are manufactured by a reputable company are typically inexpensive and already used by many programmers. As such, the ActiveX controls have already been tested by many programmers and are known to work without bugs.

- *Minimizing learning time.* No matter what the purpose of each OCX ActiveX control, you use them all in the same way (as you'll soon see in this chapter). In other words, once you learn how to use one particular OCX ActiveX control, you know the principle of working with OCX ActiveX controls. Any other OCX that you'll ever use in your program works in the same way. That is, you plug the OCX ActiveX control into your program in the same way, and you "operate" the control in the same way (for example, setting the properties of the control during design time and runtime, applying the methods of the control, attaching code to the events of the control). This means that once you know how to use an OCX ActiveX control, the learning time for studying another OCX ActiveX control is very short (because you already know how to use OCX ActiveX technology).

Note

In this chapter you'll write a program called MyUSAMap. One of the features of this program is that it plays sound. This means that you need a sound card installed in your PC. It is recommended that you read the material of this chapter even if you don't have a sound card in your PC. This way, you'll learn what it takes to play sound files from within your Visual Basic programs.

19

Downloading the MapUSA Program and Its Associated ActiveX Controls

Before starting to design the MyUSAMap program yourself, let's load a copy of it from the Internet:

Note

The MapUSA program and the OCX ActiveX controls that the program uses are copyright TegoSoft Inc.

Note

> Even if you currently do not have an Internet access, it is highly
> recommended that you at least browse through this chapter. This way,
> you'll learn what it takes to implement impressive programs that use
> the powerful OCX ActiveX technology.

☐ Use your Internet connection to connect to the Internet.

☐ Use your Internet browser program to log into the following Internet URL address:

    `http://www.tegosoft.com/bkvbusamap.html`

☐ Follow the directions given on the preceding HTML page to download the TegoUSA.EXE
file.

☐ Follow the directions given on the preceding HTML page to install the TegoUSA.EXE
file.

That's it. You now have the MapUSA program installed in your PC.

Executing the MapUSA Program

Now execute the MapUSA program and see it in action:

☐ Execute the MapUSA program. Once you've installed the TegoUSA.EXE that you downloaded successfully, the MapUSA program is installed in the C:\ProgramFiles\
TegoSoft\USAmap directory. You can execute the MapUSA.EXE program by using the
Windows Explorer to double-click the MapUSA.EXE file. Alternatively, you can click the
Start button that is located on the status bar of Windows, select Programs, select USAmap
from the list of program groups that pops up, and finally, select the MapUSA program in
the USAmap group.

As a result, the window shown in Figure 19.1 appears.

As you can see from Figure 19.1, the MapUSA program displays a map of the USA. If you
have a sound card installed in your PC, you can hear the national anthem of the USA played
in the background.

Figure 19.1.

The window of the MapUSA program.

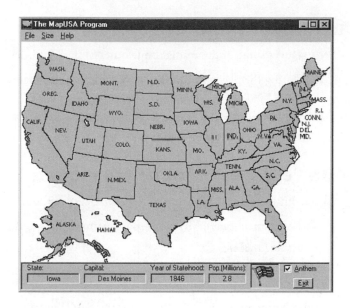

Sound Playback Features

Let's go over some of the sound playback features of the MapUSA program:

☐ Click the Anthem check box that is located at the lower-right side of the MapUSA's window.

   As a result, the check mark is removed from the Anthem check box, and the national anthem is stopped playing.

☐ Again, click the Anthem check box that is located at the lower-right side of the MapUSA's window.

   As a result, the check mark is placed in the Anthem check box, and the national anthem continues the playback.

The thing to note when checking and unchecking the Anthem check box is that when you start playing again, the Anthem continues playing from the last point that was played (in other words, the playback resumes).

19

Animation Features

Let's go over some of the animation features of the MapUSA program:

■ During the playback of the anthem, a US flag animates to the left of the Anthem check box.

■ When you stop the playback (by unchecking the Anthem check box), the flag becomes a small picture of the USA.

Map Features—Mouse Movement Events

Check out the mapping features of the MapUSA program:

☐ Without pressing any of the mouse buttons, move the mouse cursor over the various states.

```
State: Indiana
Capital: Indianapolis
Year of Statehood: 1816 (the year the state of Indiana joined the union).
Population in Millions: 5.5
```

In a similar manner, you can display information about any of the other 50 states.

The most important thing to note when you move the mouse cursor is that the program reports the correct information about the state no matter how irregular the shape of the state is. For example, look at the state of Texas which has a nonrectanglular shape. As long as the mouse cursor is in Texas, the program reports information about Texas.

Map Features—Mouse Click Events

Let's see a Click event in action:

☐ Click in any of the states.

Depending on the particular state in which you clicked, a message box appears with the information about the state. Again, it does not matter how irregular the shape of the state is. As long as you clicked in the state, the MapUSA program detects the event.

Window Features

Try out the window features of the MapUSA program:

☐ Place the mouse cursor on any of the edges of the window of the program, press the left button of the mouse, and while keeping the left button of the mouse down, drag the mouse.

As you drag the mouse, the size of the program's window changes accordingly.

Note that the USA map changes according to the size of the program's window. If you make the window smaller, the size of the USA map becomes smaller. If you make the window larger, the size of the USA map becomes larger. More importantly, no matter how large or small the map, the program always reports the correct information when you move the mouse over a certain state (or when you click the mouse in a certain state). In other words, the mouse movement and Click events are based on the shape of the state (not on the particular coordinates of the state).

Menus

Take a look at the menus of the MapUSA program:

☐ Select the File menu.

> *As a response, the File menu drops down.*

As you can see, the File menu has the Exit menu in it. When you click the Exit menu item, the program terminates. (Another way to terminate the program is by clicking the Exit button that is located on the lower-right side of the window's program.)

The MapUSA program also has a Size menu:

☐ Select the Size menu.

> *As a result, the Size menu drops down and you can see the menu items: Normal, Small, and Large.*

If you select Large, the window size becomes large. If you select Small, the window size becomes small. If you select Normal, the window returns to its default size.

The last menu is the Help menu. This menu includes the About menu item. When you click the About menu item, an About dialog box appears:

☐ Experiment with the MapUSA program, then click its Exit button (on the lower-right side of the window) to terminate the program.

Now that you understand what the MapUSA program is supposed to do, let's design it.

Creating the Project of the MyUSAMap Program

As usual, you'll start by creating a new Standard EXE project, and then you'll save the form and project files:

☐ Create the C:\VB5Prg\Ch19 directory. You'll save your work in this directory.

19

☐ Select New Project from the File menu of Visual Basic, select the Standard EXE icon from the New Project window, and click the OK button of the New Project window.

As a result, a new Form1 appears in the desktop of Visual Basic.

☐ Select Save Form1 As from the File menu of Visual Basic and then use the Save File As dialog box to save the form as MyUSAMap.Frm in the C:\VB5Prg\Ch19 directory.

☐ Select Save Project As from the File menu of Visual Basic and then use the Save project As dialog box to save the project file as MyUSAMap.Vbp in the C:\VB5Prg\Ch19 directory.

☐ In the general declarations section of the form, type the following code:

```
' All Variables MUST be declared
Option Explicit
```

From now on, you must declare variables before using them in the program.

Using Only the Necessary ActiveX Controls

Depending on the current settings of your Visual Basic, the Toolbox window may include various ActiveX controls. The icons that appear in the Toolbox window represent the controls that your project includes. It is important to include in your project only these controls that are used in your project. Why? Because when you distribute your final program, the files that are distributed with your program should only include these ActiveX controls that your project uses.

Start by first removing all the ActiveX controls from your project:

☐ Select Components from the Project menu of Visual Basic.

Visual Basic responds by displaying the Components window.

☐ The Components window has several tabs on top. Make sure that the Controls tab is selected (because you want to display the Controls page of the Components window).

☐ Place a check mark in the Selected Items Only check box (located on the lower-right portion of the Components window).

The Components window should now list all the ActiveX controls that are currently part of the project.

If the list is empty, it means that no ActiveX controls are used. In this case, click the OK button of the Components window.

If you see a list of ActiveX controls in the Components window, these ActiveX controls are part on the project (and their corresponding icons currently appear in the Toolbox window). In this case, remove the check mark that appears to the left of the item in the list. Keep removing the check marks from all the items in the list, then click the OK button of the Components window.

Take a look at Figure 19.2, which shows the Toolbox window when no ActiveX controls are included in the project. As you can see, you have in the Toolbox window controls such as the CommandButton, Scrollbars, OptionButton, CheckBox, and so on.

Figure 19.2.
*The icons of the
standard controls
of Visual Basic.*

Adding the OCX ActiveX Controls to the MyUSAMap Project

19

The MyUSAMap project uses two OCX ActiveX controls: TegoMM32.ocx and Tegousa3.ocx. These two OCX files were copied to your Windows System directory when you installed the TegoUSA.EXE file that you downloaded from the TegoSoft Web site.

Note

If you installed Windows 95 in the C:\Windows directory, the Windows System directory is C:\Windows\System.

If you installed Windows NT 4 in the C:\WinNT directory, the Windows System directory is C:\WinNT\System32.

Now add the two OCX ActiveX controls to the MyUSAMap project:

☐ Select Components from the Project menu of Visual Basic.

As a result, the Components window appears.

☐ Make sure that the Components window displays the Controls page (by clicking the Controls tab of the Components window).

☐ If the Selected Items Only check box has a check mark in it, remove the check mark.

As a result, the Components window displays all the OCX ActiveX controls that are currently registered in the PC.

☐ Scroll the list in the Components window (which is arranged alphabetically) until you see the TegoSoft multimedia control item. If you see this item, it means that the OCX is registered. In this case, place a check mark to the left of the item.

☐ If you do not see the TegoSoft multimedia control item, it means that the OCX is currently not registered. In this case, click the Browse button of the Components window, use the Add ActiveX Control dialog box to select the TegoMM32.OCX file that resides in the Windows System directory, and then click the Open button.

Now repeat the preceding steps to add the TegoSoft USA Map Control (which is the TegoUSA3.OCX file) to the MyUSAMap project:

☐ Scroll the list in the Components window (which is arranged alphabetically) until you see the TegoSoft USA Map Control item. If you see this item, it means that the OCX is registered. In this case, place a check mark to the left of the item.

☐ If you do not see the TegoSoft USA Map Control item, it means that the OCX is currently not registered. In this case, click the Browse button of the Components window, use the Add ActiveX Control dialog box to select the TegoUSA3.OCX file that resides in the Windows System directory, and then click the Open button.

After you click the OK button of the Components window, the Toolbox window should now look like the one in Figure 19.3.

Save your work:

☐ Select Save Project from the File menu of Visual Basic.

Figure 19.3.

The Toolbox window with the icons of the multimedia and USA Map controls.

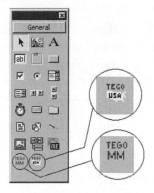

> **Note**
>
> When you place the mouse cursor (without pressing any of the mouse buttons) on the icon of the TegoSoft multimedia control, a yellow rectangle appears with the text Tegomm in it.
>
> When you place the mouse cursor (without pressing any of the mouse buttons) on the icon of the TegoSoft Map USA control, a yellow rectangle appears with the text TegoUSA in it.
>
> This way, you can easily verify that you located the icons of the controls in the Toolbox window. (You may have to move the Toolbox window and make its size larger to be able to see all the controls that the Toolbox window now includes.)

19

Placing the ActiveX Controls in the Form

Now place the two ActiveX controls that you added to the MyUSAMap project in the form of the project:

☐ Make sure that the Form1 is the selected window, then double-click the icon of the TegoUSA in the Toolbox.

As a result, the Missing License window appears. The Missing License window appears to remind you that you are not a licensed user of the OCX control. This means that you are not allowed to distribute the OCX file with your applications. (To be able to use the OCX control in your applications and to have a license to distribute the OCX file with your application, you need to purchase the OCX Control Kit; see disk offer at the end of this book.)

> **Note**
>
> As stated, the purpose of the Missing License window is to remind you that you are not licensed to distribute the OCX controls. During the development of the program, the OCX controls will occasionally remind you again by displaying the Missing License window.

☐ Make sure that the Name property of the TegoUSA control is TegoUSA1.

☐ Set the properties of Form1 as follows:

Name: frmMyUSAMap
Caption: The My USA Map Program
Height: 6360
Width: 7815

Save your work:

☐ Select Save Project from the File menu of Visual Basic.

Let's see your work in action:

☐ Execute the MyUSAMap program.

The window of the MyUSAMap program appears, as shown in Figure 19.4. As you can see, the width of the window has the width of the USA map, so the entire width of the map fits in the window of the program. The height of the window is larger than the height of the USA map so that you'll have free space form to place additional controls in the form.

Figure 19.4.

The window of the MyUSAMap program after placing the TegoUSA ActiveX control in the form of the program.

☐ Use the mouse to drag the left edge of the window to the left.

As a result, the width of the window is smaller and the USA map does not fit in the window. When you make the width of the window larger, the USA map does not stretch itself to fit the new width of the window. You'll correct this in the next section.

☐ Click the X icon that appears on the upper-right corner of the window to terminate the program.

Sizing the MAP According to the Window's Size

As previously discussed, the frmMyUSAMap form should have a status bar at the bottom of the form. Add this status bar:

☐ Place Picture control in the frmMyUSAMap form.

☐ Set the Name property of the Picture control that you placed in the frmMyUSAMap form to picStatusBar.

☐ Set the Align property of the picStatusBar Picture control to 2-Align Bottom.

As a response, the picStatusBar Picture control aligns itself at the bottom of the frmMyUSAMap form.

☐ Make sure that the BorderStyle property of the picStatusBar Picture control is set to 1-Fixed Single (because you want the status bar to have a fixed single frame).

☐ Drag the upper edge of the picStatusBar Picture control upward so that the upper edge of the picStatusBar Picture control touches the lower part of the USA map (see Figure 19.5). (You may have to scroll down the window that contains the frmMyUSAMap form, so that you will be able to see the bottom of the form.)

Save your work:

☐ Select Save Project from the File menu of visual Basic.

Now add code that causes the USA map to resize itself automatically during runtime regardless of the size of the window of the program.

☐ Add code in the Form_Resize() procedure.

After adding the code, the Form_Resize() procedure should look as follows:

```
Private Sub Form_Resize()
   ' Size the map control to the size of the form.
   TegoUSA1.Width = Me.ScaleWidth
```

19

```
        If Me.ScaleHeight > picStatusBar.Height Then
            TegoUSA1.Height = Me.ScaleHeight - picStatusBar.Height
        End If
    End Sub
```

Figure 19.5.

*Placing the status
bar in the
frmMyUSAMap
form.*

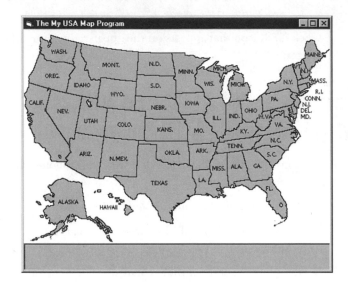

Save your work:

☐ Select Save Project from the File menu of Visual Basic.

The Form_Resize() procedure is automatically executed when the user resizes the window of the program. (This procedure is also executed when the window is displayed for the first time.)

You typed code that sets the Width property of the TegoUSA1 control to the width of the form:

```
TegoUSA1.Width = Me.ScaleWidth
```

Me represents the form in which code is executed. Currently, the Form_Resize() procedure is executed, and this procedure is in the frmMyUSAMap form. In this case, Me represents the frmMyUSAMap form.

Then you executed an If...Else statement:

```
If Me.ScaleHeight > picStatusBar.Height Then
    TegoUSA1.Height = Me.ScaleHeight - picStatusBar.Height
End If
```

The If statement checks whether the Height property of the frmMyUSAMap form is larger than the Height property of the status bar. If this condition is satisfied, the code under the If statement is executed. This code sets the Height property of the TegoUSA1 control as follows:

```
TegoUSA1.Height = Me.ScaleHeight - picStatusBar.Height
```

In other words, the height of the map will be set to the height of the window minus the height of the status bar.

Putting it all together, the width and height of the map were adjusted so that the map always stretches over the entire width of the window and over the entire height of the window (minus the height of the status bar).

It was necessary to use an If statement, because you do not want to assign a negative height to the Height property of the TegoUSA1 control.

Let's see your code in action:

☐ Execute the MyUSAMap program.

☐ Use the mouse to drag any of the edges of the program's window, and make the width of the window larger or smaller. Also make the height of the window larger or smaller. No matter how small or large you make the window of the program, the USA map always fits nicely in the window of the program.

☐ Experiment with the MyUSAMap program, then click the X icon that is located on the upper-right corner of the window to terminate the program.

19

Implementing the Exit Button

Now implement the Exit button of the program:

☐ Click (do not double-click) the icon of the CommandButton in the Toolbox window. Then place the mouse cursor in the status bar of the frmMyUSAMap form, and while keeping the left button of the mouse down, move the mouse.

As a response, a CommandButton is placed in the status bar.

☐ Set the properties of the CommandButton as follows: Name should be cmdExit, and Caption should be E&xit.

☐ Attach the following code to the Click event of the cmdExit button:

```
Private Sub cmdExit_Click()
    ' Terminate the program.
    Unload Me
End Sub
```

The code that you typed is automatically executed when the user clicks the Exit button. This code executes the Unload method on the frmMyUSAMap form. Because the frmMyUSAMap form is the only form in the project, unloading this form causes the termination of the program. (As an alternative, you could have typed the statement End in the cmdExit_Click() procedure; this means that when the user clicks the Exit button, the End statement causes the termination of the program.)

Placing the Anthem Check Box in the Status Bar

Place the Anthem check box in the status bar:

☐ Click (do not double-click) the icon of the CheckBox control in the Toolbox window. Then place the mouse cursor in the status bar, press the left button of the mouse, and while pressing the left button of the mouse, move the mouse in the status bar.

As a response, a check box is placed in the status bar.

☐ Set the properties of the check box that you placed in the status bar as follows:

Name: chkAnthem
Caption: &Anthem
Value: 1-Checked

Your frmMyUSAMap form should now look like the one in Figure 19.6. Note that if you need additional room for placing the Exit button and check box, as shown in Figure 19.6, you may have to make the status bar wider. You accomplish this by first dragging the bottom edge of the frmMyUSAMap form downward (to make the height of the form larger), and then dragging the upper edge of the picStatusBar Picture control upward until it touches the lower edge of the USA map. The beauty of the code that you typed in the Form_Resize() procedure is that this code is independent of the sizes of the form or the status bar. Thus, during design time, if needed, you can change the sizes of the form and the status bar.

Figure 19.6.

The frmMyUSAMap form with the Anthem check box in it (during design time) .

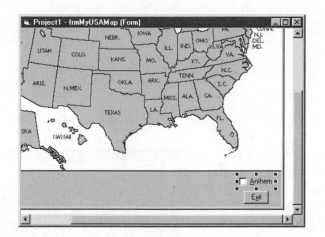

Placing a Multimedia ActiveX Control in the Form

Place the multimedia control in the frmMyUSAMap form:

☐ Make sure that the frmMyUSAMap form is the selected window and then double-click the icon of the TegoSoft multimedia control in the Toolbox window.

As a response, the multimedia control is placed in the frmMyUSAMap form (see Figure 19.7).

19

Figure 19.7.

The frmMyUSAMap form with the TegoSoft multimedia control in it.

Save your work:

☐ Select Save Project from the File menu of Visual Basic.

Let's see your work in action:

☐ Execute the MyUSAMap program.

The window of the MyUSAMap program appears, as shown in Figure 19.8.

Figure 19.8.

The window of the MyUSAMap program with the multimedia control in it.

The thing to note about the window of the MyUSAMap program shown in Figure 19.8 is that the buttons of the multimedia control are all dimmed. This is so because you have not yet attached any code that enables the multimedia control to play sound.

As a matter of fact, in the final form of the MyUSAMap program, the multimedia control is invisible (you'll be instructed to make this control invisible later in this chapter). For now, let's start programming the multimedia ActiveX control while the control is visible.

Playing Different Types of Multimedia Files

The multimedia control that you placed in the frmMyUSAMap form is capable of playing various types of multimedia files—for example, WAV files, MIDI files, CD audio, and

Movie AVI files. In the MyUSAMap program, the multimedia control is used for playing a MIDI sound file. This means that you need a MIDI sound file for the MyUSAMap program. In particular, you now need the MIDI sound file of the national anthem:

☐ Copy the USAAnth.Mid file from the C:\ProgramFiles\TegoSoft\USAMap directory to the C:\VB5Prg\Ch19 directory. You have copied the MIDI file to the directory where the MyUSAMap program resides.

Enabling the Multimedia Control to Play Sound

Now write code that enables the multimedia control to play the MIDI file:

☐ Make sure that the Name property of the multimedia control that you placed in the frmMyUSAMap form is Tegomm1.

☐ Add code to the Form_Load() procedure of the frmMyUSAMap form. After adding the code, the Form_Load() procedure should look as follows:

```
Private Sub Form_Load()
Dim DirPath
Tegomm1.DeviceType = "Sequencer"
DirPath = App.Path
If Right(DirPath, 1) <> "\" Then
    DirPath = DirPath + "\"
End If
Tegomm1.filename = DirPath + "USAAnth.MID"
Tegomm1.Command = "Open"
End Sub
```

☐ Select Save Project from the File menu of Visual Basic to save your work.

The Form_Load() procedure is automatically executed when the MyUSAMap program starts, so this procedure is a good focal point for writing initialization code. The code that you type enables the Tegomm1 control to play the MIDI file.

You declare a local variable called DirPath:

```
Dim DirPath
```

You then set the DeviceType property of the multimedia control as follows:

```
Tegomm1.DeviceType = "Sequencer"
```

When you set the DeviceType property to Sequencer, you set the multimedia control to play MIDI files. Recall that the objective now is to play the USAAnth.MID MIDI file. That's the reason you set the DeviceType property of the Tegomm1 control to Sequencer.

19

You then assign the return value of App.Path to the DirPath variable as follows:

```
DirPath = App.Path
```

App.Path is automatically updated with the name of the directory where the program resides. If, for example, the MyUSAMap program resides in the C:\VB5Prg\Ch19 directory, App.Path returns the string C:\VB5Prg\Ch19.

You want the string that is currently stored in the DirPath variable to end with the backslash character (\). Execute the following If...Else statement:

```
If Right(DirPath, 1) <> "\" Then
   DirPath = DirPath + "\"
End If
```

The Right() function is used as follows:

- The first parameter is DirPath, which is the string that the Right() function examines.

- The second parameter of Right() is 1. This means that the Right() function returns a string that is 1 character long. The returned string is extracted from the right side of the string that is supplied as the first parameter of the Right() function.

  For example,

  ```
  Right("ABCD", 1) returns D.
  Right("ABCD", 2) returns CD.
  Right("ABCD", 3) returns BCD.
  Right("ABCD", 4) returns ABCD.
  ```

To summarize, the If...Else statement that you execute checks whether the last character is the backslash character. If it is not, a backslash is added to the end of the string.

Note

> You need to check for the existence of the backslash character because the App.Path method is not consistent.
>
> For example, if your user will place the final program in the root directory of the C drive, App.Path returns C:\ (with the backslash as the last character of the string). If the program resides in a subdirectory, App.Path returns a string without the backslash as the last character. By using the If...Else statement, you make sure that no matter what App.Path returns, the DirPath variable will always have a backslash as its last character.

The next statement that you type in the `Form_Load()` procedure sets the filename property of the Tegomm1 control as follows:

```
Tegomm1.filename = DirPath + "USAAnth.MID"
```

In the preceding statement, you set the filename property to the exact path and filename of the sound file to be played.

Finally, you execute the `Open` command as follows:

```
Tegomm1.Command = "Open"
```

Note

As you can see from the code in the `Form_Load()` procedure, to make the multimedia control ready to play MIDI sound files, you have to set the following properties:

```
Tegomm1.DeviceType = "Sequencer"
Tegomm1.filename = DirPath + "USAAnth.MID"
```

Then you execute the `Open` method:

```
Tegomm1.Command = "Open"
```

Let's see your code in action:

☐ Execute the MyUSAMap program.

The window of the MyUSAMap program appears, as shown in Figure 19.9. The thing to note about the current status of the MyUSAMap program is that now some of the buttons of the multimedia control are not dimmed (compare Figure 19.9 with Figure 19.8).

☐ Click the third button from the left on the multimedia control.

As a response, the USAAnth.MID MIDI files is played through the sound card.

☐ Experiment with the buttons of the multimedia control (see Figure 19.10).

Note that depending on the particular device that the multimedia control is playing, some of the buttons of the control are always dimmed. For example, when you use the control to play a movie file, the Next Frame and Previous Frame buttons are available (these buttons let you move forward and backward frame after frame in the movie). However, these buttons are always dimmed for the MIDI device. (These buttons are also dimmed when you use the multimedia control to play a WAV sound file.)

19

Figure 19.9.

The window of the MyUSAMap program with the enabled multimedia control in it, ready to play the sound file.

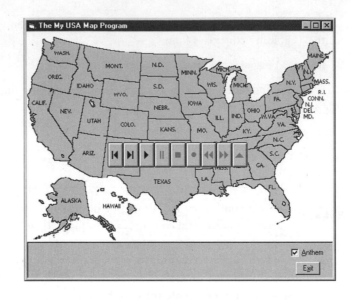

Figure 19.10.

The nine buttons of the multimedia control.

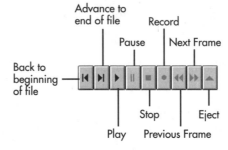

☐ Click the Exit button of the MyUSAMap program to terminate the program.

Automatic Playback (Without Using the Control's Buttons)

So far, the MyUSAMap program lets the user play the sound MIDI file by displaying the multimedia control, and the user has to click the Play button to play the sound MIDI file. However, the program should play the sound MIDI file in an endless loop without the user having to click the buttons of the multimedia control. In fact, the multimedia control should be invisible at runtime.

☐ Set the Visible property of the Tegomm1 control to False.

☐ Select Save Project from the File menu of Visual Basic to save your work.

☐ Execute the MyUSAMap program.

As you can see, now the multimedia control is invisible.

☐ Click the Exit button of the MyUSAMap program to terminate the program.

The idea now is to cause the playback of the sound MIDI file for as long as there is a check mark in the chkAnthem check box.

☐ Add code in the Form_Load() procedure. After adding the code, the Form_Load() procedure should look as follows:

```
Private Sub Form_Load()
Dim DirPath
Tegomm1.DeviceType = "Sequencer"
DirPath = App.Path

If Right(DirPath, 1) <> "\" Then
    DirPath = DirPath + "\"
End If

Tegomm1.filename = DirPath + "USAAnth.MID"
Tegomm1.Command = "Open"

If chkAnthem.Value = 1 Then
    Tegomm1.TimeFormat = "Milliseconds"
    Tegomm1.From = 3000
    Tegomm1.Command = "Play"
End If
End Sub
```

You added the following If…Else statements:

```
If chkAnthem.Value = 1 Then
    Tegomm1.TimeFormat = "Milliseconds"
    Tegomm1.From = 3000
    Tegomm1.Command = "Play"
End If
```

The If statement checks the Value property of the chkAnthem check box. If there is a check mark in the check box, the If condition is satisfied and the code under the If statement is executed. This code sets the TimeFormat to Milliseconds:

```
Tegomm1.TimeFormat = "Milliseconds"
```

Then the From property is set to 3000:

```
Tegomm1.From = 3000
```

19

The Play command is executed:

```
Tegomm1.Command = "Play"
```

As it turns out, the beginning of the MIDI file includes three seconds of silence, and the rest of the file includes the notes of the MIDI song. You want to start the playback immediately, so you first set the From property to 3000 milliseconds and then execute the Play method. The TimeFormat property specifies that the units of time are in milliseconds.

Putting it all together, when you start the MyUSAMap program, the program checks whether there is a check mark in the chkAnthem check box. If there is, the playback starts immediately.

☐ Execute the MyUSAMap program and verify that upon starting the playback, the MIDI file is played.

☐ Click the Exit button of the MyUSAMap program to terminate the program.

Playing in an Endless Loop

In the current state of the MyUSAMap program, when you start the program, the MIDI sound file plays immediately. The MIDI file is played in its entirety and then the playback stops. The idea now is to start the playback again (if the chkAnthem check box has a check mark in it). Add code that causes the playback to start all over again after the entire MIDI file is played:

☐ Add code to the Tegomm1_Done() procedure. After adding the code, the Tegomm1_Done() event should look as follows:

```
Private Sub Tegomm1_Done()
If chkAnthem.Value = 1 Then
    If Tegomm1.Position = Tegomm1.Length Then
        Tegomm1.Command = "Prev"
        '''Tegomm1.From = 3000
        Tegomm1.Command = "Play"
    End If
End If
End Sub
```

The Done event of the multimedia control occurs automatically when the multimedia control completes a command. You want to trap the completion of the Play command. That is, previously, the Play command was executed, and the multimedia control plays the file. Upon completing playing the entire file, the Done event occurs automatically. In the Tegomm1_Done() procedure, you can write code that examines whether the Done event occurred due to the completion of the playback. This is accomplished with the inner If…Else statement that you typed in the Tegomm1_Done() procedure:

```
If Tegomm1.Position = Tegomm1.Length Then
   Tegomm1.Command = "Prev"
   '''Tegomm1.From = 3000
   Tegomm1.Command = "Play"
End If
```

The `If` condition is satisfied provided that the Position property of the Tegomm1 control is equal to the Length property of the Tegomm1 control. The Position property represents the current position of the file, and the Length property represents the length of the file.

To summarize, if the current position of the file is equal to the length of the file, it means that the entire file was played, and the code under the inner `If` condition starts the playback again. You issue the `Prev` command to rewind the file to the beginning of the file:

```
Tegomm1.Command = "Prev"
```

Then you issue the `Play` command:

```
Tegomm1.Command = "Play"
```

Note that the first three seconds of the MIDI file is silence. Upon completing the playback, there will be three seconds of silence, and then the user will hear the music again. If you want the playback to start immediately, you have to include the following statement:

```
Tegomm1.From = 3000
```

(You commented the preceding statement in the `Tegomm1_Done()` procedure so there will be a three-second delay. If you do not want the three-second delay, simply uncomment the statement that sets the From property of the multimedia control.)

You enclose the code that you typed in the `Tegomm1_Done()` procedure with the following `If…Else` statement:

```
If chkAnthem.Value = 1 Then
   ...
   ...
   ...
End If
```

In other words, the playback will start all over again provided that there is a check mark in the chkAnthem check box.

☐ Select Save Project from the File menu of Visual Basic to save your work.

☐ Execute the MyUSAMap program and verify that upon completing the playback, if there is a check box in the Anthem check box, the playback starts again. (Recall that there is a three-second silence at the beginning of the song, so be patient after the playback is completed.)

☐ Click the Exit button of the MyUSAMap program to terminate the program.

19

Stopping and Continuing the Playback

You set the Value property of the chkAnthem check box to 1 at design time. This means that upon starting the program, there is a check mark in the Anthem check box, and the code that you typed in the Form_Load() procedure causes the playback of the MIDI file.

During the execution of the MyUSAMap program, the user can place and remove the check mark from the Anthem check box, and as a result, the playback should stop or continue accordingly. You'll now add the code that stops and continues the playback when the user places and removes the check mark from the Anthem check box.

☐ Type the following code in the chkAnthem_Click() procedure:

```
Private Sub chkAnthem_Click()
If chkAnthem.Value = 0 Then
    Tegomm1.Command = "Stop"
End If

If chkAnthem.Value = 1 Then
    If Tegomm1.Position = 0 Then
        Tegomm1.From = 3000
    End If
    Tegomm1.Command = "Play"
End If
End Sub
```

The chkAnthem_Click() procedure is executed automatically when the user clicks the check box. The first If…Else statement that you typed in the chkAnthem_Click() procedure causes the playback to stop when there is no check mark in the check box:

```
If chkAnthem.Value = 0 Then
    Tegomm1.Command = "Stop"
End If
```

The second If…Else statement is as follows:

```
If chkAnthem.Value = 1 Then
    If Tegomm1.Position <= 0 Then
        Tegomm1.From = 3000
    End If
    Tegomm1.Command = "Play"
End If
```

That is, if there is check mark in the check box, the Play command is issued (and this will start the playback). An inner If statement is executed to see if the current playback is less than three seconds. If so, the From property of the multimedia control is set to 3000. Thus, if the user happens to place a check mark during the first three-second silence, the playback will start immediately.

☐ Select Save Project from the File menu of Visual Basic to save your work.

☐ Execute the MyUSAMap program.

☐ Place and remove the check mark from the Anthem check box and verify that the playback stops and continues.

☐ Experiment with the MyUSAMap program, then click its Exit button to terminate the program.

Flag Animation During the Playback

You completed the sound part of the MyUSAMap program. You can now add the flag animation to the program. That is, during the playback, a picture of a waving flag will be displayed. During the implementation of the animation, you'll learn how to determine whether playback is in progress.

The two BMP pictures that are used for the flag animation are shown in Figures 19.11 and 19.12.

Figure 19.11.
Frame 1 of the flag animation.

19

At first glance, the two flags shown in Figures 19.11 and 19.12 look the same. However, if you take a close look at these two figures, you'll realize that these flags are not identical. In fact, if you display these flags one after the other, it will look as if the flag is waving in the wind.

You'll now implement the flag animation in the MyUSAMap program.

Figure 19.12.

Frame 2 of the flag animation.

Note

In the following sections, you need two BMP pictures: Flag01.BMP and Flag02.bmp. You can generate these BMP pictures with a program such as Paint. Make sure that the size of each of these BMP pictures is approximately 32 pixels by 32 pixels. Save the pictures as Flag01.BMP and Flag02.BMP.

For the sake of experimenting, instead of using pictures of flags, you can draw pictures that are easier to draw. For example, Flag01.BMP could be a small picture (approximately 32 pixels by 32 pixels) of the number 1. Flag02.BMP could be a small picture of the number 2. During the animation, instead of seeing a flag waving in the wind, you would see the pictures of the numbers 1 and 2 alternating (1, 2, 1, 2, and so on).

If you do not have the talent to draw flags but wish to be more creative, create a picture of a smiling face and save it as Flag01.BMP. Then create a picture of a nonsmiling face and save it as Flag02.BMP. During the animation, instead of seeing the flag waving in the wind, you'll see alternating faces: Smile, Cry, Smile, Cry, and so on.

☐ Click (do not double-click) the icon of the image control in the Toolbox window. Place the mouse cursor in the status bar, press the left button of the mouse, and while keeping the left button of the mouse down, move the mouse.

As a response, an image control is placed in the status bar (see Figure 19.13).

Figure 19.13.

Placing the image control in the status bar.

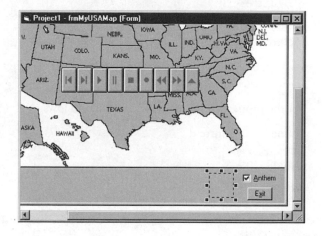

☐ Set the properties of the image control that you placed in the status bar as follows:

Name: imgMap
Stretch: False
Picture: Ctrusa.ico
Visible: False

The Ctrusa.ico file is supplied with your Visual Basic. You may find the file in the \Icons\Flags subdirectory of the directory where you installed your Visual Basic. If for some reason you do not have this file, use another ICO file. After setting the Picture property of the imgMap image control to the Ctrusa.Ico file, the frmMyUSAMap form should look like the one in Figure 19.14.

Now place three additional image controls in the status bar:

☐ Place an image control on top of the imgMap image control that you already placed in the status bar.

☐ Set the properties of the image control as follows:

Name: imgFlag01
Stretch: False
Visible: False
Picture: Flag01.BMP

19

☐ Place an image control on top of the imgMap image control that you placed already in the status bar.

☐ Set the properties of the image control as follows:

Name: imgFlag02
Stretch: False
Visible: False
Picture: Flag02.BMP

☐ Place an image control in the status bar on top of the other image controls that you placed in the status bar.

☐ Set the properties of the image control as follows:

Name: imgCurrent
Stretch: False
Visible: True
Picture: (none)

Figure 19.14.

The status bar of the frmMyUSAMap form with the Ctrusa.ico picture in the imgMap image control.

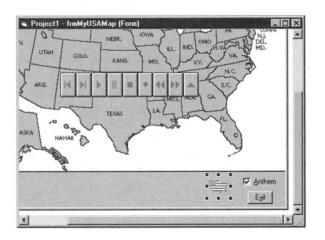

To summarize, you now have four image controls, one on top of the other. Only the imgCurrent image control has its Visible property set to True.

You'll now write code that accomplishes the following: When there is no playback in progress, imgCurrent will display the contents of the imgMap image control. Recall that you set the Picture property of the imgCurrent image to Ctrusa.ICO. So, during nonplayback, imgCurrent will display the Ctrusa.ICO picture.

During playback, imgCurrent will display the contents of the imgFlag01 Image (which you already set to Flag01,BMP) and then the contents of the imgFlag02 Image (which you already set to Flag02.BMP).

☐ Place a Timer control in the frmMyUSAMap form. (It does not matter where in the form you place the Timer, because the Timer control is always invisible during runtime.)

☐ Set the properties of the Timer as follows:

Name: Timer1
Enabled: True
Interval: 250

☐ Type the following code in the Timer1_Timer() procedure:

```
Private Sub Timer1_Timer()
Static FlagStatus
If Tegomm1.Mode = 525 Then
   imgCurrent.Picture = imgMap.Picture
Else
   If FlagStatus = 0 Then
      imgCurrent.Picture = imgFlag01.Picture
      FlagStatus = 1
   Else
      imgCurrent.Picture = imgFlag02.Picture
      FlagStatus = 0
   End If
End If
End Sub
```

☐ Select Save Project from the File menu of Visual Basic to save your work.

The code that you typed in the Timer1_Timer() procedure declares a static variable called FlagStatus:

```
Static FlagStatus
```

Then an If statement is executed:

```
If Tegomm1.Mode = 525 Then
   …
   …Playback is not in progress
   …
Else
   …
   …Playback is in progress
   …
End If
```

The Mode property of the multimedia control reports the mode of the control. When the Mode property is equal to 525, it means that playback is not in progress. When playback is

19

not in progress, the code under the If statement is executed. When playback is in progress, the code under the Else is executed.

The Timer1_Timer()procedure is executed automatically every 250 milliseconds (because you set the Interval property of the Timer1 timer control to 250).

If playback is not in progress, the following statement is executed:

```
imgCurrent.Picture = imgMap.Picture
```

The preceding statement sets the Picture property of the imgCurrent image to the Picture property of the imgMap image. This means that when there is no playback in progress, the Ctrusa.Ico picture is displayed.

When there is playback in progress, the following If…Else is executed:

```
If FlagStatus = 0 Then
   imgCurrent.Picture = imgFlag01.Picture
   FlagStatus = 1
Else
   imgCurrent.Picture = imgFlag02.Picture
   FlagStatus = 0
End If
```

The preceding If…Else checks the value of the FlagStatus variable, and if it is 0, the Picture property of the imgCurrent image is assigned with the Picture property of the imgFlag01 image. Then FlagStatus is set to 1. On the next execution of the Timer1_Timer() procedure, FlagStatus is equal to 1, because as a static variable, FlagStatus retains its value from the last execution of the Timer1_Timer() procedure. Now the Flag02.BMP picture is displayed, and FlagStatus is set back to 0. On the next execution of Timer1_Timer(), Flag01.BMP is displayed, and so on, In short, as long as playback is in progress, the following sequence of pictures is displayed: Flag01.BMP, Flag02.BMP, Flag01.BMP, Flag02.BMP, and so on.

Let's see your code in action:

☐ Execute the MyUSAMap program.

During playback, the flag animation is performed.

☐ Remove the check mark from the Anthem check box.

As you can see, when no playback is in progress, the Ctrusa.Ico picture is displayed.

☐ Experiment with the MyUSAMap program and then click its Exit button to terminate the program.

Placing the Labels of the State Information

The next step is to place the labels that will be used for displaying the state information. (Recall that as the user moves the mouse over a state, the labels of the status bar should display information about the state.)

☐ Place four label controls in the status bar. These labels will be used to display information about the state. Set the properties of the labels as follows:

Name: lblState
Caption: Make it empty
BorderStyle: 1-Fixed Single

Name: lblCapital
Caption: Make it empty
BorderStyle: 1-Fixed Single

Name: lblYearOfStatehood
Caption: Make it empty
BorderStyle: 1-Fixed Single

Name: lblPopulation
Caption: Make it empty
BorderStyle: 1-Fixed Single

The frmMyUSAMap form with the four labels on its status bar is shown in Figure 19.15.

Figure 19.15.

The frmMyUSAMap form with the four labels on its status bar.

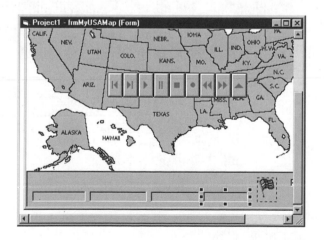

19

☐ Place four labels above the labels that you placed in the previous step. These four labels will serve as headers for the four labels that you placed in the previous step. Set the properties of these four labels as follows:

Name: lblStateHeader
Caption: State:
BorderStyle: 0-None

Name: lblCapitalHeader
Caption: Capital:
BorderStyle: 0-None

Name: lblYearOfStatehoodHeader
Caption: Year of Statehood:
BorderStyle: 0-None

Name: lblPopHeader
Caption: Pop (Millions):
BorderStyle: 0-None

The frmMyUSAMap form with the four header labels on its status bar is shown in Figure 19.16.

Figure 19.16.

The frmMyUSAMap form with the four header labels on its status bar.

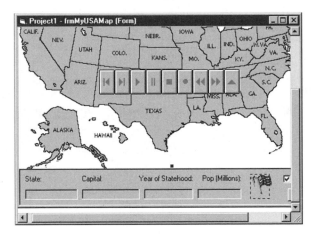

Displaying State Information According to the Mouse Location

Now that you have the labels in the status bar, you can place state information in these labels, writing code that displays the state information according to the mouse location. For example, if the mouse is currently located on the state of California, the labels will display information about California.

☐ Add code to the general declarations section of the frmMyUSAMap form. After adding the code, the general declarations section should look like this:

```
' All variables  MUST be declared
Option Explicit
' Declare arrays for storage of information
' about the 50 states.
Dim gCapital(50) As String
Dim gYearOfStatehood(50) As String
Dim gPopulation(50) As String
```

You declared three arrays. The first array is called gCapital. This array can hold a maximum of 51 elements. The first element of the array is gCapital(0), the second element of the array is gCapital(1), and so on. The last element is the 51st element: gCapital(50).

Similarly, you added the gYearOfStatehood() and gPopulation() arrays:

☐ Add the following code to the end of the Form_Load() procedure:

```
Private Sub Form_Load()
...
...
...
UpdateArrays
End Sub
```

You execute the UpdateArrays procedure as the last statement in the Form_Load() procedure.

The UpdateArrays procedure does not exist yet. In the next step, you write the code of the UpdateArrays procedure:

☐ Display the code window of the frmMyUSAMap form, select Add Procedure from the Tools menu, and then set the Add procedure dialog box that pops up as follows:

Name: UpdateArrays
Type: Sub (Select the Sub radio button)
Scope: Public (Select the Public radio button).

19

☐ Click the OK button of the Add Procedure dialog box.

> *As a result, Visual Basic adds the* UpdateArrays *procedure to the general area of the frmMyUSAMap form.*

☐ Type the following code in the UpdateArrays procedure:

```
Public Sub UpdateArrays()
    ' Store information about State #0 (Border).
    gCapital(0) = ""
    gYearOfStatehood(0) = ""
    gPopulation(0) = ""

    ' Store information about State #1 (Alabama).
    gCapital(1) = "Montgomery"
    gYearOfStatehood(1) = "1819"
    gPopulation(1) = "4.0"

    ' Store information about State #2 (Alaska).
    gCapital(2) = "Juneau"
    gYearOfStatehood(2) = "1959"
    gPopulation(2) = "0.6"

    ' Store information about State #3 (Arizona).
    gCapital(3) = "Phoenix"
    gYearOfStatehood(3) = "1912"
    gPopulation(3) = "3.7"
End Sub
```

☐ Add the following code in the TegoUSA1_MouseMoveOnMap() procedure:

```
Private Sub TegoUSA1_MouseMoveOnMap(ByVal StateId As Integer, _
                                    ByVal x As Integer, _
                                    ByVal y As Integer, _
                                    ByVal Button As Integer)

    ' Update the lblState, lblCapital, lblYearOfStatehood,
    ' and lblPopulation labels.
    lblState.Caption = TegoUSA1.GetStateName(StateId)
    lblCapital.Caption = gCapital(StateId)
    lblYearOfStatehood.Caption = gYearOfStatehood(StateId)
    lblPopulation.Caption = gPopulation(StateId)
End Sub
```

☐ Select Save Project from the File menu of Visual Basic to save your work.

As you might have guessed, the MouseMoveOnMap event occurs when the mouse is moved over the map. When the user moves the mouse cursor over the USA map, the TegoUSA1_MouseMoveOnMap() procedure is executed automatically.

Take a look at the parameters of the TegoUSA1_MouseMoveOnMap() procedure:

```
Private Sub TegoUSA1_MouseMoveOnMap(ByVal StateId As Integer, _
                                    ByVal x As Integer, _
                                    ByVal y As Integer, _
                                    ByVal Button As Integer)
```

The first parameter of the procedure is `StateId`. This is the ID of the state. When the mouse cursor is on the border of a state (or in the ocean), the `StateId` is autmatically set to 0. When the mouse cursor is on the state of Alabama, the `StateId` is automatically set to 1, and so on. Table 19.1 lists the `StatedId` values for the 50 states.

Table 19.1. State information.

StateId	State	Capital	Year of Statehood	Population
0	(Border)	(none)	(none)	(none)
1	Alabama	Montgomery	1819	4.0
2	Alaska	Juneau	1959	0.6
3	Arizona	Phoenix	1912	3.7
4	Arkansas	Little Rock	1836	2.4
5	California	Sacramento	1850	29.8
6	Colorado	Denver	1876	3.3
7	Connecticut	Hartford	1788	3.3
8	Delaware	Dover	1787	0.7
9	Florida	Tallahassee	1845	12.9
10	Georgia	Atlanta	1788	6.5
11	Hawaii	Honolulu	1959	1.1
12	Idaho	Boise	1890	1.0
13	Illinois	Springfield	1818	11.4
14	Indiana	Indianapolis	1816	5.5
15	Iowa	Des Moines	1846	2.8
16	Kansas	Topeka	1861	2.5
17	Kentucky	Frankfort	1792	3.7
18	Louisiana	Baton Rouge	1812	4.2
19	Maine	Augusta	1820	1.2
20	Maryland	Annapolis	1788	4.8
21	Massachusetts	Boston	1788	6.0
22	Michigan	Lansing	1837	9.3
23	Minnesota	St. Paul	1858	4.4
24	Mississippi	Jackson	1817	2.6
25	Missouri	Jefferson City	1821	5.1

19

continues

Table 19.1. continued

StateId	State	Capital	Year of Statehood	Population
26	Montana	Helena	1889	0.8
27	Nebraska	Lincoln	1867	1.6
28	Nevada	Carson City	1864	1.2
29	New Hampshire	Concord	1788	1.1
30	New Jersey	Trenton	1787	7.7
31	New Mexico	Santa Fe	1912	1.5
32	New York	Albany	1788	18.0
33	North Carolina	Raleigh	1789	6.6
34	North Dakota	Bismarck	1889	0.6
35	Ohio	Columbus	1803	10.8
36	Oklahoma	Oklahoma City	1907	3.15
37	Oregon	Salem	1859	2.8
38	Pennsylvania	Harrisburg	1787	11.9
39	Rhode Island	Providence	1790	1.0
40	South Carolina	Columbia	1788	3.5
41	South Dakota	Pierre	1889	0.7
42	Tennessee	Nashville	1796	4.9
43	Texas	Austin	1845	17.0
44	Utah	Salt Lake City	1896	1.7
45	Vermont	Montpelier	1791	0.6
46	Virginia	Richmond	1788	6.2
47	Washington	Olympia	1889	4.9
48	West Virginia	Charleston	1863	1.8
49	Wisconsin	Madison	1848	4.9
50	Wyoming	Cheyenne	1890	0.5

The code that you typed in the TegoUSA1_MouseMoveOnMap() procedure sets the Caption properties of the labels as follows:

```
lblState.Caption = TegoUSA1.GetStateName(StateId)
lblCapital.Caption = gCapital(StateId)
lblYearOfStatehood.Caption = gYearOfStatehood(StateId)
lblPopulation.Caption = gPopulation(StateId)
```

The GetStateName() method of the TegoUSA1 control returns the name of the state. Which state? The state whose StateId is mentioned in the parameter of the GetStateName() method.

The Captions of the other labels are updated with the values of the arrays. For example, if the mouse cursor is currently on the state whose StateId is 1, the Caption property of the lblCaption label is updates with the element gCapital(1):

```
lblCapital.Caption = gCapital(StateId)
```

☐ Execute the MyUSAMap program.

☐ Move the mouse over the states and notice that the State label is updated accordingly.

In the UpdateArrays procedure you updated the elements 0,1,2 and 3. Thus, the rest of the labels on the status bar are updated only if you place the mouse cursor on these states. If you wish, you can consult Table 19.1 and fill the other elements of the array. For example, the next statements in the UpdateArray procedure should be

```
' Store information about State #4 (Arkansas).
gCapital(4) = " Arkansas "
gYearOfStatehood(4) = "1836"
gPopulation(4) = "2.4"
```

In a similar manner, if you wish, you can fill the rest of the elements of the arrays. (For the sake of learning the material of this chapter, you do not have to fill the rest of the elements of the arrays.)

Clicking the States

Now add code that displays information when the user clicks the states:

☐ Add the following code in the TegoUSA1_ClickMap() procedure:

```
Private Sub TegoUSA1_ClickMap(ByVal StateId As Integer)
    Dim Msg
    Dim Title
    Dim CR
    CR = Chr(13) + Chr(10)

    ' If the user did not click inside a state,
    ' terminate this procedure.
    If StateId = 0 Then Exit Sub

    ' Prepare the title of the message box.
    Title = "The MapUSA Program"

    ' Prepare the message of the message box.
    Msg = "State: " + TegoUSA1.GetStateName(StateId)
    Msg = Msg + CR
    Msg = Msg + "Capital: " + gCapital(StateId)
```

```
          Msg = Msg + CR
          Msg = Msg + "Year of Statehood: " + gYearOfStatehood(StateId)
          Msg = Msg + CR
          Msg = Msg + "Population (in Millions): " + gPopulation(StateId)

          ' Display the message box.
          MsgBox Msg, vbOKOnly + vbInformation, Title
     End Sub
```

☐ Select Save Project from the File menu of Visual Basic to save your work.

When you click a state, the TegoUSA1_ClickMap() *procedure is executed automatically. The parameter of this procedure is updated automatically with the* StateId *of the state that was clicked. The code that you typed displays a message box that displays information about the state that was clicked.*

(Of course, the information about the capital, year of statehood, and population will be displayed only for the states for which you updated their corresponding array elements in the UpdateArrays procedure.)

☐ Execute the MyUSAMap program, click the various states, and note that the message box displays the correct state on which you clicked.

☐ Experiment with the MyUSAMap program and then click its Exit button to terminate the program.

Attaching Menus to the MyUSAMap Program

You can now attach menus to the frmMyUSAMap form. For example, you can attach an Exit menu item. Then attach code to the Exit menu item that will cause the program to terminate when the user selects the Exit menu item.

You can also design a Size menu to the frmMyUSAMap form. The Size menu can have the following menu items: Normal, Small, and Large. When the user selects the Small item, the window of the program should become small. When the user selects the Large item, the window of the program should become large. When the user selects the Normal item, the window of the program should be restored to its original size.

You can accomplish this by declaring the following global variables in the general declarations section:

```
' Declare variables to hold the default
' width and height of the form.
Dim gDefaultWidth
Dim gDefaultHeight
```

Then in the `Form_Load()` procedure, you update the values of the global variables as follows:

```
gDefaultWidth = Me.Width
gDefaultHeight = Me.Height
```

That is, you assign the Width and the Height properties of the frmMyUSAMap form to the global variables that you declared.

Finally, you can attach code to the corresponding menu items. If the Small menu item has the Name mnuSmall, the `mnuSmall_Click()` procedure is as follows:

```
Private Sub mnuSmall_Click()
    ' Set the WindowState property of the form to Normal.
    Me.WindowState = 0
    ' Set the size of the form to one third of the default size.
    Me.Width = gDefaultWidth / 2
    Me.Height = gDefaultHeight / 2
End Sub
```

In the preceding code, you set the Width and Height properties of the window to half the original size.

If the Large menu item has the Name mnuLarge, the `mnuLarge_Click()` procedure is as follows:

```
Private Sub mnyLarge_Click()
    ' Maximize the form.
    Me.WindowState = 2
End Sub
```

In the preceding code, you set the WindowState property of the window of the program to 2. This causes the window to be maximized.

Finally, if the Normal menu item has the Name mnuNormal, the `mnuNormal_Click()` procedure is as follows:

```
Private Sub mnuNormal_Click()
    ' Set the WindowState property of the form to Normal.
    Me.WindowState = 0

    ' Set the size of the form to the default size.
    Me.Width = gDefaultWidth
    Me.Height = gDefaultHeight
End Sub
```

The preceding code sets the Width and Height properties of the program's window to the original values (to the values that you updated in the `Form_Load()` procedure).

DirectSound Technology

The MyUSAMap program that you implemented in this chapter demonstrates how your Visual Basic programs can play MIDI sound files. In a similar manner, the TegoSoft multimedia control can also play other types of multimedia files (WAV sound files, CD audio, and Movie AVI files).

Sound cards are very popular, and today many PCs have sound cards installed in them. In fact, sound cards became so popular that a new technology called DirectSound evolved. You will not be instructed to implement a DirectSound program in this chapter, but you should be aware of this fascinating and powerful technology.

DirectSound Features

When using DirectSound technology, you can play WAV sound files (just as you can play WAV files with the standard multimedia technology). However, when using DirectSound, you have the following important additional features:

- *You can play several WAV files simultaneously.* You simply specify the names of the WAV files that you want to play, and the sound card plays the sound files simultaneously.

- *Volume control.* With DirectSound, you can adjust the volume of the sound files. When you play several sound files simultaneously, you can adjust the volume of the individual sound files. As you can imagine, you can create some amazing sound special effects with this feature. For example, you can display images that make sounds. As the user gets closer to the image that makes the sound, the volume becomes louder, and as the user gets away from the image that makes the sound, the sound becomes weaker.

- *Panning Control.* You can distribute different amounts of sound to the left and right speakers of the sound card. For example, you can play 30 percent of the volume through the left speaker and 70 percent of the volume through the right speaker. This volume distribution is called *panning*. As you can imagine, you can create some amazing sound effects with the panning feature. For example, you can display pictures of several images that make sound. As the user gets further away from one image and gets closer to another image, the volume from one object becomes weaker and the sound from the other object becomes louder. Furthermore, depending on the user's current position, the sound that the left and right speakers produce can be made weaker or stronger proportionally to the user's current position. For example, if the user's current position is to the left of an object that produces sound, the right speaker plays the sound. If the user is to the right of the object, the left speaker produces sound.

  With the volume control and panning features of DirectSound, you can create some additional amazing sound effects. Consider, for example, displaying projectile traveling from left to right on your screen. You can add synchronized sound to the animation that makes the sound of projectiles flying from left to right by first playing 100 percent of the volume through the left speaker. As the projectile flies to the right, you weaken the sound through the left speaker and start making the sound through the right speaker louder.

■ *Playback speed.* You can change the playback speed of the sound. When playing several sound files, you can change the playback speed of the individual sound files.

Again, when using an OCX ActiveX control, you can implement DirectSound technology in your program with great ease. It is recommended that you execute some DirectSound Demo programs by loading them from the following Internet URL addresses. This way, you'll be able to hear DirectSound in action:

☐ Use your Internet connection to connect to the Internet.

☐ Use your Internet browser program to log into the following Internet URL address:

```
http://www.tegosoft.com/bkinstdx.html
```

☐ Follow the directions given on the preceding HTML page to download the MixerDX2.EXE file and save it on your hard drive.

☐ Follow the directions given on the preceding HTML page to install the MixerDX2.EXE file.

Note

To be able to see DirectSound in action, you have to install DirectX. Follow the directions in the preceding HTML page to install DirectX. DirectX is discussed later in this chapter.

19

That's it. You now have the mixer program installed in your PC.

☐ Execute the mixer program that you downloaded and installed.

The window of the mixer program is shown in Figure 19.17.

☐ Experiment with the mixer program. In particular, load several WAV files, play them simultaneously, change the playback speed of the WAV files, change the volume of the WAV sound files, and pan the sound files to the right and left speakers. (All these operations are accomplished by using the scroll bars of the mixer program, as shown in Figure 19.17.)

Figure 19.17.

A mixer program that illustrates the power of DirectSound to play several sound files simultaneously.

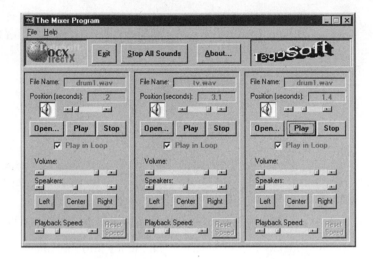

DirectX Technology

DirectSound is actually a part of a technology called DirectX. The two main components of DirectX are

- DirectSound
- DirectDraw

You already saw the power of DirectSound in action. Just as DirectSound lets you use the sound card in the most powerful manner, DirectDraw lets you use the video card in the most powerful manner. To understand the importance of DirectDraw, let's review the device independence feature of Windows.

The Device Independence Feature of Windows

One of the main features that made Windows so popular is its device independence. When you write a Windows program (such as with Visual Basic), you, the programmer, do not have to worry about things such as which video card is used, which printer is used, which sound card is used, or any of the other peripherals of the PC. For example, when your program issues a print command to the printer, the printer should print no matter who is the manufacturer of the printer. Windows converts the print command of your program to a print command that is understood by the printer. This conversion is performed with the help of the driver program of the printer. How does Windows know to perform this conversion? When the owner of the PC installed the printer, Windows either accepted or rejected the printer (together with the driver of the printer). Thereafter, Windows knows which printer to use and can convert any print command from any Windows program to a command understood by the printer. The same goes for other peripherals. There are many types of mouse devices in the market, but your program does not care which particular mouse device is installed in the PC. As long as the mouse was accepted by Windows, Windows will respect mouse move events, mouse clicks, and so on.

When it comes to a device such as the printer, the extra time that it takes to convert print commands from the program to commands understood by the printer is insignificant. A printer (even a laser printer) is a mechanical device. The time it takes to rotate mechanical wheels, and to push papers is much longer than the time it takes to convert software commands. However, when it comes to a device such as the video card, it's a different story. Typically, you want your video card to react immediately to video commands from the program. When your program moves pictures on the screen, Windows first has to convert the commands to commands understood by the video card. However, due to the fact that Windows has to "consult" the driver of the video card and convert the commands to commands understood by the video card, a lot of time is spent during the conversion. This causes annoying flickering and delays when moving graphic objects on the screen.

The old DOS operating system does a much better job when it comes to video cards. In DOS programs, the programs can access the memory of the video card *directly*. That is, the video card has memory cells, where each memory cell corresponds to one pixel on the screen. This memory cell determines the location and color of the pixel. (Depending on the particular video card, the number of memory cells that correspond to a single pixel vary—the more colors the video card supports, the more memory cells are needed to describe one pixel.) In any case, in DOS, the DOS program can access the memory of the video card directly. The moment the program changes the contents of a memory cell on the video card, the pixel that corresponds to the memory cell changes almost instantaneously. This is why some powerful game programs are DOS programs, not Windows programs. (The problem with DOS, however, is that this operating system is device-dependent. A program that works for one video card does not work on another video card from a different manufacturer or even a different model from the same manufacturer.)

Microsoft realized the limitation of Windows and released the DirectX technology. As implied by its name, DirectDraw (which is that portion of DirectX that is responsible for accessing the video card) performs an almost direct access of the video card. In essence, DirectX includes a large collection of video card drivers. When the program draws something into the screen, due to DirectDraw, the commands are "converted" very fast and the drawing accomplished immediately, without flickering.

Windows is also called Graphical Operating System. Graphical Operating System means that the operating system uses graphic objects such as CommandButtons, scroll bars, check boxes, and so on. It does not mean that Windows was designed to perform fast graphical

19

operations such as moving graphic objects. Rather, it means that the operating system uses graphic objects. In fact, as previously discussed, Windows is not the right operating system for performing fast graphics operations.

The graphics limitation of Windows was removed after the introduction of DirectX. Combining Windows and DirectX gives one of the most powerful tools for performing fast graphic operations. With the help of DirectX ActiveX controls, you can develop amazing Visual Basic programs with great ease.

Take a look at some DirectX programs in action:

☐ Use your Internet connection to connect to the Internet.

☐ Use your Internet browser program to log into the following Internet URL address:

    `http://www.tegosoft.com/bk3dsound.html`

☐ Follow the directions given on the preceding HTML page to download the 3DSnd.EXE file and save it on your hard drive.

☐ Follow the directions given on the preceding HTML page to install the 3DSnd.EXE file.

The 3-D Sound program that you installed in the previous step utilizes both DirectSound and DirectDraw technologies. The 3-D Sound lets the user use the mouse and the keyboard to travel in a 3-D picture, encountering various animated objects (see Figures 19.18, 19.19, and 19.20). As the user gets closer or farther away from the object, the sound that the objects make gets louder or softer. For example, when the user is between the elephant and the horse, the user hears both animal sounds. Similarly, when the user gets closer to the belly dancer, the dancer's music gets louder. The program gives a very realistic feeling of traveling in a real world that has animated objected and real sound in it. This type of program is therefore appropriately referred to as *virtual reality*.

Figure 19.18.

When traveling in the 3-D picture, the user encounters an animated elephant.

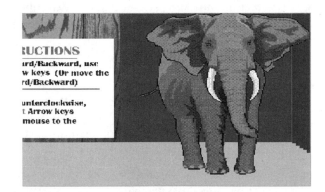

Figure 19.19.
When traveling in the 3-D picture, the user encounters a belly dancer.

Figure 19.20.
When traveling in the 3-D picture, the user encounters an animated horse.

19

3-D Virtual Reality Programs

As stated, a program that lets users feel as if they are moving in a real world is called a 3-D virtual reality program. Typically, the user uses the mouse or the keyboard to move in the 3-D picture. Often, a 3-D virtual reality program also enables the user to use various tools (for example, a gun to shoot bad creatures, a pencil to write, and so on).

It is obvious from the description of the 3-D virtual reality program that a DirectX technology is needed. Note the huge amount of graphic operations that are performed during the execution of the program: The program has to display new 3-D pictures for each movement of the mouse or the keyboard. That is, the PC has to compute the next 3-D picture to be displayed, which is a small deviation from the current picture being displayed. This must be performed very fast so that the user will get the feeling of smooth moving. Furthermore, the user can encounter animated objects, the user can interact with the objects (using tools such as a gun or pencil), and the PC also has to take care of sound playback (which in the case of

DirectSound means that several sounds are played simultaneously). The walls of the 3-D pictures can be made of any material (wood, marble, and so on). This adds additional graphic burden on the PC, which has to display these textured walls. Don't forget that as the user gets closer or farther away from an object, the object is displayed differently (larger or smaller depending on the user's distance from the object). The volume of the sound depends on the distance of the user from the object that makes the sound). No doubt, the PC has to work hard and fast to perform all these operations. Indeed, Windows DirectX is the perfect tool to accomplish this.

To see such a 3-D virtual reality program that uses DirectX in action:

☐ Use your Internet connection to connect to the Internet.

☐ Use your Internet browser program to log into the following Internet URL address:

`http://www.tegosoft.com/bkdown3dvr.html`

☐ Follow the directions given on the preceding HTML page to download the Teg3D.exe file and save it on your hard drive.

☐ Follow the directions given on the preceding HTML page to install the Teg3D.exe file.

Figures 19.21 through 19.24 show some of the things that the user encounters while traveling in the 3-D world.

Figure 19.21.

A waving flag in one of the rooms of the 3-D virtual reality program. The user can see what is going on in the adjacent room through the window.

Figure 19.22.
One of the rooms of the 3-D virtual reality program has a TV in it. The TV displays a sport show (pictures and sound).

Figure 19.23.
One of the rooms of the 3-D virtual reality program shows a basketball player dribbling a basketball.

Figure 19.24.
The Presidents room has pictures of Presidents on the walls.

19

Note

There are many applications where DirectSound and 3-D virtual reality are applicable. Of course, the first application that comes to mind is game application. However, the popularity of DirectX is increasing, and many programmers apply this technology for many other types of programming. For example, this technology is frequently used in business applications for demonstrating products (hardware products where the "real" product can be displayed as well as software products). A virtual showroom can be easily implemented with DirectX technology. DirectX is, of course, helpful in education applications, advertising applications, and many other types of applications.

Summary

In this chapter you learned to play MIDI sound file. You learned how to play the sound using the buttons of the multimedia controls, you then set the Visible property of the multimedia to False, and you played the MIDI file by executing the `Play` method. You also learned how to play sound in an endless loop and how to detect whether playback is in progress.

In this chapter you also learned about sophisticated technologies such as DirectSound and DirectDraw (which are part of DirectX). Writing DirectX programs with pure Visual Basic code will be a job that may consume a tremendous amount of time. With the help of OCX ActiveX controls, you can plug these controls into your projects and implement Visual Basic programs that utilize these technologies with great ease.

Q&A

Q Should I use the buttons of the multimedia control for playing, or should I make the multimedia control invisible (as it was done in the MyUSAMap program)?

A In the MyUSAMap program it was appropriate to make the multimedia control invisible (because the sound file is played according to the status of the Anthem check box, and the user does not have to click a Play button to play the file). In other applications, it may be appropriate to play the file only if the user clicks a Play button. In this case, you can make the multimedia control visible, and the user will have to click the Play button (third button from the left in Figure 19.9) to play the file. Alternatively, you can place a CommandButton in the form. If you set, for example, the Name property of the CommandButton to cmdPlay, you can attach the following code to the `cmdPlay_Click()` procedure:

```
Private Sub cmdPlay_Click()
    Tegomm1.Command = "Play"
End Sub
```

So, clicking the cmdPlay button will cause the multimedia control to play. In a similar manner, you can place another button that will serve as the Stop button and attach the following code to the `Click` event of the cmdStop button:

```
Tegomm1.Command = "Stop"
```

Quiz

1. The `Done` event of the multimedia control occurs when
   a. The file was played in its entirety.
   b. The multimedia control completed executing a command.
   c. There is no such event.

2. The `MouseMoveOnMap` event of the MapUSA control is used to detect
   a. On which state the mouse cursor is located
   b. On which state the mouse was clicked
   c. No such event

Exercise

Modify the MyUSAMap program so that the flag animation behaves as follows:

When there is playback in progress, the Ctrusa.Ico picture is displayed.

When there is no playback in progress, the flag animation is performed.

Quiz Answers

1. Both a and b. The `Done` event occurs when the multimedia control completed executing a command. For example, when the `Play` command is completed, the `Done` event occurs. (The `Play` command is completed when the entire file is played, so answer a is also correct.)

2. a

19

Exercise Answer

Currently, the code in the `Timer1_Timer()` procedure is as follows:

```
Private Sub Timer1_Timer()
Static FlagStatus
If Tegomm1.Mode = 525 Then
   imgCurrent.Picture = imgMap.Picture
Else
   If FlagStatus = 0 Then
      imgCurrent.Picture = imgFlag01.Picture
      FlagStatus = 1
   Else
      imgCurrent.Picture = imgFlag02.Picture
      FlagStatus = 0
   End If
End If
End Sub
```

Note the `If` statement that you use:

```
If Tegomm1.Mode = 525 Then
```

When the Mode property of the multimedia control is equal to 525, it means that no playback is in progress.

☐ Change the `If` statement so that it will look as follows:

```
    If Tegomm1.Mode = 526 Then
```

When the Mode property of the multimedia control is equal to 526, it means that playback is in progress.

Now when playback is in progress, the Ctrusa.Ico picture is displayed (because the code under the `If` is executed), and when no playback is in progress, the code under the `Else` is executed (a code that displays the flag animation).

☐ Select Save Project from the File menu of Visual Basic to save your work.

☐ Experiment with the MyUSAMap program, and verify that when no playback is in progress, the flag animation is performed, and when playback is in progress, the Ctrusa.Ico picture is displayed.

☐ Click the Exit button of the MyUSAMap program to terminate the program.

Day 20

Using Windows API

In this chapter you'll learn how to use Windows API functions from within your Visual Basic programs. This enables you to take advantage of the powerful Windows API functions from within your Visual Basic programs.

Visual Basic Functions

During the course of this book, you used many of the Visual Basic functions. For example, the Str() function converts a number to a string. The MsgBox() function displays a message box, and depending on the button that the user clicked inside the message box, the MsgBox() function returns a value that represents the clicked button.

What if the particular task that you are trying to implement is not provided as one of the functions of Visual Basic? In this case, you may find that the particular task can be achieved with Windows API functions, as explained later in this chapter.

DLLs

A *dynamic linked library (DLL)* file is a file that can have an EXE file extension (such as MyFile.EXE), or a DLL file extension (such as MyFile.DLL). The DLL file contains functions. Let's assume that a certain DLL file contains a function called MyFunction(). Let's assume also that the MyFunction() function takes one parameter and returns a value. (Just as the Str() function of Visual Basic takes a number as its parameter and returns a string that represents the number.) You can now write a Visual Basic program that uses the MyFunction() function that resides inside the MyFile.DLL file. In this case, your Visual Basic program can use the MyFunction() function in the same manner that it uses the Str() function. In other words, by using DLL files, you can increase the collection of functions that your Visual Basic program can use.

The beauty of DLL files is that many programs can use the same DLL functions simultaneously.

You can write a Visual Basic program that instructs the program to use a certain function from a certain DLL file. During the execution of your Visual Basic program, your program will load the code that corresponds to the function into memory, and now your program can use the DLL function. You can understand why these files are called dynamic linked libraries. These files are libraries of functions. The library is loaded (linked) into your program on the need-to-use basis (dynamically). The DLL file is not part of the EXE file of your program.

Furthermore, you can write another Visual Basic that uses the same DLL function (or a different function from the same DLL file). When you execute the program, you'll have two different programs running simultaneously, and both programs use the same DLL file! In fact, you can have many more programs utilizing the same DLL file.

To summarize, a DLL file is a file that includes functions in it. The functions are available for use from any program that wishes to use the functions of the DLL file.

Windows API Function

As you operate Windows, you notice that it has many features. You can move the mouse, click the mouse, select menus, and so on. Of course, as an operating system, Windows can do many other tasks. Windows saves files, loads files, displays icons, manages the hardware of the PC, and performs thousands of other important operations.

Windows itself is a program. Of course, as a Windows user, you do not tend to think of Windows as a program. Rather, you think of Windows as a mechanism that lets you execute programs (and of course as a mechanism to develop programs with programming languages such as Visual Basic). As it turns out, much of the functionality of Windows is carried out with the use of DLL files. That is, when Windows needs to perform a certain task, Windows uses a function that resides inside a DLL file.

You already learned that many programs can use the same function from the same DLL file simultaneously. This means that your Visual Basic program can also use functions from the same DLL files that Windows uses! Let's examine the advantages of using functions from DLL files that Windows uses:

- The DLL files of Windows already reside in your user PC. That is, your users are assumed to have Windows installed on their PCs. This means that you do not have to distribute the DLL files of Windows (which are very large), because your users have these DLL files already.

- The functions of the DLL files work well. After all, Windows uses these functions. So, what is good for Windows is definitely good for your program. In other words, you have to assume that the DLL functions of Windows are bug-free, and you have to assume that the functions were written in the most efficient way possible for Windows.

- One of the main reasons you would want to use functions from the DLL files of Windows is that Windows uses many operating system-related tasks that your program may want to use. As stated, Windows performs thousands of tasks. Many of these tasks are operating system-related tasks. For example, suppose that you want to write a program that causes the PC to restart (reboot itself). As you know, during the operation of Windows, it may ask you to reboot the PC (for example, after you install a new driver, Windows reboots itself). If you want to include a rebooting mechanism in your program, you can use the same DLL function that Windows uses to reboot the PC.

Now that you see that there are many good reasons to use the same DLL functions that Windows uses, let's write a program that uses functions from the Windows DLL file and see how this is accomplished.

20

Note

Microsoft designed Windows in a way so that Windows itself uses functions from DLL files. Furthermore, Microsoft designed these DLL files in a way that other programs (such as your Visual Basic program) will be able to use functions from the Windows DLL files. These functions are called Windows API functions.

Creating the MyApi Program

You'll now create a program called MyApi. This program illustrates how you can use Windows API functions from within your Visual Basic programs:

☐ Create the C:\VB5Prg\Ch20 directory. You'll save your work in this directory.

☐ Create a new Standard EXE project from the File menu of Visual Basic.

☐ Select Save Form1 As from the File menu of Visual Basic and save the form as MyApi.Frm in the C:\VB5Prg\Ch20 directory.

☐ Select Save Project As from the File menu of Visual Basic and save the project file as MyApi.Vbp in the C:\VB5Prg\Ch20 directory.

☐ Implement the frmMyApi form as specified in Table 20.1. When you complete building the form, it should look like the form shown in Figure 20.1.

Table 20.1. The properties table of the frmMyApi form.

Object	Property	Setting
Form	**Name**	**frmMyApi**
	Caption	The MyApi Program
CommandButton	**Name**	**cmdBeep**
	Caption	&Beep
CommandButton	**Name**	**cmdExit**
	Caption	E&xit

Figure 20.1.

The frmMyApi form with the Beep button in it (design mode).

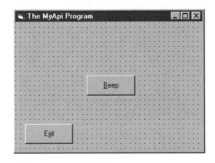

☐ Add the following code to the general declarations section of the frmMyApi form:

```
' All variables MUST be declared
Option Explicit
```

☐ Attach the following code to the Click event of the cmdExit button:

```
Private Sub cmdExit_Click()

    End

End Sub
```

Now when the user clicks the Exit button, the MyApi program terminates itself.

Adding a New BAS Module to the Project

So far, the MyApi.Vbp project includes a single form in it, the frmMyApi form (see Figure 20.2, which shows the Project window). Recall that to display the Project window, you can select Project Explorer from the View menu of Visual Basic.

Figure 20.2.

The MyApi.Vbp project currently includes a single form in it.

You'll now add a new BAS module to the MyApi project:

☐ Select Add Module from the Project menu of Visual Basic.

As a response, Visual Basic displays the Add Module window (see Figure 20.3).

Figure 20.3.

Adding a new BAS module to the MyApi.Vbp project.

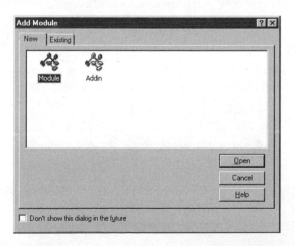

20

☐ Make sure that the New tab of the Add Module window is selected, select the Module icon in the Add Module page, and then click the Open button.

As a result, a new BAS module is added to the project.

The new module that Visual Basic added is called Module1, so change the name of the module to MyApi.Bas as follows:

☐ Select Save Module1 As from the File menu of Visual Basic and then use the Save File As dialog box to save the file as MyApi.Bas in the C:\VB5Prg\Ch20 directory.

Take a look at the Project window. As you can see (see Figure 20.4), now the project includes the frmMyApi form and the MyApi.Bas module.

Figure 20.4.

The MyApi.Vbp project now includes the frmMyApi form and the MyApi.Bas module.

Declaring the API Function

The objective now is to execute a Windows API function from within the MyApi program. This means that you must tell the program the name of the API function and the name of the DLL file where this function resides. You also have to tell Visual Basic how this function works (that is, its parameters and its returned value). This process of telling Visual Basic the details of the API function is called declaring the API function.

You added the MyApi.Bas module because you are going to add the declaration of the API function in the general declarations section of the new module that you added.

☐ Add code to the general declarations section of the MyApi.Bas module. After adding the code, the general declarations section of the MyApi.Bas module should look as follows:

```
'All variables must be declared
Option Explicit

' Declare the MessageBeep API function
Declare Function MessageBeep Lib "user32" _
          (ByVal wType As Long) As Long
```

☐ Select Save Project from the File menu of Visual Basic to save your work.

As you might have guessed from the look of frmMyApi form, you are going to implement a Beep button. That is, when the user clicks the Beep button, the program will beep.

You added the following code to the general declarations section of the MyApi.Bas module:

```
Declare Function MessageBeep Lib "user32" _
          (ByVal wType As Long) As Long
```

The preceding is the declaration of the API function. You start the declaration with the keyword Declare.

Next you type the word Function (because the declaration is a declaration of a function). This means that the API function returns a value.

Then you type the word MessageBeep. MessageBeep is the name of the API function.

Then you type the words Lib "user32".

This means that MessageBeep is a function that resides in a library (Lib). The name of the library file is Use32. Take a look in your Windows System directory. If you are using Windows 95 and you installed Windows in the C:\Windows directory, the Windows System directory is C:\Windows\System. If you are using Windows NT and you installed Windows NT in the C:\WinNT directory, the Windows System directory is C:\WinNT\System32. You can see the User32.DLL file. So, the declaration tells your program that the MessageBeep() DLL function resides in the User32.DLL file.

You then type (ByVal wType As Long). This means that there is one parameter to the function. The type of the parameter is As Long.

Finally (after the parenthesis of the parameter), you type As Long. This means that the function returns a number which is As Long.

(Later in this chapter you'll learn how to find the declarations of other Windows API functions.)

20

Executing the MessageBeep() API Function

You'll now write code that executes the MessageBeep() API function. The most important thing to note when executing an API function is that the statement that executes the API function must match the declaration of the API function. This will now be demonstrated:

☐ Add the following code to the cmdBeep_Click() procedure:

```
Private Sub cmdBeep_Click()

Dim Dummy

Dummy = MessageBeep(1)

End Sub
```

☐ Select Save Project from the File menu of Visual Basic to save your work.

You declare a local variable called Dummy:

```
Dim Dummy
```

Then you execute the MessageBeep() function as follows:

```
Dummy = MessageBeep(1)
```

You assign the returned value of MessageBeep() to the variable Dummy. You'll never again use the value of Dummy in this procedure, but to be consistent with the declaration of the function (which says that the function returns a value), you assign the returned value to a variable.

The MessageBeep() API function takes one parameter. The exact value of the parameter determines how the beep will be played.

☐ Execute the MyApi program.

☐ Click the Beep button. Verify that when you click the Beep button, the program beeps.

☐ Experiment with the MyApi program, then click its Exit button to terminate the program.

Sure, you could have used the Visual Basic Beep statement as follows:

```
Private Sub cmdBeep_Click()

    Beep

End Sub
```

but the objective of the exercise is to demonstrate the use of a Windows API function.

Depending on how your sound card is configured, the beep that you hear may be played through the sound card, not through the PC speaker. For experimenting purposes, change the code in the cmdBeep_Click() procedure to the following:

```
Private Sub cmdBeep_Click()

Dim Dummy


Dummy = MessageBeep(-1)

End Sub
```

☐ Execute the MyApi program and verify that you hear the PC speaker beep every time you click the Beep button.

Typically, when you supply -1 as the parameter of the MessageBeep() function, you are forcing the MessageBeep() to play the beep through the PC speaker. In this case, the beep duration is very small (and you can hardly hear it). To make sure that you hear the PC speaker beeps, change the code in the cmdBeep_Click() procedure as following:

```
Private Sub cmdBeep_Click()

Dim Dummy
Dim I

For I = 0 To 100
    Dummy = MessageBeep(1)
Next

End Sub
```

You add a For loop that causes the PC to beep 100 times. If the beep is played through the PC speaker, it is very short, and you will be able to hear many beeps, one after the other. (When the beep is played through the sound card, the duration of the beep is long, and by the time the beep is played, the For loop finished executing the loop, so you hear a single beep through the sound card.)

Finding the Windows Directory

As an example of another Windows API function, let's use an API function that finds the directory where Windows is installed.

☐ Place a CommandButton in the frmMyApi form.

☐ Set the properties of the CommandButton as follows: Name should be cmdWhereWindows, and Caption should be Where is &Windows?.

Your frmMyApi form should now look like the one in Figure 20.5.

Figure 20.5.

*The frmMyApi form
with the Where is
Windows? button.*

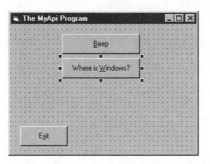

20

☐ Add code to the general declarations section of the MyApi.Bas module. After adding the code, the general declarations section of the MyApi.Bas module should look as follows:

```
'All variables must be declared
Option Explicit

' Declare the MessageBeep API function
Declare Function MessageBeep Lib "user32" _
        (ByVal wType As Long) As Long
```

```
' Declare the GetWindowsDirectory API function
Declare Function GetWindowsDirectory Lib "kernel32" _
     Alias "GetWindowsDirectoryA" _
    (ByVal lpBuffer As String, ByVal nSize As Long) _
     As Long
```

The new declaration that you added looks a little more complicated than the declaration of the MessageBeep() API function.

The name of the Windows API function is GetWindowsDirectory(). As you can see from the declaration, this function is from the kernel32 file.

You see the Alias line in the declaration. This line has to be there (and later in this chapter you'll learn how to find the declaration of API functions, so you'll see that this line has to be there).

There are two parameters to this API function:

```
(ByVal lpBuffer As String, ByVal nSize As Long)
```

The first parameter is a string, and the second parameter is a Long number.

The returned value of this API function is Long.

☐ Select Save Project from the File menu of Visual Basic to save your work.

Attaching Code to the Click Event of the Where is Windows? Button

You'll now add code to the Click event of the cmdWhereWindows button.

☐ Add the following code to the cmdWhereWindows_Click() procedure:

```
Private Sub cmdWhereWindows_Click()

Dim Result
Dim WindowsDirectory As String

' Fill 144 spaces in the WindowsDirectory string
WindowsDirectory = Space(144)

' Extract the Windows directory
Result = GetWindowsDirectory(WindowsDirectory, 144)

If Result = 0 Then
   MsgBox "Cannot get the Windows Directory"
Else
   WindowsDirectory = Trim(WindowsDirectory)
   MsgBox "Windows Directory: " & WindowsDirectory
End If

End Sub
```

☐ Select Save Project from the File menu of Visual Basic to save your work.

The code that you typed declares two local variables:

```
Dim Result
Dim WindowsDirectory As String
```

You then fill the WindowsDirectory variable with 144 spaces:

```
' Fill 144 spaces in the WindowsDirectory string
WindowsDirectory = Space(144)
```

Note the use of the Space() function: If you want to fill the variable MyVariable with 5 spaces, you use the following statement:

```
MyVariable = Space(5)
```

The preceding statement produces the same result as the following statement:

```
MyVariable = "     "
```

You then execute the GetWindowsDirectory() API function as follows:

```
' Extract the Windows directory
Result = GetWindowsDirectory(WindowsDirectory, 144)
```

The result of the execution is assigned to the Result variable. Result does not contain the directory where Windows resides; rather, Result is a number that represents the success or failure of the execution of the GetWindowsDirectory() function. If Result is equal to 0, it means that for some reason, the GetWindowsDirectory() function failed to find the Windows directory.

Now take a look at the parameters of the GetWindowsDirectory() function. The second parameter is 144. This means that the string that will hold the name of the Windows directory is 144 characters long.

The first parameter of the GetWindowsDirectory is the WindowsDirectory variable. You are used to thinking of a parameter of a function as the "input" of the function. However, in this case, the first parameter is used as the "output" of the function. The GetWindowsDirectory() API function will fill the string that you provided as its first parameter with the name of the Windows directory. It was necessary to fill 144 spaces in the string prior to executing the GetWindowsDirectory() function, because when the function updates this string, this string better have memory cells allocated for it already. (Of course, you could have filled the string with 144 nonspace characters, but the Space() function is a convenient way to fill 144 characters in one shot.)

You then execute an If...Else statement:

```
If Result = 0 Then
   MsgBox "Cannot get the Windows Directory"
Else
```

20

```
   WindowsDirectory = Trim(WindowsDirectory)
   MsgBox "Windows Directory: " & WindowsDirectory
End If
```

If `Result` is equal to 0, it means that the `GetWindowsDirectory()` function failed, and hence you display a message box that tells the user that the Windows directory cannot be extracted:

```
MsgBox "Cannot get the Windows Directory"
```

If `Result` is not equal to 0, the code under the `Else` is executed. This code displays the value of the `WindowsDirectory` variable:

```
WindowsDirectory = Trim(WindowsDirectory)
MsgBox "Windows Directory: " & WindowsDirectory
```

`WindowsDirectory` initially holds 144 spaces. You first use the `Trim()` function to remove the extra spaces. (Most probably, the Windows directory is a string of about 10 characters. However, the original `WindowsDirectory` is a string that has 144 characters.)

To summarize, you first initialize the `WindowsDirectory` variable to a string that has 144 characters in it. Then you supply this string as the first parameter of the `GetWindowsDirectory()` function. As a result, this API function fills the string with the name of the Windows directory. As you can see, when using API functions, the functions are used in a "strange" way (at least from the point of view of Visual Basic—if you are a C++ programmer, you'll find nothing strange in this way of executing the function). Well, that's the way the API function was declared, so there is nothing you can do about it. You must use the function in the way the designers of the API function designed it.

☐ Execute the MyApi program and verify that after you click the Where is Windows? button, a message box appears with the directory were Windows is installed.

Placing the Exit Windows Button

You'll now place the Exit Windows button in the frmMyApi form.

☐ Place a `CommandButton` in the frmMyApi form.

☐ Set the properties of the `CommandButton` as follows:

    Name: cmdExitWindows
    Caption: &Exit Windows

Your frmMyApi form should now look like the one in Figure 20.6.

Figure 20.6.

The frmMyApi form with the Exit Windows button in it.

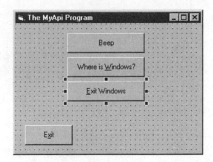

How Do You Know to Declare API Functions?

You saw the `MessageBeep()` API function in action, and you saw the `GetWindowsDirectory()` API function in action. Suppose you want to use the API function that causes the PC to reboot. How will you know which API function to use? More important, what does the declaration of this API look like?

Take a look in the directory where you installed your Visual Basic program. One of the subdirectories is \Winapi. One of the files in the \Winapi subdirectories is the Apiload.exe file.

☐ Use the Windows Explorer program to double-click the Apiload.exe program. (Alternatively, you can execute the Apiload.exe program by clicking the Start button of Windows, selecting Programs, selecting the Programs item from the menu that pops up, selecting the Visual Basic item from the list of program groups, and finally, selecting the API Text Viewer that appears as one of the items in the Visual Basic group of programs.)

   As a result, the API Viewer window appears (see Figure 20.7).

You use the API Viewer window to find how to declare API functions. Let's see this in action:

☐ Select Load Text File from the File menu of the API Viewer window.

   As a result, the Select a Text API File dialog box appears.

☐ Select the Win32api.txt file from the \Winapi subdirectory.

   As a result, the Available Items list is now filled with items.

☐ Make sure that the API Type list box is set to Declares.

   The Available Items list now includes a list of API declarations.

20

Figure 20.7.

The API Viewer window.

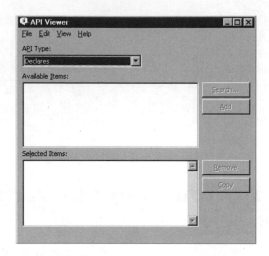

☐ Search for the ExitWindowsEx item. Then make sure that the ExitWindowsEx item is highlighted.

☐ Click the Add button of the Text API Viewer window.

> *As a result, the declaration of the ExitWindowsEx API function appears in the Selected Items list (the lower portion of the window).*

☐ Use the mouse to highlight the contents of the Selected Items list, then click the Copy button.

> *As a result, the highlighted text is copied into the Clipboard.*

☐ Place the mouse cursor in the general declarations section of the MyApi.Bas module. Then Paste the contents of the Clipboard (by pressing Ctrl+V).

> *As a result, the general declarations area of the MyApi.Bas module now looks as follows:*

```
'All variables must be declared
Option Explicit

' Declare the MessageBeep API function
Declare Function MessageBeep Lib "user32" _
            (ByVal wType As Long) As Long

' Declare the GetWindowsDirectory API function
Declare Function GetWindowsDirectory Lib "kernel32" _
     Alias "GetWindowsDirectoryA" _
     (ByVal lpBuffer As String, ByVal nSize As Long) _
     As Long

' Declare the ExitWindowsEx API function
Declare Function ExitWindowsEx Lib "user32" _
        (ByVal uFlags As Long, ByVal dwReserved As Long) _
        As Long
```

As it turns out, you also need to use a declaration of a constant.

☐ Go back to the Text API Viewer window, and set the API Type list to Constants. (You changed the API Type to Constants, because you now want to display the list of constants.)

☐ Visual Basic may prompt you with a dialog box, asking whether you want to convert the loaded API file to a database. Click the Yes button. As a response, Visual Basic displays the Select a Name for the New Database dialog box. Save the database as Win32api.MDB in the \Winapi directory. The process of converting the text file to a database will take some time, but it's worth it. The next time you start the API Viewer program, select Load Database File from the File menu of the API Viewer and select the file Win32api.MDB. Now, the program works with a database file (not a text file), so listing the items, scrolling the items, and searching for an item will be much faster.

In any case, the API Viewer program now lists the constants.

☐ Scroll the list of constants until you see the EWX_SHUTDOWN=1 item. Highlight the item and then click the Add button.

> *As a response, the* EWX_SHUTDOWN=1 *item appears on the Selected Items list of the API Viewer window.*

☐ Highlight the item in the Selected Items list and click the Copy button.

> *As a response, the item is copied into the Clipboard.*

☐ Place the mouse cursor in the general declarations section of the MyApi.Bas module and paste the contents of the Clipboard (by pressing Ctrl+V, for example).

> *Now the general declarations section of the MyApi.Bas module looks as follows:*

```
'All variables must be declared
Option Explicit
' Declare the MessageBeep API function
Declare Function MessageBeep Lib "user32" _
            (ByVal wType As Long) As Long

' Declare the GetWindowsDirectory API function
Declare Function GetWindowsDirectory Lib "kernel32" _
    Alias "GetWindowsDirectoryA" _
    (ByVal lpBuffer As String, ByVal nSize As Long) _
    As Long

' Declare the ExitWindowsEx API function
Declare Function ExitWindowsEx Lib "user32" _
        (ByVal uFlags As Long, ByVal dwReserved As Long) _
        As Long

Public Const EWX_SHUTDOWN = 1
```

☐ Select Save Project from the File menu of Visual Basic to save your work.

20

Attaching Code to the `Click` Event of the cmdExitWindows Button

You'll now attach code to the `Click` event of the cmdExitWindows button.

☐ Type the following code in the `cmdExitWindows_Click()` procedure:

```
Private Sub cmdExitWindows_Click()

Dim Dummy
Dim Answer

Answer = _
    MsgBox("Are you sure you want to exit Windows", _
           vbYesNo)

If Answer = vbYes Then

    Dummy = ExitWindowsEx(EWX_SHUTDOWN, 0)

End If

End Sub
```

☐ Select Save Project from the File menu of Visual Basic to save your work.

The code that you typed in the `cmdExitWindows_Click()` procedure declares a local variable called `Dummy` and a local variable called `Answer`.

You are just about to let the user exit Windows. That is, the user clicked the Exit Windows button, and as a response, Windows will be terminated. You have to admit that's a rather drastic action! So, it is a good idea to make sure that your user knows what's about to happen. You therefore display a message box that asks the user to confirm the Windows exit.

If the user clicks the Yes button of the message box, the code under the `If` statement is executed:

```
Dummy = ExitWindowsEx(EWX_SHUTDOWN, 0)
```

Note that you are not making any use of the returned value of the `ExitWindowsEx()` function (that's the reason you assigned the returned value to a variable called `Dummy`).

The `ExitWindowsEx()` API function will shut down the PC, because you supplied `EWX_SHUTDOWN` as the first parameter of the `ExitWindowsEx()` function. (The second parameter of the `ExitWindowsEx()` function is 0.)

Recall that you declared in the general declarations section of the MyApi.Bas module the `EWX_SHUTDOWN` constant as follows:

```
Public Const EWX_SHUTDOWN = 1
```

This means that `EWX_SHUTDOWN` is equal to 1. So the following statement

```
Dummy = ExitWindowsEx(EWX_SHUTDOWN, 0)
```

has the same result as executing the statement

```
Dummy = ExitWindowsEx(1, 0)
```

In the following step, you are going to try the MyApi prorgam (and as you know, this program will shut down Windows). Make sure that you close all applications. Make sure also to save the MyApi.Vbp project.

☐ Execute the MyApi program.

☐ Click the Exit Windows button.

> *As a response, you'll see a message box that asks you to confirm the Windows exit.*

☐ Click the Yes button and verify that Windows shut down.

Summary

In this chapter you learned how to use Windows API functions from within your Visual Basic programs. As you saw in the MyApi program that you implemented in this chapter, you must first declare the function. Once you declare the function, you can use it like any other regular Visual Basic function. This way, you can increase the number of functions that Visual Basic can use.

You learned how to use the API Viewer. It is a tool that lets you copy declarations of Windows API functions. This tool, however, does not teach you the exact meaning and purpose of the API functions. Sometimes, the name of the API function gives a clue as to the purpose of the function. The exact meaning of the Windows API functions can be found in the help files of other Microsoft products, such as Visual C++.

20

Q&A

Q Should I use Windows API functions often?

A You should use Windows API functions if the task that you are trying to implement is not available as a regular Visual Basic function or statement. Of course, the task that you want to implement may not be available as a Windows API function.

Quiz

1. You can use functions from DLL files that are not Windows DLL files.

    a. True

    b. False

2. If Visual Basic uses a function from the DLL files of Windows, Windows itself will not be able to use that function for as long as your program is running.

    a. True

    b. False

Exercise

Add a button to the frmMyApi form. When the user clicks the button, a message box will appear. The message box should display the name of the Windows System directory.

Quiz Answers

1. True. It is possible to use functions from other DLL files as long as you know the declarations of the functions. Whoever wrote the DLL must tell you how to declare the functions of the DLL in the general declarations section of the BAS module of your Visual Basic project.

2. False. Many programs (including Windows) can use the same DLL files simultaneously.

Exercise Answer

Here is how you implement a button that lets the user display the Windows System directory.

☐ Add a CommandButton in the frmMyApi form.

☐ Set the properties of the button as follows: the Name should be cmdWhereSystem, and the Caption should be Where is &System?

Your form should now look like the one in Figure 20.8.

☐ Attach code in the general declarations section of the MyApi.Bas module. After attaching the code, the general declarations section of the MyApi.Bas module should look as follows:

```
'All variables must be declared
Option Explicit
```

```
' Declare the MessageBeep API function
Declare Function MessageBeep Lib "user32" _
            (ByVal wType As Long) As Long

' Declare the GetWindowsDirectory API function
Declare Function GetWindowsDirectory Lib "kernel32" _
    Alias "GetWindowsDirectoryA" _
    (ByVal lpBuffer As String, ByVal nSize As Long) _
    As Long

' Declare the ExitWindowsEx API function
Declare Function ExitWindowsEx Lib "user32" _
        (ByVal uFlags As Long, ByVal dwReserved As Long) _
        As Long

Public Const EWX_SHUTDOWN = 1

' Declare the GetSystemDirectory API function
Declare Function GetSystemDirectory _
    Lib "kernel32" _
    Alias "GetSystemDirectoryA" _
    (ByVal lpBuffer As String, ByVal nSize As Long) _
    As Long
```

You added the declaration of the GetSystemDirectory() API function.

Figure 20.8.

The frmMyApi form with the Where is System? button.

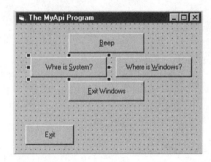

☐ Add the following code to the cmdWhereSystem_Click() procedure as follows:

```
Private Sub cmdWhereSystem_Click()

Dim Result
Dim SystemDirectory As String

' Fill 144 spaces in the SystemDirectory string
SystemDirectory = Space(144)

' Extract the System directory
Result = GetSystemDirectory(SystemDirectory, 144)

If Result = 0 Then
    MsgBox "Cannot get the System Directory"
```

20

```
     Else
        SystemDirectory = Trim(SystemDirectory)
        MsgBox "System Directory: " & SystemDirectory
     End If

  End Sub
```

☐ Select Save Project from the File menu of Visual Basic to save your work.

The code that you typed in the cmdWhereSystem_Click() directory is very similar to the code that you previously typed in the cmdWhereWindows_Click() procedure. The only difference is that now you are extracting the System directory.

☐ Execute the MyApi program by clicking the Where is System button and verifying that a message box appears with the name of the Windows System directory.

☐ Experiment with the MyApi program, then click its Exit button to terminate the program.

Day 21

Building Your Own OCX ActiveX Controls

During the course of this book you learned to write Visual Basic programs. Occasionally, you were instructed to use an OCX ActiveX control in your program. In this chapter you'll learn how to design and implement your own OCX controls.

Note

Visual Basic 5 comes in several editions: Learning edition (which used to be called the Standard edition), Professional edition, and Enterprise edition.

The Professional edition and Enterprise edition have additional software in them (software that does not come with the Learning edition). For example, currently, the software that enables you to create your own OCX ActiveX controls with Visual Basic is included only in the Professional and Enterprise editions.

> To implement the programs of this chapter, you need to use a Visual Basic edition that enables you to create OCX ActiveX controls. Even if you do not have this software, it is highly recommended that you at least browse through this chapter. This way, you'll learn about the OCX ActiveX creation feature of Visual Basic.

Implementing Your Own OCX ActiveX Control with Visual Basic

If you find yourself writing Visual Basic programs that have repeated code in them, consider writing an OCX ActiveX control. For example, suppose that your programs always ask your user to enter a number between 1 and 10, and based on the number that your user entered, the program does something. Assuming that for some reason many of your programs need this feature, you may find yourself writing the same code in every program that needs this feature. Of course, when you implement a new program that needs this feature, you will probably go back to a program that you wrote already, and you will copy and paste code from that program to your new program. This is fine, but what if you decide to improve the code, or if you discover that the code has a little bug in it that needs to be fixed? In this case, you have to go back to all the programs that use this code and make corrections to the code. So, if you already have 10 programs that use this code, you have to go back to 10 programs and make corrections in each one of them. This is no fun!

You already learned in this book that you can use the same form in many programs. For example, the code that takes a number from the user, and does something with the number, may reside in a separate form. Every program that needs this feature will use the same form. If there is a need to correct the code, you only have to correct the code in one place (in the form that contains the code of this feature). Because all the 10 programs that you already wrote use the same form, the 10 programs are automatically fixed once you fix the form. Of course, if you already converted your 10 projects to EXE program files (by selecting Make EXE file from the File menu of Visual Basic), you have to create 10 new EXE program files (because the old EXE files do not include the fixed form in them). This, however, is not such a difficult task.

Using a separate form to accomplish a particular task is a commonly used Visual Basic programming technique. However, the code that you have in the separate form is usable only from within Visual Basic programs. Other programming languages cannot use the Visual Basic form.

Nowadays, many programming languages use OCX ActiveX controls—for example, Visual Basic, Visual C++, Borland C++, and many others. If the particular feature that you are implementing is a desired feature that will be useful for programming languages other than Visual Basic, you can implement the feature with an OCX ActiveX control. This way, your Visual Basic programs will be able to use the OCX ActiveX control, as well as any other programming language that is capable of using an OCX ActiveX control.

Creating the Project of the MyActX OCX ActiveX Control

You'll now implement your own OCX ActiveX control:

☐ Create the C:\VB5Prg\Ch21 directory. You'll save your work in this directory.

☐ Start Visual Basic and then select New Project from the File menu of Visual Basic.

Visual Basic responds by displaying the New Project window shown in Figure 21.1.

Figure 21.1.

The New Project window.

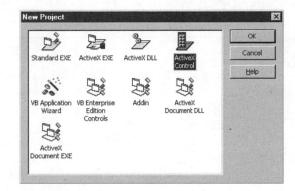

When starting a regular Visual Basic project, you have to select the Standard EXE icon in the New Project window, and then you have to click the Open button. Now you are designing an OCX ActiveX control, so you have to select the ActiveX Control icon in the New Project window:

☐ Select the ActiveX Control icon in the New Project window and then click the Open button.

Visual Basic responds by displaying the UserControl window shown in Figure 21.2.

21

Figure 21.2.

The UserControl window.

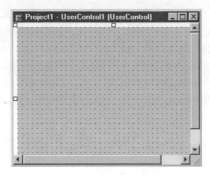

Before doing anything else, let's save the project:

☐ Make sure that the UserControl window is the active window and then select Save UserControl1 As from the File menu of Visual Basic.

As a response, Visual Basic displays the Save File As dialog box.

☐ Use the Save File As dialog box to save the UserControl window as MyActX.Ctl in the C:\VB5Prg\Ch21 directory.

Note

> Do not save your files with the default filenames that Visual Basic suggests. The default filename that Visual Basic suggests to save the UserControl is UserControl1.Ctl. However, you are now experimenting with creating an OCX ActiveX control, so a more appropriate filename is MyActX.Ctl.

So far, you saved the UserControl window as MyActX.Ctl. Now let's save the project:

☐ Select Save Project As from the File menu of Visual Basic.

As a response, Visual Basic displays the Save Project As dialog box.

☐ Use the Save Project As dialog box to save the project file as MyActX.Vbp in the C:\VB5Prg\ Ch21 directory.

Identifying and Describing the OCX ActiveX Control

As you'll soon see, after you complete designing the MyActX OCX ActiveX control, you'll end up with a file called MyActX.OCX. As previously stated, this OCX ActiveX control will be useful from within Visual Basic programs, as well as other programming languages that support OCX ActiveX controls (for example, Visual C++). Whoever uses this control will have to pick up the control from a list of OCX ActiveX controls and will place the control in the Toolbox window (of Visual Basic, Visual C++, or whatever programming language is used). Thus, you have to identify the ActiveX control and describe its purpose (so that whoever wants to use the control will be able to identify this OCX ActiveX control). Here is how you accomplish this:

☐ Select Project1 Properties from the Project menu of Visual Basic.

   As a response, Visual Basic displays the Project Properties window.

☐ Make sure that the General tab of the Project Properties window is selected (see Figure 21.3).

Figure 21.3.

The Project Properties window.

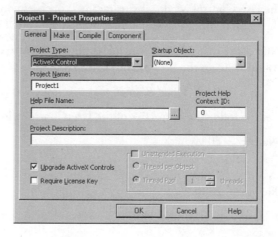

Note in Figure 21.3 that the Project Type is set to ActiveX Control. Indeed, this is the type of project that you are now designing, so leave the Project Type setting at its current setting (ActiveX Control).

Now take a look at the Project Name setting in the Project Properties window. The current setting of Project Name is Project1.

☐ In the Project name text box of the Project Properties window, type `MyActX`.

Take a look at the Project Description setting in the Project Properties window. The current setting of Project Description is empty.

☐ In the Project Description text box of the Project Properties window, type `MyActX Experimenting`.

☐ Click the OK button of the Project Properties window.

21

Later in this chapter (when you use the ActiveX control that you are now designing), you'll
see the settings of the previous steps in action.

Customizing the UserControl Window

You'll now customize the UserControl MyActX window (the window of the OCX ActiveX
control). As you'll soon see, the MyActX window represents the OCX ActiveX control that
you are now designing.

You customize the MyActX window in the same manner you customize a regular form of a
Standard EXE program. That is, you can place objects in the UserControl window, you set
the properties of the UserControl window and the properties of the objects that you place
in the UserControl window by using the Properties window, and you attach code to events
in the same manner that you attach code in a regular form.

☐ Make sure that the UserControl window is the active window and then select Properties
Window from the View menu of Visual Basic.

   As a response, Visual Basic displays the Properties window of the UserControl window.

☐ Set the following properties of the UserControl window:

   Name: ctlMyActX
   BackColor: Red
   Width: 3000
   Height: 2000

The UserControl window should now look like the one in Figure 21.4.

Figure 21.4.

*The UserControl
window after setting
several of its
properties.*

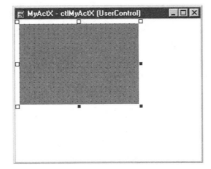

Note

> You were instructed to set the BackColor property of the control to red. Why? Soon you are going to place the ActiveX control that you are designing in a regular form (just as you place a Label control, or a scroll bar in a regular form). By setting the BackColor property of the control to red, you'll be able to tell immediately which part of the form is the ActiveX control and which part is the form. Typically, however, you make the background color of ActiveX controls gray like the color of the CommandButtons.

Placing CommandButtons in the UserControl Window

You'll now place CommandButtons in the UserControl window:

☐ If currently the Toolbox window is not displayed on the desktop of Visual Basic, display it by selecting Toolbox from the View menu.

☐ Make sure that the UserControl window is the active window, then double-click the icon of the CommandButton in the Toolbox window.

As a response, a CommandButton appears in the UserControl window.

☐ Set the Name property of the CommandButton to cmdSayHello.

☐ Set the Caption property of the cmdSayHello button to &Say Hello.

☐ Drag the cmdSayHello button to the location shown in Figure 21.5.

Let's place another CommandButton in the window of the control:

☐ Make sure that the UserControl window is the active window, then double-click the icon of the CommandButton in the Toolbox window.

As a response, a CommandButton appears in the UserControl window.

☐ Set the Name property of the CommandButton to cmdClear.

☐ Set the Caption property of the cmdClear button to &Clear.

☐ Drag the cmdClear button to the location shown in Figure 21.5.

Your UserControl window should now look like the one in Figure 21.5.

21

Figure 21.5.

The UserControl window with the Say Hello and Clear buttons in it.

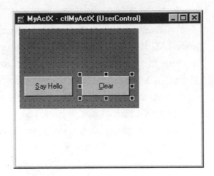

Placing a Text Box in the UserControl Window

You'll now place a TextBox in the UserControl window.

☐ Make sure that the UserControl window is the active window, then double-click the icon of the TextBox in the Toolbox window.

    As a response, a TextBox control appears in the UserControl window.

☐ Set the Name property of the TextBox to txtHello.

☐ Empty the Text property of the txtHello TextBox.

☐ Drag the txtHello TextBox to the location shown in Figure 21.6.

Your UserControl window should now look like the one in Figure 21.6.

Figure 21.6.

The UserControl window with the TextBox in it.

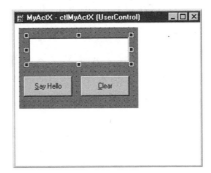

Save your work:

☐ Select Save Project from the File menu of Visual Basic.

Attaching Code to the `Click` Event of the Say Hello Button

You'll now attach code to the `Click` event of the cmdSayHello button:

☐ Double-click the Say Hello button.

> *As a response, Visual Basic displays the* `cmdSayHello_Click()` *procedure ready to be edited by you. (As you can see, attaching code to the events of objects in the UserControl window is the same as attaching code to events of objects in regular forms.)*

☐ Type code in the `cmdSayHello_Click()` procedure. After typing the code, the `cmdSayHello_Click()` procedure should look as follows:

```
Private Sub cmdSayHello_Click()

    txtHello.Text = "Hello!"

End Sub
```

The code that you typed sets the Text property of the txtHello TextBox to `"Hello!"`. So, clicking the Say Hello button causes the text `Hello!` to be displayed in the TextBox.

You'll now attach code to the `Click` event of the Clear button:

☐ Double-click the Clear button.

> *As a response, Visual Basic displays the* `cmdClear_Click()` *procedure ready to be edited by you.*

☐ Type code in the `cmdClear_Click()` procedure. After typing the code, the `cmdClear_Click()` procedure should look as follows:

```
Private Sub cmdClear_Click()

    txtHello.Text = ""

End Sub
```

The code that you typed clears the Text property of the txtHello TextBox. So, clicking the Clear button deletes any text from the TextBox.

21

Save your work:

☐ Select Save Project from the File menu of Visual Basic.

Creating the OCX File

That's it! You completed the implementation of the OCX ActiveX control. Now it is time to create the MyActX.OCX file:

☐ Select Make MyActX.OCX from the File menu of Visual Basic.

Visual Basic responds by displaying the Make Project dialog box.

☐ Use the Make Project dialog box to save the file as MyActX.OCX in the C:\VB5Prg\Ch21 directory.

As a result, the file MyActX.OCX now resides in the C:\VB5Prg\Ch21 directory.

☐ Select Save project from the File menu of Visual Basic to save your work.

Note

> If you try to execute the MyActX control (by selecting Start from the Run menu), you'll get an error message, telling you that you cannot run the control.
>
> This of course makes sense! You cannot "run," for example, the Label control, the Scroll bar control, or any other control. In a similar manner, you cannot run the MyActX control.

Seeing the MyActX OCX ActiveX Control in Action

As stated, you cannot "run" the control. How will you see the OCX ActiveX control that you designed in action? In the same manner that you see the label control in action. That is, you have to place the control in a form of a Standard EXE project and then execute the Standard EXE program.

> **Note**
>
> In the following sections, you are instructed to terminate the current project (the MyActX.Vbp project) and to start a new Standard EXE project. During the implementation of the Standard EXE project, you'll be instructed to place the MyActX OCX ActiveX control in the Toolbox window and then to place the MyActX control in the form of the Standard EXE project.
>
> In the case of the MyActX control, this control is very simple, and you hope not to make any errors during the implementation of the control. However, when you implement a more complex control, chances are that you'll make mistakes. Furthermore, you probably want to implement some code in the control, then test your implementation by placing it in a regular Standard EXE project, then implement more code in the control, then test it again, and so on. As you can see, there will be a lot of time spent on loading the MyActX.Vbp project, then loading the Standard EXE project, then loading the MyActX.Vbp project again, and so on. The designers of Visual Basic incorporated a very useful feature into Visual Basic—the feature that enables you to load several projects simultaneously! This way, when designing OCX ActiveX controls, you typically have two projects loaded: the project of the ActiveX control, and the project of the Standard EXE program that is used to test the ActiveX control.
>
> For the sake of simplicity, you'll start designing the test program as a single project. (Later in this chapter, you will be instructed to load the two projects simultaneously.)

As previously stated, you'll now design a Standard EXE program that will use the MyActX.OCX control. Forget for a moment that you designed the MyActX control. As far as the Standard EXE project is concerned, it does not matter who designed the MyActX control. In fact, it does not matter how this ActiveX control was created. This ActiveX control may have been designed using Visual Basic (as indeed is the case here), or it may have been designed using another programming language such as Visual C++. From the point of view of the Standard EXE program that you are now going to implement, the MyActX.OCX is a regular OCX control that can be used.

☐ Select Save Project from the File menu of Visual Basic.

☐ Select Exit from the File menu of Visual Basic.

Visual Basic responds by terminating itself.

21

Now start Visual Basic:

☐ Click the Start button that resides on the status bar of Windows, select Programs from the menu that pops up, select the Visual Basic item, and select the Visual Basic item from the group of Visual Basic programs.

   As a result, Visual Basic starts.

☐ Create a new Standard EXE project.

☐ Select Save Form1 As from the File menu of Visual Basic and save the form as TestActX.Frm in the C:\Vb5Prg\Ch21 directory.

☐ Select Save Project As from the File menu of Visual Basic and save the project as TestActX.Vbp in the C:\Vb5Prg\Ch21 directory.

Designing the Form of the TestActX Program

You'll now design the form of the TestActX program:

☐ Set the Name property of the form to frmTestActX.

☐ Set the Caption property of the form to `Testing the OCX ActiveX Control`.

☐ Place a CommandButton in the `frmTestActX` form and set its properties as follows: Name should be cmdExit, and Caption should be E&xit.

The frmTestActX form should now look like the one in Figure 21.7.

Figure 21.7.
The frmTestActX from with its Exit button (design mode).

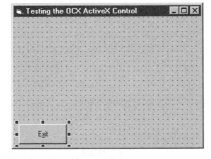

Attaching Code to the `Click` Event of the Exit button

You'll now attach code to the `Click` event of the Exit button:

☐ Double-click the Exit button and then attach the following code to the `cmdExit_Click()` procedure:

```
Private Sub cmdExit_Click()

    End

End Sub
```

☐ Select Save Project from the File menu of Visual Basic.

☐ Just to make sure that everything is working as expected, execute the TestActX program and then click the Exit button.

The TestActX program responds by terminating itself.

Note

In the previous step, you were instructed to execute the TestActX program and verify that it is working as expected. The TestActX program is a very simple program, and chances are that you did not make any mistakes in its implementation. In the following steps, you are going to place the MyActX OCX ActiveX control in the frmTestActX form, then execute the TestActX program again. If something goes wrong during the execution of the TestActX program, you will know it is because there is something wrong with the ActiveX control. In the case of the simple Exit button, this step of executing the TestActX program prior to placing the MyActX control in it may look redundant. However, in your future projects, your TestActX program may be more complex, and by executing it prior to the introduction of the MyActX control in the program, you are making sure that if there is a problem, you'll know what caused it.

Placing the Icon of the **MyActX** Control in the Toolbox Window

21

Take a look in the Toolbox window. The icon of the MyActX OCX ActiveX control does not appear in the Toolbox window. You'll now add the icon of the MyActX control in the Toolbox window:

☐ Select Components from the Project menu of Visual Basic.

Visual Basic responds by displaying the Components window (see Figure 21.8).

Figure 21.8.

The Components window.

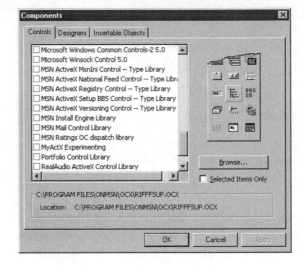

☐ Scroll down the list of components until you see the MyActX Experimenting item (in Figure 21.8, you can see this item as the third item from the bottom of the list).

☐ Place a check mark in the check box to the left of the MyActX Experimenting item of the Components window.

Your Components window should now look like the one in Figure 21.9.

Figure 21.9.

The Components window with a check mark to the left of the MyActX Experimenting item.

Note that at the bottom of the Components window, you can see the location of the MyActX control. (The bottom of the Components window displays the location of the currently selected item in the list.) As shown in Figure 21.9, the location of the MyActX control is C:\VB5Prg\Ch21 directory, and the name of the OCX file is MyActX.OCX.

☐ Click the OK button of the Components window.

As a result, the icon of the MyActX OCX Control now appears in the Toolbox (see Figure 21.10).

Figure 21.10.

The icon of MyActX control in the Toolbox window.

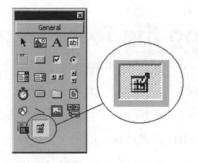

 Note

When you place the mouse cursor (without clicking any of the mouse buttons) on the icon of the MyActX control in the Toolbox, you see a yellow rectangle with the text CtlMyActX in it.

Placing the MyActX Control as the Test Program

You'll now place the MyActX control in the frmTestActX form:

☐ Make sure that the frmTestActX form is the selected window and then double-click the icon of the MyActX control in the Toolbox window.

As a response, the MyActX control appears in the frmTestActX form (see Figure 21.11).

Save your work:

☐ Select Save Project from the File menu of Visual Basic.

21

Figure 21.11.
The form of the test program with the MyActX control in it.

Executing the Test Program

Let's see the test program in action:

☐ Execute the TestActX program.

>   *As a response, the window of the TestActX program appears, as shown in Figure 21.12.*

☐ Click the Say Hello button.

>   *The TestActX program responds by displaying the text Hello! in the text box.*

Figure 21.12.
The window of the TestActX program.

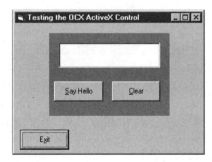

☐ Click the Clear button.

>   *The TestActX program responds by clearing the text from the text box.*

☐ Experiment with the TestActX program and then click its Exit button to terminate the program.

☐ Select Exit from the File menu of Visual Basic to terminate the Visual Basic program.

Loading the OCX Project and Test Project Simultaneously

In the following sections, you are going to make a little change to the OCX ActiveX control, then make a little change to the test program and see the changes that you made to the OCX ActiveX control and the test program in action. Then you are going to make additional modifications to both the ActiveX and test program, and so on. This means that you have to keep starting Visual Basic, loading the appropriate project, then exiting Visual Basic, loading the other project, and so on. You have to do this for each little change that you make in the ActiveX project or the test program. This process of going back and forth between the ActiveX project and the test program can make you crazy. Fortunately, the designers of Visual Basic designed it in a way that lets you load more than one project onto the desktop of Visual Basic. Let's see this in action:

☐ Start Visual Basic.

☐ Select Open Project from the File menu of Visual Basic and then select the MyActX.Vbp project from the C:\VB5Prg\Ch21 directory.

Visual Basic responds by loading the OCX ActiveX project.

At this point, Visual Basic has one project loaded, the MyActX.Vbp OCX ActiveX project. Let's load the test program project:

☐ Select Add Project from the File menu of Visual Basic.

Visual Basic responds by displaying the Add Project window. Note that the Add Project window has the Existing tab.

☐ Click the Existing tab.

Visual Basic responds by displaying the Existing page.

☐ Use the Existing page to load the TestActX.Vbp project from the C:\VB5Prg\Ch21 directory.

Visual Basic may prompt you with a dialog box telling you that the version of the OCX is being upgraded. If you receive this message, click the OK button of the dialog box.

Now there are two projects loaded: the MyActX.Vbp project and the TestActX.Vbp project.

☐ Select Project Explorer from the View menu of Visual Basic.

Visual Basic responds by displaying the Project window (see Figure 21.13).

21

As you can see from Figure 21.13, the Project window reports that indeed there are two projects currently loaded.

Figure 21.13.

The Project window reports that there are two projects currently loaded.

Creating a Project Group

During the course of developing the two projects (the ActiveX project and the test program project), you will have to repeat the preceding steps and load these two projects. Hence, it is more convenient to save the two projects as one group. This way, instead of having to load the two projects into Visual Basic, you have to load one project that is basically the two projects together. Here is how you accomplish this:

☐ Select Save Project Group As from the File menu of Visual Basic.

Visual Basic displays the Save Project Group As dialog box.

☐ Use the Save Project Group As dialog box to save the group as MyGroup.Vbg in the C:\VB5Prg\Ch21 directory.

Before continuing with the subject of enhancing the ActiveX control, let's see the project group in action:

☐ Select Exit from the File menu of Visual Basic to terminate Visual Basic.

Visual Basic responds by terminating itself.

Now let's load the project group:

☐ Start Visual Basic.

☐ Select Open Project from the File menu of Visual Basic. Then select the MyGroup.Vbg file from the C:\VB5Prg\Ch21 directory. (If Visual Basic prompts you with a message about the version of the OCX control, click the OK button of the message box.)

As you can see, in "one shot" you loaded the ActiveX project as well as the test program project.

The Resize Event of the Control

You'll now learn about the Resize property of the control.

☐ Display the Project window, highlight the ctlMyActX item in the Project window, then click the View Code icon at the top of the Project window.

As a response, the code window of the ctlMyActX control appears.

☐ Set the upper-left list box of the code window to UserControl and set the upper-right list box of the code window to Resize.

Visual Basic responds by displaying the UserControl_Resize() procedure ready to be edited by you.

☐ Type code in the UserControl_Resize() procedure. After typing the code, the UserControl_Resize() procedure should look as follows:

```
Private Sub UserControl_Resize()

    Static IWasResized As Integer

    IWasResized = IWasResized + 1

    Debug.Print "IWasResized = " & IWasResized

End Sub
```

Save your work:

☐ Select Save Project Group from the File menu of Visual Basic.

The code that you typed in the UserControl_Resize() procedure declares a Static variable:

```
Static IWasResized As Integer
```

So, upon executing the UserControl_Resize() procedure for the first time, the IWasResized variable is equal to 0.

You then execute the following statement:

```
IWasResized = IWasResized + 1
```

Now IWasResized is equal to 1 (0+1=1).

Finally, you execute the following statement:

```
Debug.Print "IWasResized = " & IWasResized
```

The preceding statement prints in the Debug window. Note the use of the & character. The statement

21

```
Debug.Print "IWasResized = " & IWasResized
```

produces the same result as the statement

```
Debug.Print "IWasResized = " + Str(IWasResized)
```

As you can see, using the & character to add strings saves you some typing.

To summarize, upon executing the UserControl_Resize() procedure, the Debug window (a special window that is used for the purpose of learning and debugging your program) will print the value of the IWasResized variable.

Note

During the course of the rest of this chapter, you'll be instructed to add code and objects to the code window and the windows of the two projects. Make sure that you are adding the code or objects to the proper project. When in doubt, simply select Project Explorer from the View menu of Visual Basic. This displays the project window. Then select the project of your choice and click the View Code icon or View Object icon to view the code or object of your choice.

Let's see the UserControl_Resize() procedure in action:

☐ Place a CommandButton in the frmTestActX form.

☐ Set the properties of the CommandButton that you placed in the frmTestActX form as follows (see Figure 21.14): Name should be cmdIncrease, and Caption should be &Increase.

☐ Place another CommandButton in the frmTestActX form.

☐ Set the properties of the CommandButton that you placed in the frmTestActX form as follows (see Figure 21.14): Name shoudl be cmdDecrease, and Caption should be &Decrease.

☐ Add the following code in the cmdIncrease_Click() procedure:

```
Private Sub cmdIncrease_Click()

    ctlMyActX1.Height = ctlMyActX1.Height * 2

End Sub
```

Figure 21.14.

The frmTestActX form with the Increase and Decrease buttons.

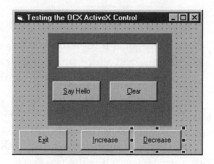

The code that you typed is executed when the user clicks the Increase button. This code causes the Height property of the ctlMyActX1 control to double its size.

☐ Add the following code in the cmdDecrease_Click() procedure:

```
Private Sub cmdDecrease_Click()

    ctlMyActX1.Height = ctlMyActX1.Height / 2

End Sub
```

The code that you typed is executed when the user clicks the Decrease button. This code causes the Height property of the ctlMyActX1 control to be half its size.

Before executing the TestActX program, let's add the Option Explicit statement to both projects. Recall from previous chapters of this book that adding the Option Explicit statement is a good idea, because this way, Visual Basic checks that every variable you use in the program was declared. If you type a name of a variable with an error, Visual Basic will prompt you with an error message, telling you that the variable was not declared.

☐ Add the Option Explicit statement to the general declarations section of the MyActX window so that it looks as follows:

```
'All variables MUST be declared
Option Explicit
```

☐ Add the Option Explicit statement to the general declarations section of the TestActX form, so that it looks as follows:

```
'All variables MUST be declared
Option Explicit
```

Save your work:

☐ Select Save Project Group from the File menu of Visual Basic.

21

Note

Sometimes you will see the ActiveX control in the frmTestActX form with diagonal lines across the control. Basically, this is a visual indication that you added some code or object(s) to the UserControl, and currently the MyActX control in the frmTestActX form is not the latest state of the control (the latest state of the control is in the UserControl window). In this case, simply make the MyActX control in the frmTestActX form the active object, then click the Delete key on your keyboard. This deletes the ActiveX control from the frmTestActX form. Now, while the frmTestActX window is the selected window, double-click the icon of the MyActX control in the Toolbox window. This places a fresh (and updated) version of the ActiveX control in the frmTestActX form. Occasionally, after you delete the MyActX control from the frmTestActX form, the icon of the MyActX control will be dimmed in the Toolbox window. In this case, display the UserControl window and click the X icon that is located on the upper-right corner of the UserControl window to close the UserControl window. This will close the UserControl window and will cause the icon of the control to be available in the Toolbox window. To redisplay the UserControl window, select the Project Window from the View menu, highlight the ctlMyActX item that appears under the MyActX.Vbp project, and click the View Object icon that appears at the top of the Project window.

As you can see, if for some reason Visual Basic got out of sequence, it is very easy to refresh the status of the ActiveX control in the frmTestActX form.

Let's see your code in action:

☐ Select Start from the Run menu of Visual Basic.

The window of the TestActX control appears, as shown in Figure 21.15.

Note that the Immediate window displays the value of the IWasResized variable.

☐ Click the Increase and Decrease buttons and note that the height of the MyActX1 control increases and decreases. Note that the Immediate window reports the value of the IWasResized variable. Every time you increase or decrease the Height property, the IWasResized variable increased by 1.

Figure 21.15.

The TestActX program. The Immediate window displays the value of the `IWasResized` *variable.*

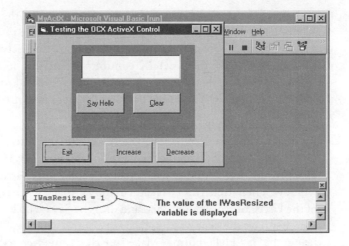

☐ Experiment with the TestActX program, then click its Exit button.

The `UserControl_Resize()` procedure is a very important procedure. Let's make sure that you understand the significance of the experiment that you performed in the previous steps. The code of the Increase and Decrease buttons changes the Height property of the MyActX1 control. This causes the automatic execution of the `UserControl_Resize()` procedure. So, every time you click the Increase or Decrease button, the `UserControl_Resize()` procedure is executed, and the value of `IWasResized` is increased (because this is the code that you typed in the `UserControl_Resize()` procedure).

In fact, you can prove to yourself that the `UserControl_Resize()` procedure is executed during design time as well:

☐ If you do not see the Immediate window, select Immediate Window from the View menu.

  Visual Basic responds by displaying the Immediate window.

☐ Use the mouse to resize the size of the UserControl window that is located in the frmTestActX form and note the Immediate window. Every time you resize the ctlMyActX1 control (the control that is located in the frmTestActX form), the `IWasResized` variable increases by 1. This means that every time you resize the ctlMyActX1 control, the `UserControl_Resize()` procedure is executed.

Why is the `UserControl_Resize()` procedure so important? Suppose that you place an object such as a button or a text box in the UserControl window. The user of the MyActX control places the control in a form (just as you did when you placed the MyActX control in the

21

frmTestActX form). Suppose that the user wants to make the size of the MyActX control smaller or larger in the frmTestActX form. The buttons, text boxes, and other controls that were placed in the UserControl window should resize themselves accordingly. That is, if the user chooses to make the MyActX control smaller, the objects that you placed in the UserControl window should change accordingly. Where will you write the code that changes the size of the objects? Yes, in the UserControl_Resize() procedure. Let's see how this is accomplished:

☐ At design time, size and move the objects in the UserControl window so that the UserControl window will look like the one in Figure 21.16. That is, move the txtHello TextBox so that its upper-left corner is at the upper-left corner of the UserControl window. Then stretch the txtHello TextBox so that it will have the same width as the width of the UserControl window. Size and drag the Say Hello button and the Clear button so that they have the same width as the UserControl window. Place the Clear button directly below the Say Hello button. Make sure that some free red area exists below the Clear button. (In a later section in this chapter, you'll need the free area below the Clear button.)

Figure 21.16.

The UserControl window with the new sizes and locations of the text box and buttons.

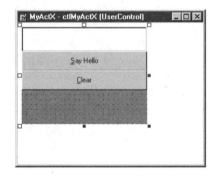

☐ Execute the TestActX program.

   The window of the TestActX program appears with the MyActX control in it. The text box, Say Hello and Clear buttons are stretched over the entire width of the MyActX control.

☐ Click the Exit button of the TestActX program to terminate the program.

☐ Now, in the frmTestActX form, drag the left edge of the control to the right (so that there is a red area to the right of the text box, Say Hello and Clear buttons). In other words, now these objects are not stretched over the entire width of the control (see Figure 21.17).

Figure 21.17.
*Making the MyActX
control in the
frmTestActX form
wider (design time).*

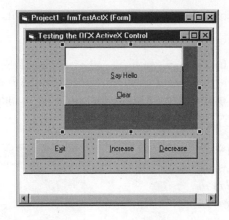

☐ Execute the TestActX program.

> *The window of the TestActX program appears with the MyActX control in it. The text box,
> Say Hello and Clear buttons are not stretched over the entire width of the MyActX control
> (see Figure 21.18).*

Figure 21.18.
*The window of the
TestActX program
after making the
MyActX control in the
frmTestActX form
wider.*

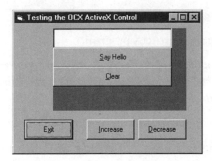

21

☐ Terminate the TestActX program by clicking its Exit button.

Let's perform another experiment:

☐ In the frmTestActX form, drag the left edge of the control to the left so that the right edge of the MyActX control is approximately at the middle of the buttons. (In other words, the width of the MyActX control is not wide enough to display the entire buttons and text box; see Figure 21.19.)

Figure 21.19.

Making the width of MyActX control in the frmTestActX form smaller (design time).

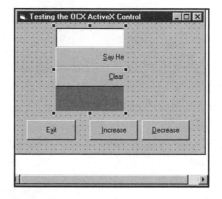

☐ Execute the TestActX program.

The window of the TestActX program appears with the MyActX control in it. Only half the text box, Say Hello and Clear buttons are shown, because during design time, you made the width of the MyActX control smaller (see Figure 21.20).

☐ Terminate the TestActX program by clicking its Exit button.

At first glance, it looks as if there is nothing wrong with the current state of the MyActX control. That is, you made it wider, so naturally, the text box and the buttons will not be stretched over the entire width of the control. You also made the width of the control smaller, so naturally, the text box and buttons do not fit in the control. The problem is that this is not a behavior of a professional ActiveX control. Remember, you are designing the ActiveX control. Users of your ActiveX control may make the control as wide as they want (you have no control over this). It is your role as the designer of the ActiveX control to design it so that it will look the same no matter how wide the user made the control.

Figure 21.20.

The window of the TestActX program after making the MyActX control in the frmTestActX form wider.

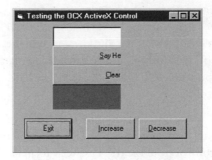

The idea now is to write code so that no matter how the user placed and sized the ActiveX control in the frmTestActX form, the text box and button will always be stretched over the entire width of the control!

☐ Modify the code in the `UserControl_Resize()` procedure of the UserControl window so that it will look as follows:

```
Private Sub UserControl_Resize()

        '''Static IWasResized As Integer
        '''IWasResized = IWasResized + 1

        '''Debug.Print "IWasResized = " & IWasResized

        txtHello.Top = 0
        txtHello.Left = 0
        txtHello.Width = ScaleWidth
        txtHello.Height = 500

        cmdSayHello.Top = txtHello.Height
        cmdSayHello.Left = 0
        cmdSayHello.Width = ScaleWidth
        cmdSayHello.Height = 500

        cmdClear.Top = txtHello.Height + cmdSayHello.Height
        cmdClear.Left = 0
        cmdClear.Width = ScaleWidth
        cmdClear.Height = 500

End Sub
```

Save your work:

☐ Select Project Group from the File menu of Visual Basic.

21

You commented out the previous code that you typed in the `UserControl_Resize()` procedure. Then you typed code that sets the txtHello text box, Say Hello button and Clear button one below the other, and the width of these controls are set to ScaleWidth (which is the width of the control). In other words, no matter what the width of the control, the text box and buttons will always be one below the other, filling the entire width of the UserControl.

Now let's make modification to the frmTestActX form. Again, if the control in the frmTestActX form appears with diagonal lines on its surface, you have to delete the current MyActX control from the frmTestActX form and place a new updated MyActX control in the frmTestActX form. (This was described in an earlier Note box in this chapter.)

☐ Delete the cmdIncrease button.

☐ Delete the cmdDecrease button.

☐ Once you delete these buttons, the code that you attached to these controls is automatically moved to the general area of the frmTestActX form. You can delete these procedures from the general area.

☐ Use the mouse to drag the left edge of the ctlMyActX1 in the frmTestActX form to make the width of the control smaller, as shown in Figure 21.21.

Figure 21.21.

The frmTestActX form after making the width of the control smaller (design mode).

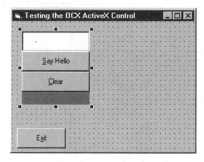

Note that as you increase and decrease the width of the ctlMyActX1 control in the frmTestActX form, the text box and buttons resize themselves, so that no matter what the width of the control, these objects are always stretched over the entire width of the control. (You already proved to yourself that the `UserControl_Resize()` procedure is automatically executed when you resize the control in the frmTestActX form during design time. This is the reason you see the result of the execution of the `UserControl_Resize()`procedure.)

☐ Execute the TestActX program.

As you can see, the text box and buttons are stretched over the entire width of the control, and they are aligned one below the other (see Figure 21.22).

☐ Select the Exit button of the TestActX program to terminate the program.

Figure 21.22.

The window of the TestActX program after making the width of the ctlMyActX1 control smaller.

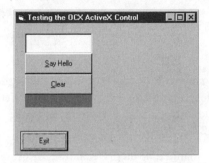

☐ Use the mouse to drag the left edge of the ctlMyActX1 in the frmTestActX form to make the control wider, as shown in Figure 21.23.

Figure 21.23.

The frmTestActX form after making the control wider (design mode).

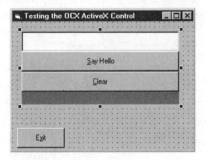

☐ Execute the TestActX program.

As you can see, the text box and buttons are stretched over the entire width of the control, and they are aligned one below the other (see Figure 21.24).

☐ Select the Exit button of the TestActX program to terminate the program.

21

Figure 21.24.

*The window of the
TestActX program
after making the
ctlMyActX1 control
wider.*

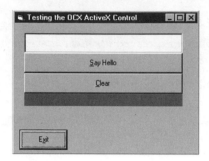

In short, no matter how large or small you make the width of the control in the frmTestActX form, the text box and the buttons are always stretched over the entire width of the control. This is valid during design time (refer to Figure 21.21) as well as during runtime (refer to Figure 21.22).

In a similar manner, if you place pictures by using image controls in your ActiveX controls, you should resize the picture controls according to the size of the control by writing the appropriate code in the UserControl_Resize() procedure. Although the code that you typed in the UserControl_Resize() procedure takes care of the width of the objects in the control, typically you should also write code that makes the height of the objects smaller or larger according to the ScaleHeight (the height) of the control.

Note

As you can see, the previous discussion of the UserControl_Resize() procedure takes care of cosmetic aspects of the ActiveX control that you are designing. Indeed, your ActiveX control should have the following two main features:

■ The ActiveX control should perform some useful function that is desired in many programs.

■ The ActiveX control should look like a professional ActiveX. This means, for example, that no matter how the user of the control resizes the control, the control should always look the same.

Adding a Property to the Control

So far, there is no connection between the MyActX ActiveX control and the TestActX program. That is, the TestActX program cannot read, for example, the text that is displayed in the TextBox of the control.

You'll now enhance the MyActX control. In particular, you'll add a property to the MyActX control. The TestActX test program will then read the value of the property and also write (set) the value of this property.

☐ Display the code window of the UserControl window.

☐ Select Add Procedure from the Tools menu of Visual Basic.

Visual Basic responds by displaying the Add Procedure dialog box.

☐ Set the Add Procedure dialog box as follows: Name should be Caption. (This is the name of the property that you are now adding to the control.)

☐ Select the Property radio button (because you are now adding a property).

☐ Select the Public radio button (because you want the property that you are now adding to be visible from all procedures).

Your Add Procedure dialog box should now look like the one in Figure 21.25.

Figure 21.25.

Adding the Caption property.

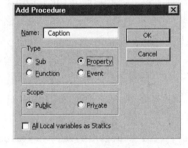

☐ Click the OK button of the Add procedure dialog box.

As a result, two procedures are automatically added to the general section of the UserControl code window as follows:

```
Public Property Get Caption() As Variant

End Property
Public Property Let Caption(ByVal vNewValue As Variant)

End Property
```

☐ The first procedure that was added is Get Caption(). You now have to change the first line of the procedure so that it will look as follows:

```
Public Property Get Caption() As String

End Property
```

In other words, you change the returned value from As Variant to As String. Why? Because the Caption property that you are now adding is a property that holds a string.

☐ Type code in the Get Caption() procedure so that it will look as follows:

```
Public Property Get Caption() As String

    Caption = txtHello.Text

End Property
```

Save your work:

☐ Select Save Project Group from the File menu of Visual Basic.

When the TestActX program reads the value of the Caption property of the control, the Get Caption() procedure is executed automatically. Now take a look at the code that you typed in the Get Caption() procedure:

```
Caption = txtHello.Text
```

When the TestActX program reads the Caption property of the control, it will read the Text property of the txtHello text box.

When you added the Caption property, two procedures were added: Get Caption and Let Caption. You already changed the first line of the Get Caption procedure, and you added code to this procedure. Now let's change the Let Caption procedure:

In the general area of the UserControl code window you see the Let Caption procedure as follows:

```
Public Property Let Caption(ByVal vNewValue As Variant)

End Property
```

☐ Change the first line of the Let Caption procedure so that it will look as follows:

```
Public Property Let Caption(ByVal NewCaption As String)

End Property
```

In the preceding, you change the parameter of the procedure from vNewValue to NewCaption. You also changed the type from As Variant to As String.

☐ Add code to the Let Caption procedure so that it will look as follows:

```
Public Property Let Caption(ByVal NewCaption As String)

    txtHello.Text = NewCaption
    PropertyChanged "Caption"

End Property
```

The Let Caption procedure is automatically executed when the user sets the Caption property of the MyActX control. The code that you typed sets the Text property of the txtHello text box with the contents of the NewCaption parameter:

```
txtHello.Text = NewCaption
```

(Note that NewCaption is the parameter of the Let Caption procedure.)

When the user changes the Caption property of the control, Let Caption is executed, and its parameter NewCaption is automatically set to the value of the Caption property. This value is assigned to the text property of the Text box.

You also execute the statement

```
PropertyChanged "Caption"
```

The preceding statement is needed; it basically tells the control to perform all the necessary tasks that are needed to be performed when a property is changed.

Let's see the Caption property of the MyActX control in action:

☐ Make the height of the frmTestActX form larger, because you are now going to add additional controls in the from (see Figure 21.26).

☐ Add a CommandButton in the frmTestActX form.

☐ Set the properties of the CommandButton as follows: Name should be cmdReadCaptionProperty, and Captions should be &Read Caption Property->.

☐ Add a label control in the frmTestActX form.

☐ Set the properties of the Label as follows:

Name: lblCaptionProperty
Caption: Make it empty
BorderStyle: 1-Fixed Single

Your frmTestActX form should now look like the one in Figure 21.26.

☐ Type the following code in the cmdReadCaptionProperty_Click() of the frmTestActX form:

```
Private Sub cmdReadCaptionProperty_Click()

    lblCaptionProperty = ctlMyActX1.Caption

End Sub
```

21

When the user clicks the cmdReadCaptionProperty button, the cmdReadCaptionProperty_Click() procedure is executed. The code of this property fills the lblCaptionProperty label with the contents of the Caption property of the control. As you know, the Caption property of the control is filled with the Text property of the text box. So, whatever is in the TextBox will appear in the lblCaptionProperty label.

☐ Add the following code to the lblCaptionProperty_Click() procedure of the frmTestActX form:

```
Private Sub lblCaptionProperty_Click()

    ctlMyActX1.Caption = "Teach Yourself VB 5 in 21 Days"

    ctlMyActX1.Caption = ctlMyActX1.Caption + _
                         " - Gurewich and Gurewich"

End Sub
```

When the user clicks the label, the text box of the control will display the text:

"Teach Yourself VB 5 in 21 Days - Gurewich and Gurewich"

Save your work:

☐ Select Project Group from the File menu of Visual Basic.

Seeing the Caption Property in Action...

You can now execute the TestActX program, and see the Caption property of the MyActX OCX ActiveX control in action as follows:

☐ Execute the TestActX program.

☐ Click the Say Hello button.

> *As a response, the text box of the control now has in it the text* Hello!.

☐ Click the Read Caption property.

> *As a response, the label of the frmTestActX form now has the text* Hello! *in it.*

As you know, the code that you typed sets the Caption property of the MyActX control to the Text property of the text box. After you clicked the Say Hello button, the Caption property of the MyActX control is equal to Hello!. After you clicked the Read Caption Property button, the label has the text Hello! in it (because this is the current value of the Caption property).

Okay, you verified that the test program can read the Caption property of the MyActX control. Now let's verify that the test program can set the Caption property of the MyActX control:

☐ Click the label control.

> *As a response, the following text appears in the text box of the control (see Figure 21.26):*

```
Teach Yourself VB 5 in 21 Days - Gurewich and Gurewich
```

In other words, the code that you typed in `lblCaptionProperty_Click()` works. It sets the Caption property of the MyActX control successfully.

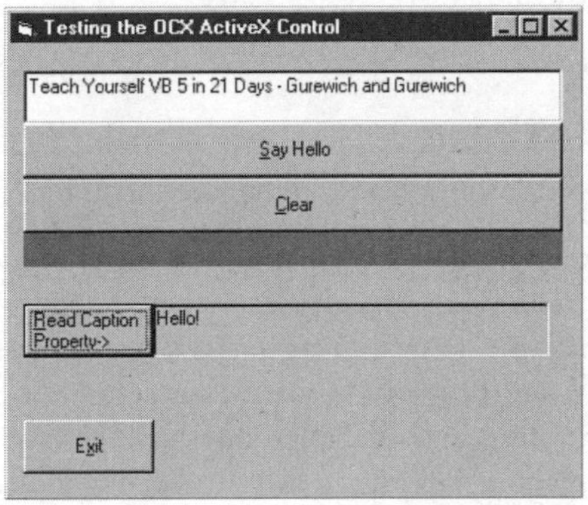

Figure 21.26.

Setting the Caption property of the MyActX control.

Setting Default Property for the Caption Property of the MyActX Control

When you place controls in a form, typically some of the control's properties have default properties. For example, when you place a CommandButton in a form, Visual Basic sets the Name property of the CommandButton to CommandButton1, and Visual Basic also sets the Caption property of the CommandButton to CommandButton1. If you now place a second CommandButton in the form (without first changing any of the first CommandButton's properties), Visual Basic sets the Name property of the second CommandButton to CommandButton2 and the Caption property to CommandButton2.

As another example, if you place a label control in a form, the default setting of the Name property is Label1, and the default setting of the Caption property is also Label1.

21

It would be nice if you could make the MyActX control behave in the same way. When you designed the MyActX control, you set its Name property to ctlMyActX. As a result, when you placed this control in the frmTestActX form, the default Name property is ctlMyActX1. If you place a second MyActX control in the frmTestActX form, Visual Basic will set the Name property to ctlMyActx2, and so on. But the Caption property of the control is empty. You'll now type code that sets the default value of the Caption property of the MyActX control.

☐ Type the following code in the UserControl_InitProperties() procedure:

```
Private Sub UserControl_InitProperties()

    Caption = Extender.Name

End Sub
```

Save your work:

☐ Select Project Group from the File menu of Visual Basic.

The preceding code sets the Caption property to the Extender.Name property. Basically, the Extender represents the control itself. When you place the first control in a form, Extender.Name is equal to ctlMyActX1; when you place a second control in the form, the default Name property is ctlMyActx2; and so on. You set the Caption property to Extender.Name, so the default property of the Caption property for the first MyActX control that you place in a dorm is ctlMyActX1; if you place a second control in a form, the default Caption property is ctlMyActX2; and so on.

Note that you used the UserControl_InitProperties() procedure. As implied by its name, this procedure is automatically executed to initialize properties of the control. You typed code that initializes the Caption property of the control.

Let's see the initial value of the Caption property in action:

☐ Delete the ctlMyActX1 control from the frmTestActX form (because you want to place a fresh control in the frmTestActX form).

☐ Using the Toolbox window, place a MyActX control in the frmTestActX from. Again, if the icon of the MyActX control in the Toolbox window is dimmed, close the UserControl window.

☐ Using the Toolbox window, place a second MyActX control in the frmTestActX form.

As a result, the frmTestActX form now includes two MyActX controls (see Figure 21.27).

Figure 21.27.

The MyActX controls in the frmTestActX form with the default setting for their Caption properties.

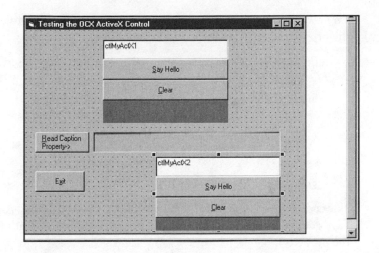

Take a look at Figure 21.27, which shows the frmTestActX form. The form now includes two MyActX controls. The first MyActX control has its Name property set to ctlMyActX1. The second MyActX control has its name set to ctlMyActX2. The important thing to note now is that the Caption property of the first MyActX control is ctlMyActX1, and the Caption property of the second MyActX control is set to ctlMyActX2. This is so because of the code that you typed in the `UserControl_InitPorperties()` procedure.

Saving the Current Settings of the Properties

You'll now write code that saves the current settings of the control's properties. Before writing this code, let's perform the following experiment:

☐ Select Save Project Group from the File menu of Visual Basic.

Visual Basic responds by saving the project group.

☐ Select Exit from the File menu of Visual Basic.

Visual Basic responds by terminating itself.

☐ Start Visual Basic.

☐ Load the MyGroup.Vbg project group from the C:\VB5Prg\Ch21 directory.

As a response, the two projects are loaded (the project of the MyActX control and the project of the test program). But guess what? The Caption properties of the MyActX controls are empty! This is so because you did not write code that makes the properties persistent.

21

To make the properties persistent (so that when you load the project again, the last values of the properties are set), add the following code:

☐ In the `UserControl_WriteProperties()` procedure of the UserControl add the following code:

```
Private Sub UserControl_WriteProperties(PropBag _
                              As PropertyBag)


    PropBag.WriteProperty "Caption", Caption, _
                          Extender.Name

End Sub
```

The code that you typed uses the `WriteProperty` method on the `PropBag` object. As you might have guessed, that's the way to make a property persistent (that's how you save the value of the property).

The first parameter of `WriteProperty` is `"Caption"`. This is the name of the property that you are saving.

The second parameter of `WriteProperty` is `Caption`. `Caption` represents the value of the Caption property, so the second parameter is the value of the property that you are saving.

The third parameter of the `WriteProperty` method is the default value of the property that you are saving.

If you now save the project group, exit Visual Basic, then start Visual Basic and load the project group, you'll discover that the last properties that you set for the Caption properties are not shown. Why? Because you did not yet write code that causes Visual Basic to read the saved properties and set the properties according to the values that were saved.

☐ Add the following code to the `UserControl_ReadProperties()` procedure:

```
Private Sub UserControl_ReadProperties(PropBag As
                              PropertyBag)

    Caption = PropBag.ReadProperty("Caption", _
              Extender.Name)

End Sub
```

The code that you typed is the counterpart of the `UserControl_WriteProperties()` procedure. In other words, the `UserControl_ReadProperties()` procedure is the procedure that is responsible for reading and setting values of properties that were previously saved (with the `UserControl_WriteProperties()` procedure).

Let's see your code in action:

☐ Select Save Project Group from the File menu of Visual Basic to save your work.

☐ Delete the two MyActX controls from the frmTestActX form. Then place two new MyActX controls in the frmTestActX form. (Now you have two fresh updated controls in the frmTestActX form.)

Note that the Caption property of the first MyActX control that you placed is ctlMyActX1. Note that the Caption property of the second MyActX control that you placed is ctlMyActX2.

☐ Select Save Project Group from the File menu of Visual Basic to save your work.

☐ Terminate Visual Basic. Now start Visual Basic again, and then load the MyGroup.Vbg project group from the C:\VB5Prg/Ch21 directory.

☐ Display the frmTestActX form, and verify that the Caption property of the first control is ctlNyActX1 and that the Caption property of the second MyActX control is ctlMyActX2.

This verifies that you saved and then loaded the Caption properties of the controls as expected.

☐ Set the Caption property of the first MyActX control to First Control.

☐ Set the Caption property of the second MyActX control to Second Control.

☐ Select Save Project Group from the File menu of Visual Basic to save your work.

☐ Terminate Visual Basic. Then start Visual Basic again, load the MyGroup.Vbg project group from the C:\VB5Prg/Ch21 directory.

☐ Display the frmTestActX form, and verify that the Caption property of the first control is First Control and that the Caption property of the second MyActX control is Second Control.

> *This again verifies that you saved and then loaded the Caption properties of the controls as expected.*

You placed the second MyActX control in the frmTestActX form for the sole purpose of seeing the default Caption property in action. However, for the rest of the exercises of this chapter you do not need a second MyActX control. So, delete the second MyActX control from the frmTestActX form:

☐ Make sure that the second MyActX control that you placed in the frmTestActX form is the selected object and then press the Delete button on your keyboard.

> *As a result, the second MyActX control is deleted.*

21

Adding an Event

You'll now add an event to the MyActX control:

☐ Display the code window of the frmTestActX form and take a look at the list of events that the MyActX control has.

As shown in Figure 21.28, currently the ctlMyActX1 control has only four events:

■ DragDrop

■ DragOver

■ Got Focus

■ LostFocus

Figure 21.28.

The four events of the MyActX control.

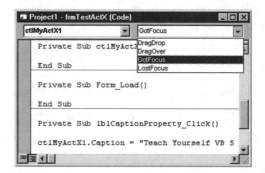

You'll now add a new event to the MyActX control.

☐ Add code in the general declarations section of the UserControl. After adding the code, the general declarations section of the UserControl should look as follows:

```
'All variables MUST be declared
Option Explicit
' Adding an event
Public Event ClickTheRed()
```

You added the following statement:

```
Public Event ClickTheRed()
```

The preceding declares a new event called ClickTheRed.

☐ Add the following code in the UserControl_MouseUp() procedure of UserControl:

```
Private Sub UserControl_MouseUp(Button As Integer, _
                                Shift As Integer, _
                                X As Single, _
                                Y As Single)

        RaiseEvent ClickTheRed

    End Sub
```

The code that you typed is executed automatically when the mouse button is released while the mouse cursor is over the control's area. When the user pushes down the mouse button (while the mouse cursor is over the control) and then releases the mouse button, the MouseUp event occurs. The code that you typed in the UserControl_MouseUp() procedure of the UserControl causes the ClickTheRed event to occur:

```
RaiseEvent ClickTheRed
```

That's all! The MyActX control now has a new event called ClickTheRed. Let's see this new event:

☐ Display the code window of the frmTestActX form and take a look at the list of events that the MyActX control has.

As shown in Figure 21.29, now the ctlMyActX1 control has five events:

■ ClickTheRed

■ DragDrop

■ DragOver

■ Got Focus

■ LostFocus

Figure 21.29.

The five events of the ctlMyActX1 control. The new ClickTheRed *event is shown.*

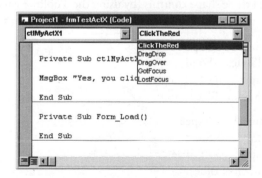

21

☐ Add code in the ctlMyActX1_ClickTheRed() procedure of the frmTestActX form. After adding the code, the ctlMyActX1_ClickTheRed() procedure should look as follows:

```
Private Sub ctlMyActX1_ClickTheRed()

    MsgBox "Yes, you clicked the red!!!"

End Sub
```

The code that you typed in the ctlMyActX1_ClickTheRed() procedure displays a message box. So, when the ClickTheRed event occurs, a message box is displayed.

Save your work:

☐ Select Save Project Group from the File menu of Visual Basic.

Let's see your new event in action:

☐ Execute the TestActX program.

☐ Click in the red area of the control.

> *As a result, the ClickTheRed event occurs. This causes the execution of the ctlMyActX1_ClickTheRed() procedure, and as a result, a message box appears. The message box displays the message:*

```
MsgBox "Yes, you clicked the red!!!"
```

☐ Click the Exit button of the TestActX program to terminate the program.

Adding Shapes in the Red Area

You'll now add several shapes in the red free area of the UserControl:

☐ Add three shape controls (by using the Toolbox window) in the free red area of the User Control. Set the properties of the shape controls as follows:

Name: Shape1
FillStyle: 0-Solid
Shape: 0 - Rectangle
FillColor: Black

Name: Shape2
FillStyle: 0-Solid
Shape: 3 - Circle
FillColor: Blue

Name: Shape3
FillStyle: 0-Solid
Shape: 2 - Oval
FillColor: Green

The UserControl should now look like the one in Figure 21.30.

Figure 21.30.

The UserControl with the three shape controls in the red area.

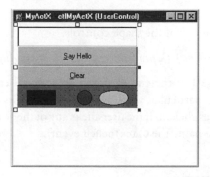

☐ Delete the ctlMyActX1 control that is located in the frmTestActX form. Close the UserControl window and then place a new fresh MyActX control in the frmTestActX form.

Your new frmTestActX form should now look like the one in Figure 21.31.

Figure 21.31.

The frmTestActX form with the new updated ctlMyActX1 control. Note the three shape controls that are located in the red area of the control.

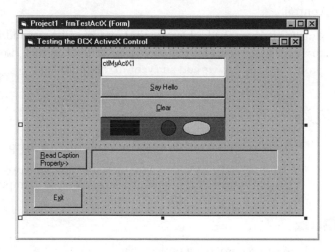

21

☐ Execute the TestActX program.

☐ Click in the red area.

As expected, the message box appears (because the ClickTheRed event occurred and this caused the automatic execution of the ctlMyActX1_ClickTheRed() procedure). As you recall, you typed code in the ctlMyActX1_ClickTheRed() procedure that displays a message box.

☐ Click in any of the shape controls.

The TestActX program responds by again displaying the message box.

In Exercise 1 at the end of this chapter you'll enhance the performances of the MyActX control. In particular, you'll add code that causes the ClickTheRed event to occur only if the red area was clicked. If the user clicks any of the shapes, the ClickTheRed event does not occur (hence the name the ClickTheRed event).

Summary

In this chapter you implemented an OCX ActiveX control from start to finish. You learned how to load two projects into Visual Basic. As you saw, this feature is very helpful when implementing ActiveX controls, because you need two projects to be loaded simultaneously: the project of the ActiveX control, and a project that implements a test program that tests the control.

You learned how to add objects in the UserControl, how to add properties to the control, how to set default values for the properties of the controls, how to save and load persistent properties, and how to add an event to the control.

Q&A

Q Should I build my own ActiveX controls for my programs?

A If you anticipate that your ActiveX control will be used by several of your current programs (or future programs), it makes sense to implement an ActiveX control.

Quiz

1. A project group is a project that
   a. Includes several projects
   b. Requires the participation of several programmers

2. The `UserControl_ReadProperties()` procedure of the UserControl serves the purpose of _____.

3. The `UserControl_WriteProperties()` procedure of the UserControl serves the purpose of _____.

4. The `UserControl_Resize()` procedure of the UserControl serves the purpose of _____.

Exercises

1. Enhance the MyActX control so that the `ClickTheRed` event occurs only if the user clicks the red area.

2. Can you find a way to press the mouse button while the mouse cursor is in the shape control, and then to release the mouse button, and yet the `ClickTheRed` event will occur? (This exercise should be performed without writing any code. Just execute the TestActX program after implementing the enhancement of Exercise 1.)

Quiz Answers

1. a

2. The `UserControl_ReadProperties()` procedure of the UserControl serves the purpose of reading the persistent properties of the control.

3. The `UserControl_WriteProperties()` procedure of the UserControl serves the purpose of writing (saving) the persistent properties of the control.

4. The `UserControl_Resize()` procedure of the UserControl serves the purpose of writing code that is executed when the control is resized. The `UserControl_Resize()` procedure is automatically executed when the control is resized during runtime, as well as during design time of the test program.

Exercise Answers

1. As your last enhancement to the MyActX control, you'll now add code that causes the `ClickTheRed` event to occur only if the user clicks the red area. If the user clicks in any of the shape controls, the `ClickTheRed` event will not occur. (As you saw, currently when the user clicks in any of the Shapes of the MyActX control, the `ClickTheRed` event occurs.)

   ☐ Modify the code of the `UserControl_MouseUp()` procedure of the UserControl so that it will look as follows:

```
Private Sub UserControl_MouseUp(Button As Integer, _
                         Shift As Integer, _
                         X As Single, _
                         Y As Single)
```

21

```
If Point(X, Y) = RGB(255, 0, 0) Then
   RaiseEvent ClickTheRed
End If
```

End Sub

The RaiseEvent *statement is now enclosed within an* If *statement. This* If *statement compares the returned value of* Point(X, Y) *with the color* RGB(255,0,0):

```
If Point(X, Y) = RGB(255, 0, 0) Then
     RaiseEvent ClickTheRed
End If
```

Point(X,Y) returns the color of the pixel located at coordinates X,Y. X,Y are parameters of the UserControl_MouseUp() procedure. X,Y represent the mouse coordinates at the time the mouse button was released.

RGB(255,0,0) represents the red color.

So, putting it all together, the If condition is satisfied, provided that the mouse was released while the mouse cursor was on a red pixel. Only then is the ClickTheRed event fired.

Let's see your code in action:

☐ Delete the ctlMyActX1 control that is located in the frmTestActX form. Close the UserControl window and then place a new fresh MyActX control in the frmTestActX form.

☐ Execute the TestActX program.

☐ Click in the red area.

As expected, the message box appears, because the ClickTheRed *event occurred, and this caused the automatic execution of the* ctlMyActX1_ClickTheRed() *procedure. (As you recall, you typed code in the* ctlMyActX1_ClickTheRed() *procedure that displays a message box.)*

☐ Click in any of the shape controls.

The TestActX program does not display the message box (because none of the shapes is red).

☐ Experiment with the TestActX program, then click its Exit button to terminate the program.

2. The ClickTheRed event occurs because the UserControl_MouseUp() procedure of the UserControl was executed. Furthermore, the ClickTheRed event will occur only if the mouse button was released while the mouse cursor was located on a red pixel.

To summarize, as long as you release the mouse button while the mouse cursor is on a red pixel, the ClickTheRed event will occur.

☐ Execute the TestActX program.

☐ Place the mouse cursor in a shape.

☐ While the mouse cursor is in the shape, press the mouse button and then release the mouse button.

As you can see, the message box does not appear, because the mouse button was released while the mouse cursor was in the shape (which is not a red pixel). (Recall that you added an If statement in Exercise 1 that causes the ClickTheRed event to be fired only if the mouse button was released while the mouse cursor is on a red pixel.)

Now try this:

☐ While running the TestActX program, place the mouse cursor in a shape.

☐ While the mouse cursor is in the shape, press the mouse button and do not release it.

☐ While the mouse button is still down, move the mouse so that the mouse cursor will be outside the shape and on a red pixel.

As you can see, the message box appears (which is an indication that the ClickTheRed event occurred). Indeed, all the conditions are satisfied for the ClickTheRed event to occur: the mouse button was pressed down while the mouse cursor was in the area of the control, and then the mouse button was released while the mouse cursor was on a red pixel.

21

Appendix **A**

Adding Your Own Custom Property to a Form

As you know, a form has many properties (for example, Caption, Width, Height, Color). These properties are standard properties; every Visual Basic form has them.

In this appendix, you'll learn how to add your own custom property to a form. As you'll soon see, after you add a custom property to a form, you can use this property as if it were a regular property. That is, you can set the value of the property, and you can read the value of the property in the same way you read and set the values of regular properties.

The Stars Program

You'll now write the Stars program. The Stars program illustrates how to write code that adds a custom property to a form.

The Visual Implementation of the Stars Program

Start by implementing the program:

☐ Create the C:\VB5Prg\AppendA directory. You'll save your work into this directory.

☐ Start a new Standard EXE project, save the form of the project as STARS.FRM in the C:\VB5Prg\AppendA directory, and save the project file as STARS.VBP in the C:\VB5Prg\AppendA directory.

☐ Build the frmStars form in accordance with Table A.1.

The completed form should look like the one shown in Figure A.1.

Table A.1. The properties table of the frmStars form.

Object	Property	Setting
Form	**Name**	**frmStars**
	Caption	The Stars Program
CommandButton	**Name**	**cmdExit**
	Caption	E&xit
TextBox	**Name**	**txtStars**
	Enabled	False
	Text	(Make it empty)
	MultiLine	True

Figure A.1.

The frmStars form in design mode.

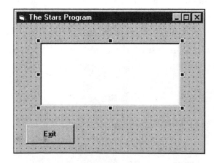

Entering the Code of the Stars Program

Next, enter the code:

☐ Enter the following code in the general declarations section of the frmStars form:

```
' All variables MUST be declared.
Option Explicit
```

☐ Enter the following code in the cmdExit_Click() procedure of the frmStars form:

```
Private Sub cmdExit_Click ()

    End

End Sub
```

☐ Execute the Stars program just to make sure that you designed the form and entered the code correctly. For example, make sure that the text box is disabled.

☐ Click the Exit button.

The program responds by terminating itself.

Writing the Code that Adds a Custom Property to the Form

You'll now write the code that is responsible for adding a custom property to the frmStars form. You'll name the custom property NumberOfStars, and you'll define the functionality of the NumberOfStars property as follows:

■ The NumberOfStars property will hold a numeric number (an integer).

■ The value stored in the NumberOfStars property will determine how many stars (asterisks) will be displayed in the txtStars text box. For example, if someone sets the NumberOfStars property to 7, the txtStars text box will automatically be filled with 7 stars.

Now that you know what the NumberOfStars property should do, implement this property.

Declaring a Variable for the NumberOfStars Property

Before you write the code that adds the NumberOfStars property to the frmStars form, you need to declare a variable for the NumberOfStars property. This variable will be used to hold the value of the NumberOfStars property.

☐ Add code to the general declarations section of the frmStars form that declares an Integer variable called gNumStars. After you write this code, the general declarations section of the frmStars form should look as follows:

```
' All variables MUST be declared.
Option Explicit

' Declare a variable for the NumberOfStars custom
' property.
Dim gNumStars As Integer
```

Don't get confused! The property name will be NumberOfStars. The variable name that you just declared is gNumStars. gNumStars will be used for holding the value of the NumberOfStars property.

The reason for declaring gNumStars in the general declarations section of the form is that you want gNumStars to be visible in all the procedures of the form.

Writing the Property Procedures for the NumberOfStars Custom Property

At this point you have a variable called gNumStars that will be used for storing the value of the NumberOfStars property. Now, you'll write the procedures that actually implement the NumberOfStars property.

☐ Display the code window of the frmStars form (that is, select Project Explorer from the View menu, select frmStars in the Project window, and then click the View Code icon).

☐ Select Add Procedure from the Tools menu.

Visual Basic responds by displaying the Add Procedure dialog box (see Figure A.2).

Figure A.2.
The Add Procedure dialog box.

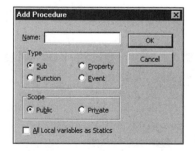

☐ Type `NumberOfStars` in the Name edit box (because that's the name of the property you are now adding).

☐ Click the Property radio button (because you are now adding a property).

☐ Make sure that the Scope is set to Public (because you want other forms and modules in the program to be able to access the NumberOfStars property of the frmStars form).

Your Insert Procedure dialog box should now look like the one in Figure A.3.

Figure A.3.

Adding the NumberOfStars property to the frmStars form.

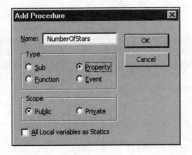

☐ Click the OK button of the Add Procedure dialog box.

Visual Basic responds by adding two property procedures in the code window. They look as follows:

```
Public Property Get NumberOfStars()

End Property
```

and:

```
Public Property Let NumberOfStars(vNewValue)

End Property
```

☐ Write the following code in the `Property Get NumberOfStars()` procedure:

```
Public Property Get NumberOfStars()

    ' Someone is trying to get the value of
    ' the NumberOfStars custom property, so return
    ' the value of the gNumStars variable.
    NumberOfStars = gNumStars

End Property
```

The `Property Get NumberOfStars()` procedure is automatically executed when someone tries to get the value of the NumberOfStars property. The statement that you typed in this procedure:

```
NumberOfStars = gNumStars
```

simply returns the value of the gNumStars variable. Therefore, whoever tries to read the value of the NumberOfStars property is provided with the current value of the gNumStars variable.

☐ Write the following code in the `Property Let NumberOfStars()` procedure:

```
Public Property Let NumberOfStars(vNewValue)

    ' Someone is trying to set the value of the
    ' NumberOfStars custom property with a new
    ' value, so set the value of gNumStars
    ' with the new value.
    gNumStars = vNewValue

    ' Fill the txtStars text box with X number of stars
    ' (where X is the current value of the NumberOfStars
    ' property).
    txtStars.Text = String(gNumStars, "*")

End Property
```

The `Property Let NumberOfStars()` procedure is automatically executed when someone tries to set the value of the NumberOfStars property with a new value. The first statement that you typed in the procedure:

```
gNumStars = vNewValue
```

sets gNumStars (the variable of the NumberOfStars property) with the new value of the property. The new value of the property is vNewValue (the parameter of the procedure).

The second statement that you typed in the procedure:

```
txtStars.Text = String(gNumStars, "*")
```

uses the `String()` function to fill the txtStars text box with gNumStars stars. Therefore, when someone sets the NumberOfStars property to a certain value, the txtStars text box will be filled with a number of stars equal to the new value of the property.

For example, if someone sets the NumberOfStars property to 10, the txtStars text box will be automatically filled with 10 stars.

That's it! You have finished adding the NumberOfStars property to the frmStars form. In the following section you'll test the NumberOfStars property.

☐ Save your work!

Testing the NumberOfStars Property

You have finished the implementation of the NumberOfStars custom property. This means that now you (or any other programmer) can write code that uses the NumberOfStars property as if it were a regular property.

Let's test the NumberOfStars property by adding two controls to the frmNumberOfStars form: a horizontal scroll bar and a pushbutton. The code that you'll attach to the scroll bar will enable the user to set the value of the NumberOfStars property, and the code that you'll attach to the pushbutton will enable the user to read the value of the NumberOfStars property.

☐ Add a horizontal scroll bar to the frmStars form and set its properties as follows: The Name property should be hsbNumStars, the Max property should be 200, and the Min property should be 0.

☐ Add a command button to the frmStars form and set its properties as follows: The Name property should be cmdDisplayNumStars and the Caption property should be &Display Number of Stars.

☐ Add a label control to the frmStars form and set its properties as follows: The Name property should be lblNumStars, and the Caption property should be Number of Stars.

Your frmStars form should now look like the one in Figure A.4.

Figure A.4.

The frmStars form after you've added to it a horizontal scroll bar, a pushbutton, and a label.

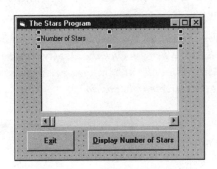

☐ Enter the following code in the hsbNumStars_Change() procedure of the frmStars form:

```
Private Sub hsbNumStars_Change()

    ' Set the value of the NumberOfStars custom
    ' property to the current position of the
    ' scroll bar.
    frmStars.NumberOfStars = hsbNumStars.Value

End Sub
```

☐ Enter the following code in the hsbNumStars_Scroll() procedure of the frmStars form:

```
Private Sub hsbNumStars_Scroll()

    hsbNumStars_Change

End Sub
```

☐ Enter the following code in the cmdDisplayNumStars_Click() procedure of the frmStars form:

```
Private Sub cmdDisplayNumStars_Click()

' Display the current value of the
' NumberOfStars custom property.
MsgBox frmStars.NumberOfStars

End Sub
```

☐ Save your work!

The code you attached to the Change event and Scroll event of the hsbNumStars scroll bar sets the value of the NumberOfStars property according to the position of the scroll bar. The code you attached to the Click event of the cmdDisplayNumStars pushbutton uses the MsgBox statement to display the current value of the NumberOfStars property. To see this code in action do the following:

☐ Execute the Stars program and experiment with the horizontal scroll bar and the pushbutton.

As you can see, the text box is filled with stars in accordance with the thumb position of the scroll bar. When you click the Display Number of Stars pushbutton, the program displays the current number of stars. Figure A.5 shows the Stars program when the scroll bar thumb is at the extreme-right position.

Figure A.5.

The Stars program, when the scroll bar thumb is at the rightmost position.

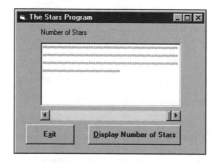

A

Summary

In this appendix you learned how to add a custom property to a form. As you have seen, after you finish writing the code that adds the property to the form, you can use the property just as you use other standard properties.

INDEX

Symbols

Q-R

HTML 3.2 & CGI Unleashed, Professional Reference Edition

John December

Readers will learn the logistics of how to create compelling, information-rich Web pages that grab readers' attention and keep users returning for more. This comprehensive professional instruction and reference guide for the World Wide Web covers all aspects of the development processes, implementation, tools, and programming.

The CD-ROM features coverage of planning, analysis, design, HTML implementation, and gateway programming.

Covers the new HTML 3.2 specification, plus new topics like Java, JavaScript, and ActiveX.

Features coverage of planning, analysis, design, HTML implementation, and gateway programming.

Covers HTML 3.2 and CGI   *Internet-Programming*
Price: $59.99 USA/$84.95 CDN   *User Level: Accomplished-Expert*
ISBN: 1-57521-177-7   *900 pages* $7\frac{3}{8} \times 9\frac{1}{8}$ *9/01/96*

Perl 5 Unleashed

Husain, et al.

Perl 5 Unleashed is for the programmer who wants to get the most out of Perl. This comprehensive book provides in-depth coverage on all Perl programming topics, including using Perl in Web pages. This is the reference Perl programmers will turn to for the best coverage of Perl.

Includes coverage of these and other Perl topics: scalar values, lists and array variables, reading and writing files, subroutines, control structures, Internet scripting, system functions, debugging, and many more.

CD-ROM includes source code from the book, programming and administration tools, and libraries.

Covers Version 5   *Programming*
Price: $49.99 USA/$70.95 CDN   *User Level: Intermediate-Advanced*
ISBN: 0-672-30891-6   *800 pages* $7\frac{3}{8} \times 9\frac{1}{8}$ *10/1/96*

HTML, Java, CGI, VRML, SGML Web Publishing Unleashed

William Stanek

Includes sections on how to organize and plan your information, design pages, and become familiar with hypertext and hypermedia. Choose from a range of applications and technologies, including Java, SGML, VRML, and the newest HTML and Netscape extensions.

The CD-ROM contains software, templates, and examples to help you become a successful Web publisher.

Teaches you how to convey information on the Web using the latest technology, including Java.

Readers learn how to integrate multimedia and interactivity into their Web publications.

Covers the World Wide Web   *Internet-Web Publishing*
Price: $49.99 USA/$67.99 CDN   *User Level: Casual-Expert*
ISBN: 1-57521-051-7   *960 pages* $7\frac{3}{8} \times 9\frac{1}{8}$ *03/01/96*

CGI Developer's Guide

Eugene Eric Kim

This book is one of the first books to provide comprehensive information on developing with CGI (the Common Gateway Interface). It covers many of the aspects of CGI, including interactivity, performance, portability, and security. After reading this book, the reader will be able to write robust, secure, and efficient CGI programs.

The CD-ROM includes source code, sample utilities, and Internet tools.

Covers client/server programming, working with gateways, and using Netscape.

Readers will master forms, image maps, dynamic displays, database manipulation, and animation.

Covers CGI	*Internet-Programming*
Price: $45.00 USA/$63.95 CDN	*User Level: Accomplished-Expert*
ISBN: 1-57521-087-8	*498 pages 7³⁄₈ × 9¹⁄₈ 06/01/96*

Sams Teach Yourself Web Publishing with HTML 3.2 in a Week, Third Edition

Laura Lemay

This is the updated edition of Lemay's previous bestseller, *Teach Yourself Web Publishing with HTML in 14 Days, Premier Edition*. In it readers will find all the advanced topics and updates—including adding audio, video, and animation—to Web page creation.

Explores the use of CGI scripts, tables, HTML 3.2, the Netscape and Internet Explorer extensions, Java applets and JavaScript, and VRML.

Covers HTML 3.2	*Internet-Web Publishing*
Price: $29.99 USA/ $42.95 CDN	*User Level: New-Casual-Accomplished*
ISBN: 1-57521-192-0	*600 pages 7³⁄₈ × 9¹⁄₈ 09/01/96*

Web Programming with Visual Basic

Craig Eddy & Brad Haasch

This book is a reference that quickly and efficiently shows the experienced developer how to develop Web applications using the 32-bit power of Visual Basic 4. It includes an introduction and overview of Web programming, then quickly delves into the specifics, teaching readers how to incorporate animation, sound, and more into their Web applications. The CD-ROM contains all the examples from the book, plus additional Visual Basic programs.

Includes coverage of Netscape Navigator and how to create CGI applications with Visual Basic.

Discusses spiders, agents, crawlers, and other Internet aids.

Covers Visual Basic	*Internet-Programming*
Price: $39.99 USA/$56.95 CDN	*User Level: Accomplished-Expert*
ISBN: 1-57521-106-8	*400 pages 7³⁄₈ × 9¹⁄₈ 08/01/96*

Web Programming with Java

Harris and Jones

This book gets readers on the road to developing robust, real-world Java applications. Various cutting-edge applications are presented, allowing the reader to quickly learn all aspects of programming Java for the Internet.

The CD-ROM contains source code and powerful utilities.

Readers will be able to create live, interactive Web pages.

Covers Java
Price: $39.99 USA/$56.95CDN
ISBN: 1-57521-113-0

Internet-Programming
User Level: Accomplished-Expert
500 pages   7³⁄₈ × 9¹⁄₈   09/01/96

Sams Teach Yourself CGI Programming with Perl 5 in a Week

Eric Herrmann

This book is a step-by-step tutorial of how to create, use, and maintain Common Gateway Interfaces (CGI). It describes effective ways of using CGI as an integral part of Web development.

Adds interactivity and flexibility to the information that can be provided through your Web site.

Includes references to major protocols such as NCSA HTTP, CERN HTTP, and SHTTP.

Covers PERL 4.0, 5.0, and CGI
Price: $39.99 USA/$53.99 CDN
ISBN: 1-57521-009-6

Internet-Programming
User Level: Casual-Accomplished
544 pages   7³⁄₈ × 9¹⁄₈   01/01/96

Add to Your Sams Library Today with the Best Books for Programming, Operating Systems, and New Technologies

The easiest way to order is to pick up the phone and call

1-800-428-5331

between 9:00 a.m. and 5:00 p.m. EST.
For faster service please have your credit card available.

ISBN	Quantity	Description of Item	Unit Cost	Total Cost
1-57521-177-7		HTML 3.2 & CGI Unleashed, Professional Reference Edition	$59.99	
0-672-30891-6		Perl 5 Unleashed	$49.99	
1-57521-051-7		HTML, Java, CGI, VRML, SGML Web Publishing Unleashed	$49.99	
1-57521-087-8		CGI Developer's Guide	$45.00	
1-57521-192-0		Sams Teach Yourself Web Publishing with HTML 3.2 in a Week, Third Edition	$29.99	
1-57521-106-8		Web Programming with Visual Basic	$39.99	
1-57521-113-0		Web Programming with Java	$39.99	
1-57521-009-6		Sams Teach Yourself CGI Programming with Perl 5 in a Week	$39.99	
		Shipping and Handling: See information below.		
		TOTAL		

Shipping and Handling: $4.00 for the first book, and $1.75 for each additional book. Floppy disk: add $1.75 for shipping and handling. If you need to have it NOW, we can ship product to you in 24 hours for an additional charge of approximately $18.00, and you will receive your item overnight or in two days. Overseas shipping and handling adds $2.00 per book and $8.00 for up to three disks. Prices subject to change. Call for availability and pricing information on latest editions.

201 W. 103rd Street, Indianapolis, Indiana 46290

1-800-428-5331 — Orders

Book ISBN 1-672-30978-5

Special Disk Offer

The Full Version of the TegoSoft OCX Control Kit

You can order the full version of the TegoSoft OCX Control Kit directly from TegoSoft, Inc.

The TegoSoft OCX Control Kit includes a variety of powerful OCX controls for Visual Basic (as well as many other programming languages that support OCX controls).

Here are some of the OCX ActiveX Controls that are included in the TegoSoft OCX Control Kit:

- An advanced multimedia OCX control (to play WAV, MIDI, CD audio, and movie files)
- An advanced animation OCX control and a sprite OCX control
- 3-D controls (for example, 3-D buttons, 3-D spin)
- A spy OCX control (which lets you intercept Windows messages of other applications)
- Gadget OCX controls
- A PC speaker OCX control (which enables you to play WAV files through the PC speaker without a sound card and without any drivers)
- Other powerful OCX controls

The price of the TegoSoft OCX Control Kit is $29.95. Please add $5.00 for shipping and handling. New York State residents, please add appropriate sales tax.

When ordering from outside the U.S.A., your check or money order must be in U.S. dollars and drawn from a U.S. bank.

To order by mail, send check or money order to

TegoSoft, Inc.
Attn.: OCX-Kit-VB521
Box 389
Bellmore, NY 11710
Phone: 516-783-4824
Web Site: http://www.tegosoft.com
E-mail: ts@tegosoft.com

You can also order the Download version of the product with a credit card (see details on how to order in the TegoSoft Web Site: http://www.tegosoft.com). *Note:* The Download version is identical in contents to the Disk version.

Create programs that use databases and SQL.

Add Field

Name:
PartNum

Type:
Text

Size:
10

○ FixedField
● VariableField

☐ AutoIncrField
☑ AllowZeroLength
☐ Required

OrdinalPosition:

ValidationText:

ValidationRule:

DefaultValue:

OK

Close

Implement Multiple Document Interface (MDI) applications.

The MapUSA Program

File Size Help

State: Capital: Year of Statehood: Pop.(Millions):
Iowa   Des Moines   1846   2.8   ☑ Anthem Exit

Learn to use powerful popular OCX ActiveX controls that let you implement powerful Windows programs with great ease.

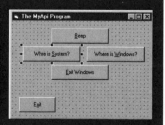

The MyApi Program

Beep

Where is System?   Where is Windows?

Exit Windows

Exit